PRINCIPLES OF MANAGEMENT

THE IRWIN SERIES IN MANAGEMENT

CONSULTING EDITOR   JOHN F. MEE   *Indiana University*

PRINCIPLES OF MANAGEMENT

GEORGE R. TERRY, Ph.D.

George A. Ball Distinguished Professor of Business
College of Business
Ball State University

 1972 · SIXTH EDITION

Richard D. Irwin, Inc. *Homewood, Illinois 60430*
IRWIN-DORSEY LIMITED *Georgetown, Ontario*

Sixth Edition

First Printing, March 1972

Library of Congress Catalog Card No. 72–180501
Printed in the United States of America

Preface

MANAGEMENT CONTINUES to be highly dynamic. More perhaps than ever before, past beliefs about management are being modified, present concepts are being challenged, and new ideas and frames of reference are being developed. This background of change suggests the writing of a sixth edition of *Principles of Management.*

With this evolution of management thinking, a vital and current need is to bring together and synchronize relevant modern management thinking into a readily understood, simple format, thus providing a practical, inclusive, and unified concept of management. To this end, the present revision features a modified management-process approach which consists of the popular and familiar—planning, organizing, actuating, and controlling—modified by appropriate current management thought. For example, included are the use of management by objectives in applying the process approach, the quantitative techniques helpful in planning and controlling, and the latest behavioral developments improving organizing and actuating efforts.

It is firmly believed that the modified process approach serves admirably as a basic structure for management study and is an effective nucleus about which current management study can take place. Further, it provides the student an awareness of the scope and extensiveness of thought being given to management study.

Yet with all the current change, the function of management remains the same—to accomplish desired results. Likewise, the basic purpose of this book is the same as that initially stated in the first edition back in 1953; namely, to help in acquiring knowledge and in developing skill in management. More specifically to this end, this book is intended to disseminate a better understanding of management and its universality, to demonstrate its fundamental importance in all activities, to encourage its effective practice, to stimulate managerial thinking, to clarify managerial concepts and terminology, and to spread the human and material benefits resulting from its enlightened application. The view is taken that management is a distinct entity; knowledge in it can be acquired, and effective instruction in it can be supplied.

Written for basic management study, this book is intended to serve the beginning student, to assist the active manager, and to provide a helpful review to the experienced manager. Supplied is a comprehensive and teachable book about which both teacher and student can be enthusiastic.

Specific outstanding features of this sixth edition include broader coverage of the social implications and responsibilities of being a manager today; more discussion of the managerial importance of environment—both internal and external; more material on management philosophy; and more attention given the impact of values upon managerial practices. There are new chapters on considerations affecting the scope of management, analyzing management problems, management organizing, management actuating, leading, and management in the future. The section on evaluating managers is expanded; and the updated treatments of objective setting, communicating, implementing plans, exercising authority, handling organization change, and using motivational controlling are significant additions in this edition.

However, with all this additional coverage, the book is reduced in length. Total chapters now number 27, a reduction of 4 chapters in comparison with the 31 of the previous edition. With 6 new chapters, and 10 chapters given a major rewrite, about 60 percent of the book is new. It represents a concise, completely modern, and instructionally effective basic management volume.

A better sequence and pattern in presenting the material is followed. The major parts include approaching the study of management, facilitating managerial activities, planning, organizing, actuating, controlling, and forthcoming developments in management. The style of writing has been reworked to gain greater sharpness and clarity. Helpful examples and the discussion of the latest significant developments in management are included to expedite ease of reading and to increase the reader's enthusiasm for the subject of management. The annotated bibliography, brought up to date, continues to be featured in this book.

Thought-provoking questions and case problems follow each chapter. Carefully screened, only those proven to be most helpful have been retained. Specifically, about one half of the questions and two thirds of the cases are brand new. Selection was based on the experience of adopters of the book plus new material developed during the past several years from my own consulting assignments and those of close business associates.

Many practitioners, educators, and students helped directly and indirectly in formulating my thoughts concerning this revision. The opportunities of exchanging ideas with faculty members and students, of discussing certain managerial concepts with experts of various disciplines affecting management, and of being a part of management in action on selected assignments, have supplied support and motivation for carrying out the revision work. The list of these active and provocative management devotees is too long to include here. Special thanks, however, are extended to Dr. John F. Mee, Dean, Division of General and Technical Studies, and Mead Johnson Professor of Management, Indiana University, who, very cooperative and generous of his time, gave outstanding and valuable suggestions. Also, Dr. Edward Reighard, Fresno State College, Fresno, California, provided pertinent, thoughtful, and detailed suggestions designed to improve the book's coverage and content. His ideas proved particularly helpful, and deep appreciation is acknowledged for his assistance. Many thanks are also extended to E. M. Terry who provided needed editorial research assistance.

February 1972   GEORGE R. TERRY

Contents

ix

of planning. Disadvantages of planning. Feasible boundaries of planning. Information and planning. Facts and planning. Planning premises. Variety of planning premises. Economic forecasts. Technological forecasts. Sociological factors. Governmental controls and fiscal action. Industry demand. Public attitudes and behavior. Individual firm's data. Research. Ethics and planning. Ethics—internal and external.

deviation. Controlling quality. Inspection control. Statistical quality control. The basis of statistical quality control. Control charts.

Personal time use by manager. Time use and new product introduction. Time use and production control. Routing. Scheduling. Dispatching. Controlling of cost. Overhead cost. Methods of distributing overhead costs. Comparing cost performance with standard. Correcting cost deviations. Cost-effectiveness method and value analysis. Fixed and variable costs. Solving break-even point problems. Algebraic solution. Graphic solution. Utilizing break-even point analysis. Budgetary controlling. Fundamental budgetary considerations. Formulating the budget. Applying budgetary control. Types of budgeting. Budget period. Advantages and disadvantages of budgetary control. Human behavior and budgeting.

Part VII FORTHCOMING DEVELOPMENTS
IN MANAGEMENT

Management thought. More involvement. Management as a resource. Management scope broadened. Social environment. Organization observations. Mass nonroutine tasks. Challenge of manpower use. Manager obsolescence. Manager of the future.

part I

Approaching the study of management

To stimulate interest and to provide adequate orientation, our study of management begins with presenting basic concepts which establish a helpful background and a framework within which management is normally conducted.

Emphasis is placed on the fact that management's reason for being is to accomplish desired results; that it is influenced by the manager's philosophy and values; that it is conditioned by environmental factors both internal and external to the enterprise; and that it is viewed in many different ways by students and practitioners.

The purpose of Part I is to give the reader an "attitudinal fix" concerning management so that its study is enhanced and made enjoyable and profitable.

Also, developed in this part is the central theme of this book. It is that management study is expedited by considering it as a distinct process modified by the approach of results management and other approaches (or schools) of management believed especially effective and highly contributive to the individual situation or area being managed. Specifically, what might be termed the eclectic-process school of management is followed. This approach brings reality to management theory and training and thus avoids the attempt to explain management by an oversimplified general theory which loses reality with actual management. The chapters are:

1. *Basic concepts*
2. *Considerations affecting the scope of management*
3. *Management objectives*
4. *Schools of management thought*
5. *The modified process approach*

1

Basic concepts

One of the chief objectives of education should be to widen the windows through which we view the world.
ARNOLD GLASOW

MANAGEMENT deals with establishing and achieving objectives. It is man's main means for utilizing material resources and the talents of people in the quest and attainment of stated goals. Management is found to some degree in almost every human activity—be it in the factory, office, school, bank, government, armed forces, church, labor union, home, hotel, or hospital. There is a universality of management among enterprises. At the top levels of enterprises, for example, the management problems have certain similarities and the basic efforts spent to solve them have a general likeness.

Major objectives are commonly provided by others, but in such cases the objectives usually are stated in very broad terms and require elaboration and refinement to be understood by management members. More often than not, managers set forth their objectives, as illustrated by precise statements of the problems to be solved or hurdles to be overcome in outlining the work to be done. From the practical and operating viewpoint, a manager is expected to spell out his objectives, giving adequate regard for the various constraints within which the goals must be achieved.

To achieve an objective there is inevitably the bringing together of the basic resources available to man—namely men, materials, machines, methods, money, and markets. Commonly referred to as the six M's of management, these resources are coordinated, that is, they are brought together and related harmoniously so that the sought end result may be

3

accomplished, all within the predetermined constraints of time, effort, and cost.

WHAT IS MANAGEMENT?

Management is defined in various ways depending upon the viewpoints, beliefs, and comprehension of the definer. To illustrate, some define management as "the force that runs a business and is responsible for its success or failure." Others claim, "management is the performance of conceiving and achieving desired results by means of group efforts consisting of utilizing human talent and resources." Still others

FIGURE 1–1. The meaning of management

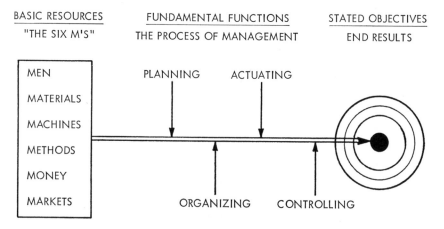

state that management is simply "getting things done through people," while others claim that it can be summarized as "planning and implementing." An additional definition is "management is the satisfying of economic and social needs by being productive for the human being, for the economy, and for society." Some state, "management is a resource used by everybody to achieve goals."[1] All these definitions have merit; they highlight important aspects of management. However, for purposes of this book the following definition is used. *Management is a distinct process consisting of planning, organizing, actuating, and controlling, performed to determine and accomplish stated objectives by the use of human beings and other resources.* In other words there are distinguishing activities which make up a management process. Fur-

---

[1] See also p. 8.

ther, these activities are performed to accomplish stated objectives and they are performed by people with the help of other resources.

It is helpful to remember that management is an activity; those who perform this activity are managers or management members. In a very real sense, management is an abstraction designed to convert disorganized resources into useful and effective goal accomplishments. This is achieved by utilizing nonhuman resources effectively and by working with people and motivating them in order to bring out their full capabilities and give reality to their dreams of having a richer, fuller life. Management is the most comprehensive, most demanding, most crucial, and most subtle of all human activities.

The preferred definition of management given above is shown graphically by Figure 1–1. The basic resources are subjected to the fundamental functions of management—planning, organizing, actuating, and controlling in order that the stated objectives are achieved. This approach to management study is developed fully in Chapter 5. Discussion is delayed to this chapter so that important considerations affecting management, no matter how it is defined, can be clarified and in this way the full significance and use of management can be better appreciated.

PEOPLE, IDEAS, RESOURCES, OBJECTIVES

At this point it will be helpful to bring into our discussion the concept of PIRO (People, Ideas, Resources, and Objectives). These are basic in management. They are what a manager works with, but not what he does which, as stated above, are the fundamental functions of planning, organizing, actuating, and controlling.

People are by far the most important resource available to a manager. In the final analysis management is by, through, and for people. Its raison d'être is people. A manager knows that to achieve a stated objective, people require leadership, they need to be persuaded, inspired, communicated with, and be able to perform work tasks that are satisfactory and satisfying. Ideas are among the most precious possessions of a manager for they represent the fundamental notions and conceptual thinking required of a manager. Questions such as what objectives to seek, what resources to allocate, what priorities, sequences, and timing to follow, and what problems to analyze are answered by the use of ideas and mental efforts of the manager. Resources, other than people, are essential to the manager's success. The manager must define liaison lines to facilitate coordination of resources and establish proper and up-to-date relationships among them. Objectives give purpose to the manager's use of people, ideas, and resources. There is a goal to reach, a mission to fulfill. A manager is goal-oriented. Figure 1–2 diagrams these PIRO concepts. In the center are the four basic conceptual elements. For each one, illustrative actions are suggested.

FIGURE 1–2. People, ideas, resources, and objectives (PIRO) are basic in management

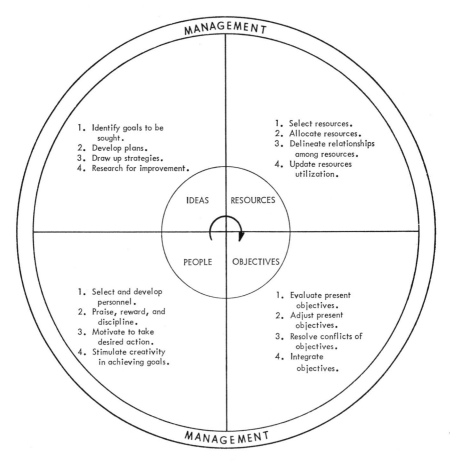

IMPORTANCE AND ROLE OF MANAGEMENT

Few enterprises can long be successful that do not utilize effective management. To a great extent the establishment and the accomplishment of many economic, social, and political goals rest upon the competency of the manager. The task of making a better economic life possible, improving social standards, or achieving more efficient government is the challenge to modern managerial ability.

Management provides effectiveness to human efforts. It helps achieve better equipment, plants, offices, products, services, and human relations. It keeps abreast of changing conditions, and it supplies foresight and imagination. Improvement and progress are its constant watchwords.

Management brings order to endeavors. By means of management, apparently isolated events or factual information or beliefs are brought together and significant relationships discerned. These relationships bear on the immediate problem, point out future hurdles to be overcome, and assist in determining a solution to the problem.

Furthermore, it is being more widely recognized that management is the critical ingredient in a nation's growth. Both economic and social development are brought about by management. To develop an undeveloped nation, for example, necessitates management know-how. National development is not solely one of transferring capital, technology, and education to the undeveloped nation. As expressed by a manager in Chile:

Perhaps it is time to alter our concept of undevelopment and think in terms of management. This would focus our attention on helping mismanaged areas to improve their organizations and knowledge. No amount of capital investment will succeed in furthering human progress if such wealth producing resources are mishandled or undermined through lack of fundamental concepts.[2]

In essence, undeveloped countries are undermanaged ones. Supplying capital and technology provides economic wealth, but supplying management provides the generation and direction of effective human energies. Management know-how utilizes the available resources effectively toward achievement of basic needs.

In addition, there is no substitute for management. To determine worthwhile goals, carefully select and utilize resources efficiently by means of applying planning, organizing, actuating, and controlling require a high degree of judgment and the exercise of great courage. From time to time, gadgets and aids are offered to replace management, but actually at best they assist and do not represent management. Serious consideration of such devices usually points out the need for more managerial judgment and courage to be used. Nothing takes the place of management.

---

[2] J. Ross, "The Profit Motive and Its Potential for New Economics," *Proceedings*, International Management Congress, CIOS XIII, 1963, p. 16.

CHANGE IN MANAGEMENT

Another basic concept of management appropriate for inclusion in these introductory comments is that change constantly challenges the manager. Some of this change is evolutionary, some revolutionary, some recognizable, some nonrecognizable. Both forces within an enterprise as well as forces outside the enterprise cause managers to act and react in initiating changes in their immediate working environment.

Change invalidates existing operations. Goals are not being accomplished in the best manner, problems develop, and frequently because of the lack of time, only patched-up solutions are followed. The result is that the mode of management is superficial in nature and temporary in effectiveness. A complete overhaul of managerial operations should take place.

Change is inevitable; the challenge is to seize the opportunity that change presents and shape it for human progress. It appears quite likely that we are just beginning to see the real effects of change in our society; the pace probably will accelerate in ways that few really understand or know what to do about. Both technology and social changes have overtaken the fiction writers and it is a bit jolting to realize that 95 percent of all the professors, engineers, and scientists in existence since the beginning of history are alive and working today. The volume of their work is overwhelming and seems to ensure that change will continue at an even greater rate in the future.

Resources are being added to and altered at an amazing rate. Compared with the past, significant changes, for example, have taken place in the people resource. The present work force has more education, is younger, and is guided by economic and social standards unheard of several decades ago. In the case of materials, there are currently nearly twice the number that existed just fifteen years ago. And new machines as well as methods are appearing with such rapidity that obsolescence has become a major difficulty.

Furthermore, numerous changes are taking place in the implementation of management itself. New concepts are being developed, new ideas being evaluated, and the manner of carrying out the management function is being radically altered. To illustrate, some believe that management should be viewed as the important resource for all achievement and recommend abandonment of its traditional, "you tell 'em—authoritative hierarchy" concept. In other words, management is a resource to nearly all achievement and every member of an enterprise performs the management functions to accomplish his goals. The view is rapidly gaining followers and is in contrast to the traditional viewpoint of looking upon management as basically a system of authority. Also, participation in managerial decision making by those affected by the decision is now widely advocated and practiced by many managers. Inclusion of these and other newer managerial concepts are featured in this book.

Management is dynamic. A manager cannot hope to operate in a period of "no change." He must anticipate change and manage within this dynamic economy of developments and unforeseen events. What is the best way to do this? Probably by accepting that (1) his key operating mode is flexibility, and (2) his essential resource is people with knowledge. People are the most flexible of all the resources which a manager employs. Knowledge gives people insight into change and the consequences of change. Hence, the manager alert to change strives to attract co-peers who are as flexible as the events of the times, are open-minded, and not those devoted completely to a particular discipline of thinking, or "hung up" on a specific conclusion to a specific problem.

When more managers can adapt to the changing nature of our economic and social requirements, many pertinent questions raised today will be answered. At that time, we will have found the right method for the attainment of fair profits, the alleviation of poverty and hunger, the provision of jobs for all who seek employment, and work environments where people can find their dignity.

OPPORTUNITIES IN MANAGEMENT

Management offers abundant opportunities. The choice of careers is broadening steadily and covers a wide range of talent and ability. Every major activity in every enterprise involves management personnel. Women, as well as men, and members of minority groups are occupying positions of managerial importance.

Just what are the chances of getting into management? Very good. Management ability will be in increasing demand. With the growth in the U.S. economy, improvement in government and social order, and the maintenance of a strong national defense, the need for people with management knowledge and skill will be tremendous. Of all the men and women gainfully employed in the United States, approximately one out of every ten, or 10 percent, are classified as executives, managers, and officials. Hence, assuming a total national work force of 100 million, there are roughly 10 million management jobs in the United States. This means that during next year, about 250,000 management jobs will have to be filled, assuming an average working span of 40 years.

It is of interest to note that by adding the census classifications of professional and technical people to that of the managerial group, we have one of the largest segments in the U.S. labor force. This composite group accounts for the bulk of the American business wage and salary bill. It is also among the fastest growing groups in the United States.

PRINCIPLES OF MANAGEMENT

Another basic concept in management is that there are principles of management. Some prefer to call them propositions. A principle can be defined as *a fundamental statement or truth providing a guide to thought or action.* The fundamental statement applies to a series of phenomena under consideration and signifies what results to expect when the principle is applied. Hence, by means of principles of management, a manager can avoid fundamental mistakes in his work and with justified confidence can reasonably foretell the results of many of his efforts. Principles of management are to the manager as a table of strengths of materials is to a civil engineer. The table represents to a civil engineer fundamental truths, expressed as data, based on years of experience and testing. He can predetermine the safe allowable load for a steel girder of a building simply by using the table and analyzing the design drawings and specifications.

Actually, the discovery and statements of principles are a product of any well-developed science. In the study and comprehension of any body of knowledge, particular bits of knowledge are relatively nothing; they are rapidly aging facts. Principles are enduring. In fact, every field of learning has its principles which represent the distillation of basic truths in that area as man knows and understands them. There are basic principles of management that are reasonably well established, accepted, and used. Management is not a confused hodgepodge that defies logical analysis. These principles cover many facets of management.

It can be stated that the principles of management represent the current development of management. As more and more reliable knowledge is gained about it, new principles will emerge and at the same time, other management principles will be modified, and some discarded as not being truly representative of management knowledge.

APPLYING PRINCIPLES OF MANAGEMENT

Principles are basic; yet they are not absolute. They are neither laws, nor dogmas, and they should not be considered too rigid. Principles are working hypotheses. Principles should be (1) practical, which means they can be put to use no matter how remote or distant in time the applications are, (2) relevant to a basic and broad precept, thus providing an inclusive perceptive, and (3) consistent in that for identical sets of circumstances similar results will occur.

Principles only describe and predict. They do not state what ought to be until the user employs them with his particular set of values. Difficulty in applying a principle of management, most frequently stems from the faulty interpretation of the facts involved and the relative importance given them. It is a matter of a human being's prudence, morality, and making of difficult value judgments. This means that management principles have some flexibility in that their application should take into account the particular, special, or changing conditions. For example, consider the statement: "For maximum managerial efficiency, total costs should be kept to a minimum." Perhaps this is valid for most cases, but should it still be used as a guide in cases of emergency or in the efforts of defending our country against an invader? In these instances, perhaps maximum management efficiency is not the important goal. The chief consideration is: Knowledge of a principle is helpful, but one must use judgment regarding when and how to apply it.

The use of management principles is intended to simplify management work. The modern tendency is to request just the gist of the subject. "Just provide the main points" is a common everyday request. So it is with the study of management. Both the practitioner and the student want the prime keys to successful managerial work. They ask: "What are the principles of management that can be memorized?" Such an approach to management is deceptive, limited, and excessively exacting; and use of such an approach jeopardizes the full comprehension of management. Principles provide the basic bench marks from which a comprehensive mastery of a subject area may be stated. To reiterate, principles are guides; they assist in the comprehension and application of management, but they are capsules of what is believed to be the most effective management wisdom.

CHARACTERISTICS OF MANAGEMENT

To better comprehend management and its unique nature, ten selected characteristics of management will now be discussed. Portions of the following have been implied in the above material, but a listing such as the following will be beneficial to the beginning student of management.

1. Management Is Purposeful. Management deals with the achievement of something specific expressed as an objective. Commonly, managerial success is measured by the extent to which the objectives are achieved. Management exists because it is an effective means of getting needed work accomplished. The fact that an executive has a number of subordinates reporting to him does not *ipso factor,* make him a manager. A qualification is that the efforts of the group contribute to specific accomplishments.

2. Management Makes Things Happen.   Managers focus their attention and efforts on bringing about successful action. They know where to start, what to do to keep things moving, and how to follow through. Successful managers have an urge for accomplishment.

Management is acceptable because by its means things are accomplished that people know should be done and that they want done, but they realize probably won't be done if management is absent. This means that in some cases the person practicing management may find he is not "winning a popularity contest," but members of his group respect him. The management member gets along with people by not only liking them, but also by being firm, helpful, and expectant of the best. The people, in turn, are glad that they have the management member they do because they are getting somewhere.

3. Management Is Accomplished by, with, and through the Efforts of Others.   To participate in management necessitates relinquishing the normal tendency to perform all things yourself and get tasks accomplished by, with, and through the efforts of the group members. This is far more difficult than it sounds. The usual pattern is for a person to acquire ability in a specialized type of work and win promotions and progress by acquiring increasing knowledge and skill in this given field of specialization. But the time comes when further progress requires shifting from the role of a specialist to that of a management member. The prime measure of success now becomes setting or securing agreement on the proper goals and getting others to accomplish these specific goals. How successfully this deliberate shift is made determines the potentialities of the new manager.

It is important that the specialist, upon entering managerial work, recognize this distinction. All too frequently the salesman promoted to district sales manager remains a salesman; the employee training expert advanced to assistant personnel manager continues to be a training expert; and the time-study engineer promoted to plant manager fails to manage the plant, continuing essential as the time-study engineer.

4. Management Effectiveness Requires the Use of Certain Knowledge, Skill, and Practice.   There is a vast difference between getting salesmen to sell and knowing how to sell; between getting employees to utilize training and knowing how to train; and between getting operators to produce the products of an enterprise and knowing the details of how to perform the various jobs.

Technical skill is extremely important for accomplishing an assigned problem, but basically the role of the management member does not require specialized technical expertness. Many managers were technical experts or specialists before entering management work. In an age of specialization this is quite common. The technical skill and background may add greatly to a future manager's ability. However, the important consideration is that upon entering management work, another specialty is required—to manage effectively.

5. Management Is an Activity, Not a Person or Group of Persons. The word "managing" is a more precise and descriptive term than management. Popular usage, however, has made management the widely accepted term. It is therefore erroneous to refer to an economic class, a social class, or a political class as management, although this usage has popular appeal. Management is not people, it is an activity like walking, reading, swimming, or running. People who perform management can be designated as managers, members of management, or executive leaders. In addition, management is a distinct activity. It can be studied, knowledge about it obtained, and skill in its application acquired.

6. Management Is Aided, Not Replaced by the Computer. The computer is an extremely powerful tool of management. It can widen a manager's vision and sharpen his insight by supplying information for key decisions and facilitating the use of quantitative management methods. The computer has enabled the manager to conduct analyses far beyond the normal human being's analytical capacities. It is no exaggeration to state that the computer has probably contributed more to our current management development than any other single entity. And it will continue to contribute much more in the future. Present computer capability outdates present managerial ability to use the computer fully and effectively. Managers are being forced to reexamine their analytical and judgment processes in view of the almost unbelievable data processing and feedback facilities of a modern computer.

However, a manager must supply the judgment, imagination, interpretation, and evaluation of what the data mean in a specific individual case. The computer forces us to think, to set the criteria. Essentially it carries out orders. Its user must clarify the objectives, determine what assumptions ought to be considered, and interpret the answers supplied. Due to the low probability of success, it is doubtful that General George Washington would have crossed the Delaware River had he relied on a computer to help him decide. The use of leaky boats, at night, during a snow storm, to face a numerically superior enemy would have negated the expedition. The overwhelming odds were that the mission could not succeed. However—despite such rationale—General Washington believed he could succeed, seized the initiative, assumed the risk, and won his objective.

7. *Management Is Usually Associated with Efforts of a Group.* The management-group association is the viewpoint adopted in this book. This group emphasis rests on the fundamental fact that an enterprise comes into existence to attain certain goals which are achieved more readily by a group than by one person alone. For example, by means of a group, resources can be amplified, members dispersed in time and space, and a continuity of effort maintained. People become members of an enterprise in order to satisfy their needs and because they feel their gains will outweigh their losses or burdens as members of a group. However, it is also true that management is applicable to an individual's efforts. A person manages his personal affairs. But the wider and more important reference is to a group.

8. *Management Is an Outstanding Means for Exerting Real Impact upon Human Life.* Management influences its environment. If a manager so desires, he can do much to improve the surroundings of himself and his co-workers, to stimulate men and women to better things, and to make favorable actions take place. Past and present frustrations and disappointments need not be accepted at face value and passively viewed as inevitable. A manager can achieve progress; he can bring vision, hope, action, and achievement for the better things of life. Impact upon its environment is a vital characteristic of management.

9. *Management Is Intangible.* It has been called the unseen force—its presence evidenced by the results of its efforts—orderliness, enthusiastic employees, buoyant spirit, and adequate work output. But for the most part these results are unnoticed. Strange as it may seem, in some instances the identity of management is brought in bold relief by its absence or by the presence of its direct opposite, *mis*management. The results of mismanagement are quickly noticed; and thus, the identity of management is brought into clear focus.

10. *Those Practicing Management Are Not Necessarily the Same as Owners.* A manager and an owner are not necessarily synonymous. True, in some enterprises the managers and the owners are identical, but in many cases the managers are an entirely separate group, distinct and apart from the owners. There is, in fact, a managerial group

in present-day society. Management members manage the enterprise for the owners who have title to or who possess economic wealth.

MANAGEMENT TERMINOLOGY

Before closing this chapter, it is well to point out that there is a vocabulary of management but it is not as clear and uniformly followed as may be desired. Unfortunately, as yet there is no standard terminology widely recognized and used in the field of management. This poses difficulties for the student of management who will find, in the general literature, different terms used for the same identity. Also the same management term is used for many different entities. For example, the term "management" is confused with managerial principles and managerial philosophy. The terms "policies" and "procedures" are employed to cover almost any managerial practice, and "organization" covers a multitude of notions. "Staff" is a greatly overused term in current management literature and its meaning is omnibus as is also the common term "cost."

But the present state of affairs is not all bad. Progress toward a useful and simplified management vocabulary has been made during the past several decades. However, much remains to be done. A commendable effort is the work of the Society for Advancement of Management (SAM), National Research Committee in compiling a glossary of terms in general use in the personnel and industrial relations area of management.[3] Other efforts have been undertaken with varying degrees of success.

It appears reasonable to expect terminology differences in a growing field like management, especially as more and more thought is being given to its meaning, application, and study. In this book, the concepts of management are presented in simple language with the ordinary or predominant meaning of common terms being followed. At the same time, an effort has been made to sharpen the concept of each respective term where possible and to avoid misleading management terminology.

QUESTIONS

1. Name the three characteristics of management you believe are most important. Substantiate your answer.

[3] See the 59-page booklet, *Glossary of Personnel Management and Industrial Relations Terms* (New York: The Society for Advancement of Management, National Research Committee, John F. Mee, Chairman, 1959). Also A. E. Benn, *The Management Dictionary* (New York: Exposition Press, Inc., 1952).

2. Define management.
3. How can the modern manager cope with the problem of change with which he is constantly confronted?
4. Justify the viewpoint that management is important in our contemporary society.
5. Discuss the subject, "Change in Management."
6. Discuss the importance of management.
7. Comment critically on the statement: "The success of any one of several promising current research projects to eliminate management from our society will at long last bring sought-for satisfactions to our citizens and an enlightened way of living."
8. As you see it, what is meant by a "principle of management"? Does it have practical value? Discuss.
9. Identify each of the following fully: (*a*) the six M's of management, (*b*) the concept of PIRO, and (*c*) management terminology.
10. If a student memorizes all the available principles of management, does this accomplishment mean he is a potentially competent manager? Discuss.
11. What is your understanding of the statement: "Management is a resource."
12. Explain Figure 1–2 in your own words.
13. Discuss the opportunities available in management.
14. As you see it, what is the effect upon and the relationship of the computer to management?

CASE 1–1. THE CROWN COMPANY

Paul Moody, a management trainee, has been asked by the president of this company to prepare a chart showing graphically the meaning of management including its components and their operations. The president intends to use this chart for a forthcoming speech he is to deliver at a meeting of a local community service club.

After giving the assignment some study, Paul Moody submitted two charts as illustrated by the accompanying drawings.

Questions

1. Interpret the meaning of each chart.
2. Which chart do you prefer? Why?
3. For each chart suggest modifications to improve it. Justify your suggestions.

CHART 1

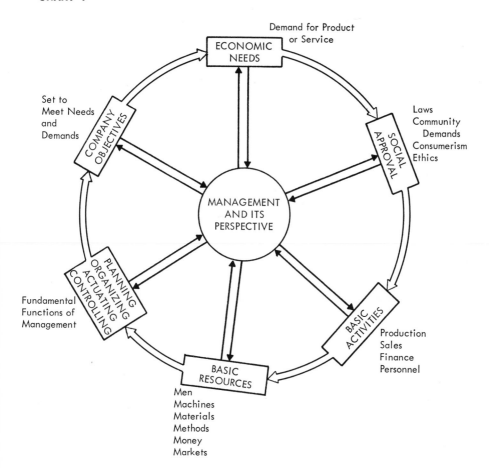

CHART 2

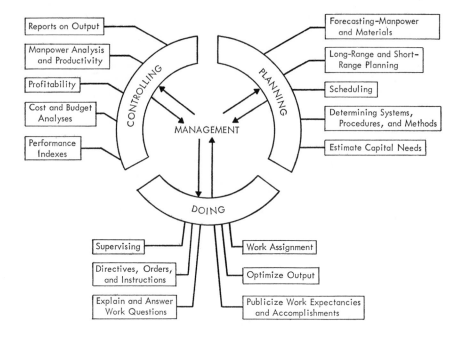

Reports on Output

Manpower Analysis and Productivity

Profitability

Cost and Budget Analyses

Performance Indexes

CONTROLLING

PLANNING

MANAGEMENT

Forecasting–Manpower and Materials

Long-Range and Short–Range Planning

Scheduling

Determining Systems, Procedures, and Methods

Estimate Capital Needs

DOING

Supervising

Directives, Orders, and Instructions

Explain and Answer Work Questions

Work Assignment

Optimize Output

Publicize Work Expectancies and Accomplishments

2

Considerations affecting the scope of management

What could be more satisfying than to be engaged in work in which every capacity or talent one may have is needed, every lesson one may have learned is used, every value one cares about is furthered.

JOHN W. GARDNER

MODERN MANAGEMENT is being challenged by forces developing out of a changing environment. Important among these forces are the generation of tremendous amounts of knowledge, the development of almost unbelievable technology, the wide alterations in the general environment in which management operates, and the deluge of changing human values. They are exerting strong pressures on management; in fact, the diversity and the newness of these developments are so great that they are literally rocking our society. It is folly to attempt to ignore these forces. The challenge and the need are to recognize them in our managerial efforts in order that the attainment of a better and more equitable way of life in the future is a realistic possibility.

THE CONGLOMERATE LOOK

To enrich its utility and adaptability, management is drawing and using more and more from the various sciences. Initially, in the development of management the emphasis was upon the economic aspects of problems. Attention was directed to questions of cost, efficiency, and measured accomplishments. With time, however, other viewpoints have been added until today disciplines contributing to management include psychology, sociology, anthropology, ecology, mathematics, political science, biology, and geography. Some of these have developed to the point where they are referred to as separate schools of management thought or theory.[1]

It should be clearly stated that management draws from and uses these disciplines, but management is not inclusive of all these disciplines. If it were inclusive, such a subject area would truly stagger the imagination. It would be beyond the capacity of the human mind to comprehend since it would represent nearly the totality of knowledge.

Management of the future will continue to seek knowledge and ideas believed to be helpful from whatever discipline appears feasible. At some distant date, management may be drawing knowledge from nearly all the disciplines known to man. But in utilizing these various disciplines, management will tend to integrate them and also to apply them to a specific problem. Thus, management probably will be viewed more and more as the important medium serving as the integrator and the applicator of total knowledge.

This brings us back, so to speak, to the idea that any segment of knowledge is in the ultimate related to other knowledge. All knowledge is interrelated. Since management is broad and universal in its concept, it appears that drawing from and utilizing many disciplines is proper and such practice will bring the best knowledge known to answer a managerial problem with the best answer. Of course, in these efforts there are difficulties and areas of controversy, but most of these deal with how and where the discipline under question should be used, not in the fact that the discipline may well have something of help to offer and should be employed.

Actually, managers need all the help they can get. The problems are seldom of any one given field of study. For example, a business corporation is not simply an economic entity, but a social institution as well. And while great advances have been made in engineering and industrial technology, we have not as yet made similar headway in human relations. It takes a long while for the habits and attitudes of people to catch up with their technology. Further, the task of motivating employees so that they gain a sense of accomplishment from their work and apply themselves with gusto to the task at hand remains a problem

---

[1] See Chapter 4.

faced by many management members. Hence, to perform his work, the modern manager employs a number of disciplines. The net effect is to give management a conglomerate look.

THE WHY AND THE MEANS OF MANAGEMENT

As the integration and application of total knowledge becomes more prominent in management, we shall see greater and greater emphasis being given to the why of management and the goal sought. Soft-pedaled will be the means of accomplishment. In other words, overall managerial evaluation will be more in terms of whether the goals sought are worthwhile, and less on the means of achievement. Credence will be given the saying, "Your goal is bad if you know more about how to reach it than why."

This view follows not only because pushing back the horizons of knowledge used in management entails concepts of reasons why, relative worth, and man and the better life, but also because the present know-how of management is at such a peak that we have the means to solve almost any problem we make up our minds to solve. Modern management has tremendous ability to accomplish stated goals including having a man walk on the moon. Many experts say that with the support of science and technology managers today have the knowledge and ability to achieve virtually any desired result. Some feel we have a surplus of management means. The challenge is to use these means for worthwhile endeavors. Specifically, what goals should managers seek and are these goals the ones most desired when they are achieved?

PHILOSOPHY OF MANAGEMENT

To answer satisfactorily the why of management brings up the subject of the philosophy of management and its subsequent values as well as the environment in which the management operates. A philosophy of management can be viewed as a way of management thinking. To illustrate, management philosophy in the United States began with thinking about separating inefficiency from work efforts at the operating level by workmen performing assigned tasks.

No one can manage without having a philosophy of management either implied or implicit. He cannot manage without some basic concepts he believes in, which he can refer to and use as guidelines. That is to say, a manager cannot operate in a vacuum. There is some system of thought that prevails in his management efforts. A manager is required to exercise thinking, make decisions, and take actions. As a result, he builds a pattern of judgments, measures, tests, and uses criteria which reveal his true motives, the real objectives that he seeks, psychological and social relations deemed appropriate, and the general economic atmosphere that he prefers. To ignore management philosophy is to deny that character, emotions, and values are related to a manager's ideas, and that his mental and physical processes have influence upon his managerial behavior.

USE OF MANAGEMENT PHILOSOPHY

There are major advantages to a manager in having and using a philosophy of management including the following:

1. *Helps win effective support and followers.* People know what a manager stands for and what overall actions he is most likely to take. They know why he acts as he does, and they have confidence in what is being done.
2. *Provides bench marks and a foundation for managerial thinking.* Where scientific and social conditions are changing rapidly, the importance of a body of basic knowledge and beliefs constituting a philosophy is apparent. New management challenges to which there are no tailor-made solutions must be met. Here a management philosophy is especially useful.
3. *Supplies a framework within which a manager can commence his thinking.* Normally this will not only orient but will also stimulate the thinking process to effective and satisfactory developments.

Over the decades, various philosophies of management have developed, flourished, and given way to new philosophies or have been modified by the contemporary thought of a particular era. No exhaustive treatment of these philosophies will be attempted here, but several will be mentioned in order to indicate briefly the nature of their respective makeups.

Some managers base their work on the belief in rugged individualism. Immense self-reliance, sanctity of decision unity, and outstanding personal abilities appear necessary for this particular philosophy to be used. The strong-willed and powerful industrialists at the turn and beginning of the 20th century are examples of advocates of this particular philosophy. More specifically, Henry Ford and his gospel of production may be cited.

During recent years, however, management followers giving emphasis to the group have increased tremendously. Here a fundamental belief is to consider the group in all managerial decisions and actions. This has resulted in such activities as planning by groups, decision making by groups, extensive use of committees, and consideration for a mutuality of interests between management and nonmanagement members. Likewise, social constraints, behavior, and influence have been given greater recognition.

Further, the influence of technological and environmental changes—especially fuller utilization of the computer, automatic devices, government climate, and the U.S. historical perspective in which management concepts have developed, are other important ingredients that have helped shape other systems of thought for accomplishing desired results and resolving problems. As both these ingredients change as well as man's viewpoints toward them, certain philosophies flourish while others shrivel. The entire setting and background is one of dynamics.

SIGNIFICANT CHANGES IN MANAGEMENT PHILOSOPHY

It will be helpful to include what represented the prevailing philosophy during the middle portion of the century and contrast it with what is now developing during the last portion of that century. The former can be characterized as being activities oriented—stress being given to what must be done. In addition, the question of who decides what issues and enforces the decisions was viewed as a key consideration. The modus operandi of the manager was the power over people position. The manager "ran the whole show" and among his many activities were prescribing the organization structure, setting the tasks of nonmanagement people, delegating decision-making power, determining the best way to perform the work, and exercising tight controls. These concepts are depicted by the top illustration of Figure 2–1.

In contrast, the emerging management philosophy is much broader than that of its predecessor and is more relevant to the current technological changes and opportunities as well as to the changing environmental and cultural conditions. Emphasis upon the decision-making power of the manager is being reduced and the emerging philosophy is oriented around the results desired. In other words, *results oriented,* not activities oriented is the coming theme. See bottom illustration of Figure 2–1. Management is viewed as a resource providing power through people's participation. By utilizing the full resources of its people, an enterprise shapes its future and its destiny. Goal setting and creativity

FIGURE 2–1. Old and new general philosophies of management

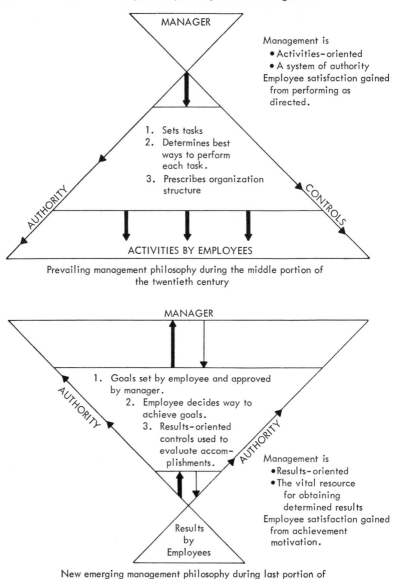

MANAGER

Management is
  • Activities-oriented
  • A system of authority
Employee satisfaction gained
  from performing as
  directed.

1. Sets tasks
2. Determines best
   ways to perform
   each task.
3. Prescribes organization
   structure

AUTHORITY   CONTROLS

ACTIVITIES BY EMPLOYEES

Prevailing management philosophy during the middle portion of
the twentieth century

MANAGER

1. Goals set by employee and approved
   by manager.
2. Employee decides way to
   achieve goals.
3. Results-oriented
   controls used to
   evaluate accom-
   plishments.

AUTHORITY   AUTHORITY

Management is
  • Results-oriented
  • The vital resource
    for obtaining
    determined results
Employee satisfaction gained
  from achievement
  motivation.

Results
by
Employees

New emerging management philosophy during last portion of
the twentieth century

and assistance to achieve that goal are given much attention. The decision-making right stems from the objective; personnel work for objectives—not simply to achieve certain activities; managers develop
self-commitment and self-direction for results; personnel have a part in

determining the methods of work; and control is evaluated by results rather than by activities.[2]

It should be observed that a given enterprise is neither wholly activities oriented nor wholly results oriented, but the enterprise tends to be predominantly one or the other. What determines the characteristic is the type of managers and employees. For example, if there is a lack among employees of self-commitment and self-direction for results, influence to bring about these characteristics should be supplied. On the other hand, if these personal characteristics exist among the members, the results-oriented approach should be used, i.e., management as a resource emphasized.

VALUE AND VALUE SYSTEMS

A value entails some evaluation of moral or social good expressed as a concept not merely of the desired, but also of the desirable. It is commonly thought of as a "concept of the desirable," which has many connotations. For purposes here, we can say that the value of a manager is the relative esteem, estimated worth, or excellence attributed to a belief or a preference. Values are assimilated to the extent that they appear to satisfy our needs. We learn them from personal interaction of various groups in which we are a part, such as the home, the school, the church, and the place of work. Values are not only important to managerial life but also to private life.

Values stem from personal choice based on beliefs, opinions, prejudices, and standards. They are dynamic; people seek values, test them, and change them. However, the process is slow, for it is a human tendency to repeat and continue ways of life as long as it is possible to do so. It has been stated many times that values are tested by every generation. By critically analyzing our values and value positions, we deepen our understanding of situations and our own reactions and behaviors. Examining one's values is one of the best ways to keep mentally alive, alert, and flexible.

What a manager believes in and stands for is the result of what he acquired in the course of his development, what he reflects of his influence, and the mores and values of the culture of which he is a part. A manager may, for example, believe strongly in the Protestant ethic, which can be summarized as the bourgeois virtues of hard work, perseverance, frugality, pride of workmanship, obedience to constituted authority, and loyalty to employer. These concepts represent strong basic

---

[2] Results management is discussed fully in Chapter 3, p. 49.

values to him. In marked contrast, some people, including managers, believe in the Mediterranean ethic, which in essence states that a man should expend only enough effort to earn what he needs to enjoy the good life and such worldly pleasures as may appeal to him.

Figure 2–2 lists two columns of values headed *A* and *B*. They represent extreme opposites in values or bipolar values. For example, a certain manager's values may be best represented by those listed in column *A*, another by those listed in column *B*. Many managers would be classified as intermediary to *A* and *B*. To characterize by a particular set of values is to generalize and such characterization would neither apply uniformly to all cultures nor to the institutions within any culture. Rather the

FIGURE 2–2. Example of bipolar values

Column A	*Column B*
1. Conservative, traditional, against innovation	1. Liberal, progressive, revolutionary
2. Repression and restraint	2. Spontaneity and exhibition stressed
3. Law and justice emphasized	3. Mercy and compassion stressed
4. Emphasis on duty, discipline, conscience	4. Emphasis on zest for life, not guilt stressed
5. Sacrifice, fear of pleasure	5. Leisure welcomed
6. Distrust of research and inquiry	6. Encourage creativity and inquiry
7. Build, produce, save	7. Enjoy, appreciate, consume
8. Competition stressed	8. Cooperation stressed
9. Sex differences maximized, especially in dress	9. Sex differences minimized, especially in dress
10. Rational, abstract, cause and effect relationships	10. Emotion, intuition, and instinct

evaluation should be considered as representative of somewhat enduring regularities in feelings and values.

By way of explanation, let us state that culture can be viewed as a way of life. In the broad sense, culture refers to learned behavior or predominant patterns of life. In the more concentrated sense, culture can be thought of as a system of values and sanctions of society. Culture determines what is desirable and defines what is possible by means of its institutions. An institution is an establishment of public character affecting a community, i.e., marriage is an institution, competition is an institution in some economies. Both culture and institutions can and do vary among people, communities, and nations. Actually an institution serves as a cultural unit by means of which influence is applied upon an individual or, of special interest here, upon a manager. An institution serves as an equilibrating mechanism between the value structure and the environment. It is both a determining and a determined medium and as such, merits consideration in managerial activities.

Returning to Figure 2–2, the current trend of American management and society is toward values of *Column B*. Since the Great Depression days of the early thirties, *Column B* has been increasingly more popular. We can see this in everyday events. Historically the trend can be substantiated by evidence of the New Deal laws, the "great society," Medicare, increasing fringe benefits, civil rights, and antipoverty legislation.

Additional examples of values concern the effect of increasing corporate size, the responsibility of an American manager in a foreign country, and the relationship between government and business. Specifically with expansion, mergers, and acquisitions taking place, are some business enterprises becoming so large and powerful that there is no effective control over their activities? What social values are in order regarding this concentration of power? Regarding the American manager in a foreign country, what should be the relationship of profit to national interests? What should the manager do in terms of what values? Furthermore, what values are pertinent in the relationship between government and business? What role, if any, should government play? In brief, what values should be used?

From what has been stated, it follows that value systems are complex. What is vital to one manager may be given little consideration by another manager. The accomplishments of most enterprises stem ultimately from the different values which the various management personnel bring to the enterprise. Usually several values must be accepted simultaneously, and this may cause conflict. To avoid such conflict, a manager usually recognizes a scale, or rank, of values. That is, of his values he will choose one as dominant, with all his other values subordinate. Self-interest, for example, may be viewed above all others, and sacrifice of respect for excellence or of efficiency would be made in order to satisfy the self-interest value.

VALUES AND MANAGEMENT

Values are the basis for a management philosophy. That is, the acceptance of various different values by a manager helps formulate his management philosophy. Values reveal what is really important to a manager, what is truly meaningful to him, and what will temper his managerial thrusts.

Since an individual reacts to basic values considered important to him, it is vital for a manager to know the values of his associates. With such knowledge he can better inspire and motivate and make his managerial efforts more meaningful. Every person operates according to a system of values. In most cases, these are visible as shown by the time and energy expended in using and following them and the satisfactions foregone in their behalf. To do away with values and act strictly on impulse puts one at odds with others and makes managing difficult, if not impossible.

ENVIRONMENTAL FACTORS AND MANAGEMENT

What is outside an organism—neither governing it directly nor governed by it directly—is technically known as environment. In management there is environment surrounding and affecting the individual worker's efforts. Likewise, there is environment surrounding an enterprise. That is, management is not performed solely as an internal activity within an enterprise. External factors, making up the external environment in which the enterprise operates, must also be taken into account in the practice of management. A manager of a Chicago electronics plant transferred to another plant may initially be less efficient. The manager has not changed, but the environment has. Or suppose the manager transferred to a government executive job. Again the manager remains the same, but the environment within which the manager operates has changed.

The crucial external factors which directly influence the internal management of an enterprise are many. In this discussion we will include five such factors, generally believed most important. They are (1) economic, (2) political and legal, (3) social, (4) technological, and (5) educational. The setting of these factors in relation to the total framework of attaining results is shown by Figure 2–3. Beginning at the left, a manager draws upon the basic resources of men, materials, machines, methods, and money and subjects them first to his management philosophy and then to the management process. However, both his philosophy and the application of the management process are affected by environmental factors which condition, constrain, and influence his managerial decisions and actions. This leads to management effectiveness of attaining the right work, at the right place, at the right time, and with the right method. From this, management results bringing benefits and satisfactions to the individual, group, company, and community, are obtained.

The environmental factors included here are complex and to comprehend them thoroughly requires much study. However, our interest here is confined to that portion of the factor that influences management effectiveness directly. This simplifies our task and helps to gain some practical insight into the environmental effect upon management. The

FIGURE 2–3. The management process in its total framework of attaining results

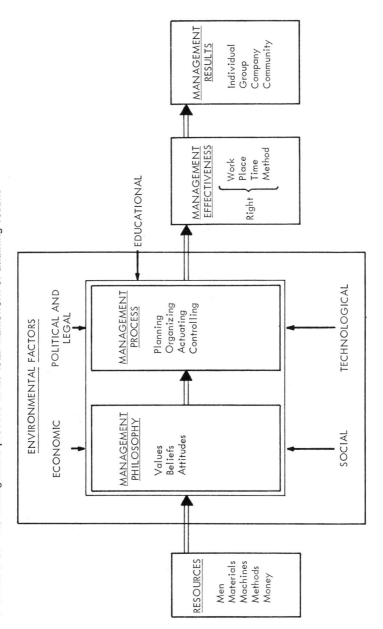

general identity of each of the selected environmental factors includes:

1. Economic Factor.   This includes the basic economic system whether private or public ownership prevails, the fiscal policy of government expenditures, the organization of capital markets, the size of the market, and total purchasing power of the population. Also of interest are the controls over commercial banks' operations, credit, discounting, availability of power, water, and transportation as well as labor skills and productivity.

2. Political and Legal Factor.   Covered are the relevant political climate and legal rules prevailing. The general tax, its degree of enforcement, political stability, effectiveness of pressure groups, police protection, existence of trading restrictions, flexibility of law, and legal changes are among the types of considerations included under this factor.

3. Social Factor. It encompasses the general social status given management members, what is acceptable regarding personal achievement in the culture, the dominant view with regard to wealth, and the degree of rational risk taking which meets approval. Also included are the extent of management-union cooperation, the prevalent views on the use of authority, the possibilities of social class mobility, up or down, and the approved means for achieving such movement.

4. Technological Factor.   This consists of ways, especially the application of new ways, to transfer resources into a product or service. Included are the discovery and use of new materials, new methods, and new machines. As used here, it is inclusive of new knowledge which because of its extreme importance, some prefer to designate as a separate factor. Automation and the widespread use of computers are also important facets of the technological factor.

5. Educational Factor.   This factor is made up of the general attitude toward education, the literacy level, and the practicality of education offered. Further, the number and types of persons obtaining higher education as well as the availability of specialized vocational and technical training are included.

SOCIAL RESPONSIBILITY AND MANAGEMENT

During the decade of the 60s, we saw increasing emphasis accorded to the social responsibility of management. In business, for example, we have historically expected social progress, but until lately it was commonly thought of as a by-product of economic efficiency. Now, however, the general philosophy is changing to the belief that business is a part of a total society and has the obligation to help solve broad and important social problems even if it means that business profits are retarded. This social action, so say many, is not an elective; business managers must make the changes to solve our social ills or change will be forced upon them. The social problems are so great that left unsolved, they will bring down the entire structure of business and of society as we know them today.

The issues are clear and familiar. Putting a stop to the poisoning of our environment and squandering of natural resources, implementing the betterment of cultures, and improving race relationships rank high on the list of social desires. Business must have more direct concern for that part of society which exists beyond its plant doors. The need is to cultivate and interact with dynamic self-generative interdisciplinary programs with relevance to problems of tomorrow.

People are turning to business managers to solve these social ills because these managers have the technical know-how and the power to solve them. But the "look to business" is far from unanimous. Opponents point out that it is improper to place public problems on corporate managers. Such men may not possess the proper skills required in matters of politics and social sciences. Further, they are not accountable to all the people and to permit any group to decide what is best for society may culminate in a highly undesirable paternalistic ruling class running the country.

However, management of the future will find a way to resolve the opposing viewpoints. Public expectations of social responsibility will be met and integrated, without conflict, and with full accounting to management's responsibility to the private corporate owners. The manager will perform his efforts with respect to the prevailing norms of society and the interests of owners. The stakes are too high to ignore the basic challenges.

THE SCIENCE OF MANAGEMENT

Before closing this chapter, let us discuss the science and the art of management, which are additional considerations affecting the scope of management. There is a science of management. It may be incomplete in the eyes of many, but we do have a body of knowledge about management. This knowledge is objective, it is free from prejudice, and represents what is believed to be the best thinking on the subject of management. Science is *a body of systematized knowledge accumulated and accepted with reference to the understanding of general truths concerning a particular phenomenon, subject, or object of study.*

The science of management is neither as comprehensive nor as accurate as a so-called physical science, such as chemistry or physics. In these areas, accurate prediction is possible so that once certain actions are started, they cannot be regulated or duly influenced by human beings. In other words, a physical science deals with physical, material, nonhuman entities. In contrast, management deals with not only nonhuman but human entities as well. It is the inclusion and the effect of the human being in managerial knowledge that raises questions in some minds about management qualifying as a science. As yet it cannot be stated as a finality that a person will think, act, or react in a definite manner under certain given circumstances. Although great advances are being made in the science of management, it seems reasonable to state that management will approach, but probably never fully qualify as a pure science in the same sense as the well-known physical sciences. Perhaps the appropriate term "pseudoscience" or the generic term "social science" should be used to identify management. Such an identity more accurately represents the true context of management and demonstrates understanding of what management is all about.

THE ART OF MANAGEMENT

There is also the art of management. The meaning of art is *the bringing about of a desired result through the application of skill.* That is, art has to do with the applying of knowledge or science or of expertness in performance. This is especially important in management because in many instances much creativeness and adroitness are necessary in applying the managerial efforts. Management is one of the most creative of all arts. It is the art of arts because it is the organizer and utilizer of human talent.

The development of the science of management can and does include knowledge about management applications. For a given situation, science can reduce the amount of managerial art required, but it never eliminates it. The art of management is always present. The science and the art of management are the two sides of the same coin. An increase in science brings about an increase in art, at least to the degree that the science increase is applied. Managers confront problems from time to time for which there is relatively little management science. In such cases the manager must rely greatly upon his hunches, beliefs, creativity, and the skillful application of them; that is, he must place great emphasis upon his art of management.

To reduce to simplest terms, a science teaches one "to know," and an art, "to do." For example, astronomy is the science, while navigation is the art. Science and art are complementary fields of endeavor; they are not mutually exclusive. The medical doctor acquires the knowledge or science of chemistry, biology, and anatomy. But excellence in absorbing these funds of knowledge does not make him an excellent physician. He has to apply his wealth of knowledge expertly, and his skill in perceiving how and when to use his knowledge is essential to his success as a practicing physician.

There is an old saying that "knowledge is power." This is only partially true. Knowledge can be power, but to state that it is ignores the importance of art. To be correct the saying should be "applied knowledge is power." Everyday observations reveal that many people have abundant knowledge but actually use little of it. They have never developed the needed art to apply what they know.

MANAGERIAL SCIENCE AND ART

In any given case, management can be dominated by science with a sound artistic veneer, or it can be made up of a strong folklore with slight sprinklings of management science. In any event, both science and art are needed. There is knowledge about management, and it should be obtained and digested in order to achieve highest competency in management. Likewise, there is skillful application of the knowledge of management, and excellent accomplishment in this area is to be sought.

In essence, a manager is a scientist and an artist. He needs a systematized body of knowledge which provides fundamental truths he can utilize in his work. At the same time he must inspire, cajole, flatter, teach, and induce others—talented and nontalented—to serve in unison and contribute their best individual and specialized efforts toward a given goal. Some believe that art is superior to science because art starts from the beginning whereas science usually builds on its predecessors. The man who built the first automobile was a genius, but now many engineers can build one. Also, the man who writes a great play or applies his knowledge of management to bring about effectively a service which mankind wants is making a unique art of creation and is often hindered, rather than helped, by the past.

In a certain sense it can be said that the art of management begins where the science of management stops. Facts are first used, "knowns" are given preference, and data on tangibles initially considered. These scientific aids are pursued to their limits, but often, in any given case, they may seem inadequate. It is then that the manager must turn to his artistic managerial ability to perform his job. Deciding to move ahead at one time rather than another time, to act even though all desirable data are lacking, or even to take action are illustrative of involvement of the art of management.

Although perhaps academic, to distinguish between science and art as they apply to management serves to show better the underlying managerial approach and mode of operations. For this purpose Figure 2–4 has been included.

FIGURE 2–4. Comparison between science and art as used in management

Science	*Art*
Advances by knowledge	Advances by practice
Proves	Feels
Predicts	Guesses
Defines	Describes
Measures	Opines
Impresses	Expresses

As the science of management increases, so should the art of management. A balance between the two is needed. Science should not be outweighed or art slighted. And it is equally shortsighted to emphasize art at the expense of science. The fact is that to be useful, knowledge or science must be applied; that is, art must be present. The real need in this respect appears to be greater emphasis given the art of management so that the science and the art of management advance together.

QUESTIONS

1. In the future will greater emphasis be on the why of management or the means of management? Justify your answer.
2. What is meant by environment and of what importance is it in the study of management?
3. What is the meaning of each of the following: (*a*) culture of society, (*b*) a value that a person has, (*c*) science of management, and (*d*) Protestant ethic.
4. Discuss Figure 2–1 pointing out what is conveyed and its importance to management study.
5. Give some examples of values that a manager might have and point out the influence, if any, that they might have upon his managerial efforts.

6. Do you agree with this statement: "Management in its broader sense can be considered as inclusive of many different disciplines such as psychology, sociology, and mathematics." Justify your answer.
7. Discuss fully the social factors affecting environment.
8. Discuss the importance and role of "philosophy of management" in the study of management.
9. Of what importance are the values of a manager and of a nonmanager in management?
10. In your opinion do managers of private business enterprises have social responsibility? Justify your answer.
11. Distinguish carefully between the science of management and the art of management. In your opinion which is more important? Why?
12. As you see it, is internal or external environment of greater importance to the manager of today? Why?
13. In your opinion what will be some major factors in the philosophy of a manager in the year 2000? Elaborate on your answer.
14. Do you agree with this statement: "As the future manager becomes more involved with problems pertaining to external environment, he will develop his science of management more diligently." Justify your answer.

CASE 2–1. PRESIDENT JOHN B. WILLIS

INTERVIEWER CARL ROWE: Mr. Willis, as president of the Willis Products Company and a man who has been quite outspoken on current controversial issues, it is a pleasure to have this opportunity to interview you.

WILLIS: It is my pleasure to be here.

ROWE: You have stated that broad and profound developments—economic, social, and technological—have been transforming our entire society during the past two decades. These changes are also affecting management. Would you care to comment?

WILLIS: Yes. In my opinion we are having sort of a revolution of affluence—a higher standard of living, plenty of goods and services available, large diversity and choice. As an executive I believe this has come about largely because business has satisfied public demand. We are not perfect, but we are now being told that business is largely responsible for the present ills of our society from poverty to pollution.

ROWE: You do not believe that business is.

WILLIS: No, of course not. We in management have made mistakes and we cannot avoid sharing the blame for some of the things that have gone wrong. I feel managers can do a great deal now to set things right, but it is a task for everyone. All of us, me, you, the man in the street, and the housewife must make contributions in effort, motivation, and willingness to pay for those cures.

People complain of dirty cities and then throw debris into the streets. Government regulates and forces restrictions on manufacturing methods. Many employees think in terms of a quick buck, not in the quality of their workmanship.

ROWE: You're saying it is not management's fault at all?

WILLIS: No, I'm saying our problems are bigger than any one faction. We all have responsibility in this, everyone of us. I'm tired of listening to people who accept no responsibility themselves. I believe we should speak out against abuse from those who have no accountability for their actions, against those who play on the emotions of the public and against critics who point out only their side of the problem.

ROWE: Well, people are taking a keen interest in current problems, aren't they? What about consumerism, for example?

WILLIS: Consumerism is part of the much deeper doubts all about us, along with the cry for a better quality of life, fear of loss of individuality, and the demands of minority groups. The business community, I believe, can probably do more to resolve our problems than any other institution. But we can't do it alone. We need the help and cooperation of government and of consumers.

ROWE: What do you need? Why doesn't enlightened management go ahead and solve our problems?

WILLIS: It is easier said than done, Mr. Rowe. All of us must decide what we want and be willing to pay for it. Correcting our ills will not come easily or cheaply. We in business need adequate earnings for they are the key to getting the job done. We all lose when inadequate earnings are realized. Better earnings are essential to make better services and products possible. With adequate means, the needs of either the individual consumer or society as a whole can be met.

I am not advocating that managers in business become social workers. Certainly our decision making must include consideration for the social impact of our decisions. We must think not only in terms of economic soundness, but also in the protection and advancement of human values. In the final analysis the best way to meet society's total needs is to provide high quality goods and services and strive to improve our environment so that no one can criticize us.

ROWE: Thank you, Mr. Willis, for sharing your thoughts with us.

WILLIS: Thank you. I appreciate the opportunity to express my views.

Questions

1. In general, do you agree with the viewpoints expressed by Mr. Willis? Why?
2. What attitude are you inclined to follow regarding a manager's social

responsibilities? His philosophy including technical and political environmental considerations?

3. What important values would you say Mr. Willis has? Discuss.

CASE 2–2. MR. RAIN'S LETTER

Dear Professor Tanlinger:

Your recent paper, "Management VEP," pertaining to management values, environment, and philosophy proved to be most interesting reading. It was thoughtful of you to send me a copy and I do appreciate it.

Reading your paper has sparked several thoughts. I agree that management is changing, but I also sense that people in management, or wherever you find them, change only under force of circumstances imposed. Rarely is changing of their own choosing. For the most part, managers stay with the tried and proven.

As the democratizing process accompanying enlargement of management usefulness takes place as you predict, people of lesser stature will be involved in its sphere. I'm not sure whether the effect of this will be good or bad. For the short range I'm inclined to say it will dilute the caliber of management we have enjoyed.

I say this for several reasons. One is that top management success of the future will demand almost complete absorption of a human being's time and energy. An evangelical zeal for managerial work will be a compulsive requirement. People geared to and harnessed by demands of friends and family will find management too demanding. Also, as you attempt to take into account the influence of all the factors of external environment, it would seem that you are making the work of a manager too complicated and spreading his efforts far too thin for effectiveness.

I seriously doubt that a manager can be all things to all people. To attempt the impossible is downright foolish. There is no simple all-inclusive solution to man's problems.

The following excerpt taken from a newspaper is a statement made by Mr. George B. Beitzel, vice president and general manager, Data Processing Group, IMB Corp., in an address to the American Bankers Association, New York City, during May, 1971: "The faster the pace of change, the more rapidly the future invades our lives. To control the future, to shape it to our needs—rather than let it overwhelm us—we must, in fact, invent it. And we can do this by determining our alternative courses of action a further distance ahead."

I like that and I believe it again emphasizes the importance of management and especially planning. The question then becomes: Just what does one do to help mankind become more aware of his destiny? I would say we need a giant with intense interest in mankind and with the art to give his managerial utopia voice.

Best personal wishes and continue your excellent work.

Sincerely,

Edward F. Rain

Questions

1. What ideas or suggestions in Mr. Rain's letter do you feel have special merit? Justify your viewpoints.
2. Using the material of Chapter 2 of this book as a base, what are your reactions to the major statements made in this letter?
3. If you were Professor Tanlinger what major responses would you include in a reply to the above letter? Discuss.

3

Management objectives

Daring ideas are like chessmen moved forward; they may be beaten, but they may start a winning game.

GOETHE

IF THERE IS no purpose why individuals should try to cooperate and get something accomplished, there is no justification for management. An objective is mandatory for a sense of attainment to exist. Having purpose, management revolves around objectives. Effective management practices are related to the selection and identity of the objectives being sought. Centuries ago Seneca stated, "If a man does not know to what port he is steering, no wind is favorable to him." No one quibbles with these words. Lack of objectives or failure to keep them clearly in mind makes the task of managing unnecessarily difficult—if managing in its true meaning is performed at all.

These statements may sound like truisms. One can reason, for example, "Certainly every manager knows what he is trying to achieve—that's fundamental." Fundamental, of course, but from the practical viewpoint, objectives tend to get lost in the shuffle of managerial activity, their identities become obscured, activity is mistaken for accomplishment, and precedent or habit emphasizing what to do completely overshadows what is to be accomplished. Always good questions in management are: "What is the manager trying to accomplish? Why is he trying to accomplish this?"

MANAGERIAL OBJECTIVE DEFINED

A managerial objective is the intended goal which prescribes definite scope and suggests direction to efforts of a manager. Note that this definition includes the following four concepts: (1) goal, (2) scope, (3) definiteness, and (4) direction. From the manager's viewpoint, objectives are commonly thought of as values to be attained. However, as an individual, a manager can have an objective in the form of a personal aspiration which may be of a mental or intangible form. The scope or range of the intended goal is included in the meaning of managerial objective. The prescribed boundaries for a given enterprise might well include more than one statement as the intended goal. Frequently this is the case. Also, a managerial objective connotes definiteness. Purposes stated in vague and double-meaning terms such as "make as many as you can" and "finish the work quickly" have minimum managerial value because they are subject to various interpretations and frequently result in confusion and turmoil. Finally, direction is indicated by the objective in that it shows, in general, the results to be sought and segregates these sought-for results from the mass of possible goals.

IMPORTANCE OF OBJECTIVES

Objectives have inherent power within themselves to stimulate action. When known or defined, they help identify what is to be done and minimize forgetfulness and misunderstanding. Objectives give meaning to the famous saying, "Little is denied to well-directed labor; little is ever attained without it." Too often, efforts are wasted because we expend our energies on a mass of uncertain directives and interpersonal conflicts. A primary need of most enterprises is a single target or several major ones toward which the efforts of all members, and particularly the leaders, are directed with the greatest force.

Consider Sears, Roebuck and Company, which has grown from being a small catalog merchant into a giant distributor serving the public with a broad range of goods and services. Part of its outstanding success has been its ability to update its objectives. Today it operates, for example, mail-order plants, retail stores, a life insurance business, an auto, fire, and casualty insurance business, an acceptance corporation, and a motor club. The managers of Sears have not been content with objectives that perpetuate the company's existent form. Objectives have assisted greatly in achieving wanted growth. Throughout this company's history, its managers have continuously redefined their objectives and lived by them.

The importance of objectives is widely accepted; most managers agree that they are vital. Inappropriate and inadequate objectives can retard the management and suffocate the operations of any organization. The difficulty is in managers knowing what their current objectives are, in identifying them both to themselves and to their associates, in updating them and in using them effectively in their management work. Too frequently, objectives are not stated, are overlooked, forgotten, or ignored. Objectives have been called the neglected area of management. It is common for a manager to find that the details of an immediate operation have occupied so much of his time that he has lost sight of the basic overall objective of the main problem at hand. A profitable suggestion to any manager is to sit back periodically and reiterate his objectives and then determine whether he is actually working toward these goals.

PRINCIPLE OF OBJECTIVES

Objectives are basic in management and a prerequisite to the determining of any course of action; they should be (1) clearly defined, preferably quantified, and measurable, (2) realistic in that they are attainable with some reach or difficulty, and (3) understood in that they are specific and known by all members of an enterprise affected by them.

TESTS OF GOOD OBJECTIVES

Management objectives should be set with great care. They serve best and stand a better chance of being fulfilled when the following considerations are taken into account:

1. Objectives Should Be the Result of Participation by Those Responsible for Carrying Them Out. Those near the situation probably know best what is achievable. When persons have helped formulate objectives, they have a strong commitment to achieve them. In addition, they gain a feeling of belonging and of importance.

This also means that top management members must participate in the setting of objectives. Such members should not accept proposals or decisions from their subordinates with no review or question. A recommended arrangement is for the subordinate to supply information to his superior on what the objectives should be. These suggestions are then jointly discussed, altered if believed necessary, and the final objectives determined. When a serious crisis is faced, it may be necessary to impose objectives from the top managers, but the reason for this approach should be explained and the opportunity for the subordinate to assist in determining how to achieve the stated objective should be followed.

2. All Objectives within an Enterprise Should Support the Overall Enterprise Objectives. In other words, objectives should be mutually consistent through an organization. The sales department, for example, should not have a variety of products as its objective while the production department has two or three products as its goal. The test of goal consistency helps attain unity of efforts and compatibility of goals. The emphasis is upon what to reach, not how to reach it. The former is the target, the latter the means to hit the target. Unfortunately, in considering objectives it is a common mistake to define areas of activity instead of goals. Illustrative is "to reduce costs" which points out a general area of activity. A manager may succeed in reducing them too much at a consequent sacrifice of service, or he may concentrate on the wrong activities for the cost reduction.

3. Objectives Should Have Some "Reach." Most people are more satisfied and they work better when there is a reasonable challenge. People want to exert themselves and to enjoy a feeling of accomplishment.

4. Objectives Should Be Clearly Stated and Be Realistic. Specific figures measurable in an objective manner are preferable. Considering again, "to reduce costs" might better be stated as "to reduce 'X' units of 'Y' products by 'Z' cost." Also agreement on the measurement factors, including what information and who keeps the records, should be reached. A simply stated objective can be remembered by the people responsible for carrying it out—a condition far more desirable than long, detailed, written statements of objectives. An objective should be realistic in view of both the internal and the external environment constraints present in a given case. It is well to guard against trying to gain too much in too short a time. The goal must be reasonable to the person responsible for its attainment.

5. Objectives Should Be Contemporary as Well as Innovative. The successful manager keeps objectives up-to-date, reviews them periodically, and makes revisions when it is believed advantageous to do so. In a number of cases the decision will be to continue with the same objective. However, in these times of rapid change, no updating or the lack of any innovation in objective setting may be a possible danger signal for present management.

6. Objectives Established for Each Management Member Should Be Limited in Number. Too many cause confusion and neglect; too few permit waste and inefficiency. Four or five objectives per management member is maximum. If there are more objectives, they should be consolidated in some way. Too many objectives diminish the relative importance of the really major ones and emphasize unduly those of minor status.

7. *Objectives Should Be Ranked according to Their Relative Importance.* This places the needed emphasis upon major objectives. Giving every management member a percentage value for each objective that concerns him helps to allocate his efforts effectively. However, a reasonable accomplishment of all his objectives in each period must be attained; otherwise he is not in control of his operation. Thus, the entire management effort is improved. Also, note that it is human nature to delay the accomplishment of the more difficult objectives and to gain satisfaction from completing other objectives even though they are minor ones.

8. *Objectives Should Be in Balance within a Given Enterprise.* The various objectives should not collectively point to an excess on either side of a major company condition. For example, the objective for customer service may be overstressed to the detriment of the objective for realizing adequate earnings. Likewise, the objective of management development should be in balance with the growth objective of the overall organization.

TYPE AND CLASSIFICATION OF OBJECTIVES

The need for balance among objectives within an enterprise suggests the requirement of attaining harmony among them. Before discussing this harmonizing effect, let us first review the important types of objectives of which there are many. Included here are the more common: (1) to provide good products and services, (2) to stay ahead of competition, (3) to provide for the welfare of employees, (4) to grow, (5) to be efficient, (6) to eliminate the pollution of air and rivers, (7) to clean up our highways and streets, and keep them clean, and (8) to disseminate new knowledge. Such statements, due to their lack of preciseness, are inadequate for managerial purposes, but they are objectives.

Existing facilities, technological skills, financial capacity, and market conditions prescribe many objectives of an organization. In turn, these may suggest specific key areas for which subobjectives can be derived and the extent of their accomplishment evaluated. For example, the managers of the General Electric Company identify eight areas which are believed vital in maintaining and advancing the leadership, strength, and competitive ability of that company. These key result areas are:

1. Profitability
2. Market position
3. Productivity
4. Product leadership
5. Personnel development
6. Employee attitudes
7. Public responsibility
8. Balance between short-range and long-range plans

Establishing goals for each of these areas, implementing them, and evaluating the results achieved, constitute an important part of the company's management efforts.

To assist management study, objectives can be classified as (1) primary, (2) secondary, (3) individual, and (4) social. Providing salable goods and services for the market illustrates primary objectives which are normally thought of as being related to a company, not an individual. By providing such goods and services, consumers are offered what they want, and rewards can be given to participating members of the company. The primary goal of a mattress manufacturer is to provide a line of mattresses which are deemed desirable on the market; the primary goal of a department of this manufacturer is to produce a certain mattress part. Primary goals can be traced, in this manner, to the level of the work assignment performed by the individual member.

Secondary objectives assist in attaining primary objectives and identify targets for efforts designed to increase efficiency and economy in the work performance. Goals dealing with analysis, advice, and interpretation are illustrative. Their contribution is indirect in that they provide supportive efforts to those directed by the primary objectives. Secondary objectives like primary objectives are impersonal in nature.

Individual objectives, as implied by its name, are those of the individual members of an organization. Depending upon the viewpoint taken, they are attained by subordinating them to the primary or secondary objectives or by having such objectives realistically fostering the achievement of individual objectives. Most individual objectives are either economic, i.e. money or material needs goals, or psychologic—status, recognition, or nonfinancial rewards desired in return for the use of their personal resources. The specific nature of the needs an individual attempts to satisfy by working within an organization and the relationships between inducements by an organization and individual contributions are interdependent and quite complex.[1]

---

[1] See Chapter 19, Management Actuating.

Simple illustrations of individual objectives of top managers are shown by the goal to achieve bigness and by the goal to maintain their managerial positions. In the first case, the year-to-year profits might be bypassed in order to increase the long-run capital value of the enterprise. The manager secures considerable satisfaction and is completely contented to see the enterprise acquire great stature. In the second case, dealing with maintenance of their positions, moderate degrees of risks are not assumed, conservative plans are followed, and most actions follow a well-beaten path which by only the remotest chance will disturb the present security of the managers. This "management maintenance" objective, sometimes referred to as "satisfying," may be found where present operations are considered satisfactory by the owners, where the additional gains mean little to the managers, or where the failure of a new project might jeopardize the manager's position. Such an objective usually is not publicized yet underlies most managerial action, especially at the top level.

Social objectives deal with the goals of an organization toward society. Collectively they are sometimes referred to as "the corporate citizenship concept." Included are obligations to abide by requirements established by the community, such as those pertaining to health, safety, labor practices, and price regulation. Further, they include goals intended to further social and physical improvement of the community and to contribute to desirable civic activities. It should be noted that business companies achieving their primary goals contribute to their respective communities by creating needed economic wealth, employment, and financial support to the community.

HARMONIZING OBJECTIVES

The significance of different types of objectives is that harmony among them should exist if a unity of effort is to be won. Particularly is this true of so-called internal objectives—those within a given enterprise. However, these internal objectives must also be compatible with external objectives—those dealing with factors outside a given enterprise in order for the enterprise to function smoothly in the society, technology, and environment within which it exists. The discussion here will be directed to objectives (1) of enterprises in general, (2) of managers within a given enterprise, and (3) of nonmanagers of the same company.

Goals of enterprises in general should be within the constraints recognized, demanded, and established by society. Whether they are or not is a question determined by the values of society, but certainly an objective not in keeping with society's moral and economic beliefs can be classified as undesirable. And such goals do exist; some, for very short periods; others, for quite extended lengths of time.

Of major significance in management is harmony between the overall objectives of the enterprise and the managerial objectives within that enterprise. In addition, harmony among goals of managers within the enterprise is vital; they should not be at cross-purposes. Each manager's goal should supplement and assist the goals of his colleagues. There is nothing wrong with having the same objective for more than one manager of a given enterprise. Some overlap of objectives usually exists; it is a normal state of affairs.

Likewise, the objectives of individuals or nonmanagement members should be harmonized with those of the manager. When this is accomplished, genuine teamwork is enjoyed, and human relations are aided materially. For example, if the aim of a manager is to contribute a needed service and this corresponds to his subordinate's goal, the needed foundation is present for getting things accomplished effectively by this subordinate in this enterprise. The integration of managers' and individuals' goals aids in achieving greater work satisfaction at all levels. Reconciling a manager's objectives and an individual's goals, however, is no easy task. Helpful suggestions include getting the individual to:

1. Visualize in the work of the enterprise an opportunity to satisfy his work interests, to use his capacities, and progress toward his career goals.
2. Develop an overall understanding of the enterprise's activities in order to anticipate improvements for accomplishing work and to meet the requirements of the enterprise.
3. Analyze work assignments and promotional opportunities with reference to reasonable expectancy of his goals.
4. Determine periodically his changing interests and abilities in light of the plans and changes taking place within the enterprise.

Likewise the manager should:

1. Recognize the capacity of the employee to contribute toward realization of managerial goals.
2. Encourage self-development of the employee for exceeding ordinary job performance.
3. Relate the employee's work contributions to that of other members of the enterprise and to the end product or service supplied.
4. Demonstrate that the employee advances only to the extent that he

contributes directly and ultimately to the accomplishment of stated goals.

It is claimed by some management students that a key consideration in harmonizing objectives is to get important members of a group to place team goals before their personal goals. We know that most individual goals will be surrendered if group goals, or those established by the manager, are a sufficiently rewarding substitute for the individual goals. Where the managerial goals are strong enough to persuade the individuals to abandon or modify his individual goals, wonders can be accomplished.

In summary, the harmonizing of objectives means that they blend with each other. The goals of an enterprise should be in keeping with those acceptable, but not identical, to all enterprises in general. And, for any given enterprise, all managerial objectives should blend into the overall objectives of the enterprise and, wherever possible, should, in the interest of teamwork, either encompass the individual goals or win substitution of the managerial for the individual goals. The blending of managerial goals suggests a hierarchy of objectives.

HIERARCHY OF OBJECTIVES

For every enterprise there exists a hierarchy of objectives. This can encompass objectives dealing with enterprises in general, such as those concerning customers' aims, as well as those of the public or society as a whole. However, it more commonly connotes only objectives within the enterprise, and includes these at the different organizational levels of the enterprise. This concept will be followed in this discussion.

At the top organizational level and providing the goal for the entire effort is the major objective, or objectives, as the case might be. Subordinate to, but definitely related to, the major objectives are objectives including departmental objectives that set forth the goal of particular segments or organizational units of the enterprise. These department objectives, in turn, have subordinate group objectives, which in a similar manner are subsequently broken down into unit objectives and finally into individual objectives.

Figure 3–1 shows the various levels of objectives in diagrammatic form. As illustrated, the major objective is to "beat Z Company in production and sales." To the production department this means achieving a high volume of output interpreted in terms of the department objective to "manufacture 100,000 complete units A-6243 by Novem-

FIGURE 3–1. Illustrating a hierarchy of objectives

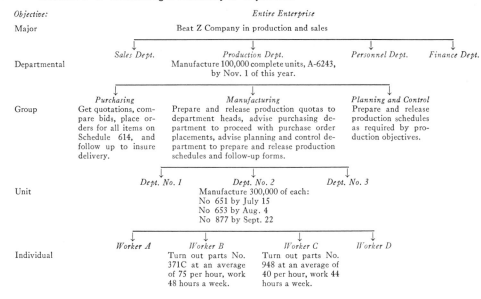

ber 1 of this year." This departmental objective can be stated at the group level; for example, purchasing, as "get quotations, compare bids, place orders for all items on Schedule 614, and follow up to insure delivery." Figure 3–1 indicates other group objectives along with unit and also individual objectives.

The accomplishment of each subsidiary objective should contribute to the achievement of its respective immediate superior objective, thus providing a thoroughly integrated and harmonious pattern of objectives to all members of the enterprise. For maximum effectiveness, an objective must be meaningful and timely to the individual. To tell an individual operating a lathe that the objective of the company is to "beat Z Company in production and sales" means little to him until that objective is translated into meaningful terms in his immediate task. Specifically, it is necessary to point out in clear and precise language what his individual goal is.

PROFITS AND OBJECTIVES

Because many feel that the major management objective applicable to *all* enterprises is to realize a financial profit, a discussion of this subject is warranted. Not *all* enterprises are interested in making a profit. For example, churches, hospitals, schools, charitable institutions, and government agencies are not concerned basically with the acquisition of profits. The nonprofit enterprises customarily rely on gifts, endowments, receipts from money-raising projects, certain charges, assessments, or taxes which are needed "to keep the enterprise going." The basic managerial objective in such enterprises is the providing of a service that is useful and socially desirable. However, the kind of service these enterprises render and how well they render it are important factors in determining the amount of financial support they win.

But the question may be asked: Is not the major managerial objective of *business* enterprises, or at least most of them, the achievement of profits? Here again the answer is no.

Actually, it is impractical to pursue financial profits as the sole basic goal. Profits are residual in nature and come into existence as the result of other endeavors. A manager cannot go out and directly secure profits; he must do something else which might result in a realization of profits. In this sense profits can be thought of as an indirect goal, a possible and hoped for by-product of other direct efforts. Profits lie at the final link of a long chain of interrelated events. The president of a large department store has the objective to acquire 300,000 satisfied customers. This emphasizes service, and when accomplished, a satisfactory amount of profits is most likely to accrue.

This does not imply, however, that profits, i.e., total income minus total expenses, are not important. Under the competitive system, it is true that a business enterprise must show profits to survive, to pay reasonable returns to its owners, to improve and develop its facilities, to contribute to its community, and to pay its share of the cost of government. Essentially the making of a profit is needed to meet necessary obligations and to continue offering a fundamental service. However, emphasis upon profits alone can misguide the manager. For instance, it could lead to a "penny-wise, pound-foolish" attitude in that machines are not adequately maintained, only products with high margins are promoted, research is ignored or eliminated, and short-range operations are stressed—the "get it and get out" type of attitude and thought prevailing.

RESULTS MANAGEMENT

Objectives are not only a basis for directing efforts but can be a tool for generating the will-to-do, enthusiasm, and teamwork by the members of an organization. However, in numerous cases the objectives fail to provide this added spark to attain objectives. Why? Mainly, because the manager does not clearly communicate the objective, the scope within which the subordinate has to exercise decision making is too narrow, or the major problem areas are not given preferred attention. To correct these shortcomings, we can utilize participation in formulating an objective by the users of that objective. Encouraging the user to participate in decision making has won great favor. Why not encourage him to participate in objective setting?

Actually this participative objective-setting approach is winning many followers. It has developed into an entire approach to management. Sometimes referred to as management by objectives, management by mission, goals management, or as we prefer to call it, *results management*, because results are emphasized, not the activities performed. Results are the criteria that determine the success of the management member.

Under results management each employee participates in the determining of his own objectives as well as the means by which he hopes to achieve these objectives. Developed within the overall boundaries set forth by his superior, subsequently the objectives and plans for attaining them are discussed by the initiator and his superior, altered if necessary, and finally adopted, if mutually agreed upon. The specific expected results serve as the guides for directing the operations, and also as the standards of performance against which the subordinate is appraised. Following results management tends to make each employee a manager of his own particular work. It diminishes the authoritarian practice of deciding and telling subordinates exactly what to do. The individual has a greater part in his own work decisions and purposes. Results orientation is stressed, activities orientation is minimized. Better management is achieved.

Let us look more closely at the built-in high motivational elements of results management. The employee starts with a self-appraisal of his performances, abilities, and potential. He begins to know better his strengths and weaknesses, to gain confidence in himself, to receive feedback on what he is accomplishing, to know why he is doing what he is, and to be a self-directed and self-improved member. By participating in establishing his own goals, an employee is encouraged to think about his work, to capitalize on his experiences, and to believe in his objectives. In addition, results management motivates from within, the individual has a closer feeling of what the end results should and can be, he senses that he is an important part of getting the work achieved, and he views himself as a vital part of the team effort. All these qualities make for effective management.

THE ZEIGARNIK EFFECT

For results management to be successful, at least some of the employees must have a sense of achievement and sufficient background and experience to formulate and implement objectives intelligently. These requirements are usually met with the higher educational level of people today and their deep desire to be "a part of the action." Another factor, however, must be noted. It is the "Zeigarnik effect" which is a compulsion in some individuals to complete a task or accomplish a given result. A psychologist, B. Zeigarnik, reported her research in 1927 and found that some people have a high Zeigarnik effect, others have a low one.

This is important in results management for it means that the setting of an objective does not result in its achievement unless the person or persons involved have a sufficient compulsion for closure of actions to attain the goal. We require members with a need for achievement and at the start of activities will push the tasks to completion. That is, our demands are for personnel motivated by the Zeigarnik effect; they realize great personal satisfaction from accomplishment of completed tasks. In fact, accomplishments preoccupy them. In contrast, others have weak or very little compulsion to finish work assignments. Activities preoccupy them.

Without a sufficient number of persons having a high Zeigarnik effect, the use of results management, and in fact most participative management programs and practices will prove disappointing. Unless a company has hired or developed managers and employees with high Zeigarnik effects, it will find that the more conventional types of management, emphasizing authoritarian practices should be followed.

DETERMINING OBJECTIVES FOR RESULTS MANAGEMENT

For convenience, either the "top-down" or the "bottom-up" approach can be used in determining objectives for results management. The former is exemplified by the practice of a president of a company who near the end of each year writes his vice presidents asking:

1. What were your outstanding accomplishments during the past twelve months?
2. What major accomplishments do you contemplate during the coming new year?
3. Are these accomplishments measurable? If so, explain how you will measure them.

Similar requests are sent by each vice president to his key people, who in turn do the same, and so on down to the bottom level. The replies form the basis for establishing the objectives. Each superior reviews the replies of his subordinates and working together with them sets pertinent goals with the knowledge, understanding, and acceptance of both superior and subordinates. In turn, each superior consults with his responsible superior and goals are established for this next higher level. The process is repeated for successively higher levels up to the president.

In contrast, the bottom-up approach starts with individuals stating their objectives and submitting them for modification and mutual approval with their respective superior. In turn, each superior consolidates and drafts his objectives and then submits them to his superior for discussion, modification, and mutual approval. The process is continued until the chief executive decides, in counsel with his chief associates, the top or company objectives. Then, these objectives are given to departmental managers who determine their respective departmental objectives that must be achieved to accomplish the overall goal. After approval by the chief executive, the departmental goals become the required objectives of these respective units and the stated accomplishment against which the departmental manager will be measured. In like manner, objectives are established for members at each level throughout the entire enterprise. In establishing the objectives the superior's evaluation of them is quite important. For example, the future period must be specific; the task required to meet the objective must be practical, sufficient, and obtainable; the method of measuring accomplishment must be clearly stated, i.e., in dollars, hours paid, or labor efficiency; and the objectives must be compatible with the overall enterprise plans for the period, i.e., there is a hierarchy of objectives.

QUESTIONS

1. Other than profit, discuss some major objectives that the manager of an enterprise might establish.
2. Point out the major significance between the management of a manager who is results oriented and one who is activities oriented.
3. What is your reaction to the following statement: "Since most managers agree that objectives are essential in management, it is academic to discuss objectives in the typical management course." Why?
4. Distinguish carefully between the two concepts in each of the following pairs: (*a*) profit and bottom-up approach, (*b*) individual objectives and social objectives, and (*c*) a primary objective and a secondary objective.
5. Do statements of objectives supply a manager with clear targets toward which he can direct his efforts? Defend your answer.

6. Relate an experience of your own (or of a friend) which demonstrates that lack of knowing what was to be accomplished resulted in poor management.
7. From your own observations or experience, relate an example of an enterprise showing an ability to update its objectives.
8. Briefly discuss the subject of the hierarchy of objectives and its importance in management.
9. Relate the importance you attach to the harmonizing of objectives in acquiring effective management.
10. Discuss results management indicating what it is, how used, its effectiveness, and whether you favor its use.
11. Discuss the built-in motivational elements of results management.
12. Select three widely separate enterprises, such as a hospital, manufacturing concern, sales agency, hotel, government agency, club, and school, and for each one find out the major managerial objective by communicating with a member of that enterprise. What conclusions do you draw from this experience and also from the information obtained?
13. Discuss the Zeigarnik effect explaining what it is and its importance to the manager.
14. What three criteria for determining or testing objectives would you favor as the manager of the systems and data processing department of a large corporation? Justify your selection.

CASE 3–1. HERBHILL MANUFACTURING COMPANY

At the present time three types of plastic covers are molded (1) A-19, (2) B-12, and (3) C-55. Type A-19 has four metal insert bushings, type B-12 has no bushings, and type C-55 has from 12 to 32 bushings depending upon the individual design. The molding machines are operated by men with a wide range in seniority with the company. The general practice has been to let the men pick the type cover they wanted to make and the machine they wanted to operate. From this the result has been that men with the most seniority mold covers A-19 primarily because they require less finger dexterity. Covers C-55 were molded by experienced molders with good finger dexterity. All covers B-12 are molded by the least seriority members and each operates two machines rather than one machine as is the case with the other molders.

The process manager, All Brazer, suggests that the present floor plan of the molding machines be revised to improve efficiency and reduce cost. Currently there are two rows of machines numbered 1 through 8 on one side and 9 through 18 on the other row. Machines 2, 3, 6, and 7 mold A-19 covers; machines 1, 4, 5, and 8 mold C-55 covers; machines 9 through 18 are used for B-12 covers. Al Brazer wants to locate all machines molding A-19 together in one area and the same for those molding C-55 covers. This will not only streamline the handling of materials to the machines, but will reduce present walking time by the operators in getting material to and from the machines, and also will place the finished covers closer to the in-process banks. He estimates by following his suggestion a savings of $17,400 per year will be realized.

Yesterday at a management meeting, Mr. Brazer's proposal was brought up for discussion. The superintendent of production pointed out that he had talked with the foreman of the molding department and was informed that if adopted, the proposal would greatly disturb the molders. Each one is satisfied with the machine he is working with and its location. There are very few complaints now from this department and he strongly recommends that the floor plan not be disturbed. It was suggested by the personnel manager that the molders be asked their opinions about the proposed change. They might come up with a better idea. In his opinion, if costs can be reduced, they should be. A $17,400 yearly savings should be pursued.

The assistant sales manager added that the projected sales curve for covers showed that type B-12 would be the outstanding seller in the immediate years ahead. It was probable that both A-19 and C-55 would level out at their present sales, although there was no certainty about this. At this point, the president of the company stated that he has been giving serious thought to the company getting out of the plastic cover business. "It doesn't come up to our requirements. The margin is very low and the market extremely competitive. We are losing money on the B-12 type and I favor eliminating that type from our line right away. Greater volume on this won't help us, we'll simply lose more as we manufacture more of them." The assistant sales manager countered that the company should have the B-12 type to satisfy their customers who also purchase the other type covers and wish to deal with one source for covers.

Questions

1. What is the problem of this company?
2. What action do you recommend be taken? Why?

CASE 3–2. ELLIOTT CORPORATION

On the business page of the local newspaper this item appeared:

Elliott Corporation announced today purchase of Dolin Products, Inc. This is the third acquisition completed by Elliott during the past 14 months. Dolin

Products, Inc., one of the largest poultry processors in the south, will increase Elliott's annual sales to nearly $400 million. Terms of the transaction were not disclosed.

A management team from Elliott Corporation consisting of Ray Conklin, general manager, Harry Petroski, personnel manager, and Philip Hutton, vice president of finance, visited the Dolin Products plant to discuss possible future management activities and changes to be made as a result of the acquisition. The official spokesman of Dolin Products was Mr. Victor Wade, general manager. The company had been owned by a family none of whom took an active part in its management. Mr. Wade has managed the company almost entirely by himself. He is a forceful, energetic leader. Resourceful and ambitious, he has shown good profits to its owners who have respected his wishes and have never interfered with his efforts. He receives a good salary plus a percentage of the net profits of the company. He has a reputation for being firm and running "a tight ship," but he is also fair and assumes full responsibility for the plant with little or no "buck passing."

During the visit, members of the Elliott management team stated that in all their plants, results management was used. Excellent achievements were being won. They stated their intention was to use a similar approach here at Dolin Products. A number of committees and meetings were also utilized. It was their firm belief that such actions as these were vital in their past success.

WADE: It won't work here, but of course, you fellows own the plant now and can do what you like.

PETROSKI: Why won't it work here, Mr. Wade?

WADE: It just won't, that's all. You can't turn the management of a plant like this over to them. They just can't handle it. They don't have the know-how and they don't have the experience. And I doubt if they have the interest. I've been in this business for over sixteen years and I know what I'm talking about.

HUTTON: You have an excellent profits record, Mr. Wade. You must be doing many things correctly.

WADE: Well the former owners were always pleased.

PETROSKI: You do have some help in running the plant, don't you?

WADE: Of course, what do you think I am? Superman? A tyrant?

PETROSKI: Oh no. I was interested in how much participation you permit others to have in your organization.

WADE: Suppose it looks like we must work overtime. They are not just told—you're working overtime tonight. We talk it over, if they want to O.K., if they don't, that's all right too. I'd say every employee in this plant is told everything he or she needs to know to do the job they were hired to do. An employee doesn't need to know everything that's going on. That's not what he was hired for.

CONKLIN: Do you have work expectancies or what you expect each employee to accomplish?

WADE: Yes, sir. Yes, sir. We have very fair work standards. You can ask anyone out on the floor and they'll tell you the same thing. We expect them to meet standard; if they don't they are not with us very long. We pay top wages in the community. I get very few gripes. Every employee knows where he stands. He knows what is expected of him and that, gentlemen, is the way to run a business, in my opinion. At least, that's what my granddaddy used to say. Once in awhile we get a troublemaker who isn't satisfied with anything you do. We either set him straight or ask him to leave.

CONKLIN: Do you have many like that?

WADE: No, when we do it is usually a new employee who doesn't like the work or doesn't want to work. We get maybe six or eight like that a year.

HUTTON: Your record of profits intrigues me, Mr. Wade. Yours is an outstanding accomplishment.

WADE: Well, thank you. I can continue to show good profits. This is a good business and we have good employees.

Questions

1. What approach to management are you inclined to support—that of Elliott Corporation or of Dolin Products, Inc.? Why?
2. What is your general evaluation of Mr. Victor Wade?
3. What action do you recommend be taken by the management team of Elliott Corporation? Justify your answer.

4

Schools of
management thought

*To be a success, devote three or four hours a day to being
an executive and the rest of the time to thinking.*
FELIX FRANKFURTER

AS THE INTEREST, need, and importance of management have grown, different major strands of beliefs and viewpoints making up management's development have come into being. This is a normal state of affairs, for any area as vital as management with its involvement in fundamental issues affecting people, philosophy, values, environment, and human wants will attract the attention of scholars and practitioners in such areas as business, economics, psychology, sociology, anthropology, politics, and mathematics. As a result, various schools of management thought—each employing certain beliefs, views, and discipline—have come into existence. To comprehend better the various management thoughts as they exist today, let us briefly review their historical development. This will provide a helpful perspective.

EARLY DEVELOPMENT OF MANAGEMENT THOUGHT

Early civilizations west of Mesopotamia and the writings of the Egyptians extending back to around 1200 B.C. indicate knowledge and use of management for guiding political affairs. Likewise, the history of ancient Greece and that of the Roman Empire gives much evidence of managerial knowledge, especially in the area of courts, operation of government practices, army organization, unity of group efforts, and establishing authority. In addition, throughout the history of Western civilization the church has contributed to the knowledge of management by means of developing a worldwide organization structure and by the effective use of authority in managerial work.

Until about the middle of the 18th century, the people of western Europe used basically the same methods and implements of production that had been used for nearly 20 centuries. Then, within a few decades a series of inventions was discovered, and the whole picture of industrial activity was enormously altered. This new period, commonly referred to as the Industrial Revolution, brought about the greater utilization of machines, the centralization of production activities, the establishment of new employer-employee relationships, and the separation of consumers from producers. Under these new conditions, the customary means of establishing and achieving objectives were not entirely satisfactory. The belief grew that better management must be developed.

A number of men contributed to this movement. For example, Charles Babbage, a professor of mathematics at Cambridge University in England, advocated as early as the first half of the 19th century that accurate data obtained from rigid investigation be utilized in the managing of an enterprise. He wanted work measurement, cost determination, and wage incentives. The following quotation is of interest:

> Babbage found, by visiting many factories in England and France, that manufacturers were wholly unscientific—that most of their work was guesswork. He found, to his great surprise, that factories were run by traditional methods. He discovered that manufacturers made little use of science or mathematics, and that they relied upon old opinions instead of investigations and accurate knowledge.[1]

Frederick W. Taylor (1856–1917) contributed enormously to the fund of management knowledge. He believed a major difficulty was the lack of an expression by managers of what they expected and of the employees knowing and understanding what this expectancy was. The answer to this question was needed: *What constitutes an honest day's work?* If this could be determined, it would serve as a basis of mutual understanding and form a center around which better management could be built. Hence, Taylor conducted extensive studies of all components of production: observing, measuring when possible, and relating the contributions of each component. His was a precise analytic approach of proving or disproving definite hypotheses or assumptions by means of controlled experimentation. His approach was applying the scientific method to management. The result became known as "scien-

---

[1] Herbert N. Casson, *Creative Thinkers* (New York: B. C. Forbes Publishing Co., 1929), p. 180.

tific management." As explained by Taylor, it was based on four principles:

1. The development of the best method. This included the analysis of each job to determine the "one best way" of performing it. The proper method was recorded and followed. The employee was paid on financial incentive basis, being given a higher rate for work above the standard.

2. The selection and development of workmen. This included prescribed selection techniques to determine the right man to do a particular job and training him in the prescribed best method.

3. The relating and bringing together of the best method and the selected and trained workman. It was Taylor's belief that this would cause significant changes in managers' thinking, but nonmanagers would show little resistance primarily because of the greater earnings they would receive.

4. The close cooperation of managers and men. Essentially this included division of work and gave managers the responsibility for the planning and preparation of work.

Henri Fayol, a French contemporary of Taylor, also made valuable contributions to management thought and development. Fayol was a successful industrialist of a steel and coal combine. He was a vital management pioneer in that he made universal generalizations about management based on his keen insight and practical management experience. He provided a broad and inclusive perspective of management and supplied a framework about which management thought could be developed. He was the pioneer of the concept of viewing management as being made up of functions. Although his book, written in French, first appeared in 1916, his contributions were somewhat beclouded until 1949, when the English translation of his book became widely available.

Fayol's efforts dealt with "classical administration" in that the focus was upon the firm as a whole, not upon a single segment of it such as production, the lathe department, or a job within the lathe department, as was the case with scientific management. Also, unlike scientific management, the thinking was more deductive and less inductive. Rationalism and logical consistency were emphasized, but emotional needs and the individual's desire to act responsibly were mostly ignored.

CURRENT DEVELOPMENT OF MANAGEMENT THOUGHT

During the early 1930s, increasing stress was being given to the idea that people are the important consideration in management, that objectives are established and achieved with and through people. Hence, an important concept in the study of management should be human beings, their work environment, and interpersonal relations. These considerations were stressed in the famous Hawthorne studies in the Hawthorne plant of Western Electric and are generally considered the classical initiation of a new development in management thought. The importance of leadership and of human relations was emphasized, and the strong belief developed that the contributions of the behavioral sciences such as psychology and sociology were essential in management study.

This line of thinking has uncovered a rich influence helpful in management efforts. We now realize that human information and human tools are required to solve human problems. A person reacts to an event in terms that the meaning of the event had for him. This, in turn, depends upon his hopes, values, and fears, conditioned mainly by his group and family experiences and the influence of his total work environment including the attitudes, rules, and sentiments making for social stability and acceptance.

About 1950, another approach to management started to win favor. It is the use of mathematics in management or the emphasis given to quantitative methods of analysis. Numerical data had long been used in management, but the application of mathematics and statistics represented a new approach to the subject. These quantitative approaches take many different forms. For example, mathematical symbols and relationships, as exemplified by algebraic equations, can be employed to represent basic relationships of factors bearing on a problem and to solve this problem in terms of selective objectives. In addition, the sampling theory of statistics can be extremely helpful in solving certain types of management problems. Likewise, the theory of probability can be used advantageously in reaching certain managerial decisions.

Other developments have come into the limelight during the past several decades. They include concentration on decision making whereby how the decision is made, who makes it, the environment affecting it, and its implementation are believed of prime importance. Another is to study management by means of the systems approach. In essence the belief here is that for a given entity, all activities are interrelated and can be identified as interdependent systems forming a pattern or network of related activities. By use of these networks, the true meaning and directing of the various work activities are best comprehended and utilized.

SCHOOLS OF MANAGEMENT THOUGHT

From these various developments of management study have evolved different thought patterns about management. Today there are a number of schools of management thought. Included here and probably of greatest significance are the following: (1) management by custom school, (2) scientific management school, (3) human behavior school, (4) social system school, (5) systems management school, (6) decisional management school, (7) quantitative measurement school, and (8) management process school. To some degree the names are self-explanatory. Some are relatively broad in their scope; others tend to relatively specialized areas. Some are closely related; others have little relationship among them. Some tend to elaborate or extend further the developments of previously held concepts; others take basic portions of different schools and along with new core ideas weave a composite new approach, while still others strike out in new directions, employing entirely different concepts and tools.

A cursory review of these various schools reveals that they place emphasis upon different values and beliefs, but in some instances they provide confirmation of a particular concept as representing truth by revealing identical results, or nearly so, as those obtained when different viewpoints are followed. On the other hand, some of the schools can give rise to controversy about a particular management practice. However, the similarities or the differences, as the case might be, seem analogous to the well-known story of the three blind men describing the elephant. Each related what he believed the elephant was like. Likewise, each school's advocates are viewing management as they conceive it to be. The perfection or shortcoming might be in their conception of total management.

MANAGEMENT BY CUSTOM SCHOOL

Some believe that current managerial tasks should basically be thought of and performed in the manner similar to those of the recent past. That is, the management is guided by custom or tradition. The line of thought adopted and the securing of information believed needed and its handling are obtained by reviewing what was done in the past by managers under similar circumstances. "How would my predecessor have solved such a problem?" is a typical approach used in the custom school. It is also exemplified by observing what leading

managers are doing in circumstances similar to yours and then following this example by applying the same techniques and actions in your
managerial work. Sometimes this school is called the empirical school
because it contributes generalizations and masses of practical management information. Normally this is written in a descriptive or even
narrative form and is structured around a given core idea.

The management by custom school includes the studies of the biog-
raphies of outstanding managers and the studies of the histories of
phenomenal companies. Answers to what objectives were sought, what
practices did the managers follow, and what results were achieved are
made and these serve to build a fund of knowledge for the practicing
manager to apply. In addition, certain elements of the case study approach suggest use of the custom approach, but definitely not the
exclusive approach. A case study is a written description of a company's
situation presumably requiring managerial action. The situation is
analyzed, key issues discussed, significant relations revealed, and finally
a recommended solution is evolved. The case study approach helps develop skill in problem determination and in analytical ability. It also
suggests that if a manager is faced with an actual situation closely
resembling the one described and discussed, his best recommendation
and solution may well be the one developed for the case study. To this
degree it can be considered to promote use of the custom management
school.[2]

Favorable results are obtained by following the custom school. It is
practiced by current managers, chiefly because it is simple, gives a feeling of assurance, and keeps a manager informed on activities outside
his enterprise. Detailed information on progress in other firms can be
of considerable help in solving managerial problems. It maintains the
customary way of performing managerial tasks. In fact, in a very real
sense, the chief implication may well be to maintain the status quo,
don't disturb things, and continue to manage the enterprise through
the same means it always has been managed. That, in the mind of the
custom manager, is the safest and surest key to managerial stability
and success.

Little effort is made to blaze new trails. Anything different that is
tried out is not too far removed from the traditional dictates. This
means that mediocre results are commonly obtained. Not even the best
of tradition or what others are doing is assured. What the leader or the

---

[2] See also case study discussion in Chapter 6, p. 107.

majority practice cannot always be evaluated as best for an individual concern. What fits one enterprise might not fit another at all, and comparing past management issues with those of the present and future can be questionable. But critical examination of what other managers have done and careful evaluation of it can be of assistance. Few deny that disseminations by "old pros" of how they handled difficult managerial problems can be extremely helpful.

SCIENTIFIC MANAGEMENT SCHOOL

The chief characteristic of this school is the use of the scientific method to discover new knowledge about management. This method can be described as one of controlled experimentation. It is made up of well-defined steps which must be followed in proper sequence. Briefly stated, the scientific method confirms or disproves a proposition. The experiment or test is conducted under carefully controlled conditions. While the experiment is being carried out, observations are made and records maintained to indicate precisely the what, when, and how of all happenings included within the experiment. The data are then sorted into common groups, or classified, in order to expedite their interpretation. From the classified data, carefully worded statements are made which constitute the answer to the originally posed proposition. The definite steps in the scientific method are shown in Figure 4–1.

The scientific method can be viewed as an attitude to be taken toward problems, or an instrument by means of which answers based on effective factual data are obtained. The essence of the scientific management school is the development of the inquiring mind with the resultant intelligent searching for more knowledge, more facts, and more relationships. Imagination, originality, and an ability to think up new ideas are required. The derived tentative solution is directly influenced by the ingenuity and adroitness of the scientific person, and considerable resourcefulness is utilized in carrying out the various steps.

The scientific manager strives to discover causal relationships—that is, in the knowledge that certain things when present or taking place are accompanied causally by other things which are present or will take place. This should not be confused with the identity of the cause and of the effect. All causes result from effects; and vice versa, effects result from causes. To isolate either cause or effect ultimately resolves into thinking in circles, for cause and effect are inseparably related. Furthermore, the scientific manager knows there is little practical value attached to cause or to effect information; the valid, useful knowledge

FIGURE 4–1. The steps of the scientific method

1. *Identify the proposition.* This defines the objective and points the entire investigation to a specific goal.
2. *Acquire preliminary observations about the proposition.* This is exploratory, supplies acquaintance with existent knowledge, and provides helpful background material.
3. *State tentative solution to proposition.* The hypothesis, so stated, will be confirmed or disproved by controlled experimentation. All factors affecting the proposition will be kept constant throughout the test, except one factor which, permitted to vary, will reveal its relationship to the proposition. Considerable creativity is required to formulate the tentative solution by thinking beyond what is presently available. Also, history reveals that many major discoveries result from seeking the answer to one proposition and winding up with an unexpected answer to another proposition.
4. *Investigate the proposition thoroughly, using both current knowledge and controlled experiments.* The degree of relationship, or total lack of it, between the data and the tentative solution is sought. Used are both analysis and synthesis. Analysis means to break down the entity into its components and examine each component by itself and also in relation to its remaining components. Synthesis means to combine, build up, or put together the various entities being considered. In addition, controlled experiments are set up to provide data on the specific proposition under discussion. Sufficient tests must be run to establish consistency of results.
5. *Classify data obtained.* Classification expedites the handling of data. The classes selected depend upon the proposition and its tentative answer. For example, data on published books can be classified by publisher, size, or subject. For a manufacturer of bookcases, the size of book would be the most meaningful, whereas for a library, the subject would be selected.
6. *State tentative answer to proposition.* This is accomplished by careful interpretation of the classified data. For this purpose, two types of reasoning are used: (*a*) inductive reasoning and (*b*) deductive reasoning. The former is reasoning from the results of a relatively few but adequate parts, in this case tests, to the probable results of many tests concerning the same phenomenon. In contrast, deductive reasoning is reasoning from the truth of an entirety, revealed by many tests, to a portion or segment of that entity.
7. *Adjust and state answer to proposition.* To help insure validity and completeness, the tentative answer is tried out under the prescribed conditions and the results are noted. If needed, the answer is adjusted and then clearly stated, care being taken to relate it to the originally stated proposition of step No. 1.

is relationships and this knowledge is supplied through application of the scientific method.

The scientific management school has contributed tremendous management knowledge to mankind. Its value, however, is not confined to its own school, for its line of thought can be and is used in other schools of management, notably in the human behavior, social system, and process schools. Success for the scientific manager necessitates a propensity for progress; there is a constant seeking to improve the managerial work. Informed advocates of scientific management firmly believe better management is possible and seek to find it but realize that it is never permanently attained because the continuous new knowledge paves the way for constant improvement. Scientific management enjoys wide usage but is by no means universal.

PRINCIPLE OF SCIENTIFIC MANAGEMENT

The use of thorough investigation, controlled experimentation, and careful interpretation of the resultant data provides a reliable basis for the determination and evaluation of new facts used by managers.

PRINCIPLE OF ANALYSIS AND SYNTHESIS

Segregating a problem into its components and, in contrast, combining various entities under consideration assist in identifying and in establishing the relative importance of each factor of that problem.

HUMAN BEHAVIOR SCHOOL OF MANAGEMENT

Important in the belief of this school is that the focal point of managerial action is the behavior of the human being and human beings. What is achieved, how it is achieved, and why it is achieved is viewed in relation to its impact and influence upon people who, it is believed, are the really important entity of management. Followers of this school say, "Management does not do; it gets others to do." Voluminous writings of this school show the need for the manager to use the best human relations practices. Among the more common topics are human relations, motivation, leadership, training, and communication.

This school is a development from the application of the behavioral sciences, especially psychology and social psychology, to management. The individual is viewed as a sociopsychological being, and the question facing the manager ranges from understanding and securing the best efforts from an employee by satisfying his psychological needs to comprehending the whole gamut of psychological behavior of groups as representing the totality of management.

Figure 4–2 illustrates the pragmatic concepts of psychology widely used in the human behavior school. Both clinical and experimental approaches are used in order to discover new avenues of learning, motivating, adjusting, and achieving.

Significant contributions by this school have been made; for example, the emphasis upon the use of participation and the ways to handle organization conflict. Also this school gives greater recognition to the influence of the environment and constraints affecting behavior. This has led to fruitful discoveries regarding the needs and motivations of men at work, the use of authority, the importance of irrationality in people's behavior, and the informal relationships existing within a work environment. On the other hand, one might ask whether the field of human behavior is inclusive to or covers the entire area of management. Perhaps, in addition to insight into human behavior, knowledge of things exemplified by technology, machines, and buildings is helpful in determining and achieving objectives beneficial to mankind.

FIGURE 4–2

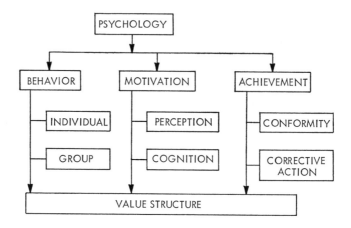

THE SOCIAL SYSTEM SCHOOL

This approach views management as a social system or, what is more specific, as a system of cultural interrelationships. This school is sociologically oriented and deals with identifying the various social groups as well as their cultural relationships and, in addition, integrating these groups into a complete social system. Both the social system school and the human behavior school stem from the development of behavioral sciences applied to management.

Fundamental to most of the social system school's belief is the need to solve through cooperation the various limitations which man and his environs may have. Many followers of this school utilize the concept of a social unit and consider it ideally as one in which people communicate effectively with each other and willingly contribute toward achievement of a common goal. In many cases, constraints are those of a single enterprise and hence the name, organization-behavior, to designate this approach has come into common use. The social system, however, need not be confined to a single enterprise. Sometimes the consideration is for a large segment of society, or even the entire social entity. When this is done, the school is ecologically influenced in that it is concerned with the relationships among (1) the organization, (2) the internal and external environment, and (3) forces bringing about change and adjustments. Some students of management believe there is an ecological school of management thought. It begins with basic units—customers, students, soldiers—and then adds the elements of operations required to accomplish the goals. Such a school has interesting possibilities but as yet is not prominent.

It is generally recognized that an ideal social system is a long-sought, probably never attained, goal. Ordinarily a social system develops conflicts, cohesions, and interactions among its members. There are group feelings, perceptions, and identifications as well as culturally patterned responses, all of which makes for problems of power control and reconciliation of interests. These forces are neither confined to formal leadership, organization relationships, and group reactions, nor to forces within the particular system. But they are conditioned by informal organization—the leadership and group relationships coming into being as a result of social forces which can help or hinder the official or formal purposes. In addition, activities within the system are affected by social forces outside that social system, for example, by members of a community that are not employees of the enterprise, such as trade unions and government agencies. Furthermore, consideration for ethics, or what is morally right, is brought to light by the social system school. While personal conduct and moral duty are just that—personal— nevertheless it becomes meaningful in relationship to a group or groups, and it is greatly group-influenced. Ethics of a manager cannot be confined to his personal activities; what he does affects more than his personal life.

Figure 4–3 shows the integrated concepts of sociology as currently applied to management. As indicated in the figure, sociology, or the study of the human habitat in a social society, affects organization structure, the community, and interactions among institutions of a society. These, in turn, can be divided into subunits helpful in managerial study. For example, organization structure is divided into formal and informal structures.

The social system school stresses the interaction and cooperation of people making up a social system. It utilizes nonrational as well as rational organization behavior and the development of understanding based on empirical investigations. Advocated is the attainment of cooperative relationships among the members of the organization. The decision reached should be in keeping with what has been termed the "balanced best interests" of the group. This means that the course of action should not be based on the wants and desires of one group alone, but should reflect the interests of all parties. The thesis is that an enterprise is likely to prosper most if it recognizes the social demands of the society in which it is operating.

FIGURE 4–3

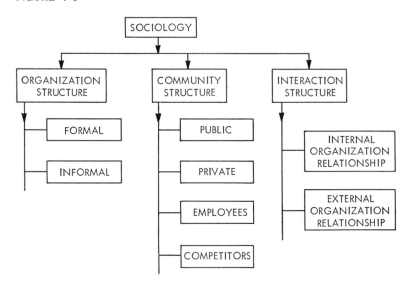

SYSTEMS MANAGEMENT SCHOOL

As suggested by its name, systems are the focal parts around which this school of management is built. A system can be thought of as an organized whole made up of parts connected in some fashion and directed to some purpose. That is, the parts are not a hit-or-miss conglomeration of separate elements but are of a definite order characterized by organization and unity. Systems are basic to most activities. Analysis reveals that an activity is in reality the result of many other subactivities, and in turn, these subactivities of many sub-subactivities. To illustrate, the activities of the human body can be considered a system and a result of many subsystems, including the digestive system, the circulatory system, and the nervous system. In turn, each of these result from lesser subsystems, for example, the digestive system from the food mastication system, stomach system, and intestinal system.

A manager must operate systems that are quite complex, but these systems offer an effective vehicle of thought. Each system has an input, a process, and an output, and is a self-contained unit, but it is also related to a system of a wider and higher order as well as to its own subsystems that represent the integration of several systems of the lower order. Thinking in terms of systems simplifies, to some degree, the conception of the multitudinous activities with which a manager must work, and it also enables the manager to see better the nature of the complex problems that he faces. Developing a systematic framework for describing relationships of the empirical world dealing with management is the concern of the systems school. This leads logically to the evolving of interdisciplinary knowledge and emphasizes the inter-relationships of formerly isolated disciplines. If management draws from and is affected by such disciplines as economics, engineering, psychology, sociology, and anthropology, then the systems followers claim their approach is proper and that it is feasible to blend these contributions into a unity that is both correct and meaningful.

An enterprise is looked upon as a man-made system, the internal parts of which work together to achieve established goals, the external parts to achieve interplay with its environment, including customers, the general public, suppliers, and government. The manager integrates his available facilities toward goal achievement by means of systems which relate needed activities required for the end result. The systems serve as the media through which the manager operates. For example, American Motors Corporation, a pioneer of the systems approach, uses a physical distribution system for managing materials usage and movement from the time raw materials are received until they are delivered to the customer. Profits can be maximized through daily tradeoffs such as using more air freight, but offsetting its higher cost by lowering inventory cost. The inclusiveness of the systems approach makes such a gain feasible. In contrast, separate decisions by the transportation manager and by the inventory control manager may negate this possible advantage.

The systems school violates the traditional departmentation by function, i.e., by production, sales, and finance. Systems cut across departmental lines and relates activities in a heretofore unorthodox manner. The organization is designed in keeping with its individual systems requirements. Figure 4–4 offers a suggestion along this line. The president has an executive committee which, upon advice and information from product, market, and finance research, decides what products or services the enterprise will provide. Wtih this established, the system to produce and sell the output is designed by the Systems Design Unit which takes into account the constraints, policies, and practices to be followed. Next, the allocation of resources is worked out, by the group with the same name, as required by the major systems to be followed.

It is then turned over to the Operations Group and assigned to either the Major Product Systems or Facilitating Systems subgroups. The latter includes those organized to produce a service or an assistance necessary in carrying out the major system. That is, facilitating helps the major products group do its work.

FIGURE 4–4. Systems management organization chart

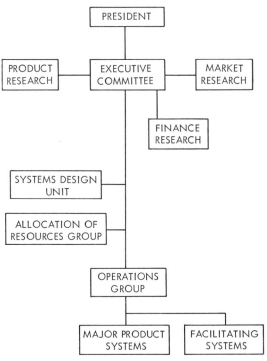

Systems management implementation is assisted by the use of the computer. Masses of data can be processed to help determine the relationships among various parts and the change brought about in one part due to a change in another. Such information has great value even though the system design itself is the creation of the human mind. Also, it should be added that systems management enables a manager to use broad concepts; to envision wide, sweeping areas; and to push back the constraints. The "big picture" is emphasized. In turn, this emits more meaningful and inclusive relationships, revealing more precisely how the various parts act and react to bring out designated actions. To illustrate, large engineering projects such as those for a building complex, for missiles, and for spacecrafts are quite complex but can be handled by integrating the several systems and subsystems of the total system. The problems of production and reliability for each component pose special hurdles in themselves; yet the bringing together of all these components and the successful performance of the particular product must be properly integrated with all other products of the total system. In spacecraft, for example, the craft itself, the tracking system, the ground facilities, and the operating personnel must function as an integrated unit.

DECISIONAL MANAGEMENT SCHOOL

Focus here is upon the managerial decisions. This, claim the followers of this school, is the real job of the manager. The decision of what to achieve and how to achieve it are the vital characteristics and challenges of the manager. The decision maker is the manager. The approach is sometimes limited to the economic rationale of the marginal utility and economic behaviors under uncertainities. In other instances, the area of consideration is broadened to include any event that takes place within the enterprise or any impact from the outside which in some direct or indirect way might influence the decision reached. The problem, risks, and predicted outcome of each alternative are customarily followed. In its early stages, the preponderance of work was on efforts performed to evaluate alternatives. Today, this is no longer true.

Almost all human activity is now considered legitimate for a decision-making study. To illustrate, decisional adherents have grappled with decisions pertaining to the diagnosis and the resulting prescriptions for improving communication, incentives, reactions of the individual to a group, and the analysis of human values with respect to stated objectives. In these efforts, the school has widened its interest and influence. It appears that it cannot be considered a specialized treatment and concentration on decision making as such but is more of an examination of the entire enterprise via the decision-making approach. This trend is plausible since decision making is vital in management.

Decision making is a part of every school of management thought. That it is vital in management there can be no question. However, the query can be made whether decision making alone is the proper and best medium for the understanding and application of management. In a given case, what decision-making basis includes all the important aspects of the issue to be decided? Furthermore, does the decision finalize the sought action or does it commence the action? If the latter, the means for implementation must be determined. Many believe that a managerial decision includes not only what to do but how and when to do it as well. Also, like some of the other management schools, the decisional school cuts across traditional boundaries of the segments of an organization. The inclusive factors to be resolved by the decision can be quite diverse. In modern management, decision conceptualization is neither confined to a limited area nor is it determined by a simple exercise in common sense.

THE QUANTITATIVE MEASUREMENT SCHOOL

This school includes those who see management as a logical entity, the actions of which can be expressed in terms of mathematical symbols, relationships, and measurable data. It is important to state that this school is primarily concerned with decision making. The techniques followed are ultimately for this purpose.

The quantitative measurement school has great usefulness. It forces the user to define precisely his objectives, problem, and problem area. In addition, orderly thinking, logical methodology, and recognition of definite constraints are encouraged. There is no doubt that it supplies a powerful tool for solving complex problems and has influenced the rearrangement of information sources to provide more meaningful quantitative data. The approach is especially effective when applied to the measurable physical problems of management—such as inventory, material, and production control—rather than to problems where measurement is difficult such as for human behavior. It is important to know what is being measured. Risk is not eliminated by use of this approach, but assistance is provided to enable a manager to assume the correct risk.

Two characteristics feature the quantitative school: (1) optimizing input-output, and (2) the use of mathematical models. By optimizing is meant that which within current knowledge is desirable for a selected factor being chosen from an entirety such as an entire organization, department, or work group; any alternative would be less desirable. When viewing this entirety, a manager is normally interested in optimizing a certain sought quantity or a selected factor. Usually optimizing is a condition of either maximizing or minimizing a definite factor related to the entirety's operations. Maximizing is usually associated with sales, gross margin, machine utilization, or productivity. In contrast, minimizing is typical of costs or inventory, i.e., to seek a minimum amount.

The entirety selected represents the total operations within which the quantitative approach will be used. This practice has advantages in that it (1) makes for decisions for the entirety, not for just a segment of it, (2) recognizes the impact of decisions on the various components, and (3) promotes concentration of managerial efforts on vital areas rather than spreading such efforts too thinly.

Commonly the optimizing is sought from the viewpoint of an entire enterprise. Actually this is a fleeting ideal. It means that all resources must be combined in exactly the correct balance and that this balance be maintained. The complexity of the operations and their dynamics make enterprise optimization extremely difficult. To overcome this, an approach called suboptimization is used. Here the attempt is made to consider a specific portion of the entire enterprise and to determine the conditions necessary to optimize this portion. The common portions of most enterprises are (1) input, (2) process, and (3) output. Common to each of these portions is inventory consisting, in the case of production, of (1) raw materials being received, (2) materials processed, and (3) products finished.

Suppose our objective is to maximize production profits. To achieve this we optimize production. To this end, we suboptimize input, process, and output. Step number one: input, or raw materials being received, can be suboptimized and will depend upon forecast demand, inventory carrying cost, and ordering processing cost. Likewise, step number two: process, or materials processed, can be suboptimized independently by adequate consideration to production capacity, machine setup cost, and processing cost for each product. Lastly, number three: suboptimization of output, or products finished, is obtained by considering product demand and transportation cost. Thus by suboptimization of the production components, optimization of production is approached. The result is not a certainty because of inventory costs, but satisfactory results can be determined quite accurately.

Use of a mathematical model makes the optimizing work feasible. A mathematical model can be defined as an abstract presentation of symbolic character showing all pertinent factors quantitatively and reflecting the relative influence of each factor upon the entire situation represented and the impact of a change in any one, or group, of the factors upon the remaining factors and upon the total. The mathematical model can be a single equation or a series of equations, depending upon the complexity and number of factors involved. If in a given problem there are, say, ten different factors, each of a different weight and each differently related to the remaining nine factors, the mathematical model can be quite complicated.

Different alternatives can be determined from the mathematical model by calculations based on quantitative evaluation of the factors and of their group interactions. As noted above, commonly sought is optimization in relation to a selected factor or factors included in the model. For this work, calculus, a fundamental branch of mathematics, is employed.

Calculus determines the rate of change of one factor with respect to another factor and is based on the concept of dependency of one factor upon the other factor, or factors. In mathematical parlance one factor is designated as the dependent variable, the other the independent variable. Thus, through calculus, we can calculate the rate of change in a dependent variable in relation to a change in an independent variable. The point at which this rate of change is zero represents either a maximization or a minimization in the relationships of the two variables for the following reason. If the rate of change is a positive amount, the relationship is increasing at that point; if negative, the opposite is true. When the change is neither positive or negative, i.e., is zero, the rate of change has ceased at that point; so it must represent either a maximum or a minimum in the relationship between the dependent variable and the independent variable.

ILLUSTRATION OF MATHEMATICAL MODEL

A simple illustration will prove helpful. Assume we have created the mathematical model in the form of a single equation:

$$Y = 15X - \tfrac{3}{2}X^2 \tag{1}$$

where Y is gross profits and X is the number of different products handled. This equation says that the gross profits, Y, are equal to 15 times the number of products handled, $15X$, less $\tfrac{3}{2}$ times the number of products handled squared (or multiplied by itself, i.e., X times X equals X^2) making the total expression, $\tfrac{3}{2}X^2$. Gross profits, Y, are dependent upon number of products handled, X, and this relationship is represented by the equation (1) above.

What happens to Y when there are changes in X? We can calculate a table of values showing the answer by substituting values for X in Eq. (1) and solving for respective values of Y. Starting with X equal to zero, or no products, we have, by substituting in the equation, the values of Y, the gross profits,

$$Y = 15 \times 0 - \tfrac{3}{2} \times 0 \times 0$$

or

$$Y = 0$$

When $X = 1$,

$$Y = 15 \times 1 - \tfrac{3}{2} \times 1 \times 1$$
$$Y = 13.5$$

Continuing when X equals 2, and so forth, we can determine the following table of values for X and Y:

X	0	1	2	3	4	5	6	7	8	9	10
Y	0	13.5	24.0	31.5	36.0	37.5	36.0	31.5	24.0	13.5	0

Figure 4–5 shows these values in graphic form. Observe that when X

FIGURE 4–5. Graphic representation of equation, $Y = 15X - \tfrac{3}{2}X^2$

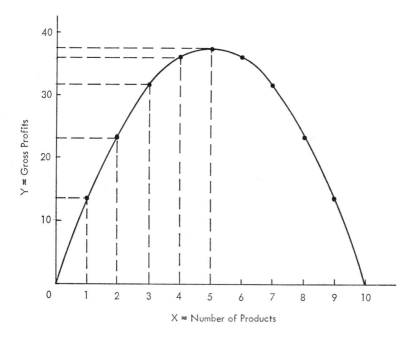

$Y =$ Gross Profits

$X =$ Number of Products

equals 5, the maximum value of Y is obtained, or stated differently, gross profits are maximized when the number of different products handled equals 5.

The same information can be found more easily and quickly using calculus.

$$Y = 15X - \tfrac{3}{2}X^2 \tag{1}$$

The rate of change of Y with respect to X, expressed as dY/dX, is

$$dY/dX = 15 - 3X \tag{2}$$

Equating this rate of change to zero for optimization, the equation becomes

$$0 = 15 - 3X \tag{3}$$

or

$$X = 5$$

The transition from Equation (1) to Equation (2) above represents the use of calculus. It is not our purpose here to present all the details of calculus, but inclusion of several general rules to aid in understanding are given in Figure 4–6.

FIGURE 4–6. Some general, helpful rules for determining derivatives as used in calculus

1. The derivative of one variable is equal to its exponent times the variable to the exponent of one less than the initial exponent.

   Example 1: $Y = X^2$
   $dY/dX = 2$ times X^1
   $\quad\quad\quad = 2X$

   Example 2: $Y = X$
   $dY/dX = 1$ times X^0
   $\quad\quad\quad = 1$ (Any variable with the exponent of 0 is equal to 1.)

2. The derivative of a sum of variables is the sum of its derivatives.

   Example 3: $Y = X^4 + X^3 - X^2$
   $\quad\quad\quad\quad dY/dX = 4X^3 + 3X^2 - 2X^1$

3. The derivative of any constant is zero.

   Example 4: $Y = X^2 + 2$
   $\quad\quad\quad\quad dY/dX = 2X^1 + 0$
   $\quad\quad\quad\quad\quad\quad = 2X$

4. The derivative of a variable dependent upon several independent variables is the derivative of the dependent variable to the first independent variable, and the derivative of the dependent variable to the second independent variable, etc., considering, for each derivative, all independent variables as constants except the one being derived.

   Example 5: $Y = 3X^3 + 2R + 4$
   $\quad\quad\quad\quad dY/dX = 9X^2 + 0 + 0$
   $\quad\quad\quad\quad\quad\quad = 9X^2$
   $\quad\quad\quad\quad dX/dR = 0 + 2 + 0$
   $\quad\quad\quad\quad\quad\quad = 2$

MODELS AND MANAGEMENT

Mathematical models are abstract concepts and they do not and cannot depict reality wholly and precisely. They are limited by factors that are interrelated and can be quantified, i.e., are measurable. In essence they reveal that these factors, interacting in this relationship, can bring about these alternative results. As such, the derived alternatives can be evaluated and predetermined without actually experimenting with various combinations of the real factors on a trial-and-error basis.

The building of the model requires much ingenuity and complete understanding of the problem—what constraints must be observed, what factors must be considered, and how the factors are related. The processing of the model is a technical task, albeit a very important one. In extremely complicated cases the computer can be used. Also, it should be noted that the results must be interpreted in relation to the problem.

In addition to mathematical models used in management, there are also graphs, charts, special formats such as rows and columns of matrix algebra, and physical models. Physical models have been popular with engineers and designers for years. Accurate models of new aircraft designs tested in wind tunnels are examples of physical models used by the aerodynamicist.

MANAGEMENT PROCESS SCHOOL

To complete the presentation of the various important schools of management thought, brief comments about the management process schools will now be made. This school provides the framework for the structuring of this entire book and is fully discussed in the following chapter along with the justifications for using it as the core for both the effective study and the comprehensive presentation of basic modern management.

Followers of the management process school view management as the performance of certain activities or basic management functions that constitute a process. Emphasized are the visualization and determination of all proposed managerial actions, the effective utilization of people working in groups, helping people to be satisfied members of a satisfied work group, and the applying of periodic checkups to insure stated goals are being accomplished.

The management process is broad in scope. It regards the management process as universal. Recognition is given to differences among enterprises and levels, but fundamentally the identity of the manager's work—performing the management process—is always present. This school draws from those with long experience in management, and the information gained in this experience is codified by management fundamental functions in order to provide a helpful and orderly framework for management thought. In addition, pertinent and helpful knowledge is utilized from different sciences in order to supply a thoroughly comprehensive and modern means for stimulating progress and study of management.

QUESTIONS

1. Relate your understanding of the custom school of management, being careful to point out its favorable features as well as its shortcomings.
2. What are the significant differences in the contributions to management thought by each of the following pairs: (*a*) Frederick W. Taylor and Henri Fayol, and (*b*) Hawthorne studies and the use of mathematics in management.
3. A 12-year-old boy asks you what is meant by the systems management school. Outline your answer.
4. Identify each of the following fully: (*a*) optimization, (*b*) scientific management, (*c*) mathematical model, and (*d*) hypothesis of scientific method.
5. Comment fully on the following: "In the highest and most thorough type of application of quantitative measurements to management, a manager is able to eliminate risk. It is for this reason that quantitative measurements have found favor in the management field."
6. Is Frederick W. Taylor's thesis to determine the "one best way" to perform a job obsoleted by the use of results management? Why?
7. Briefly relate the pattern of thought employed by members of the social system school of management.
8. George Munson, now 52 years of age, has followed custom management in his job as production manager for a long time. He states that he is not against any of the other and more recent approaches but clings to custom management because he is achieving his objectives very satisfactorily by its use. Do you feel that George Munson should change to any other school of management? Why?
9. Assume you have just been appointed general manager of a motel. How would you apply systems management to your new job? Repeat the question using scientific management.
10. Draw the graphic representation of the equation $Y = (7 - X)^2 + 1$.
11. As an advocate of the human behavior school of management, how would you justify your favoring this approach?
12. Explain Figure 4–3 in your own words.
13. Visit the manager of a well-known enterprise located near your home.

Find out what school of management he follows and his reasons for doing so. What conclusions do you draw from your interview?

14. Discuss the use and limitations of mathematical models in management.

CASE 4–1. CREEDS OF MANAGERS

The managers of various companies, institutions, and organizations have formulated management creeds intended to set forth the purpose, philosophy, internal environment, and guides helpful in carrying out their managerial tasks. Following are excerpts from three such creeds.

Company A. We believe that everyone—manager, nonmanager, vendor, customer, and stockholder—should have the opportunity to benefit from their contact with our company. Our leadership and positive direction contribute to the basic spirit behind our operation. Proper rewards go to all who have any part in the development of the company. We maintain written descriptions of each job, yet we strive to avoid limiting a person's initiative to a circumscribed area. We have profit goals, but they are strictly in accordance with standards of quality and integrity. Basically our philosophy can be expressed in two words, *mutual benefit.* We endoctrinate our personnel to accomplish this belief. We expect our managers to manage in keeping with this basic premise. Of course, anyone with different ideas is expected to bring them to the attention of appropriate people in our company.

Company B. Our objective is to manufacture and sell products useful to society so that each member of society can enjoy a worthwhile living and benefit mankind. For our efforts we expect an adequate return. Public acceptance is not measured in terms of what people want, but by what is satisfactory for each individual and for each group from the viewpoint of all mankind. Results through measurement of performance is mandatory. All factors of management should be measured even though some may require a rather flexible measuring unit. Every employee is encouraged to speak out on any subject that concerns the company's welfare. We believe every employee should strive to be a good corporate citizen assuming his or her full responsibility in the communities in which we operate.

Company C. Our company is a living enterprise existing to perform a needed service. We exist for the benefit of employees, customers, owners, and the public and its interests, rights, and obligations are inseparable. Each employee strives for a high degree of competence and performance in his job and to attain a high order of corporate citizenship. Our greatest assets are human assets and we encourage progress, by keeping each employee fully informed, developed, and properly assigned in order that his life and work is given mutually recognized meaning, dignity, satisfaction, and purpose. These goals are, in our opinion, won in large measure by the manager managing his group's efforts, being a good listener, making constructive suggestions, giving praises when due, and promoting qualified existing personnel whenever the opportunity is present. We limit our sales of products not produced by us to 20 percent of our total sales. We strive for a net profit of 11 percent of sales. As an overall guide, we ask ourselves these two questions: Is is fair to all concerned? Will it benefit all concerned?

Questions

1. What thoughts or content appear to be common to all three creeds?
2. Which of the three creeds do you prefer? Discuss.
3. For each company, using its creed as a base, suggest the school or schools of management which the company probably follows.
4. Which company would you prefer to work for? Why?

5

The modified process approach

Prejudice is a mist which in our journey through the world often dims the brightest and obscures the best of all the good and glorious objects that meet us on our way.

SHAFTSBURY

IN PREVIOUS PAGES of this book, management has been called an activity. It consists of what a manager does to qualify as a manager. What a manager does is distinct and is made up of several fundamental activities that constitute a unique process—the management process. Those who view the management process as the essential core of their management thinking constitute the management process school. Attention is now directed to a detailed discussion of this management process followed by certain recommended modifications resulting in the modified process approach to management study.

To begin, such pertinent questions as the following will be posed: What specific activity or activities does a manager perform? What is the significance of this activity or activities in the affairs of men? What is common about the managerial work of a production manager, a sales manager, a dean of a college, a hospital manager, and the squadron commander of an air force unit? What beliefs, attitudes, and thought patterns are encompassed in the management process school?

THE FUNDAMENTAL FUNCTIONS OF MANAGEMENT

Assume a manager and a group of employees. The very first thing to be decided is what objectives are to be accomplished. As indicated in

Chapter 3, this may be decided in a number of ways including by the top manager himself, by the top manager with his top associates, or by participation in decision making as exemplified by the results management approach. With the objectives established, the next step is to accomplish them. The initial task is to decide what work needs to be done, when and how it will be done, what the necessary work components should be, the contributions of each such component, and the manner of accomplishing them. In essence, a plan or a predetermined integrated pattern of future activities is drawn up. This requires an ability to foresee, to visualize, to look ahead purposefully. In short, *planning* is necessary. This is a fundamental function of management.

The direction and makeup of action having been determined, the next step, in order to accomplish the work, is to distribute or allocate the necessary component activities among the members of the group. This distribution is guided by consideration for such things as the nature of the component activities, the people of the group, and the physical facilities available. These component activities are grouped and assigned so that accomplishment with minimum expenditure or maximum employee work satisfaction is attained, or in accordance with some similar worthwhile endeavor. Should the group be deficient in either number or quality of necessary management members, such members are secured. Each member assigned to a component activity is faced with the situation of his relation to his group and that of his group to other groups of the enterprise. Typical are the questions of who decides what issues and when? This work of task-allocating and relationship-establishing and relationship-maintaining by the manager is known as *organizing*. It may be thought of as making the plan, created by the manager, meaningful to each member of the group. Organizing is a fundamental function of management.

To carry out physically the activities resulting from the planning and organizing steps, it is necessary for the manager to take measures that will start and continue actions as long as they are needed in order to accomplish the task by the members of the group. The measures selected will depend upon the particular members of the group, the component activity to be done, and the manager's judgment. Among the more common measures utilized by the manager to put the group into action will be leading, developing managers, instructing, helping members to improve themselves and their work through their own creativity, and compensating. This work is referred to as *actuating*. It is a fundamental function of management. The word actuate means literally "move to action," and its use is thus appropriate for this managerial function that deals with either the supplying of stimulative power to the group members or maintaining a work environment within which the members want to perform their best.

Managers have always found it desirable to check up or follow up what is being done in order to make sure that the work of others is progressing satisfactorily toward the predetermined objective. The establishing of a sound plan, the allotting of component activities required by this plan, and the successful actuating of each member do not assure that the undertaking will be a success. Discrepancies, imponderables, misunderstandings, and unexpected hindrances may arise. Such contingencies must be known quickly to the manager so that corrective action may be taken. Answers are sought to the questions: How well should the work be done? How well is it being done? This function by the manager constitutes *controlling*. It is a fundamental function of management. The actual performance is usually evaluated by comparing accomplishment with a standard or established base line of reference. Corrective action might consist of any or all of the following: changing the means of actuating one or more of the group members, reassigning component duties, adjusting the relationships among the group members, altering the managerial plan, and modifying the objectives.

THE PROCESS OF MANAGEMENT

These four fundamental functions of management—planning, organizing, actuating, and controlling—constitute the process of management. They are the means by which a manager manages. They are the distinguishing marks between a manager and a nonmanager.

A summary statement of these fundamental functions of management can be presented as (1) *planning* to determine the objectives and the courses of action to be followed, (2) *organizing* to distribute the work among the group and to establish and recognize needed relationships and authority, (3) *actuating* the members of the group to carry out their prescribed tasks enthusiastically, and (4) *controlling* the activities to conform with the plans. These concepts are shown in Figure 5–1.

A graphic representation of the management process is shown by Figure 5–2. The objective, represented by the rectangle on the right, is accomplished through the efforts of the group members. For this purpose, a manager performs *planning,* represented by the left portion of the figure. In this effort, the best course of action is selected and de-

FIGURE 5-1. How the fundamental functions of management are used

Function	*Question*	*Result*
Planning.............	What is the need? What courses of action should be adopted and how and when should they be followed?	Objectives, policies, procedures, and methods
Organizing...........	Where should actions take place and who should do what work?	Work division, work assignment, and authority utilization
Actuating............	Why and how should group members perform their respective tasks?	Leadership, creativity, development, rewards, and incentives
Controlling...........	Are the actions being performed —when, where, and how—in accordance with plans?	Reports, comparisons, costs, and budgets

veloped. Proceeding to the right on the figure, *organizing* is represented by the small areas denoting the distribution of the necessary component activities derived from the plan. This distribution plus utilization of the authority required to get the specific work performed are included under *organizing.* The lines on the figure extending from these various organizational concepts to the objective represent *actuating,* which is undertaken by the manager in order to execute through others the plan to be implemented. Lastly, the vertical arrows labeled *controlling* represent the managerial effort to insure that the activities by others are in keeping with the prescribed plan, thus accomplishing the objective.

These concepts become more meaningful with the study of Figure 5–3 shown on page 86. Here are listed the more important activities for each fundamental function of management. Some of the terms shown in this figure have not yet been defined in this book, but the illustration is included here because it shows effectively an overall and inclusive view of management. The terms are completely discussed in the following chapters of this book.

INTERRELATIONSHIP AMONG FUNCTIONS

In actual practice, these four fundamental functions of management are inextricably interwoven and interrelated; the performance of one function does not cease entirely before the next is started. And they normally are not carried out in a particular sequence but as the situation being considered seems to require. In establishing a new enterprise, the order of the functions probably will be as outlined in this discussion, but

FIGURE 5-2. The vital process of management consists of planning, organizing, actuating, and controlling

PLANNING
What is to be
done where?
When? And
how?
(P)

ORGANIZING
Who is to do what? With how much
authority and under what physical
environment?
(O)

ACTUATING
Getting the
employee to
want to do
his prescribed
work
willingly
and with
enthusiastic
cooperation
(A)

CONTROLLING
Following up to see
that the planned work
is being properly carried
out, and, if not, to apply
the proper remedial
measures
(C)

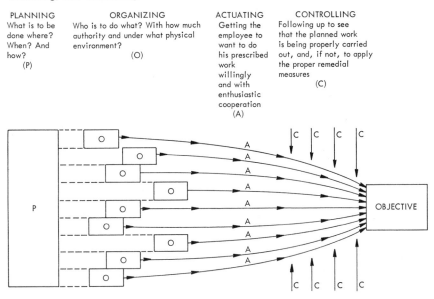

for a going concern a manager may perform, for example, controlling at a given time and follow this by actuating, then by planning.

The sequence should be suited to the specific objective. Typically, a manager is involved with many goals, and he may be at different stages in the process with each one. To the layman this may give the impression of inefficiency or a lack of order, whereas actually the manager may be acting quite purposefully and forcefully. In the long run, greater emphasis is usually placed on certain functions than on others, depending upon the individual situation. Also, it should be noted that some functions must be performed before others can be put into action. Effective actuating, for example, requires that persons either have been assigned activities or have determined their own in keeping with overall plans and objectives. Likewise, controlling cannot be exercised in a vacuum; there must be something to control.

As a matter of fact, there is planning involved in the work of organizing, of actuating, and of controlling. Likewise, the elements of organizing are employed in effective planning, actuating, and controlling. Each fundamental function of management affects the others, and they are all intimately interrelated to form the management process.

Figure 5-4 illustrates the extent of each fundamental function at each

FIGURE 5–3. Important activities of each fundamental function of management

	The work of the manager		
Planning	*Organizing*	*Actuating*	*Controlling*
1. Clarify, amplify, and determine objectives	1. Break down work into operative duties	1. Practice participation by all affected by the decision or act.	1. Compare results with plans in general
2. Forecast	2. Group operative duties into operative positions	2. Lead and challenge others to do their best	2. Appraise results against performance standards
3. Establish the conditions and assumptions under which the work will be done	3. Assemble operative positions into manageable and related units	3. Guide subordinates to meet performance standards	3. Devise effective media for measuring operations
4. Select and state tasks to accomplish objectives	4. Define position requirements	4. Develop subordinates to realize full potentials	4. Make known the measuring media
5. Establish an overall plan of accomplishment	5. Select and place individual on proper job	5. Stress creativity to find out new and better ways to manage and to accomplish the work.	5. Transfer detailed data into form showing comparisons and variances
6. Establish policies, procedures, standards, and methods of accomplishment	6. Utilize and see that proper authority is used for each management member	6. Praise and reprimand fairly	6. Suggest corrective actions, if needed
7. Anticipate possible future problems	7. Provide personnel facilities and other resources	7. Reward by recognition and pay for work well done	7. Inform responsible members of interpretations
8. Modify plans in light of control results.	8. Adjust the organization in light of control results	8. Revise actuation efforts in light of control results	8. Adjust controlling in light of control results

level of management. Note that all managers at all levels perform all four managerial functions. However, generally speaking, there is a tendency for planning and organizing to be relatively most prominent at the upper-management level and for actuating and controlling to occupy relatively major importance at the lower-management level.

For convenience, we now repeat the definition of management, using

FIGURE 5–4

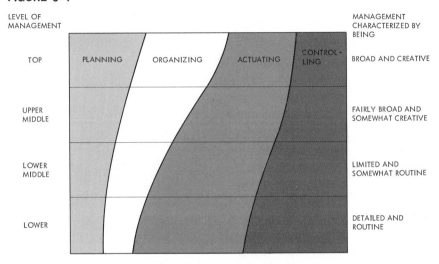

LEVEL OF MANAGEMENT					MANAGEMENT CHARACTERIZED BY BEING
TOP	PLANNING	ORGANIZING	ACTUATING	CONTROL-LING	BROAD AND CREATIVE
UPPER MIDDLE					FAIRLY BROAD AND SOMEWHAT CREATIVE
LOWER MIDDLE					LIMITED AND SOMEWHAT ROUTINE
LOWER					DETAILED AND ROUTINE

the process of management approach just described as first stated in the beginning of this book.[1] *Management is a distinct process consisting of planning, organizing, actuating, and controlling, performed to determine and accomplish stated objectives by the use of human beings and other resources.*

UNIVERSALITY OF THE MANAGEMENT PROCESS

The management process has universal application; this is significant. It means that the fundamental functions of planning, organizing, actuating, and controlling are basic and are performed by the manager, regardless of the type of enterprise, the major activity, or the level at which the manager works. Erroneously, and all too frequently, management is thought of as existing only in the top-managerial level and not in all levels down to the supervisory level of management. The fact is,

---

[1] See p. 4.

however, that when acting in their respective managerial capacities, not only the company president but also the office supervisor perform the fundamental functions of management. The difference lies in such things as the breadth of the objectives, the actions which comprise the plans, the magnitude of the decisions made, the organization relationships affected, the amount of leadership required, and the complexity of measuring the actual efficiency of the performance.

Since the management process is universal, what is meaningful about one manager's work applies likewise to that of all managers. The management process represents the common fabric of similarity among managers and serves to expedite the study of management. It is universally found wherever men work together to achieve common objectives. It is, for example, used successfully by the executive in the United States, the businessman in Japan, the government official in Turkey, and the military officer of France.

There is ample evidence to show that these managerial functions can be applied effectively by the same managers to different enterprises. Familiarity with the background, technology, and environment of the new enterprise probably helps the new manager to arrive at more effective decisions than he otherwise might make. However, the important observation is that basically he performs the same type of activities whether he manages in, say, enterprise *A* or *B*. By way of illustration, the manager of an electrical appliance manufacturer switched to a company constructing ships and enjoyed outstanding success. Many managers in industry are called to serve in government posts, and it is worth noting that they are called, not because of their intimate knowledge of government, but because they can apply effectively the fundamental management functions. And the same is true for management members in the educational field going into business enterprises and public utility managers leaving their chosen field and admirably serving charitable enterprises.

ADDITIONAL CONSIDERATIONS OF THE MANAGEMENT PROCESS

It is possible to extend the number of functions making up the management process beyond these four. The additions are many, and over a period, suggestions to add any of the following have been made: advocating, authorizing, changing, choosing, confirming, coordinating, counseling, directing, evaluating, improving, integrating, leading, measuring, modernizing, motivating, recommending, representing, specifying, and staffing. A manager does these, but the addition of any of these terms seems unnecessary and undesirable. Of course, any or all of these could be added, but such action would make the process approach somewhat unwieldly and difficult to handle. Also, some of the suggested additions are simply different terms for the four designated as making up the process. For example, measuring in the sense of measuring results is similar to controlling. Further, in most cases the additional function is implied in the concept of the functions of the process as stated. Leading is actually a part of, and is included in, the meaning of actuating. And the same is true of counseling. In addition, the stated four functions adequately identify the management process and represent a number that is easy to remember and limit discussion of the management process to an acceptable length.

ADVANTAGES OFFERED BY THE MANAGEMENT PROCESS SCHOOL

As stated in the last part of Chapter 4, the management process approach provides the framework for structuring this book. Justification for this lies in the fact that:

1. The management process school offers a broad, easy-to-understand, conceptual framework of management. The entire scope of management is included, thus helping to provide a totality concept of management. This approach has fostered the idea that management is a separate and distinct discipline that can be identified, taught, and practiced. It has emphasized and given specific meaning to the oft-used expression "the managerial viewpoint."

2. An excellent foundation for the study of management is provided. It is inclusive and applies to every type of enterprise and to every level within a given enterprise. It supplies helpful guidance for management education, development, and progress. The process school promotes understanding of what management really is. Misleading, incorrect, and incomplete concepts have been minimized by its use. The student can work from the general to the specific, and from the known to the unknown—practices which educators agree are probably most effective.

3. Utilization of contributions by other schools of management is entirely feasible. In the quest for the best management possible, it appears that we should utilize the best approach for the problem at hand. For example, if a task of decision making requires measurable physical factors, a mathematics approach probably can be most helpful. If the task is one of motivation, contributions from the human behavior

school would seem appropriate. More will be said about this in the pages immediately following.

4. The management process school stresses both the determination and the achievement of the objective. Some schools are very effective in the work of determining objectives, but they offer little help in the implementation of resources to achieve these objectives. In contrast, other schools are strong in the implementation phase of management but weak in, and in some instances void of, objective-determinative work.

5. The management process school is serviceable to practitioners of management. It helps the manager put his knowledge to use; it assists in determining a course of action when needed. The approach is straight-forward, practical, and proven by wide experience. Management as a vibrant, living, and helpful entity is fostered. It is neither a mental exercise for exercise's sake nor is it hid in an academic closet buried beneath dull, complicated, and theoretical assumptions.

6. Genuine assistance in determining and implementing a needed course of action is supplied by the process school. Its pattern of management thought enables a manager to ferret out and to understand the problem. Is it primarily one of planning, organizing, actuating, or controlling? Or is it a combination of several or of all these? What specific component of a fundamental function is deficient? Answering these questions makes it possible for the management efforts to be concentrated on critical areas and thus emphasize the purposive aspect of management.

7. Flexibility is provided by the management process school. There is room for innovating and achieving improvement. The school has the qualities of consistency and rigorousness so essential for a dependable management thought program. Yet, it is not rigid, either in demanding that variable forces be compressed or measured by specific and some-times inconvenient media, or in insisting that a patterned sequence of steps must be followed. The process school is applicable to a variety of situations. It gives its user needed leeway to suit a particular set of circumstances.

8. The art of management is recognized by the management process school. How best to apply the management knowledge in a practical situation in the right place and at the right time is encouraged.

9. Principles derived from distillation of fundamental truths or man-agement generalizations are encouraged by the management process school. These principles serve as guides and provide needed bench marks

for useful management research, give increased meaning to management, and assist in management application.

10. The acquisition of a helpful and purposeful philosophy of management is encouraged and expedited. The very nature of the management process school places a philosophy about management in a preeminent position. The process school is not mechanistic; it does not proceed in any automatic manner. At each phase of its application it requires drawing from the manager's values, beliefs, and understanding of the goals, resources, and environments with which he is working.

RECOMMENDED SCHOOL OF MANAGEMENT TO FOLLOW—THE MODIFIED PROCESS SCHOOL

In Chapter 4 various schools of management were discussed at some length. Following this, and in this chapter, a comprehensive discussion of the process school was given. Further, it was stated that this book follows the process school pattern, and the inherent advantages of this school have just been offered. All this may be interpreted to mean that the management process school is the school to follow. This is a reasonable deduction, but such a conclusion requires some modifications.

Figure 5–5 is of special interest. It shows the relative contribution to

FIGURE 5–5.   Relative contribution to fundamental functions of management by selected schools of management

School of Management	*Fundamental Functions of Management*			
	Planning	*Organizing*	*Actuating*	*Controlling*
Custom.......................	L	L	L	M
Scientific.....................	H	L	L	M
Human behavior...............	L	M	H	L
Social system.................	L	H	H	L
Systems......................	H	L	L	H
Decisional....................	M	L	L	M
Quantitative measurement........	H	L	L	H
Process.......................	H	H	H	H

Code: L = Low, M = Medium, H = High.

each fundamental function by the various schools of management. The ratings are indicative only, but they reveal that important contributions to each management function are offered in varying degrees by the different schools. For example, high contribution to planning has been made by the systems school and the quantitative measurement school.

These data suggest utilizing contributions by all schools to attain the best planning, the best organizing, the best actuating, the best controlling, and the best management. In essence, this means improving the process school. It has the scope, fundamental nature, and flexibility to make this possible. The result is a modified process management school.

The recommendation here is that the basic framework offered by the process school should be followed with use of the other schools when the individual situation suggests valuable contributions can be gained from them. That is, the recommended approach can be termed *the eclectic-process school of management,* featuring the basic framework of the process approach modified by certain theories from other appropriate schools of management thought. Eclectic means "consisting of what is selected" and this term has been interpreted to indicate taking the best from what is available in management thought and working it into a single theory molded around the process framework as the central core.

FIGURE 5–6.   Modified process management school

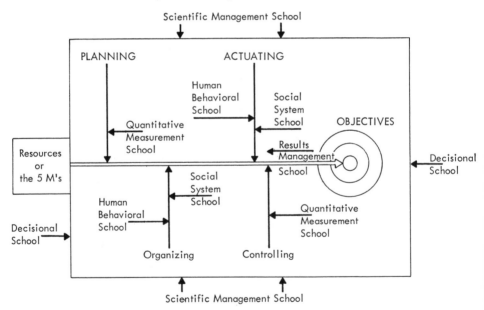

This modified process approach brings reality to management theory. In practice a manager recognizes that he must adapt any theory to meet his specific needs. From the situation of a given case, a conflict of theories may arise. In such instances the manager evaluates the impact of his following certain approaches, tries to minimize the conflict, and determines a course of action that to him appears best to meet the individual requirements. In essence, he usually looks to more than one oversimplified general theory for parts of his total answer.

Figure 5–6 shows a graphical interpretation of this modified process approach. The resources consisting of the five Ms are subjected to the four fundamental functions of management in order to achieve the objective. Contributing to planning efforts is the quantitative measurement school which offers for some situations excellent techniques helpful in planning, such as precision forecasting and revealing possible outcomes for different tentative plans. Likewise, both organizing and actuating efforts utilize outstanding and pertinent contributions of the human behavior school and the social systems school as indicated in the sketch. Further, controlling is improved by modifications of the quantitative measurement school which add desirable precision and accuracy to these efforts. In addition, results management, which can be considered an approach to management, is employed to determine the objectives. As discussed in Chapter 3, results management modifies the older concept of who is responsible for planning, organizing, actuating, and controlling and, in addition, supplies excellent actuating stimulation for all members of an enterprise.

With further reference to Figure 5–6, the entire process is affected by the scientific management and decisional management schools. Contributions of the former greatly assist in finding answers to problems in each of the fundamental functions of management. And decision making is required of anyone engaged in the management process. How to better these decision-making efforts is drawn from the decisional school.

It is difficult to show the place of the systems school on Figure 5–6. But in this school we can note that for each majority activity, a system is identified and utilized. To obtain that system's objective, the resources used are subjected to planning, organizing, actuating, and controlling. Likewise for another system, its objective is obtained by applying planning, organizing, actuating, and controlling to the resources of that system. Figure 5–7 shows planning, organizing, actuating, and controlling being used for systems X, Y, and Z to achieve their respective goals. System X might be for materials, system Y for marketing, and system Z for costs. In brief, the system is the vehicle of thought and establishes the overall constraints of the activities to which planning, organizing. actuating, and controlling are applied.

To reiterate, the result of these modifications is an eclectic conceptual management framework. Essentially process in makeup, it draws from the other management schools to evolve the most effective thought pattern of management yet devised by man. It is believed that this modified process school extracts the best of current management thinking and synthesizes it into an effective unity. Furthermore, following the modified approach means that this book is not simply a process management book or a principles book, but a composite of the best of current basic management thinking brought together in a single volume, which is believed best for the beginning study of management. Minimized are the chances of the management scholar getting trapped within one

FIGURE 5–7. Process plus systems management school

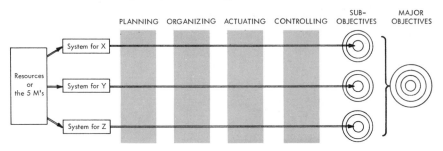

set of assumptions or another, and thus needlessly constraining his whole management outlook. In the final analysis, the ultimate criterion is the degree to which the school assists in attaining the stated management goal.

QUESTIONS

1. A follower of the process school of management states that its most outstanding advantages are: (*a*) an effective and practical framework for management study is provided, (*b*) flexibility is offered, and (*c*) the art of management is recognized and promoted. Do you feel these are advantages and, if so, are they outstanding? Substantiate your answer.
2. Do you agree with this statement: "If management is a process should not the fundamental functions be carried out according to a logical sequence so that orderliness and effectiveness are present?" Why?
3. Do you view use of the management process as more or less mechanical in its application and operation? Justify your answer.
4. Refer to Figure 5–6, and in your own words, explain the meaning of this illustration.
5. Name the fundamental functions of management and discuss each briefly.
6. Douglas Duncan believes that two additional functions, improving and specifying, should be added to the four fundamental functions as stated in this book. What is your reaction to his suggestion? Justify your answer.
7. Discuss your understanding of the eclectic-process school of management.
8. The process of management is cited to supply excellent assistance in find-

ing and understanding the problem to be solved. In your opinion would the human behavior school and the quantitative measurement school be equally effective in this respect? Why?

9. In your opinion should a person necessarily have a background in the general area of endeavor in which he is a manager? Discuss.

10. For each of the following pairs, point out the differences, if any, between the two terms: (*a*) organizing and managing, (*b*) a fundamental function of management and a conceptual framework of management, and (*c*) a resource and a process.

11. Discuss the universality of the management process.

12. What is the modified process of management approach?

13. Give an example from your own experience showing the interrelations between organizing and actuating. Between planning and controlling.

14. Based on your personal experience and reading, do you feel that any one of the fundamental functions of management is of greatest importance? Elaborate on your answer.

CASE 5–1. RYAN CANDY COMPANY

About two months ago, Joseph Wheeling was transferred from the company's New York plant to its Chicago plant and promoted to Administrative Assistant to the General Manager. Top officials were not pleased with the operation in the Chicago plant, which was the largest of the company's six manufacturing plants. The company manufactures and sells several different brands of popular 10¢ candy bars. Since his arrival at the Chicago plant, Mr. Wheeling has busied himself studying and reviewing various reports on the Chicago operations, interviewed many management and nonmanagement members of the plant, and observed a number of operators.

He has just formulated from all the information collected the following pertinent facts organized around ten topics as follows:

1. The management team. Not much enthusiasm and little will to achieve. Heads of receiving, mixing and cooking, quality control, packaging, shipping, accounting, engineering, purchasing, and personnel seem satisfactory, but not outstanding. They follow authoritative management for the most part, yet are reluctant to exercise authority. Plant is loosely run. All state they feel Mr. George Meadows is O.K. as the general manager, but none believe he is outstanding in his work performance.

2. Profit trend. Downward for the past four years. Prior to this an average net income of about 8 percent experienced. Mr. Meadows says it is due to higher wages and material cost. Says we should raise our prices. But if we do, retail price will probably become 15¢ and put us at competitive disadvantage, as I see it.

3. Supervisors. All but two of the eleven total came up from the ranks. They know the technical aspects of the work. Impression gained is that they are mediocre in performance, are reluctant to discuss any problem they have of supervision. Seem to have a fear that they might lose their jobs.

4. Personnel. Mixed ethnically and about 20 percent of work force from minority groups. Turnover is high in certain departments. Of the total 464 employees on payroll, one fourth, or 116 employees have been with the company less than one year. Personnel appears to keep busy most of the day—little loafing on the job.

5. Productivity. Appears low. Some work standards have been the same for the past ten years. Current production level is 91.6 percent of what is expected, but no strong measure to raise it to required 100 percent is in evidence.

6. Wages. All available data I have been able to gather show that wages are on par with what is being paid for comparable jobs in the area.

7. Machines and equipment. Some very old machines are in use, but appear to be trouble free up to now. No complaints from employees about them. Have no data on newer machine productivity compared to what we are accomplishing.

8. Sales. For the most part have been steady for past five years for each of the different candy bars. But sales of the candy bar industry show average annual increase of 4.7 percent during this same period. Local sales manager claims new packaging and increased store displays are needed, but home office in New York says "No."

9. Finances. Chicago plant is in good shape financially. Liquidity is satisfactory, bills are paid; both accounts receivable and accounts payable are in favorable position.

10. Community relations. Company rated neutral as a place to work. Little participation in civic affairs by the company. Mr. Meadows supports the corporate citizen idea but feels getting his management team members active in civic affairs is "pretty much a waste of time."

Questions

1. What is the problem faced by Ryan Candy Company?
2. Based on information compiled by Joseph Wheeling, what recommended plan of action should be made? Why?
3. What major difficulties do you envision in putting your recommended action into use? Discuss.

part **II**

Facilitating managerial activities

To make the modified process of management feasible, there are important activities which must be present. Some consider these facilitating activities as a part of management itself; we segregate them here to point out clearly their identities and contributions in managerial efforts.

Typically, a manager encounters problems in his efforts to accomplish his desired results. Analyzing such a problem to determine its identity and possible solution facilitate the use of management. Discussed in some detail is decision making which is required for planning, organizing, actuating, and controlling to exist. Also, communicating, which gives life and understanding to all management actions, is presented. For Part II, these four chapters are:

6. *Analyzing management problems*
7. *Managerial decision making*
8. *Managerial decision making (continued)*
9. *Communicating*

6

Analyzing management problems

Every man is worth just as much as the things he busies himself with.

MARCUS AURELIUS

IN ESTABLISHING and achieving objectives, needs must be identified, confidence won, scarce resources assembled, progress maintained, and obstacles eliminated. In surmounting these difficulties, problems arise. That is, a manager encounters situations slowing, interrupting, or preventing the achievement of tasks designed to bring about the desired results.

All managers must deal with problems which exist because most goals we want to achieve will just not be achieved unless we strive to make them a reality. Further, progress is won by improving what we are now doing. And here, again, to improve upon what we are now accomplishing raises problems. The typical manager looks for problems if they are not brought to him. The constant urge to produce a better product or service, to improve product design, reduce selling price, serve more people, and finance more economically are common examples.

This means that, in a sense, a manager is oriented around problems. He manages for some purpose—some desired result. If his work were not purposeful, there would be no problem.

Some view problems as opportunities. This is good because problems provide the chance to improve. We progress by solving pertinent problems, by seizing the opportunity to correct errors and making the total effort the best we possibly can. This necessity to overcome obstacles to goal achievement can be viewed as a favorable circumstance because most progress is stimulated by opposition. The field of medicine, for example, has advanced by combatting disease, education by combatting ignorance, and law enforcement by combatting crime. In similar manner, management has gone forward by combatting problems. Problems are the diet upon which a manager thrives. By successfully resolving problems, the manager not only serves his enterprise but also achieves personal growth and advancement. One of the greatest contributions of executive leaders is to provide fresh thinking to problems.

COMMON PROBLEM AREAS FOR MANAGERS

Among the broad problem areas faced from time to time by many managers are the following: the development and improvement of long- and short-term objectives for the entire enterprise and for each major part of it; the improvement of resources, including manpower, facilities, and finance, and better allocation and evaluation of their respective adequacies; the clarification of managerial ethics which prevails in the enterprise's relationships with outsiders; and the effectiveness of presently used communicative means and how improvement in the media may be obtained.

More specifically, common managerial problem areas, arranged alphabetically, include the following:

1. *Costs:* Utilization of standard cost plan, distribution of cost data, better use of cost information.
2. *Decision making:* Adequacy of present techniques, use of latest techniques, developing skill in ascertaining alternative actions.
3. *Employee training:* Sufficiency of present efforts, utilizing advanced techniques, advisability of changing supervisory training.
4. *Financing:* Securing short-term loans on better terms, increasing the working capital, planning future money needs.
5. *Information distribution:* Providing adequate and complete oral and written information to all personnel so that they are fully informed and can do their respective jobs better.
6. *Inventory records:* Improvements to reduce inventory losses, correlation with sales and manufacturing data, simplification needed.
7. *Markets:* Efforts to find out what buyers want, determining market potentials, finding areas of greatest sales opportunities.
8. *Morale:* Determining what employees think of their company, areas in which morale can be improved, possible improvements that can be started.

9. *Plant location:* Utilization of centralized or decentralized arrangement, build or rent, reduction of maintenance costs.
10. *Pricing:* Appraisal of present prices, probable effect on volume due to price change, competitive pricing.
11. *Production planning:* Determination and achievement of economic runs; maintenance of proper inventories of raw, in-process, and finished goods; increasing machine and equipment utilization.
12. *Products and services:* Development that meets favorably the requirements of the market and of the enterprise.
13. *Quality control:* Economical maintenance of higher quality standards, training personnel for this work, availability of qualified people.
14. *Recruitment and selection:* Finding and attracting the best prospective employees, effectiveness of interviews and tests.
15. *Reports:* Improvement in format and writing style, distribution and evaluation of reports, and data supplied.
16. *Sales effectiveness:* Reducing time required for processing a sales order, establishing sales quotas, improving sales reports.
17. *Social responsibility:* Contributing managerial talent to projects designed to improve social relationships, better understanding among people, and satisfactory environmental conditions.
18. *Supervising:* Guiding and directing efforts of employees and other resources to accomplish stated work outputs.
19. *Wage and salary administration:* Improving equitableness of present plan, winning greater acceptance for it, adequacy of plan in the future.
20. *Waste elimination:* Employee awareness of waste, data on extent of waste material, means of reducing waste, effectiveness of waste campaigns.

PROBLEM ANALYSIS

Problem analysis consists of two parts (1) problem identification and (2) problem solution. Before a problem can be solved, it must be identified. A problem *is a deviation from some standard or desired level of dimension, important enough to be solved, and to which a person is committed to find a solution.* The importance of problem identification is given by an old truism which states, "A problem well stated is half solved." Problem identification is one of the most difficult tasks that a manager faces. It is helped by the manager's acquisition of knowledge and his improvement of skill. However, in this regard, most agree that certain kinds of knowledge are most beneficial in developing better ways of thinking, which is a vital skill in efforts to learn more about problem situations faced as a manager.

Observe also the important contribution of results management to the problem identification. A person has no problem with no objective. A problem is what is keeping a person from achieving his objective. Therefore when results are stressed, as in results management, the obstacle or problem preventing the results achievement is highlighted. Remove this obstacle and the sought objective will be won. As mentioned previously, in this approach the result serves as the standard of performance.

Problem solution is the end result of problem analysis. It follows problem identification. It is mandatory to know what the problem is, or even if you have one, before you can begin to draw up a solution for it. Like problem identification, the superior solution is aided greatly by the manager's adequate knowledge, skill, and thinking.

PROBLEM ANALYSIS AND THE MANAGEMENT PROCESS

To enable managers to identify and understand their current problems and to assist in providing a course of action to follow, the framework provided by the management process is extremely helpful. It is sufficiently flexible to be used in a variety of situations, is relatively simple to apply, and provides the needed overall viewpoint.

The obtaining of data on all aspects of the enterprise's operations over a period will probably be by departments. Applying measures of efficiency to these data reveals various trouble spots throughout the enterprise. The problem analyst, however, should avoid classifying the data by departments. This relates problems to isolated units of the entire enterprise and leads to the fallacious conclusion that the problem and its solution lies within the realm of that particular unit. In some cases this assumption may be reasonably correct, but in many others, it will not be true. Problems have a way of cutting across departmental boundaries and commonly are not properly identified or solved by a "department-by-department" approach. The problems simply do not fit departmental categories and will not be completely solved by tackling them one by one.

Use of the process management approach provides the needed perspective. Departmental activities are interrelated and an impact on the enterprise is quite likely to produce ripples of reaction in various departments and many of the trouble spots within these departments are probably interrelated to one another. These trouble spots, such as rising production cost, declining sales, and slow collection payments, are in essence symptoms rather than the problem to be solved. They have come into being as the result of some higher, more fundamental weakness. The challenge is to find out the cause or the problem permitting these symptoms to emerge. The process of management provides an adequate way to generalize and bring together these underlying symptoms. In other words, the process approach offers a logical system of inquiry and also frequently suggests additional analyses overlooked during the initial stages of examining the basic data.

FIGURE 6–1. Possible managerial actions to solve management problems arranged by fundamental functions of the management process

I. Planning
    1. Objectives of individuals
    2. Objectives of the enterprise
    3. Policies covering authority, prices, attitude toward competition
    4. Procedures—specific means of handling paper and products
    5. Internal programs
II. Organizing
    1. Span of authority
    2. Delegation of authority
    3. Use of staff and service groups
    4. Informal groups
    5. Integration of structural activities
III. Actuating
    1. Leading
    2. Developing and evaluating employees
    3. Fulfilling personal needs through work satisfaction
    4. Job enrichment and enlargement
    5. Supervising
IV. Controlling
    1. Establishing standards of performance
    2. Measuring work performance
    3. Improving rate of return on investment
    4. Developing adequate budgeting
    5. Employing better cost and quality controls

In addition the major problems are expressed in terms of management when the process approach is used. This suggests what managerial action may be taken to solve the problem. Figure 6–1 includes suggestions under each major function.

Specifically, do the symptoms suggest improvement is needed in planning? In organizing? In actuating and controlling? Studying the trouble spots in light of these fundamental functions of management reveals comprehensive and inclusive suggestions to not only identify, but also to correct the total problem.

Statements of problems as "we need better managers," or "our problem is lack of sales," reflect a superficial attack on symptoms. Usually evidence can be found to support such a statement and the investigation ends prematurely. Subsequently, efforts to correct things fall short. What is required is a comprehensive, diagnostic approach such as the process of management provides.

Problem solving by the manager must be objective; possible causes are not supported with arguments prompted by subjective feelings of the manager. It is also well to include the ideas and suggestions of others. Excellent solutions emerge from groups working constructively as a team. Additional guidelines for problem solving are to:

1. *Review quickly all the elements of the problem so that a composite entity of the entire problem is obtained.* This focuses attention upon the "big picture" and avoids seeing the problem as a mosaic of numerous individual considerations. Also pertinent relationships are more easily disclosed, the memory is relieved, and the mental capacity is enlarged.

2. *Try a change in the manner in which the problem is expressed.* Switching from verbal terms to a mathematical model, graph, or numbers to represent the problem may shed new and wanted light on the task. If dealing with nonverbal terms, try stating the problem in simple action terms.

3. *Consider the problem environment and try rearranging the space and time characteristics of the problem.* This can help in revealing known and common patterns that originally are hidden by an unfamiliar arrangement. Stating the identical relationships in a different and perhaps more normal manner can contribute to the solution.

4. *Evaluate your own ideas and those of others constructively.* Guard against complacency in accepting your own ideas. They may be brilliant, but also consider the insights of others wrestling with the same or similar problems.

5. *Discuss problem with others.* Following this guideline forces one to restate all the aspects of the problem and in so doing brings out considerations requiring attention which the tentative solution does not include. This practice necessitates a relating of the fundamentals so that the listener knows what is being considered. By such communication, obscure and inconsistent points are uncovered, and furthermore, the listener, by his questions, reveals gaps which appear inconsistent and inadequate, thus pointing out areas for bettering the problem solution.

MANAGEMENT PROBLEMS AND CONTROLLING

Although all the fundamental functions of management are important in problem identification and problem solution, controlling is especially so. A management problem can be thought of as the difference between the desired level dimension and the present level dimension, or stated differently, the deviation between what should be and what actually is. In other words, the amount by which we are off the planned target represents the problem. This represents the imbalance which the manager needs first to identify and then decide what action to take to correct.

In addition, controlling identifies and locates precisely the deviation or deviations. With such information, rationality, represented by analysis and synthesis, can then be followed to find the possible cause or causes of such deviations and hence of the problem. The cause is a change or an action from the plan being followed that has taken place to produce the unwanted effect. Every problem has a cause. There are always one or more things that have brought about the cause, as distinguished from that thing or things that have not brought about the cause. Care should be taken to avoid the common tendency to jump to conclusions by accepting the first deviating thing and justifying it, at least tentatively, as the sole responsible one.

PROBLEM SOLVING METHODS

There are five major approaches to management problem solving. As shown on Figure 6–2, they include (1) routine, (2) scientific, (3) decisional, (4) creative, and (5) quantitative approaches. Referring to this figure, we start at the top with a desired result. As clearly indicated in this chapter, as soon as a manager begins his efforts to accomplish a desired result, management problems will appear to impede his actions. By what means can the manager solve these problems?

First, he can employ the routine approach. This includes solving the problem via traditional means, or doing what has always been done when a problem of this type is confronted. Reference is simply made to habit or history and the same answer used before is used now. It is also possible to use standard operating procedures (SOP), which are written forms telling the manager what to do under certain described conditions. Usually SOPs are in the format of a manual. Another means under the routine approach is to abide by superior's order. Here the manager has actually no choice at all. He follows the edict of his superior.

The scientific approach is a widespread means of solving problems.

As pointed out in Chapter 4 (see pages 63–64), the scientific method consists of a controlled experimentation to prove or disprove an assumed answer, or hypothesis. The steps taken, in sequence, are indicated on Figure 6–2.

FIGURE 6–2. Approaches to management problem solving

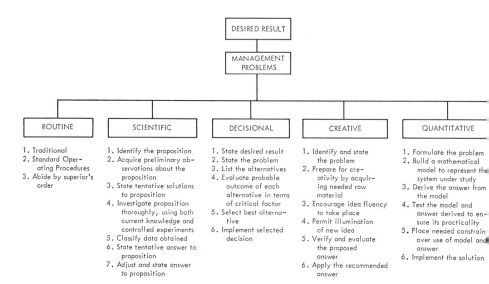

The third approach is decisional, one of the most common and popular of all the approaches. To gain the desired result, a decision is made. Hopefully this decision will solve the management problem which is the barrier to obtain the desired result. For clarity, it is essential that the desired result be stated first and then the problem. Confusion is common in this portion of the decisional approach. For example, suppose you are fullback on a football offense team. The play called is for you to carry the ball on a delayed buck through the center of the line. What is the problem? If you answer, "to get through the line," that is wrong. That's the end result. The problem or barrier is the opposing team's defense—all eleven players. They are trying to keep you from gaining yardage. Eliminate or neutralize the defense and you will achieve the end result. It helps to state the desired result as a noun, the problem as a verb. Using a verb implies action—acquire, remove, sell, or prevent.

For any given situation, several decisions leading to alternative actions are possible. Any of these alternatives are possible to resolve the problem. The alternatives, resulting from a situation requiring a decision, are identified and one of them is selected as being the best, based on the probable predicted outcome of that alternative. Usually the evaluation is on the basis of what is the least costly, conforms with legal requirements, is the quickest, the best quality, or the best quantity. The basis used is referred to as the critical factor. It is not the same in every case, but will vary depending upon the individual requirements. The final step is to implement the selected decision.

The creative approach is the fourth method of problem solving to be discussed. This method utilizes the ability to evolve new workable ideas and to implement them. A positive attitude, imagination, and the ability to put together new relationships along heretofore unconventional lines are basic requirements for applying this method. The gist is to create and apply new ideas—those never used before or known. It represents a brand new way of achieving the desired result and is not determined judicially, that is, by making logical analysis or rational comparisons. As indicated in Figure 6–2, the sequence to follow for the creative method is: (1) identify and state the problem, (2) prepare for creativity by acquiring needed raw materials, (3) encourage idea fluency to take place, (4) permit illumination of new idea, (5) verify and evaluate the proposed answer, and (6) apply the recommended answer.[1]

The last method to be discussed is the quantitative approach. As stated in Chapter 4, the emphasis here is on the mathematical modeling of systems. Comparison of various feasible actions such as cost reduction, revenues, and rates of return on investment are expressed by measurable values. The relationship of the factors for any given action is stated in mathematical form, i.e., by a formula or an equation. By substituting different mathematical values for the variables of the equation, different results are obtained and evaluated in keeping with the requirements of the stated problem. The computer is of great assistance in using this method, especially where the mathematical model is complex or the volume of the calculations is large. Shown in Figure 6–2 are the steps to follow. They include (1) formulate the problem, (2) build a mathematical model to represent the system under study, (3) derive the answer from the model, (4) test the model and answer derived to ensure their practicality, (5) place needed constraints over use of model and answer, and (6) implement the solution.

CASE STUDY

A case study is a presentation of a situation involving problems to be solved. Basically it is descriptive, not analytical, i.e., it does not neces-

---

[1] See also Chapter 21, creating and innovating ideas.

sarily try to explain what is being observed or reported. Case studies reveal the complexity of the environment in which problems requiring solution exist. They necessitate the solver to face up to the uncertainties of the practical world and to develop skill in applying the knowledge he has.

A major task of working with case studies is problem identification. Frequently, it requires deep and concentrated thought. The key issues are not always easy to locate and identify. But reference to the fundamental functions of the management process serve as useful guides. Once the problem is known, efforts can be directed to its solution.

Criticism is sometimes voiced that the case study does not include all the facts. This is true; few case studies do include all the facts. But managers seldom have all the facts, a concept itself subject to wide interpretation by the case solver. So while not perfect, case studies do have a definite sense of reality. Attempting to determine a solution without full knowledge may be frustrating, but actually it is part of the essence of managerial problem solving.

Any of the above described five methods of problem solving can be used for a case study and different approaches for different problems of a case may be followed. In other words, for a particular case perhaps the superior solution is found via the creative approach that recommends an entirely new set of actions be taken to solve the problem. Or in another case or for a part of the case, the quantitative approach may supply what appears to be the best answer, precisely stated and fairly simple to implement.

However, in most instances, the usual suggestion is to view the case study as requiring the development of an orderly analysis. When this viewpoint is followed, the problem solving consists of evaluating the facts, organizing such facts into meaningful patterns, weighing the important facts against the unimportant facts, formulating alternative courses of action, evaluating these alternative courses, and finally, choosing the final solution.

Different alternatives may be selected as the recommended one to follow by two managers of equal competence. How is this possible? Does it mean that there is no single correct and best solution to a case study? Precisely. What exact actions a manager takes in a given circumstance are greatly influenced by the manager himself. As already stated, his goals, attitudes, philosophy, and values exert influence on what he thinks and does. However, it is possible to say that some recommendations appear superior to others because the answer shows a better understanding of the real issue involved, or the analyst supports and justifies his position more adequately, or the solution appears more feasible and workable under the given circumstances.

The following steps may be followed in analyzing a case study. This outline is suggestive only, some may prefer to approach case studies in a different manner.

1. Identify the Central Issues. Focus on what seems to be the key problems. Separate superficial issues from the key problems. The superficial issues are usually just symptoms of deeper, ingrained problems. Use the planning, organizing, actuating, and controlling framework to assist in identifying what the central issues are. Then concentrate your thoughts around the suggested central theme.

2. Organize the Pertinent Facts. This is accomplished by utilizing the central issues as centers around which substantiating and relevant facts are organized. Put the facts in a different format if this will assist understanding of them. Use of charts and matrix forms, for example, are helpful.

3. Determine the Alternatives. There is always more than one possible answer. Think and imagine until at least three or four possibilities are evolved. In some case studies the alternatives are quite clear while in others some deep thinking and probing are required.

4. Evaluate the Alternatives. Basically this is a matter of relating certain important facts in support of a certain alternative, and repeating for each alternative. Some facts will support a given alternative, others will indicate why the alternative should not be followed. Also some facts will suggest the consequences of choosing one alternative over another. Judgment and experience will also assist in evaluating the alternatives.

5. Select the Alternative Recommended. All things considered, what appears to be the strongest, most appropriate, and most feasible alternative is selected and recommended. This selection is a natural outgrowth of step No. 4 above. By this means the case solver is aware of the strengths as well as the limitations of his choice.

POTENTIAL-PROBLEM ANALYSIS

Actions to minimize or possibly to prevent the effects of potential problems are among the most rewarding that a manager can take. However, any standardized practices in this respect are rare in management today. This follows for several reasons. First, managers are more concerned with correcting present-day problems than with minimizing or preventing tomorrow's problems. Praise and recognition are rarely, if ever, bestowed on managers for things that do not happen. Also, there is a tendency for human beings to believe they fully understand all the implications of a proposed plan, especially if they agree with the intent of the plan. The potential problem remains invisible until the planned activities take form and content. At that time the opportunity for prevention is passed; the problem exists and must be solved. In addition, the critical consequences of a managerial action may be inadequately analyzed. The possibility for failure or results somewhat less than expectancy are simply ignored perhaps because "such thinking is negative" or the analysis of such consequences are unsavory and disagreeable to face. Last, there is the persistent conviction by management members that plans they suggest are nearly infallible; otherwise they would not recommend them. They reason that "there is little use in looking for trouble." But experience demonstrates that actions do go wrong, troubles do arise. It appears wise to probe for possible errors and to evaluate their effects.

Despite all these handicaps, it is possible to adopt a rational analysis of potential problems. Such an anlysis consists of first listing all the potential problems from the proposed action. Sources for such problems include situations where there is no outstanding desired alternative action, responsibility is difficult to fix, a given sequence must be followed, the action is new or unfamiliar, or the scheduling is tight. Next, describe each potential problem. This helps to identify accurately each problem, revealing precisely the what, where, and when of it. Following this, the classification of potential problems by their degree of risk is suggested. Further, for each high-risk problem identify its possible causes. In this way a priority of problems is determined and concentration on those most threatening to the management plan can be followed. The setting forth of possible causes of these major problems shows what the manager may have to cope with. He doesn't know for sure since he is dealing with possibilities only. The small-risk problem will be accepted and the chance is taken that they will not occur. Next, assess the probability of occurrence to the causes of each major potential problem. In essence, for each major problem this points to the major causes which merit the most watching. And logically, efforts are then taken to minimize the effects of these major causes. Efforts in widely different areas may have to be taken since causes commonly are from multiple sources. And finally, decide how to handle the most serious potential problems. This supplies contingency actions to adopt at once should any of the potential problems become a reality. Such actions are rewarding when the potential problem could bring about chaotic conditions and the removal of its causes or reduction of its probability appear slim.

QUESTIONS

1. List six specific problems of managers and discuss two of them in some detail.
2. In what specific ways can the use of results management applied to the management process be helpful in problem identification? In problem solving?
3. Should the problem be stated first, then the end results sought, or the reverse, the end results first and then the problem? Substantiate your answer and include an example to demonstrate your answer.
4. Define each of the following: (*a*) problem, (*b*) routine approach to solving management problem, and (*c*) problem solution.
5. Explain Figure 6–2 in your own words.
6. Give an example from your own observation of progress being stimulated by opposition.
7. Justify the statement that controlling is especially effective in problem identification and problem solution.
8. What management importance do you infer from the statement, "The typical manager looks for problems if they are not brought to him." Elaborate on your answer.
9. Discuss the subject, problem analysis and the management process.
10. What is meant by problem analysis in management? Should a manager favor its use? Why?
11. Enumerate the five methods for solving problems. Which one are you inclined to favor? Why?
12. List the symptoms and their related problems for three situations you have experienced or read about. Suggest for one of these situations, how the process of management would assist in problem identification and solution.
13. Enumerate and discuss the suggested five steps for analyzing a case study.
14. How do you explain the lack of potential-problem analysis in today's management?

CASE 6–1. KISH INVESTMENTS, INC.

A few years ago a loan for a contemplated shopping center development in Honeysuckle, Illinois, was made by Kish Investments, Inc. The project failed to mature and as foreclosure on the loan, the corporation received the land to be used for the project. In an attempt to utilize it, the corporation submitted a proposition for a joint venture to Wells Buildings, Inc. After several months, their response was received. The following is a summary of their report.

Overall impression:

Honeysuckle is a stagnant community of about 6800 people. There appears to be a housing shortage and a definite need for some rental units. Currently there is a limited number of apartments, but on the whole the town is oriented to single-family living. Local officials indicated that 24 units would sell, but did not advise anything over this amount.

The land in question is good, being located in the growth area of the town; the high school is across the street and a new junior high is two blocks away. Actually the land is outside the corporate limits of Honeysuckle and is therefore not subject to zoning limitations. Most of the land is about two feet below the level of the highway, but drainage does not appear to be a problem. Homes in the immediate area are in the $15,000–18,000 category.

Interviews:

Philip Wolf, manager of the chamber of commerce, said, "Honeysuckle isn't the place for multi-family dwellings. Over on Redbud Lane, the Grandeur Apartment Complex of 30 units is bankrupt. I'd say it was due to poor management and high rents and the fact that local people just don't want to live in apartments."

Thoughts expressed by Duane Barber, manager, American Savings and Loan Association include: (1) the town needs low-rental units, (2) the area has a low per capita income, and (3) housing for the elderly is definitely not recommended.

Jack Berkely, manager Second National Bank, expressed the opinion that Honeysuckle could use nice apartments for around $120 a month tops. The land in question is ideal and the location is good. Suggest starting with 24 units.

The personnel manager of Page Products, Inc., the only manufacturing plant in town indicated that they planned no expansion and knew of no other company contemplating coming into Honeysuckle.

Apartments in area:

The Grandeur Apartment Complex, 30 units, one-bedroom unit rents for $125 a month, two-bedrooms unit $145 a month. One year lease required. Apartments are carpeted and include range and refrigerator. Gained the impression that place was poorly managed. Complex is bankrupt.

Four one-bedroom units at 500 N. Pine Street are fully occupied, nice, rent for $150 a month. Owner is talking of adding 12 similar units.

Across the street from the land under question are four two-bedroom units over a retail store. Appeared well maintained, full occupied; rent is $145 a month.

Questions

1. What conclusions do you draw from the information supplied by the report of Wells Buildings, Inc.?
2. Has the manager of Kish Investments, Inc. analyzed his problem? Discuss.
3. What recommended action would you offer Kish Investments, Inc.? Why?

CASE 6–2. CONWAY COMPANY

Mr. Alfred M. Rice, president, recognized the need for improving his company executive group and personal performance. Associates of Mr. Rice shared his belief and concurred in his decision to call in Mr. James Lee, a management consultant for professional help. Within several weeks, Mr. Lee arrived at Conway Company and during the afternoon of the first day had a long interview with Mr. Rice. During this time, Mr. Rice answered a number of questions posed by Mr. Lee. They were primarily designed to give him background information about the company.

Subsequently, Mr. Lee talked with all the company's top and middle managers. He was interested in finding out what they believed the problems were that the company faced, their ideas of what actions should be taken, and the probable hurdles in implementing the suggested actions. From this Mr. Lee senses that all the management members needed a greater perspective, to see their jobs and their departmental effort in relationship to the total company effort. Further, they needed to be informed about the company's plans for all phases of the business.

Accordingly, Mr. Lee recommended interaction among the top managers and among top and middle managers by means of a series of scheduled meetings at which appropriate top managers discussed the plans and problems of the company as they saw them. At each meeting, a question and answer session was featured. From these meetings, individual study, and observation, Mr. Lee suggested that each department manager hold for his group "Roadblock Meetings," the purpose of which was: (1) to identify roadblocks preventing the manager from doing the most effective job he could, and (2) to suggest practical ways that these roadblocks could be eliminated. The recommendation was approved and in the meetings that followed some 850 roadblocks were identified. There was of course some duplication in these, but the range varied from "improving our managerial leadership" to "making every

Conway employee cost conscious and reduce present overall cost by 5 percent."

In the opinion of Mr. Lee the situation was now ripe for problem-solving conferences. Again Mr. Rice agreed. Three-day conferences were scheduled. They featured sessions conducted by specialists in developing effective human relations with emphasis upon implementing change and maintaining motivation. Also, unstructured sessions for developing plans to eliminate selected roadblocks from the departmental meetings discussed above were held. A separate meeting for each selected road-block took place concurrently and the manager was free to attend the one of his choice.

Armed with the problem identification and suggestions for its solution, each manager was encouraged to dispel roadblocks in his area of operation. To assist in these efforts, a task force was appointed consisting of two outside specialists and three key company executives. Care was taken that the operating manager remained the manager of his unit and continued to decide what corrective action would be taken.

After being in operation for three months, a total of 307 roadblocks had been reviewed, of which 123 were acted upon. Mr. Lee cautioned that it would require time to realize full benefits from the program. In his words, "The important thing is to keep it alive and continue to work together in identifying and solving problems that keep you from achieving your goals. How this is done is just as important as what is done."

Questions

1. What is your reaction to the help supplied by Mr. Lee? Discuss.
2. Would you say the program followed has elements of a results management-modified process management approach? Elaborate on your answer.
3. Are you of the opinion that a program such as Conway Company followed could be applied successfully in most enterprises today? Why?

7

Managerial decision making

The more decisions that you are forced to make alone, the more you are aware of your freedom to choose.
THORNTON WILDER

DECISIONS ARE BASIC to management in action. From the popular point of view, the manager is the one who decides what is to be done. Decisions are expected of a manager. To make management meaningful, decisions must be made. In the process school of management, for example, decisions are mandatory for planning, organizing, actuating, and controlling to have significance. Decision making permeates each of management's fundamental functions, exists in every part of an enterprise, and deals with every possible subject. Decision making is a major facilitator of managerial activities.

THE MEANING OF DECISION MAKING

Decision making is always related to a problem, a difficulty, or conflict. By means of a decision and its implementation it is hoped that an answer to the problem or a resolution of the conflict will be gained.

Not all problems, however, are of a decision-making variety. Some are essentially problems dealing with information. For example, the problem of when will the course Personnel Management be offered in a given university is essentially a problem of information. There is no resolution of conflict to be made. Secure the needed information, and you secure the answer. In addition, some problems necessitate information and prediction. You have the information, but this is insufficient; it must be used in a prediction. For example, the course Personnel Management will next be offered by a given university a year from the present semester. Can you take the course at that time? This question requires a prediction about the future. You know the course will be offered, and you predict that you can and will take it a year from now because you will be in school and want to take this course.

Decision making concerns problems that go beyond the need for information and prediction. Decision problems necessitate a choice; several possibilities are available from which we must make a selection. We have the information and predictive material but still do not have the answer of what to do. In our illustration, other courses are being offered at the same future time as Personnel Management. Alternatives include a course in Business Policy, Accounting III, or Finance II. Which course will you take? Consideration is given to many questions such as: Which course is required for my major? Which course will probably be most helpful to me? Which course will I enjoy the most? Which course does my counselor suggest? Then you decide.

Literally, decision making means "to cut off" or, in practical content, to come to a conclusion. As stated in Webster's, it is "the act of determining in one's own mind upon an opinion or course of action." Stated formally, decision making can be defined as *the selection based on some criteria of one behavior alternative from two or more possible alternatives.*

DECISION MAKING AND ALTERNATIVES

For decision making to exist, there must be two or more alternatives present. If there is only one choice there is no decision to be made. Figure 7–1 shows a situation for which there are five possible behavior alternatives, A_1, A_2, A_3, A_4, and A_5. Moving to the right on the figure, of these five alternatives, three are available for choice. A_2, for example, is outside the sphere of discretion and hence is eliminated; the decision maker is unaware of A_5. The possible outcomes for each available alternative are predicted, followed by an evaluation of each outcome in terms of relative desirability. To illustrate, for A_3, the outcomes are A_3O_1, A_3O_2, and A_3O_3. Comparing the outcomes of the various available alternatives, A_3O_1, A_3O_2, and A_3O_3 are considered most favorable, and hence A_3 is the decision followed. The decision is based on the criterion or basis believed important in the particular situation and represents a choice, from a group of alternatives, or what the manager feels is the

FIGURE 7–1

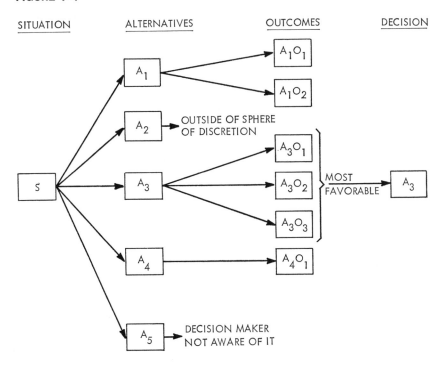

best action to be taken for the particular state of affairs as he sees them. In other words the alternative is selected by considering all he knows about all the alternatives. He believes the one selected to be the most compatible with the attainment of the objective under the given conditions.

OBSERVATIONS ON SELECTION OF ALTERNATIVE

It is a simple matter to state that alternatives are evaluated in terms of their respective probable outcomes, but to determine the relative merits usually poses real difficulties. The requirement is to make comparisons based on values, be they economic, psychological, social, or political. And conflict among these values is quite likely. There are normally both desirable and undesirable aspects in every alternative, but these conflicting values must be reconciled in some manner satisfactory to the manager.

Many problems requiring a decision are not solved by a simple "Yes" or "No." There is a little "Yes" and a little "No" in most decisions. In other words, decision making is not a matter of black or white, but mostly in-between, or gray. It is appropriate to visualize a strip one-mile wide labeled "black" and another strip one-mile wide labeled "white." Between these strips is another strip 1000-miles wide of "gray" and it is within this wide gray band with all the degrees and combinations of black and white that most decisions exist.

Help in decision making is gained by concentrating on the really important facets of the problem. This is a common mark of most successful managers. It also helps to eliminate the least attractive alternatives as well as those which are impractical for the manager to follow with his particular resources. Also to be observed is that in any given case none of the alternatives may be entirely satisfactory, but they are the best in that given case.

Furthermore, the alternative selected by the manager may prove to be inadequate, owing to his inability to see the future without error. In decision making the manager is dealing with future values which for the most part are unknown. Efforts are made to reduce the element of chance due to futurity, but it can never be reduced to zero.

In most cases there are limitations of the decision maker's knowledge which condition the alternative selected. A manager's ability to decide is bounded by the scope of his comprehension and understanding of the area for which the decision is being made. A decision can only be as good as the decider's values permit him to see the problem and to conceive what might possibly be done about it. Generally speaking, in most decision making, some alternatives are ignored simply because the decision-maker's knowledge does not permit him to be aware of them. This condition was included in Figure 7–1.

In contrast, it should be noted that normally the alternatives must be within certain stated constraints. The financial position of an enterprise may eliminate consideration of a decision necessitating large capital expenditures. And all managerial decisions are constrained by the abilities of employees to carry out the decisions. Furthermore, it is common for trade unions, through collective bargaining, to establish various constraints which the manager recognizes in his decision-making work. Likewise, governments through their various regulatory measures place constraints upon much managerial decision making. There are also constraints placed upon decision making by factors external to the enterprise, including the public, technology, other enterprises, and world affairs.

Frequently, aid in evaluating alternatives is gained from answers to specific and pertinent questions. Consider the case of a production con-

FIGURE 7–2.   Decision making for special handling of production order

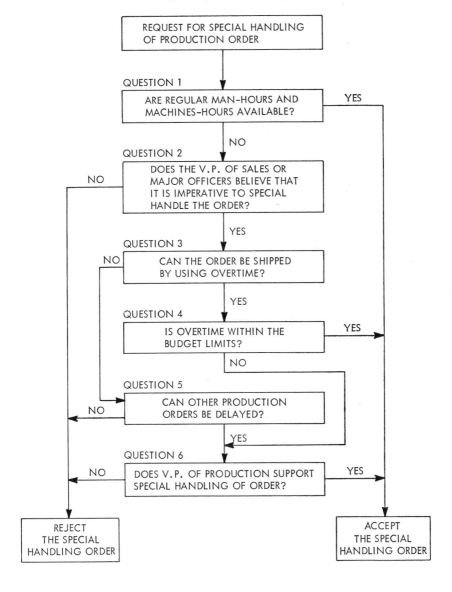

trol manager deciding on a request for special handling of a production order. The decision whether to use special handling or not is arrived at by answering questions such as those shown in chart form by Figure 7–2. The first question is "Are regular man-hours and machine-hours available for this activity?" An answer of "Yes" leads to special handling of the order as shown by the line at the right of the drawing. In contrast, an answer of "No" to the second question leads to rejection of the special handling.

Lastly, it should be noted that the selection of the alternative can be strongly influenced by following the practice of a leader. In such instances, the managers of a well-known company set the precedent and others calmly follow. Also, in many instances, and, especially at the top management levels, the decision has already been tacitly accepted when the formal investigation for formulating a decision is launched. That is, by the time a formal study is launched about a problem, the fundamental decision has unwittingly been reached; determining the means of implementation is the main issue. When this condition exists, the decision-making process is reduced to a corroboratory ex post facto analysis. Influences such as these—follow-the-leader and acceptance prior to determination—tend to make for "patterned" decisions.

JUDGMENT AND DECISION MAKING

Important in decision making is judgment. When values are clear, information is adequate, and risks are reasonably predictive, the decision making may appear to be void of judgment. But such is not the case because, in selecting the alternative, comparison of values and relations of things must be mentally formulated and asserted. Consider, in contrast, the situation where value comparisons are difficult, information spotty, and risks are mostly unknown. Here the presence and need for judgment is more evident. In fact, under such conditions, judgment becomes the medium by which conflicting values are resolved, risks assessed, and alternatives evaluated.

FIGURE 7–3. The spectrum of decisions

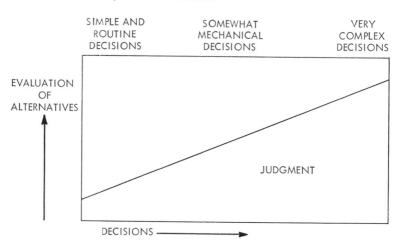

Figure 7–3 shows these concepts in which might be termed "the spectrum of decisions." Evaluation of alternatives is represented by the vertical scale; decisions are represented on the horizontal scale. On the left or lower end of the spectrum are the simple, routine decisions—those requiring easy comparison of alternatives; toward the middle are the more complex decisions; at the right or upper end are the extremely complex decisions. Judgment is present throughout the entire spectrum but at the lower left end is relatively small. In moving to the right, or going up the spectrum, more and more judgment is injected into the decision making.

TYPES OF DECISIONS

Managers are called upon to decide issues in many different areas. To illustrate, for common major business functions, important types of decisions include the following.

1. Production decisions relating to:
   - 1.1 Volume of output
   - 1.2 Location of plant
   - 1.3 Layout of plant
   - 1.4 Methods of production
   - 1.5 Allocation of facilities
   - 1.6 Balancing of production line
   - 1.7 Purchasing practices
   - 1.8 Amount of inventory
   - 1.9 Wage payment plan
   - 1.10 Extent of technical research

2. Sales decisions relating to:
   - 2.1 Determination of markets
   - 2.2 Location of sales offices
   - 2.3 Packaging of the products
   - 2.4 Brand name used
   - 2.5 Marketing channels employed
   - 2.6 Price
   - 2.7 Extent and kind of advertising
   - 2.8 Sales compensation methods
   - 2.9 Sales promotional efforts
   - 2.10 Use and extent of marketing research

3. Finance decisions relating to:
   - 3.1 Capital structure
   - 3.2 Credit terms
   - 3.3 Amounts of working capital
   - 3.4 Securing of new funds
   - 3.5 Payment of dividends
   - 3.6 Refinancing plans
   - 3.7 Determining cost of operations
   - 3.8 Office systems
   - 3.9 Mergers
   - 3.10 Liquidation

4. Personnel decisions relating to:

    4.1 Sources of labor supply
    4.2 Selection techniques
    4.3 Extent and kind of training
    4.4 Job analysis and evaluation
    4.5 Negotiations with unions
    4.6 Handling tardiness and absenteeism

    4.7 Use of suggestion system
    4.8 Pension plans
    4.9 Safety promotion
    4.10 Relations of company with outside groups

Decisions can be classified in any number of ways. One classification, by its degree of uncertainty, is especially helpful. Usually decisions of a

FIGURE 7–4. Classification of decisions by the extent of uncertainty involved

	Risk	*Characteristics*
1. High certainty	Low	Repeated sufficiently to reduce uncertainty to a minimum. Decisions are of a routine nature, usually affect a small group only, and are easy to apply. Prediction of decision outcome is nearly perfect.
2. Fair amount of certainty	Medium	Reasonable estimates of uncertainty are possible. Decisions affect two or three departments at maximum.
3. Considerable uncertainty	Above average	Little surety of hoped-for results from decisions. Includes large areas of activity.
4. Great uncertainty	High	Situations cover very broad areas and many nonpredictable factors.

high certainty are made at the lower organization levels and decisions involving great uncertainty are made at the higher levels. In the words of Aristotle, "Every situation has its own degree of certainty, and a well-trained man accepts that degree and does not look for a greater one." Figure 7–4 illustrates different types of decisions according to the extent of uncertainty involved.

The higher the certainty, the more simple, routine, and repetitive the decision making. Decisions of this type can be standardized by establishing prescribed means for performing certain work. When this practice is followed, there is reasonable predictability of activities covered by such decisions. This kind of decision making is found when decisions pertain to easily observed operations and involve quantity and quality measurements.

PROBABILITY AND DECISION MAKING

Many management decisions involve uncertainty in various degrees but normally not total ignorance. Managers have long sought to minimize the uncertainty in their decisions. To this end they utilize research of various kinds including material, product, process, and market. Also, insurance is employed extensively. Another method is to deal systematically with the uncertainty by evaluating the probabilities of an event happening as revealed by the application of the probability theory wherever possible. Briefly measurable units of the phenomena are used to determine mathematically the chances of a certain outcome taking place from these phenomena.

In one sense, probability denotes the extent of an individual's belief in the truth of a declared statement. Basically it consists of figuring the odds. Illustrative is the belief that there is an 80 percent chance, or 4 to 1 odds, that it will not snow in Chicago on October 1. The person is not certain of his belief, but the probability of its being true is 80 percent. In another sense, probability means the relative frequency with which a specific event occurs when an action is repeated many times. For example, the probability of drawing the ace of spades from a deck of cards is $1/52$, or 1 time in 52 on the average. This is the common concept that mathematicians use in applying the theory of probability.

In connection with decisions and probability, the mathematical theorem developed by Thomas Bayes of the 18th century is helpful. In effect this theorem states that the knowledge of a certain probability of an event occurring can be modified should additional evidence which seems to differ from the first be obtained. An adjusted, or new probability, is derived by means of the Bayesian formula which is written mathematically as:

$$ P\left(\frac{E_1}{E_0}\right) = \frac{PE_1 \times P\left(\frac{E_0}{E_1}\right)}{PE_1 \times P\left(\frac{E_0}{E_1}\right) + PE_2 \times P\left(\frac{E_0}{E_2}\right)} $$

where

$$P\left(\frac{E_1}{E_0}\right) = \text{the adjusted probability due to additional knowl-}$$
edge

PE_1 = the initial probability of the first operation or by the first party

$$P\left(\frac{E_0}{E_1}\right) = \text{the probability of the second operation or by the}$$
second party

PE_2 = the coefficient of the initial probability of the first operation made by the first party. Mathematical value is $(1 - PE_1)$

$$P\left(\frac{E_0}{E_2}\right) = \text{the probability of the second operation or by the}$$
second party being, or is, erroneous.

An example will clarify how this theorem is used. Assume a business man wants to expand his manufacturing facilities and he estimates the price for his major product will not increase. Based on his knowledge of market conditions, experience, and talks with friends, he feels he can be about 65 percent certain of price stability, but he wants to be at least 80 percent sure before going ahead with the expansion. He engages the help of a management consultant who utilizes all relevant information and analyses to the product under discussion to determine the probability of price not increasing. The consultant concludes that price will not increase and further estimates that his conclusion has a 75 percent probability of being correct, and that if there is an increase, the probability is 25 percent that the consultant would be in error; that is, he would predict no rise in price. Substituting appropriate values in the formula above gives:

$$\begin{aligned}
P\left(\frac{E_1}{E_0}\right) &= \frac{0.65 \times 0.75}{0.65 \times 0.75 + 0.35 \times 0.25} \\
&= \frac{0.4875}{0.5750} \\
&= 84.8\%
\end{aligned}$$

In other words, the business man can be 84.8 percent sure that the price of his product will not increase.

The use of probability in management decision making is increasing. To calculate the likelihood of certain events and to supply an estimate of the gain or loss from a decision assists the manager in selecting the best decision for a given set of circumstances. In addition, knowledge of probability helps shape effective conclusions from evidence that appears at first to be insufficient or inadequate. This involves sampling and the use of small amounts of data to represent their totality.

DECISION TREE

A technique helpful in decision making is the decision tree. It is a representation in diagram form of a number of possible future events that may effect a decision. Relative values for the predicted outcomes of each decision are considered. The outcome having the highest value indicates the course most likely to produce the highest dollar return. From a decision point the decision tree approach links a number of possible actions and possible events by means of straight lines so that the total effect resembles a tree lying on its side. See Figure 7–5.

In this illustration a manufacturer has the alternatives of acquiring

FIGURE 7–5. A decision tree

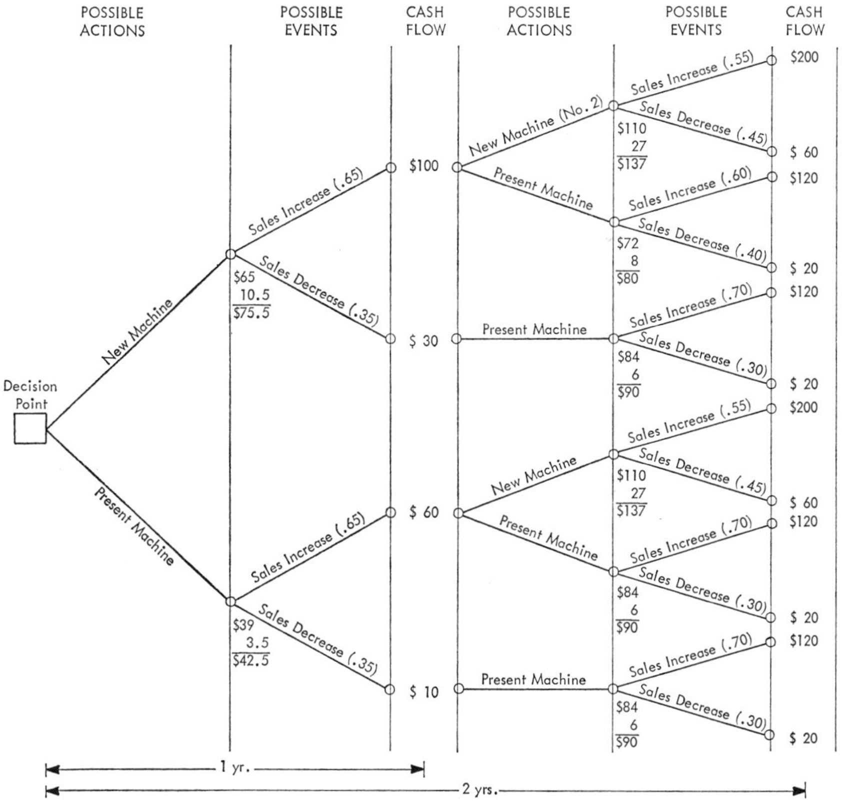

Note: All dollar figures in terms of thousands of dollars.

a new machine or keeping the present machine. These two possible actions are shown emerging from the decision point at the left of the drawing. We can assume that sales of material parts made on this machine may increase or decrease with respective probabilities of 0.65 and 0.35 as indicated on the diagram. For simplicity of analysis, we will use estimated net cash flows which will result for the several outcomes. To illustrate, the estimated net cash flow for a new machine and a sales increase is $100,000, for a new machine and for sales decrease the amount is $30,000. By the manufacturer running the present machine and sales increasing (lower left of Fig. 7–5), the net cash flow is estimated at $60,000, whereas, for sales decreasing the amount is $10,000. These data are for one year's operations.

Multiplying the probabilities by the net cash flow and summing them gives the total expected value the manufacturer can expect from any possible action. In Figure 7–5, this is $75,500 for the new machine (0.65 × $100,000 plus 0.35 × $30,000) and $42,500 for the present machine (0.65 × $60,000 plus 0.35 × $10,000). The better decision is to use the new machine as the expected value from it is greater than that from the present machine. The decision tree approach enables the decision maker to evaluate alternatives in terms of the best estimates of future results.

Extending the analysis we continue the diagram as shown by the right portion of Figure 7–5. For example, at the decision point of the new machine-sales increase (top of illustration) at the beginning of the second year the manufacturer has the alternative of buying another new machine (machine number 2) to replace the one he acquired last year or continue with the then present one. For a sales decrease forecast it is assumed continuation of the then present machine will be followed. For the new machine (number 2) the probabilities for sales increase and for sales decrease are shown under the possible events column to the right. Likewise, alternatives and subsequent probability values are shown for all other points included in the diagram. Again, working from right to left, and using the estimated net cash flow data for the end of the second year, the total expected value for new machine (number 2) and sales increase is $110,000 (0.55 ×$200,000), for sales decrease $27,000 (0.45 × $60,000), or a total of $137,000. Comparable data are shown on the diagram. From these data we would decide to (1) buy the new machine at the beginning of the first year and again buy a new machine at the beginning of the second year. This would probably give us a two-year total expected value of $137,000. Based on the data used in this illustration we would get this same result

($137,000) by using the old machine at the beginning of the first year and using a new machine at the beginning of the second year. Actually this would be the more economical decision as it would entail less expenditure since only one new machine is acquired.

Analysis for the third year might result in a changed pattern for the manufacturer. Decision trees are helpful not only in decision making, but also in planning. However, the technique becomes rather cumbersome for periods exceeding three years and also estimates of probabilities and of net cash flows are quite speculative for too distant periods.

WHO SHOULD MAKE DECISIONS

For any given situation, the decision is the result of efforts by one person or of a group. Which approach is used depends upon the circumstances. The individual approach is common when the decision is fairly easy to reach. Likewise, when the group has little knowledge or background in the subject area or the issue is of an emergency nature, the individual approach is probably superior. In contrast, decisions by a group are growing in popularity. The use of results management is illustrative, for in this approach the employee decides his objectives which are reviewed and approved by his superiors. Also, the use of participation in management usually means participation in decision making, or decisions by the group. Group decision making helps to develop the members of the group and gives them a chance to voice their opinions concerning matters that affect their work.

But it should also be observed that decision making is essentially a lonely task. It is human to want to enjoy support from the outside and to share the risk of error. Few like to face important issues entirely alone, especially when what is decided may be contrary to the deep desires of subordinates and thus risk their devotion and loyalty. Figure 7–6 is a

FIGURE 7–6

Group decision	
is	*is not*
Being fair to all members of the group	Giving each individual what he wants
A means of getting together different attitudes	Manipulating group members
Letting a member tell what he thinks should be done to solve a problem	Selling the ideas of the superior manager to the members of the group
Group discipline through social pressure	Throwing discipline to the winds
Problem solving cooperatively	Seeking mere advice through consultative supervision

comparison chart spelling out what group decision is and what it is not.

In the interest of clarity, it is appropriate to state that decision making consists basically of several steps including: (1) determine alternatives, (2) evaluate each alternative, and (3) select the alternative which becomes the decision.[1] When the individual approach is followed, the individual decision maker himself performs all the steps. Referring to Figure 7–7 and reading across the top, when decision making is indi-

FIGURE 7–7

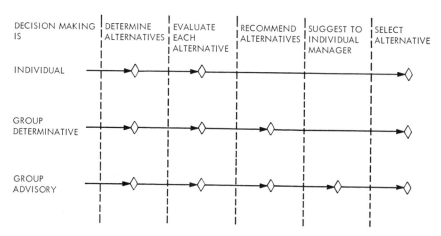

vidual, the steps are to determine, evaluate, and select. When the group approach is practiced, additional steps are injected between the evaluating and selecting steps. For a group the steps are to determine, evaluate, recommend, and either select directly the alternative or suggest to an individual manager who selects the alternative to be chosen. The former arrangement, in which the group selects the alternative, may be termed *group determinative* decision making; the latter arrangement, in which the group suggests its recommendation to an individual manager who then selects the alternative to be followed, may be termed *group advisory* decision making. In this latter type, the individual manager can modify or even reject the group's recommendation. In some cases the individual manager's selection of the group's recommendation may be

---

[1] Some managers prefer to list five steps for decision making, including: (1) define the problem, (2) analyze the problem, (3) determine alternatives, (4) suggest alternative to adopt, and (5) put it into action. This is more complete since it points out the need to define and analyze the problem before determining alternatives and also gives stress to putting the selected alternative into action. However, the three steps listed in the text above suffice to distinguish between individual and group decision making.

almost routine; especially is this true if the group predominantly favors one alternative that is entirely agreeable to the individual manager.

DECISIONS BY INDIVIDUAL

The one-manager decision-making setup is in keeping with the popular concept of a manager. This arrangement stems from the one-man owner beginning of many enterprises. They were established by one man who made all the decisions, or at least all the major ones. As the enterprise grew, the tendency was for this individual to continue to handle most of the decision making because he believed secretly that

FIGURE 7–8. What a manager's subordinates should be told about a crisis decision

The manager should
1. Tell why he made the decision without giving them prior notice.
2. Relate expectancies in the execution of the decision.
3. Discuss the extent to which particular activities or interests were considered before he made the decision.
4. Tell them the flexibility they have in carrying out his decision.
5. Be sure they understand (a) an emergency came up, (b) he had to decide quickly, and (c) he is relying on them to make his decision effective.

others in the enterprise were perhaps less competent than he, that decisions by others might prove costly, or that to permit others to make decisions might mean a loss of prestige or power by him. Many managers want to be the ones that decide, at least in the ultimate or upon important issues.

The decision to meet an emergency is typically of the individual manager type. In an emergency there isn't time to talk it over, seek advice, or resolve many different ideas of what might be done. The decision must be made without delay. However, before implementing the decision, or at least in its very early stages of implementation, the manager should communicate with those to be affected by the decision in order to help them understand the decision and know the circumstances that caused such action to be taken. Figure 7–8 gives suggestions for what the manager who makes a crisis decision should do in relationship with his subordinates.

In many respects crisis decisions test the true measure of a manager's ability. There are always emergencies, but there is cause for real concern if emergency decision making is the order rather than the exception.

Whether to make or defer an emergency decision is a question depending mainly on the consequences of not acting. There can be no uniform set of rules to cover emergency decision making; yet reason cannot be abandoned. History is rich with stories of men who have risen to the challenge requiring emergency decisions. Julius Caesar, the Duke of Wellington, General Robert E. Lee, General Dwight D. Eisenhower, and Admiral Nimitz are a few from the long list of such decision makers. These were men who interpreted facts imaginatively, recognized opportunity, and understood decision making.

Many reason that decision making involving highly technical considerations can best be done by the scientist qualified in the given technical area. Is not the expert the one to make the decision, they argue. Who understands better all the scientific ramifications than he? In contrast, others contend that not all scientists are effective in decision making. They qualify their statements too much, may not be fully informed, or are inexperienced in dealing with people. Hence, the argument goes, decisions relating to technology should be made by groups. But here again questions arise such as: What persons should constitute the group? Should it be determinative or advisory? With the tremendous scientific progress to be made over the next several decades and with scientists called upon to fill greater and greater roles, the traditional concepts of individual and of group decision making may undergo drastic revision.

DECISIONS BY GROUP

Many favor group decision making, believing it gives those who will be affected by a decision a chance to participate in its formulation and helps to develop the members of the group. A person is more inclined to follow a decision enthusiastically if he had some part in shaping it. And group decisions help satisfy individual needs, such as a sense of feeling wanted, of being important, and being "in the know." Also, at its best, decision making should involve vigorous discussion of the various alternatives, a condition fulfilled by the group decision approach.

Some advocates of group decision making, especially that of the advisory group, feel that assistance can and should be obtained from others, but also feel that the task of selecting the alternative should remain basically an individual task. Their viewpoints go along the following lines. The manager must accept and retain his decision-making task in order to retain his managerial status. The real purpose of seeking suggestions from others is to gain a better understanding of the issue to be decided. Further, the decision maker can evaluate best the suggestions and opinions offered in terms of their real meaning and consequence to the particular group or the enterprise.

In this age of great technological change, the issues to be decided have grown beyond the expertise of the top manager in many companies. The input of many people is called for, each unique in knowledge and experience. This sharing of decision-making responsibilities establishes interdependence among the parties. Thus, group cooperation is enhanced and the old authoritarian concept of decision making is reduced.

However, in actual practice group decision making is subject to a great many limitations. Some members will contribute far more than others, and both the status and power of some members will exceed that of other members. Furthermore, in some instances, certain members seldom differ with the opinions expressed by other group members; and in other instances, when they do differ, they can exercise little influence upon what is finally decided.

There is also the question of the degree of freedom which the manager permits. If he is subordinate-centered, he will define fairly broad limits and expect the group members to make their decision within these limits. Then he follows the decision usually with very minor, if any, adjustments. Various degrees of decisional freedom can be followed as indicated by Figure 7–9. At the top is the subordinate-centered, great freedom arrangement. In contrast, the bottom or the situation where the manager makes the decision and tells the group members what it is, represents the area of no freedom and symbolizes one type of the individual manager approach to decision making.

In addition, the manager frequently finds that after talking it over he still must make the decision; that is, the deciding of what to do still is up to him—the decision does not evolve from the group discussion. He may have won approval of many proposed decisions and received excellent suggestions for the modifications of others, but in the final analysis, he must decide what to do. In many instances, from all the information submitted plus his own ideas and individual experiences, he is able to create a new course which is neither a compromise nor simply a fusion of the material submitted but a new approach which appears ideally suited for the particular problem.

Committees, the membership of which may vary widely, commonly make up the group to do the deciding. While a committee is satisfactory, its decisions evolve as the result of compromise and are based not on the best but on the average on which the committee members can agree. There can be an element of procrastination in their decisions in that they omit controversial elements, which subsequently appear for debate. Furthermore, from the very nature of a committee it follows that there is some lack of fixed responsibility for specific

FIGURE 7–9. Relative degrees of decision making

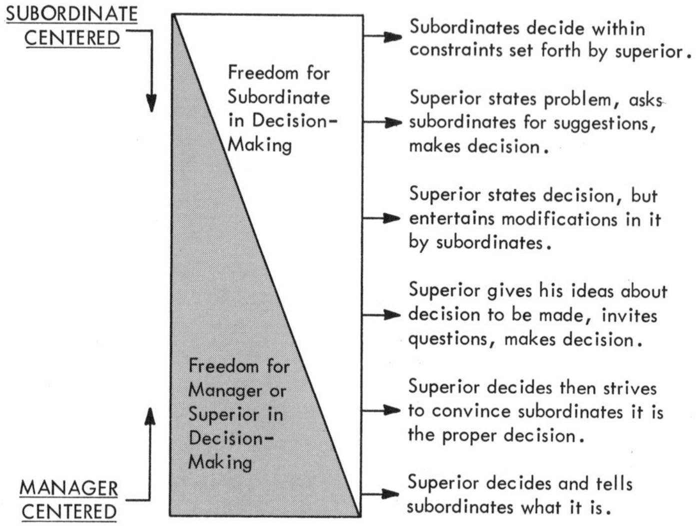

contributions. A committee may accept this responsibility, but inherently it is divided among its members.[2]

IMPLEMENTING THE DECISION

The successful manager not only knows how to make good decisions but also to construct an effective plan for carrying out the decision. Some executives have trouble getting their decisions implemented, thus to a degree voiding the goodness of the decision formulated. And as we shall see in the next chapter, some techniques of decision making emphasize the determining of the decision with little or no attention being given to the decision's implementation. Thus, when such techniques are followed, the determining of the decision's implementation is especially important.[3]

---

[2] Committees are discussed in detail in Chapter 17, pp. 393–97.
[3] See page 141.

Effective implementation of a decision necessitates a questioning attitude toward every detail of the decision and toward the steps required to carry it out. The sequence of the steps, the responsibilities of the individuals involved, and the controls to be practiced must be spelled out precisely. It is helpful to pinpoint in advance difficulties likely to be encountered and to make provisions for handling these difficulties.

Further, the decision and how it is to be implemented must be communicated to those who will be involved or affected by the decision. To neglect the human beings intended to carry out the decision is to court considerable difficulty, if not total failure. The reason for the decision, the action called for, what adjustments are required, each individual's role, and what results are expected are among the major types of information that should be communicated.

In addition, participation in the decision making helps formulate acceptable means for putting the decision into effect. The task of adequate communication is lightened by employee participation for through the decisions employees become familiar with what is decided and why, as well as the hoped-for gains to be made by implementing the decision. In many cases the participants' most helpful contributions are in determining how to implement the decision. Their intimate knowledge of both the work and other members of the work force make this so.

AIDS FOR THE DECISION MAKER

Decision making is difficult. There are times when a decision maker is disposed to feel that no matter which route he takes he probably will wish he had taken another. But management requires decisions, and a manager cannot have the fatal disposition noted by Herman Melville of "sailing around an island without landing, and talking around a subject without getting at it."

In the work of decision making, the following aids are helpful:

1. *Aim Every Decision to Contribute toward Goal Achievement.* Knowledge of the stated goal helps to simplify the task of decision making. Both the practicability and the applicability of the decision are vital. If the objective is complicated or involved, write it out. Recognize the assumptions made, the constraints identified, and the major reasons for the alternative selected.

2. *Use Creativity in the Decision Making.* The best answer may be something never done before or a combination of familiar ideas

grouped together in a new way. More than straight, cold logic may be helpful. Imagination and inventiveness are usually excellent keys to the development of possible alternatives and courses of action. Include practical compromises.

3. Remember That Decision Making Is Mental Action; It Must Be Transferred into Physical Action. The actual work that appears to make up decision making consists of many and perhaps rambling mental concepts and ideas thought of discursively. Decision-making difficulty is not having an excess of issues to decide nor is it having too little time, but it is surmounting mental hurdles and getting from mental to physical action. Remember too that the decision must be implemented.

4. Recognize That a Decision Will Bring Change by Means of a Chain of Actions. All functions of an enterprise are interrelated. Adding or modifying an existent activity brings about changes in many or all the other activities. Through decision making, try to attain improvement. The chain of actions set off by a decision commonly extends beyond the boundaries of the originally intended realm of influences. Be prepared to defend, modify, or delete a decision in view of the chain of actions it brings about. For this purpose it is advisable to review a potential decision on these points: (*a*) what can go wrong with this decision, (*b*) how serious would each of these situations be, (*c*) can the decision be modified to lessen the possible impact of each such error, (*d*) what is the estimated expenditure to minimize these possible mistakes and is it worth it, and (*e*) how long should the proposed decision be in effect to determine its correctness; that is, when is it time to modify or reverse the decision.

5. Maintain a Stability about the Decisions Used. Excessive reopening of decisions can be a source of great frustration, and it gives cause for alarm. When new facts or perspectives warrant, it is satisfactory to reconsider the decision, but this should not be done to the point where the regularized procedures for conducting the affairs of the enterprise are hindered or, what is worse, placed in jeopardy. Do not adopt incomplete decisions or constantly modify existent ones because of what is considered a better solution.

6. Use Trial Runs to Determine the Feasibility of Most New Decisions. A sample installation requires only a minimum of resources and reveals how things will probably shape up. After the weak points have been discovered, the decision can be changed accordingly and the corrected action expanded. Also, in some cases, it is possible to divide the decision with respective subsequent actions into phases. After each phase, both the preceding and succeeding steps can be reviewed, improved if necessary, and then the next phase of the decision implemented. This approach avoids full decision commitment at the start without retrieval.

7. *Take Sufficient Time for Decision Making.* A manager is usually not required to make snap decisions. Rapidly shifting conditions may permit little time for reflection, but this does not mean that hastily conceived decisive action is necessitated. Immediate action does not imply sudden decisions. Normally it is helpful to mull over various ideas and possibilities so that the subject can be given adequate thought and the various ramifications identified and properly evaluated. To this end, and if possible, request time to think it over and ask for a list of the topics or problems to be decided well in advance of the deadline dates. However, don't delve into so many aspects of a situation that confusion rather than clarity is present. It is well to note a famous saying in this respect: "He who considers too much will perform little."

8. *Make the Decisions—Never Default.* Face up to the decision for action. The worst decision is to decide not to decide. If letting things continue as they are, or doing nothing, is believed the best decision, know why this is so. Drifting can get a manager into a lot of trouble. Do not strive unnecessarily and uneconomically for the perfect answer. Costly delay is suffered in trying to get a 95 percent correct answer up to 99 percent correct. Almost every problem has a short, but limited, answer. It can serve as a beginning. Needless delay may result in a waiver of decision making, and others may assume this function. Furthermore, one must practice decision making to gain proficiency in it. Observing or studying what others decide appears to have very limited value in developing decision-making ability. Seize opportunities for decision making. There are ample events for such a practice—events in the home, office, shop, factory, club, or school.

9. *Institute Follow-Up to Each Decision.* This is important, not only to see that the decision is carried out, but also to appraise the results from the decision. Expect some wrong decisions. As Theodore Roosevelt said. "He who makes no mistakes makes no progress." This does not advocate irresponsibility but rather decision-making action guided by reasonable care and prudence. Correct the bad decision as quickly as possible. The tragedy of a bad decision occurs when a manager is compelled to live with an error or commits the same error in another decision.

10. *Recognize That Everybody Will Not Be Pleased with The*

Decision. Most decisions cannot be in keeping with everyone who is interested, concerned, or affected by the decision. There is almost always someone who feels a different decision would be better. After the decision is reached, the challenge is to explain the decision and win cooperation of the entire group.

QUESTIONS

1. For each of the following problems state whether it is one of information, prediction, or decision, along with the reasons for your answers: (*a*) Should Mr. Kay, the assistant controller, be promoted to controller? (*b*) What paper forms are used in company M for controlling production? (*c*) Will the 3:15 P.M. flight get Mr. Snyder to New Orleans in time for his meeting? and (*d*) Which manufacturing process is better for order RM 361?
2. Explain what each of the following means: (*a*) group advisory decision making, (*b*) most decisions consist of a little "yes" and a little "no," and (*c*) a decision tree.
3. In your opinion what is the effect upon decision making when results management is used to modify the process of management approach?
4. As you see it, which is better, a decision reached by an individual or by a group? Discuss.
5. Explain Figure 7–5 in your own words.
6. Define each of the following: (*a*) patterned decision, (*b*) crisis decision, (*c*) uncertainty of decision, and (*d*) routine decision.
7. Do you agree with this statement, "All decision making contains some degree of judgment." Justify your answer.
8. Discuss briefly three ways in which decisions can be made more effective.
9. Are you of the opinion that limitations of the decision maker's knowledge affect the alternative selected? Justify your viewpoint by relating several examples from your own experience.
10. As a member of a group, such as of school, business, church, or community, what amount of freedom or relative degree of decision making (see Figure 7–9) does the formal manager of this group practice? Why in your opinion does he follow this practice? Elaborate on your answer.
11. Rodney Faber, a manager, faces a very difficult situation about which to make a decision. He does not know what to do. Consulting with his immediate subordinates, he finds that they do not know what to decide any more than he does. Rodney decides to not decide, hoping that with time the situation will either ease or suggest what decision to make. Is this action of Rodney Faber's good or bad? Why?
12. Discuss the subject of probability and its use in decision making.
13. In view of the fact that effective decision making requires sufficient time, are crisis decisions usually effective? Justify your answer using an example to illustrate your viewpoint.
14. Discuss the subject "Implementing the Decision."

CASE 7–1. GIFFORD COMPANY

For years employees of Gifford Company selected the period for their annual vacation. Most selected a time during June, July, or August, but a few selected early spring or late fall. An employee received 2-weeks' paid vacation after 2-years' service and up to 15-years' service. Three weeks were given for 15 years up to 25 years. After 25 years an employee was given 4 weeks. About 85 percent of the employees were female, and since the majority of them worked only 5 to 6 years due to marriage or for family reasons, most vacations were of 2-weeks' duration.

Mr. Wilbur Lasser, director of personnel, suggested to the executive committee of the company that a change in vacation practice be adopted by closing the office and plant for a 2-week period during July. To justify his proposal, Mr. Lasser pointed out that the present arrangement was becoming untenable and there are always disappointments by some who do not get to go at a time in keeping with their first choice. One period for all is the simple and fair solution. Further, data developed with Mr. Frey, the works manager, show it would be less costly to close the plant for 2 weeks. Those entitled to more than 2 weeks would be compensated at their regular rate for the additional time, i.e., a person entitled to 3-weeks' vacation would receive 2-weeks' vacation and an extra week's pay.

A member of the executive committee raised the question whether the matter should be submitted to the employees for them to decide or at least to give their suggestions and preferences. For the committee to decide and authorize its implementation may give rise to employee ill feelings and much unrest. The controller, a member of the executive committee, said he did not believe that would be the case. It must be recognized, as Mr. Lasser pointed out, that not all employees are getting to go on their vacations when they want to. We are not pleasing everybody now and we will not do so under any plan, whether we ask the employees' opinions or do not. We should simply develop the plan, announce it, and give the valid reasons for adopting it.

Mr. Frey, also a committee member, pointed out that another consideration must be viewed. It is that the company requires employees to work regularly scheduled workdays before and after the vacation period to receive vacation pay. For example, if the vacation is July 12–23, eligibility requirements call for working Friday, July 9, and Monday, July 26. Otherwise some will try to stretch the authorized 2-week period.

Mr. Lasser added that this requirement is already in effect. But he added there is another point to be considered. Suppose Independence Day is included in the 2-week period. Do we pay holiday pay for this day or give the preceding Friday or the following Monday in exchange for the holiday. I guess what I am trying to say is, do we give 10 full working days as the prescribed vacation period?

Well, I believe that's another reason for our discussing this vacation business thoroughly, stated Mr. Frey. It must be carefully worked out before we announce it.

Questions

1. What vacation arrangement do you favor for the Gifford Company? Justify your answer.
2. What is your general opinion of Mr. Frey's comments?
3. What action do you recommend the company take with respect to its vacation arrangement and how should it be implemented? Discuss fully.

CASE 7–2.   EAST BEND HEAT TREATERS, INC.

The service rendered by this company consists of heat treating machined metal parts and foundry castings in order to give them required hardness or desired internal structure, in keeping with the use to which they would be applied. Over the years, Mr. Orwell Busch built the business to its present level, which consists of annual sales of about $500,000; number of employees, 37; average profits after taxes, $32,000 (last three years); and number of "regular" customers, 207. The selling and interviews with customers were handled personally by Mr. Busch. The shop was managed by Mr. Charles Bertnicki, a competent shop man who came up through the ranks at the plant, as did also his five foremen. Mr. Bertnicki works closely with Mr. Busch, who makes all the major decisions and is the real head of the corporation.

A month ago Mr. Busch suffered a fatal heart attack. He was 55 years old. His will specified his 57 percent ownership of the corporation be given to his wife, Amelia, age 52, who never had been active in the business and knows very little about it. Her lawyer suggested that she get someone to manage the corporation and stated that perhaps some present member of the corporation should be selected. Mrs. Busch talked with Mr. Bertnicki, who said he did not feel he knew enough about the sales end of the business, he didn't like selling, and he would not be interested in assuming the responsibility of managing the corporation.

Mr. Henry M. Dellwood, an officer of a real estate company and owner of 40 percent of the stock of East Bend Heat Treaters, Inc., advised Mrs. Busch to find a new manager from outside the corporation. He stated he would like to retain his interest in the corporation but admitted he did not consider himself capable to assume its management.

In conversation with Mr. Timothy O'Leary, a local banker, Mrs. Busch was advised to sell the business and to accept "almost any price for it within reason." Mrs. Busch countered that she needed the business income and doubted that the return on her proceeds from sale of the business invested in securities would supply her with ample income. It is Mr. O'Leary's opinion that a total net amount from the sale of the business would be in the $125 to $150 thousand range. He believes the business might be merged into another corporation, but if such could be arranged, Mrs. Busch would be better off getting her money out of it now, rather than own a portion of a merged corporation. He strongly urges Mrs. Busch not to try to manage the business herself, as she knows nothing about the business and could detract rather than add to the attractiveness of the corporation to an interested buyer. However, Mrs. Busch stated that in times of necessity one can do things formerly believed impossible and since the business means a great deal to her, she feels with time she could learn to manage it reasonably well.

Questions

1. What is your general opinion of Mr. O'Leary?
2. In your opinion, how did the corporation get into the situation giving rise to this problem?
3. In addition to the possible decisions suggested, what other possibilities are open to Mrs. Busch?
4. What decision do you believe Mrs. Busch should make? Why?

8

Managerial decision making (continued)

Good judgment like wisdom requires careful appraisal of all three sides of the decision cube. Only a human computer with five sensory inputs, electro-biochemical memory core, plus a volition-laden imagination can do this. Industry hasn't been able to produce a like system yet. It is called the Model 1 Homo Sapiens.

W. SIDNEY TAYLOR

CONTINUING THE DISCUSSION of making managerial decisions, we now turn our attention to the various bases for decision making, why different bases are used, and when and what each contributes. The importance and pervasiveness of decision making in management have stimulated much thinking as to the basis and the way in which it can and should be performed. The span of techniques extends, on the one end, from guesses, to the other end, where complex mathematical analyses are employed. From the practical viewpoint there is neither one best technique or combination that should be used under all circumstances. The selection is individual and usually is predicated upon the manager's background, his knowledge, and the facilities available.

BASES FOR DECISION MAKING

For purposes here we have selected a total of ten bases. They are classified into two main groups: *nonquantitative* or *nonmathematical;* and *quantitative* or *mathematical* as follows:

Nonquantitative

1. Intuition   3. Experience
2. Facts   4. Considered opinions

Quantitative

5. Operations research   8. Monte Carlo
6. Linear programming   9. Queueing
7. Simulation   10. Gaming

As we shall see a manager may make a decision by a nonquantitative means or he can use a quantitative means which is quite another way.

The nonquantitative means are helpful not only for problems dealing with objectives—that is, decisions dealing with end results—but also for issues requiring determination of courses of action—so-called decisions covering the means to accomplish the end results. In application the nonquantitative techniques are highly personal in nature, are widely known, and are considered by many as the natural way to make a decision.

In contrast, when the quantitative bases are used, the end results are usually either given or assumed in broad terms. The decision to be made is how best to reach this goal. In other words, what the end results are to be is not a question to be decided; but the means of attaining the end results is. For example, the goal from an end-results decision is to minimize inventory within stated limits or constraints. The means for determining this goal is answered by quantitative techniques, and the means designated is precise. Employing a quantitative basis is relatively personal in selecting or creating the mathematical representation to be used, but the processing of the quantitative data is impersonal yet cannot be followed in a mechanical way.

The concept of decision-making bases for end results and for means (to accomplish end results) is illustrated in Figure 8–1. At the left of the figure, the bases of intuition, facts, experience, and considered opinions are useful for decisions regarding both means and end results, as illustrated by the connecting lines between appropriate rectangles. In contrast, the techniques of operations research, linear programming, simulation, Monte Carlo, queueing, and gaming are useful for decisions regarding the means to be used for accomplishing the end results or goal.

It is interesting to observe these bases of decision making in relation to the different schools of management thought discussed in Chapter 4. Figure 8–2 gives this information.

FIGURE 8–1. Various bases for decision making and their relationship, respectively, to decisions regarding means and end results

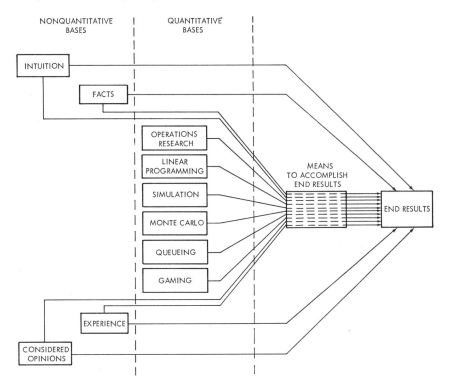

The data shown are indicative only. They represent the preponderance of evidence. In many instances it is not a "yes" or a "no" answer as to whether a certain basis is used in a particular school. One might argue, for example, that intuition is employed in the quantitative measurement school, for in this school, one must decide which of many quantitative techniques to employ and have a belief and feel toward the units to be manipulated. But fundamentally the decision basis is not intuitive but predominantly a quantitative type such as operations research and linear programming.

INTUITION

This is the first of the nonquantitative bases to be discussed. Decision making based on intuition is characterized by the use of hunches or "inner feelings" of the person reaching the decision. Suggestions, influ-

FIGURE 8–2. Different bases of decision making related to selected schools of management thought

		School of management thought						
Decision-making bases	Custom	Scien-tific	Human behavior	Social system	Systems	Deci-sional	Quanti-tative measure-ment	Process
Intuition...............	x	x	x	x	..	x	..	x
Facts..................	x	x	x	x	x	x	x	x
Experience.............	x	x	x	x	x	x	x	x
Considered opinions.......	x	x	x	x	x	x	x	x
Operations research.......	..	..	..	..	..	x	x	..
Linear programming.......	..	..	..	..	..	x	x	..
Simulation..............	..	x	..	..	x	x	x	..
Monte Carlo.............	..	x	..	..	x	x	x	..
Queueing...............	..	..	..	..	..	x	x	..
Gaming................	..	..	x	x	..	x	x	x

ences, preferences, and the psychological makeup of the deciding individual play an important part; the subjective element is vital.

Quite probably the intuitive decision maker is influenced *unconsciously* by his past knowledge, training, and background. But these influences are not habitually utilized by him. The common explanation by the decider is usually "It's just the way I feel about it." No set pattern of decisions is usually made by a person using intuition as a basis. Each problem is apparently individually handled and given an individual decision. However, some consistency in the type of decisions reached can usually be observed.

The intuitive decision maker is usually an activist, moves fast, incisely questions about situations, and finds unique solutions to difficult problems. He leans heavily upon instincts, on his personal feel for a situation, but he tempers his actions with realism. He has the ability to sense opportunities and, by sheer conviction of belief, is able to push forward major decisions. He may be never fully aware of exactly how or why he takes the particular action he does. He is not rational in the usual meaning of that word, but he does bring to his work place each day a form of thought process conditioned by his experiences.

At one time, intuition was considered a precious mental faculty which provided a direct line to the essence of truth. With the advances in the use of other decision-making bases, intuition is sometimes scorned as having little or no validity. This is unfortunate because intuition is an indispensable asset in decision making. In most management problems there are incommensurables consisting of intertwining tangles of human values, needs, and emotions. Intuition is basic. The fact that it has been abused is no basis for discarding it. In the words of Susanne K. Langer, a contemporary philosopher, "Intuition is the basic process of all understanding, just as operative in discursive thought as in clear sense perception and immediate judgment. Intuition is, moreover, the beginning and end of logic; all discursive reasoning would be frustrated without it."

Intuition as a basis of decision making has advantages in that (1) decisions can be reached within a relatively short period of time, (2) a generally satisfactory means for decisive action on problems having limited influence is supplied, and (3) decision-making ability is utilized. On the other hand, the shortcomings include (1) the decision may prove bad, that is, the hunch was incorrect; (2) the means for substantiating the decision to compeers of the decider are unavailable; and (3) other bases for reaching decisions may be unduly minimized or even neglected.

FACTS

Facts are popularly regarded as constituting an excellent basis upon which decisions can be made. The statement that "a decision should be based on adequate facts" is widely accepted. When facts are employed, the decision has its roots, so to speak, in the factual data; and this implies that the premises upon which the decision is based are sound, solid, and of the proper sort. Furthermore, decisions based on adequate facts give the feeling that they are intensely applicable to the particular situation.

The steadily increasing number of computers being installed adds greater and greater emphasis to the use of facts in decision making. Information as a management tool has already acquired high status, and the activities in this area are well-defined and employ the use of highly sophisticated techniques and equipment.[1]

"Adequate facts," however, are not always available. To secure them may cost too much, present too difficult a task, or require too much time. Complete factual information is an ideal to be sought, but perhaps seldom achieved. A manager frequently finds that he is forced to make a decision without as many facts as he might deem adequate. Nevertheless, he uses what data he has but appreciates their deficiency. Furthermore, in arriving at a decision, facts must be carefully diagnosed, classi-

---

[1] See also Chapter 10, p. 201.

fied, and interpreted. The process of relating facts in their correct perspective, in applying proper weights, and in extracting the essential information induces the subjective element of the decision maker and requires an ability, training, and skill wholly apart from that simply of collecting all facts that are available.

In other words, facts alone are seldom sufficient to reach a decision. Imagination, experience, and beliefs are usually required to interpret the facts in their proper perspective and to utilize them advantageously. Facts should give the decision maker confidence and courage to go ahead when his imagination and experience tell him a certain decision is the thing to do. There is always the element of the unknown, no matter what decision-making technique is followed. Facts might reduce, but they never eliminate the unknown. And this is good because it makes the job of the manager exciting.

Costs, an important type of facts, are employed by many managers as a basis for decision making. Cost facts are common to most activities with which the manager deals. Examples include dealing with facts from marginal cost analysis, break-even point cost charts, and cost allocation theories and practices. Cost is so widespread in decision making that some believe "all decisions are cost decisions." But the manager also faces decision-making situations in which it is difficult to utilize cost data. Which of three candidates to select for a new management job is an example.

Facts help assure consistency. Factual data on progress reports, sales accomplishments, and production operations assist in arriving at helpful decisions. Evaluation of accomplishment suggests whether any new decision needs to be made, but the facts seldom tell in detail what the new decision should be.

EXPERIENCE

When a decision must be reached, it is common practice to draw assistance from past events. Having participated in or witnessed a situation similar to the one being decided provides an intimacy and understanding of the issue and suggests possible actions which might be taken. A person sees and understands things in terms of concepts with which he is familiar. He forgoes and in some cases resists approaches which are foreign to his individual experience.

Experience furnishes guides for decision making. It helps answer the question of what to do in particular types of situations. Perhaps the chief value of experience in decision making is developing an ability to discriminate and to generalize past situations. Thus, similar situations along with their decisions, as well as unlike situations and their decisions, can be recognized and evaluated.

Experience may tend to emphasize excessive conservatism in decision making, but this need not follow. "Nothing succeeds like success," but in a rapidly changing economy past success in decision making does not insure future success, nor by the same reasoning does it necessarily follow that an experience-based decision that failed in the past must be avoided, in total, in the future. Experience can be extensive but an incomplete and expensive basis for decision making. Ordinarily a good cause is required in order to vary from established custom. However, astutely applied, this can make for very effective decision making. A manager should use experience, but he need not be blindly bound by it.

Decisions based on experience utilize practical knowledge. Presumably the best portions of the decision-maker's background are used. Also, the decision includes "tried-and-true" ingredients and enjoys acceptance by others. In contrast, decisions based on experience may be predicated on events which are outmoded. The time element is important. The dictates of the experience of last year might be inappropriate today. In addition, the experiences of the decision maker may be somewhat limited, and hence the decision is derived from too narrow a background. It is also possible to overemphasize the traditional and maintain too rigidly the status quo, with the result that progress and improvement are unduly retarded.

CONSIDERED OPINIONS

Many managers rely upon considered opinions in their decision making. This particular basis is distinguished by the use of logic behind the decision—logic which is made explicit and derived from careful analysis of the situation. Furthermore, quantification of the tentative decision is employed. To do this, varying amounts of statistics are collected and related to the decision. For the most part the statistics substantiation is technically valid and acceptable, but there are instances when inappropriate statistical techniques are followed in collecting the data or a very small and sometimes nonrepresentative portion of the data collected is actually utilized.

Considered opinions have won acceptance as managers have given more attention to the group and its acceptance of decisions. Also some managers frequently seek some logical analyses of their decision-making problems, they want some rational process, even though it be small, in their decision making. A simple example will illustrate to what extent rationalization may enter into a considered opinions decision.

Suppose a company general sales manager has decided to reduce his sales cost by dropping sales service to one of two marginal customers. During the past eight years, such a customer, A, has purchased $40,000, while another such customer, B, over the last five years has purchased $25,000. The data are shown by Figure 8–3.

FIGURE 8–3. Sales to two marginal customers for selected years

Sales	Customer A	Customer B
Last year........................	$ 3,500	$ 9,300
2 years ago......................	5,600	7,200
3 years ago......................	6,400	4,000
4 years ago......................	5,900	3,000
5 years ago......................	7,200	1,500
6 years ago......................	5,400	—
7 years ago......................	3,000	—
8 years ago......................	3,000	—
Total......................	$40,000	$25,000
Average per year.................	$ 5,000	$ 5,000

These data help sharpen up the difference between the customers. Eliminating either customer would not represent an average loss of $5,000. Customer A would probably cost the least, customer B, the most. Also the purchasing trend of customer B is increasing while that of customer A is decreasing. Other considerations, especially opinions of the sales manager's colleagues would also be taken into account, but the decision here could well be to retain customer B and eliminate customer A.

QUANTITATIVE TECHNIQUES FOR DECISION MAKING

These techniques for the most part involve problem conception, hypothesis, definition, experiment, and a trading-off among alternatives. The assumptions made are of special importance and usually are carefully defined. The processing toward the answer is rational, orderly patterns of behavior are assumed, and logical explanations and predictions are utilized. Management skill is enhanced because the quantitative techniques seek to support this skill by bringing maximum rationality to it.

The development of the quantitative techniques has come about with improvement in the measurement of the values of the elements involved, with the availability of the computer, and with the desirability for a more logical and systematic approach to current complex managerial problems. The following discussion of these techniques is fundamental, stressing what the technique is, how used, and the types of applications for which it appears most appropriate.

OPERATIONS RESEARCH

The term operations research has grown to mean different things to different people. Some consider it as one technique; others use it to designate most of the quantitative techniques. It originated during World War II, when persons of special competence were assigned the problem of how to get the most out of Great Britain's limited air power during the early years of the war. Later such problems as determining the best pattern for a convoy of ships and the optimum rapidity for operating certain weapons were solved using this technique. The name "operational research" in Great Britain became operations research in the United States, probably because it applied to many operations.

Operations research consists of bringing together available data on a specific problem, processing these data, and from them resolving quantitative reports on the relative merits of various potential courses of action. As indicated in Chapter 4 the concepts of optimization, input-output, and mathematical model are utilized. The model is frequently a series of complex equations of highly involved relationships and applies to a problem that could not be worked by other quantitative techniques. Specifically the steps of operations include (1) precise statement of the problem, (2) collection of relevant data, (3) creation of a valid mathematical model for the pertinent forces or values involved, (4) substitution of data in the model and calculation of results under varying circumstances, (5) selection of the optimum course of action, and (6) follow-up on the model validity with availability of new data.

Problems best suited for operations research are those involving recurring decisions. Generally the problem concerns time, cost, or amount of profits which are to be optimized. Consider the problem of inventory. Operations research can determine the lowest amount of materials to satisfy production requirements, when and what to order, and the manner in which to dispose of an inventory most profitably. In the area of shipping, the elimination of backlogs and the location of production centers for minimum shipping costs are illustrative of operations research application. The evaluation of the economic value of new plant investment, of adding or subtracting products, and of cash flow and cash requirements are further examples.

By means of operations research every important variable, probability, and reasonable outcome for a given decision or set of decisions can be determined before the action is adopted. Operations research not only points out the significant relationships of activities taking place as they do but also predicts events when certain actions are taken. Usually the basic problem is to improve present operations by using the available facilities, but operations research will reveal what, if any, equipment can be improved for better results. These advantages are appealing; yet on the other hand, the amount of data required can be tremendous and the interpretation of these data into a mathematical form commonly is an extremely difficult and time-consuming task. Use of a computer is normally required to make the technique feasible.

LINEAR PROGRAMMING

Usually either matrix algebra or linear mathematical equations are used in this technique. For linear programming to be applicable the following conditions must be satisfied. First, an objective is to be optimized—either a maximum or a minimum value is sought and is expressed in terms of money—profits or cost, time, or quantity. Second, the variables or forces affecting the outcome have linear or straight-line relationship, meaning if one unit requires 5 minutes to produce, then ten units will require 50 minutes. Mathematically, this is defined as the condition where none of the independent variables have exponents greater than 1; i.e., there are no second or third powers, such as X^2 or X^3, in the equation. Third, obstacles or restrictions on the relationships of the variables exist. Without the restriction, linear programming would be unnecessary, since the objective could be obtained unencumbered. The computation is by means of "iteration," a method by which a mechanical rule determines, at the end of each step, what the next step should be. Hence, the value from each step leads on closer and closer to the correct answer.

LINEAR PROGRAMMING—MATRIX ALGEBRA EXAMPLES

Assume a corporation has three factories and five warehouses. Costs of shipping differ among the fifteen different routes from the factories to the warehouses. Monthly capacities of the factories are 300, 375, and

450 units, respectively. The warehouses, located near large market centers, have the following monthly requirements: 150, 180, 210, 240, and 270 units, respectively. Each warehouse must be supplied with the units required; yet total shipping costs should be kept at a minimum. The problem is: How should production be distributed to the warehouses?

The arrangement of the given data, as shown in Figure 8–4, is known as a distribution matrix. Actually it is a type of model. The shipping costs per unit for each of the fifteen routes between three factories, X, Y, and Z, and five warehouses, A, B, C, D, and E are

FIGURE 8–4. Distribution matrix showing data for transportation problem

Factories	Warehouses						Capacities in units	
	A	B	C	D	E	Slack		
X	37	27	28	34	31	0	300	Row
Y	29	31	32	27	29	0	375	Row
Z	33	26	35	30	30	0	450	Row
Requirements in units.....	150	180	210	240	270	75	1125	
	Column	Column	Column	Column	Column	Column		

shown in the figure by the number in the lower right box of each cell. The shipping cost from factory X to warehouse A, for example, is 37 cents per unit; from factory Z to warehouse D, the cost is 30 cents per unit. Row refers to data horizontally or across the matrix, column to data vertically or down the matrix. The factory capacities are shown at the extreme right of each horizontal row; the warehouse requirements are shown at the bottom of each column.

Observe that the total warehouse requirement, 1050 units, is less than the factory capacities, 1125 units, meaning that a capacity of 75 units (1125 less 1050) will not be used. To show this condition in the matrix, we add a "slack" column with zero cost from each factory since these slack sales requirements will not be produced and hence not transported.

To start, we will use the "northwest corner" approach, which means beginning with the northwest, or upper left, corner of the matrix, AX, work down the column, completely meeting the requirements of warehouse *A;* then shift to the next column representing warehouse *B* and complete its requirements, always being alert to, and keeping within, the corresponding factory capacities for each row. We continue this process until we finish in the southeast corner, *EZ.* Such a distribution, which we will term "first distribution," is shown in Figure 8–5.

Each row and each column must have at least one value in it to meet the capacities and the requirements of the problem. Also for the answer to be valid, its number of values or entries cannot exceed the quantity

FIGURE 8–5. First distribution or tentative solution to transportation problem

Factories	Warehouses						Capacities in units	
	A	*B*	*C*	*D*	*E*	*Slack*		
X	150 | 37	150 | 27	| 28	| 34	| 31	| 0	300	Row
Y	| 29	30 | 31	210 | 32	135 | 27	| 29	| 0	375	Row
Z	| 33	| 26	| 35	105 | 30	270 | 30	75 | 0	450	Row
Requirements in units. . . .	150	180	210	240	270	75	1125	
	Column	Column	Column	Column	Column	Column		

equal to 1 less than the sum of the rows and the columns. Sometimes a solution with less than this number of entries is obtained. In Figure 8–5, there are 8 entries; the sum of the rows and the columns, or 3 plus 6, equals 9. This amount less 1, or (9 less 1), equals 8, or in this example equals the number of entries. This shows that the problem can be solved by this approach.

Referring to Figure 8–5, the question is: Can this distribution be improved? That is, can entries be shifted so as to reduce the total cost? Note the qualification "total" cost. What we seek is the combination or pattern of shipments giving the lowest cost within the constraints enumerated. The solution is therefore not a matter of simply picking out the lowest cost shipping routes. We can find out if this northwest corner, or first distribution, is the best by a number of ways, but one simple and effective way is to evaluate each of the blank cells to determine if cost reduction would result by assigning an entry to any one of them. We must maintain the overall balance which this first distribution shows in order to keep within the specifications of the problem. Considering cell XC, if we add one unit to it, we must subtract one unit out of YC to maintain the condition of column C. In turn, this will mean adding one unit to YB to maintain the condition of row Y and this, in turn, subtracting one unit from cell XB. By these moves the overall balance is maintained, but what happens to cost? One unit added to XC will increase cost 28 cents; subtracted from YC will decrease cost 32 cents; added to YB will increase cost 31 cents; subtracted from XB will decrease cost 27 cents. The net change in cost, therefore, is zero ($\$0.28 - 0.32 + 0.31 - 0.27$); so there is no cost advantage in making an entry in XC.

FIGURE 8–6

XC	XD	XE	$X\ Slack$	YA	YE	$Y\ Slack$	ZA	ZB	ZC
+28	+34	+31	+ 0	+29	+29	+ 0	+33	+26	+35
−32	−27	−30	− 0	−37	−30	− 0	−37	−31	−32
+31	+31	+30	+30	+27	+30	+30	+27	+27	+27
−27	−27	−27	−27	−31	−27	−27	−31	−30	−30
0	+11	+31	+31	−12	+ 2	+ 3	+27	− 8	0
		−27	−27				−30		
		+ 8	+ 7				−11		

This procedure is repeated for each blank cell of the first distribution of Figure 8–5. In doing this, the shortest loop from the unfilled cell back to the unfilled cell is used. Also, in this loop only right angle turns are permitted and such turns must be made only at filled cells. Any filled cells can be skipped over to form the required loop. Again, these conditions are required in order to maintain the balance required and to stay within the confines of the stated problem. The calculated data, in cents, for all blank cells are shown in Figure 8–6.

The deduction from these data is that the unfilled cell YA offers highest cost reduction opportunity. For each unit put in YA, total costs are reduced 12 cents. How many units can we transfer to cell YA? The answer is 30 units as revealed by analysis of the loop utilized to get units in cell YA from the first distribution. The total number of moves is therefore YB to YA, 30 units; XA to XB, 30 units making the new total 120 units in XA and 180 units in XB; the new total of YB is zero since the 30 units were moved to YA. This transferring or moving units into cell YA results in a second distribution, the remaining cells of the matrix staying the same as in the first distribution.

The process of evaluating each unfilled cell of the second distribution is now performed. It will be found that cell XC offers the greatest opportunity to reduce total costs. The data, in cents, are shown in Figure

FIGURE 8–7

XC	XD	XE	X Slack	YB	YE	Y Slack	ZA	ZB	ZC
+28	+34	+31	+ 0	+31	+29	+ 0	+33	+26	+35
−32	−27	−30	− 0	−29	−30	− 0	−29	−27	−32
+29	+29	+30	+30	+37	+30	+30	+27	+37	+27
−37	−37	−27	−27	−27	−27	−27	−30	−29	−30
−12	− 1	+29	+29	+12	+ 2	+ 3	+ 1	+27	0
		−37	−37					−30	
		− 4	− 5					+ 4	

8–7. By the same reasoning as above, the maximum number of units that can be transferred to this cell are carried out and the resultant third distribution is evolved and analyzed for cost reduction opportunity in any of its blank cells. The process is repeated until a distribution is

FIGURE 8–8. Final solution to transportation problem

Factories	Warehouses						Capacities in units	
	A	B	C	D	E	Slack		
X		15 / 27	210 / 28	/ 34	/ 31	75 / 0	300	Row
	/ 37							
Y	150 / 29	/ 31	/ 32	225 / 27	/ 29	/ 0	375	Row
Z	/ 33	165 / 26	/ 35	15 / 30	270 / 30	/ 0	450	Row
Requirements in units...	150	180	210	240	270	75	1125	
	Column	Column	Column	Column	Column	Column		

reached that has no blank cells offering cost reduction opportunity. For the example under discussion this is shown in Figure 8–8. This answer to our problem is precise and it represents the best arrangement to obtain total minimum distribution costs. No other arrangement will result in a lower total cost. The total cost can be calculated as follows:

Units		Cost/unit		Total cost
150	×	$0.29	....	$ 43.50
15	×	.27	....	4.05
165	×	.26	....	42.90
210	×	.28	....	58.80
225	×	.27	....	60.75
15	×	.30	....	4.50
270	×	.30	....	81.00
		Total	....	$295.50

VAM METHOD FOR LINEAR PROGRAMMING

The above method is acceptable, but less time-consuming approaches are available, among which the VAM (Vogel Approximation Method) merits inclusion in this discussion. The steps taken in this method include:

1. For each row and each column, find and post differences between the two lowest cell costs. Include and consider slack the same as any other cost.
2. Choose the largest difference of a row or column.
3. Assign maximum possible quantity to available lowest cost cell in the selected row or column.
4. If row or column is satisfied, eliminate that difference and consider all other unfilled cell costs in that row or column as no longer available by filling them in with a zero.
5. After each assignment, calculate new differences for effective rows and columns.

An example will clarify how this is done. For simplicity let us consider the same problem as above. Figure 8–9 shows the data. For step No. 1, the differences between the two lowest cell costs for each row and column are indicated under cycle 1 on the figure. For row X, the difference is 27 (27 — 0); likewise for row Y, it is 27. We will select the first, or row X, indicated by the circled 27, but either row X or row Y could be used. For row X we assign the maximum quantity possible in the cell of the lowest cost. This is X *Slack* and this entry eliminates the *Slack* column from further consideration in the problem. Next, the differences for cycle 2 are calculated and these are entered under cycle 2 in the figure. For this cycle, the difference of 4 for column A, indicated by the circled 4, is selected and 150 units assigned in cell *YA,* the lowest cost cell of that column. The procedure is continued until all assignments have been made.

In this case the identical result is obtained with that of the initial method discussed above. This may or may not happen in similar prob-

FIGURE 8–9. VAM method for determining initial solution to transportation problem

Factories	Warehouses A	Warehouses B	Warehouses C	Warehouses D	Warehouses E	Warehouses Slack	Capacities in Units		Cycle 1	Cycle 2	Cycle 3	Cycle 4	Cycle 5	Cycle 6	Cycle 7
X	0 [37]	15 [27]	210 [28]	0 [34]	0 [31]	75 [0]	300	Row	(27)	1	1	(4)	—	—	—
Y	150 [29]	0 [31]	0 [32]	225 [27]	0 [29]	0 [0]	375	Row	27	2	2	2	2	2	—
Z	0 [33]	165 [26]	0 [35]	15 [30]	270 [30]	0 [0]	450	Row	26	4	4	4	4	0	0
Requirements in units	150	180	210	240	270	75	1125								

Cycle	A	B	C	D	E	Slack
	Column	Column	Column	Column	Column	Column
1	4	1	4	3	1	0
2	(4)	1	4	3	1	—
3	—	1	(4)	3	1	—
4	—	1	—	3	1	—
5	—	(5)	—	3	1	—
6	—	—	—	(3)	1	—
7	—	—	—	—	—	—

lems of this type. VAM gives an approximate solution, which should always be checked by means of the blank cell evaluation method as described above in order to ensure that the VAM result is the lowest total cost answer. We did this in the previous method; so there is no need to check our VAM results in this particular illustration.

LINEAR PROGRAMMING—GRAPHIC EXAMPLE

Some problems suitable for linear programming analysis can best be solved by use of the graphic method. When the problem can be expressed in two dimensions only, a graphic solution involving straight lines (linear) is feasible; when three dimensions are involved, a graphic solution including planes, not lines, can be derived. The example here will be characteristic of the type of two dimensions only.

Consider a radio manufacturer producing two different product models, A and B. The data, shown per unit, are as follows:

Model	Revenue	Production time in hours per unit		
		Subassembly	Final assembly	Trim
A	$20	1.0	0.7	0.5
B	30	1.3	2.0	None

The following maximum hours are available for the production of these products:

Subassembly .... 1300 hours
Final assembly .... 1400 hours
Trim .... 500 hours

We want to find the combination of models A and B that will produce the maximum revenue.

First, let us show graphically the constraints within which the products must be produced. Referring to Figure 8–10, units of A will be shown on the vertical axis and those of B on the horizontal axis. For product A, the subassembly time per unit is 1.0 hours. If we produced no B products and devoted all our available subassembly time to product A, we could produce 1300 units of product A (1300 divided by 1.0). Contrariwise, if we produced no A products and used all our subassembly time for B products, we could produce 1000 units of product B (1300 divided by 1.3 hours). The line representing the relationship between A and B is indicated by line (1) in Figure 8–10. It is a straight line because the constraints are linear; it intercepts the A-axis at 1300 and the B-axis at 1000. In a like manner we can determine line (2) on Figure 8–10 for the final-assembly work. And line (3) represents the trim work. It is a straight horizontal line with an intercept of 1000 units on the A-axis because trim time does not affect B. It is all applied to A; so the maximum A production, due to this constraint, is 1000 units (500 divided by 0.5).

The solution to our problem has now been reduced to knowledge

FIGURE 8–10. Linear programming graphic solution

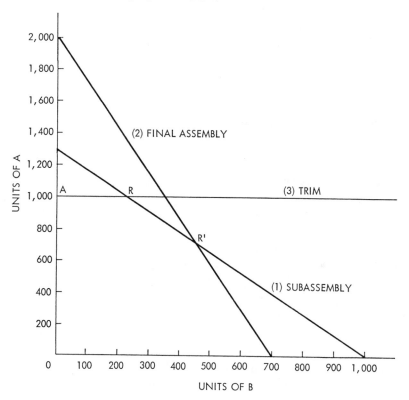

that it lies somewhere within the area bounded by the vertical axis, the line $ARR'B$, and the horizontal axis. These represent the outer constraints within which the total product mix must be made. The sought-for maximum revenue combination of A and B does not lie along the vertical axis up to point A on the graph because we can produce up to that point without constraint. And the same reasoning applies to the horizontal axis; that is, we can produce up to point B on the graph. The answer, therefore, lies on line $ARR'B$. Calculating the revenue for production combinations represented by points *A, R, R′*, and *B*, we get the results shown in Figure 8–11.

FIGURE 8–11

Point	Product A		Product B		Total revenue
	No. of units	Revenue per unit	No. of Units	Revenue per unit	
A...................	1000	$20	0	$ 0	$20,000
R...................	1000	20	230	30	26,900
R′..................	715	20	450	30	27,800
B...................	0	0	700	30	21,000

The maximum total revenue occurs at point *R′*. Points to either side of *R′* on line *ARR′B* will show less revenue than the amount at point *R′*. The answer to our problem is, therefore, to produce 715 units of *A* and 450 units of *B*.

LINEAR PROGRAMMING—ALGEBRA EXAMPLE

The above graphic solution is actually a problem in product mix, which is a common type of problem for which linear programming is suited. Blending of gasoline is a similar and common example of this type application. Actually, product mix is a part of a larger category of problems under the heading of allocation. These problems involve assigning resources such as men, machines, materials, and money in a way that will result in maximum efficiency within the constraints of the particular case. Characteristically, alternate uses of the facilities are restricted. There is not enough of each one, and the best way to use the existing facilities is the problem. Stated differently, there is a given or fixed amount of work to be accomplished for which several resources are required. What is the best combination or quantity mix of these required resources?

Let us consider a simple problem involving product mix which illustrates the allocation aspect. A manufacturer processes peanuts and cashews, packages them in one-pound bags, and employs two different mixes. The one mix is .5 peanuts and .5 cashews; the other mix is .7 peanuts and .3 cashews. From the former a profit is realized of 5 cents a bag; from the latter, 4 cents a bag. The manufacturer's facilities limit daily capacity to 200 pounds of peanuts and 100 pounds of cashews, and he must supply some of each mix to satisfy the market demands.

First set up these data in a matrix-type form to visualize the facts easily. Figure 8–12 shows such a matrix. From these data we can state,

FIGURE 8–12

Item	Mix A	Mix B	Restrictions
Peanuts.........................	.5 pound	.7 pound	200 pounds
Cashews.........................	.5 pound	.3 pound	100 pounds
Profit (per pound bag)...........	$0.05	$0.04	

reading across the peanut row, that .5 pound of mix A plus .7 pound of mix B equals, and cannot be more than, 200 pounds, the peanut capacity. Likewise, reading across the cashew row, .5 pound of mix A plus .3 pound of mix B equals, and cannot be more than, 100 pounds, the cashew capacity. Expressed algebraically:

$$.5A + .7B = 200 \tag{1}$$

and

$$.5A + .3B = 100 \tag{2}$$

Here we have two equations with two unknowns. To solve, we subtract one from the other to eliminate one of the unknowns, and then calculate the value of the remaining unknown as follows:

$$
\begin{array}{rll}
& .5A + .7B = 200 & (1) \\
\text{less} & .5A + .3B = 100 & (2) \\
\hline
\text{remainder} & 0 + .4B = 100 & \\
& B = 250 &
\end{array}
$$

Substituting this value for B in one of the equations, say equation (1),

$$
\begin{aligned}
.5A + .7 \times 250 &= 200 \\
.5A &= 25 \\
A &= 50
\end{aligned}
$$

This means the manufacturer should process 250 one-pound bags of mix B, for which profit per bag is 4 cents and 50 one-pound bags of mix A, for which profit per bag is 5 cents. For this product mix which is best in keeping with the problem restraints, the total profit realized is $12.50 (250 × $0.04 plus 50 × $0.05).

SIMULATION

Another quantitative technique for decision making is simulation. By its use, helpful decisions to certain types of problems are obtained, and it has increased in popularity since the availability of high-speed computers to perform many of the necessary calculations. The idea of simulation is to make a dry run of the problem at hand by carrying through the experiment or process completely to observe the effect of variables upon the finished result. A model based on empirical data is set up and then subjected to the same influences as it is in actual practice. In simulation these influences are measured quantities, and their occurrence is determined by the use of random number tables which synthesize the happenings on a strictly chance basis. In other words, the approach is to duplicate systematically what happens in reality by setting up a model and putting it through the same paces or influences that affect it in real life.

It should be noted that simulation models are empirical; they are not mathematical in the same concept that models of operations research are mathematical formulae into which values are substituted to calculate the answer. The model in simulation is a quantitative representation of the behavioral characteristics, interactions, and intangible and non-logical attributes of the entity under study. Further, in simulation it is possible to trace from the model the activities as relationships and variables change, that is, as the characteristic activities take place. This is not true in the case of solving equations for an optimization objective. In fact, the simulation model is not used for optimization. It serves basically for the systematic trial-and-error approach to complex problems.

Chance behaves in an unexpected manner. Machines break down, bottlenecks pop up in key operations, and important suppliers fail in critical shipments. Chance events take place in the best of managed enterprises. This is because there are several variables interacting and thus affecting the outcome. Some of these usually involve probability distribution; they are not constant through time or space. Such variables are called *stochastic.*

In simulation we construct distributions empirically from actual or logically assumed data and then at random generate an artificial sequence of events against which the behavior of the distribution can be evaluated. Many random sequence generations, taken from the probability distribution applicable to the process being studied, tend to disclose the behavior of the process. Mathematics is not used in simulation to represent a general solution; rather an approximate solution is determined by systematically running the simulated process a large number of times with the alternatives under test.

Hence, it is also feasible to test changes in relationships of important variables of a problem before actual installation of the assumed set of forces or conditions. With such comparisons, the accomplishment of goals; the determination of how much "off-target"; and the change in the pattern of actions and results, or what is sometimes called the change in the "configuration of the totality," being considered can be quickly assessed. If required, simulation can be broad in scope; it can encompass a maze of different activities. This provides insight into the total, or multicomponent, concept of an extensive area.

MONTE CARLO

This technique is a form of simulation, but it also includes probability factors. The simulation is guided by random sampling to take into account the probability of the event happening. In other words, random sampling is employed to simulate the natural events in order to determine the nature of the probability of events under study. A table of random numbers is employed to obtain the random sample. Monte Carlo is predictive and tells what will probably happen in actual events without analyzing comparable existing events. The possible applications are numerous. The technique is easy to comprehend and to use. Figure 8–13 shows the basic pattern followed.

Monte Carlo can be employed to answer problems having these typical questions: What are the chances of an event, or combinations of events, occurring in a given process? Based on this frequency and time of occurrence, what decision in relation to possible alternatives should be followed? What is the current chance of a breakdown of a given machine?

Applications of Monte Carlo include the determination of the quantity to produce of a special material for a given order so as to minimize excess. Determining the factors that affect the excess and then calculating the probability of these factors occurring in the proper proportions to get just the quantity desired is the essence of one suitable approach. In addition, Monte Carlo can be used to determine the amount of stock most feasible to produce for a good, repeat customer in order to get satisfactory production runs. Surplus from one production run is stored, but the approximate certainty of the time and quantity of its future sale to the good customer can be calculated. Likewise, and in the same vein, Monte Carlo is helpful in determining the optimum manpower level that will balance overtime cost with excess manning costs. Another application is the calculating of the optimum period between maintenance inspections for certain equipment, and the sequence of orders to minimize time in process.

FIGURE 8–13. Basic pattern of Monte Carlo technique

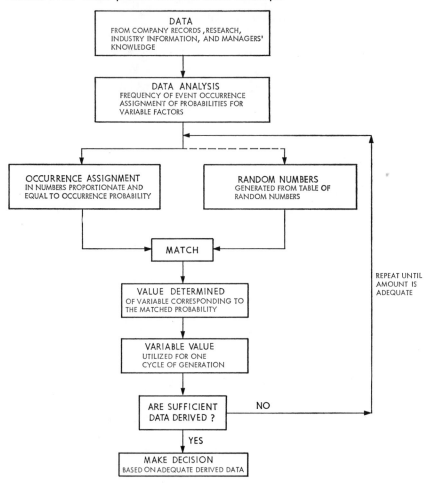

QUEUEING

Problems occur in management that arise due to (1) men, machines, or materials made to wait because of insufficient facilities to handle them immediately or (2) less than maximum facilities utilization is taking place because of the arrival sequence of resources using the facilities. There is lost time, unused labor, and excessive cost caused by waiting lines, or queues. To minimize these losses is the objective of queueing. Representative is the situation at a check-out counter in a supermarket, material waiting for machining (line balancing), airplanes circling an airport waiting for landing directions, and ramp design and toll gate provisions for expressways. Queueing is concerned with flow and, in addition to the above examples, includes flow of communication and of materials. Hence, it includes reconsideration of paper-work processes and of material handlings.

Normally this technique involves a balancing of expenditures of existing queues with the cost of providing additional facilities. The Monte Carlo approach is commonly used to ascertain the arrival rates at facilities and thus reveal the expected delays. This is especially useful where the queue is not constant. Computer mathematical analysis is resorted to, and it is common for complex equations or models to be required.

Under given conditions, queueing has shown that for 29 patrons arriving randomly each hour at a post office stamp window, each patron taking two minutes to transact his business, there will be an average waiting line of 28 patrons and an average wait of 58 minutes. If an additional stamp window is opened, the average waiting line is reduced to less than one patron. The 26 patron-hours saved, $(28 - 1) \times 58/60$, are won at the additional cost of just one additional window attendant, truly a worthwhile gain.

GAMING

To give reality to the situation, gaming can be utilized. Actually this is a type of simulation. The theory of games was developed by scientists Von Neumann and Morgenstern. Advocates of gaming state that it is helpful when the problem is concerned fundamentally with the actions of competitors. That is, if company A alters its plans and manufactures a product in greater quantities, how will the competitors to company A meet this new condition? The theory of games implies use of the strategy of least regret. In other words, the course that will cause company A the minimum amount of trouble is determined and can be followed if and when its competitors do the smartest action possible for them to do. In this manner, the planning of company A can be made the most beneficial to company A.

One approach in using "business games" is to begin with each decision maker in an identical position as shown by a balance sheet revealing the current condition of his enterprise. Auxiliary information to supply a needed background is provided. Decisions are made which affect the balance sheet. For example, it is decided to invest so much money in research, so many units will be manufactured, and the selling price is adjusted. Periodically subsequent decisions are determined, keeping in mind the results derived from the previous decision and also the effect of the decisions of competitors.

Although commonly thought of as a management-training device, business games can also be considered a type of quantitative decision-making technique. Although the mathematics is relatively simple since basic ratios, projections, and statistics are employed, the data are used in every phase of the game. The decisions are expressed in quantitative terms, such as a certain number of sales obtained, units purchased, or inventory added. "Playing the game" provides the manager with practice, insight, and the opportunity to improve his managerial actions. And he decides his courses of action from typical situations that he experiences in his everyday managerial activity.

QUESTIONS

1. With the increase of technology, emphasis upon measured attributes such as quantified objectives and uses of computers, do you feel that in the future, decision making based on intuition will decrease in usage and importance? Elaborate on your answer.
2. How do you account for the development and wide usage of the quantitative techniques in managerial decision making? As you see it, will their usage increase or decrease in the future? Why?
3. Suppose you could use only three decision-making bases. Which three would you utilize? Justify your answer.
4. As a manager you must make a decision for a difficult situation that you have never before faced. What nonquantitative base or bases for your decision making would you employ? Substantiate your answer.
5. Relate on experience in which you reached a decision by intuition. By experience. Which do you believe is better? Why?
6. Referring to Figure 8–8, suppose an operation required on model B only is added to the problem. This operation requires 1 hour and there is a maximum of 350 hours available for this work. What combination of models A and B will now provide the maximum revenue? Explain how you derive your answer.
7. Discuss considered opinions as a base for managerial decision making.
8. Do you feel that quantitative means for decision making can be employed advantageously for managerial problems of a social type, i.e., for problems of urban redevelopment, pollution of air and water, and providing adequate school facilities? Discuss fully.
9. With reference to operations research, what are (*a*) the steps taken in applying it, and (*b*) the advantages in using it?
10. What is simulation? Is it similar to the technique of operations research? Discuss.
11. Describe Figure 8–7 in your own words, explaining how this arrangement of data was obtained by VAM.

12. Identify each of the following fully: (*a*) linear equation, (*b*) configuration of the totality, (*c*) matrix distribution, and (*d*) stochastic variables.
13. In general, what types of problems would you say are best suited for the technique of simulation? Linear programming? Gaming?
14. Compare Monte Carlo with queueing, noting the similarities as well as the differences, and relate for what types of problems each may be used.

CASE 8–1. BRAWLEY PRODUCTS COMPANY

The output of four factories is distributed through three warehouses of this company. Capacities of the factories are F_1, 60 tons; F_2, 180 tons; F_3, 126 tons; and F_4, 114 tons. The capacity of each warehouse is 150 tons. The freight rates are as follows:

From	To	Cost per ton	From	To	Cost per ton
F_1	W_1	$60	F_3	W_1	$54
	W_2	36		W_2	48
	W_3	18		W_3	36
F_2	W_1	24	F_4	W_1	30
	W_2	42		W_2	42
	W_3	48		W_3	54

Questions

1. Arrange data in matrix form.
2. What factory should ship what quantities to what warehouses in order to minimize total freight costs to the company?

CASE 8–2. MILLS MACHINE COMPANY

Two products, *BR* and *MT,* present a problem to the company. Both require processing time in Departments 11 and 22. Product *BR* requires 12 hours in Department 11 while Product *MT* requires only 4 hours in this department. On the other hand, Product *BR* requires only 4 hours in Department 22 while Product *MT* requires 8 hours in this same department. Product BR contributes $100 profit per unit and Product *MT* contributes $60 per unit. There are 60 available hours for both these products in Department 11 and 40 hours available in Department 22.

Questions

1. By means of linear programming—graphic approach, find the optimum product mix to maximize profits.
2. Determine the total contribution to profits of this mix.

CASE 8–3. SUPREME FOODS, INC.

Peanuts and cashews mixed to form a one pound package is a popular item at the various outlets supplied by this company. One such one pound mix called "Deluxe" consists by weight of 70 percent peanuts and 30 percent cashews. From this mix the company realizes a profit of 11¢. Another mix, "Topper" is one pound and has more cashews. It consists of 60 percent peanuts and 40 percent cashews. From this mix a profit of 19¢ is realized by the company. To meet the market requirements, a minimum of 200 pounds of each mix must be supplied daily by the company which has facilities to handle 400 pounds of peanuts and 200 pounds of cashews daily. The company can sell all it can package.

Questions

1. What number of one pound units of Deluxe and of Topper do you recommend the company package?
2. For this recommendation what will be the company's profit?
3. Assume the company could package the peanuts and cashews in any combination of Deluxe and Topper that it wished. Is your answer to question No. 2 above the maximum profits that can be realized? Explain.

9

Communicating

*The exact contrary of what is generally believed is often
the truth.*

JEAN DE LA BRUYÈRE

ONE OF THE MOST important facilitators of managerial activities is communication because a manager is required to exchange facts, ideas, and experiences with others. Always present is the need for communicating effectively; each such opportunity represents a chance to improve managerial competency. Others know the manager primarily by what he is able to communicate to them. Better communicating helps obtain better job performance and improved results.

COMMUNICATING AND MANAGEMENT

Adequate communicating supplies the needed sharing and exchanging of information among all management members. Within any enterprise managers must communicate with other managers; there are times in which each needs to know what the other has done, is doing, or is planning to do. Plans to be followed by the finance manager, for example, may influence what actions the sales manager takes. Specifically, communicating enables the manager to obtain data for decision making, to assist in identifying problems, to know what actions are probably needed to achieve certain goals, to determine what degree of unified effort among employees is being carried out, and to know if achievements within and without the company are acceptable. Information must be known by the proper managers at the right time and place.

167

Communication is a means, not an end. It serves as the lubricant, fostering the smooth operation of the management process. Communication helps managerial planning to be performed effectively, managerial organizing to be carried out effectively, managerial actuating to be followed effectively, and managerial controlling to be applied effectively. Management is inclusive of communication, not communication of management.

Successful communication is the result of and not the cause of competent management. Conceivably one might be an excellent communicator but a poor manager. However, a competent manager is nearly always a good communicator. Actually, communication should never be thought of as an independent activity. It is an essential ingredient of almost everything a manager does.

From time to time what is assumed to be a problem in poor communication is actually a case of inept management. Excellent communicative efforts and the use of various devices and gimmicks will fall short of expectancy and may result in total failure if the management is ineffective. Communicating poor plans or utilizing a badly conceived organization structure, for example, are not corrected by astute and sophisticated communicating. Excellent execution of the entire management process, especially that of actuating which gives emphasis to the purpose and intent of communicating, is vital.

KEEPING OTHERS INFORMED

In addition to intramanagement and operational communication, a system of communication to keep employees informed is essential. By keeping employees informed, management develops rapport and influences productive actions. An employee who understands his job, knows his employer, and has a sense of loyalty about what he is trying to accomplish will contribute effectively and be a valuable member of the company team. Hence, management effectiveness is enhanced by good employee communication.

An employee likes to be in the know—it is natural for him to have curiosity about his place of employment and to want to have information about events that may possibly affect him. Four major areas about which information should be communicated will be included here. First, information dealing with special situations within the enterprise including the securing of a large order, the opening of a new plant, and new management member acquisitions. Also, information about company policies and practices and especially any change in either of them. Employees want to know about their chances for advancement, for pay increases, for transferring of job, and the opportunity for growth and development. They want to know under what policies they operate and what practices are followed in everyday work operations. Third, employees usually have many questions about their employer. What are the products or services and what is the general outlook of the company's future. Information about the company is a large category of employee communication. Lastly, the relationship of the employee to the total environment—economic, social, and technological—merits inclusion. Communication in this area gives needed background information. Such means help employees gain an understanding of the conditions of the system and the environment in which they are working and to see the relationship of these forces to their experience and to their employer.

It is also vital to keep customers, government, and the general public informed on certain matters. This is recommended to help keep customers "sold" and satisfied, maintain good relationships with government representatives, and develop public goodwill. A company seeking to improve its community and public interests and responsibilities and producing desirable products and services for the market can be aided by good external communication. Also a positive disposition toward the company by the general public can be won by proper communicative efforts. By such means, friendly, confident feelings toward the company and its products are accomplished.

TYPES OF MANAGERIAL COMMUNICATION

There are five types of managerial communication that warrant discussion here. First is the *formal communication* which follows the chain of command of the formal organization. For any such communication the path of transmission is prescribed, the format designated, and official sanction is provided. Second is the *informal communication,* commonly referred to as the grapevine. Most managers use it to supplement formal communication. They do this by finding out how the informal operates within their particular organization, identifying its major connections, and providing constructive information for it to handle. The grapevine can be very effective. Third is *nonformal communication*. It exists due to unintended conditions of the formal organization that cause unanticipated behavior to take place. That is, the formal organization itself tends to generate unanticipated behavior.[1] Nonformal communication is effec-

---

[1] See also the discussion on nonformal organization, Chapter 14, p. 315–16.

tive, nearly always exists in a large group working together, and tends to be continuous and permanent. Sometimes it is referred to as being parallel to the midnight requisition concept in the armed forces. Fourth is the *technical communication* which is employed by people working in the same area. Representative is the communication among people working with the computer. This type of communication is specialized, effective, and somewhat limited. Fifth, and last, is *procedural and rules communication*. Such communication is commonly set forth as a manual of the particular organization. It informs about specific policies and rules and when they are applicable. Formal communication channels are not utilized. While somewhat rigid, such communication does contribute to efficiency. Rules, for example, are specific and authoritative guides for action, making it unnecessary for a manager to decide each issue each time it happens. Rules require little or no interpretation and cover numerous situations.

THE COMMUNICATING PROCESS

In a very real sense communicating is a process affecting all society. Not only does it enable one person to know and to get along with his fellow men, but it also provides a means to record knowledge and pass it along to future generations. Communication provides the means for both individual and group progress.

Our major interest here concerns communicating as it is related to management. In this regard communicating can be viewed as *a continuing and thinking process dealing with the transmission and interchange with understanding of ideas, facts, and courses of action.*

Further, communication is purposeful. Whenever there is a desire or need for communicating, the idea or information is transmitted *in order to serve a specific response.* In some instances this requires little preparation, but in most communication in management, careful preparation is needed. Hence, the first thing to determine in a management communication is the exact purpose in terms of receiver response. This requires some thinking. For example, is the response intended to be used to help reach a decision, persuade the recipient to a new point of view, or build a favorable attitude toward a given concept? Next, the communication should be planned with stated purpose in mind and in a format believed effective to get understanding and an honest response from the receiver. To illustrate, if the communication is to inform about a forthcoming meeting, certain data should be included and the message put in a given format. However, if the purpose is to build goodwill, the communication must be planned with this purpose in mind and certain data included. In this case the format may be far different. Lastly, preparation of the communication should include provision to receive an effective expression by the receiver. The better the understanding of the receiver's thoughts and behavior by the sender of the communication, the more effective the presentation can be. A communication is adopted to the needs and interests of the receiver in order to reach him and to cause him to react in a manner that accomplishes the purpose of the sender.

THE ANATOMY OF COMMUNICATING

In communicating there is always a giver, a message, and a receiver. A condition or event stimulates the giver and he becomes aware of its existence. Out of this, comes the need to transmit his idea or feeling about this event to someone. Wanting to share his idea provides the need for communicating. To do so he must decide what to communicate that will accomplish his purpose. Accordingly he arranges words and symbols in some meaningful sequence keeping in mind that he seeks a favorable response from the receiver. The message is then transmitted to the receiver who perceives the words or symbols and translates them into his accustomed patterns. The meaning of the message is thus obtained and hopefully the receiver responds. For him to do so, he selects a reply message to satisfy his desire, arranges it in what he believes is an effective format and transmits it to the giver. In return this reply stimulates the initial giver and others to have responses. Thus, the process of communicating continues, each time a giver sends a message the receiver or another person may respond by further communicating ideas and facts.

This leads to the observation that in much communicating the process followed is two-way, meaning that to obtain the thought or idea being conveyed, when one speaks, another listens, or when one writes, another reads. However, communication itself may be multiway depending upon the type of communication being used. Types of communication were enumerated near the beginning of this chapter.[2]

To reiterate, a manager tells, informs, and requests, but for communication to be effective, he must also listen, ask, read, reply, and interpret. When communication moves freely in both directions, greater exchange of ideas and concepts is won and the way is open for greater understanding. Mutual acceptance and a willingness to receive or transmit must be

---

[2] P. 169.

present. In fact this back-and-forth exchange of ideas is implied by the "com" (meaning "with") at the start of the word communication. It is an error for a manager to assume that his communicating job is to hand it out; the other fellow is supposed to do all the listening and reading.

This interaction of communication has been called the communication equation. Using verbal communication for illustrative purposes, this equation is as follows:

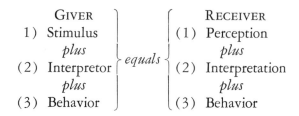

The giver first has a stimulus or fact that motivates him to attempt to influence the receiver. Next, the giver must interpret this fact, and third, when the interpretation is completed, the giver expresses himself by behavior consisting of talking, gesturing, writing, or a number of different ways.

From the receiver's point of view the initial step is that of perception. This includes his hearing or receiving the message. It covers his apprehension of the information being transmitted. The next step of the receiver is interpretation, which is influenced by many different factors. Lastly, the reactions of the receiver take place. Here we are interested in what behavior he shows, such as the expressions made—shaking his head, nodding approval, or stating that he agrees.

LANGUAGE AND COMMUNICATING

Language can be thought of as a set of symbols for conveying ideas from one person to another. It results from human beings living together. As the need to communicate arose, language was developed. A variety of symbols are used including color, signs, emblems, characters, noise, numbers, and alphabetical letters. Normally in the selection of symbols the user tries to follow the predominant custom for communicating within the given field, and keeps in mind what the selected symbols will mean to the receiver.

Figure 9–1 shows some of the symbols in common use today. If you were a proofreader, the top line would show different symbols which convey definite meanings to you. The second line is meaningful to a musician. To him, these marks stand for concepts just as much as alphabetic letters do in a written word. Going down the lines in the illustration, the third line is that of the telegraphic operator, and following in sequence the symbols are in mathematics, electronic tape, shorthand, electrical networks, and stock exchange ticker tape.

Alphabetical letters arranged into words are among the most common symbols used. A word is simply a symbol of an idea or object. The

FIGURE 9–1. Communication utilizes a wide variety of symbols

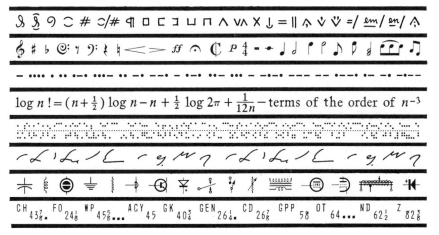

$$\log n\,! = (n+\tfrac{1}{2})\,\log n - n + \tfrac{1}{2}\,\log 2\pi + \tfrac{1}{12n} - \text{terms of the order of } n^{-3}$$

word "pencil" symbolizes a particular object, and to English-speaking people it means that particular object alone. That is, a word is not a person or thing but a *label which represents* a person or thing that can be distinguished. Broadly speaking, there are two classifications of words: (1) extensional and (2) intensional. The former includes words for persons, places, objects, materials, and fixed-label concepts, such as units of measurement. "Girl," "Ohio," "watch," "copper," and "inch" are examples. Extensional words are definite and refer to standards which are widely accepted. Sometimes these words are referred to as those standing for objects that can be pointed to or brought in to clarify the meaning of the word. There is little misunderstanding about the meaning of extensional words.

In contrast, intensional words do not refer to something that can be pointed out. They neither always connote an identical meaning to different persons nor the same meaning to the same person at all times, and this is where difficulty arises in communication. To illustrate, the word "easy" is subject to different meanings. "The examination is easy" can connote different meanings to different students, and "he is an easy boss" implies a different meaning to the word "easy" than that of the previous example.

The meaning of words is influenced by association. For example, the word "pay" brings to mind different words to different persons. To the executive it might suggest "bonus," "checking account," "dollars," "twice a month," or "bills." To clerks of the personnel department, "starting," "promotion," "job evaluation," or "increase" may be thought of; while to another employee it may be associated with "food," "clothes," "car," "family," "date," or "blonde."

Word differences constitute a serious obstacle to mutual understanding. Barriers exist simply because different evaluations and meanings are given the words used, and this condition tends to remain even when both sides are trying hard to communicate effectively. In addition, the tone of voice, gestures, and context influence the meaning conveyed. A word spoken in a context of anger can have an entirely different meaning from the same word spoken in friendliness. The statement "All right, I'll show you how to do the work" can be said with various points of voice inflection, emphasis, and gestures so that different meanings are imparted to the listener—for instance, a feeling of encouragement or, in contrast, a feeling of impatience.

BLUEPRINT DRAWINGS

A special type of symbols for communicative purposes is illustrated by blueprint drawings. They communicate accurately information that is difficult, if not almost impossible, to convey by most other communication media. Furthermore, blueprint drawings are in common use not only by factory employees but also by industrial salesmen, purchasing agents, estimators, product designers, and research people.

The standard arrangement of a blueprint drawing shows (1) top, (2) front, and (3) end view, with the top immediately above the front view and the end view immediately to the right of the front view. Figure 9–2 shows this typical arrangement. The dimensions of the object, such as length, height, and width are shown, as well as a "title block" to indicate pertinent information, such as name, part number, drawing number, drawn by, checked by, approved by, type of material used, tolerances, and the type and date of changes made on the print. See lower portion of the illustration.

Visible edges are shown by solid lines, invisible edges by dotted or

FIGURE 9–2. Blueprint of a slider block

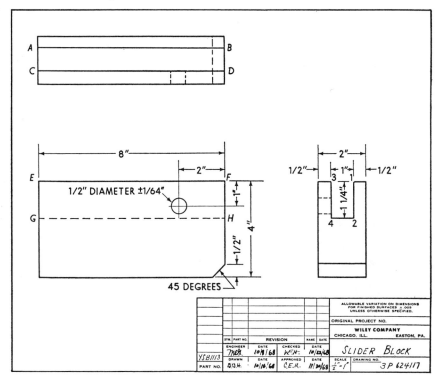

broken lines. The dimensions of circular locations are shown from a center line; for example, in Figure 9–2, front view, the center of the half-inch-diameter hole is located two inches from the right edge of the slider block and one inch down from the top edge, E-F. Degrees are used to indicate the dimensions of angles as indicated in the illustration. The permissible deviations or variations from the stated dimensions are shown either (1) in the title block or (2) on the drawing itself. To show details of the interior, a sectional view is used. This represents what would be seen if a section or a part of the object were cut away.

MAJOR BARRIERS TO EFFECTIVE COMMUNICATION

More often than we care to admit, what we transmit is not fully understood by the receiver precisely in the terms intended. Why is this so? There are many reasons. First, it is human nature to condition communication in terms of what has happened to us in the past, and lacking a past to go on, we guess or take a chance on what to say or write. The average person gives meanings to communication in line with his personal interpretations and, furthermore, defends and clings to them because they are his. In some cases he may not be dealing with reality, and as a result, the communication is affected accordingly. Also, there is reluctance on the part of some management members to share important information with their associates and subordinates. Why such behavior? Because by sharing they believe they lose a sense of superiority. If others are as well informed on some important matter as they are, they feel highly insecure. They have neither fully accepted the importance of communicating in management nor the essentiality of developing subordinates in managerial work. In addition, most people have certain

FIGURE 9–3. Common barriers to communication

1. The identity and the interpretation of facts by the giver.
2. The willingness and ability of the receiver to perceive the communication.
3. The attitudes of the giver and the receiver toward each other, their superiors, their peers, their subordinates, and the communication subject.
4. The general view taken by the giver and the receiver toward the situation in which the communication occurs.
5. The mutual acceptance of the communication medium by the giver and the receiver.

expectations; they unconsciously think in terms of what they expect. If a communication is not in keeping with what a person expects, he may become disturbed and actually reject the objectionable part of the communication. This bears truth to the oft quoted statement, "He hears only what he wants to hear." Figure 9–3 lists common communication barriers.

In addition, there is the tendency for a communication to be altered as it travels from one organization level to another. Due to individual interpretation, a communication issued at the top management level may be considerably altered by the time it reaches the bottom level or, vice versa, from the bottom to the top. A subordinate is always influenced by his immediate superior. As a consequence, communication from the bottom upward tends to be deleted of unpleasant realities—it is sweetened and explained. If things go wrong, it is not policy, attitudes, aims, or methods that perhaps should be changed; it is simply that "understanding by the employees is insufficient." Hence, members of the higher echelons of management may not be provided the information as it actually is. A frown by the boss gives cause for worrying about what it really means. Ill health? Bad business conditions? Loss of key man? Some feel a management member can spend so much of his time trying to figure out his superiors that he neglects communication with his subordinates; the net result is poor communication. Limited study shows that the flow of communication downward from the top to bottom levels of an organization indicates a startling state of affairs. The pattern found is shown graphically by Figure 9–4.

FIGURE 9–4. Communication is altered in its distribution

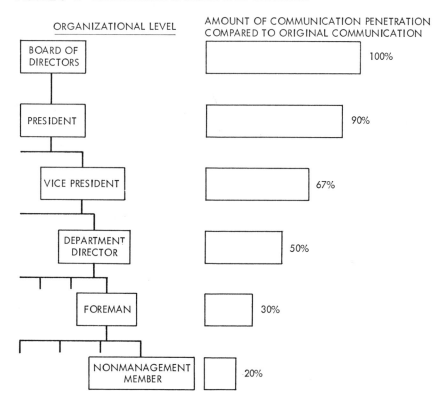

IMPROVING COMMUNICATING

The first step in improving communicating is to believe in its essentiality in management. By means of communication a manager finds out about problems, draws up plans, assists employees to satisfy their basic wants, gives instructions, and checks on results. Recognition of its importance is basic for effective communication to be achieved and maintained. Each manager is obligated to state every communication clearly, to listen sympathetically, to respond considerately, and to act promptly.

Once its importance is fully accepted, the manager's task of improving his efforts at keeping others informed boils down to (1) expressing himself clearly, and (2) achieving good listenership and readership. With reference to the former, before a manager can communicate effectively he must clearly envision and know completely that which he is trying to pass on to others. Generally speaking, the communicator should have a greater amount of information than is needed for the communication. He should possess some reserve or fund of knowledge to handle any unexpected questions or requests for further information. In addition a plan for the communicating should be followed. What to communicate is vital, but consideration for how and when to communicate are also essential. Take time to plan effective communication. This planning precedes establishing any kind of physical action.

Also seek to establish a work environment that encourages upward communication. The results-management approach to the management process is a modern way to achieve this condition. As stated in Chapter 3, results management encourages each management member to manage his own unit of operations with full authority and responsibility, emphasis being on the results he achieves. With such an arrangement, communicating from the bottom up is encouraged and is closely tied to efforts taking place to accomplish the sought-for results. Upward communication is also encouraged by the manager expressing an interest in the problems and views of his subordinates, and by not discriminating against anyone because of the information given to him. The manager must be ready to accept criticism and use it constructively and to act promptly on unhappy news.

It is also well to remember, "One picture is worth one thousand words." Hence, use appropriate illustrations and charts to get your idea across. Be sure the visual is relevant to the idea being communicated. If possible add glamour to the communication. Simply to state, "The government is spending one billion dollars for this project," is dull and it doesn't evince real understanding by the receiver. In contrast, the following is exciting and penetrating: "The government is spending one billion dollars—the equivalent amount for a man working 40 hours a week, 50 weeks a year, at $5.00 an hour for 100,000 years. If he started with the year 1, he would have less than 2 percent of his job completed today."

The second basic key to improving communicating is achieving good listenership as well as readership. It follows that if from communicating we want the receiver to understand us and to react to what is said or written, then he must listen or read so he knows what is transmitted. Many management members spend one half of their time listening and reading. One may learn a great deal he didn't know by these means. The problem is that we retain only a small portion of what we hear or read, and that for but a brief time. For example, estimates are that immediately after listening, a person remembers only one half of what he has heard, and two weeks later he remembers only one fourth of it. This is explained, in part, by the fact that the brain functions much faster than the average of 100 words per minute of a speaker. As a result the mind wanders, and gets off the subject of the communication. In addition, too many communications contain too many words. The receiver loses interest because of the mere quantity to which he is subjected. And likewise, if too many messages are directed to him, he becomes harassed; the listenership and readership pace becomes irksome.

Improvements can be won in a number of different ways. In the case of verbal communication, the listener can utilize the time differential between the time it takes the speaker to say words and the shorter time it takes the listener to "think them." To do this the listener can judge if the speaker seems qualified to talk on the subject, weigh the evidence presented, note his major points, and summarize for himself what is being stated. In addition, it helps to study the receiver and be familiar with his needs and reactions. By talking or writing in terms of his interest, we can improve listenership and readership. If we fail to do this, our communicating may never register in the illusive mind we are attempting to reach. Further, listening and reading take energy and require effort. They cannot be hurried. It is well to take sufficient time to formulate a reply. Whenever possible deal with one subject in one communication. This avoids getting spread too thinly in communicative efforts, as well as gaining better understanding and precision of the subject covered.

Word choice is another important consideration in improving listenership and readership. Selection of the proper word can be difficult. Failure to recognize the variety of meanings that words convey, use of trite expressions, and inclusion of negative and unfavorable words weaken a communication. Figure 9–5 shows some guides to follow in this respect.

FORMAL COMMUNICATION MEDIA

For communicative purposes a manager has a number of formal media available to him. Formal media are those established and sanc-

FIGURE 9–5. Suggestions for word choice

1. Use specific, definite words

Specific	*General*
refrigerator	product
table	thing
private office	your place
mail	send

2. Avoid trite expressions, such as

I beg to advise
We are happy to inform you
As per statement attached herewith
We have your kind favor of

3. Use a single word for a group of words

Use	*Do not use*
like	in the nature of
before	prior to
now	at the present time
since	in view of the fact that

4. Use pleasant, positive terms

Use	*Do not use*
cooperation	unfair
benefit	inconvenient
accuracy	Prohibit
generous	neglect

tioned by provision of the company's formal organization and represent officially recognized and approved media. Illustrative are:

1. Interviews—regular and special.
2. Departmental meetings.
3. Mass meetings.
4. Conferences.
5. Telephone calls.
6. Company newspapers.
7. Company magazines.
8. Company handbooks.
9. Information booklets on products, selling, and display materials.
10. Employee-benefit publications—pension plans, insurance, and savings.
11. Special-purpose publications—executives' messages and company policies.
12. Payroll inserts.
13. Plant bulletin boards.
14. Posters.

15. Annual report to employees.
16. Supervisory publications.
17. Direct-mail letters.
18. Film strips, slides, and motion pictures.

Studies conducted to find out the relative effectiveness of various media reveal some interesting data. Among the speediest disseminators of information are (1) the grapevine and (2) the supervisor, in the case of nonmanagers, or immediate superior management member, in the case of managers.[3] Memos, letters, and bulletin boards are relatively the least effective for most communication. In general, face-to-face communication carries the message much better than printed media. Also, the fewer the organizational restraints, the faster the communication. For example, having to clear information with higher authorities tends to slow up the communication process. The impact of communication is greatly increased when the release is from as close to the top management level as possible, thus giving the communication official flavor.

SELECTED MEDIA

Several of these formal media warrant discussion because of their wide application. A brief treatment of group meetings, orders, instructions, and reports will be given.

Group meetings have grown to occupy a major role in communication. Some have described them as a way of managerial life and facetiously state that a manager who isn't at a meeting is likely to either be coming from or going to one. Meetings provide participation, give members a sense of belonging and of importance, and are excellent distributors of information. They do, however, have some drawbacks. Commonly, only a few members make any real contributions, many come to the meetings without any real preparation and are content to rely on the others. Also, meetings take considerable time and even though a strong man is at the helm, discussions tend to get off the subject. Further, meetings give excessive advantage to the quick, glib, politic, convincing speaker who may neither offer the best idea nor supply the best comments. Suggestions for making meetings effective are listed in Figure 9–6.

Orders are essential to the execution of management. They tell *what* is to be done, *who* is to do it, and *when, where, how,* and *why*.

[3] See page 169 for discussion of the grapevine.

However, in certain cases, some of these components may be implied or may be omitted; for example, the order, "Effective November 27, Charles E. Hunter will become foreman of Department 17," answers the *what, who, when,* and *where,* but the *how* and the *why* are omitted. An order should be subjected only to the interpretation intended by the giver. In many companies a verbal order is confirmed in writing so that its issuance can be verified and a record maintained. The obli-

FIGURE 9–6. Fourteen ways for a chairman to build helpful meetings

1. Don't call a meeting to decide something you can and should decide yourself, or when a series of telephone calls to individuals will adequately serve the purpose.
2. About three days in advance of the meeting, send out notices giving the time and place of the meeting, appropriate material or research data, the agenda to be covered, and the approximate time the meeting will require, establishing a definite starting time.
3. Indicate clearly the purpose of the meeting to all members, that is, whether to supply advice, arrive at a decision, or accept or reject a certain proposal to be presented.
4. The day before the meeting review your notes for completeness. Give thought to possible questions that might be raised.
5. Make certain all members are informed of the meeting.
6. Encourage each member to participate.
7. Ask questions that cannot be answered with a "Yes" or "No."
8. Employ generous amounts of visual material but don't usurp all the time with a show.
9. Get all members to express themselves; do not permit one member to monopolize the discussion.
10. Be specific; make the discussions apply to the particular issues.
11. Keep to the agenda; let each member have a chance to express himself, but get them back to the subject at hand if they wander, and sum up succinctly immediately following what they have stated.
12. Do not permit telephone calls to be transferred to the meeting room while committee is in session.
13. Present facts first, then proposals for solutions.
14. Write up all proceedings of the meeting and distribute copies to all group members and to the superior to whom the group reports.

gation for the order's execution should be definite and mutually known. Belief by the recipient in the meaning and intent of the order is paramount and to gain such belief an explanation or the "reason why" for the order is effective. People usually are willing to follow an order when they clearly see the gains from such action, especially if the gain is to them or for a purpose in which they believe. In contrast, fear of consequences if the order is not followed is likewise a powerful force. The power to enforce should be behind every order; but in many instances, potential enforcement is most effective as a threat rather than actual execution. Also in some instances, the recipient's faith in a particular leader may be so great that the following of his orders is adopted enthusiastically.

Instructions stress the how-to-do-it aspect, and their use helps to insure correct and orderly execution of the work. An instruction can be defined as *oral or written information on a recommended manner in which a particular kind of task is to be performed.* With reference to written instructions, all elements of the work performance are included. Written instructions are not easy to compose. Required are detailed data and a skill in seeing the task from the recipient's or other person's viewpoint. Clarity of expression and a sequence of steps to follow are of major consideration. The use of written instructions is on the increase and for good reasons. First, such instructions supply standardized and approved means of performing specific tasks. In the case of tasks which repeat from job to job, the work can be performed without separate and individual managerial action. And the availability of how-to-do-it information is increased, thus making the indoctrination and training of employees less difficult. On the other hand, written instructions are costly to prepare, inject rigidity into the handling of the work, and stifle creativity.

Defined as *a factual presentation of information directed to a particular audience for a specific purpose,* a report is oral or written and used mainly for subjects of a technical or operational nature. Most serve either as (1) informational reports or (2) investigational reports. The former stress data on developments, trends, and favorable-attitude growth. The latter are concerned with analysis and interpretation of data, presenting recommendations, and suggested solutions to stated problems.

The systematic working over of the various stages from investigation to presentation is fundamental for preparing reports that will provide satisfactory communication. Preparing the report from a detailed outline is extremely helpful. Subject headings throughout a report are useful. Flexibility in their use should be followed; yet some standardization in their use makes for consistency and ease of comprehending the communication. Reports can be very costly and control over their number and content should be followed.

QUESTIONS

1. Enumerate the four major areas in which employees should be informed. Elaborate on one of these areas, pointing out its importance in management.

2. What is the meaning of each of the following: (*a*) nonformal communication, (*b*) communication barrier, (*c*) symbols of communication, and (*d*) intensional words.

3. What significance do you attach to the statement, "Communication is a necessary adjunct to management, not management itself." Discuss.

4. Recall a situation in which you have been a participant and in which communication was ineffective, resulting in some embarrassing or dire consequence. Suggest effective communicating for this situation that would have avoided the dire consequence.

5. In your opinion does the use of results management aid or hinder communication? Justify your answer, using an example to illustrate your views.

6. With reference to Figure 9–6 select six ways you feel are most important. Justify your selections.

7. What are some ways that improved listenership and readership can be obtained? Discuss one of the ways you state in some detail.

8. Have each one of a small group of friends write down five words that come to mind as you read off the following words: (*a*) rock, (*b*) football, (*c*) clinic, (*d*) president, and (*e*) music. Analyze the results. What do they mean from the viewpoint of acquiring effective communication?

9. Discuss the subject of language and communicating.

10. Does explanation and discussion of an order to a recipient tend to weaken the effectiveness of an order? Explain.

11. Listen to a speech on TV tonight. What considerations did the speaker give to his audience?

12. What media of communication would you use for each of the following and give reasons for your choice: (*a*) You want to invite the 19 members of your office to an open house at your new home; (*b*) As a typist in a large department store you feel you are underpaid and intend to let your boss know about this; (*c*) As personnel manager in your firm, you need to inform the employees of a new fringe benefit program your company is providing beginning in about six weeks; (*d*) You are a senior partner in a public accounting firm and want to squelch rumors that your company is merging with a competitive public accounting firm; and (*e*) By a telephone call you have been informed that your immediate superior will be hospitalized for three weeks and you are to take charge.

13. Discuss the change of communication in its normal distribution throughout an enterprise.

14. Write concise but complete instructions for one of the following: (1) tying a bow tie, (2) winding and setting a watch, (3) writing themes or papers in a specific course, (4) starting and driving an automobile, (5) installing the film in a movie projector, and (6) washing the inside and outside of a house window.

CASE 9–1.   OXFORD COMPANY

Mr. Melvin Snyder, factory superintendent, takes trips through the factory at different hours and on different days. He likes to talk with the operative employees and ask them questions about their work, their families, the material they are using, and the machine being operated. He believes such conversation makes for better morale and also lets him know what is taking place in the shop.

Every Monday morning at the weekly production meeting, he will bring up some aspect of information picked up from the previous week's shop visits and ask for an explanation of it. Usually his production management personnel will answer him, but Mr. Snyder will continue, asking about other bits of information he received until his associates are unable to answer or inform him that he has erroneous information. Mr. Snyder, however, insists that the operative employees are telling him the truth and sometimes he points out that the same information is given him by different employees in different departments. Some of his associates have suggested that they accompany Mr. Snyder during his shop tours, but he will have no part of this, stating that the operators will not talk when their immediate superior or more than one management member is with him. He claims the friendly sincere atmosphere he has achieved with many of the men and women in the shop is a definite advantage, helps communication, and he doesn't want to jeopardize it in any way.

Mr. Snyder is not entirely satisfied with his production management associates. In his judgment his production control manager, Benjamin Lake, just doesn't seem to comprehend what he is told. Mr. Snyder admits the manufacturing work is getting quite complicated, but it irks him when Benny just stands there and replies "Yes," "Yes," "Yes." Mr. Snyder has noticed that Benny says he understands a request or a suggestion or a change given to him, but then proceeds to go about his work as if nothing had been said to him. Mr. Snyder would like to promote the assistant production control manager, Tom Roth, to the production control manager's job, but he doesn't know as yet what to do with Benny.

This morning while on a plant tour, he talked with a production control clerk who told him Tom was leaving the company for a better paying job. In reply to Mr. Snyder's question, "Where's he going?" he was told, "He's going to work for his father-in-law who owns a trucking business."

That afternoon, My. Snyder summoned Benny Lake to his office.

SNYDER: Benny, I understand Tom is leaving the company. Is that true?

LAKE: Yes, sir. That is what he told me a couple days ago.

SNYDER: How come you did not tell me?

LAKE: Well, sir, I thought he might change his mind. It's not certain yet as I understand it.

SNYDER: It doesn't sound good to me.

LAKE: If he does leave, we will just have to do the best we can without him. And we have some capable people in production control. I didn't want to bother you with problems of my department, Mr. Snyder.

SNYDER: Bother? That's no bother. I want to know about matters like this.

LAKE: Yes, sir.

Questions

1. What is the problem the company faces? Discuss.
2. Are Mr. Snyder's actions generally good or generally bad for the company? Why?
3. What action do you recommend the company take? Be sure to include how you would implement your proposed action.

CASE 9–2. NORTHERN STATE UNIVERSITY

A new ice-skating rink has been completed by the athletic department of Northern State University. The rink is mainly for students and faculty of the university, but since the university is an important part of the local community, it was decided by university officials to permit the general public to use the rink at certain times throughout the week.

In keeping with this decision, the following ice-skating rink schedule was determined and mailed along with a friendly letter to students, faculty, and other members of the community in which the university is located.

ICE-SKATING RINK SCHEDULE

Public sessions at which time rink is available to the public in addition to Northern State University personnel:

	Afternoon	*Evening*
Wednesday	3:00–6:00	7:30–10:00
Friday	3:00–6:00	7:30–10:00
Saturday	2:00–5:00	7:30–10:00
Sunday	1:00–5:00	7:00–10:00

Ice hockey scrimmage and instruction will be held on Thursday evenings, 6:00–8:00, and Saturday evenings, 5:00–7:00. A charge of $1.00 per person per session will be made in addition to the regular admission fee.

Monday and Tuesday evenings, 8:00–10:30: Special private ice-skating sessions for Northern State University students only. No faculty, no public, no children.

Wednesday evening, 7:30–11:00: Public skating with the last hour from 10:00–11:00 reserved for Northern State University personnel only.

Thursday evening, 8:00–10:00: Adult lesson night and Northern State University ice-skating session. No public. Eskimo Ice Skating Club meets and skates at the rink this evening from 6:00–8:00, and they will help any members of Northern State University faculty and student body who are interested in learning to skate.

Ice-skating lessons, private and group, for all ages and abilities, are available at the rink with excellent teaching staff. Times will be arranged.

Wednesday and Friday from 10:00 A.M. to 2:00 P.M. skating is permitted, provided there are at least two skaters on the rink.

Admission rates for students and faculty are one half of the public rates which are: under 18 years—40¢, 18 years and over —80¢.

Questions

1. Rewrite the above schedule in the same or different form so that the information is conveyed better to the reader.
2. Is the present schedule probably meeting the needs of the university? Of the community? Discuss.
3. In general, what changes in the schedule do you believe might be in order? Discuss.

part **|||**

Planning

This is the first fundamental function of management to be discussed in detail. Planning provides, prior to activity, the guides and courses for action required by managers in order to achieve goals.

Among the important and interesting major topics covered in this part of the book are the meaning of management planning; premises and constraints utilized; the considerations of managerial ethics; types of plans in use; long- and short-range planning; the implementation of planning; and strategies to follow.

The four chapters devoted to planning include:

10. *Management planning*
11. *Managerial classifications of planning*
12. *Long- and short-range planning*
13. *Implementing managerial planning*

10

Management planning

Some men see things as they are and ask, "Why?" I dream things that never were and ask, "Why not?"
ROBERT F. KENNEDY

EVERY ENTERPRISE that wants and strives for survival, growth, and a healthy mode of operations must place heavy emphasis upon planning. It is the planner who seeks improvements, listens for and nurtures new ideas into practical applications, and gets away—at least in theory—from day-to-day operating problems and sees the possibility or the image of future time, space, and quality. The planner is the one with the greatest opportunity to bring together all the resources of an enterprise into a more effective entity. In short, planning is indispensable. It is the intellectual arm of our future growth.

PLANNING AND THE MODIFIED MANAGEMENT PROCESS

To reiterate, planning is a fundamental function of management. Planning is vital in management. For a new project, it is the logical managerial starting area, and it is important for any activity. What we plan affects how we organize and vice versa. As a matter of fact, planning for organizing, planning for actuating, and planning for controlling are requisites of effective management.

It can be reasoned that planning is basic to the other fundamental management functions. Without the activities determined by planning, there would be nothing to organize, no one to actuate, and no need to control. For example, actuating is most remunerative when it assists in bringing reality to the planning, and controlling is carried out to make sure that the plans are being realized as intended. In fact, a manager performs organizing, actuating, and controlling to realize the objectives and the means of achieving them as set up by his planning efforts.

On the other hand, it is true that some goals are achieved with relatively little planning. They are in the minority. A manager charged with the need to accomplish definite results cannot wait and hope that the favorable will happen. He must aim his efforts toward achieving the desired results.

MEANING AND CHARACTERISTICS OF PLANNING

Planning is the selecting and relating of facts and the making and using of assumptions regarding the future in the visualization and formulation of proposed activities believed necessary to achieve desired results. It is the determining in advance what is to be done and how it is to be done. One can look upon planning as being made up of a bundle of decisions.

Planning has five characteristics of special interest to the management student. They are:

1. Planning Includes Personal or Organizational Identification. A plan is a blueprint for action and, to be complete, includes the future course of action that will be taken by the planner or a designated person within the enterprise. In other words, how the plan is to be implemented, and by whom, is a part of every plan. It is not a carefully detailed dream of what action might be desirable.

2. Planning Relates to Conditions of Relative Certainty and Uncertainty. The probability of an event or events happening, or relative certainty, is dominant for certain conditions for which planning is created. In contrast, other conditions represent the situation of relative uncertainty or the probability of an event or events not happening. To illustrate, for the former, planning what machines to use, for how long, and during what periods to process a batch of production orders represents a condition of relative certainty. There is little likelihood that the actual processing will differ from the plan developed. There is relative certainty in the facts. However, much planning today is made for actions to take place in an environment conditioned by an increasing complexity and interdependency of difficult variables. To take these various forces into account in planning has given a new dimension to planning, namely the condition of relative uncertainty. We cannot be sure that all the cosideration included in a plan will act in the manner assumed and bring about the results planned for. Advanced planning techniques are being extended and in this area, computer technology has contributed enormously.

3. Planning Is Intellectual in Nature. It is basically mental work. Reflective thinking, imagination, and foresight are utilized. The planner visualizes his proposed patterns of activities, deals with intangibles, and tempers his planning efforts with his experience and knowledge.

4. Planning Involves the Future. It deals with futurity of present decisions. By means of planning, management members try to look ahead, anticipate eventualities, prepare for contingencies, map out activities, and provide an orderly sequence for achieving the objectives.

5. Planning Is Pervasive and Continuous. Every manager has a planning function to perform because he is a manager and planning is a fundamental management function. The pervasiveness of planning, however, is commonly overlooked, the error being that planning is concentrated among top-level managers. Also, planning is continuous; it is a never-ending activity of a manager. Variables are present and must be appraised periodically. All plans are tentative and subject to revision and amendment as new facts become known and as the variables are reevaluated.

PLANNING AND TIME

Managers have found that certain aspects with respect to time and their relationships with planning are of prime importance. Included here are several of the more basic observations to be noted. First, planning should precede the actual physical doing of an action. That is, it is better to formulate a definite plan of what you are going to do before you start to do it. Too frequently in actual situations, physical efforts are expended before the proposed action is adequately planned, the questionable justification being there isn't time for planning, or action must be taken immediately.

PRINCIPLE OF PLANNING

To accomplish a goal most effectively, adequate planning, or mental effort, should take place before the doing, or physical effort.

There is also a proper time for most actions. This usually depends upon the relative importance of the particular objective being sought, the internal and external environmental conditions and whether they are favorable or not to the sought goal, and the general attitude of the employees toward the plan. Help in recognizing the proper time is provided by preparing one's mind to look ahead so that possible changes can be anticipated and scheduled for future periods. Planning aids in these efforts and further helps to uncover opportunities of the present and future.

In addition, there is the time concept of phasing which is a part of many plans. Phases identify the successive time periods for activities, as set forth by the plan, to take place. By using phasing, a complex plan can be reduced to a simple series of actions, each one of which is easily understood and effectively handled. Also, in many cases phasing helps insure acceptance of the plan by all who will be affected by it.

FIGURE 10–1.   A chart used for scheduling

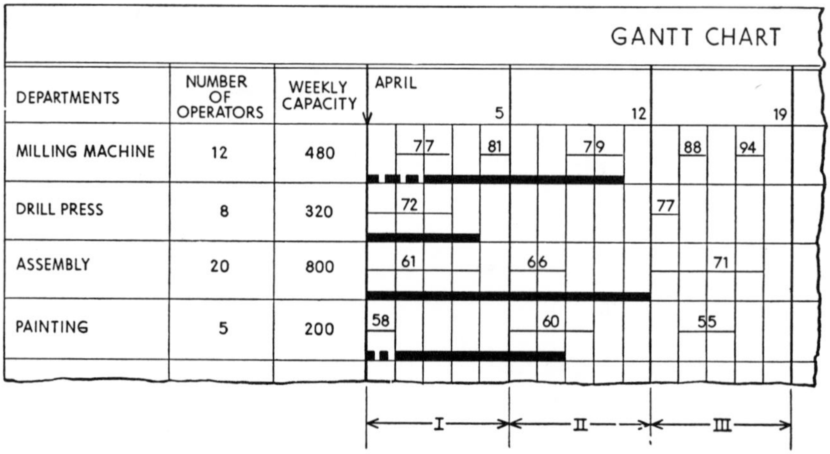

GANTT CHART

DEPARTMENTS	NUMBER OF OPERATORS	WEEKLY CAPACITY	APRIL			
			5	12		19
MILLING MACHINE	12	480	77 81	79	88 94	
DRILL PRESS	8	320	72	77		
ASSEMBLY	20	800	61	66	71	
PAINTING	5	200	58	60	55	

|←——— I ———→|←—— II ——→|←—— III ——→|

Another basic relationship between planning and time is scheduling, which is the assigning of specific time periods to each work component and to the total work project. Scheduling gives vitality and a practical meaning to a plan. Consider the illustration shown by Figure 10–1. This is a simple plan with scheduling, emphasizing the work-time relationship. It is known as a Gantt chart, having been devised by Henry L. Gantt, a prominent management scholar and practitioner around the beginning of the 20th century. Departments are listed on the left, along with the number of operators and their weekly capacity. Each main column of the chart, identified by I, II, and III for clarity, represents one week; and the small numbers at the right of each column indicate the week ending as of that date. To illustrate, column I represents the week ending April 5. Opposite each department heading are two lines, a light line and a heavy line. The position and length of the light line in a column represents the starting and ending times for work (by shop order number) in the respective department. For example, in the milling machine department, during the week ending April 5, order No. 77 is scheduled to start Tuesday morning and to be finished Wednesday night; order No. 81 is to be run all day Friday. For the week ending April 12, it is planned to run order No. 79 from Wednesday morning to Thursday night. The heavy line opposite each department represents the cumulative time scheduled for the respective department. Hence, for the milling department, the heavy line is seven days long, representing the total times scheduled for order Nos. 77, 81, 79, 88, and 94, as shown by the light lines opposite the milling machine department. The dotted heavy line indicates work scheduled but not yet completed. The "V" mark at the top of the chart indicates the effective date of the chart. In the illustration, this is the end of March 31, and the data shown are effective as of that time. The milling department is behind schedule two days, as indicated by the dotted heavy line. Subsequent changes can be drawn on the chart; it is unnecessary to redraw the entire chart. Note that values per day differ for departments. One day in milling machine represents 96 hours of work, while one day in the drill press represents 64 hours. The chart quickly reveals the amount and the "limits" of time available by departments. For example, an additional order requiring 480 hours of assembly work, or three days (480 divided by 160), could be scheduled for one day, Friday, during the week ending April 5 and two days, Wednesday and Thursday, during the week ending April 12. The earliest date this assembly order could be completed would therefore be April 11, assuming previously scheduled orders as shown by the chart are not changed to give priority to this new order.

Many adaptations of the Gantt chart idea are in use today. They may not be identified as Gantt charts, but they all emphasize the importance of time values in planning. Observe that the determining of the particular activities and their sequence are normally included in the meaning of planning, but not of scheduling. The former has the broader connotation.

PATTERNS OF PLANNING

The patterns of planning among enterprises differ quite widely. For example, some stress strong and persistent growth, while that of others includes little intention to change future events. One enterprise may conduct elaborate planning with the aim of increasing its share of the market, entering new fields or markets, or making major organizational changes. Its planning calls for active product development and adoption of new manufacturing techniques. In contrast, in another enterprise, the planning is simply to maintain the present position of the company. Here "survival today" is emphasized, the reasoning being that an enterprise must survive today if it is to survive in the future.

Generally speaking, there are three divergent and current patterns in planning practice which include (1) satisficing, (2) optimizing, and (3) adaptivizing.[1] The first emphasizes the satus quo; seldom are breaks with the past produced. Obvious deficiencies are corrected, but the customary and current way of conducting affairs is preserved. Survival is of major importance; growth and development are secondary and frequently ignored.

The pattern of optimizing stresses doing as well as possible. For this goal a type of operations research may be followed or various judgment considerations may be employed in these optimizing efforts. Truly optimum plans are not always attained, but close approximations of them are. Furthermore, in these efforts, valuable by-products of the behavior of important forces are gained, and this knowledge is helpful in further study and research.

Adaptivizing describes the planning pattern whereby operations can be adapted to short-run and also to major future changes. Basically a reduction in the variations of the expected behavior of essential forces affecting the plan are sought. To illustrate, a company with a product having highly cyclical demand determines its operations to conform as best it can with this fluctuation. But under such conditions, its facilities and personnel cannot be effectively employed. To improve its situation the company might seek another highly cyclical product line of the same general technological requirements with demand fluctuations opposite to those of its present product line. By this means, variation in annual sales would be reduced to a fraction of their former amount. By adaptivizing or adjusting production requirements and outputs, the planning is simplified from the overall viewpoint.

ADVANTAGES OF PLANNING

To expedite quick comprehension the following 8 major advantages of planning are listed. Planning is advantageous in that it:

1. Makes for Purposeful and Orderly Activities. All efforts are

---

[1] From an excellent article by Russell L. Ackoff, "The Meaning of Strategic Planning," *McKinsey Quarterly* (Summer 1966).

pointed toward desired results and an effective sequence of efforts is accomplished. Unproductive work is minimized. Usefulness of the achievement is stressed. As far as effort is concerned, a man running in circles can be working as hard as a man running down the street. The difference is in the usefulness of the achievements. Planning distinguishes between action and accomplishment.

2. *Points Out Need for Future Change.* Planning helps to visualize future possibilities and to appraise new key future fields for possible participation. It enables the manager to avoid entropy or the tendency to let things "run down" and to see things as they might be, not as they are. A manager can be awakened to opportunities through planning.

3. *Answers "What If" Questions.* Such answers permit a manager to see through a complexity of variables that affect what action he decides to take. Typical questions are "What would happen to our employees if we automated production line No. 27?" "What would happen to our sales if we limited orders to $50 and over?" "What would happen to our budget if we called in the bonds and issued more preferred stock?" Models can be built and computers used to process answers to such questions. Or intuition, judgment, and various "studies of the situation" can be employed.

4. *Provides a Basis for Control.* The twin of planning is controlling which is performed to make sure the planning is bringing about the results sought. Quite a number of new techniques combine the planning-controlling functions, as illustrated by budgeting. By means of planning, deadlines are determined for the starting and completing of each activity, the setting of standards of performance is promoted, and maximum expenditures are set. These serve as bases for controlling. A plan must establish such help for controlling. If it is demonstrated that a certain plan cannot be implemented, then the plan must be modified to provide one which can be implemented.

5. *Encourages Achievement.* The act of putting thoughts down on paper and evolving a plan provides the planner with guidance and a drive to achieve. Spelling out desired results and how to achieve them are of themselves positive forces toward good management. Planning reduces random activity, needless overlapping efforts, and irrelevant actions.

6. *Compels Visualization of Entirety.* This overall comprehension is valuable, for it enables the manager to see important relationships, gain a fuller understanding of each activity, and appreciate the basis upon which his managerial actions are supported. Isolation and

confusion are reduced. Through planning, a constructive identification with the problems and the potentialities of the enterprise as a whole is gained.

7. Increases and Balances Utilization of Facilities.   Many managers point out that planning provides for a greater utilization of available facilities of an enterprise. For any given period of time the best use is made of what is available. Also, activities are balanced both in amount and in timing, thus ensuring needed support among them. The result is that the best possible use is made of available facilities.

8. Assists Manager in Gaining Status.   Proper planning helps a manager to provide confident and aggressive leadership. It enables him to manage his affairs at hand rather than allow the affairs to dilute and negate his efforts. In the viewpoint of some managers, planning is an organized approach to future problems. Thinking out things ahead of time provides long-term, stable guides. To do otherwise is to manage as a result of events rather than by managerial foresight, influence, and action.

DISADVANTAGES OF PLANNING

Planning as a fundamental function of management is essential, but there are disadvantages or limitations to its use. Again a listing will be used to show these disadvantages. Observe that the seriousness of any of these disadvantages will vary depending upon the individual considerations in each case.

1. Planning Is Limited by the Accuracy of Information and Future Facts.   The usefulness of a plan is affected by both the current and the subsequent correctness of the assumptions regarding the future which were used in formulating the plan. No manager can predict completely and accurately the events of the future. If conditions under which the plan was formulated or must be implemented change significantly from those assumed by the planner, much of the value of the plan may be lost. Plans should be evaluated in light of current operating conditions, and the usefulness of any plan based on unreliable forecasts is open to question.

2. Planning Costs Too Much.   There are those who argue against planning, saying that the cost of planning work is in excess of its actual contribution. They believe that the money could better be spent in actually performing the physical work to be done. Planning expenditures can be high, but like all functions, planning must justify its existence; and the amount and extent of planning activities must be in keeping with the individual circumstances.

3. *Planning Has Psychological Barriers.* A prevalent barrier is that people have more regard for the present than for the future. The present is more desirable and has certainty. The future means change and adjustments to new situations and conditions. The feeling by some, oddly and erroneously, is that if planning is soft-pedaled, the changes and the possible dangers of the future will in some way or other be minimized. Planning, they believe, tends to accelerate change and unrest.

4. *Planning Stifles Initiative.* Some feel that planning forces managers into a rigid or straight-jacket mode of executing their work. It is contended these rigidities may tend to make the managerial work more difficult than it need be. Instead of helping, they actually hinder. There are elements of truth in these arguments, but as already implied, the most effective plans provide some degree of elasticity and interpretation in their application. Where every last detail is carefully planned and spelled out, the situation may be such that minute planning was deemed necessary, as for example in the case of performing a major surgical operation.

5. *Planning Delays Actions.* Emergencies and sudden uprisings of unusual and difficult situations demand on-the-spot decisions. Action is required now, spending valuable time thinking over the situation and designing a plan cannot be followed. That such conditions do arise is without question. But in all events, at least a modicum of planning is desirable for, as stated above, activity does not necessarily mean useful accomplishment. It appears foolhardy to start a course of action without giving some attention to what the desired results are, how best to achieve them with available facilities, and the probable consequences of the adopted course.

6. *Planning Is Overdone by Planners.* Some critics state that those performing planning tend to overdo their contribution. This is evidenced by the preparation of elaborate reports and instructions beyond any practical need and the refusal to take risks mandatory for his managerial work, attempting instead, through planning, to eliminate all risks. Excessive time and money are spent on securing information and trying to fit all of it into a neat, compact plan. Likewise, seemingly endless follow-ups of results are practiced. In essence, lacking is a realistic recognition that getting along with the work by reasonable means is fundamental to the manager's purpose.

7. *Planning Has Limited Practical Value.* Some contend planning is not only too theoretical, but other means are more practical. For example, they believe effective results are obtained by a muddling-through type of operation in which each situation is tackled when and if it appears pertinent to the immediate problem. In this way, opportunism can be utilized to full advantage. Also, they note that planning results in few plans that are followed consistently and exclusively to specific ends.

FEASIBLE BOUNDARIES OF PLANNING

In his planning work a manager makes use of premises. He does this to reduce the uncertainty inherent in the future, to have an identifiable foundation upon which to form a structure upon which planning can be based, and to give his planning reality and acceptance. Since planning deals with the future, a manager in order to manage, assumes that certain entities will act in certain ways, that certain forces will be present to known degrees, or that specific conditions will be absent during the future period under consideration. To illustrate, forecasts of economic activity, predictions of governmental actions, prophesies of consumer behavior, and estimates of future company sales can and are used as bases for planning work.

In addition, constraints contribute to the defining of boundaries within which planning is performed. Typical constraints include the basic resources at the disposal of the manager, his evaluation of them, his managerial philosophy, his attitudes toward society in general and toward his associates, as well as his ethical beliefs. Constraints are established more by intuition, judgment, attitude, and belief than is the case with premises. The planner's attitude about management, what is important and what is not important to him, to his fellow human beings, and to society, is especially significant in establishing constraints. In addition, the manager's background and basic management training influence the constraints that he establishes for himself. The statement is sometimes made that plans formulated by a manager reflect his character, his behavior pattern, his concept, and his caliber of management. This effect stems mainly from his managerial planning constraints.

By using premises and constraints, a manager is able to plan—and further he places boundaries within which the planning efforts are to be performed. Premises and constraints tend to confine planning within areas considered appropriate and feasible by the planner. As already stated, they help to establish a framework within which the planning is done. In essence, the planning is contingent upon the premises and the constraints used.

INFORMATION AND PLANNING

To establish his planning premises and constraints, a manager needs information. There is a truism in management that one never has *all* the information to cover *all* facets and contingencies of a plan. The manager's planning efforts must always be partly rational and partly visceral. Personal courage, personal commitment, and personal responsibility are required for the premise establishing the planning to take shape.

With reference to his enterprise, the informational needs of a planner can be classified into three types: (1) environmental, (2) competitive, and (3) internal.[2] The first, or environmental, includes data pertaining to economic, social, and political aspects of the climate in which the enterprise must operate in the future. Examples include data on price levels, wages, availability of labor, foreign trade, population, and unemployment. Competitive information deals with performance in the past and with present activity of the enterprise, as well as with knowledge about competitors' plans. Representative of competitors' information is the enterprise's share of the market, return on investment, management changes, new products to be introduced, marketing patterns to be followed, new facilities, and research and development efforts of competing firms. The last classification, internal information, embraces identification of the enterprise's strengths and weaknesses that can be utilized in charting the enterprise's future plans. Included are cost data, cost behaviors to volume changes, degree of productivity, manpower resources, community standing, and public relations.

FACTS AND PLANNING

From the stockpile of available information, the planner seeks to ferret our facts that appear relevant to his planning task at hand. A fact is an occurrence, quality, or relation that is manifestly real or actual. It represents a thing done or existing. Obviously not all information is made up of facts.

---

[2] Adapted from an excellent article by D. Ronald Daniel, "Management Information Crisis," *Harvard Business Review* (September–October 1961), pp. 111–21.

Emphasis should be placed on the importance of the use of facts in the establishing of premises and the formulating of the plan. Too many times what is accepted without question as fact turns out to be opinions, hopes, premises, or estimates of the planner. What one would like to have exist as a planning premise is sometimes confused with what actually exists. Also, one may be hasty in concluding that there are no facts available about a certain area of activity and proceed to a plan based on judgment, intuition, past experience, or some cultural pattern when actually facts are available and could be found if a diligent and consistent search were made for them. In some cases, the facts may be unpleasant and difficult to believe and accept. Nevertheless they should be included in the planning work if practical and effective plans are to be evolved.

PRINCIPLE OF FACTS AND PLANNING

To design an effective plan, it is necessary to obtain all the available pertinent facts, face the facts, and in the plan include the action that the facts dictate.

PLANNING PREMISES

Premises are assumptions providing a background against which estimated events affecting the planning will take place. The selection of planning premises and their use depend upon the skill, perception, and experience of the planner. Some premises seem more appropriate than others, but for any given case final judgment must await the results obtained. The difficulty usually faced by the planner is twofold: (1) selecting what premise to use and (2) evaluating the essential assistance obtained from the use of the premise. If the assumption is one for which statistical or quantitative data are available, that is, gross national product, dollar sales, or costs of financing, a corollary to the second difficulty mentioned above is how to manipulate or make use of the data so that the derivations from them are meaningful to the planning efforts and are statistically correct.

Within any one enterprise, agreement regarding the planning premises is vital in order to achieve proper coordination and integration among the various plans. Obviously, one manager of a company using the premise of retrenchment over the next several years and another manager basing his plans on an expansion of the company's facilities could result in confused and extremely costly operations. However, different premises can be used. In some instances this approach serves as a check upon past plans, or more commonly it is helpful to draw up different plans for consideration.

The makeup of planning premises changes, and it is sometimes difficult to keep a set of premises up to date. This is the result of both the actions of the future and the importance of a premise upon the plan. In addition, every major plan adopted by an enterprise tends to become a planning premise. This stems from the interrelatedness of plans and their dependence upon each other. If a company adopts a plan to market a new line of products, that plan will become an important premise in the determination of other plans where the presence of this new product line is significant.

VARIETY OF PLANNING PREMISES

There are many kinds of planning premises. It is beyond the scope of this book to try to list them, much less to present a discussion of each type. Some are of major importance, and others are minor; some are tangible, while others are intangible; and some are primarily external to the enterprise, while others concern conditions primarily internal to the firm. Care must be exercised to include those premises which have or might have a significant bearing on the plans. In some instances the use of a certain premise may be advantageous to a particular type of enterprise only. However, planning premises having a universal character and those to be discussed are applicable to nearly every enterprise. They include economic forecasts, technological forecasts, sociological factors, governmental controls and fiscal action, industry demand, public attitudes, and the individual firm's data.

ECONOMIC FORECASTS

Forecasts vary considerably in the periods covered, some are for one year, others are for five or even ten years. The period selected depends upon the needs and the type of activity in which the enterprise is engaged. Some forecasts are more or less informal hunches by managers quite close to the operating scenes. Sometimes these considered guesses prove excellent determinants of future events. In contrast, many forecasts are formidable statistical studies that analyze masses of data to arrive at a measured forecast. Most statistical forecasts are based upon the behavior through time of selected economic values such as gross national income, business capital expenditures, bank debits, retail sales, freight carloadings, employment, and new incorporations. By studying and analyzing these data, qualified statements regarding the future are made. Among the more common techniques used to interpret the data and to formulate forecasts are *trajectory,* in which the past trend of the data is projected into the future; *cyclic,* which assumes for the most part that patterns of events are stable and repeat themselves over fairly definite periods; *associative,* by which relationship between events is established—if one type of event is present, the other type will also appear shortly; and what might be termed *persistency,* which predicts basically no change in events from what they currently are, an approach which is popular for situations relatively stable and, in the nature of things, slow to change.

FIGURE 10–2

> Nearly a billion dollar increase in sales volume for food manufacturers is estimated for the forthcoming year. During the same time, these manufacturers are expected to spend nearly $550 million for new plants and capital equipment. This is approximately 10 percent over the expenditures of last year, when they amounted to $508 million.
>
> Convenience foods—frozen and otherwise—are the pacemakers in the upward food trend. Dehydrated milk has made rapid gains by the new instant dry milk. Also instant coffee continues to win new users. Currently nearly 30 percent of the coffee sales in the New York and Philadelphia trading areas are accounted for by instant coffee. Bakery mixes have skyrocketed in sales. Vegetables packaged in plastic bags for convenient finished cooking have set new sales records.
>
> Plant executives continue to favor fewer and larger plants. Continuous operation with instrument controls and unit-load materials handling are favored. It is predicted that 10 years hence companies who do not follow these manufacturing trends will have a slim chance for survival unless they sell a high-price specialty product to a limited market.

Source: Adapted from *Food Engineering* (New York: McGraw-Hill Publishing Co.).

Figure 10–2 shows an excerpt from a forecast concerning the food manufacturing industry. This study provides predictions, as well as past behaviors, from which the manager may make comparisons and reasonable interpretations.

It is well to note that all forecasts contain some guesswork. Since they deal with the uncertain future, some predicted statements may not prove true with the passing of time, and important events may not have been included. But forecasting helps forecasting. As Elbert Hubbard expressed it: "Go as far as you can see, and when you get there you'll see farther."

TECHNOLOGICAL FORECASTS

The ability to take into account technological changes is becoming increasingly important in managerial planning. One of the most powerful factors influencing the growth or the decline of an enterprise is technological change, some of which has a high degree of uncertainty. The effects of technology are far reaching having severe interactions with economic, social, and political factors and modifying them significantly. For example, from the social viewpoint, technology brings about labor displacement and new educational and training needs. Some technological change is taking place all the time as exemplified by routine product refinement and technical modifications of processes and tools.

To cope with these changes pose tremendous tasks. It is important to know the major directions of technologic change and the approximate scope of these activities. Also, knowledge of natural resources is helpful. In addition, keeping up to date on technical processes and evaluating new concepts in this area are basic requirements. Frequently, information on who is using what technology and evaluating this usage can be of great assistance. We know that a particular technical growth follows a typical cycle of four steps: (1) invention (2) rapid growth, (3) consolidation, and (4) maturity. Being able to identify where on this growth cycle a certain technology entity is, aids in drawing up forecasts about it.

It appears that the formulation for effective technological forecasts rests upon three bases. First, have strong research efforts and effective research policies. Second, evaluate periodically technology competition to know what others are doing, their successes or failures, and in what ways these developments might aid or harm you. Third, make appraisals of radical technological developments and estimate what these developments might mean to your particular company. Technological forecasts are not precise, the field is too dynamic. What will be technically feasible three or five years from now is unknown, but as stated above, the direction and probable range can be estimated. The use of mathematical formulas are ineffective for technological forecasts. What is required is human judgment, knowledge of the technological field under study, and an understanding of its economic, social, and political implications.

SOCIOLOGICAL FACTORS

Planning premises are conditioned importantly by various key social factors and institutions. This area is frequently less common than economic and technical forms of premises, but it merits inclusion and is becoming part of the planning agenda of more and more managers. The distribution of present and future populations with respect to size, age, sex, location, and ethnic structure are significant in much planning. The emphasis that different members of society or of a community place upon personal needs, entertainment, home, and community can have an important bearing upon the premise selected, its makeup, and the weight given it in the formulation of plans.

Further, the attitude of prospective buyers toward such things as foreign versus domestic products, types of available public transportation, communication, and health should be considered. Their inclusion, for certain types of projects, appears essential if the plan is to encompass real and practical circumstances. Also, among the sociological environments to forecast are labor relations and education. Indicative of the former are the availability of skilled labor, extent of trade unionism, hiring and layoff practices, and types of fringe benefits. Collectively these constitute a background from and against which premises used in planning should be drawn. For example, in the field of education, the number of college graduates, professional people, and scientists and their views toward foreign affairs, their research work, and their level of living must be taken into account in order to obtain best results from planning.

GOVERNMENTAL CONTROLS AND FISCAL ACTION

Few enterprises escape the influence of governmental actions, and it is therefore appropriate to consider such actions as a cardinal premise of planning activities. Governmental services, international affairs, protective measures, and regulations are so extensive and affect so many different activities of an enterprise that it is essential to keep in mind the effects of legislation in formulating any plan.

The degree of governmental influence differs widely among various types of enterprise. The pattern of the laws dealing with government-enterprise relations is mixed and represents an inconsistent picture. Certain laws, for example, encourage competition, while others give noncompeting efforts a nod of approval. Some legal measures aid and others regulate the efforts of the group. Governmental regulations for protecting public health imposed upon a food manufacturer may be far different and more numerous than those applicable to a manufacturer of metal stampings. Likewise, a supplier of chemicals to the government soon discovers that rigid specifications must be met and definite ways of handling the paper work, of inspecting, and of shipping must be carried out.

There are also the areas of foreign markets, tariffs, international monetary stability, and foreign aid programs. For them, what effect and what premises should be taken into account in the planning effort? Furthermore, the application of current governmental controls and the makeup of probable future controls are vital. Such questions as the following confront the planner: Will more or will fewer controls be used? Are the present regulations likely to be interpreted differently in the near future? Will the present regulations continue to be administered by the same commission, board, department, or governmental unit? Tentative answers to these questions are assumed in the planning premises.

Governmental fiscal actions merit special mention. Government is a dominant figure in income distribution and investment activities. It is thus necessary for a manager to premise governmental fiscal actions in developing his plans. Taxes, for example, represent a sizable amount of expenditure to many enterprises and consumers. In formulating current plans a manager must make some assumptions regarding taxes. Should he plan on a continuation of the present tax rates, or prepare for higher rates, or perhaps even on lower rates? Likewise, governmental fiscal action of regulation over credit affects planning premises. Federal reserve banks by their market operations of government securities, by their modifying of the reserve amounts, and by their changing of the discount rates affect credit. When credit is readily available, purchasing of goods and services is stimulated; and, in contrast, when credit is scarce, buying is discouraged. Therefore, credit availability, throttled by government, can exert tremendous influence upon a company's operations. The amount and purpose of government expenditures can seriously affect a manager's planning activities. He may make the planning premise that the government will continue to purchase large quantities of "X" material from his enterprise and accordingly plan for enlarging and improving his facilities for the manufacture of this material. However, a reversal in the government's purchasing and cancellation of orders for reasons not foreseen by either government authorities or the manager can result in serious difficulty and require major adjustments in operations without delay.

INDUSTRY DEMAND

The main purpose of establishing premises with respect to industry demand is to define the kind of market demand that the individual firm faces for its products or services. Logically the industry demand is first estimated, followed by sales estimates for the individual firm in that industry. Many statistical series are available to predict probable demand for a given industry. Population, employment, and prices are among the more common. For some industries special studies are available, providing quite comprehensive and factual information. Most of these have been prepared by either trade associations or the government.

A basic indicator for showing the probable future situation and growth or decline for an industry demand is population in terms of totals, composition, and location. The correlation between population and industry demand may not be precisely known or constant, but for many products and services, population is a major demand determinate. When population as a whole is classified by specific age segments, the information becomes even more significant, because demands can differ greatly among age groups. For example, the products and services purchased by those in the 22- to 44-year age bracket are different from those purchased by the 65 and over group. Available data reveal that during the period 1975–85, the 18- to 21-year-old group will increase by more than 42 percent—15.3 million persons in 1975 and 21.8 million in 1985. Also observe that these data have high certainty and they are not dependent upon future birth rates; these persons are in schools today.

Employment is another bellwether for estimating industry demand. People plus employment mean buyers with income to purchase the goods and services being offered. With reliable population data and the assumption that the government will not permit unemployment beyond a given level—if necessary it will expand public works and public employment—usable information about employment can be developed and associated with probable effects upon industry demand.

Prices are another important consideration. The planner is concerned about levels of prices. Typical questions include: Will prices rise? If so, at what approximate rate? Can it be reasonably assumed that prices will stabilize at their current levels? Economic history shows that during the past several decades there has been great depreciation in the value of money. This has been true in all countries. The reasons for this are numerous and extremely complex; they represent the many considerations that enter into the decision to trade—either buying or selling of a given product or service at a particular time and place. Predicting price levels for a long period of time is extremely hazardous; but for short periods, perhaps up to a year, fairly satisfactory estimates are possible.

PUBLIC ATTITUDES AND BEHAVIOR

This classification includes a number of considerations. Attitude toward government control of prices, the meaning of a "fair" profit, deceptive business practices, bigness in business, freedom of job selection, and participation in an enterprise's ownership are typical to name a few. Factors such as these color the environment and affect the premise and the relative importance given to it. They are difficult to handle because measurable data on them are scarce and careful estimates and judgments about them commonly must be made.

The attitude of an individual as reflected by his behavior, especially at the marketplace, is widely used in planning efforts. Trying to discover fragments of certainty in the uncertainty of consumer buying behavior has been a major goal of planners for many years. Efforts to shed light in this area include a variety of approaches and investigations. Most but certainly not all of this work has been directed to the domestic, not the industrial, consumer. Consumer panels, surveys, motivation studies, test groups, and consumer budgets are among the more common approaches. All decisions to do or not to do, to buy or not to buy, resolve ultimately to the human being—hence, the interest in finding out how the consumer acts and why he acts as he does.

One of the enlightening studies in this area is based on the theory that the most reliable predictors of change in a mobile society are people who can be classed as highly mobile. That is to say, certain people are the most alert, most responsive, and most active. These "high mobiles" set the pace for changing of values. They initiate changes—try new ventures, change occupations, get exposed to new ideas, advance in their jobs, and try out foreign cookbooks. Value patterns shift, and study of these high mobiles provides clues and reasons for these changing social values. By properly qualifying and applying these data, predictive power regarding consumer behavior can be gained.[3]

INDIVIDUAL FIRM'S DATA

With reasonably accurate information of the future concerning the industry demand and consumer buying behavior, the manager of an individual firm can formulate forecasts of his company's sales. Frequently, the manager is familiar with the relationship of his firm's position to the industry in which it operates so that he can usually select

---

[3] See the booklet, *America's Tastemakers* (Princeton, N.J.: Opinion Research Corp., April 1959.).

his planning premises without undue hardship and within a reasonable degree of accuracy. Furthermore, he can employ his intimate knowledge of his competitors and customers. A considerable amount of helpful information affecting sales can be obtained from talks at business luncheons, informal conferences, published financial statements, local business news items, and reports from salesmen and public relations men. Additional data of the individual firm are compiled from records and reports maintained, from observing, and from asking questions.

What might be termed "the middle-sized companies" approach offers possibilities to the individual firm in the industrial field. Figure 10–3

FIGURE 10–3. Data on U.S. manufacturing industries

Plants by number of employees	*Establishments*		*Expenditures by plants in operation*		*Value added by manufacturing*		*Total payroll*		*Total employment*	
	Number	*%*	*$000*	*%*	*$000*	*%*	*$000*	*%*	*Number*	*%*
Small, under 100.......	260,233	90.7	1,509,565	19.3	25,219,894	21.6	14,011,653	22.2	4,030,445	25.0
Medium, 100–999......	24,576	8.6	3,164,379	40.5	48,432,595	41.4	25,437,168	40.4	6,512,600	41.6
Large, 1,000 or more....	2,008	0.7	3,144,175	40.2	43,259,999	37.0	23,544,462	37.4	5,108,211	32.6
Total................	286,817	100.0	7,818,117	100.0	116,912,488	100.0	62,993,283	100.0	15,651,256	100.0

shows pertinent data on U.S. manufacturing industries. They have been grouped according to number of employees: small—those with under 100 employees; medium—those with 100–999 employees; and large —those with 1,000 or more employees. Study of the data shows that this middle group constitutes only 8.6 percent of the total number of establishments, yet accounts for over 40 percent of capital expenditures made by all manufacturers. In addition, these middle-sized companies are relatively easy to market to because they have large demands and the ability to buy. Furthermore, their size suggests only two or three key men making the purchasing decisions.

RESEARCH

For centuries man has sought more and more information in order to work out solutions to his problems and at times has resorted to consulting oracles, reading crystal balls, and just plain searching and hard thinking. Particularly helpful in our time is research and it is destined to increase in importance.

What is research? It is work formally applied and executed with the intent of adding to human knowledge. The name itself means to search and search again. A more formal definition may be stated: *Research is an attitude of mind and includes the application of the scientific method*

and mathematical methods to entities with the ultimate goal of reveal-
ing meaningful relationships and universal social and physical laws re-
garding man and his environment. Interestingly a researcher not only
deals with problems expertly, but he deliberately and competently
formulates problems. Well-stated questions and the suggestions for
new ways to deal with old problems mark the real advances in research. Actually, problems must be created with some frequency to
assure continued progress.

Research has been used to assist managers in practically all fields of
endeavor. To illustrate, new uses as well as substitutes for existing
materials, products, and processes have been pointed out by research as
well as the reduction of costs and the improvement of quality and
performance. Research of marketing, for example, has grown tremendously during the past several decades. It is recognized that the things a
buyer likes about a product or service, what he dislikes, the effectiveness
of selling efforts, the buyer's behavior habits, and his economic ability
to purchase are fundamental to marketing success, which governs ultimately all activities of an enterprise. Typical of the questions that
marketing research answers are:

On the product:
1. What do buyers want from the product?
2. How should it be packaged?
3. Do buyers purchase in single or multiple units?
4. What is the proper price range?

On the market:
1. How large is the current market? The potential market?
2. What channel or channels of distribution are best for this product?
3. What types of market outlets should be used?
4. To what extent is competition active in this field?

On selling:
1. What are the most effective sales appeals for this product?
2. What is the effect of price change on sales, i.e., what is the elasticity of demand for the product?
3. Are the relationships with the market outlets good?
4. Are the sales territories properly allocated?

On advertising:
1. Do a satisfactory number of current buyers and prospective buyers
   see or hear our advertisements?
2. What medium is most effective in reaching the market for this
   product?

3.   What are the most effective appeals that can be used?
4.   To what extent is advertising helping sales?

On public opinion:

1.   What does the public think of the company?
2.   What steps might be taken to influence favorably the public's attitude?
3.   Where does the company stand relative to its competitors?
4.   Is the company gaining or losing in public favor?

In some instances, research is concerned with what is commonly termed *pure* research, that is, research pursued without regard for specific application. Pure research is important because it provides the fundamental principles and knowledge upon which further research can be pursued. It is research for research's sake. In contrast, the term *applied* research is used to denote research conducted for a definite purpose. Actually the two are interrelated, because pure research sometimes does not lead to the sought-for basic knowledge but to a desirable commercial application. Likewise, some applied research fails to find the answer to the specific problem but reveals fundamental knowledge heretofore unknown.

Extensive research is conducted by several foundations, governmental units, and private enterprises whose names, in many cases, remain anonymous in publications of the research discoveries. Also, a great deal of pure research is conducted by private companies, and in some instances applied research is conducted by universities and research foundations. Many of the larger universities in the United States have established special units to conduct pertinent research studies in selected management fields.

ETHICS AND PLANNING

A suitable definition of ethics is: *Ethics deals with personal conduct and moral duty and concerns human relations with respect to right and wrong.* Ethics concerns morals and philosophy. It deals with the behavior of individuals and the standards governing the interrelationships between individuals.

Violation of civil law tends to encourage the violation of moral law. Statutes which in effect encourage lying, cheating, and irresponsibility promote these vices as a way of life and encourage the pragmatic idea that anything an individual can get away with is right. The result is crime, corruption in public life, disrespect for authority, and disregard of properties. The true test of right is based on moral principles which are the product of social forces and human experiences over thousands of years.

Planning is influenced by the planner's ethics. What he believes "is right" and the correct action morally to take in a given circumstance shapes his planning in important ways. Ethics is related to an individual. The ethical standards followed by the individual manager help determine the ethics of his enterprise or of his industry. His code of conduct influences what degree of ethical behavior or unethical behavior is followed. But it is difficult to answer such questions as: When does business aggressiveness become bad ethics? What is the boundary between honorable self-interest and moral or legal dishonesty?

It is the belief of some that the character of an action can be evaluated by two major means: (1) the intention or subjective means and (2) the result or objective means. In some instances these two differ tremendously; in others, they do not. Suppose a manager with the good intention of giving a reward for a job well done presents a $500 bonus to a salesman with the result that the salesman decides to lay off several weeks to spend his bonus, thus causing inconvenience and loss of sales to his employer. Was this action by the manager ethically satisfactory in that it was generous and thoughtful, or was it wrong because it resulted in inconvenience and loss? Consider an opposite case in which an employment manager, wishing to get rid of an undesirable employee, wrote a letter of praise recommending this employee to a prospective employer. Subsequently, the employee is offered and accepts the new job and proves to be an entirely proficient, satisfactory, and valuable worker. Was the employment manager's action ethical because the results were beneficial, or was the action bad because the manager had purposely misstated facts as he knew them. Fortunately, good intentions and good results commonly exist together.

Also, ethical issues arise dealing with conflict of interest. This condition arises when a manager is simultaneously a member of several groups that have conflicting goals. Consider the case of a manager of one company having a financial interest in a second company that purchases from the first company. Should the manager demand the best for his employing company even though such demands reduce the profits of the second or supplying company? Or should he grant special favors to the supplying company? We can also include his acceptance of special favors in the form of gifts and gratuities from the second company. It is "right" for the manager to do so? Is he obligated by acceptance of such favors, does he violate his duties to his employer by such actions, and to what extent is there.a conflict of interest in such practices?

ETHICS—INTERNAL AND EXTERNAL

It is also helpful to discuss ethics in planning from the viewpoints of (1) internal ethics, or those within an enterprise, and (2) external ethics, or those with the enterprise and outside entities such as other enterprises, consumers, suppliers, and government agencies. With reference to the former, a manager must be honest with himself, since his greatest asset is his character. And he should be honest and straightforward with others, treating them in the same manner in which he wishes to be treated. Fairness in dealings with his compeers and subordinates is mandatory; he should never discriminate by dispensing special favors as privileges, whether for remuneration or not. Information coming to him confidentially should neither be revealed nor used to the disadvantage of any of his fellow employees. He should ensure his employees' right to privacy.

With reference to external ethics, the same suggestions stated above can be followed. Sincere efforts must be made, especially in planning, not to injure any outsider's rights, treat him unjustly, or injure his person or property. Corruption wherever discovered should be exposed. Determining what is right in external ethics poses some difficulties. To illustrate, consider the task of a businessman proving superiority of his product or service over that of a competitor. Upon what ethical basis can differences between competitive products be accurately measured, by what authority, and for what wanted purposes? Exaggerated claims, misleading comparisons, and tricky statements harshly asserted in print, radio, and television suggest possible violations of ethical conduct. Likewise, illustrations and copy employing lewdness and vulgarity appearing in home-consumed media seen by both sexes of all ages create problems of good taste and raise the question of who benefits from such actions and why. Specifically, is a manager ethically justified in including such actions in his planning and in promoting them?

PRINCIPLE OF ETHICS

Proper ethics in management requires a manager to be honest with himself and with society, and to deal honorably with others just as he would like to be dealt with.

Assistance in improving the ethics of business is provided by the Better Business Bureaus, organized in 1914. They are nonprofit, independent corporations established and maintained by businessmen to construct and promote programs of self-regulation in business transactions. There is no affiliation with any government agency. Located in nearly 100 cities throughout the entire United States, these bureaus provide assistance in writing needed codes to cope with local unethical trade practices, promoting honesty and dependability in advertising, providing control over certain types of peddling, the supplying of talks and information to schools on the subject of better business practices, sponsoring programs for consumer education on the operation of the competitive system, and the recording of all complaints and their disposition in a file which is convenient for reference regarding the record of a specific individual or company.[4]

QUESTIONS

1. Does planning insure usefulness of achievements? Why?
2. Justify your reaction to the following: "To plan means essentially to time; hence activities for which time measurements cannot be obtained cannot, and in fact should not, be planned."
3. Explain the meaning of the statement, "Every major plan adopted by an enterprise tends to become a planning premise."
4. Discuss the use and importance of technological forecasts in managerial planning efforts.
5. Clearly distinguish between the two concepts in each of the following pairs: (*a*) satisficing as a pattern in planning practice and forecasting, (*b*) "what if" questions and pure research, (*c*) planning premises and planning constraints, and (*d*) planning and decision making.
6. Why perform planning if nobody, not even a manager, can be certain of events in the future? Elaborate on your answer.
7. What is meant by sociological factors in establishing planning premises? Select one such factor and explain how it may affect the premises used.
8. How is it possible for a manager to overplan? Discuss. In your opinion, is overplanning common in management? Substantiate your answer.
9. What is ethics? In what way or ways is it important in management?
10. What is the meaning and importance of each of the following: (*a*) phasing in planning, (*b*) environmental informational needs for planning, and (*c*) the planning pattern of adaptivizing.
11. Discuss public attitudes and behavior as they influence managerial planning.

---

[4] For a comprehensive discussion of the Better Business Bureaus and their activities, see *A Guide for Retail Advertising and Selling* (5th ed.; New York: Association of Better Business Bureaus, Inc., 1956).

12. As a practicing manager discuss the importance you would attach to "what is right" in your work.
13. Discuss the continuity of planning, pointing out its importance in management. Use an illustration in your answer.
14. For an enterprise with which you are familiar, or of which you have been an employee, relate an example of planning that was performed. In your opinion how effectively was this planning conducted? Discuss.

CASE 10–1. WATSON CORPORATION

The president of Watson Corporation, manufacturers of plastic zippers and fasteners, feels his company should obtain a substantial increase in sales. His sales manager assures him that the market for the company's products is tremendous and much of it is still untapped. The president also realizes that to meet present-day costs and operate on a sound financial basis, sales of the company must be increased.

In response to his request, the sales manager has drawn up a sales plan covering a four-year period. Using current sales as a base, the plan projects a sales increase of 10 percent the first six months, 15 percent the second six months, and 15 percent for each of the following three years. In discussing these increases with the president it was agreed that they would require stretching, but were attainable.

Marketing was conducted through selected sales representatives who were chosen in accordance with high standards demands by the company. Representatives were paid a commission on net delivered sales. All major marketing areas were covered by the representatives, and it was a normal practice for the company to grant the representative exclusive representation in a given area. Most of the representatives carried two or three other noncompetitive products—a common practice to which the company did not object, but in fact, accepted as a general and realistic marketing condition. The company enjoyed a reputation for making high-quality products. It had a good name in the trade and was generally considered an excellent firm with which to do business. In fact, manufacturers' representatives sought to handle the company's products.

To increase sales, the company plans to increase its advertising and promotional efforts, the increased cost of which is estimated as 1.2 percent of projected sales. Changes in the representative's commission were also to be made. Comparison between the previous and proposed compensation arrangements is:

Previous compensation plan		Proposed compensation plan	
Monthly sales	*Commission*	*Monthly sales*	*Commission*
Under 5,000...............	4.5%	Under 10,000...............	4 %
5–10,000...............	5	10–15,000...............	5
10–20,000...............	5.5	15–20,000...............	7.5
20–30,000...............	6	20–30,000...............	9

With the exception of several in relatively remote areas, all the representatives were called upon personally by either the sales manager or his assistant and the increased advertising and promotional efforts as well as the revised commission plan were thoroughly explained. Reports to the president by the sales manager and his assistant showed enthusiastic cooperation by the manufacturer's representatives to the new plan.

Now, after one year experience with the new plan, there has been little increase in sales. Data are as follows:

Three years ago................................	$4,957,247.94
Two years ago.................................	5,301,601.08
One year ago..................................	5,183,853.53
For year just ending...........................	5,227,725.66

Monthly sales for the past year are as follows:

January................................	$ 541,541.40
February..............................	496,119.07
March.................................	388,750.51
April..................................	461,978.80
May...................................	424,636.34
June...................................	445,806.56
July....................................	370,651.73
August................................	394,906.19
September.............................	435,789.20
October...............................	443,923.51
November.............................	417,589.64
December.............................	406,032.70
Total............................	$5,227,725.66

The president is extremely disturbed by these results and is determined to better the company's sales and to improve its financial strength.

QUESTIONS

1. Comment fully on the company's decision to change the sales representatives sales quota and commission rate.
2. In your opinion, what are or might be some specific reasons for the lack of any appreciable increase in the company's sales? Discuss.
3. What action should the president now take? Why?

CASE 10–2. ADLER ADVERTISING AGENCY

MR. LEWIS KEITH: You certainly have excellent experience to offer, Mr. Anderson. As I stated, we have an opening for an account executive and you favorably impress me. May I ask you one more question before you talk with our Mr. Fairfax, who I have already told you has the final approval in our hiring of an account executive.

MR. PETER ANDERSON: Go ahead, shoot. If I can answer it, I will.

KEITH: I'd like to know why you are leaving your present job. Betz, Mystrom, and Schweitzer is an excellent agency.

ANDERSON: Yes, it has a good reputation. But I am going to be transferred to another account with whom I don't want to work. We're losing the Belmont account effective in about . . . a . . . 'er . . . seven weeks. It will be announced in about a month. Dick Griffin, our account executive on Belmont, will take over my present job and so I will be on a different account which is not to my liking.

KEITH: You're losing Belmont?

ANDERSON: Yes.

KEITH: Is Belmont coming out with some new product that makes for a conflict of interests with your agency's present accounts?

ANDERSON: No, not that I know of. They have a new sales manager, "Zeke" Kurch, who insists on changes in the present advertising campaigns they are running.

KEITH: Zeke Kurch. I don't know him. He's new, isn't he?

ANDERSON: Yes, they got him from Portlands in Cincinnati. Portlands, you know, is quite an aggressive competitor of Belmont. From what I hear, he is difficult to work with and insists on making a lot of changes. He is trying to make a name for himself, I guess. But I can tell you this: Any mistake in Belmont advertising is made to look like our agency's doings. Kurch sees to that.

KEITH: I see. Well, Mr. Anderson, it was nice talking with you. I'll take you over to Mr. Fairfax's office and he'll see you.

ANDERSON: Thank you very much, Mr. Keith.

Belmont is a major account that Adler Advertising Agency would like to get. Mr. Keith reported the possibility of the Belmont account to his superiors. It was news to them and they intend to try and pick up the business. The following day Mr. Keith wrote a letter to Mr. Anderson telling him Adler Agency would advise him later if he was to be hired. Following this, Mr. Keith informed his superiors that he intends to reject applicant Anderson on the grounds that he cannot be trusted with confidential information.

Questions

1. What ethical constraints are present in this case?
2. Comment on the actions by Mr. Anderson.
3. As president of Adler Advertising Agency what action would you take? Why? As Mr. Keith? Why?

11

Managerial classification of planning

It is ridiculous to forget that you and your business are each implanted in the society of the moment. We cannot ignore the world of our time. We had better understand it.

J. IRWIN MILLER

NUMEROUS CLASSIFICATIONS of planning exist. There is, for example, repeat planning which evolves plans used again and again; single-use planning which produces plans that are used up when the goal is accomplished; and physical planning which deals with arrangements of buildings and equipment, or of spatial design. In addition, planning can be functional, individual, departmental, and comprehensive. The list could be extended almost indefinitely.

MAJOR CLASSIFICATIONS OF MANAGERIAL PLANNING

For purposes of this book certain classifications of planning have been selected. Since common usage identifies the type of plan, not the planning, we will make reference to these different types of planning by means of the plans which they bring about. Included in our selected list of plans are (1) objective, (2) policy, (3) procedure, (4) method, (5) standard, (6) budget, (7) program, and (8) techno-factor. These are of great importance in management and serve to provide a cross section of planning as it is used by the manager. A concise statement about each will now be presented. Following this a discussion of each type will be offered.

An objective can be considered a plan in that it has to do with future activities, requires foresight and imagination in determining, and is an integral part of all planning activities. To determine and identify the desired result requires at least a modicum of planning. All planning, in fact, deals with objectives, and vis-à-vis, objectives result from planning.

A policy is a statement or understanding that outlines the guiding course to be followed in both mental and physical actions by a manager. Broad boundaries are set up by policies, thus permitting initiative and judgment by the manager in interpreting a particular policy. Planning includes the formulation and use of policies since they assist in determining what must be done in order to accomplish the work. Examples of policies include promoting employees from within the enterprise, paying low base wages with high bonus payments, and producing only small, high-volume products.

Another kind of plan is *a procedure.* This deals with the selection and use of a specific course of action in keeping with established policies. Procedures provide chronological sequence to tasks and fix the path of a chain of such tasks across but within the policies and toward the predetermined goal. Compared to policies, procedures are more definite and apply to specific activities for the accomplishment of a certain well-defined goal.

Planning the manner in which each task of a procedure is to be performed by an individual employee results in *a method.* Method plans are quite common in manufacturing enterprises and indicate the "best way" to perform the task. By the use of method planning, a manager expects to gain improvement in efficiency, to compare accomplishments of individual employees, to have a practical basis for training employees, and to accomplish uniformity of quality in the products and services provided.

A *standard* provides a norm or base of reference. It can be thought of as something to strive for or as a model for comparison. Standards are basic in preparing schedules. They also supply the means for identification, comparison, and the determination of whether a factor is above, below, or on a par with an established and accepted base of that factor.

A budget is an important category of plans. In some instances, a budget represents the most important plan of an enterprise. A budget consists of logically arranged data representing reasonable expectancies for a given period. The target of what is to be achieved is evolved for each segment of the enterprise, and further, all such targets are coordinated into a comprehensive plan.

A program is also a plan. Programs can be thought of as planned

FIGURE 11-1.   The meaning and relationship of selected categories of plans

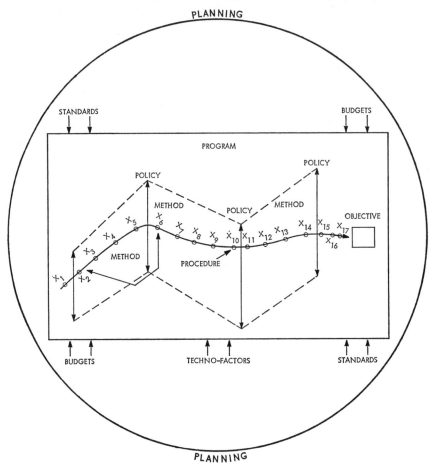

actions, integrated into a unity and designed to bring about a stated objective. Programs vary greatly as to type and makeup. They normally provide an outline of the actions to be taken, the facilities included, the commitments and the assumptions involved, and the areas in which efforts are to be directed.

A *techno-factor* is a relatively new type of plan of a somewhat technical nature and dealing with a selected factor such as time, cost, or material flow. In many cases a graphic chart is constructed to visualize the details of the plan as illustrated by a PERT network or a RAMP chart.

Efforts to clarify the meaning of these categories of plans are illustrated by Figures 11-1 and 11-2. In the former, or graphic illustration of Figure 11-1, the large circle represents the sphere of planning. As

FIGURE 11–2. Comparable information concerning selected categories of plans

Kind of plan	Distinguishing attribute	Chief characteristics	Required for use	Common erroneous situation
Objective.......	Provides target for direction and guidance of activities	Comprehensive	Interpretation for each operative level	Not precisely known or stated
Policy..........	Sets up the overall boundaries for activities	Broad, general, comprehensive	Interpretation, judgment	Improper identification for every managerial decision
Procedure.......	Defines chronological series of tasks	Tailor-made to achieve specific work	Compliance with slight interpretation required	Once established tends to remain
Method.........	Prescribes course of action to accomplish a task	Specific and detailed in how a task is to be done	Compliance	Ignored or insufficient planning directed to it
Standard........	Gives level of expected achievement	Tailor-made for specific work	Compliance	Not brought up to date in line with current operations
Budget.........	For a given period, consolidates many operational expectancies into a concise format	Tailor-made for specific work	Compliance with slight interpretation required	Difficult to modify as situations require
Program........	Integrates diverse but related activities into a unity	Comprehensive, covers relatively large scope of facilities and activities	Interpretation, judgment, and managerial competency	Used to identify any type of plan
Techno-factor...	Assists in visualizing probable effect of selected factor	Comprehensive for selected factor	Interpretation	Believed to be rigid plan

a result of planning, an objective, represented by the small block on the right, is included within the circle. The large rectangle within the circle designates a program. It encompasses the objective, is inclusive, and takes into account a relatively large undertaking. Standards, budgets, and techno-factors are also included within the circle of planning and, in the figure, provide respectively satisfactory levels and a desired balance of activities for the program to attain. Actually standards, budgets, and techno-factors can and are utilized in connection with plans other than programs. Policies are represented by the four vertical lines. They serve as guides for specific areas. The arrowheads on the ends of these vertical lines designate the boundaries or prescribed limits within which all activities are to take place. The horizontal line labeled "procedure" marks the specific fixed course of action to reach the objective. The procedure is made up of a series of tasks shown by marks X_1, X_2, X_3, etc., representing chronologically the various tasks to be performed. The procedure stays within the area limits established by the policies but cuts across these areas in establishing the path to the objective. The manner of performing each specific task of the procedure, such as X_1, X_2, or X_3, represents the respective methods.

Figure 11–2 shows tabulated key information about these categories of plans. To illustrate, for a procedure the distinguishing attribute is that it defines a chronological series of tasks, its chief characteristic is that it is tailor-made to achieve specific work, its use requires compliance with slight interpretations, and once established it tends to remain.

BALANCE AND INTEGRATION OF PLANS

The extent, amount of detail, and kind of plans to be employed in any given set of circumstances depend mainly upon the actions being planned and the manager's judgment, experience, and skill in planning. There is no precise rule to follow. What may prove highly effective in one case will be inadequate in another. Some managers will tend, for example, to stress programs and procedures, others, techno-factors, while still others will emphasize policies and budgets.

Even though individual considerations enter into the picture, it is important that a balance be maintained among the various plans of an enterprise and that these plans be integrated. Individual considerations should not result in isolated planning endeavors. Within any enterprise, all plans are interdependent. For example, a policy is related to other policies and also to programs, a procedure to another procedure as well as to policies, and a standard to a method. Failure to recognize this interdependence can cause much difficulty in planning. The isolated plan is an extremely restricted plan.

Hence, for maximum benefits, plans within an enterprise must be integrated and, in effect, support each other and contain a consistency of purpose and intent. In many respects the plans of an enterprise are as strong as their weakest link. For example, a well-thought-out program is only as effective as the policies and procedures with which it is integrated. In other words, the results of effective planning arise from an adequate integration of plans.

Furthermore, in the typical going enterprise, planning is in the nature of a cumulative, bit-by-bit activity. That is, a going enterprise has plans, and the planning function adds to these existent plans. And current plans frequently serve as guides in the development of additional plans. These characteristics stress the need for achieving balance and integration among plans.

POLICY

We will now discuss fully each of the selected classifications of planning. First is policy. Objectives are not included here since they were discussed fully in Chapter 3. *A policy is a verbal, written, or implied overall guide setting up boundaries that supply the general limits and direction in which managerial action will take place.* Management policies reveal the manager's intentions for future time periods and are decided prior to the need for knowledge of such intentions. They are broad, comprehensive, elastic, dynamic guides and require interpretation in their use. A policy defines the area in which decisions are to be made, but it does not give the decision. Policies spell out the sanctioned, general direction and areas to be followed. By keeping within these predetermined boundaries, but with freedom to decide within the stated areas, the manager performs his work in keeping with the overall planning of the enterprise of which he is a part.

Policy is extremely important in management. It is under policy that other plans are developed including procedures, methods, standards, budgets, programs, and techno-factors. Hence, within any given enterprise, policy has a very significant effect upon all plans.

POLICY FORMULATION

A well-formulated policy requires time to develop and it is well to consider all contingencies in formulating a policy. Hastily conceived policies usually prove unsatisfactory. High priority to policy formulation is suggested both during the establishment of an original enterprise and when changes in planning are to be made in an existing enterprise.

Several pointers in policy formulation should be kept in mind. First, good policies tend to be broad; they leave room for judgment, but do not require complex interpretation. Within an enterprise, policies should be consistent; no company should have two policies that say opposite things. Another consideration is to establish a sufficient number of policies to cover the areas deemed important. At the start, a company normally has enough to serve as needed bench marks in various areas. With time, more are added, and they should neither overlap existing policies nor leave any neglected gaps. Also, in formulating policies, the view should be taken that they are designed to be used as important plans of a manager. They are not drawn up to be broken or considered mere wishful thinking. In addition, sound policies will reflect and develop the unique personality or image of an enterprise. Effective policies possess individuality. They assist in giving an enterprise individual differences that distinguish it from others. Lastly, good policies are current. As conditions change for a company, policies need to be changed to fit the new condition.

FIGURE 11–3. Important considerations in policy formulation

1. The use of a policy should help in achieving the objective, and a policy should be built from facts, not personal reflections or opportunistic decisions.
2. A policy should permit interpretation; it should not prescribe detailed procedure.
3. The formulator's thoughts and ideas of the content of the policy should be conditioned by the suggestions and reactions of those who will be affected by the policy.
4. Wherever necessary to cover anticipated conditions, policies should be established, but care must be exercised to avoid having policies that are seldom, if ever, used.
5. Every policy should be expressed in definite and precise wording that is fully understood by every member of the enterprise.
6. All policies must conform to external factors such as laws and measures in the public interest.

In many enterprises the members of the board of directors and top management members establish the basic policies. Sometimes an executive committee assumes this task and submits its recommendations to the board or top manager. However, many policies dealing with the intermediate and lower organization levels are commonly formulated by managers in the respective areas.

When results management is followed, it is common to give those establishing goals considerable participation in policy formulation. This follows, because the attainment of the goals which the manager defines and holds himself responsible to attain, are greatly influenced by the policies to be followed.

Further, participation by nonmanagement members in policy formulation is recommended. Employees are consulted regarding their ideas and beliefs on a policy that is to be either established, modified, or abolished. In many cases the action taken is best described as a simultaneous working-down from the top managers, revealing what they perceive are the policy needs, and a working-up from the employees of the areas which will be affected by the policy. Figure 11–3 gives six important considerations in policy formulation.

WHY MANAGERS USE POLICIES

Policies provide the basis for the answers to many managerial problems. The question of what to do in a given case of a particular enterprise is answered, in part, by a thorough study of the policies. Hence, at all organizational levels better understanding of what is to be accomplished, as well as the means of accomplishment, is fostered by the use of sound policies. Confidence of the manager is enhanced, since a manager operating within a policy gains assurance that his actions are in keeping with the wishes of, and will be backed up by, his superiors.

Furthermore, the policies of an enterprise give meaning to the objective. The goal might be expressed in rather general terms which have small significance to the members of the enterprise. However, the policies translate the goal into terms which are comprehensible, individual, and intimate to the employees. And from a practical viewpoint, it is much less difficult to find out the policies than the objectives of an enterprise. In many instances, the first concrete evidence of a change in objective is revision of the present policies and the addition of new policies.

Policies implement the utilization of authority so that effective group action can be attained. By the presence of good policies, those having authority are encouraged to use it. This follows because, in effect, a policy informs (regarding what is to be attained) by making known the general areas within which activities are to take place.

Policies also encourage management development because *policies develop those who apply them.* Policies require interpretation and make it feasible for a manager to think *for,* not *by,* himself. Policies encourage the development of sound judgment and the exercise of managerial activities in keeping with prescribed limits. Policies force positive, wanted action. They are not confined to the prevention of bad action.

TYPES OF POLICIES AND EXAMPLES

While there are many kinds or types of policies, a helpful classification is that based on the source of the policy, that is (1) external, (2) internal, and (3) appealed. The first group, external policies, include those policies arising to meet the various controls and requests of forces outside the enterprise, such as government, trade associations, and trade unions. The second group, internal policies, includes those started by the managers at any level of management in order to have needed guides established for their own and their subordinates' use in managing the enterprise. The third, appealed policies, come into being from the appeal of an exceptional case by a manager to his superior regarding how to handle the case. As such cases are decided, precedents develop and constitute additional policies or important modifications to existent policies. When many policies are being made by appeal, it may indicate an insufficient number of existent policies.

Another classification of policies is that based on the organizational

FIGURE 11–4

Type of policy	*Mainly used by*	*Extent of influence*	*Scope*	*Importance*
Basic............	Top managers	Affect every unit of the organization	Very broad	Greatest
General..........	Middle managers	Sometimes apply to all but frequently to large segments of the organization only	Specific and somewhat limited	Medium
Departmental.....	Foremen and supervisors	Apply to activities of department for meeting everyday requirements	Definite and limited nature	Least

levels of managers. That is to say, there are policies which are used primarily by top managers, other policies by the middle managers, and still other policies which are applicable chiefly to supervisors and group leaders. Various nomenclatures have been used to designate policies of different levels, but the terms *basic, general,* and *departmental* are satisfactory. Figure 11–4 shows these three types of policies along with relevant information.

Another common classification of policies is by major functions of an enterprise: production policies, sales policies, financial policies, and personnel policies. Examples of each of these are shown in Figure 11–5.

An example of a policy pertaining to capital assets states:

It is the policy of this company to maintain a program for the acquisition and disposal of capital assets to insure a return of at least 22 percent on its investment. To this end the following guidelines will be used: (1) capital assets will be acquired on the basis of profitability, competitive position, and legal requirements; (2) capitalization and depreciation will be calculated within the limits of the provisions of the company's accounting manual; (3) obsolete or surplus capital assets will be disposed of as quickly as possible; (4) detailed records maintained on capital assets shall show their acquisition, location, and disposition; and (5) physical inventories will be made semiannually by the Controller.

Note that this policy, like all policies, provides guides only. It does not specify what capital assets to acquire, how to depreciate them, or when to dispose of them.

FIGURE 11–5. Policies classified by major functions of an enterprise

Production policies:
1. Locate branch plants in cities of less than 100,000 population.
2. Mechanize when machine will pay for itself within three years.
3. Follow wide spans of authority in organizing.
4. Complete all shop production orders within 60 days from receipt in shop.

Sales policies:
1. Sell a variety of types, sizes, and qualities of products.
2. Distribute products in Midwest area only.
3. Keep total expenditures for sales and advertising expenses within 15 percent of gross dollar sales.
4. Advertise exclusively on television.

Finance policies:
1. Utilize long-term creditors for sources of capital.
2. Practice paying out a stable dividend rate.
3. Invest capital not needed for immediate operations in bonds.
4. Extend credit to rated firms only.

Personnel policies:
1. Specify high school graduation as minimum educational requirement for hiring of new employees.
2. Train employees for possible promotion.
3. Promote from within the company work force.
4. Compensate employees at higher than comparable "going wages."

A manufacturing company sets forth its policy regarding promotions and transfers of employees in these words:

It is our policy to "promote from within" whenever qualified employees are available for vacancies in our organization. Diligent application to their present assignments, special preparation for positions immediately ahead, and length of service are considered in the selection of those for promotion. Employees on their present jobs a reasonable length of time may request transfers to other assignments in the company if they feel that different work will be better suited to their qualifications.

Observe again that this policy statement provides the overall guides to be followed. It does not give a precise means of how "to promote from within," or of handling transfers. Such work is the duty of the individual charged with the particular activity, but guides or areas within which to operate are provided by the policy.

POLICIES—WRITTEN AND UNWRITTEN

Preferably policies should be in writing. Some managers feel that a policy actually does not exist unless it is written. Although many companies do not put all their policies in writing, the tendency to do so is

FIGURE 11–6

Advantages of written policies are:
1. Managers are required to think through the policy's meaning, content, and intended use.
2. The policy is explicit and misunderstandings are reduced to a minimum.
3. Equitable and consistent treatment of problems is most likely to be obtained.
4. Unalterable transmission of policies is insured.
5. Authorization of policy, helpful in many cases, is provided.
6. A convenient and authoritative reference of policies can be supplied to all concerned with their use.

Disadvantages of written policies are:
1. Policies become too widely distributed and frequently are placed in the hands of persons who are not concerned with their use.
2. It is difficult to write a policy accurately and adequately—there may be uncertainty as to what the policy should be, and there is the constant danger of misinterpretation of certain words and phrases.
3. Flexibility in the use of the policy may become hampered—too rigid a course for practical management is defined.
4. Changes in policies to cope with changing conditions may be difficult to establish.
5. If confidential material is involved, nonwritten policies may be preferred for reasons of security and secrecy.

increasing. Verbal policies are frequently too nebulous and lead to excessive misunderstanding for satisfactory use.

Written policies are especially desirable for (1) subjects of a highly controversial nature; (2) situations where the distance between top and lower levels of management is quite deep, thus making personal and informal association and communication difficult and infrequent; and (3) preciseness of the policy statement so that an adequate and a complete understanding is conveyed. The writing should feature a matter-of-fact style and convey the feeling of wanting to share information and to be of genuine assistance. Sometimes the practice is followed of including statements of procedures to be used in carrying out the stated policy. Figure 11–6 lists the outstanding advantages as well as the disadvantages of putting policies in writing. In the great majority of cases the advantages outweigh the disadvantages.

Many policies are not expressed either in written or verbal form. They exist by inference or by means of consistent managerial behavior in certain subject areas. They may have little, if any, official approval, but they are operative. Such policies are termed *implied policies* and may be favorable or unfavorable to the enterprise. They result from tacit agreement or from the lack of any vigorous formal policy formulation efforts. Usually secrecy, difficulty of expressing, or reluctance to limit freedom of the manager's action are the chief reasons for the existence of implied policies.

EVALUATING POLICIES

Policies become antique, and to maintain their effectiveness they should be periodically reappraised, realigned, and restated in line with current opportunities and conditions. However, some managers feel that frequent requests for modification in a policy indicate its failure either in content or in usage. This may be true; yet it is difficult to attribute disagreement, conflict, and waste solely to poor policy, but policy can be a major contributing cause. The entire management process should be reviewed and studied for possible improvement.

The ultimate proof of a policy's correctness is in the desirable results which it helps the manager bring about in actual performance. Conducting interviews with managers and nonmanagers to ascertain the relationship between practices and policies is one effective approach. Another is to determine how useful the policy actually is by finding out how frequently it is used and what confidence the managers have in it. Policies not used regularly or not believed in suggest corrective action, such as elimination or restatement, possibly as a part of a more important policy. A simple check of current policies against objectives often reveals whether the policies are helping, or hindering, in the efforts to reach the objectives. Also, the "trial approach" can be employed. Here, a proposed revised policy can be applied to past problems to determine how it might have worked out. As an alternate, but similar, approach, hypothetical situations requiring the use of the present and the revised policy can be assumed and comparisons made between the probable assistance supplied by the two policies.

From the overall viewpoint, it is well to get opinions and facts both for and against an existent policy in order to uncover, for example, whether the stated policies and what is actually being done are compatible or in conflict. Furthermore, a review will reveal whether the ultimate aims are clearly known, whether activities are pointing to the established objectives, and whether all policies are integrated making, in effect, a unit or a whole from all the constituent or separate policies.

PROCEDURE

A procedure is specific and tailor-made to achieve certain work. Procedures exist in every part of an enterprise; they are a highly important category of plans. They have received considerable attention in the fields of office management, production, and sales engineering. Formally defined: *A procedure is a series of related tasks that make up the chronological sequence and the established way of performing the work to be accomplished.* The chronological sequence of tasks is a distinguishing mark of any procedure.

A procedure includes how each of its tasks will take place, when it will take place, and by whom it is to be performed. The best way from the viewpoint of time, effort, and money expenditures is usually represented by the procedure. However, this is not always the case. In some instances, the influence of certain environmental factors, such as competition, taxes, or the equipment available, may alter the procedure somewhat from the theoretically most efficient way of handling the work.

Normally time limits are placed on each step of a procedure to insure that each task as well as the the end result will be accomplished when desired. Procedures are usually thought of as applying to repetitive work, and in the typical enterprise, much work is of this type. Once the procedure for handling such work is established, the procedure can be used over and over again, thus sparing the manager the problems of deciding the course of action to be followed for much of the work.

A purchasing procedure is shown graphically by Figure 11–7. In this illustration two main categories of purchases are recognized (1) stock orders and (2) special orders. For each group, the procedure starts with three steps—recognition of need for the material, description of the material needed, and transmission of purchasing requisition for the material. Stock orders are handled on stock replacement purchases by means of blanket purchase orders. In contrast, special orders are handled on individually placed purchase orders. All requisitions are sent to the purchasing department for negotiation of supplier. For stock orders, the approved sources and their immediate past performances are checked, and if found O.K., the order is written and placed. In the case of special orders, bids are requested, proposals received and analyzed, sources

FIGURE 11–7. A purchasing procedure

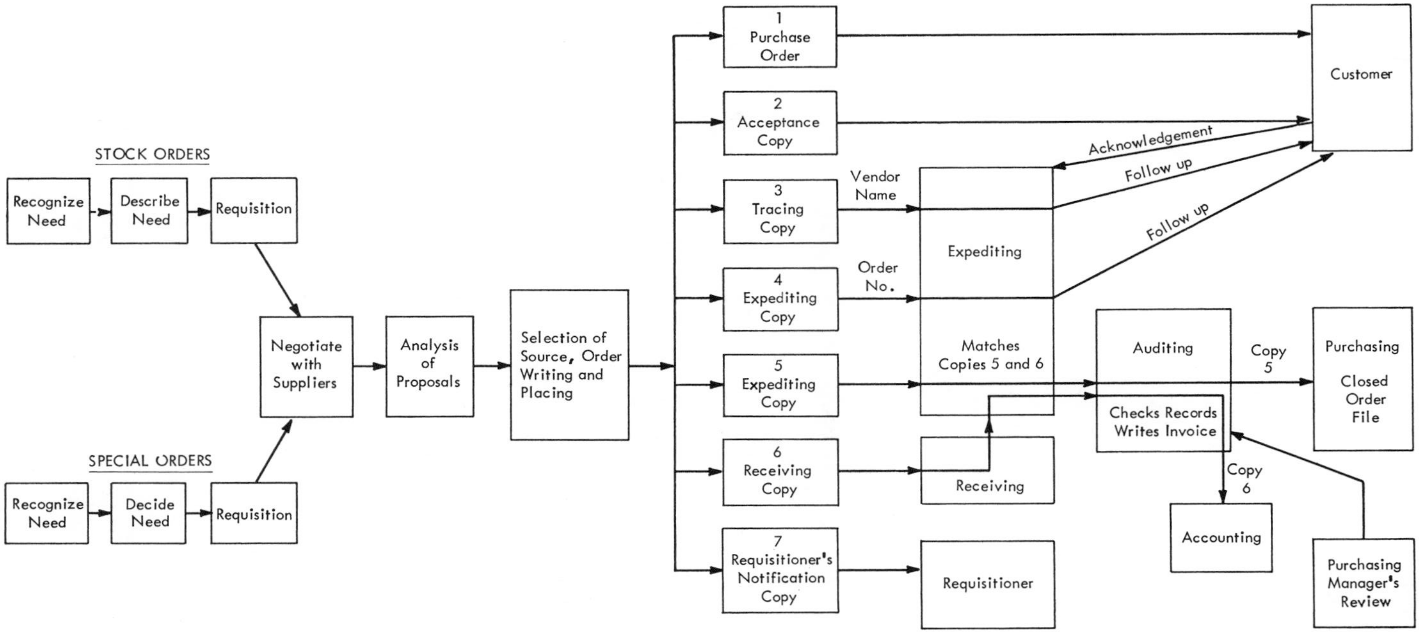

selected, the purchase order written and placed. As indicated in Figure 11–7, seven copies of the purchase order are made. Copies 1 and 2 are sent to supplier who returns Copy 2 which goes to the Expediting Department. Copies 3, 4, and 5 go to the Expediting Department, Copy 6 to Receiving Department, and Copy 7 to Requisitioner which lets him know the material has been ordered. Copies 3 and 4 are used to expedite the order with the supplier. When order is received, the Receiving Department sends its copy to Expediting which matches Copies 5 and 6, sending them to the Auditing Department, which checks the records, writes the invoice, and sends Copy 5 to Purchasing for its closed order file and Copy 6 to Accounting authorizing payment to vendor. In addition, as shown in the illustration, the records of Auditing are reviewed by the Purchasing Manager to reveal the status of his purchasing efforts. By following these several related tasks indicated by Figure 11–7 the identity of the purchasing procedure is revealed.

DESIRABLE CHARACTERISTICS OF PROCEDURES

Procedures should be based on adequate facts with proper consideration given to the objectives, physical facilities, the personnel, and the type of work. A procedure that is best for a given enterprise may not be best for another simply because significant differences among the factors affecting the procedure may be present. The end result governs what steps are taken and is of prime consideration. The steps should be complementary and lead cumulatively to the accomplishment of the desired goal. Each step should fulfill a definite need, and be in proper relationship to the remaining steps of the procedure.

A procedure should possess stability in that it provides a steadfastness of the established course, with changes made only when fundamental modifications in the factors affecting the operation of the procedure occur. Stable objectives are paramount for stable procedures. On the other hand, flexibility of procedures is desirable in order to cope with a crisis or emergency, special demands, or adjustment to a temporary condition. However, emergencies may become too commonplace, and the benefits from the use of stable procedures are lost. The problem is essentially one of maintaining a proper balance between the stability and the flexibility of the procedure.

Also there is a tendency for procedures to remain once they are started in an enterprise. New procedures are commonly added to the existent ones instead of reworking and modifying existing procedures, or eliminating those no longer needed as a result of change and in view of current requirements. The results are that some procedures that are useless continue and much costly duplication of efforts is permitted to exist. Again, the solution is to review periodically all procedures within an enterprise and to ascertain if they are needed under present operating conditions. If not, they should either be eliminated or modified as the facts in the case indicate.

METHOD

Fundamental to every action is a method which can be defined as *a prescribed manner for performing a given task with adequate consideration to the objective, facilities available, and total expenditures of time, money, and effort.* A method deals with a task comprising one step of a procedure and specifies how this one step is to be performed. It normally is confined within one department and frequently to the efforts of one employee while engaged in the specified work. A method is more limited in scope than a procedure. Referring again to Figure 11–7, the manner of writing seven copies, for example, constitutes a method. In it would be prescribed such things as the arrangement of the work area and the work, the operation of the machine, the necessary details to observe, and the use of certain printed paper forms.

METHODS IMPROVEMENT

The determination of the method to be employed in any given case depends mainly upon the manager's experience, knowledge, and creativeness. Historically, Frank B. Gilbreth and his wife, Lillian M. Gilbreth, American management pioneers, stressed the importance of methods in management. The Gilbreths developed what is today known as "motion study," which is conducted to find a better way of performing work. Analysis of methods shows that the greatest output is achieved when the task is carefully defined, performed in a definite manner, and within a definite period of time. Methods have been a focal point for improvement and for quite logical reasons. In the first place, of all planning efforts, methods are probably the easiest to comprehend. Second, methods are tangible to a greater degree than other plans, and third, they are more intimately associated with the employee who is normally most interested in his own work and improvements in it.

WORK SIMPLIFICATION—METHODS

Efforts to improve the manner of work performance are commonly termed work simplification. As its name implies, work simplification deals with the simplifying of work. *Work simplification is applying common sense for finding the most economical use of human efforts, materials, machines, time, and space so that easier and better ways of doing work can be employed.*

In the interest of clarity and brevity, work simplication can be said to consist of five major steps, which are:

1. Select the Work to Which Work Simplification Will Be Applied. This includes bottleneck tasks or those which represent a relatively expensive or time-consuming task.

2. Analyze the Work Selected, Carefully and in Detail. Each component is identified and carefully examined. Various charts are commonly used to depict pertinent facts about the present work method.

3. Utilize the Questioning Attitude for Each Component. Used are the basic questions of why is this component performed, what is performed, where, when, by whom, and how. Answers to these questions suggest possible means for improvement.

4. Seek Improvements. These are gained by (*a*) eliminating, (*b*) combining, (*c*) rearranging, or (*d*) simplifying the present components. Also, can mechanical means replace present manual means? Can the current machine method be improved? How is the best way to reduce the operator's physical effort and fatigue?

5. Put Improved Course of Action into Effect. Implementing the improved method is the final and a very important step.

Observe that work simplification determines what components are essential and results in work performance that includes only those essential components carried out in the most economical manner. That is, work simplification results in performing only the necessary components in an efficient manner. Note also that *work simplification is not speedup.* Speedup is the hurrying of the work performance and includes the essential and nonessential operations, it implies no analytical study to determine how time, space, or human effort can be better utilized.

The key to successful work simplification is participation by those performing the work being simplified. Give the employee help and encouragement in applying the five work simplification steps listed above. Let him improve his own job as he sees fit to improve it. Work simplification is as much an attitude of mind as it is a science. Fundamental to its success is the belief that *there is always a better way.* Amazing results have been credited to the use of work simplification. Savings in effort and time frequently reach 40–50 percent, and in certain instances they are as high as 80–85 percent of the initial work performance requirements.

PRINCIPLE OF WORK SIMPLIFICATION

Waste in performing work can be eliminated by diligent application of work simplification, which stresses making every component of the work productive by the application of common sense aided primarily by participation with know-how of and by employees.

WORK SIMPLIFICATION—PROCEDURES

Work simplification is not confined to methods; it applies to other plans, for example, to procedures. Normally, it is advisable to simplify

FIGURE 11–8. Overlapping consecutive tasks permit shorter overall completion time

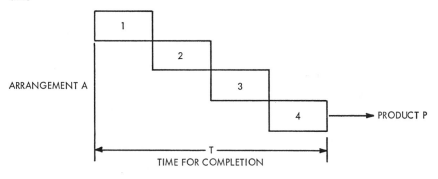

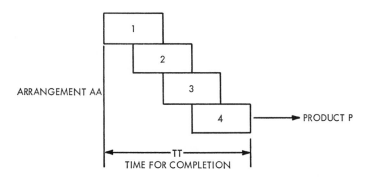

the plan of the broader scope first, for example, the procedures and then the methods. To reverse this order might mean that method plans are improved only to find later that these methods are unnecessary after improving the procedure plans.

An important principle to follow in improving procedures is to arrange and perform the series of tasks in a shingling, or overlapping, pattern. On page 237, Figure 11–8 shows an arrangement 'A" for assembling product "P" by performing four consecutive tasks—Nos. 1, 2, 3, and 4. None of the products completed by task No. 1 are subjected to task No. 2 until all No. 1's are completed, and so on down through task No. 4. Total time for completion is "T." In contrast, with an overlapping pattern for the consecutive tasks, arrangement "AA," task No. 2 is started on completed products of task No. 1 before all No. 1's are completed and so forth through task No. 4. With this arrangement the total time for completion is "TT." Ideally a successive task should start at a time which will permit its completion once it has started; that is, it need not be temporarily stopped due to the rate of output of the preceding task.

PRINCIPLE OF OVERLAP

The minimum overall time required to perform a group of successive tasks on one product is obtained by performing the tasks arranged with a maximum overlapping.

STANDARD

A standard is a type of plan. It is *a unit of measurement established to serve as a criterion or level of reference.* For example, a standard cost of $5.00 for one item of "A" is a measurement of expenditure and represents the amount of cost to which the cost of other items of "A" can be referred or of other items comparable to "A." Standards are essential in planning schedules, determining requirements, and achieving proper balance and relationship among the basic resources of an enterprise. To illustrate, it is difficult to plan the work of eight men unless the standard of what should reasonably be expected of one man is known. In addition, a standard forms the basis of controlling. What is accomplished, or the standard, is a fundamental step in controlling.[1]

Standards assist measurement in that they record the number of times a unit is used or taken in a given application. Further, they pro-

---

[1] This is discussed in Chapter 5, p. 83. A complete treatment of controlling is contained in Chapter 23.

vide an expression of a level of performance which is usually termed normal. Standards apply to all resources that a manager utilizes. Uniformity of products is also an important purpose of standards. This makes not only for manufacturing efficiency, but also expedites inspection and desirable practices in product design. In addition, standards are helpful in describing and identifying products, processes, and activities, the pertinent characteristics being set forth in terms, tests, and measurements as set forth by standards. Especially is this important in production and sales. Finally, standards assist in settling disputes because they serve as base or reference levels and thus help to clarify the issue and suggest investigative courses to pursue.

THE ESTABLISHMENT OF STANDARDS

A standard is usually established by using one of the following sources: (1) past experience, (2) appraisal, or (3) scientific method. In establishing standards by past experience, a manager uses past records, memory, and knowledge acquired from his intimate work with the particular factor or with one he believes is similar to it.

Standards set by appraisal are arrived at through guesses or estimates of what the standard probably should be. This means is resorted to when available time is short, the work is temporary, or the cost of determining more accurate standards is prohibitive.

The scientific method, widely used for the setting of standards, is to be perferred because it utilizes factual data in a carefully prescribed and proved manner.[2] Included are so-called synthetic standards arrived at by detailed study and interpolation of existing data. Representative are time standards set by Methods Time Measurement (MTM) or Work Factor approaches. Common media used to express standards are shown in Figure 11–9.

Nearly all companies carry on some work involving the setting of standards and develop standards strictly for their own use. Many standards, in fact, are of this sort. However, in the interests of communication, trade, and general welfare, it is desirable to have uniform standards, at least for many common items and activities. To this end, technical societies, trade associations, and government agencies have served as a clearinghouse or a group approach to a common standard problem. In this work, the American Standards Association (ASA) has been very active. The ASA is a federation of technical societies, trade associations, and several agencies of the federal government.

---

[2] The scientific method is discussed in Chapter 4.

FIGURE 11-9. Common media for expressing standards

1. *Written description* giving in detail the complete specifications covering all pertinent requirements stated precisely and accurately.
2. *Verbal statement* including a representation by spoken words of the important factors making up the standard.
3. *Legal regulations,* usually enforced by a recognized authority, stating a range or area within which the standard must conform.
4. *Typical sample* providing an exact representation of the particular item or unit; in some cases a scaled model is used.
5. *Customary procedure,* either written or verbal, setting forth the generally accepted or habitual practice followed.

FLEXIBILITY OF STANDARDS

Standards tend to stabilize plans; yet they contain some element of flexibility necessary to adjust them to the needs of current managerial efforts and changing conditions. This does not mean that standards should be changed to meet current whims or altered within relatively short periods of time. Quite the contrary, stability must be maintained, but this does not mean that a rigid, never-changing practice must be followed. The needed flexibility is assured by making provisions for finding out how satisfactory the established standards are and reviewing periodically technological and economic changes which might affect the standard. Normally some deviation from the standard is permissible in view of practical considerations. This deviation is referred to as tolerance.

Within a given enterprise, standards are interdependent. That is, for a company the standard for a material is definitely related to the standard for its inspection; and in the same manner, the design standards are related to the manufacturing standards and, in turn, to the sales standards. This means that, within an enterprise, a change in one standard frequently requires a compatible change in another standard or standards. A manager should review all standards, within meaningful limits, when any one standard is changed. It should also be noted that usually the standard employed represents what is believed best for the intended purpose at a given time. It does not necessarily represent a level of perfection.

STANDARDIZATION

Standardization is the establishment and use of definite sizes, types, styles, measures, etc., based on standards. It is the logical result of the application of standards to the various factors of an enterprise. Standardization helps make permanent the progress achieved in that the best and the most practical is utilized. Standardization assists planning and lessens controlling, since the activities are standardized in conformity with their respective established standards. Generally speaking, the greater the standardization of component activities, the less the extent of planning and controlling needed. Some standardization appears essential for managerial economies. But also practiced is either "simplification," whereby reduction of sizes, styles, and processes is accomplished as a result of observation and experience, or "diversification," in which the handling of various species and varieties is followed.

PRINCIPLES OF STANDARDIZATION

Standardization provides predetermined patterns and levels for performances which aid planning, contribute to efficiency, and expedite controlling.

The fact that parts can be standardized does not necessarily mean that all finished products made from these parts are identical. In such cases, the standardization usually applies to *selected parts* of the product, and these parts are combined with the parts not under standardization in various combinations so that a substantial amount of variety and flexibility in finished products is possible.

Standardization has its social implications. Some argue that its effects are socially beneficial, while others vehemently disagree. Proponents point out that (1) work specialization is here to stay, regardless of standardization; (2) the employee can exercise greater choice of employer since similar jobs are offered by many enterprises; (3) useful employment for those who neither have nor desire much skill is provided; and (4) the employee can concentrate his efforts, attain high proficiency, and enjoy greater safety. In contrast, those disapproving of standardization believe (1) the initiative of the employee is reduced, (2) the work under standardization is highly repetitive and dull, (3) any versatility of the employee is sacrificed, and (4) the self-reliability, personal dignity, and status of the employee is reduced.

BUDGET

A budget is a plan for income or outgo, or both, of money, personnel, purchased items, sales items, or any other entity about which the manager believes the determining of the future course of action will assist in his managerial efforts. Budgets are comprehensive in that they include an entire enterprise or they can be drawn up for any segment of it. At the same time they establish goals for each activity, so they are relatively detailed. Budgets always apply to a certain time period, and again, the data making up the budget are normally segregated by small time periods, such as hours or days in a monthly budget or weeks and months in a yearly budget.

The initial creating of a budget for a specific unit normally poses real difficulties. However, the continuing of a budget is relatively simple, since past budgets serve as excellent guides. But the budget, like all plans, is forward looking; nothing can be done about the past; and what you are doing in budgeting is planning for things that are to happen. The best budget makers profit from experience. It usually requires much time to develop skill in budget preparation for a specific area of operations. In fact, the first budgets drawn up commonly have weaknesses which subsequent events reveal. Modifications can be made until the budget is developed into a reasonably accurate plan. Budget makers tend to tighten up or reduce the allotments slightly each time a new budget is made out. This is favorable since it tends to emphasize improvement; but if carried to extremes, it has the effect of discouraging work efforts because the employee may feel that the goals set forth by the budget cannot be attained.

Budgets are plans, but their use for controlling is so great that many think of them as control media. The term, budgeting, designates controlling based on a budget. The budget comes first; just as in any planning-controlling endeavor, the planning precedes the controlling. Comparison of actual to planned expenditures by items represents the common format of budgetary control. In addition, a budget can be used to authorize expenditures in that a department head can spend the amount budgeted for each item without asking permission. In this sense, budgetary controlling is being practiced. Budgets are so closely, and in most instances so completely, identified with controlling that further discussion of them has been included in Part VI of this book.[3]

PROGRAM

A program is a plan frequently encompassing a relatively large undertaking, although not all of them can be so classified. The term itself is used in many different ways, and this unfortunately leads to

---

[3] Budgetary controlling is discussed in Chapter 26.

misunderstanding. A program can be defined as a comprehensive plan that includes future use of different resources in an integrated pattern and establishes a sequence of required actions and time schedules for each in order to achieve stated objectives. The makeup of a program can include objectives, policies, procedures, methods, standards, and budgets, but it does not necessarily have to include all these categories of plans. Programs outline the actions to be taken, by whom, when, and where. The assumptions, commitments, and areas to be affected are also set forth.

To illustrate, consider the work of a telephone company to provide plant expansion, service modernization, and operations improvement. These objectives necessitate effective utilization of different resources, such as buildings, carrier systems, dial switchboards, cable, trucks, and sundry tools. To perform this work on a time basis, communication designs must be created, checked, and rechecked. Materials must be acquired from the proper sources and delivered to the proper places when needed. Manpower must be trained, assigned, and dispersed. All the components must be kept in balance and scheduled to take place in accordance with a master timetable. This requires managerial efficiency, and the first step is to draw all these future actions into a comprehensive plan which we can designate as a program.

The increasing practice of considering large segments of an enterprise for management analysis instead of isolated components has stressed the use of programs. A production program, for example, can include the designation of materials, the processes to be followed, the machines to be used, the skills to be utilized, the production schedules to be met, and the warehouses to which shipments are to be made. This entire gamut of materials acquisition to completed shipments as a single entity represents a program in modern management.

TECHNO-FACTOR

Utilizing a technical approach to a selected factor such as time, cost, or material flow, techno-factor represents a relatively new type of plan. A number of such plans are already being used and it seems quite likely that more will be seen in the future. They provide assistance to the manager that no other type of plan supplies. The first to be discussed is PERT (Program Evaluation Review Technique).

Introduced in 1958, PERT was originated to achieve a reduction in the time span projected for the Polaris Ballistic Missile Project of the U.S. Navy. PERT includes not only planning but also controlling.

Justification for including it under planning in this book is that it starts with the formulating with respect to time of the interrelated activities making up the overall program. From this planning effort, changes or adjustments as required can be made in order to ensure that the plan is carried out. This latter effort is the controlling aspect of PERT.

The basic analytical device of PERT is a network consisting of a pictorial description of the necessary work. This network is made up of activities and events that comprise a project. Figure 11–10 illustrates a

FIGURE 11–10. A PERT network. The heavy line indicates the critical path

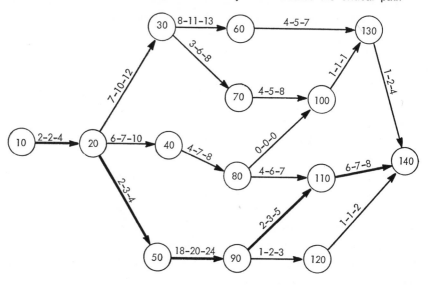

PERT network. An activity is shown by an arrow; an event, by a circle. The former represents work required to accomplish an event. Estimates of time to complete each activity are indicated on the network. For example, the activity from event 30 to event 60 is estimated at 8–11–13, which means, respectively, the optimistic, most likely, and the pessimistic times for completion of this activity. Only activities consume time, events cannot.

To accomplish the project objective represented by event 140 in Figure 11–10 it is necessary to start with event 10 and accomplish a series of events related in a pattern as indicated by the network. All networks start with one event and end with one event. An event is accomplished when all activities leading to it are completed, and no activity can begin until all preceding activities have been accomplished.

A network path is a series of related events and activities from the beginning to the end event of the network. We are interested in the network path that requires the *longest* time because this path time-controls the project; that is, any delay along this network path will delay completion of the entire project. This path is called the critical path. There are also semicritical paths and slack paths requiring successively shorter time periods for completion than the critical path. By means of a trade-off of resources from one of the paths to the critical path, the elapsed time of the latter may be reduced.

There are different formats for calculating pertinent data of a network. Commonly, an average value is determined for the estimated times for each activity. This is termed the expected time. Subsequently, the earliest expected time to achieve the activity from the entire network viewpoint is calculated. This value is the sum of the expected times along the longest path from the start of the network to the event in question. Finally, the latest allowable time is determined. This is the time by which an event must be accomplished to meet the scheduled completion date for the entire project. It is the value found by subtracting from the scheduled length of the project the length of the longest path backward from the finish of the project to the event in question.

When these calculations are made for the network shown in Figure 11–10, the critical path is found to be that indicated by the heavy line, that is, 10–20–50–90–110–140. All the other activities take less time so there is nothing to be gained by shifting or trading off among the activities. Either manual or computer calculating methods can be followed. The former is practical up to about 100 events. In some of the large governmental projects over 20,000 events have been involved.

PERT is advantageous for nonrepetitive, nonroutine projects. It is being used in research and development projects, the conducting of new-product developments, the preparation of building bids and proposals, periodic maintenance shutdowns, pilot plant runs, and the construction of buildings, bridges, and power stations. PERT helps (1) to focus attention on potential problems in projects, (2) to reasonably predict the attainment of project objectives, (3) to evaluate progress toward this attainment, and (4) to indicate feasible adjustments in related activities to improve overall project accomplishment.

Another techno-factor plan is PERT–COST which is similar to PERT but with the data referring to cost rather than time. Cost expenditure is normally contingent upon more variable factors than time expenditure, and hence, cost results are more difficult to plan for. In PERT–COST, the planning and controlling efforts are directed toward expenditures of money and provide an effective management tool for the modern manager. PERT–COST seems destined to increase in importance, although its predecessor, PERT, is currently much better known and more widely used.

RAMP (Review Analysis of Multiple Projects) is another example of a techno-factor plan. It refers to multiple related projects rather than to a single project as does PERT. With respect to time constraint, it helps guide the activities of several projects simultaneously. To illustrate, a contractor building several buildings can use RAMP for the several buildings and know the critical areas and activities to watch carefully from the viewpoint of all the buildings considered as a unit, not each building considered separately.

Rhochrematics is still another techno-factor worthy of mention. It deals with the management of material flow and includes the concept of integrating the management of all material flow from its original source through production facilities to final consumers. It is very helpful in automation studies. The traditional concept of considering autonomous, but related, units in accomplishing material flow is abandoned. Rhochrematics includes an efficient system of interactions among information, manpower, money, and materials. Its proponents claim better customer service at lower costs, better integration of the production process, and better use of working capital. The development of rhochrematics depends upon improved accounting data and mathematical techniques for computer use. It can be considered a specialized application of the systems concept of management discussed in Chapter 4.

QUESTIONS

1. What is the meaning of each of the following: (*a*) implied policy, (*b*) synthetic standard, (*c*) work simplification, and (*d*) rhochrematics?
2. Discuss several important reasons why managers use policies.
3. Is there any significant effect upon policy, procedure, method, or standard when the approach of results management conditions the planning efforts? Elaborate on your answer.
4. Explain Figure 11–7 in your own words.
5. In your opinion are managerial policies motivational to those who use them? Justify your answer.
6. As a manager, what importance do you attach to the statement, "Procedures have a tendency to remain once they are started in an enterprise."
7. What is PERT? Of what value and help is it to a manager?
8. Carefully distinguish between the two concepts in each of the following pairs: (*a*) a policy and a procedure, (*b*) a procedure and a method, (*c*) a practice and a policy, and (*d*) a techno-factor and a principle.

9. What is a program and why does a manager use it? Use an example to illustrate your answer.
10. Enumerate and discuss four major purposes of standards. Discuss one of the purposes thoroughly.
11. Discuss four major considerations to take into account in formulating policies.
12. Do you agree with the statement, "Method is the most important type of plan that a manager uses. Method is fundamental to all work accomplishment. Other plans expedite the effective use of methods." Substantiate your answer.
13. From your general observations of business, give two examples of standardization being used in an industry of your choice.
14. List some of the important policies of your university, business, or club. Classify them according to basic, general, and departmental groups. In your opinion, which policies are most effective? Why?

CASE 11-1. SCHREIBER ENGINE COMPANY

Two divisions of this company are being consolidated. The general manager of Division 3 is retiring and the general manager of Division 4 is to become the general manager of Division 11, the consolidation of Divisions 3 and 4. Each division had a relatively large engineering department and these were brought together with the former director of engineering of old Division 3 appointed to head engineering of new Division 11.

The procedure followed for projects by the engineering department of old Division 3 was quite simple. To begin work on a project all that was required was (1) a brief description of the project on the total projects report of the department and (2) assignment of a project number. All projects were initiated by memo from the general manager. A project cost report was issued to management each month showing the expenditure for the month and total-to-date expenditure by project. The projects remained in an active status until work was discontinued usually by written request in the form of a memo from the general manager. Several projects had been active for as long as 12 years.

In contrast, old Division 4 had a much more detailed procedure for initiating, approving, and reporting engineering projects. The projects could be initiated by any management member of sales, production, or production services, as well as anyone in the engineering department. Initially screened by a product and services committee consisting of the president, works manager, the vice president of finance, and the sales manager, projects o.k.'d were then routed to the sales department for a sales estimate, to the engineering department for a cost estimate, and then submitted to the executive committee for final approval. A cost report on all engineering projects being worked on by engineering personnel was issued twice each month showing the activity in each project for the current period and the total to date. The accompanying exhibit shows a portion of this report.

EXHIBIT 1

	Project no.	Auth. $	Engg. hrs.	Engg. $	Labor hrs.	Labor $	Plant over-head	Other exp.	Total actual exp.	Sales realiz.	Auth. $ bal.	% exp.
	2748 1H Gear box											
6/14	Total	2000	7	28	172	611	0	0	639	0	—	32
6/14	Total to date	2000	126	504	258	952	0	0	1456	0	544	73

The new general manager of Division 11 believed the contribution to profits by the engineering department should be improved. He favored adopting the engineering procedure used by old Division 4. But he insisted that the project cost reports be improved. He claimed the present report is too complicated, making it difficult to interpret the data.

Questions

1. Do you feel that the procedure advocated by the new general manager of Division 11 is adequate? Elaborate on your answer.
2. Suggest an improved procedure the company might follow.
3. Draw your suggested format for the engineering project cost report, pointing out improvements to be gained by the company adopting it.

CASE 11–2. THE WINTERS COMPANY

A study of the records of the Winters Company reveals that differences in accounts payable exist between what the vendor claims is due and what Winters claims is due the vendor. The differences seem to originate when the company receives and subsequently returns defective, damaged, or incorrect material from suppliers. In addition, errors occur in quantities received and invoiced as well as in the prices and extensions on invoices. Also, in some instances adjustments, such as freight and allowances in purchases, are found by Winters' office personnel.

A common procedure followed by many companies is to handle these differences and adjustments by receiving a credit memorandum from the vendor, after notice is given the vendor of the differences. A few firms do issue their own debit memoranda, which are notices to others that their account is being debited with the particular charge. However, the plan followed by the Winters Company upon finding any adjustment is to issue what is known as a Special Charge, which is an invoice usually sent before the credit is received from the vendor. If possible, permission is obtained from the vendor by telephone before the Special Charge is sent. The managers of Winters Company believed the idea behind the present practice is good because it puts the supplier on notice as soon as possible and it helps to control the goods sent back and the corresponding money due the company, as this is deducted from the amount of future payments. In addition, it is a source of entry for the company's records.

However, the present procedure for handling adjustments is not functioning properly. Many errors and duplications occur. Many of the vendors complain to the company and ask for an explanation of the Special Charge. To correct these errors, a credit memorandum is used, making additional entries and payments necessary.

The form of invoice for the Special Charge is a single white copy with the name and address of the company preprinted on it. Consecutive numbers are not preprinted on it. Information—such as reasons for the charge, the related invoice number and date, and the correct values —is filled in by the typist based on data given her. The authorization for the issuance is not indicated since the error can be discovered by any of a number of company departments, i.e., receiving, pricing, purchasing, or accounting departments. However, most of the Special Charges are authorized and sent out by five management members of the company. For additional copies of Special Charges, two blank yellow second sheets are used. The white copy is mailed to the vendor; the yellow copies are given to the bookkeeping and disbursement departments, respectively, for entry and record purposes.

Questions

1. Does the company have a planning problem? Discuss.
2. Outline your recommendations to the company and justify your proposal adequately.

12

Long- and short-range planning

He who can see three days ahead will be rich for three thousand years.

JAPANESE PROVERB

THE PERIOD COVERED by a plan has gained prominence in planning. As a result, much planning is now popularly designated either as long-range or short-range planning. However, in some companies, long-range planning is called strategic planning, the thought being that this term to some extent minimizes the tendency to procrastinate in the planning efforts.

LONG-RANGE AND SHORT-RANGE PLANS

Differences of opinion exist regarding the period that qualifies certain planning as long-range planning (LRP) and other planning as short-range planning (SRP). One-year budgets, certainly not new in industry, are not considered in modern parlance as long range. Some companies have developed plans covering periods 20 years ahead. The length of the planning period is partly a function of the particular enterprise. If the production cycle is long, say two years, LRP and SRP take on different meanings from those of an industry where the cycle is six weeks. Also, the relative stability of the industry's cyclical pattern may be dominant. LRP for a public utility may be quite different from that of an electronic parts manufacturer. Arbitrary, but generally accepted, practice is to regard any plan covering periods of two years or less as short range, of five years and over as long range. Plans dealing with over two years and less than five years are termed short or long depending upon the enterprise, but the designation intermediate-range planning might be more satisfactory.

Long-range planning and short-range planning are much more than the mere projecting of trends. They include, in part, future actions designed to make things happen that otherwise probably would not occur. They set the course to follow against either favorable or unfavorable conditions, be they economic, technological, sociological, or political.

To qualify as LRP or SRP, it appears that certain requirements should be met. These include:

1. The entire enterprise or a large portion of it is encompassed by the planning. Both LRP and SRP are inclusive. They are confined neither to a division or a department, nor to a particular function. Performing only financial planning, for instance, is not LRP or SRP.

2. The planning is on paper. Definiteness and refinements of the various points are assisted by reducing to a written form in black and white. Mental images and thoughts are too nebulous to qualify as either LRP or SRP.

3. The planning is being used—it is a living entity. It is not a report in the president's file, buried for an indefinite period of time.

PLANNING PERIOD DETERMINED BY COMMITMENTS

It is reasonable to expect different time periods covered by planning. The manager's planning ability, the scope of the plan undertaken, past practices, and the type of enterprise and industry are among the more common reasons contributing to this condition. Costs are also important. Usually a manager is interested in using a period sufficient to justify the dollar expenditures involved. To plan for a shorter period is risky. He would like to make certain—to the extent that planning can help him do this—that he will recover his investment, not only in capital but also in time and effort expenditures.

This leads to the importance of managerial commitments required by the plan as the determinate for the length of period covered by the planning. Another way to express this is to speak of recovery costs. How long will it take to get back the investment in equipment, sales promotions, and training of manpower required by the plan? This question can best be answered by means of planning, and the planning should include a sufficient time period to provide a complete answer.

PRINCIPLE OF COMMITMENT

The time period covered by planning should preferably include sufficient time to fulfill the managerial commitments involved.

Following the commitment idea in determining the length of planning period is sound economically, but it means that an arbitrary universal length of time for a planning period is not feasible. The periods of commitment vary considerably among enterprises. In some cases the period may be only eight weeks, whereas in another, such as in a mine, many commitments are of a long-term single-use variety. In this latter case, the planning can be definite, but it is of a do-or-die type of commitment. Furthermore, in some instances the commitment is adjusted to conform with standard practices, such as quarterly or yearly accounting periods, or to certain tax years or periods.

It is well to add that a plan really becomes a working plan when definite commitments for executing it are made. True, some plans are canceled and commitments renegotiated or accepted as a loss, but such happenings are in the minority. Also, when the production lead time is large or special equipment must be acquired, the period covered by planning tends to be carried further into the future than might otherwise be the case.

INTEGRATION OF LONG- AND SHORT-RANGE PLANNING

Long-range planning and short-range planning should be integrated, with the latter fitting in and contributing toward the achievement of the long-range goals. Examinations from time to time should reveal whether proper integration is being achieved. The necessary information should be made readily available, indicating the current progress and whether it is sufficient and in the right direction for production, marketing, financial, and personnel efforts.

The usual problem here is that short-term planning is adopted but does not contribute to the long-range plan. An immediate opportunity is seized; in the urgency of the situation, the long-range objectives are slighted or the movement of the enterprise gets "off the beam," unbalanced and unwanted situations are inherited, and "fire engine" decisions become paramount. For example, an enterprise needing added space built an addition on a parking lot adjacent to its main factory. But this addition was not in keeping with the long-range planning to construct a modern new building covering the parking lot sites. Immediate needs for production space were satisfied, but the long-range requirements were ignored.

On the other hand, there are examples where development over a short range revealed by short-range planning suggests changes be made in long-range planning. To illustrate, the financial market may change so that a debt should be refinanced at a lower rate or the maturity date should be extended, or the opportune time for issuance of a new equity is signaled by short-range planning. These conditions may suggest that the long-range planning was faulty, and this may be true. However, all planning should contain the element of flexibility, because the future is unknown. Assistance in knowing what to do is provided by both long-range planning and short-range planning.

LRP AND SRP CHARACTERISTICS

Both long-range planning and short-range planning are continuous —they are never-ending activities. A long-range program, for example, is never finalized. Yet, it is vital to establish and enforce deadlines for the sequential segments of a long- or short-range plan. The planning must be halted by an established closing date; otherwise, endless delays due to the inherent desire to "go over certain areas" and "polish up the rough spots" will take place. The plan should be recognized as a tentatively completed package as of a certain date, but with the realization that next quarter or next year are almost certain to bring along new additions or modifications. Emphasis is on the answer not to "Where do we go from *here?*" but to "Where do we go from *there?*"

Closely related to this never-ending characteristic is the fact that few, if any, plans, especially those of LRP are without error. This follows because at the time of formulation, certain information is not available, but there is a human tendency among planners to refrain from making assumptions or to supply an imperfect plan. Perfection, however, is quite elusive, and a planner can easily spend more than half of his time in trying to improve his plan from 90 to 100 percent perfection. In the interest of economy and practical management, this practice should be avoided.

SRP is usually more easily evaluated than LRP. If results are used as the measurement, certainly they are known sooner in the case of SRP than that of LRP. Also, there is more certainty about the factors affecting the result in SRP and many of these factors are tangible. Furthermore, in evaluating LRP, there is always some question of how to evaluate goal accomplishment of today in comparable terms with the means of achievement of yesterday.

Both LRP and SRP are difficult, painstaking, broad yet detailed work. Many hardships are encountered in locating and selecting significant data and in analyzing and obtaining reliable determinates. The work can be time-consuming and quite frustrating. At times, the answer may seem quite simple, as exemplified by the company who wished to expand its sales and decided to "get into a growth industry." But what is a growth industry, and which one is best suited for the individual company? Production facilities, skill of work force, competitive status, relative costs, and sales ability are but a few of the factors that must be appraised to answer such a question.

For the most part, long-range programs are perhaps more necessary for top managers in multiproduct, multiplant enterprises than in smaller companies. In the large enterprises the top managers must depend, in some degree, upon other management members in order for the huge enterprise to survive. Corporate size alone makes this necessary. Intimate knowledge of all the operations by the top manager is lessened; yet actions shaping the corporate destiny are numerous and require decisions. In contrast, the president of a small company is close to, if not right on the top of, what is going on, and he is familiar with what they want to achieve and how they are going to do it. Communication and understanding among the management team is simple and direct. A long-range plan is helpful to the small company, but usually it is relatively of less importance than it is to a large company.

ADVANTAGES OF LRP AND SRP

It seems appropriate to preface a discussion of advantages by stating that the prime merit of LRP and SRP does not lie in being able to outguess others with regard to future events. Quite the contrary, it lies in recognizing the human inability to forecast all tangible variants accurately. It is this overall quality that gives LRP and SRP their great value.

Perhaps the greatest single benefit is that the formulation and the use of LRP and SRP emphasize defining the corporate goals, and the philosophy to be followed in reaching these goals. Jumping to conclusions, as to what the goals are, without sufficient study can cause serious trouble. If the goal is "to improve profit through sales," does this mean acquire more sales at more costs, keep present sales but reduce costs, or lower sales at lower costs? Preciseness in goal identity is enhanced by LRP and SRP. Rather than the general goal, "to continue the growth and progress of the company," account would be taken of (1) the precise growth sought—how much and in what areas; (2) timing—is the target date 1975 or 1980; (3) the risk involved—does the possible gain justify the hazards to be incurred; and (4) people—what is the attitude and understanding of the work force, the community, the trade? However, it is important to observe that some companies find general goals very useful. Such goals assist in communication about them throughout the enterprise and in thinking about them before deciding upon the particular aspect to be pursued by the management team. Customarily they are supplemented by stated subgoals which are expressed exactly, preferably by quantitative means.

Also, LRP and SRP help to orient management to current conditions in that they supply a yardstick to measure achievement of goals to date. They answer the question: Where are we now? The answer includes the present status of the physical plant and equipment, marketing, advertising, engineering, organization, manufacturing effectiveness, quality control, personnel administration, and public relations. By comparing sought goals with present status, areas of strength are revealed and areas of weakness requiring correction are disclosed. Bolstering any deficiency is normally a matter of adjusting and improving what already is being done. Hence the manager can tell if the company is free of handicaps and in a position to move in the direction set forth by the planning. Also, are the current facilities and the work accomplishments competitive, is the company's organization sound and adaptable to change, and is the personnel adequate and of the proper skill to meet contemplated future needs?

Another advantage is that an overall, integrated viewpoint is gained since LRP and SRP cut across functional lines. The problems standing in the way of desired accomplishments are identified and brought into true focus. Problems with common bases are uncovered and either eliminated or minimized.

Strong managers are identified and weak managers are spotted by the formulation and implementation of planning, but this is especially so in LRP. Foresight, creativity, and genuine skill in planning is demonstrated in LRP. Also, effective follow-up can promote the competent manager and, on the other hand, provide needed assistance to develop the weak managers.

In addition, LRP and SRP provide pertinent answers to where, when, and how much financing is required for what purpose and what is the expected return. Such planning is inclusive in that it takes into account major matters of sales, production, manpower, and research for projected activities, and relates them to the financial requirements. It is not confined to financial planning only, such as cash flow requirements, acquisition of loans, or making stock available on the open market.

Lastly, the use of LRP and SRP brings attention to new techniques and developments either of a technological or of a managerial nature. Managers become aware of what is new whether it is taking place in marketing, engineering, production, or data processing. Exchange of ideas regarding improvements in their own, as well as in allied, fields is also encouraged by LRP and SRP.

PERFORMANCE OF LRP AND SRP

Special skills, such as conceptual skill, are necessary for the development of LRP and SRP. This is a high-level ability to visualize and relate concepts that never have been related before, to apply imagination effectively to scattered bits of information, to sense the real significance of new ideas and developments, or to crash barriers saturated with outmoded thoughts. The planner who is all mechanistic or all analytical in his thinking seldom evolves the most comprehensive and complete plans.

Formulating plans and using them effectively are related but separate activities; however, the same person can do both. Planning benefits not only by involvement of staff specialists in planning efforts, but also by involvement of directly responsible managers in charge of the operations for which the planning is being done. It is neither the exclusive province of staff experts nor managers of operations.[1]

Effective LRP and SRP take time, effort, and money. They are not acquired for nothing. To expect either LRP or SRP to be performed competently as a sideline by a management member is erroneous. If such is the case, other work of the manager will suffer. LRP especially requires a considerable amount of time.

Participation is an important key in the success of all planning. Outsiders, such as experts in a given area, can be brought in, but they should neither be permitted nor expected to mastermind the planning. They should suggest, contribute, and review, but should never be used to the exclusion of the enterprise's management members to formulate

---

[1] See Chapter 13 for further discussion of this subject.

the plans. All managers should be given a hand in developing the programs.

In some cases the technician in the field of mathematics or statistics and the manager do not quite understand each other. This problem may arise in developing a quantitative approach to a planning project. The technician is not fully familiar with how his studies will be used, and the manager does not understand the premises, strengths, and weaknesses of information made available to him. The answer here is better communication and more educational development designed to promote mutual understanding among technicians and decision makers.

This suggests repeating a statement made in Chapter 10, namely that many become enthralled by planning and tend to overdo the fact-gathering task to the point of excess. The availability of computers, the tremendous amount of data that can be used, and the emphasis in management literature upon sources other than standard economic data unduly influence some managerial planners in this fallacious direction. There is virtue in deciding in advance what facts are needed and where to find them. Too often all sorts of data are collected, then attention is turned to what answers can be developed from them. The excess facts may prove extremely interesting, but they have no bearing on the work to be done.

SECURING DATA, DECISIONS, AND ACTIONS

More needs to be said about the manager assessing in broad terms the current position of the enterprise in terms of its strengths and weaknesses. This includes orientation as to the type of activities or business in which the enterprise is now involved and whether these are the types of activities the enterprise should be in. Further, the enterprise's image in its community, its relationships with customers and employees, and its financial strength are the types of things that profitably can be investigated. In addition, the probable future accomplishments with the current courses of action can be assessed. That is, with the present goals, policies, methods, and personnel, where will the enterprise probably be in one, two, or five years from now? The results from this type of projected data lead logically to an evaluation of whether this is where the managers want the enterprise to be. It might well be that the present course is desirable, or study may suggest adoption of either slight modifications or even quite different objectives. Of course, this is all based on future expectations as they are seen today. That is, the answers of the managers are tentative.

The continuation, modification, elimination, or addition to the present plans suggest the future courses of action to be followed. This resolves into how are the managers going to get the enterprise where they want it? Who is going to do what? This type of work is commonly called *operational planning* and deals with the activation of the physical resources—the people, facilities, materials, methods, and the like. Compared with other types of planning, operational planning is more tangible and requires relatively less conceptual thinking for its formulation. Commonly the various operational requirements are divided into

FIGURE 12–1. Useful outline for report on long-range planning

```
A.  The industry
    1.  The company's position
    2.  Activities of competitors
B.  Sales forecasts
    1.  Present products
    2.  Modified present products
    3.  New products
C.  Capital investment needed
    1.  Sales facilities
    2.  Production facilities
    3.  Working capital
    4.  Return on invested capital
D.  Facilitating requirements
    1.  Location of sales and of production facilities
    2.  Manpower requirements
    3.  Pricing policies to follow
    4.  Financing sales to customers
E.  Consideration of special problems
F.  Appraisal of strength and weaknesses
```

segments with the assignment for each segment given to a specific person. Acceptable scheduling, or time value assignments, are worked out for each component so that the finished work will be accomplished when it is wanted. Following this, the estimated costs of the plan are calculated, both for the plan as a whole and for each major component. The financial inputs and outputs are determined as well as the kind of financing that probably should be adopted. Finally, the total packaged program is offered to the top managers for review, modification if necessary, and final approval. Typically, there is some amount of reconciliation that takes place before official top sanction is given.

A written report for presenting a long-range plan is helpful. Figure 12–1 shows a recommended outline for such a purpose. The arrangement is logical and the usual major areas are included.

PLANNING IDENTIFICATIONS

Some students of management identify planning, especially LRP and SRP, with four major areas including (1) user, (2) growth, (3) profit, and (4) executive manpower. In the first classification is included either or both product and market. The emphasis is upon how best to serve better selected product or market segments. The major efforts are made in tune with these objectives. The second area, growth, is primarily concerned with what direction the enterprise is going, what rate of expansion (or contraction) is hoped for, and what goals are to be reached at what specific times. The third, profit, deals with the profit economics of the enterprise. What is the break-even product mix, what are the cost elements and the income elements, and what mix of sales is most profitable? The last, executive manpower, deals with planning efforts determined to attract and retain needed management members. The first three of these identifications will now be discussed; the fourth is deferred to Part V, especially Chapters 20 and 22.

PRODUCT PLANNING

Product programs provide good discussional material because products are familiar objects, they have wide interest, and they illustrate many excellent examples of planning techniques. For business enterprises products are commonly the beginning area for programs. Figure 12–2 shows a useful product long-range planning approach. Referring to the figure, for each present product an estimate of the desired future sales is made. In order to achieve these desired future sales, estimates of the following are made: (1) requirements saleswise for the desired future sales of this product, (2) the technological recommendations for improved design and manufacturing cost reduction, and (3) the profit and loss statement (projected) for the improved product. From this information the decision is made whether to continue or terminate the sales of the product. A similar study is made for each present product of the company. In the case of future products, an estimate of sales is made for each one. Then the financial requirements are determined for the combined improved present products to be continued and the new products. This is achieved by means of profit and loss statements. Based upon the financial requirements projected, the program is established with the required activities being divided among sales, engineering, production, finance, and personnel departments.

Short-range planning is tied to the above format by developing a

FIGURE 12–2. An approach to long-range planning for a product

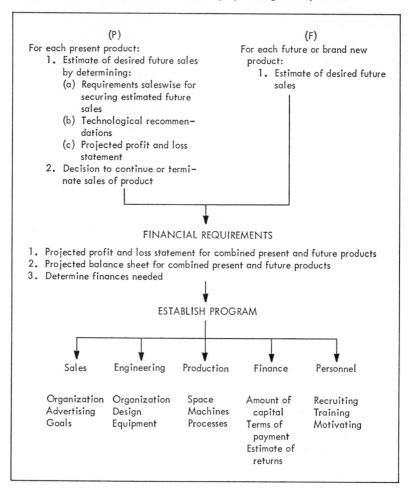

(P)
For each present product:
1. Estimate of desired future sales by determining:
   (a) Requirements saleswise for securing estimated future sales
   (b) Technological recommendations
   (c) Projected profit and loss statement
2. Decision to continue or terminate sales of product

(F)
For each future or brand new product:
1. Estimate of desired future sales

FINANCIAL REQUIREMENTS
1. Projected profit and loss statement for combined present and future products
2. Projected balance sheet for combined present and future products
3. Determine finances needed

ESTABLISH PROGRAM

Sales	Engineering	Production	Finance	Personnel
Organization	Organization	Space	Amount of capital	Recruiting
Advertising	Design	Machines	Terms of payment	Training
Goals	Equipment	Processes	Estimate of returns	Motivating

monthly, a six months', and a yearly sales forecast by products. Similar periodic statements are drawn up for activities in the other major areas of the enterprise. These forecasts serve as the intermediate goals and guide efforts along a course designed to achieve the long-range program.

GROWTH PLANNING FOR AN ENTERPRISE

Planning for growth can be considered representative of long-range planning. An enterprise can either plan for growth or just let it happen; the latter alternative is simply not compatible with effective management. The American economy has witnessed fantastic industrial growth, but not all enterprises have experienced this change. Some have done extremely well, others have plodded along, and still others have terminated their activities. And among those that have done extremely well, some have done better than others in this group.

This raises some interesting questions, such as "When does an enterprise stop growing and why?" "What makes an enterprise grow?" "How does an enterprise gear for growth?"

Consistent and desirable growth generally is the result of proper and adequate long-range planning. This is the rational way to ensure accomplishment of goals in the long run. Highly important in this concept is the strong belief and heavy commitment of top management members to growth for the enterprise and planning for that growth. How they look at the future, their acceptance of change as an opportunity for growth, and their belief in and use of planning appear essential qualities for growth to take place.

In achieving planned growth in an orderly fashion, a beginning essential is to understand exactly what the enterprise is and specifically where it is going. This is actually an assessment of what manpower, facilities, marketing know-how, reputation, good will, and other useful assets the enterprise has. In essence, the questions are in what area of endeavor is the enterprise? What economical and technological abilities does it have? What products or services are now being supplied? With such information as a background, the decision can be made of which direction the proposed growth should be and to what extent or intensity. Growth can be within the field of present experience or different fields can be sought. For example, in the former case, markets which the enterprise can serve but which are not now being served may be designated as the direction to go. Or technology now possessed may be exploited more fully, or modifications in present products or services may offer the best growth possibilities. Diversification can be sought, but basically within the area of experience. The alternative is to seek new and different fields, especially those where it is believed production and services that provide a superior appearance, performance, or assistance over anything now available can be offered. In this sense, any area where the enterprise can offer a new technology, improved product, or unique value is the direction for growth.

Knowing what the enterprise is and the precise growth direction along which it wants to advance, the next phase is to identify the major hurdles or problems that it is believed now stand or will stand in the way of accomplishing this growth. Judgment plays a big part in identifying and evaluating these hurdles. One of the biggest problems is identification of the enterprise's location in the typical growth cycle. If the enterprise is just being launched or is relatively young, the problem is commonly one of finance or of how best to market one product or a specific technology. Later in the growth cycle the major attention is focused upon improved product design, obtaining a bigger share of the market, and competing more favorably with rival enterprises. Eventually this develops into a defensive stage in which stress is placed on maintenance of the then present status. Too often, the planning of the defensive stage is ill conceived and made in desperation so that extremely complex problems arise during this period. It should be pointed out that as the growth cycle develops, old problems generate new problems so that the challenge is to cope with constantly evolving new problems. Practical solutions to these problems, or at least minimizing their effect, must be found. Generally speaking, the most common growth problems include finding competent manpower to keep the operations moving satisfactorily, maintaining communication among members of the expanding labor force, obtaining adequate financial means, and establishing adequate and proper controls over the new or expanded activities.

Further, of special interest and worthy of note here is the observation as well as the problem that few, if any, executives are qualified to manage an enterprise at every stage of its growth. Ideally, it appears to take a different kind at each stage. In the early growth period the entrepreneur is superior. But as growth is accomplished, the manager's problems assume a different character, and in these stages the need is for more of a planner—the professionally trained, more sophisticated manager. This could well be the answer to why the son of the founder of an enterprise does not seem to the founder qualified to assume top responsibilities. The son may not be qualified, but frequently the problem is the founder's failure to recognize that his successor's needs are not necessarily the identical abilities that he (the founder) possesses because the enterprise is in a different stage of development, wherein new kinds of problems and challenges must be met. For example, the present pressing need might be seeing and identifying to others what the enterprise should be doing that it is not. This type of problem may never have gained major importance during its previous history.

Returning to the consideration of growth planning for an enterprise, the next major phase is establishing goals to target the growth and to provide measurable objectives whether they be sales, income, return on investment, or the amount of service. This gives qualitative character to the goals and suggests where to concentrate efforts and where to apply limited facilities that are indispensable to planned growth. Market factors, balancing of product requirements, and financial facilitating are commonly of utmost value in this stage of development.

Lastly, the manner in which the growth will be attained, the manpower requirements, and the required finances are resolved. With major problems and quantitative goals established from previous phases, the tasks involved in attaining this growth become clearer and more definite. Should acquisitions be used? Is a merger a better way? Are new markets to be entered? What, if any, technology and new production facilities are required? Furthermore, finding qualified manpower is almost certain to be one of the most demanding tasks. Competent human resources are not easily found or acquired. New positions will be created, effective work teams must be molded, and development of mergers will occupy major attention. Worthy candidates may be found within the organization, but securing candidates from acquired companies and from the outside are common practices.

PROFIT PLANNING

Another classification is profit planning which is not always but commonly classified as short-range planning. This planning focuses on improving the profit, especially from a particular product over a relatively short period of time. Hence, as used here, it is not the same as corporate planning or a cost reduction program.

Profit planning involves streamlining activities in order to get employees profit minded and to secure maximum benefit from minimum effort and expenditure. Best results seem to be obtained by assigning a profit planner to investigate all the factors affecting the profit obtained from a single product. The planner is given the right to probe the economics, the organization, the mode of operations, the pricing, the marketing, or any other facet of making and selling the product that in his judgment affects profit accruing from that product. The concentration of profit efforts upon one product and the right of the planner to cross traditional functional boundaries of the enterprise to translate needs from one group to another and to obtain concerted profit-building efforts among those who can effect profits are the fundamental factors that contribute to the success of profit planning.

A big portion of the planner's job is to make management members aware of the untapped profit potential in the given product. He needs a local business and corporate background, a capacity to analyze problems, and the ability to innovate to improve the profit picture. He requires the knack of working with specialists and recommending improvements without telling the specialists how to do their work.

In a number of enterprises today, profit planning is still given casual treatment. Some managers remain unconvinced of the power of planning to realize a profit. They concede profit planning is logical and is an exciting concept, but feel strongly that it just does not apply in certain businesses. Profit planning can assist any business enterprise. To think otherwise is erroneous and commonly arises from two major misconceptions. First, the belief that profit planning is a job for staff experts only. Profit planning is pointless unless the direct operative managers play a principal role in the planning and are active in implementing the planning. Second, the feeling that profit planning need not really concern the nonmanagement members. Such members with their detailed knowledge of operating conditions are highly qualified to translate the profit goals of top management into specific goals, plans, and accomplishments. In fact, by their participation in the profit planning, they will become truly committed to achieving the profit goals.

Favorable results from profit planning should be forthcoming within a year. However, up to two years normally must be allowed to achieve maximum benefit. In a small enterprise, profit planning can be undertaken by a major officer who knows what an acceptable profit for a given product is, can assume the overall approach in his work, and be quietly forceful in prodding the right people of the enterprise.

QUESTIONS

1. What are the requirements for planning to qualify as long- or short-range planning?
2. Which is the more easily evaluated, LRP or SRP? Substantiate your answer.
3. Of the five characteristics of LRP and SRP given in the text, select the one you feel is most important and discuss it thoroughly.
4. Elaborate on the statement, "Planning should include a period adequate to fulfill the commitments involved."
5. Elaborate on the meaning of the following statement, "The providing of answers to the amount and to the timing of financial needs is a significant contribution of LRP and SRP, but probably of greater significance to the manager is their aid in orienting and in defining the means to reach stated goals."
6. Discuss the integration of LRP and SRP.
7. Point out the major differences between the two concepts in each of the

following pairs: (*a*) product program and LRP, (*b*) short-range program and short-range planning, and (*c*) growth cycle and growth planning.

8. What is profit planning and how is it conducted within an enterprise?
9. What interpretation do you give the statement, "Long-range planning is never finalized."
10. Discuss the subject, "The Performance of Long- and Short-Range Planning."
11. Generally speaking, should a manager strive to plan for a relatively short or a long time period? Substantiate your answer.
12. What are five important advantages of long-range planning?
13. Using an enterprise with which you are familiar either from employment or from your reading, determine whether your selected enterprise is in need of short-range planning.
14. Discuss growth planning for an enterprise.

CASE 12–1. KING FOUNDRY, INC.

Located in northern Indiana, King Foundry, Inc. produces cast-iron products primarily by two processes (1) green sand, and (2) shell mold. The former lends itself to short-run jobs and to orders for a small quantity of castings. It is the older of the two processes. The shell mold is the more advanced and represents about 80 percent of the corporation's sales. About 65 percent of the corporation's total production is purchased by an electric motor manufacturer.

It is now the middle of January and Gregory Kirkdall, the major owner and president of the corporation, is reviewing fourth quarter reports for last year's operations. He notes that for the quarter they had about $1 million in sales and showed a reasonable profit. However, he also discovers that the corporation had almost $180,000 in inventory of unfinished castings. Immediately he called for Mr. Jacob Mintz, sales and shipping manager, and Mr. Conrad Bradford, production manager, to come to his office. Mr. Mintz's duties include calling on customers, handling complaints over the telephone, and supervising the final processing of castings which entails cleaning and shipping. Mr. Bradford has charge of core assembly, production, and maintenance. He is technically proficient and is regarded as Mr. Kirkdall's right-hand man. On an informal basis Mr. Mintz and Mr. Bradford make up weekly production schedules.

When both Mr. Mintz and Mr. Bradford were in Mr. Kirkdall's office, he started the conversation.

KIRKDALL: Gentlemen, as you probably know we had a fairly good quarter ending last December 31. I want to congratulate both of you for the fine job you have done in making this possible. However, I have noted we have nearly $180,000 in unfinished castings. This is fantastic. How in the world did this happen? Is it actually that high?

BRADFORD: Yes, it is high. We have unfinished castings all over the place. The storage areas both outside and in are filled to capacity.

KIRKDALL: But how come?

MINTZ: I believe I can answer that. Our main purchaser cut his order from 35,000 units per week to about 20,000. Brad and I did not cut back on the production of electric motor housings. I made a special trip to our buyer's main office and discussed the matter quite extensively. The mutual belief was that they were experiencing a temporary slowdown which would pick up shortly. This slowdown started the latter part of October.

KIRKDALL: I see. But they aren't ordering. We know that. So why didn't we scale production down? You've seen the figures since last October and I assume followed up on them. So why . . .

MINTZ: Yes, I . . .

BRADFORD (interrupting) Pardon me, but we must keep in mind that in the planning of the production schedule we must schedule at least 12 tons of salable iron to be produced daily. Otherwise we lose money because of insufficient volume. And we believed we could afford to let the inventory for the electric motor castings build up anticipating an upswing in the economy.

KIRKDALL: I see. Well as of now, orders for the electric motor castings have not increased, have they?

MINTZ: No sir, they have not.

KIRKDALL: Seems to me we will have to make an adjustment in production.

BRADFORD: We have. Starting last week we are using more green sand and less shell mold. This is in keeping with incoming orders. We ran an average of seven tons a day last week and I estimate suffered a weekly loss of between $1800 to $2000.

Questions

1. What is the problem faced by the corporation?
2. What major factors would you say permitted and contributed to this problem? Discuss.
3. What short-range plan of action do you recommend for the corporation? Be specific.
4. What long-range plan of action do you recommend for the corporation? Be specific.

CASE 12-2. DESHLER CHEMICAL COMPANY

Nine years ago, after considerable negotiating, the city of Conroyville, Tennessee, succeeded in getting a new manufacturing company, the Deshler Chemical Company, to locate near Conroyville. The site is some two miles northwest of the city limits. The top managers of Deshler Chemical Company believed the city's packaged offer was attractive. In return for a guarantee of year-round employment for at least 50 persons, the city (1) sold the land to the company for $18,000, which, it was mutually agreed, was an attractive price, (2) constructed a plant to Deshler's specifications with the company repaying the building cost in equal monthly payments over a 12-year period with annual interest being charged at 5.5 percent on the unpaid balance, and (3) agreed to collect no property taxes for a 10-year period.

The city has grown westward during the last several years, and recent plans for civic developments include a general area which involves the Deshler Chemical Company's manufacturing operations. The city wants to develop a new park featuring boating and picnic facilities centering around Hickory Creek, but waste from the chemical plant contaminates the water. Hickory Creek adjoins the plant and was a big reason for locating the plant where it is. The creek empties into Beard River about three miles west of Conroyville's center of town. Beard River flows westward after winding through the western part of Conroyville.

The city government requests the company to install special chemical equipment to neutralize the waste materials now emptied by it into Hickory Creek. Company engineers estimate the cost of waste treatment at $750,000 for equipment and $50,000 for annual operating costs. The company contends it cannot afford such expenditures, the president stating that insistence for such an outlay by the company will result in the company abandoning the Conroyville plant and locating elsewhere.

The president further points out that the company has fulfilled every requirement of the initial agreement reached when the decision was made to locate in Conroyville. For example, the company has met all required payments, and since opening the plant has never employed fewer than 57 persons. The current employment is 63; this accounts for wage payments of approximately $400,000 per year, an amount representing nearly 16 percent of the total payrolls of the greater city area. The president also points out that the building is specially designed and built for his company's particular type of chemical manufacturing. It is not an all-purpose building and can be utilized economically only by a firm such as his own. Last year's publicly available data on the company showed total sales of $3,817,632.91 and profits after taxes of $268,956.17.

The city takes the view that the initial packaged deal was offered to give the company assistance in getting established. With nominal land costs, favorably financed building costs, and availability of admittedly high productivity labor of the area, the company should be competitive or recognize that it must prepare itself to be so. The company is a part of the community and therefore should assume its obligations as such. Pouring waste into a public stream is harmful and simply cannot continue. Any long-range view by the company's managers must concur with the correctness of the city's position. Also, in the opinion of the city officials, the threat of the company abandoning its Conroyville plant is pure bluff. A suitable building at today's prices will cost more than twice what the one in Conroyville did, efficient labor will be lost, and moving itself is costly.

Questions

1. Point out the relationship of this problem to modern management planning.
2. What suggestions can you offer to solve the impasse between the company and the city?
3. Do you feel the package deal given by the city to the company was attractive? Discuss.
4. What action do you recommend the company take? Why?

13

Implementing
managerial planning

*Kites rise against, not with the wind. No man has ever
worked his passage anywhere in a dead calm.*

JOHN NEAL

IN THIS CHAPTER is discussed the manner in which a manager performs
planning along with the activities allied to this effort. Proven guides
in this work are helpful and are included in the discussion. Answers
to questions such as the following will be given: What are the specific
steps taken in planning? What strategies might be employed? Who
should do the planning work?

MAJOR STEPS IN PLANNING

In the previous chapters on planning it was indicated that planning
is a highly individualized activity and is influenced greatly by the
pertinent characteristics of the enterprise, the wishes of top management members, the particular conditions external to the enterprise
which affect its operation, and the person or persons performing the
planning function. However, most planning work is characterized by
certain basic steps, which are enumerated and discussed as follows:

1. Clarify the Problem. Visualize the problem clearly. State it
concisely. See vividly the present condition that requires improvement
and for which the planning is being undertaken. Do not attempt to
formulate a plan until this step is completely mastered.

The following questions will help in this step:

269

a) What is the real aim or purpose of the plan to be formulated?

b) Does this aim or purpose require a brand new plan, or will a modified existent plan suffice?

c) What will the accomplishment of this aim mean to the enterprise?

d) Is the contemplated aim in conflict with any existent goals of the enterprise so that adjustments or eliminations of any present plans will be in order?

2. *Obtain Complete Informaton about the Activities Involved.* Knowledge of the activities to be planned is essential, and their effect upon other activities both internal and external to the enterprise is necessary for intelligent planning. Remember that in most cases for action to be effective, it must be based on knowledge. Experience, past solutions to problems, practices of other enterprises, observation, looking over records, and data secured from research and experiments constitute popular sources of usable information.

To assist in this step, the following questions may be asked:

a) Have all pertinent data been collected?

b) Are the data sufficiently broad to cover all activities which may be affected?

c) Have any possible sources of data been overlooked?

d) Have operating personnel been solicited for suggestions?

3. *Analyze and Classify the Information.* Each component of information is examined separately and also in relation to the whole of the information. Causal relationships are revealed, and pertinent data to the planning at hand are discovered and evaluated. Information pertaining to similar subjects is classified so that like data are together.

As a guide in this step, ask:

a) Are apparent relationships among data real and confirmed by key operating personnel?

b) Has information been tabulated or charted to facilitate analysis?

c) Are all usable data being included?

d) With further study can any steps in the present flow of work probably be eliminated?

4. *Establish Planning Premises and Constraints.* From the data pertinent to the problem as well as beliefs deemed important in the determination of the plan, certain assumptions upon which the planning will be predicted are now made. These premises and constraints will point out the background assumed to exist or take place to validate the plan. They are the backdrops on the stage of planning and should be carefully noted so that the plan can be thoroughly understood.[1]

Helpful in this step are the following questions:

a) What important assumptions regarding the future are being made in order to envolve the plan?

b) Are the premises inclusive, and do they cover all important contingencies?

c) Has all reasonably available information concerning the planning premises been obtained and evaluated?

d) What premises and constraints must be carefully watched in order to detect changes which might bring about a serious effect upon any plan based upon these assumptions?

5. Determine Alternate Plans. Usually several alternate plans exist to achieve the work to be done, and the various possibilities are evolved in this step. Ingenuity and creativeness frequently are required to arrive at several possible plans.

The following questions may be considered:

a) Are these possible plans in keeping with the basic objectives and methods of operation of top management members?

b) Will mechanization expedite the work?

c) For each plan, how much adjustment will be needed in the event it is adopted?

d) Are cost, speed, and quality requirements satisfied?

6. Choose Proposed Plan. The decision is now reached regarding which plan to adopt. Adequate consideration for expediency, adaptability, and cost must be made. The decision may be made either by an individual or by a group. In this step the choice among alternates includes that of doing nothing. When this is the decision, the planning operations terminate, of course, at this step.

Considerations contributing to the proper solution include:

a) Is the proposed plan simple or complex?

b) Will it be readily accepted by the operating personnel?

c) Does it possess flexibility to adjust to varying conditions?

d) What new equipment, space, personnel, training, and supervising will be needed?

7. Arrange Detailed Sequence and Timing for the Proposed Plan. The translation of the plan and its relation to all activities af-

---

[1] "Premises and Constraints of Planning" are included in Chapter 10.

fected by it are now worked out. The details of where the planned action should be done, by whom, and when are put in proper order for the intended purpose. The approach to be followed as well as the timing of the application of the proposed plan is vital and should be included as a part of the plan itself. This aspect of planning is discussed later in this chapter.[2]

These questions might be asked:

a)   Has a carefully worked out time schedule been established?
b)   Is the proposed installation, both in content and timing, in keeping with maximum acceptance by those affected by the plan?
c)   Are detailed instructions written to cover the plan?
d)   Are the required paper forms and supplies available?

8. *Provide Progress Checkup to Proposed Plan.* Success of the plan is measured by the results obtained. Therefore provision for adequate follow-up to determine compliance and results should be included in the planning work. Normally, of course, this is included in the fundamental function of controlling.

For this step, ask:

a)   Are records and reports included to keep operating personnel heads advised of progress?
b)   Will sufficient data over a reasonable period be collected to measure the results?
c)   In what range or within what limits will results be considered satisfactory?
d)   What remedial action is proposed if results indicate weaknesses?

BASIC QUESTIONS FOR PLANNING

Asking pertinent questions is a favorite means of stimulating thinking and providing the information needed for adequate planning. The answers to such questions disclose not only material to incorporate into the plan, but also areas for further study to make the plan complete. A number of helpful lists of such questions are available, but most of them resolve ultimately to the basic questions commonly referred to as the "Five W's and the How" questions. Effective planning involves the answering of these questions, and in turn these answers provide the

---

[2] See Pages 276–79.

basic ingredients of planning. For existent plans, these basic questions include:

1. *Why* must it be done?
2. *What* action is necessary?
3. *Where* will it take place?

4. *When* will it take place?
5. *Who* will do it?
6. *How* will it be done?[3]

To illustrate, in performing planning step number one, "Clarify the problem," the answers to basic questions, *why* must it be done, and, if justifiable, *what* action is necessary, are essential. The tie-in between the other planning steps, listed above, and these basic questions can be readily ascertained. In fact, by answering the basic questions the planner's thinking is directed into the proper area for satisfying planning efforts. The types of information revealed from these questions will now be stated briefly.

Why must it be done alerts the planner to the need for the work and encourages him to include only necessary activities. Those not needed are excluded. Activities comprising the effective plan represent the best combination of simple, well-combined, necessary activities.

The answer to the second question, *what* action is necessary, indicates the types of activities and their sequence necessary to achieve the desired result. Also included are descriptions of the facilities and equipment which will be required to carry out the proposed activities.

Number three, *where* will it take place, designates the specific physical location for the performance of each activity of the plan. All facilities must be available at the proper time in order for the planning to be meaningful.

The answer to *when* will it take place emphasizes the timing considerations. A definite beginning and ending time should be determined, not only for the entire course of action but also for each separate activity included in the plan. Maximum overlapping of required activities is usually recommended because such an arrangement requires the minimum time for completing the contemplated course of action.

Who will do it establishes assigned duties and responsibilities for the members of the group. Assignment of activities should be guided and usually made on the basis of the particular skills and abilities of the members. That is, a task requiring a special skill should not be assigned by the plan to a member who lacks that particular skill or ability. Each

---

[3] Note these same questions are used in work simplification, see p. 236.

Note also that the sequence of these questions is valid for evaluating existent plans only. For initial planning, the *what* question should be asked first, followed by the *why* question.

member should have the power to accomplish satisfactorily the duties assigned to him.

Lastly, *how* will it be done brings out the manner of getting the work accomplished and serves as a review regarding the thoroughness in answering the above five questions. This last question actually checks the entire plan for completion and for direction toward the desire goal.

The sequence of these questions should be observed. *Why* must it be done is logically the first question to ask in improving existing plans. Then ask number two, or *what* action is necessary in order to devise the most effective plan possible. The next three, *where, when,* and *who,* can then be asked; but question number six, *how,* should always be last. The inexperienced planner frequently asks the *how* question first and gets confused with the manner of doing the required work, instead of determining first *why* the work must be done and then proceeding logically in accordance with the above given listing.

RANGE OF COURSES OF ACTION

The determining of alternate plans as a major step in planning results in the planning having several possible courses of action so that a range, not just one course, of action is available. And as already noted, the application of planning must frequently be made amid highly dynamic conditions, and ample allowances for needed modifications and changes in keeping with events and circumstances as they develop should be provided. Having a range from which to select helps not only to determine the most suitable alternative, but also provides for the unexpected. After all, the "best" alternative is only best under a certain set of circumstances. Furthermore, alternatives make it possible to take advantage of opportunities.

By way of illustration, plan A may be the preferred plan because of the equipment and the time required for its execution. However, when the occasion arises for application of plan A, the conditions and setting to which the plan will be applied are so different from the premises used that plan A must be abandoned. In its place plan B, prepared originally in keeping with the new conditions, is substituted. In other words, planning for a range, not a single course, of action makes it possible for the manager to select the plan deemed best fitted to achieve the result, with due consideration given the conditions under which it must be applied.

DYNAMIC PROGRAMMING

Many problems encountered by enterprises today are of a multistage type; i.e., there are a series of sequential phases or steps making up the entire problem. Referring to Figure 13–1 the problem starts at S, and the first stage is either to decide on course of No. 1 or No. 2. Suppose the decision is to take No. 2 and subsequently No. 22 at stage 2, No. 221 at stage 3 leading to our goal, G, shown at the bottom of the

FIGURE 13–1. Dynamic programming permits reevaluation of plan at each stage before decision for subsequent stage of plan is finalized

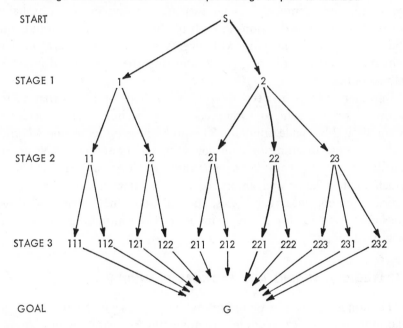

figure. To solve our problem, we plan to follow S–2–22–221–G. We have assumed that this plan is superior because it utilizes the optimum decision at every stage or phase. However, in actual practice this may not prove to be so; it depends upon the outcome or accomplishment at each phase. For example, at the accomplishment or results of 22 we may determine that 221 is not the best subsequent decision to make; it should be 222. In such an event we would be modifying our plan from its initial format. We do not know the best onward decision to stage 3 from stage 2 until activities are completed, or nearly so, at stage 2. Then the decision for stage 3 as predetermined, or a better one, can be determined in view of the unfolded current circumstances.

Dynamic Programming (DP) is intended to achieve utilization of the optimum decision at every stage of a multistage problem. This will provide the superior plan. DP takes into acount the effect of each decision at each stage of the overall problem. The cumulative effect of the path of decisions through the network of stages is the concern of DP. It permits reevaluation of the decisions as advancement along the prescribed pathway takes place. It updates and reassesses the program at the completion or near the completion of each phase.

DP has been made feasible by the modern computer. With its capacity, speed, and accuracy, it is an easy matter to reevaluate probable outcomes of various decisions at each of the stages of a plan and thus update the plan in keeping with events as they are occurring. The dynamics of all contributing forces affecting the plans are thus taken into account.

Representative of the type of problem suited for DP is that of investment, replacement, and maintenance of machines, where decisions are or should be made annually. The problem is to determine whether to buy a new machine or continue with the present one. Normally calculated are comparative expenditures of operating the machine, which include labor and amortized costs. A new machine is usually indicated when, on a year's basis, current labor, maintenance, and depreciation costs for the old machine exceed the minimum cost for the new machine.

STRATEGIC PLANNING AND TACTICAL PLANNING

The implementing of planning involves the usage of either strategic planning or of tactical planning. In any enterprise, strategy in planning consists of dealing with the enterprise's internal developments and external forces that affect the successful accomplishment of its stated objectives. Strategy normally is used with reference to fundamental issues, broad perspectives, and long-term periods, but these are not firm requirements. In contrast, tactical planning deals with determining the most efficient use of the resources that have been allotted for achieving given and specific objectives. The important differences between the two lie in the time element involved, the portion of the total enterprise activities being planned for, and the level of objectives involved. Generally speaking, the longer the time element, the more strategic the planning. Almost all long-range programs are classified strategic. Planning for an entire enterprise is strategic, whereas most product planning or advertising planning is tactical from the top-management viewpoint. An advertising manager's plan for his entire activity is strategic for him, but tactical for the corporate planner. Further, in strategic planning the emphasis commonly is upon the ends, not the means, of the activities, whereas in tactical planning, goals established by top management are accepted and ways to achieve them are sought.

One often hears the expression "Lose the battles, but win the war" as a statement of strategy being followed. This stresses the long-term period and end-result aspects of strategy. Managers are sometimes forced to decide whether to stand firm, compromise, or retreat. How many battles can be lost and yet win a war? A compromise commonly neither solves the issue nor satisfies anyone. In many cases, it is the battles, the daily struggles, that determine the ultimate success or failure of an endeavor. It would appear that some managers think exclusively in terms of strategy when some tactical planning is also needed.

While all resources are taken into account, strategy is most likely to include consideration of and adjustment to the reactions of people affected by the planning. This makes for highly practical and usually effective planning, as pointed out under step No. 7 of the major steps in planning. In this sense, the term "strategy" can be viewed as a well-thought-out approach, development, and application of the plan so that a minimum of difficulty is encountered from the reactions of fellow managers, employees, competitors, or the public.

STRATEGIES IN PLANNING

There are many strategies used in planning.[4] Their employment and evaluation depend upon the particular situation and the use to which they are put. The following list is illustrative, not inclusive, and it is intended to show the variety of the more common strategies that may be taken into account in the work of planning.

1. Camel's Head in the Tent. This stresses an infiltration approach. An entire plan may be quickly rejected; but by offering only a small portion of the plan, acceptance may be won for this portion. Subsequently other portions of the plan can be offered and accepted until the entire original plan is in operation.

2. Sowing Seed on Fertile Ground. Some members of a group are normally more receptive to the provisions of a tentative plan than are

[4] Professor L. C. Sorrell of the University of Chicago has prepared an extensive outline dealing with strategies. The listing included here has been adapted from this outline.

others. To offer the plan outright may run the risk of its rejection by the group. However, by selecting those favorable to the plan, thoroughly indoctrinating them in the merits and desirability of the plan, answering their questions about the plan, and stimulating their enthusiasm for its adoption, a group favoring the plan is developed, and its attitude is spread and shared with others of the group. Eventually, a sufficient number are favorable to the tentative plan and will accept it when presented.

3. Mass-Concentrated Offensive. This strategy is to take in one lump sum the total action believed necessary and get the proposed plan into operation as rapidly as possible. Rather than an infiltration type, mass-concentrated offensive can be termed as "earthquake" approach. When this strategy is used, the belief is that it is better to get it over with, eliminate uncertainty, and get started in the activities to be retained or inaugurated.

4. Confuse the Issue. A deliberate effort is made to divert the attention of the group by bringing in questions or stressing approaches that have no direct bearing on the real issue on hand. This may be employed when concentration is desired upon favorable issues and soft-pedaling is believed essential concerning controversial issues.

5. Use Strong Tactics Only When Necessary. Basically it is well to use no more energy or motivation than is necessary to accomplish the stated result. Strong tactics and pressures can be held in reserve and used only in those situations where their extra push is required. The revolutionary way of achieving the objective or the use of a top key executive is applied for special events where their presence and impression will carry great weight.

6. Pass the Buck . The transferring of blame or responsibility to someone else is provided by this strategy. The adopted plan makes it possible to pass unpleasant tasks willingly to others. Frequently the maneuver is handled in such a way that censure is made of the other party.

7. Time Is a Great Healer. Often the planning includes the strategy that with time many actions will take care of themselves. For some problems, time helps bring about the answer. The strategy is basically that it is a mistake to hurry or to insist that certain action take place, for by waiting the need for some of the actions will have been eliminated and many of the remaining actions will have been performed to some degree of satisfaction. This strategy is part of the same thinking expressed in the familiar "Everything comes to him who waits." Time and timing are very important elements in many planning strategies.

8. Strike While the Iron Is Hot. In other words, get on promptly with the application of the plan when acceptance to it is prevalent. Full advantage is thus taken of a favorable situation. Tomorrow may bring opposition or difficulties; so act today and avoid possible trouble. Act while the time for action is favorable is the essence of this strategy. Thus a sales manager established immediately a sales analysis unit following the suggestion made by the executive committee that such a unit might prove helpful. Had the sales manager waited until the time was more propitious for him, the committee may have changed its mind and approval of the unit may not have been won.

9. Two Heads Are Better than One. This emphasizes the obtaining of allies and applying joint action. If one executive of an organization wishes to adopt a plan regarding quality control, he may find that playing a lone hand is extremely difficult. However, should other executives be induced to join him in adopting the plan, the resultant joint action may be highly effective.

10. Divide and Rule. An old strategy is for an individual to keep members of a group separated into different factions so that overall rule can be maintained by that individual. This strategy is well-known in politics, and to a somewhat lesser degree in other fields. Its use can be highly effective, although it has its drawbacks, such as dynamic leadership being curbed and cooperative efforts among the members being stifled.

WHO PERFORMS PLANNING?

All managers perform planning. Some plan more than others because of the requirements of their respective positions. In some instances the management member does all his own planning work; in other cases, it is shared with managerial subordinates, or it can also be delegated to specific personnel. A manager can follow any of a number of possibilities.

The first possibility is that the manager does all his own planning. This requires a considerable amount of the managers' time, but it keeps *doing and planning* closely related. Usually planning under such conditions is highly practical; it provides flexibility, plans can be changed quickly; it permits closeness to immediate problems; and it develops capable managers. However, it is employed in relatively few enterprises today.

The second possibility, and probably most popular, is the manager plans but qualifies his planning by utilizing suggestions from his associates. Many managers feel that since they know the goals and have the facts at hand they are in an advantageous position to plan effectively. But they encourage contribution of ideas by associates. These contributions can be either (1) before the formulation of the plan by the manager or (2) after the formulation, indicating its good and bad points as the subordinates see them. With this approach, acceptance of a plan by subordinates is high, but the planning work of the manager is slowed down.[5]

Also, a manager can supply a broad outline of plans to subordinates, who fill in the details. Participation in planning by subordinates is stressed, and their enthusiastic support is enhanced. Also the manager's time is conserved. Where the planning duties require special or technical knowledge for full comprehension, this arrangement has its distinct advantages. However, this approach tends to be time-consuming, and it removes the manager from planning work.

Fourth, subordinates do planning and submit plans to manager for approval. This relieves the manager of most planning efforts and assists in developing subordinates. But there is risk that the plans will lack complete reality and feasibility. Also, the manager's personal contributions and importance are quite likely to be lessened.

No one of these approaches need be followed consistently. It is possible to use one approach in planning for one goal and another approach in planning for another goal. Individual circumstances and the personal wishes and abilities of the manager will determine the practice in any specific case.

PARTICIPATION IN PLANNING

The planner of today usually consults with others, thereby gaining sought-for advice, facts from many sources, opinions on different ideas of what might be done, and approval of all or of portions of a tentative plan. This approach results not only in improved plans but also in more acceptable plans than those conceived entirely by a "master mind" and distributed as the blueprints of action. Participation in planning contributes to good human relations. It helps win hearty endorsement and enthusiasm for the plan by all members of a group. This might well result in a mediocre plan bringing excellent results. Likewise, a well-conceived plan accepted halfheartedly by the work force will, at best, probably bring only average results.

---

[5] See also discussion under the heading, "Participation in Planning" immediately following.

The zenith of planning participation takes place where results management modifies the process of management approach. As pointed out in Chapter 3, under results management, with final approval by his superior, an individual manager designates those things he is going to accomplish, plans for them, and implements his own plans. His performance is appraised on the results he achieves. Obviously, this practice makes planning intimate and highly meaningful to the individual manager.[6]

Committees have been employed successfully for planning. The inherent characteristics of the committee provide an effective means for securing an understanding of plans by the various members and for gaining ideas from different parts and organizational levels of an enterprise. Ideas can be presented, suggestions discovered, and full information can be disseminated regarding current as well as tentative plans. Committee members are likely to feel a personal obligation to make the plan a success. Also, they become more interested in planning as a major function of the enterprise and in qualifying themselves to participate in the activity of planning. However, the possible tendency of a committee to discuss without completing a plan should be noted.

Many companies have a basic planning committee consisting of the chairman of the board, president, and vice presidents of the company. The duties of the members of this committee include the establishing and clarifying of major goals and plans and the refining and integrating of recommendations submitted by subplanning committees called project teams. Each project team is composed of one member from the planning committee plus other management members who represent areas of activities pertinent to the work of the project team. Representation is from across functional lines so diversified backgrounds, ideas, and opinions are considered. Responsibilities of a project team include studying basic questions suggested or inferred by the planning committee, gathering information on the pertinent subject areas, and recommending courses of actions along with alternatives and an evaluation of each.

This use of a basic planning committee supplemented by project teams emphasizes major roles by top and middle managers in planning work. They, in turn, encourage other managers to participate in planning. The specialists, technicians, and managers of facilitating, but not directly operating, functions should also play a part in the planning, but their efforts are mainly to provide help to the operating executives. Planning performed without involving operating managers usually winds up a waste of time and money.

[6] See chapter 3, pp. 49–50.

PLANNING AND OPERATING

However, there are two distinct schools of thought regarding the answer to the question "Should the performance of planning be separate from that of operating?" Some feel it is impractical to delimit the assignment of these functions. They contend that planning and doing are so closely related, especially at top-management levels, that the same executive can best perform both functions and, as a consequence, achieve the most satisfactory results. It is further argued that performance of planning and operating by the same individual is beneficial because it provides quick and needed flexibility in plans, permits closeness to immediate problems, furnishes complete familiarity with available facilities, and develops capable, well-balanced executives.

FIGURE 13–2.   Estimates of time spent on planning (by managers at various organizational levels according to period covered by plans)

Organizational level of manager	Current	1 month ahead	6 months ahead	1 year ahead	5 years ahead
President	2%	5%	20%	25%	48%
Vice president	5	15	40	30	10
Middle manager	25	50	15	10	..
Departmental	50	30	15	5	..
Supervisor	80	15	5	..	..

In contrast, many hold the opinion that planning should be performed by one person and operated by another. Members of this school believe the most effective planning evolves when the planner is free of current operating problems and can devote his entire thinking to the vital function of planning. When planning and operating are combined in one person, both suffer. In other words, planning is a speciality function and should be treated as such. A planner is an anticipator of problems and should be free to organize the probable consequences of many present or contemplated actions. This requires meditative thought, imagination, creativeness, and vision unperturbed by pressing operating problems which can probably best be solved by others. In addition, such things as consultations, keeping abreast of developments, reading literature on new techniques, and measuring results and performance in terms of objectives are important in turning out good planning work; and these activities frequently must be passed over if the planner's time is occupied with operating problems.

For various jobs in planning, a leading auto manufacturer employs people with extensive firsthand experience in other parts of its business. After a few years in planning, these employees move on to other operations. Specially trained, or so-called professional, planners are not used. The emphasis is placed on product planning. The manufacturer's executives claim this practice concerning planning keeps their program in line with developments in technology, marketing, and operating methods. Product planning becomes an integral part of their total operations, is highly practical, and is enthusiastically accepted by the non-planning employees.

The length of time covered by the plan is an important consideration in the question "Who performs the planning?" Generally speaking, plans pertaining to relatively long periods are made by top managers; those of current or short-run duration are commonly handled by managers at the lower organizational levels. Figure 13–2 has been included to illustrate this condition.

A DEPARTMENT OF MANAGERIAL PLANNING

A number of enterprises have a department of managerial planning in their organization structure. Commonly this department is established because top managers feel that the importance of planning warrants such a department; or the developments in this activity require such a department; or the general belief that the amount and caliber of planning that should be done will not be done unless a planning department exists. Also in some companies problems arising out of rapid growth and diversity of operations have suggested the establishment of a planning department. In other cases, the planning department is set up and its work limited to one class of work, for example, financial planning or facilities planning. Many companies engaged heavily in defense work have adopted this arrangement.

Generally speaking, planning departments do not mastermind the whole enterprise. They do not represent the centralization of all planning efforts. Their real job is to get others within the enterprise to plan. They achieve this purpose by suggesting what should be planned, by supplying information, by demonstrating how specific planning could be performed, and by telling others the chief executive officer wants them (others) to do planning and the planning department stands ready to offer assistance and guidance. In some respects, the members of the planning department are viewed as idea men.

However, the exact status of a planning department is not always clear cut. In extreme cases after the department has been established, it must hunt for work to do. There is no problem in most enterprises of finding planning work that ought to be done. But this approach is erroneous. The real qeustion is "What kinds of work are appropriate for a planning department?" Should it be a vehicle for gathering information; a clearinghouse for dispensing information; the recipient of specific assignments from top managers; the planner for acquisitions, new plant layouts, cost reduction opportunities; or what?

Figure 13–3 shows a portion of a memorandum on the planning function in a large university. Observe that the statement spells out the need for planning and details who handles the planning work and the practices to be followed in this respect.

While a department of management planning may not exist, there is commonly a systems and procedures department in many large enterprises. It does the planning work required for the creating, establishing, and maintaining of systems and procedures. The unit may be small, but

FIGURE 13–3. The planning function in a large university

The establishing of University needs and the accomplishing of them according to immediate and long-range goals requires planning. Planning is an imperative of any dynamic organization but in institutions of higher education planning is particularly necessary. As the responsibilities of the University continue to increase in diversity and magnitude, it is of utmost importance that the University consciously determine the directions it should take rather than react without design to forces directing change either inside or outside the institution.

There are many areas of planning. The most important is the determination of educational objectives and the means of attaining them. Other areas of planning in which the

Planning is centralized in the roles of the Department of Planning and two committees: the Faculty Planning Committee and the Administrative Planning and Policies Committee, both of which report to and through the Dean of Faculties.

The Faculty Planning Committee is responsible for initiating studies, reviewing plans and recommendations made by the respective schools and subcommittees, and making recommendations concerning long-range educational plans for the University. The Trustees, the President, or the Vice Presidents may make requests of or refer problems to the Committee for consideration and recommendations.

The reports and recommendations of the Faculty Planning Committee are submitted through the Educational Policies Committee (the senior faculty policy committee) to the Vice President and Dean of Faculties, who refers them or such parts as are pertinent to the deans of the various schools, department chairmen, the Dean of Students, Director of Admissions, Registrar, University Librarian, or other appropriate persons, committees, and agencies for discussion and comment. These comments may then be referred back to the Faculty Planning Committee for further review and comment. They are then forwarded to the Administrative Planning and Policies Committee.

The last-named Committee is responsible for ultimate review, staff approval, and forwarding, with recommendations, to the President. On review, if he approves, they are then forwarded to the Board of Trustees for final approval.

the importance of its work frequently warrants a separate unit working constructively with other organizational units. For illustrative purposes, the specific duties of a systems and procedures department in a large and well-known industrial firm include:

1. Investigate all problems of systems and procedures.
2. Write and revise, when necessary, all systems and procedures of the company and place in appropriate manuals for distribution to every management member.
3. Make annual review of all reports that are prepared by one department for its own or for another department's use.
4. Develop material for employee training designed to improve effective use of all systems and procedures.
5. Conduct a study every two years of all the company's printed and numbered paper forms.
6. Evaluate new equipment for possible application to the particular needs of each department.

The work for a systems and procedures department can originate from members designated to handle such work or it can start as a result of a suggestion from any member of the enterprise. The latter—such as an employee offering an idea that needs development or a problem that crosses departmental borders—is commonly an excellent source.

In a small enterprise, this type of work is normally shared by several management members, such as the controller, the information manager, the office manager, and the works manager. Unless cautiously handled, there is a possibility that under this dispersed arrangement the work may lose its impartial investigative and advisory effectiveness because of the load of operating routine matters by the members.

For any given enterprise, the issue is essentially "What are the planning needs and how is it best to organize to meet these needs?" Failure to define the planning needs can easily result in efforts expended in interesting and important problems, but problems which contribute little to the requirements of the enterprise. Sound planning as well as the organization for it necessitate a recognition of the need for planning, support by top managers, and the enthusiastic and intelligent participation of key people.

CHARACTERISTICS OF THE PERFORMANCE OF PLANNING

Usually there are certain difficulties associated with inaugurating planning efforts. Determining the scope and content of the planning and organizing for the work are probably of greatest concern. In this connection, it should be recognized that the first several attempts to formulate a plan may require what appears to be an excessive amount of time and extra work. But a definite start must be made. Even though imperfect, there must be a beginning if the planning is to be done. And one should not expect perfect results from the first one or two sets of plans. In addition, consideration must be included for the degree to which all management members need to be involved in their early stages of the planning efforts. Perhaps not more than two or three key persons should start the work because know-how, depth, and thoroughness are paramount.

Planning can be described as a tentative process. Initially certain concepts are visualized, but they are tentative and await the development of other components of the planning efforts. As these other components are selected or formulated, they are coordinated with the initial concepts. As a result, some of the initial concepts may be changed or eliminated, or they might remain intact. Additional concepts and refinements are added until the complete plan is created. The process consists of a "back-and-forth," tentative adding and subtracting, of concepts to form the plan. It is something like putting together a jigsaw puzzle. A start is made in one area and extended as far as possible; then efforts are shifted and concentrated to another area of the puzzle. Eventually the various separate areas are consolidated, but this may require modification, discarding and reworking certain parts in order to present the final integrated picture.

Since the performance of planning is greatly influenced by the people who perform it, the suggestion is made that in every enterprise a working climate conducive to planning should be maintained. The prevalent attitude should be one of believing in the value of planning and recognizing the need for it. The entire force should be planning conscious; continuous training in planning practices should be provided; and each one who plans should accept his responsibility for it and allocate an ample amount of his time to planning so that it can be properly performed. In essence, planning must be planned—it does not just happen.

Also, while writing of people and plans, it is well to note that the degree of success of any plan is greatly influenced by the manner in which employees do their jobs. It is of significant importance, therefore, for the planner to take into consideration the skills and limitations of the people who will carry out the plan. If they lack the required skills, adequate training or an acceptable arrangement of transferring must be worked out.

The performance of planning is an art as well as a science. The carrying out of the major steps in planning should not be thought of as being mechanistic. There is considerable skill in performing each step. Effective planning requires practice, creative thinking, insight, and a feel for the particular activity being planned. Being essentially a mental process, it is difficult to tell, for example, how plan X was determined. But plan X is available—the fruit of a manager's planning. Some have said that planning is like "shooting from the hip," or "portraying a character in a play," or "composing a hit tune"—some can do it effectively, others cannot, even though knowledge of what is supposed to be done can be enumerated logically and clearly. The details of what to do can even be memorized by the participant but yet not be performed expertly. So it is with planning, because an essential ingredient of planning lies in the skill, the expertness, and the individualism with which it is personally performed.

ADDITIONAL CONSIDERATIONS IN PERFORMANCE OF PLANNING

It is also helpful to recognize the tangible from the intangible factors involved in planning work. Preferably the two types of factors should not be mixed. Normally the tangible factors can be expressed in common measurable units, such as dollars, and comparisons and summaries made of such factors to expedite the planning. In contrast, the intangible factors can be classified as well as possible and evaluated in terms of judgment and experience or in relation to data representing specific tangible factors. For example, a company planning to offer a new product on the market can express tangible costs like shipping costs, billing expenses, and advertising expenditures in dollars, and summary figures can be used; but the intangible factors—acceptance and willingness of the public to purchase the product, propensity for repeat sales, and so forth—must be appraised by judgment and experience.

Some managers in performing planning find it helpful to work backward from the objective. This approach helps insure that the planning work is directed to the needs of the enterprise and is properly synchronized with other plans. Also difficulties to overcome will be brought out in clear relief and will not be minimized. In addition, progress in the planning can be easily gauged when this approach is followed.

In determining a plan it is helpful, in considering the alternative course of action to be selected, to concentrate attention upon the variable issues and disregard those that are constant in the alternate courses being considered. Actually it is the variables that make the differences among the alternates; the constants are really irrelevant insofar as the selection of the makeup of the plan is concerned. For instance, in making the plan for the work of a given manufacturing department, assume that the floor space allotted and its cost to the department remains constant; hence the factor of floor space can be ignored in the considerations of planning the department's work. Instead planning efforts can concentrate upon variables such as accomplishing the work by manual means versus automation.

All other things being equal, it is better to start planning with the major issues. These will exert the greatest influence upon the design of the plan and should be resolved so that the broader structure of the plan is determined in the beginning stages of the planning. This approach is illustrated by the college professor planning a new course. Normally the plan of a list of assignments and the type of examinations constitute relatively minor issues and can be deferred in the initial stages of planning. Major issues, like what is to be achieved by this course, its content, and planning the presentation of the material, should be given prior considerations.

Planning is expedited by giving emphasis to the present and the future. Commitments made from which there is no turning back and past errors in actions which cannot be retrieved are valuable for the experience and knowledge that they provide. However, to brood over past unfortunate results and to wish that such and such had not been included in the plan is nonproductive and interferes with the application of clear thinking to present and future planning. A planner should learn from past mistakes and not repeat them. The goal of planning is to determine what action should be taken now and in the future. Foresight is the prime requisite, not hindsight.

QUESTIONS

1. Enumerate the eight steps of planning.
2. Distinguish between the two concepts in each of the following pairs: (*a*) planning strategy and planning premise, (*b*) strategic planning and tactical planning, and (*c*) the strategy of "confuse the issue" and that of "time is a great healer."
3. Relate your understanding of the suggestion, "Plan for a range of courses of action."
4. In your opinion is managerial planning helped or hindered by using the results management approach in planning work? Justify your answer.
5. Explain the meaning of tactical planning and describe an example of its use in your school, place of employment, or community organization.

6. In general, which approach of a manager performing planning—do it all, none, or share it under any of several degrees—do you favor? Why?
7. What is dynamic programming and for what purpose and under what conditions do you recommend its use?
8. Based on either your experience or events about which you have heard or read, relate a strategy of planning that was or is being used. In your opinion could a better strategy be used? Explain.
9. As a top-management member, assume your choice for improving current planning in your corporation is establishing and using either a basic planning committee or a department of managerial planning. What decision would you make? Why?
10. What advantage is there to a planner to identify and keep separate in his own thinking the tangible and intangible factors involved in his planning efforts? Give an illustration to substantiate your viewpoint.
11. Generally speaking, do you favor having the planning and the doing phases of a manager's job within that job, separated between two jobs, or some other arrangement? Substantiate your answer.
12. Elaborate on the statement, "Planning is a tentative process." Illustrate your answer with an example.
13. Explain the meaning of the statement, "The constants are really irrelevant insofar as the selection of the makeup of the plan is concerned."
14. Relate an experience in either school or employment where you successfully applied the strategy of "camel's head in the tent."

CASE 13–1. WITCO COMPANY

Operating in a highly competitive market, Witco Company managers have to achieve high efficiency to survive. For one of their products, ZD-7, consideration is now being focused on automating the assembly line. After several conferences with representatives of Acme Automation Company, it appears definite that an automated assembly line is entirely feasible and will provide higher quality, and a more accurate product than what is now being assembled manually. The proposed line would require 18 employees to operate it and would increase production by 40 percent over the present level. The equipment is offered at a price of $150,000 installed with 10 months delivery time required.

Currently the company operates two assembly lines, two shifts of eight hours per day, five days a week. Output is 20 units an hour per line which requires 24 employees. The average wage rate for the assembly line is $4.25 an hour for either the first or second shift. At a meeting to discuss the question of automating the assembly line, the following conversation took place:

PRESIDENT: Now as I understand it, the assembly for our part ZD-7 can be automated. It is not a difficult problem.

ACME REP.: That is correct.

V. P. PRODUCTION: And it will require 10 months for delivery?

ACME REP.: Yes.

V. P. PRODUCTION: Can that period be shortened?

ACME REP.: I'll do all I can, but frankly I doubt it. We are very busy.

PERSONNEL MANAGER: When we talked before you mentioned something about our training responsibility for maintenance men to keep the automated line going and also for retraining our present assemblers to handle the automated line.

PRESIDENT: I understood it was automatic. Do we still have to have manual assemblers?

ACME REP.: The automated line will require bringing and taking away materials to and from the line and also some hand feeding. Regarding the training requirements, the answer is, yes, training is recommended. In this regard, my company will supply you free of charge with some material that has proven effective.

PERSONNEL MANAGER: I estimate $10,000 for training maintenance men and $25,000 for retraining the assemblers. How does that sound?

ACME REP.: A little low. We use $1,000 per assembler as a rule of thumb. I'd recommend $25,000 to cover training maintenance men. I might add that from our experience, I doubt if you'll do any more maintenance work. It's just that your present maintenance men should be trained in how to repair and keep the automated equipment in proper running order.

PRESIDENT: We will need fewer assemblers with the automated line, won't we?

V. P. PRODUCTION: Yes, I don't recall the figure, right at the moment.

PERSONNEL MANAGER: Those that are let go . . . . we are obligated to give them severance pay of one year's pay.

PRESIDENT: Well aren't we going to make every effort to use them somewhere else in the company?

V. P. PRODUCTION: Yes, of course, but that isn't easy. You get into skill requirements for the job to which they are transferred, whether they want to do the other work, what group they want to work with and all sorts of problems.

PERSONNEL MANAGER: We'll try to work that out O.K. I believe we can.

PROCESS ENGINEER: Will the automated line require the same floor space as what we have now and will the equipment follow the same sequence of steps we now perform?

ACME REP.: No, to both questions. Our automated line will require about 80 percent of the space your present line requires. We perform the sequential steps in an order best suited for automation and there are some differences from what you now have.

PROCESS ENGINEER: We'll have to do some rearranging.

ACME REP.: Yes, but it will be relatively minor.

PRESIDENT: Any more questions, gentlemen? If not, thanks for sharing your information about Acme. Meeting adjourned.

Questions

1. Other than economic considerations, what should the company managers carefully weigh in their effort to determine what should be done? Discuss fully.
2. What is your recommended action for the Witco Company? Give complete justification for your answer.

CASE 13–2. THE HODGES BUILDING

The building manager of the Hodges Building, a well-known office building, is faced with the problem of how to improve its elevator service. The building is ten floors in height, was constructed in 1926, and has been maintained in a good state of repair. The location is on a main street of Oakland, California. Complaints regarding poor elevator service have been registered by several tenants. The building manager has delayed taking any action because he believes that whatever improvement can be made should be included in the planning of the elevator service for the new five-story addition to be constructed adjacent to the present building.

Currently, two elevators serve the building; each has a capacity of 20 persons. The speed of each elevator is approximately as follows:

10 seconds per floor going up if stop is made at each floor.

50 seconds for travel from ground to 11th floor (the ground floor is considered the first floor) with no intermediate stops.

9 seconds per floor going down if stop is made at each floor.

40 seconds for travel from 11th floor to ground floor with no intermediate stops.

The manager conducted a survey of elevator traffic in the building, and typical data are as follows:

Time	Total Traffic (No. of Persons)	Destination to Floor										Service Required Is Mainly
		2	3	4	5	6	7	8	9	10	11	
7:30 A.M.- 8:30 A.M.	Average = 81	7	4	13	9	5	8	9	5	9	12	Up
8:30 A.M.- 8:45 A.M.	291	17	95	12	33	8	11	21	37	16	41	Up
8:45 A.M.- 9:00 A.M.	194	50	8	3	42	1	83	1	2	1	3	Up
9:00 A.M.- 9:15 A.M.	176	2	1	90	1	3	2	5	22	45	5	Up
9:15 A.M.- 9:30 A.M.	142	10	7	2	2	81	1	30	3	2	4	Up
9:30 A.M.-11:30 A.M.	Average = 94	3	2	14	2	16	8	3	10	29	7	Up and Down
11:30 A.M.-12:30 P.M.	Same as 8:30 A.M.- 9:30 A.M. Traffic											Down
12:30 P.M. - 1:30 P.M.	" " "											Up
1:30 P.M. - 4:30 P.M.	Average = 75	1	7	9	10	3	12	12	2	6	13	Up and Down
4:30 P.M. - 4:45 P.M.	205	36	6	7	51	4	77	10	7	5	2	Down
4:45 P.M. - 5:00 P.M.	201	5	3	86	7	4	4	20	19	37	16	Down
5:00 P.M. - 5:15 P.M.	163	15	68	7	12	6	5	9	13	14	14	Down
5:15 P.M. - 5:30 P.M.	87	4	1	14	4	13	5	5	11	17	13	Down

In other words, during the time period 7:30 A.M.–8:30 A.M., the average traffic load is 81 persons for each 15-minute period, distributed among the various floors as indicated by the above data, namely 7 for the second floor, 4 for the third floor, and so forth. Traffic builds up rapidly at 8:30 A.M., and during the 15-minute period 8:30 A.M.–8:45 A.M., the total elevator traffic load is 291 persons, of which 17 are passengers for the second floor, 95 for the third floor, and so forth. The total load for each 15-minute period is almost evenly distributed over its 15-minute period. There is also interfloor traffic at all times, but the building manager feels this is relatively minor in volume and has received no complaints on such service.

It is anticipated that elevator traffic resulting from the proposed five-story addition will be as follows:

Time	Total Persons
8:30 A.M.–8:45 A.M.	150
8:45 A.M.–9:00 A.M.	130
9:00 A.M.–9:15 A.M.	100
9:15 A.M.–9:30 A.M.	100

This pattern will be repeated between 11:30 A.M.–12:30 P.M., between 12:30 P.M.–1:30 P.M., and between 4:30 P.M.–5:30 P.M. For 15-minute periods during the day for other than times indicated, the load is assumed to be a maximum of approximately 60 persons with an average of 40 persons or less. Again the traffic load for each of these 15-minute periods is almost evenly distributed over its 15-minute period. The lobby of the proposed addition will join onto the present building lobby so that the present elevators could be used for tenants in the addition.

Questions

1. Is there reasonable justification for the complaints regarding the elevator service at the present time? Substantiate your viewpoint.
2. Will the present elevators take care of the additional traffic predicted for the new five-story addition?
3. Based on information supplied in this case, what decision do you feel the building manager should make? Why?

part IV

Organizing

The second fundamental function of management to be discussed is organizing. One of the oldest of managerial areas, it is currently being subjected to much study and research especially from the behavioral viewpoint. The modern organization is far different than its counterpart of several decades ago. New concepts of the meaning of organizing, the individual's behavior in the organization, the effect of group actions, the social and the work environments of an organization, the modern use of authority, relationships, and structure are all undergoing change, giving more and more impetus to the dynamics of organization.

Organizing is indeed an exciting area of management study. The following five chapters give a concise picture of up-to-date organizational thinking:

14

Management organizing

In order that people may be happy in their work, these three things are needed: They must be fit for it, they must not do too much of it, and they must have a sense of success in it.

JOHN RUSKIN

FROM EARLIEST TIMES some men have directed efforts of others in a team effort toward various specific goals. The total work to be done, as set forth by the plans, required the efforts of more than one person. Hence, many hands and minds were brought together and coordinated so that not only the collective actions were effective, but also that the contribution of each individual was valuable and hopefully satisfying and in keeping with the individual's respective knowledge and skill.

In presenting material on organizing we will first give helpful general information about this important fundamental function of management. Following this, the considerations of organizing generally known as formal organizing will be offered. This will give an awareness of the formal organizing theory. Using this as a base, we then proceed logically with important modifications of formal organization bringing in other theories and the important behavioral concepts and contributions. In this way, a complete picture of organization today is provided and hopefully will expedite a better understanding of it.

MEANING OF ORGANIZING

Organizing brings together the basic resources in an orderly manner and arranges people in an acceptable pattern so that they can perform the required activities. Organizing unites people in interrelated tasks. It is intended to help in getting people to work together effectively toward the accomplishment of specific goals.

The word "organizing" stems from the word "organism," which is an entity with parts so integrated that their relation to each other is governed by their relation to the whole. Organizing is followed because the work to be done requires the efforts of more than one person. When two or more persons work together toward a common goal, the relationship and interaction among them gives rise to problems such as who decides what issues, who does what work, and what action should be taken when certain conditions exist. Hence, persons working together effectively, each doing to the maximum what he can best do, and the persons achieving the total best possible results are basic in the concept of organizing. A satisfactory definition of organizing includes: *Organizing is the establishing of effective behavioral relationships among persons so that they may work together efficiently and gain personal satisfaction in doing selected tasks under given environmental conditions for the purpose of achieving some goal or objective.*

ADVANTAGES OF ORGANIZING

By proper organizing a manager hopes to have more than the sum of the individual efforts. That is, he hopes for *synergism,* which is the simultaneous action of separate or individual units which together produce a total effect greater than the sum of the individual components. Organizing is a case where, contrary to basic mathematics, the sum is greater than the sum of its individual parts. We are interested more in the potency of the mixture than in the strength of its ingredients.

Organizing can have a highly favorable effect upon managerial actuating and controlling. For example, actuating efforts are conditioned greatly by the quality of organizational efforts performed. A person placed in the wrong job for him, or reporting to a group leader whom he doesn't get along with, or with fellow employees he doesn't care to be associated with, will be extremely difficult to motivate. Here the effect of the organization upon the individual's behavior comes into full light.

Increased emphasis is being given to the actions of individuals and groups as they influence each other within the organization framework. The stress is upon interpersonal relationships. Maximization of human satisfaction as well as work productivity are sought. The constraints placed upon an employee by organization and the total organization environment in which the employee works are important facets of modern organization. Likewise, organizing has considerable effect upon controlling in that organizing establishes known constraints and expectancies which are to be achieved.

IMPORTANCE OF ORGANIZING

Organizing has always been important to man. He has dealt with the recurring issue of organization and its implications throughout all history. Organization has been pervasive in many forms of human activity because human collaboration—the dependency of people on each other —and protection against threats and antisocial behavior have encouraged intense organization activity by all mankind over the centuries. Governments, armies, businesses, and institutions of all kinds have studied organizing with the intent to improve it or to utilize it better in their particular managerial endeavors. Of all the basic management functions, organizing has been the most intensively studied, and contributions to this area are abundant.

Of great significance, however, is that organizing results in an organization structure which can be thought of as a framework which holds the various functions together according to a pattern suggesting order, logical arrangement, and harmonious relationships. Vital is the concept that organizing supplies the nucleus around which human beings can unite their efforts effectively. In other words, an important part of the task of organizing is to harmonize a group of different personalities, to fuse various interests, and to utilize abilities—all toward a given direction. Such an entity has great importance.

FORMAL ORGANIZATION

A formal organization is one formed with official sanction to achieve stated goals. It is sometimes referred to as a hierarchy of positions and tasks. There are four basic components of formal organizing: (1) the work which is divisionalized, (2) persons who are assigned to and perform this divisionalized work, (3) the environment under which the work is done, and (4) the relationships among the persons or the work-persons units.

Let us look closer at these four basic components. From the sought goals, the necessary work activities are derived. The work is divided into "packages of work" for these reasons: (1) the work is too big for performance by one person and must be divided to be performed by several people, (2) the distribution of work requires that the work be divided, and (3) the desire to achieve the advantages of work specialization necessitates that the assigned tasks require only the specialized skills of the personnel. However, specialization cannot be applied to every situation without limit, for if it is extended too far, the employee's interest, work satisfaction, and "will to do" are impaired. But in organizing, work combination, the counterpart to work division, is also done. It entails the regrouping of the divided activities into units believed more suited for effective performance from the viewpoint of the facilities and personnel available. Groupings are normally intended to be on some logical basis.

With reference to the persons who will perform the work, their experience, competency, and behavior must be taken into account in determining who should perform what specific work. It should be divided

FIGURE 14–1. Steps in formal organizing

1. Know the objectives of the organizing in the environmental situation.
2. Break down the required work into component activities.
3. Group the activities into practical units based on similarity, importance, or who will do the work.
4. Define the duties and provide the physical means for each activity or group of activities.
5. Assign qualified or potentially developable personnel.
6. Inform each member what activities he is expected to perform and his relationships to others in the enterprise.

so that the work activities assigned to each person constitute work that the person can do successfully, that is, the proper types of work in keeping with the person's ability and the proper amount of work in accordance with reasonable and equitable diligence and pursuit of accomplishment by the person. Organization that fails to include these considerations is deficient.

The environment under which the work is done includes such things as the location of the work performance, materials, and machines. Also included are the general climate of the work area, helpfulness of superiors, influence of competitive forces, activities of labor unions, and government regulations and actions.

The fourth and last component is the relationships among the persons or the work-persons units. These relationships are very important. They give rise to authority which is discussed fully in chapters 15 and 16. Figure 14–1 shows these four basic components of organizing included in the steps of formal organizing.

FUNCTION OR PEOPLE AS ORGANIZATION NUCLEUS

A controversial issue of organization is whether the organization should be built around functions or people. In the above discussion we started with the function of work and its divisions. This is the recommended procedure. Justification for this approach is that for most enterprises work activities are fairly stable and thus provide a reliable foundation on which to *start* organizing work. In contrast, the interests, abilities, and skills of people are subjected to considerable change. People tend to come and go, but the work remains relatively stable. Thus, stability is acquired by utilizing the work approach in the determining of organizational units.

PRINCIPLE OF FUNCTIONS

Functions are the main entities around which a manager builds an effective organization structure.

On the other hand, examples are available to demonstrate the use of personnel about which to cluster organizational units. Such units are frequently of most unusual combinations of activities; yet they are highly productive. With time, however, such combinations usually prove to be difficult to manage, and it is extremely arduous to replace managers for them. Combinations of this type frequently have overlaps in the assignments of personnel, with several persons nominally being charged to see that the work is performed properly but with actually no one serving in that capacity, and misunderstanding of who is to do what work being common. Work is slowed up, indecisions are rampant, and buck passing is practiced—all of which causes inefficiency and frustration. In too many such cases the organizational obstacles are not recognized but are inadvertently tolerated as inherent difficulties of managing an enterprise.

CHARACTERISTICS OF FORMAL ORGANIZING

Formal organizing theory emphasizes rationale, efficiency, logical arrangement of functions, written orders, a work-oriented behavior, attention to the number of subordinates reporting to a superior, and a definite chain of command or channel of communication from the top to the bottom level. People are placed in different organizational units (work-persons units) after study and careful consideration. Usually they are expected to accomplish certain prescribed results and are in-

FIGURE 14–2. Chart of formal organization

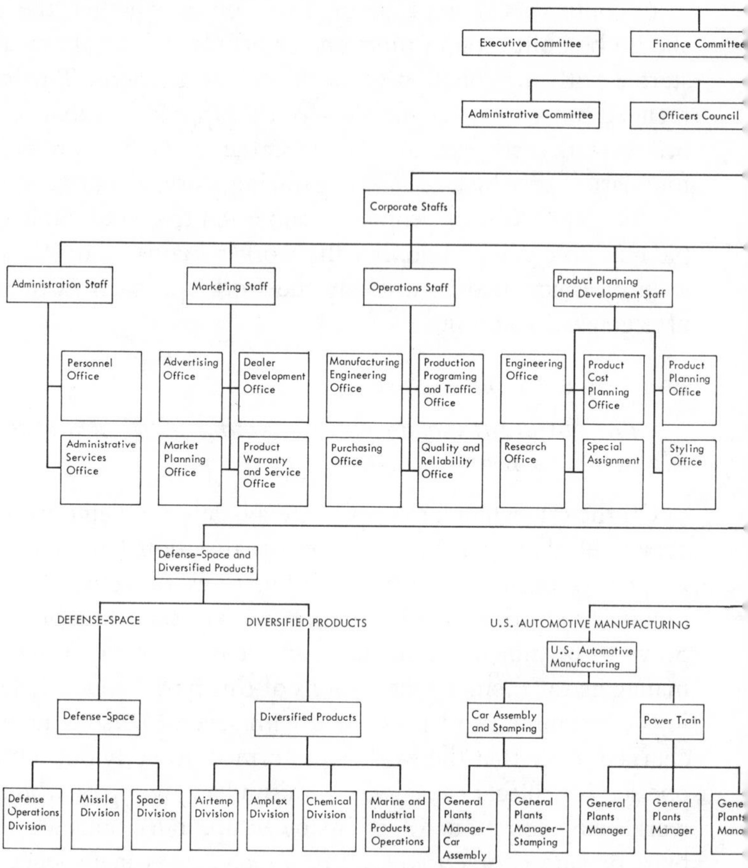

fused with a sense of duty in which self-interest and self-enrichment are prime motivators.

The belief is that for organizing to be effective, a manager must know specifically what activities he is to manage, who is to help him, to whom he reports, and who reports to him. Further, each manager is given the objectives to be obtained, and needs to be informed of the makeup of his entire group and each member of it, his place in the group, and the formal channels of communication. Likewise, the nonmanager is given a clear understanding of the requirements of his job, its limitations, and his relationships not only to the manager of his group, but also to the total work group and to members of his immediate work group.

Further, an effort is made to maintain a balance among the various types of work being done, each being given the importance that its true

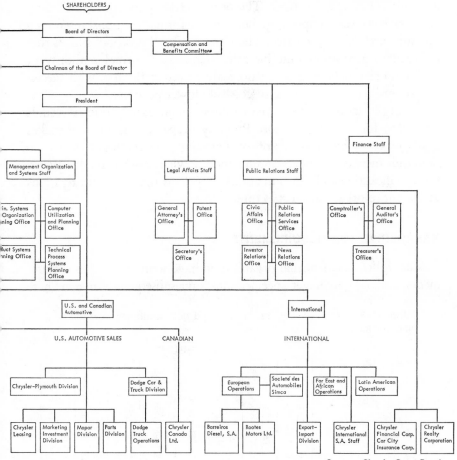

Courtesy: Chrysler Corp., Detroit.

value warrants. All activities believed necessary are included and each one is given attention in keeping with its relative importance. Thus, empire building is minimized and further, the placement of people on jobs best suited for them is enhanced.

WRITTEN TOOLS OF FORMAL ORGANIZATION

An organization chart and manual plus job requirements or job descriptions and man specifications are common written tools of formal organization. These spell out in some detail what formal relationships, requirements, and working conditions are envisioned to be. This information serves as an official guide in performing the organizing work.

Figure 14–2 shows the formal corporate organization chart of a leading automobile manufacturer. The organization units are logical, similar work has been grouped together, and the formal relationships among the units are clearly indicated. The lines joining the various blocks that represent organization unit indicate channels of formal authority or command channels. Major functions are placed at the top, with successive subordinate functions in successively lower positions.[1]

An organization manual gives supplemental and additional details about the formal organization. Properly prepared, the manual makes available complete information on pertinent matters about each position, thus increasing understanding and knowledge of the requirements, the specifications and the limitations as well as the position's relations to the entire organization structure.

MANAGERIAL JOB REQUIREMENTS

Most followers of formal organization have written (1) job requirements, and (2) manager specifications, and subsequently match these

FIGURE 14–3.   Relative degree of selected job attributes for different managerial jobs

JOB ATTRIBUTES

MANAGERIAL JOBS	ANALYTICAL ABILITY	SPECIALIZED KNOWLEDGE	SOCIAL SENSITIVITY	SELF RELIANCE	OPEN-MINDEDNESS	EMOTIONAL STABILITY	EFFECTIVENESS IN COMMUNICATION	EMPATHY WITH OTHERS
PRESIDENT	H	M	H	H	M	H	H	H
SALES MANAGER	M	M	H	H	H	H	H	H
CONTROLLER	H	H	M	H	M	M	M	M
PURCHASING AGENT	M	M	H	M	H	M	H	M
PERSONNEL MANAGER	M	M	H	M	M	M	H	H
DATA PROCESSING MANAGER	H	H	M	H	M	M	M	M

H = HIGH
M = MEDIUM

---

[1] More discussion on organization charts is included at the end of this chapter.

job and man requirements to assign managerial manpower in the organization structure.[2] To assist in writing the job and man requirements, pertinent questions are asked, such as: What do we expect the manager to do? What are the exact requirements of the manager's job (the title or name is insufficient)? What is the specific content of the job? How is the content determined and how valid is this information? What important relationships must the occupant of this managerial job maintain and develop for the best operation both for the enterprise and for the individual manager?

Job attributes can also be used to determine what the managerial job requires. Figure 14–3 shows the relative degree of selected job attributes for each of several managerial jobs. These are approximations, and the importance of each attribute required will vary with the precise job makeup and the organization in which it is located. In other words adequate consideration must be given to the individual circumstances in each case.

The format used to set forth managerial job requirements can follow several designs. Figure 14–4 shows an arrangement especially effective. The figure illustrates a particular position on the formal chart and includes a concise statement of that position. Detailed and carefully outlined information concerning this same position is shown by Figure 14–5.

From the viewpoint of management in general, a standardized managerial job makeup is a theoretical convenience, not a practical reality. In the final analysis, the makeup of a particular managerial job constitutes what is expected of the manager in a particular enterprise, and this requirement changes considerably from enterprise to enterprise. The same managerial title may be used, but the actual job content may differ widely. For example, a manager with the title "office manager" in one enterprise may be expected to perform work of much broader scope than that of the office manager in another enterprise.

For a formal organization there are a series of job descriptions covering each job. But it should be noted that few job descriptions include *all* the duties and responsibilities that the job in reality entails. Writing job descriptions is a difficult and detailed task to be all-inclusive, and whatever is put into the written description is always subject to inter-

[2] The work of placing management members in an organization can be justified as within the work of organizing. These reasons are (1) organizing stresses human and social relations, (2) the true meaning of organizing must include consideration for the management members who are so organized, and (3) management manpower is acquired and assigned for an organization unit, usually a specific one—it is not done in a vacuum, or as an isolated act.

FIGURE 14–4. Location and concise statement of a particular position in an organization structure

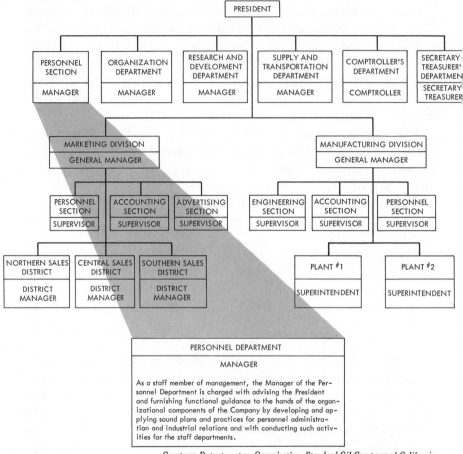

PERSONNEL DEPARTMENT

MANAGER

As a staff member of management, the Manager of the Personnel Department is charged with advising the President and furnishing functional guidance to the hands of the organizational components of the Company by developing and applying sound plans and practices for personnel administration and industrial relations and with conducting such activities for the staff departments.

Courtesy: Department on Organization, Standard Oil Company of California

pretation. Furthermore, over a period of time the typical executive alters his job content to some degree. An aggressive manager will move in and occupy areas not specifically defined as the work of another manager. It's another case of getting there "furstest with the mostest." Vacuums do not exist in most organizations for very long.

MANAGER SPECIFICATIONS

Leaving the managerial job requirements and turning now to manager specifications, we can consider first the manager skills that seem

FIGURE 14–5. A portion of the detailed information regarding a position in an organization structure

MANAGEMENT GUIDE

MANAGER, PERSONNEL DEPARTMENT

I. FUNCTION

As a staff member of management, the Manager of the Personnel Department is charged with advising the President and furnishing functional guidance to the heads of the organizational components of the Company by developing and applying sound plans and practices for personnel administration and industrial relations, and with conducting such activities for the staff departments.

II. RESPONSIBILITIES AND AUTHORITY

Within the limits of his approved program and corporate policies and control procedures, the Manager of the Personnel Department is responsible for, and has commensurate authority to accomplish, the fulfillment of the duties set forth below. He may delegate to members of his Department appropriate portions of his responsibilities together with proportionate authority for their fulfillment, but he may not delegate or relinquish his over-all responsibility for results nor any portion of his accountability.

A. Activities

1. He will formulate, or receive and recommend for approval, proposals for policies on personnel administration and industrial relations, will administer such policies when approved, and will conduct such activities for the staff departments.

2. He will establish procedures for personnel administration and industrial relations, and will establish and administer procedures for the initiation and maintenance of personnel records.

3. He will negotiate, but not sign, agreements with employee groups and labor unions, and their representatives, affecting staff department employees or employees of both the Marketing and Manufacturing Divisions, and will advise and assist in the negotiation of such agreements affecting employees of only one division, as requested.

4. He will establish and conduct a Company personnel office for the administration of personnel and industrial relations matters, and will maintain therein personnel records of members of management and home office employees.

5. He will participate in the selection of personnel for management positions, and will conduct the initial interview of applicants for such positions and for employment in the home office.

6. He will prepare, guide, and co-ordinate the personnel rating and personnel development programs, and will formulate, or receive and recommend for approval, proposals for action based thereon.

7. He will guide and co-ordinate the safety program and safety standards and practices, and will disseminate applicable safety laws and orders.

8. He will guide and co-ordinate employee benefit plans and programs, and will conduct activities pertaining thereto for the personnel of the staff departments.

B. Organization of His Department

1. He will recommend changes in the basic structure and complement of his Department.

C. Personnel of His Department

1. Having ascertained the availability of qualified talent from within the Company, he will hire personnel for, or appoint employees to, positions other than in management within the limits of his approved basic organization.

2. He will approve salary changes for personnel not subject to the provisions of the Fair Labor Standards Act who receive not over $350 per month, and will recommend salary changes for such personnel receiving in excess of that amount.

3. He will approve wage changes for personnel subject to the provisions of the Fair Labor Standards Act.

Courtesy: Department on Organization, Standard Oil Company of California to be required for managerial success. These are (1) technical, (2) human, and (3) conceptual.[3]

Technical skill includes proficiency and understanding of a specific activity involving a process, procedure, or technique. It usually consists of a specialized knowledge and ability to perform within that specialty. Technical skill enables its possessor to accomplish the mechanics demanded in performing a particular job.

Human skill, as the name suggests, includes the ability to work with others and to win cooperation from those in the work group. It includes, for example, being able to communicate ideas and beliefs to others and to understand what thoughts and attitudes others are trying to convey to you. In addition, the manager with human skill recognizes what views he brings to situations and in turn what adjustments or changes in these views might be made as a result of working with his associates.

Conceptual skill includes the ability to visualize the enterprise as a whole, to see the "big picture," to envision all the various functions involved in a given situation or circumstance. It is conceptual skill that enables an executive to recognize the interrelationships and relative values of the various factors intertwined in a managerial problem. In general, managerial jobs at low organizational levels require relatively more technical and human skill than conceptual skill, but at high organizational levels the need is relatively greater for conceptual and less for technical skill.[4]

Common traits of a manager are also used to determine manager specifications. These traits are *general,* not specific, and they are best viewed, not in any precise manner, but as a composite. A deficiency in these qualities is interpreted to mean that the candidate is unsuited for the job so specified, but at the same time favorable appraisals do not necessarily insure executive success by the candidate. For example, good judgment, winning respect of others, and ability to speak effectively may be considered necessities to a top manager. A candidate for a top management job may have all these traits, yet not fill the top position successfully. And concentrating on specific traits tends to overemphasize what managers *are.* This outlook has a place and is useful, but perhaps of equal or of more importance is what executives *do*—or the type of actions a manager must perform to do his job effectively.

---

[3] Robert L. Katz, "Skills of an Effective Administrator," *Harvard Business Review* (January–February 1955), pp. 33–42. The discussion on this topic is based upon this excellent source.

[4] The "skills required" approach is also helpful in management development work discussed in Chapter 22.

Nevertheless, the use of traits is helpful and advocates of this approach point out that the trait of adaptability is vital in a great many conditions a manager must face. Further, some believe that both the degree of adaptability and the decisiveness in carrying out this feature are of foremost importance in selecting executive candidates. Another feature is an ability to wield power and influence among members of a formally organized group. Indirectly this reveals an ability to motivate others and to get objectives accomplished through the efforts of others. Observations show that the effective manager knows his own limitations as well as those of his associates. He maintains a broad perspective; yet the major goal is constantly in mind.

Also, usually considered of importance is the ability to find, train, and develop subordinates and especially immediate assistants. Availability of an assistant to take over, if necessary, is one of the earmarks of a competent manager. This requires taking sufficient time to teach assistants the work. In addition, the attribute of concentrating on important matters rates high by many organization placement people. Furthermore, the manager is objective, not subjective; he deals with things as they are, not as he feels they should be. He recognizes the need for and knows when to compromise. Finally, the successful executive knows that there is a proper time for almost every action. Acting when the recipient is in a receptive mood is of invaluable aid in winning acceptance to managerial action. If the time isn't right, it is better to hold the proposed action in abeyance, for eventually the proper time will come, and then success is more likely.

An interesting list of fifteen managerial traits is shown by Figure 14–6. A manager cannot be selected by a scorecard, but lists of this sort serve as a general guide. To judge a human being is difficult especially when no attempt to measure him against some standardized factors is followed.[5]

From the written and specific job requirements and man requirements for managerial jobs, the formal organizer has information upon which to construct an organization structure in keeping with his wishes. As indicated above, the next step is to match as best possible the managerial job and the management member. This sounds quite simple, but it is seldom possible to find the wholly suited candidate who fulfills perfectly the specified total managerial job requirements. And even with time the "reasonably good" candidate may not match the stated job specifications.

---

[5] See Chapter 22 for further discussion of use of managerial traits.

FIGURE 14–6.   Fifteen traits of fundamental significance in the success of a manager

---

A. Inborn Traits or Basic Equipment
  1. *Intelligence* as shown by I.Q. score, scholastic achievements, and honors.
  2. *Integrity* revealed by honesty and moral soundness.
  3. *Durability* or good physical fitness to withstand the rigors of managerial work.
  4. *Sensitivity* includes possession of both empathy and sympathy, consideration of others, both on and off the job.
  5. *Self-development drive* as identified by building up a record for solving tough assignments and seizing opportunities for self improvement.

B. Acquired Traits or Skills
  6. *Motivation* revealed by the demeanor of the people around a manager, the environment he creates, the will-to-do impressed upon others.
  7. *Communication* or the quality of expressing oneself clearly and succinctly and listening effectively.
  8. *Planning and organizing* as revealed by the group doing purposeful work, jobs clearly defined, and an energetic work force.
  9. *Teaching* or the ability to bring each individual up to his highest potential.
  10. *Salesmanship* as demonstrated by success in getting others to accept his ideas

C. Inborn and Acquired Traits
  11. *Decisiveness* or being able to make up his mind about what to do in a situation and selecting a choice of action.
  12. *Flexibility* encompasses the willingness to keep trying different means and approaches until the most satisfactory means is found.
  13. *Working with people* is the means by which a manager makes his contribution.
  14. *Will to win* or an instinctive drive to excel others.
  15. *Picking other managers* or the ability to select people who will eventually move up and perhaps even beyond the selector.

Source: *Personnel*, May/June 1971.   Used with permission of American Management Association, New York.

CURRENT STATUS OF FORMAL ORGANIZATION

The preciseness of formal organization, the rationale employed, and the nature of human beings, plus the power that they gain, preclude any perfect adaption by him to formal organization. Furthermore, during the last several decades, the advance in information about human relations, the changing attitude of society to the individual and to the group, and technological innovations have brought a strong impact upon formal organization. Man's judgment, understanding, and behavior, for example, performed in what he considers to be in the best interests of the company, may not coincide with what his superior or the formal organizer had in mind that he should do. We know that a manager brings his attitude and values with him to his job and these same characteristics influence his work, perception, and beliefs utilized in applying the modified management process approach. Further, the organization environment permits the manager to develop good attributes or acquire bad ones, satisfy his social needs or block them, and provide a sense of achievement and self-assertion or frustrate the manager in seeking these desires. Hence, for practical reasons, modification in the formal organization is taking place simply because all the details cannot be formally spelled out and we are dealing with human beings who interpret what they should do, are anxious to use their ideas, want recognition, and honestly feel they are improving and making the formal organization practical and workable under today's conditions. In the vernacular, "they want a piece of the organization action."

It will be helpful to summarize the underlying assumptions of formal organization. Relatively low levels of change in product and in technical change of production methods are assumed. Expertise in human relations is somewhat scarce and social conformity and subservience prevail. In addition, important communication is predominantly from the top to bottom level. Observe that there is some change assumed even though it may be slow and small. It seems reasonable to state that formal organization might well accommodate many certain current needs, but some ingenuity of managers may be required in adapting it to a particular current condition. At any rate, the formal organization serves as a basis from which a modified, hybrid, or even a revolutionary form of organization can be evolved.

UNDERLYING REASONS FOR MODIFYING FORMAL ORGANIZATION

In all the history of organizing, there appears the eternal question of proper balance between organizational efficiency and individual freedom. Scholars have never agreed precisely on what the proper balance is or how it should be accomplished. Some have envisioned individual man as selfish and aggressive and hence advocate groups of men organized to preserve peace, order, a desirable ethical conduct, and to achieve economical and social gains. But, in any organization that defends, protects, and makes possible the achievement of greater goals than otherwise possible, can the individual uniting himself with the group remain practically as free as before? The challenge is to obtain a balance of individual initiative and freedom of action with guidance and restraint. And to do this can all the members participate satisfactorily in the decision-making process concerning that organization?

The general nature of organization gives rise to the problem for we are concerned with imponderables dealing with the interactions among the characteristics of men and the task climates provided by organization. In the overall, do we gain more from permitting motivational situations within which man behaves or from carefully defined relationships known to all and to which the individual, if necessary, must adopt? That is to say, all things considered, does man live the best life, economically, psychologically, and socially, by working and behaving within a carefully prescribed and rational work situation, or does he find more comfort in relatively unstructured situations in which people form and re-form into different work-oriented groups to perform present tasks and plan to overcome future work problems?

FIGURE 14–7

Perhaps we should approach possible modifications from the viewpoint of the objectives sought from our organizing work. In this respect Figure 14–7 depicts some of the basic issues. For example, in organizing do we want to stress change or stability, people satisfaction or task satisfaction, people to organization, or organization to people? It is possible to view change in an organization as being in any one of these three categories: (1) structure, (2) motivation, or (3) technology. A change in any one affects the other two. For example, structure change might result in motivation improvement; that is, the improved motivation comes about by resolving conflicts stemming from structural organizational relationships. In this instance, the improvement was not a matter of simply getting the employee to strive more intensely. Likewise technological change, such as computerizing much information and routine decision making, quite often results in organization structure change.

Perhaps of all the major reasons for modifying formal organization, the one of greatest importance is the influence and the importance of people upon organization. Organization requires human beings to assume obligations, make decisions, and to execute the work. Regardless of whether the discussion is about duties, organization relationships, or interactions, the important concept is that organization deals with human beings and is a means for people to work together effectively and harmoniously toward achieving stated goals. The different personalities, interests, ambitions, and abilities of these human beings are brought together and mixed by organizing so that the sum total or composite of the total members of the group is reflected by the organization structure. But in addition this sum total is modified by the interaction with one another. Cooperative patterns and various adjustments take place among the members of the group that is organized, and eventually there evolves a way of operating and collaborating which becomes "the way" approved and sanctioned by each member of the group. And this mode of operation may modify or be in addition to the basic formal organization.

It seems certain that we will have organization changes in the future. The effect of behavioral science, technology, government, and education will necessitate greater adaptability and flexibility. Some departmentation will serve as the basis of organization activities, but the basis of the pattern may shift in keeping with contemporary needs. Yet it appears that the formal organization featuring the dividing of tasks and arranging them in some pattern will remain, for this appears basic for effective group actions striving for common goals.

OTHER ORGANIZING THEORIES

Efforts to improve organization have led to many different approaches and theories of organization. Some tend to modify the formal organization, others to eliminate it. Brief comments on the fusion theory, the systems theory, and the quantitative theory of organization will be included, followed by prominent and important developments from the behavioral approach to organizing.

These theories and contributions have been developed as the result of study, experience, and viewpoints assumed. The methods used, constraints considered, along with predominant background in economics, psychology, sociology, anthropology, or mathematics, influence the theory propounded. In brief, one can view organizing essentially as either an economic, behavioral, adaptive, mathematical, or decisional entity. In the aggregate most of these theories are concerned with structure, behavior, and strategy under conditions of change and complexity brought about by technology, environment, and human behavior.

The fusion theory of organization stresses the existence and action of a fusion process in organizing. Advocates state that an organization attempts to use the individual to further its goals, and vice versa, the individual hopes to achieve his goals by using the organization. Emphasis is upon behavior, dealing largely with role, not job, modification. The individual seeks, for example, possession of means, harmony, freedom of decision, and optimum performance by a "personalizing process." In turn, the organization provides a "socializing process," illustrated by work assignment and the practice of rewards and penalties. The "fusion process" brings about the fusion of the personalizing and the socializing processes.

Under the systems theory organizing is viewed as a system of mutually dependent variables. It is similar in approach to the systems school of management thought discussed in Chapter 4. The basic parts of the organizing system are (1) the individual, (2) the formal organization or arrangement of functions, (3) the informal organization, (4) reciprocal patterns of behavior arising from role demands of the organization and role perception of the individual, and (5) the physical environment in which the work is performed.[6] The area of application of the theory can be extensive, both within and without the enterprise, or it can be intensive, applying to a specific and definite group. The terms *open system* and *closed system* identify these possibilities. Linking the basic parts are communication, balance or system parts maintained in harmonious relationship with each other, and decision making.

Another is the quantitative theory which provides an aura of objectivity to the study of organizing, even though it covers only a portion of the considerations that affect organizing work. For example, leadership, environment, and communication are excluded in the analysis. These pose difficulties in measuring, but of course, available arbitrary values can be either derived or assumed and utilized in the theory. Countable factors are employed for such factors as size of organization unit, number of decisions made by each manager, and the amount of work produced. No doubt mathematical models will be perfected for the study

---

[6] Informal organization is discussed on p. 316.

of organizing. In fact, some very interesting work is being done in this area, but as yet it does not constitute a complete theory.[7]

A most inclusive and influential effect upon organizing is the contributions of the behavioral scientists. Let us now turn our attention to this area.

NONFORMAL ORGANIZATION

Existing within formal organization is nonformal organization that permits and sometimes encourages behavior by members not intended or included in the formal organization. This nonformal behavior cannot only be desirable, which frequently it is, but it is also work oriented and contributes significantly to efficiency. Behavioral factors such as unnecessary socializing on the job, group values, and cultural likes and dislikes serve as bases for nonformal behavior in formal organization. These unintended conditions permit the examination of behavior in terms of *dysfunctions*, which are the characteristics or aspects of formal organization that cause unintended or unanticipated behavior. Dysfunctions are many, but probably structure, differentiation as to the type of decisions different members can make, and specification of work processes are of greatest importance.

Structure, for example, may give rise to communication blocks—by slighting prescribed channels or by the subordinate not revealing complete information to his superior because the subordinate believes it is to his best interest not to report bad news or poor results to his superior, especially if the superior evaluates performance of subordinates. In other words, the formal organization itself may tend to generate unanticipated behavior. Or consider the effect of formally spelled-out work processes. They can be dysfunctional in that they may not be applicable to all situations of the job, may cover the job only partially, or may conflict with orders given by a specialist. A person tends to condition any job that he occupies. He brings more than a physical body to perform prescribed work motions. Also present are impressions, interests, ambition, views, and feelings toward his job, compeers, superiors, subordinates, as well as all these toward him.

Nonformal organization always exists along with formal organization. It serves as an adjunct, is intangible, and takes on different degrees of importance depending upon the activity and the person involved. A

---

[7] For interesting accomplishments, see Rocco Carzo, Jr., and John N. Yanouzas, *Formal Organization—A Systems Approach* (Homewood, Ill.: Dorsey Press, 1967), chaps. 9, 11, and 13.

manager should be aware of the presence and influence of nonformal organization.

INFORMAL ORGANIZATIONS

There is also informal organization which is quite a different concept from either formal or nonformal organization. Whenever people work together there evolve informal groups bound together by common social, technological, work, or goal interests. Such a group constitutes an informal organization. It conditions many actions set forth by the formal and nonformal organizations and must be reckoned with in managerial organization.

The specific determinants of informal groups are usually interests, similarity of work, and physical location. Employees having common interests tend to seek each other, discuss their common interests, and socialize. Man likes to be with people he knows and, in turn, know him. Having mutual interests helps bring about this favorable condition. Performing the same type of work is a common determinant of informal groups. Here again there is a mutuality among such employees; they have job satisfactions that are common, confront similar problems, and talk about subjects high on each other's priority lists. Likewise, location is important. Frequent face-to-face meetings and being in close proximity while at work influence who is in an informal group and who is not. There are also other determinants including almost any common course which the person feels is important to him. Usually groups formed because of these "other determinants" are temporary and disintegrate after an objective or want has been satisfied or no longer exists. In contrast, groups formed because of interests, similarity of work, and physical location tend to be permanent.

Nothing destroys these informal groups for the very action of grouping people together to work toward common goals gives rise to these groups. It is in the nature of human behavior and of organization. Hence, a manager should utilize the informal organization because it is a part of his total organization facility. He should, for example, point out to the informal leader his views and support them with his reasons why, release accurate information, listen when the leader of the informal group speaks, and prior to making a decision, consult with the group on matters which are of deep concern to them.

To determine the structure of an informal group, analysis taking into account the measurement of social elements and interpersonal relationships is used. For example, an individual's expression of preference to associate with others who enhance his feeling of satisfaction and personal worth is given high priority. For survival, the informal group requires continuing relationships among its members, and it has communication of its own variety, usually entirely apart from the formal communication prescribed by the formal organization. Further, it has what might be termed a scale of status values peculiar to itself. It also has a leader. Identifying and determining the characteristics of this leader have been subjected to much study, and a considerable amount of information on this subject is available.

THE BEHAVIOR VIEWPOINT

What we are saying is that the formal organization with its hierarchy of positions and tasks, is constantly being modified by the behavior of an individual member or of a group membership. Within the formal organization are inexorable forces which give rise to the nonformal organization and the informal organization. Back of the formal organization are the invisible nonformal and informal organizations through which much of the work is accomplished and no enterprise can exist without them. In some cases only these adjunct organizations will permit timely action. A vast number of contacts are made among people in the nonformal and informal organizations to solve problems, pass information along, and to achieve certain goals. Ideally, these adjunct organizations are compatible with the formal organization. However, with their ever-shifting and undefined structures, the nonformal and informal organizations are vulnerable to manipulation and opportunism. And it is commonly difficult to detect these perversions which can do considerable harm if not corrected.

Hence, it is paramount to understand why people behave as they do and especially within the organization environment. Behavior and beliefs of people result in patterns called "cultures" by the behavioral scientists. All organizations have cultures which affect the conduct and the working of people together. A significant aspect of culture is the way it develops informally in an organization.

Much of our behavior is the result of custom. We get used to doing things in a certain manner, never really giving it much thought, let alone being rational or consciously determining a way of behavior. Customs become formulated mainly by means of experience. If we do a certain task a certain way and normally get certain acceptable results, we are inclined to do the same task in the same manner whenever it arises. In short, we develop a custom to be followed for this type of task.

Customs become established with use. Simply to define duties and authority does not make them customary behavior; they have to be accepted in actual use. Normally, if formal plans and instructions are not insisted upon by the manager, the subordinate will evolve the work pattern, and with usage this pattern will become the custom. When emphasis is placed on results and the results via custom are satisfactory, the importance of informal employee behavior in management is easily discernible.

In addition, most people have mental images of how an employee in a certain job should behave i.e., what his role is. We expect a production control manager to behave in a certain way and a sales manager to behave in a different way. These expected roles tend to influence the actions of their occupants. To fulfill expectancies, i.e., acquire acceptance socially by other members of the organization, most people strive to play the role expected of them. We dislike the director of research making light of basic research results obtained by members of his department or the company medical doctor not behaving as a true professional in his chosen line of work.

What can be done when there are honest differences in the desirability of an existent strong custom or in the formal concept of a job in comparison to the incumbent's views based on his experience and preferences? With time, these differences will probably change, but it is unrealistic to expect them either to change rapidly or perhaps to move eventually in a direction exactly in keeping with the manager's wishes. The manager may find that his best action is to get to know the members' behavior patterns better and figure out ways to utilize them. Or corrective change, as he sees it, may be preferred, but this may be unreasonably difficult, take too much time, and cost many dollars. However, if some modifications in behavior appear feasible, he may take any or all of the following actions: (1) explain what change is desired and give complete reasons for the change, (2) relate specifically how the change will benefit both the organization and the incumbent, (3) give examples and provide opportunities to demonstrate the suggested new behavior, and (4) encourage with rewards the incumbent when he adopts the new for the old behavior.

Many believe that organization enhances favorably the behavior of a person, or at least the benefits outweigh the deficits. They argue that great personalities, leaders, and truths are made more effective by organization. The development, support, and accomplishment of worthwhile goals are made possible by organization in which most members progress, the big men become bigger, and great men become greater.

Without organization, they would descend rather than ascend. Individuals are more effective and satisfied in an organizational behavior because organization supplies the needed facility for group study, cooperation, and mutual assistance, while at the same time it places the individual in a situation that challenges, stimulates, and develops his behavior so that it is favorable both to himself and to mankind.

SOCIAL REQUIREMENTS AND ORGANIZATION

The increasing attention being directed to behavioral aspects in organization has likewise brought emphasis to the societal factors of this function of management. Today organizing cannot be thought of strictly as a logical and economic activity. It is also a social entity as well as an economic arrangement. The justification for any organization is to provide goods or services required or desired by the society of which the organization is a part. And it must have the financial means to operate and survive. But in addition, if organization is to serve and be a part of society, it needs to supply not only economic wants but also social and psychological needs of its members that should come from being a part of an organization.

From the viewpoint of social-psychological behavior, organizing represents a major part of environment from which stimuli emit that affect most people. In brief, from his environment, influences affect the individual who, in turn, responds to these influences. Hence, his behavior is conditioned by the organization of which he is a part. Likewise, he affects the organization. There is interaction between the individual and the organization; he becomes imbedded in the organization and features of the organization became embedded in him. He may be stimulated by the organization to accomplish what he did not believe possible for him or, in contrast, suppressed by his organization stimuli to perform only what is required "to get by" and to say things he doesn't mean.

The pressure of social groups upon the behavior of its members can be substantial. Conformity to a group's standard is an outstanding example. The individual receives some of his job satisfactions through group responses. To get too far removed from the group's standards can mean that the group's approval and acceptance of him may be lost. Furthermore, this conformity to a group's standards is illustrated by holding factory output to an accepted level informally set by the group. The individual member who exceeds it is promptly reminded of what the acceptable level of production is. This is a social group determinative. Interestingly the reverse situation is frequently found among a group of salesmen where higher and higher sales are sought and accepted by the group as approved behavior. In fact, the behavior of low sales producers may be viewed with disdain by the group members.

Changes tend to be accepted with a minimum of resistance when the change is initiated from within the group. People usually dislike change that destroys that to which they have become accustomed, primarily because the change is likely to break up established social relationships. In other words, we usually dislike giving up known present satisfactions for unknown future satisfactions. It should also be noted that typically the group supplies many beliefs and values to its individual members. In essence, the group influences attitudes toward many matters. For example, the prevailing belief of an individual frequently stems not from his personal knowledge or conviction about a matter, but from statements and "truths" provided by the group of which he is, or wants to be, a part.

Ignoring these social considerations is, in part, the answer to why a formal arrangement of functions according to a well-conceived, rational pattern does not assure automatically that sought results will be realized or that arrangement X will prove superior to arrangement Y purely because the activities in X are grouped more effectively. The simple truth is that the effect of the human beings and their social groups play a vital role in whether the results of organizing prove a success or a failure. What employees do to and for each other, their commonness of purpose, and their ability to make sound judgments and initiate proper action are fundamental considerations in the effectiveness of an organization.

Since in the nature of things, social entities crop up and develop when people work together, it seems wise from the standpoint of management to utilize these social groups to accomplish our work goals. The first requirement to achieve this end is to view the social customs, roles, and other influential social forces as having the potential of serving the best interests of organizing. We may conclude, after careful investigation, that existent social groups should be the main entities about which an organization is constructed or, in contrast, that existent social groups should be modified to support better the formal organization. It is folly to ignore the social entities of organization or to believe that they have no effect upon organization.

ORGANIZATION CHARTS

Before closing this chapter, a few more pertinent facts about organization charts should be added to what was stated earlier. Organization charts are helpful tools of organizing. They assist in visualizing the formal organization, but their use does not insure a good organization structure.

Organization charts can be conveniently divided into (1) master charts and (2) supplementary charts. The first, or master chart, shows the entire formal organization structure. The second, or supplementary chart, is devoted exclusively to a department or major component and gives more details as to relationships and duties within that prescribed area.

The customary arrangement of an organization chart is to show the major functions at the top, with successive subordinate functions in successively lower positions. This is the arrangement shown earlier in Figure 14–2. But this is not the only way. Additional arrangements are (1) left-to-right and (2) circular. These are shown in Figure 14–8. In the left-to-right chart, the organization levels are represented by vertical columns, the flow of formal communication is from left to right. While not in common usage, the left-to-right chart offers advantages, including it (1) follows the normal reading habit of going from left to right, (2) visualizes the various organization levels clearly, (3) simplifies the understanding of how lines of command flow, (4) reveals quickly areas where organization levels are omitted by formal supervisory channels, (5) indicates relative length of lines of formal command, and (6) is compact and relatively simple to construct.

The circular chart places the supreme position in the center of concentric circles. Functions making up the structure are clustered around this center in such a manner that the closer the position of the function to the center, the more important the function. Advantages of the circular chart include that it (1) portrays the actual condition of outward flow of formal command from the chief executive in many directions; (2) shows functions of equal importance clearly; (3) utilizes one dimension—from the center out—to indicate relative functional importance (the somewhat confusing "down from where" or "over from what" is eliminated); and (4) eliminates the undesirable concepts of bottom of the chart, top of chart, and the like, since a circular chart can be viewed from any direction.

TITLES

For a single enterprise, a hierarchy of titles is expedited by use of an organization chart for it helps gain acceptance and gives meaning of the titles to all members of the enterprise. However, there are no standardized titles in relationship either to organization level or job content.

FIGURE 14–8. Left-to-right (below) and circular (facing page) arrangements of organization charts

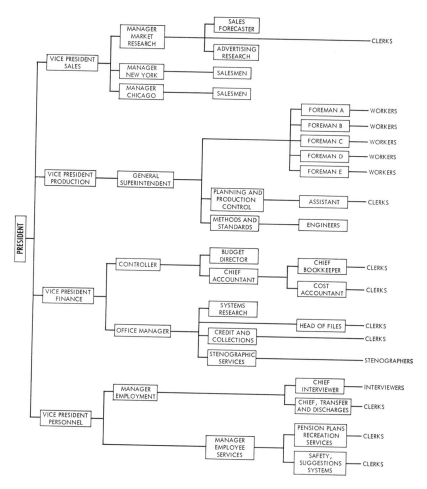

For example, the executive in charge of sales might be termed sales manager, general sales manager, director of distribution, or vice president in charge of sales. Furthermore he can be at the top or intermediate organization level, and even though he is "sales manager," he may not perform precisely the same functions as other sales managers in other enterprises.

Preferably a title should serve two purposes: (1) help identify and define the nature of the work and its relative importance, and (2) indicate that the person possessing the title is competent and qualified to perform the tasks required in that position. Unless these purposes are

FIGURE 14–8 (continued)

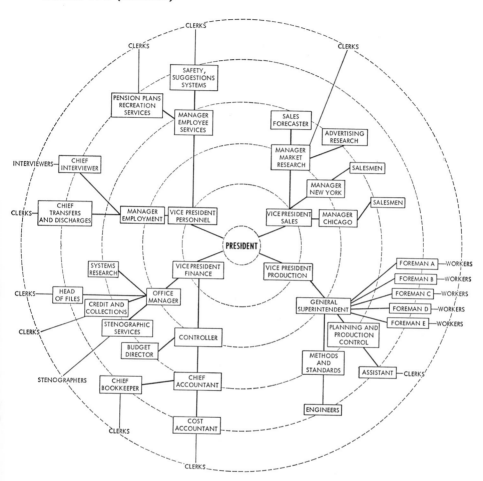

fulfilled, a title can be extremely confusing to both the work force and the general public. A title is in the nature of a confidence; it signifies trust and faith in the individual and in his ability to see that the work is satisfactorily performed. It is not an embellishment, for to have worth-while significance a title must be earned by the individual.

QUESTIONS

1. What is your reaction to the following definition: "Organizing is a mechanism of an enterprise that neutralizes those forces which prevent cooperative efforts by its employees?" Elaborate on your answer.
2. Enumerate and discuss the four basic components of formal organization.

3. Should an organization be so designed that it fits the personalities involved or should the individuals be required to adjust to the organization structure? Justify your answer.
4. With reference to Figure 14–6, rate yourself on each of the 15 traits by scoring from 5 to 1 points for each trait (5 is maximum) depending on your judgment. What interpretation do you give your results? Elaborate on your answer.
5. Discuss the general characteristics of formal organizing.
6. What is the meaning of each of the following: (*a*) manager specifications, (*b*) nonformal organization, (*c*) synergism of organizing, (*d*) left-to-right organization chart, and (*e*) dysfunctions?
7. Discuss the major reasons for wanting to change or to modify formal organizing. Do you feel formal organizing should be modified? Why?
8. Discuss the fusion theory of organizing, pointing out its salient features.
9. Discuss several social requirements of an organization, pointing out their major significance to a manager.
10. Discuss the behavioral viewpoint toward organizing and include in your answer in what ways this viewpoint influences an organizer's thoughts and actions.
11. With reference to Figure 14–2, answer the following: (*a*) Does the organization appear to be logical? (*b*) Does this chart represent the total organization of the corporation? (*c*) In your opinion would it be an improvement to (1) move the marketing staff so that it is under U.S. automotive sales? (2) combine the administrative staff and the management organization and systems staff? In each case give reasons for your answers.
12. Discuss the meaning, activity, and importance of informal organization.
13. Enumerate some social considerations pertinent in the study of organizing.
14. What is conceptual skill of a manager and how is it used in organizing?

CASE 14–1. FAIRMONT COMPANY

Vice President of Finance Walter Miles has three people reporting directly to him: the manager of general accounting, Harry Knapp; the manager of data processing, Charles Laferty; and Edward Pitts, the manager of cost accounting. Mr. Miles is known as a hard but fair manager. He listens to problems brought to him and assists his people in solving them. But he doesn't tolerate "back talk" and feels most meetings are a waste of time. He insists upon accuracy and completion of all reports and records on or before their due date. There are carefully stated job descriptions for each job and Mr. Miles follows them to the letter. His job as he sees it is to manage according to the wishes of his superior and the regulations and requirements contained in the several manuals available to all finance management personnel.

Harry Knapp follows the general mode of operations demonstrated by Mr. Miles. Although there is no official assistant to Mr. Miles, through seniority of ten years, Harry Knapp is considered next in line after Mr. Miles. Productivity is the key to success as Mr. Knapp sees it. He has work expectancies for each of his employees and evaluates each once a year to see if they need any help in attaining efficiency and to let them know they are doing all right, if such is the case. In Mr. Miles' opinion, general accounting is the best managed of his three units.

Charles Laferty has been with the company about 1½ years. He is a friend of Edward Pitts who used his influence to help Mr. Laferty get his present job. At that time, the then and still assistant of the department, James Harding, thought he should have had the job. He along with others in the department did not favor bringing in an outsider, but more important, he believed he was well qualified for the promotion as his work record was excellent. As the son-in-law of the works manager with whom Mr. Miles does not get along too well, Mr. Harding feels this is at least part of the explanation why he was not promoted.

Since joining the company, Mr. Laferty has offered several suggestions for improving his department. Mr. Miles has listened intently but to date has not given him any "go-ahead" permission. Mr. Laferty pays a great deal of attention to the suggestions offered by Mr. Pitts. They eat lunch together and their families visit each other about every other week. James Harding knows this and feels Ed Pitts is interfering in data processing work. He recognizes that cost accounting is well managed and Ed is doing acceptable work or he would not have been with the company for 7 years.

About two months ago, Mr. Laferty injured himself in a skiing accident and was absent from work for 5 weeks, during which period Jim Harding took over. His work, however, was not satisfactory in the opinion of Mr. Miles. "Jim simply doesn't follow orders" is the way Mr. Miles expressed it. Mr. Pitts made several attempts to help Jim Harding but was not warmly received. In fact, on the last occasion, Mr. Harding reported the incident to Mr. Miles who promptly told Mr. Pitts to stay in his own department. Mr. Miles was glad to see Mr. Laferty return to work.

During the next several weeks, Mr. Laferty was not physically up to par. He found it difficult to concentrate. Work in his department began to pile up and the inability to meet schedules caused inconvenience and difficulties in the other departments. Mr. Miles called Mr. Laferty to his office and told him things would have to improve quickly. James Harding, hearing of this, offered to work overtime and relieve Mr. Laferty of some of his duties. Mr. Miles did not reply to his offer.

Last Saturday morning, Edward Pitts was helping Mr. Laferty in his

office. Several other data processing personnel were also working overtime. While Mr. Laferty was checking some old records in the storage
room, James Harding walked in the department and saw Ed Pitts working there.

HARDING: You're working in my department, Mr. Pitts?

PITTS: Yes, we need some cost data processed.

HARDING: What job are you . . . .

(Laferty joins them)

HARDING (continuing): Good morning, Mr. Laferty. You're also working today and Mr. Pitts is helping you?

LAFERTY: We must get this work out.

HARDING: Well, I'm willing to help, but you didn't ask me.

Questions

1. What is the problem?
2. Will formal organizing meet the company's needs satisfactorily? Why?
3. What would you do if you were James Harding? Mr. Miles?
4. What action do you recommend the company take? Justify your answer.

CASE 14–2. PRYOR FOUNDRY, INC.

Metal castings of different sizes and shapes are made by Pryor
Foundry, Inc., located in a town of about 10,000 persons, south of Chicago. The town's population is made up of a number of different na-
tionality groups. The foundry help at Pryor Foundry, Inc. is composed
of three fairly distinct groups—German, Polish, and Romanian. Employees in the department of pattern making and designing of molds are
almost all German; those in the mold-building and casting department
are mainly Polish; and those in the cleaning and chipping department
are predominantly Romanian. There are, of course, a few others in these
three departments who are not members of any of these ethnic groups.

For each department, an informal leader exists and he assists in clarifying communications from management members and in maintaining
a satisfactory work output. When a job opening occurs within his group,
this informal leader takes it upon himself to find a man for the job—
always from his ethnic group. Management has no objection to this as
dependable help seemed to be acquired in this way and the group appeared to want it this way.

About two months ago, Arthur Leposki, engineering graduate of
Illiani University and son of an employee in the mold-building and casting department, was hired as an assistant production engineer to work
on new business development. His father had mentioned the availability

of his son to his group leader, who in turn asked the works manager that the young man be given serious consideration for the job. Included in the duties of an assistant production engineer are the following: to expedite samples through the shop, to make changes believed essential for good castings, to suggest areas where new business could be obtained, and to lower the cost on work being processed. Mr. Leposki was hired and spent the first few weeks on his new job getting acquainted with the work and the employees. He was friendly, somewhat blunt, and quite serious about his new responsibilities. After about one month, he suggested several minor changes be followed. These caused some discord among the pattern makers, and one suggestion was dropped after Mr. Leposki's superior sensed that it might lead to increasing friction at a time when production had to be maintained.

A couple of weeks later, Mr. Leposki made a most unusual request of the pattern makers. It concerned a sample run of 15 castings which were of a somewhat unprecedented design. The pattern makers, somewhat reluctantly, did exactly what Mr. Leposki requested. Subsequently, the castings were poured, cleaned, and shipped to the customer. Within 10 days, vigorous complaints from the customer were received stating the castings were not acceptable, had failed in trial runs, and already represented a $47,000 loss to them. When word of this reached the employees of the department of pattern making and designing of molds, one pattern maker remarked, "What did I tell you? The design that Polish kid insisted upon will never work. I knew that all the time. But I do what I am told. That way I keep out of trouble. You can't tell this kid of those molders anything. They are all alike—stupid, know-it-all, and noisy."

Questions

1. What is the problem faced by Pryor Foundry, Inc.?
2. From the organizational point of view, is the presence of ethnic groups in the company desirable? Discuss.
3. As Arthur Leposki, what action would you take? Why?
4. What is your recommendation to this corporation? Discuss.

15

Authority
in management

One rooster can't help another scratch the same piece of ground.

AFRICAN PROVERB

ORGANIZED MANAGERIAL ACTION requires authority. It is extremely important in all organization study and operation. Authority conditions the actions and behavior of every management member in an enterprise and represents the vital link tying together the various organization units, thus making possible the existence of the organization and the effective working together of the total personnel.

CONCEPTS OF AUTHORITY

Authority is viewed by different people in a number of different ways. One popular viewpoint is that *authority is the official and legal right to command action by others and to enforce compliance.* Authority is exercised by making decisions and seeing that they are carried out. Compliance, however, is gained in a number of ways—through persuasion, sanctions, requests, coercion, constraint, or force.

Looking more closely at this concept of authority, we can state that a person with authority influences the activity of another individual or group or causes a different behavior by the individual or group than would otherwise take place. However, a person might have this influence without having authority, that is, no official or legal right to command and enforce action by others. We say such a person has *power.* He has no authority in the formal sense, yet he does influence behavior in others. This state of affairs has brought about modifications in the concept of authority and different viewpoints toward it as it relates to organization. We discuss the most important of these concepts in the following pages.

Historically the concept of authority is from the government and the military. The reasoning goes like this. Authority comes into being from ownership, organization status, or legal decree. Ownership includes the right to put property to use and direct how it is used, an arrangement having both legal and social approval. That is, the support is by approval that evolves from property laws. An employee not following an order can be removed from company property by court action and police, if he refuses to do so. Followers of this source of authority approval also believe that authority is conferred by formal organization status position or the relationships established. Failure is usually attributed to inadequate authority, which implies a lack of power conferred by organization position. Authority by legal decree is also possible, and this is commonly found in governmental formal organization. The law grants authority so that enforcement of the statute can be and is accomplished. It vests the officeholder with the necessary power to see that compliance with the stated legal requirements is met.

With the developments of additional theories about organizing and human behavior have come different concepts of authority. For example, changes have come about by recognizing the existence of nonformal behavior and informal groups within the formal organization structure. Some of these changes are minor modifications of the classical theory concept, while others are based on entirely different premises and beliefs. It is beyond the purpose of this book to exhaust all these authority concepts, but we will note what currently appears to be of most significance.

The term "subordinate-acceptance approach" can be employed to identify a viewpoint growing in importance. In this approach it is believed that authority comes to the manager by the acceptance of his power to make and enforce decisions by his subordinates. In other words, according to this approach a manager has no authority until it is conferred upon him by his subordinates. Acceptance by the subordinates is the key in this line of explanation and reasoning. In addition, it stresses the social and ethical aspects of authority. Leadership by the manager, for example, becomes highly significant because the manager's influence depends in great measure upon his ability to win support from his subordinates through such attributes as knowledge of human relations, technical skill, and communicative ability.

Why will a subordinate accept the authority exercised over him? The reasons are many. Among the most important are to gain approval and acceptance by fellow employees, to contribute to a cause or goal considered worthwhile, to avoid possible disciplinary action, to comply with moral standards considered proper, and to gain rewards. All of these are not exclusive with the acceptance approach, but they are emphasized in this approach. As a matter of fact, most advocates of the classical approach to authority believe that a manager *should win, not order,* the support of his subordinates and that there are important psychological and social limitations to authority.

In addition, there are those who view personal acceptance, gained through popularity and satisfactory past accomplishments, as the true source of authority. The employee having long association with the activity, a practical knowledge of it, plus competence to command respect and enthusiastic cooperation frequently finds himself with authority. A brilliant researcher in marketing, for example, may be frequently approached to give factual data concerning vital markets. From the viewpoint of the formal organization, he may have little or no authority; yet his answers carry so much weight and are so consistently followed that he appears to be one with extensive authority.

The term "authority of the situation" is sometimes encountered in management literature. In nearly every enterprise, emergency and unusual events occur which are not provided for in the regular organizational setup. When such an event occurs, the person assuming authority to meet the particular circumstances is said to have derived authority from the "authority of the situation." Such authority exists during the extent of the emergency only or until the person regularly charged with the authority assumes command over the unusual event. It can exist in any type of organizing.

There is also "position authority," which is essentially the authority a person has by virtue of the superior position he occupies in the organization. Normally, subordinates recognize authority of those occupying higher hierarchical positions. And to a great extent the recognition is extended regardless of who occupies the position. If an incompetent holds the position for a period of time, some disintegration of the position authority may take place, but subsequently when a capable successor takes over, the original position authority regains its previous high level.

Since about 1950, the term "computer authority," or "technical authority," has come into use. The term is suggestive of its meaning. Computer authority stems from the decision-making power granted to processed data by a computer. But authority is a human possession, and hence, computer authority can be defined as that authority possessed by the person who either interprets computer-processed data or points out their significant managerial meanings for others.

PSYCHOLOGICAL AND SOCIAL INFLUENCES UPON AUTHORITY

From what has been stated it follows that not all authority stems from economic bases; there are also psychological and social attributes influencing the concept of authority. From the formal organization point of view, two district sales managers having identical job descriptions might be considered to have the same authority. However, the actual authority of each may be quite different in that the mode of operations, decisions made, and willingness to accept direction and order from their superior, or sales manager, may differ significantly between the two.

The basis upon which one individual influences the behavior of another has been subjected to much study from which has been identified a number of factors believed responsible. Without going into an exhaustive discussion here, we can state that the following sources appear to be most important: (1) control of sanctions, (2) personal liking, (3) expertise, (4) legitimacy, and (5) coercion. Sanction can be defined as either a reward resulting from a willingness to respond favorably to a directive or a penalty exacted for failure to accept and follow a directive. In other words, a person's behavior within an organization is affected in part by the sanction utilized for or against him. In some instances the ultimate base of the authority for the sanction exists not with the superior but in another part of the organization or outside the organization. Personal liking is self-explanatory and is simply the human preference being followed for one individual over another. Expertise is recognition of excellence in a given area of endeavor to the degree that a willingness to follow orders issued by this learned source is practiced. This was mentioned above under types of authority as exemplified by the brilliant researcher in marketing. By legitimacy is meant formal authority existing within the formal organization and includes job titles, general decision-making rights, and accepted power granted to the holder of a formally defined position. Coercion is the use of force. The subordinate is compelled or restrained by force such as law and police enforcement to abide by orders.

Note that both formal and informal leaders use these means to adjust their actual authority. Also, a manager with limited authority may become very influential through personal liking and expertise. And informal leaders may have much influence over their associates even though such leaders have no formal legitimacy.

Status is a major consideration in maintaining authority. By status is meant the totality of attributes that rank and relate members in an organization. Compliance with directives is expedited because status rationalizes degrees of inequality and generally a person is inclined to take orders from one he believes superior to himself. Status tends to reinforce the authority relationship. Among the many psychological and social factors affecting status, custom provides perhaps the best-known symbols of status. For example, persons occupying higher positions, or those of the top organization levels, usually but not always have a higher status than those in the lower positions. A certain function in a particular organization may have high status, while in another organization the same function may have a relatively small status. To illustrate, the purchasing manager may enjoy high status in a mail-order house, but very little in an automobile assembly plant. Additional means to identify status include insignias, uniforms, titles, and special facilities. Insignias in a military organization, for example, are a common denominator of status throughout the organization. Vestments of church officiants, black robes of judges, as well as uniforms of certain hospital management personnel are formal symbols of status. Scalar rank in an organization has long been indicated by titles. A person with the title of executive vice president is known to exert more authority than a person with the title of foreman or group leader. Also, special facilities provided reveal status. The ornate office, the richly upholstered chair, the more luxurious carpeting, and access to the special dining room with longer lunch periods are illustrative.

It is well to add that authority in organization is supported and sustained by society. The first years of a human's life are conditioned by his parents. The child initially resents this intervention, but gradually begins to accept the authority imposed upon him and obeys without too much question. Later this conditioning is duplicated and reinforced when he enters school and by other subsequent group experiences. All these experiences tend to reinforce the authority relationships in an organization of business, a hospital, or the armed forces. Doing what the superior says tends to be habitual for many but not all people. In addition, there are social sanctions imposed and these become the accepted way of doing things in that if they are not followed, consequences beyond the penalties imposed within the organization take place. Of course, there are differences of opinion regarding these social conditioning processes as well as questions regarding to what social forces a child should be subjected and to what extent should he accept decisions of a superior. For our purposes here, the point is simply that society does influence the authority functioning in an organization and in important ways.

LIMITS OF AUTHORITY

Traditionally we have viewed unlimited authority as an instrument of possible corruption. For centuries man has placed constraints on the acts of those in authority. In the modern business organization, for example, it is common to find that two or more management members must concur on certain issues before they are put into effect. The manager in charge of finance and the controller agree on the financing program before it is adopted, and a supervisor's recommendation for a pay increase for one of his men must normally be approved by the personnel manager to become effective.

There are specific limits of authority. No one, not even a manager, can decide and enforce an activity which is beyond the capacity, either mentally or physically, of the subordinate to perform. A manager ordering a shop employee to life manually an object weighing 1,800 pounds cannot enforce compliance with the order. Nor will the object be lifted even though the subordinate agrees with the request. Likewise, a manager cannot expect compliance to a request for a stockroom helper to operate a gear-cutting machine. Such managerial decisions should not be made, because their enforcement is beyond the capacity of the subordinates to perform.

Authority must also be in keeping with the accepted plans of an enterprise. In most cases, an objective cannot be ignored or a policy modified simply because a manager says to do so. Many management members have found that efforts to get certain changes made meet with seemingly endless difficulties. The articles of incorporation, established precedents, and long-standing implied agreements utilized in company affairs may place serious restrictions on the manager's exercise of his authority. This is not to suggest that changes cannot be made. They can, but usually not at the caprice of a manager.

In addition there are many social limitations to the use of authority by a manager. The activities being ordered must be in keeping with the group's fundamental social beliefs, codes, creeds, and habits; otherwise the effective power of the exerciser of authority is limited. These social limitations upon authority are both within and without an enterprise.

In the case of labor unions and collective bargaining, for example, the right to collective bargaining is affirmed in the United States by several federal statutes which aim to protect the interests of employers, employees, and the general public. From the viewpoint of limitation of authority of a person having property, employers, under the present labor law, cannot interfere with the employees' right to bargain or not to bargain collectively as they choose. Employers cannot interfere with the establishing or the operating of labor unions, nor can an employer refuse to bargain collectively with his employees. He is not free to do with his property as he pleases. But care must be taken to distinguish the crucial issues involved, which are who uses the property and under what conditions are they used. Property includes such things as machines, tools, and materials. It does not include employees; they are human beings.

RESPONSIBILITY DEFINED

At this point of our discussion on authority, we need to inject another important concept concerning organizing. This concept is responsibility. In the formal theory of organizing, *responsibility is the obligation of an individual to carry out assigned activities to the best of his ability.* It is what one is expected to do in order to carry out his prescribed job. Responsibility may be continuing or it may terminate with the accomplishment of a single action.

However, this concept of formal responsibility is being modified as, for example, when results management is used, the meaning of responsibility becomes: *Responsibility is the obligation of a person to achieve the results mutually determined by means of participation by his superior and himself.*

Some managers consider responsibility as having two parts or phases. The one is the obligation to carry out assigned activities to achieve results; the other is to account to a superior for the degree of success achieved in completing the prescribed work. The former is, of course, the formal organizational concept. The latter is also to a degree, but it, too, implies some of the modified organization thinking affecting organizing.

COEQUALITY OF AUTHORITY AND RESPONSIBILITY

The authority and responsibility of any manager should be coequal. In other words, responsibility is the inseparable twin of authority. Hence, a manager's authority gives him the power to make and enforce decisions concerning his assigned or defined duties and his responsibility places the obligation upon him to perform these duties by using this authority. It follows that authority and responsibility of any manager are fundamental and are very closely related.

From the management viewpoint, authority without responsibility lacks an ultimate purpose or justification for existing. Likewise, responsibility without authority to carry out the assigned duties has a hollow ring. A manager cannot perform assigned duties if he lacks the necessary authority to see that the work is accomplished. On the other hand, his failure to assume responsibility for the fulfillment of the assigned duties is equally a bad managerial situation. That is, for any manager, authority must be matched with responsibility, and vice versa, responsibility must be matched with authority.

Authority can be looked upon as the regulator. In other words, the amount and extent of authority tend to establish the amount and extent of responsibility. To illustrate, when authority is less than responsibility, the tendency is for responsibility to be reduced to the level of the authority. This follows because a manager without adequate authority to secure compliance for decisions reached in connection with fulfillment of his duties is, in the ultimate, being relieved of that responsibility by corresponding authority. Conversely, when authority is greater than responsibility, the tendency is for responsibility to be increased to the level of authority. If this does not take place, the situation, as pointed out above, is bad. Encouragement for the manager to assume more responsibility compatible with his authority is needed. A reduction in authority, however, might be in order. Authority and responsibility are teammates— one without coequality and coexistence of the other is unsound.

PRINCIPLE OF AUTHORITY AND RESPONSIBILITY

For sound organizational relationships the authority of a manager should be commensurate with his responsibility and, vice versa, his responsibility commensurate with his authority.

It is important to point out that this coequality of authority and responsibility is achieved by means of modifying the process management approach by results management. When this is done, the member's participation in determining his goals and being held to achieve them answers the problem of how to get authority to the one held responsible or vice versa, how to get responsibility to the one who has authority.

THE SOURCE OF RESPONSIBILITY

Responsibility comes into existence when a person with authority, or a manager, accepts the obligation to perform work and starts to utilize his authority. The viewpoint taken here is that authority is the essential management entity to organizing. To achieve goals, the use of authority gives rise to the acceptance of the obligations for these goal attainments and it is these obligations that give rise to responsibility.

The acceptance of an obligation to perform work can take several forms. In a business enterprise it is the employee's agreement to accept employment and perform certain services. Generally, being given the job provides the authority to perform it. In a charitable or similar enterprise, it may be a simple written agreement or an oral statement or even an act that signifies the employee's or member's acceptance of the obligation to carry out certain work.

IMPORTANCE OF FIXED RESPONSIBILITY

Fixed responsibility means that acceptance of the obligation for the performance of a function places the obligation squarely upon the person making the acceptance. It is up to this person to carry out the function promptly and efficiently. The fixation of definite responsibility is important because it helps to develop the acceptor, assists in getting the work accomplished, points out areas needing remedial action, and minimizes buckpassing. It requires the individual so designated to perform the task.

Most persons like to measure up to the requirements of their jobs. When held completely responsible for a task, a person will execute his best efforts. He wants to come through and to demonstrate that he is competent and able. Fixed responsibility tends to develop initiative, resourcefulness, and reliability. Obstacles are overcome, problems are solved, and the immediate chief interest becomes one of successfully completing the task.

The managerial coordination of tasks within an organization structure is assisted by the fixation of definite responsibility. Knowing who is responsible for what work and when helps to locate the proper person for a specific task quickly and directly. Furthermore, areas where additional help or training appear necessary can be identified with a minimum of delay.

Principle of Fixed Responsibility

For any given period, an individual will accomplish most when responsibility for the completion of a definite task is fixed upon that individual.

DELEGATION OF AUTHORITY

Delegation of authority is essential to the existence of a formal organization. Organizational units require the delegation of authority to their respective managers so that they can manage their respective units. Without delegation the chief executive, or president, would be the only management member of an enterprise. There would be only on department, and an organization structure would be absent. We can look upon delegation as a necessity wherever a manager must rely on another to help accomplish an objective.

To delegate means to grant or confer; and in this discussion, delegation means conferring authority from one executive or organizational unit to another in order *to accomplish particular assignments*. A manager does not *just delegate authority*. He delegates authority to get certain work accomplished. He does not delegate to give the delegatee a title as some symbol of authority. By means of delegation an executive extends his area of operations, for without delegation his actions are confined to what he, himself, can perform.

In management, delegating does not mean to give away or to surrender authority. A manager delegating always retains his overall authority for the assigned functions whether he wishes to or not. Delegation does not mean the permanent release from these obligations but rather the granting of rights and approval for others to operate within prescribed areas. That is to say, delegation has a dual characteristic, because as a result of delegation the subordinate receives authority from his superior, but at the same time his superior still retains all of his original authority. It is something like imparting knowledge. You share with others who then possess the knowledge, but you still retain the knowledge too.

For example, a sales manager delegates selling functions to his salesmen, but he retains authority for seeing that sufficient purchase orders are secured. In turn, the authority of the sales manager is delegated by the president of the company, who is obligated for all major functions of the company; and this authority cannot be delegated permanently to anyone. In essence, a chain of correlated authority is established, extending from each delegator to delegatee level throughout the entire formal organization structure.

Customarily, delegation is considered as being from a higher to a lower level, but it can also be from a lower to a higher level or between levels on the same plane. In other words, *delegation can be downward, upward, or sidewise*. Downward delegation of authority is illustrated by

a sales manager to his salesmen, upward delegation by state governments to the federal government, and sidewise delegation by certain
churches in a federation of churches.

IMPORTANCE OF DELEGATION

An outstanding disciple of delegation, Andrew Carnegie, made this
pertinent statement: "When a man realizes he can call others in to help
him do a job better than he can do it alone, he has taken a big step in
his life." A manager must delegate primarily because of three reasons.
First, he is in charge of more work than he personally can do. This
brings up questions of the degree to which he should delegate authority.
Second, delegating authority is the cardinal step in developing subordinates. All the benefits of executive training programs, seminars, and
workshops go for naught if authority delegation is ignored. Third,
organization depth is required by an enterprise. Managers are taken out
of an organization through promotion, illness, resignation, and business
trips. Others must be able to carry on if the need arises, and this suggests
that they are participating in the work. A manager is one in a line of
persons; he had a predecessor and sooner or later will have a successor.

Delegation of some form appears essential regardless of the concept of
organizing followed. If organizing is viewed as a dynamic aggregation
of social human beings, systems, or clusters of different projects, there
will be differences in what the members perform and in the relationships among the members. Leaders will exist, and for group action to be
fully effective, delegation will be practiced.

MEANS OF DELEGATION

In too many cases the delegation is made by the delegator simply
telling the delegatee to run the department as he sees fit. This permits
broad powers, perhaps too broad, by the subordinate. He may take over
activities not intended by the delegator, get into organizational difficulties with other subordinates, and ignore activities which others feel he
should perform. In such instances, the subordinate resorts to trial and
error and ultimately gains some delineation of his specific assignments.
This expensive and wasteful process can be shortened should he be
thoroughly familiar with traditions and policies of the enterprise, know
the likes and dislikes of his superior, and use good judgment in determining the activities to perform.

An alternative is to follow results management within the management process approach. Results management optimizes delegation of authority. Under results management the person striving to achieve mutually known goals receives authority and responsibility in keeping with his particular tasks.

Another alternative is for the superior to give written and specific delegations of authority. This clarifies the entire relationship and removes uncertainty. Such practice is advantageous both ways—to the delegator in making him think through the situation and decide what specific assignments are being made, and to the delegatee who will know specifically in what areas and to what degrees he is to operate. It is probably best to quantify the delegated authority, but this poses problems of measurement which usually are not easily overcome. Many managers prefer to have some degree of flexibility and thus adjust as conditions require. In addition, specific delegation not only keeps the delegatee fully informed but also anyone who may be called upon to work with the delegatee in fulfilling the assignments. Similarly, any subsequent changes should be transmitted to all concerned with the change in delegated authority. Figure 15–1 shows a format designed to show the authority delegated to management members.

In the case of a new activity, written delegation may pose problems. A temporary wait-and-see approach may be followed, but it appears that some statement of what constitutes the activity, what the delegatee is expected to do with it, and his relationships with other executives who are interested in the new activity should be made so that there is some definiteness at the beginning of the operation. Subsequently, modifications and additions can be made at stated intervals. Criticism has been directed to the practice of written delegations in that it reduces organization flexibility and emphasizes the parts rather than the whole of an organization structure. Unfortunately there is some justification for these views, but the underlying causes need not be permitted to exist. A tradition of organization flexibility can and should be established so that organizational changes are made when it is deemed in the best interests of achieving the work to be done.

WHY MANAGERS DON'T DELEGATE

Failure to delegate is a common problem. It does not come naturally. The reasons why managers don't delegate are numerous. Of major importance is first, *the tendency of a human being to want to do things himself*. If charged with specific activities, the normal desire is to make certain the work is performed and the best way to ensure this is to do it

FIGURE 15–1. Form to indicate authority delegated to management members

DELEGATION OF AUTHORITY

The extent of authority of various managers for each of the following expenditures is indicated by number according to this code:

1 = complete authority; 2 = complete authority after consulting with superior; 3 = flexible —depends upon individual circumstances; 4 = no authority; and 5 = committee has authority.

Expenditures	President	Vice President	Divisional Head	Department Head	Supervisor
1. Purchase of machinery					
2. Purchase of materials or supplies					
3. Repair of machinery					
4. Settlement of claims against company					
5. Settlement of claims by company					
6. Extension of credit by company					
7. Adjustment of selling price by company					
8. Adjustment of salaries					
9. Making organizational changes					
10. Giving donations or charitable contributions for company					
11. Handling payment of expense accounts					
12. Changing job classifications					
13. Hiring of personnel					
14. Promoting of personnel					
15. Firing of personnel					
16. Selecting control media to be used					

yourself. Remember too that responsibility goes with authority. The nondelegator, in essence, retains the responsibility which he commonly feels is his own possession and a mark of his self-importance.

Second, *lack of assuming the managerial role when promoted to the managerial ranks* can be cited. In many cases, persons are promoted to managerial positions partly as a result of their willingness in the past to make decisions. They were decisive. When promoted, they continued to be decisive and operate under the erroneous belief that they must be included in and make every decision in their unit.

Third, is *fear of being exposed.* Delegation may reveal managerial shortcomings being practiced. Poor operating procedures, methods, and practices come to light. This fear is understandable, but to have it, is indeed being shortsighted. Exposure of the difficulties can be the first step in correcting them at their roots. To permit the problems to continue under cover will only delay and worsen the eventual remedy that will be required.

Fourth, there is also *the unconscious acceptance of the indispensable-man theory.* In many situations the manager feels deep down that he is really an indispensable person in the organization. Of course, this is not publicly admitted, but wanting to be missed and finding things not going so smoothly when he is absent satisfies his ego and results in seriously limiting his delegating of authority. Most managers want to be remembered as outstanding in their work. Some would like to be thought of as a great tree, symbolic of strength and righteousness, standing foursquare to every wind. This is a noble aspiration, but how much better it is to be a great tree under which other great trees are nurtured and permitted to grow.

Fifth, *the desire to dominate* can be cited. For any number of reasons, some executives have an intense desire to influence others, to participate in practically every decision, to make their presence felt in every company meeting, and "to run" their organization. They like to work under pressure, to be busy with appointments, to have subordinates bring matters to them for approval. Lots of papers stacked on their desks and a large volume of correspondence give them a feeling of satisfaction and importance. Very often, organizational units dominated by such an executive accomplish a great deal of work, but this situation poses difficulties, including the replacement of a dominant executive, tendency to overwork by the executive, and nondevelopment of subordinates.

Sixth, *an unwillingness to accept calculated risks* retards delegation of authority. To delegate authority successfully it is necessary to accept the risk that a subordinate may make wrong decisions. But this risk must be

taken if experienced executives are wanted. Mistakes at the lower echelons are the calculated risks—the price one may have to pay for agility
and management-in-depth where effective managerial power is dispersed
widely and deeply throughout the company. Most present-day managers
are where they are today because somebody had faith in them and accepted the calculated risk inherent in delegating authority to subordinates.

Lastly, *the attitude toward subordinates* is vital. The executive may
feel quite frankly that the subordinate is not capable of using authority
properly. As a matter of fact, the quality of performance may suffer; but
a big part of a manager's job is to develop people under him, and delegation of authority aids in this objective. Furthermore, the attitude may
be one of fear that the subordinate, as a result of delegation, will prove
himself so capable of performing the delegator's job that he should be
given it. The fear is sometimes present that delegation makes it possible
for the subordinate to win a promotion that results in the executive losing one of his best subordinates.

GETTING MANAGER TO DELEGATE

A number of measures can be followed to alleviate the problem of
authority delegation. For convenience, the following ten points are listed
and discussed.

1. Make the Potential Delegator Feel Secure.   Typically the nondelegator is a hard worker, fully competent in his field, but he feels
insecure in his job. This is partially the reason why he surrounds himself
with mediocre people or in any event those who lack the courage to
challenge him. He wants to continue as the superior and to be looked
upon as a necessary man on the company team. To help make him feel
secure, point out clearly that his job and contribution to the group are
not being questioned. Further, help him build or acquire more influence
with his associates by granting him an impressive title or an increase
in pay, or providing him with special facilities such as an oversize office
and services of a private secretary, and a private parking space.

2. Realize the Need for Delegation.   As long as a manager is
limited to what he can accomplish himself, he will always be short of
time and limited in his achievements. A manager's need is to multiply
himself. It is nonsense to try to lead the band and play all the instru-
ments too. The only alternative is to acquire helpers, train them, and
permit them to contribute in full measure. Commonly it is convincing
to have the nondelegator take an inventory of the tasks he does person-

ally. Then have him evaluate these tasks to determine whether it seems reasonable for him to do all these tasks, especially with an organization unit beneath him.

3. Tie-In with Intelligent Planning. Authority should not be delegated to the management team before the goals are clear. To delegate without knowing and keeping in mind objectives leads to chaos. Authority is utilized to achieve goals, and the extensiveness of the authority should be in keeping with the type of activities performed in attaining the goals. This is another reason why in Chapter 3, results management modifying the process approach was recommended. Results management permits management members to set their own goals with superior approval. This very act of goal setting aids authority delegation for it brings in close focus what authority will be required to achieve the mutually agreed to goals.

4. Establish a Work Climate Free from Fear and Frustration. This is essentially psychological and social in character. The executive must have a feeling of confidence that delegation of authority will reward, not penalize, him. It must represent an opportunity for growth, not the certainty of getting bawled out. Authority delegation should have the blessing of the top managers, as evidenced in such things as a reasonable and satisfactory compensation, an impartial means for evaluating a manager's work, and a significant part of the executive development program.

5. Encourage a Deep Belief in Delegation. A manager must want to make delegation successful and strive to make it succeed. He must view delegation as the way to develop his subordinates, to liberate their energies purposively, and to build a real management team. He must realize that these goals are elusive and to win them takes time, effort, and persistence. Furthermore, he must be willing to see his subordinates make mistakes and charge the cost to management developing and to strengthening his organization.

6. Determine How the Delegator Keeps His Hand on It. Since the delegator retains his overall authority for delegated duties, he is always interested in keeping himself well enough informed to protect his own accountability and to be fairly certain of the outcome. Few delegators want to be merely the depository of the result. The delegating method followed should provide the means for informing the delegator of the status of the assignment in time to take corrective steps, if needed. There are many ways for the delegator to "keep his hand in it." The subordinate can be questioned periodically about the progress of the delegated work. Written reports can be required at prescribed times in order to reveal progress being accomplished, and these reports can include comparisons with predetermined deadlines. Also, conferences can be scheduled for the purpose of reviewing what has been and what is intended to be accomplished.

7. Determine Decisions and Tasks to Be Delegated. A simple and direct means of solving this is for the delegator to list all the various types of decisions and tasks that must be performed and then rate each one in terms of (1) their relative importance to the total enterprise and (2) the time required to perform. These data serve to determine what type of decisions and tasks should be delegated. In most cases, those that are relatively less important and most time-consuming may be delegated.

8. Choose the Delegatee Wisely. This might well be the man with unused and the not so obvious abilities. Studies indicate that nearly one half of management personnel do not utilize their full potential in performing their regular duties. Also, the group's productivity and morale generally improve when the not so obviously qualified manager is given a chance to prove himself. We tend to favor the underdog. In addition, the assignment should be measured to the man. It should be challenging but not too tough to finish.

9. Delegate Authority for Whole Job. It is advisable to give the delegatee a chance to participate in a complete undertaking. Broad rather than narrow projects best serve to whet the imagination and stimulate ingenuity. Such asignments serve as an effective means of testing a man's ability to manage and of building his confidence. Too frequently the delegated work constitutes what the delegator himself doesn't want to do. He uses delegation of authority to rid himself of unpleasant tasks, and often such delegation is performed without adequate thought.

10. Give Assistance to Delegatee. Delegation is not a matter of giving a subordinate an assignment and necessary authority and letting him on his own succeed or fail. The delegating manager does not assume the role of a helpless onlooker. Typically, the delegatee is going to require some assistance and commonly goes to the delegator for help. If the problem is clearly within the range of his delegated authority, the delegator should make the delegatee decide it for himself. An effective question to ask the subordinate is "What do you think ought to be done?" If the problem is complicated, assistance in helping the subordinate to identify and explore possible alternatives is recommended. But the delegator does not tell the subordinate the precise action to take. The delegator makes himself available for discussions, counsels the delegatee, lends encouragement, and maintains a helpful, continuing relationship with the delegatee.

DEFINITE ORGANIZATION CHANNELS

The tying and relating of the organization units by means of delegation of authority set forth channels or avenues along which formal authority is exercised over the activities of each unit. These avenues are definite and can be considered the formal channels of supervision. The relationship and the type of authority existing between organization units govern what characteristic action is to take place in any segment of a formal organization structure. These defined channels of supervision should extend from the top of a formal organization structure to the very bottom. All organization units are joined by these channels; there are no unattached, dangling units. The intent is to avoid overlapping of supervisory efforts and also so-called horizontal gaps in the organization structure. A horizontal gap is an area within any organizational level which is not connected with any supervisory channel. Horizontal gaps result in waste because the activities of individuals in such areas are not adequately managed.

PRINCIPLE OF DEFINITE SUPERVISORY CHANNELS

For any given enterprise, the various formal organization units should be connected by definite supervisory channels.

QUESTIONS

1. As you see it, what is authority and from whence does it come? Substantiate your answer.
2. Discuss the relationship of a manager's status with his maintaining authority.
3. Does society influence the functioning of authority in an organization? Elaborate on your answer.
4. Discuss two major reasons why managers don't delegate authority.
5. What is delegation of authority and why is it important in organizing?
6. Give an example to show what is meant by one individual influencing the behavior of another by means of control of sanctions.
7. Define responsibility, and discuss the implications of your definition in the study of management.
8. In order to promote greater delegation of authority, discuss the assistance provided by establishing a work climate free from fear and frustration and also delegating authority for the whole job.

9. Is the authority of a manager weakened by his use of results management? Since authority and responsibility of a manager should be coequal, is your answer the same for the question, "Is the responsibility of a manager weakened by his use of results management?" Justify your answers.
10. What are the common means of delegating authority? As a manager, which means would you follow? Why?
11. What is meant by each of the following: (1) authority by legal decree, (2) computer authority, and (3) position authority. Use examples to illustrate your answers if you wish.
12. Discuss the limitations of authority and point out their importance in management.
13. Discuss the meaning and the reasons for having fixed responsibility within an organization.
14. Are you of the opinion that in modern management the power of authority is somewhat restricted? Substantiate your answer.

CASE 15–1. AMBERG SALES COMPANY

NOVAK (sales representative): Mr. Bishop, I've decided to leave the company.

BISHOP (sales manager): Leave the company? What's the matter?

NOVAK: I just can't give my best efforts under the conditions I find I am in.

BISHOP: I don't understand. You are practically in business for yourself. You determine when you're going to work, who you're going to see within your protected sales area, the pay is good, you negotiate the price, business is good, and we all think highly of you here in the main office.

NOVAK: What you say sounds super, but it just isn't the way it works out. For instance, I worked with Allied for weeks. Talked with their engineers and finally got Amberg OK'd as an approved source. Then I negotiated price with Tom McHugh, gave him a good reduction in price, and felt certain I'd get the business. At my quoted price I stood to lose some $4,200 a year because of narrowing the spread between the sales price and the price charged to me.

BISHOP: Yes.

NOVAK: I followed up yesterday on my bid and McHugh told me he telephoned my home office and talked with Mr. Joseph Wilson (assistant sales manager) who gave him an extra 3 percent discount. Now I'll get even less commission. I thought I was the top man and had the authority in dealing with my customers. Now, Mr. Wilson is in the picture and cutting prices behind my back. I don't know where I stand.

BISHOP: Don't get upset. Joe talked with me about the Allied account and indicated McHugh had a better price from Queen City. So we decided to meet it in order to get the business.

NOVAK: He did not have any better price. He was bluffing. Besides the boys in engineering didn't want that stuff from Queen City.

BISHOP: I see. But you'll be interested in knowing that we've had reports recently of Queen City putting in prices below ours. Joe is trying to help. I am sure he felt it a good opportunity to get in with McHugh.

NOVAK: But I'm the guy to decide that. I'm the guy you are holding responsible. I'm the guy to achieve the results. It is my job to handle McHugh. As you yourself said in our sales meeting last October, the sales representative is an independent operator; he has the authority to deal with the customer on all matters of developing sales, obtaining samples, negotiating prices, and determining delivery schedules.

BISHOP: Yes. Look at it this way. It's a team effort, Novak. You know that. If we in the home office can help we are going to do it.

NOVAK: I want to handle my accounts. You are not going to make me just a peddler. I am just plain not interested in that kind of job.

Questions

1. What is the problem as you see it?
2. As Mr. Novak, what action would you now take? Why?
3. Do you feel Mr. Bishop handled the affair properly? Why?
4. What would you do now if you were Mr. Bishop? Justify your answer.

CASE 15–2. THE L.M.B. COMPANY

About 12 years ago, Mr. Bosworth started the L.M.B. Company in an alley garage with a few machines, two employees, one order, and plenty of nerve and enthusiasm. In these early days, he inspired the employees with keen understanding of their problems, active participation in all phases of the business, and in his ability to solve difficult problems confronting the small enterprise.

The company grew, and within 10 years it was employing 230 people. Mr. Bosworth believed he had too much to do, but in his own words: "There is no one around here who has sufficient understanding and background to whom I can give some of my work." Mr. Bosworth found each day too short to finish his work. He worked till 10 or 11 P.M. every night and frequently took a briefcase of work home over the weekend.

Last year at the insistence of his associates, Mr. Bosworth hired an assistant for himself. The asistant is kept extremely busy following up projects, "doing footwork," and assembling information. However, Mr. Bosworth asks his assistant his opinion on many issues, but he does not permit him to make any final decisions. The assistant's name is John Duff.

Mr. Bosworth is conscientious and has extremely high standards of performance. To his close friends he has made the statement that his assistant is satisfactory as an an assistant; he has good ideas but is too young to command the respect of the other men. Furthermore, in Mr. Bosworth's opinion, he cannot afford to take a chance with his assistant taking over important projects. Something might go wrong, and the company would suffer a severe setback.

Mr. Anthony Huss, works manager, entered Mr. Bosworth's office and the following conversation took place:

HUSS: Mr. Bosworth, it looks like something is going to have to be done about this fellow Dan Reynolds, one of the assemblers. I wish we could get rid of him.

BOSWORTH: What's he done?

HUSS: Those little parts we're running for Curtis—well, the assembly of them looked to me to be awful slow; so I asked Mike (Mike McCann, foreman of Department 16 L, light assembly) what the trouble was, and he told me some of the components were not absolutely correct and true like the blueprints call for, and as long as the parts making up the unit were off, he couldn't get out the production we want.

So I talked with the foremen in punch press, welding, and automatic screw machine and warned them to look into it and get the parts "right on the button" before shootin' 'em over to light assembly.

BOSWORTH: Yes. And what did they say?

HUSS: Oh, they said they would all right. No trouble with them. It's this guy, Dan Reynolds.

BOSWORTH: Yeah, what about him?

HUSS: Well, apparently during lunch hour or one of the breaks or sometime, the men got together—I mean some of them from punch press, some from welding, some from assembly—and got to talking about these Curtis parts. Reynolds had the nerve to tell them the parts were O.K. coming to his department. He said the trouble in putting them together is that the assemblers have no suitable fixtures and tools for this work. And the men agree with Reynolds. McCann is plenty sore and told me Reynolds should be put in his place. From his actions you'd think Reynolds believes he's the foreman. In fact, McCann told me that Reynolds was out for his (McCann's) job. The men go to Reynolds with many of their problems, shop as well as personal, and apparently listen to what he tells them. I told Mike not to worry about his job. Reynolds told me once that he never wanted a foreman's job. Some action will have to be taken about this, Mr. Bosworth. Any suggestions on what you want me to do?

BOSWORTH: I'll come out in about 15 minutes. You go back to work, and I'll see you shortly.

HUSS: Yes, sir. Thanks, Mr. Bosworth.

Questions

1. From the viewpoint of organizing, evaluate Mr. Bosworth as the chief executive of the company.
2. How do you explain the situation involving employee Dan Reynolds?
3. What action do you suggest Mr. Bosworth take? Substantiate your answer.

16

Organizational relationships

Great men never feel great;
Small men never feel small.

CHINESE PROVERB

As WE SHALL SEE in this chapter, there are many different types of authority. They are employed to make feasible the functioning of the formal organization. Different managers need different decision-making powers, both in type and amount, in order to make the group's efforts meaningful and effective in attaining the specific goals. These various types of authority, extending through the entire organization structure, give rise to various relationships existing among the managers of the organization units. These organization relationships affect significantly the *modus operandi* of the organization and are vital in the study of organization.

LINE AUTHORITY

The superior-subordinate authority relationship whereby a superior delegates authority to a subordinate who in turn delegates authority to another subordinate and so on, forms a line from the very top to the very bottom level of the organization structure. The line of authority so formed gives rise to the name "line authority." This line of authority consists of an uninterrupted series of authority steps and forms a hierarchical arrangement present in all formal organization types.

Line authority is easily understood by members of an enterprise. A superior exercises direct command over a subordinate; this is the essence of line authority. The authority relationship is thus a direct line between superior and subordinate. Each member knows from whom he receives orders and to whom he reports. A person with line authority has charge of and is responsible for the work of his unit and its *direct contribution* toward the goals of the enterprise. Line authority is sometimes called direct operative authority. Decision making is expedited since each management member has authority giving him complete charge of his particular area and when necessary he need only consult with his immediate superior.

When only line authority is employed, the formal structure is called a line organization structure. Each line manager is responsible for all activities within his particular unit. For example, he schedules the work, hires, fires, figures cost, and checks quality. He is a doer, a putting-into-action type of manager. The line type of organization is commonly used for small enterprises, especially retailers and manufacturers having perhaps seven to eight employees. It has outstanding advantages: Quick decision making is fostered; buckpassing is eliminated; excellent management training experience in direct operations is provided; and the type of authority relationships present are clearly understood. Nonetheless, this type organization has inherent disadvantages: executives tend to become overloaded with too many duties; specialization is not practiced; management members may be difficult to replace; and insufficient time and effort may be given to such activities as managerial planning, research and development, and overall controlling measures.

STAFF AUTHORITY

The use of the term "staff" gives rise to many misunderstandings in management. Literally the word means a stick carried in the hand for support. Hence, staff authority relationships *originally* were thought of as those relationships used to support line authority relationships. This concept exists today and is valid. Staff means a supporting role and function; it is intended to help the "doer." With the passing of time additional meanings of staff authority, or what this help consists of, have developed and are currently in use. In other words, there are different types of staff authority which will be discussed later in this chapter. There is also a current revival to use the term, support, instead of staff. This is desirable because support is indicative of the concept conveyed.

In most enterprises the use of staff in organization structures can be traced to the need for help in handling details, locating data required for decisions, and offering counsel on specific managerial problems. In the Armed Forces, for example, an officer commanding a large number of men does not have the time or perhaps the specialized knowledge to secure all the information necessary to arrive at decisions which are vital to a campaign being waged. Also, many executives of business corporations find the ramifications of modern business so numerous that assistance in the form of staff executives and organizational units is employed. Specialization is needed, and assistance to the doer in many different areas appears to be highly desirable.

Most staff authority relationships are characteristically a manager-to-manager authority relationship and exist among any managerial levels of an organization structure. The managerial recipient of staff authority is commonly called a staff executive or staff officer. He has charge of his respective staff organizational unit. The concept of staff authority is quite old, for staffs were employed by government and armies of nations in ancient history.

LINE AND STAFF ORGANIZATION

Most enterprises must operate amid complexities and ever-increasing advances in knowledge and technologies. These along with expansion of an enterprise make it necessary eventually to relieve management members with line authority of certain duties. The need for certain specialists is recognized. For example, the expert in establishing work standards, the legal advisor, the researcher, and the tax expert are incorporated into the formal organization structure primarily so that the line manager is relieved of certain of his duties and thus better able to concentrate his efforts on the direct doing activities in keeping with the enterprise's objectives. Hence, the line authorities are adjusted, resulting in staff authorities whose recipients are called staff managers. The line of authority remains the avenue for command or performance of the work. It consists of the authority relationships between line managers. Generally speaking, most staff managers do *not* exercise their staff authority *along* the channels of line authority but rather *to* the line of authority. Staff managers exercise their proper staff authority to help line managers who command to achieve work performance. What is a line manager and what is a staff manager depend on the type of authority possessed; line authority designates a line manager, and staff authority, a staff manager. Line authority gives rise to a line organization. The use of staff authority conditions the line organization and makes it a line-and-staff organization, which is the type most organizations are.

Figure 16–1 shows a line-and-staff organization structure. The line

FIGURE 16-1. A line-and-staff organization structure

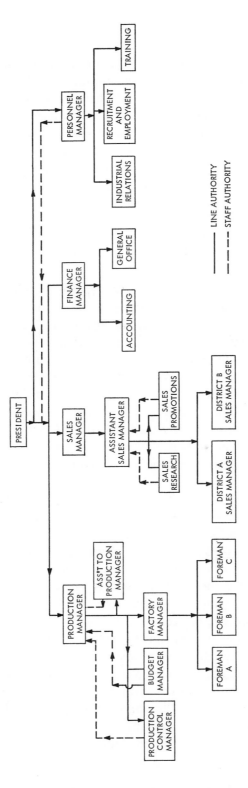

LINE AUTHORITY
STAFF AUTHORITY

PRESIDENT

PRODUCTION MANAGER

SALES MANAGER

FINANCE MANAGER

PERSONNEL MANAGER

ASS'T TO PRODUCTION MANAGER

PRODUCTION CONTROL MANAGER

BUDGET MANAGER

FACTORY MANAGER

FOREMAN A

FOREMAN B

FOREMAN C

ASSISTANT SALES MANAGER

SALES RESEARCH

SALES PROMOTIONS

DISTRICT A SALES MANAGER

DISTRICT B SALES MANAGER

ACCOUNTING

GENERAL OFFICE

INDUSTRIAL RELATIONS

RECRUITMENT AND EMPLOYMENT

TRAINING

part of this structure, which represents the line of authority, extends from the president down through the three fundamental organizational units including (1) to the production manager, factory manager, and three foremen; (2) to the sales manager, assistant sales manager, and two district sales managers; and (3) to the finance manager, accounting, and general office. As drawn in the figure, the staff portion is represented by the production control manager and the budget manager under production, the sales research and sales promotions under the assistant sales manager, and the personnel manager reporting to the president. Staff units can exist at any organization level from the very top to the lower levels.

WHAT IS LINE; WHAT IS STAFF

Although a function is of a staff type in its relation to the entire organization structure, it can, when viewed in and of itself, be of a line type organization. To illustrate, in Figure 16–1 the budget manager performs a staff function considering the entire line-and-staff organization. However, to perform these staff duties, the budget manager may require the services of two assistants who have three clerks each (not shown in the illustration). Hence, if only this budget group is viewed as a unit, the budget manager is a line manager; but if the entire organization structure is considered, the budget manager is a staff manager. His line authority within his organizational unit, that is, to his two assistants, is the only line or command authority he possesses.

This dual identification is sometimes confusing to the student of organization. To clarify this difficulty it is helpful to consider the work done by a unit from the viewpoint of the major objectives of the enterprise. If the authority over the activities is *directly related* to the major objectives' accomplishment, the units are line. In contrast, if the authority over the activities is *indirectly related* to the major objectives' accomplishment, the units are staff. In the latter case the immediate goal may be to achieve auxiliary objectives which, in turn, assist in achieving the major objectives.

Actually, from one company to another there is no uniformity regarding what unit should be line authority and what unit should be staff authority. Different activities receive different emphasis and position *depending upon the objectives of the enterprise.* For example, office work may be considered line in an insurance company, whereas it is staff in a manufacturing company.

Line includes those units that initiate and carry through to conclusion the fundamental activities; staff for the most part includes those that give help to the line. Staff includes all units of an organization which are not line.

To reiterate, in order to get a group of people to work together effectively, certain management members of the group will decide and perform certain activities while other management members will decide and perform other activities; yet all the decisions and activities must be compatible—contribute to and result in achievement of common goals. This requirement of who decides and performs what means their respective authorities must be spelled out and results in line authority and staff authority.

The identification of a manager as either line or staff is really not the important issue. What is important is to understand the function to be fulfilled through the efforts of the manager in question. What is to be accomplished? The results-oriented view tends to place line or staff managers in their true perspective in that each is important and are required to make the team complete and to attain enthusiastic and effective operations.

CONFLICTS BETWEEN THE LINE AND THE STAFF

In practice, however, the harmonious working together of a management team encounters roadblocks; there are honest differences of opinion on who should decide what, which decision is best, and who takes what action when which decision is adopted. The difficulty is commonly a combination of the failure to (1) identify and utilize the staff authority, (2) recognize the true line-staff relationship, and (3) cope with a noncooperative behavior pattern by some management members.

To illustrate, from the line manager's viewpoint, the complaint is voiced that staff people tend to grab credit for work that turns out successfully and lay the blame on line when the work does not. Staff managers tend to take advantage of the fact that they report and have frequent access to high line managers. It is easy for them to relate to the top line manager why a project is or is not successful. Another complaint is that staff assumes line authority. In their eagerness to inject their programs into what is done, they overstep their staff prerogatives and tend to "run the show." At one time most staff authority was advisory only; now a sizable portion of staff authority actually has mandatory power.[1] Furthermore, it is sometimes stated by line man-

---

[1] Discussion of different types of staff authority begins on p. 357.

agers that staff assistance is impractical, unbalanced, and fails to take into account all the ramifications of the situation. What is offered stresses too much the staff's particular specialty. The big picture is ignored.

In contrast, those with staff authority do not always hold line managers in high esteem. From the staff viewpoint, difficulties in line-staff relationships commonly include that the line managers resist most new ideas and are too cautious and conservative. At times the line manager is accused of ignoring the staff and wanting to run his department or operation as he (the line) sees fit. Line has staff to help but doesn't make full use of it or calls it in too late to realize maximum benefits. Another common theme is that staff is not given adequate authority. Staff authority managers are experts—they know more about their specialty than line, but they are not given sufficient power to enforce their decisions.

IMPROVING ORGANIZATION RELATIONSHIPS

A solution to these opposing viewpoints could take the form of a long list of things that should be done. For purposes here three suggestions, that appear major, will be mentioned. First, acquire a better understanding of the basic authority relationships in organizing. This suggests better communication and training efforts in such areas as the differentiation among various staff authorities, the importance of clearly defined authority channels, and the influence of behavior and social considerations upon the functioning of authority.

Second, develop a clear concept of what the interrelationship of those with different types of authority really is within an organization. It is not formalized statements, threats, or neatly bound manuals. It is organizing deals with people working together effectively toward a goal. Each management member has authority over certain activities—presumably those that he can best do—considering all the activities and all the managers. There are no primary and secondary managers—all have a relatively vital task to perform. This view toward managers in the organization of one enterprise is well stated in the following:

You are to become a specialist . . . and to perform . . . for the maximum benefit of the total enterprise. You will be accountable for results in your own sphere. You will coordinate your efforts with others in the organization who are also specialists in their spheres. Certain of your responsibilities, such as providing your people with adequate materials and supplies, will be performed for you by a centralized purchasing department because centralized purchasing permits economies. Other units, such as personnel, will administer company-wide plans with which you must comply; and they will also assist with recruiting and other personnel needs. We think you will find their assistance valuable because they can identify problems and recommend solutions that may escape you. If you use their services and if they fail in their responsibility, they will be accountable. If you fail to use their services, you will be accountable for failure, not only in your own sphere, but in the spheres in which other people specialize.[2]

Third, stress interdependence, not separation, of the various organizational units and their respective managements. Basically the manager of each unit does two things: (1) he takes action in some measure and over some activities and (2) in taking this action the unit supports other units in the performance of their activities. All the segments of an enterprise are fused together by means of organizing; this is one of the important purposes of organizing. Each unit should be viewed and evaluated by its contribution to the whole, not by what it achieves in its own activity alone.

This is the real essence of teamwork. Consider a football team. Not every player can carry the ball, nor is every player a good lineman. You don't want a team made up all of fleet-footed halfbacks or all of good defensive tackles and guards. Playing good, hard, aggressive football requires a combination of different skilled players, each making decisions in his prescribed area of activity and performing certain individual actions which are well coordinated and executed. The mutual goal is well-known to all the players; and each contributes what he can do best, when and where he can do it in keeping with the overall plan and the group's or team's best joint efforts. Organizing in enterprises operates in a similar manner.

TYPES OF STAFF AUTHORITY

Over a period of time the meaning of staff authority has taken on several different and important concepts. These differences in meaning have come about because of the basic needs of modern organization. These different concepts of staff authority give flexibility to the concept of line-staff relationships which are needed to bring about efficient organization. It isn't a question of either line or staff, but of line and various shades of staff authority as dictated by the organizational needs.

Staff authority is of two broad categories: (1) specialist staff and (2) personal staff. The former is made up of four different types which

---

[2] Richard C. Anderson, "Today's Thinking on Tomorrow's Managing," *Business Horizons* (Winter 1958–59), p. 22.

are advisory staff, service staff, control staff, and functional staff. The personal staff types include the assistant to and the general staff. These names are somewhat suggestive of the respective type of staff, but there is no uniformly accepted or applied terminology for these staff concepts. The common practice is to call any type of staff authority just that—staff authority—thus giving rise to much misunderstanding in organizing.

ADVISORY STAFF AUTHORITY

This type of staff authority is of a specialized counseling nature to line managers. It is the type of staff authority popularly associated with the term staff authority. An advisory staff manager studies problems, offers suggestions, and prepares plans for the use and help of the line manager. It is axiomatic that the advisory staff manager recommend without fear of losing his job—in effect to counsel and not simply to confirm and suggest only what the line man wants to hear. Usually the work of advisory staff can be accepted, modified, or rejected by the line manager. This state of affairs may tend to put the advisory staff manager on the defensive. He feels insecure unless he can convince the line manager to accept and use the recommendations offered. Advisory staff authority does not restrain line authority.

Advice is of little benefit unless it is utilized. To insure that the advisory staff will be used, the adoption of "compulsory staff service" is sometimes followed. This doctrine requires a line manager to listen to staff managers, but not necessarily to follow the advice they give. The term "compulsory staff service" is unfortunate, since it is not compulsory in the sense of using the advice. Following the doctrine, however, makes for an excellent management team, especially when the managers are competent and their morale is high.

Furthermore, it is advisable to make it possible for an advisory staff manager to talk with the line managers that will be affected by a proposed tentative recommendation before the staff manager submits it to their superior line manager. A recommendation that has cleared the managers who will be affected by it, and is so indicated by the staff manager, has an excellent chance of approval. The advisory staff man who keeps to himself, develops his recommendations secretly, and refrains from listening to willing assistance of line managers may find suspicion and a prevailing negative attitude by others toward his work. In addition, the line manager's responsibility for implementing the recommendation is increased by the burden of evaluating its soundness. A good portion of an advisory staff manager's job is to sell, not tell. And the line manager should realize that he is receiving counsel, not command.

The real purpose of advisory staff authority is not always clearly understood. The staff man's purpose is to advise, not to seek the advice of his superior on a problem. Approval or disapproval of a complete recommended solution should be the staff man's goal. Incomplete solutions and "tell me what you want and I'll write it up" are evidences of lack of true staff managerial ability. The reason for an advisory staff

FIGURE 16–2. Completed staff work doctrine of a company

1. As an advisory staff member, study your problem, prepare your answer, and present it in a *completed* form so that your superior need only approve or disapprove of your completed action.
2. Completed form means a finished, no-part-lacking presentation with all the necessary details included.
3. Refrain from piecemeal recommendations or asking your superior "what he wants done." It is your job to supply what your superior should do with the problem being studied, to give answers, not ask questions.
4. The prescribed finished format need not necessarily be followed in your first presentation; one copy will suffice, but it should be neat and complete. The requirements covering the format, type of paper, and the number of copies can be met after your superior's decision is made on the recommendation.
5. Submit your completed form only after you can answer "yes" to this question: "As the superior would I be able to approve or disapprove this recommendation as it is presented in this report?"

man is to help, to recommend, and to undo mental tangles. To take the problem to the line man and bother him with it defeats the whole purpose of the staff arrangement; and such practice is certain to impede the progress, if not actually jeopardize the standing, of the staff member. The line man wants help, not harassment.

The doctrine of "completed staff work" should be followed. This doctrine is outlined in Figure 16–2. All too frequently agreement to completed staff work is expressed but not put into practice.

SERVICE STAFF AUTHORITY

Many staff organizational units have a service relationship, not an advisory relationship, to the line. Service units perform a service consisting of activities which have been separated from the line job. The formation and use of a service unit in organization is encouraged when the concentration of certain facilities to perform designated activities permit their more economical performance. The grouping of activities is made up usually but not always of the same or similar activities.

The formation of a service staff unit generally compels the line manager to use it because to continue to perform the work in his unit would be needless duplication. Hence line authority is restricted by the existence of service staff authority, and in this respect it differs from the relationship under advisory staff authority. In other words, the manager of a service unit typically makes decisions and enforces them concerning not only action within his own unit but also action relating to his unit facilitating the activities of other organizational units. He exercises line authority outside his unit, but he has service staff authority from the overall viewpoint of the organization.

To illustrate, a factory manager may specify the product to be purchased, thus initiating the purchasing activity, but he does not buy the product. The purchasing function is performed by the purchasing department, a unit having service staff authority. And the factory manager, a line manager, is required to utilize the purchasing department. Thus, an element of compliance is present; it is not advisory only.

CONTROL STAFF AUTHORITY

Certain units have managers with staff authority who directly or indirectly exercise control over other units in an organization structure. Such managers can be designated control staff authority managers. The term "control staff" may seem poor terminology since controlling is a fundamental function of management and implies line authority. The manager with control staff authority realistically controls directly by serving as an agent for a line manager or indirectly either through policy interpretation, control through procedural compliance, or reports and their interpretation supplied to line executives. In these efforts the manager with control staff authority actually can exercise a veto over line actions. Here again is staff authority that is not of the counseling type. The control staff authority manager does not simply advise; he controls. Control staff authority restrains line authority.

Examples of control staff include the extension of credit to customers, auditing, procedure for routing, expenditures, and inspection. The manager of inspection is an excellent illustration of control staff. The top illustration of Figure 16–3 shows the organization structure of a factory manager with three foremen, A, B, and C. Each foreman performs the inspection work of his respective department. Assume there is sufficient inspection work to move it from each foreman's unit and concentrate it in an inspection unit. This is illustrated by the bottom portion of Figure 16–3. The control unit is shown by the shaded area. The authority of the manager of the inspection unit is staff, yet he decides which products are acceptable and which are not. He restrains the line authority of foremen, A, B, and C. The justification for the establishment of the inspection unit is predicated upon the following considerations: (1) the caliber of inspection is improved, (2) the cost is more economical than having it included in other units, and (3) the volume of inspection work warrants specialization in this type of work for at least one man.

FIGURE 16–3

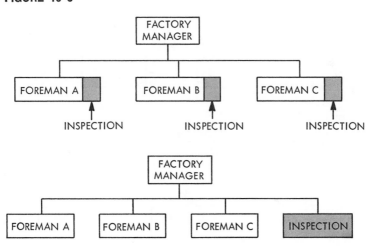

Or consider the case of a district sales manager who wishes to eliminate the use of certain records filled out by his men and turned over to the accounting department for analysis and subsequent preparation of sales reports. Objection by the manager of accounting may be made and he may request and enforce the continuation of the records on the basis that such records constitute important accounting data deemed significant for successful operation of the company. In this case, accounting serves as a control staff unit.

FUNCTIONAL STAFF AUTHORITY

For *specified activities* only, the authority of a manager may be exercised along lines other than the channels set up by the formal organization structure. This is done in the interest of convenience and efficiency. Certain authority normally exercised by a line manager and concerning the restricted areas of activities will be delegated to another manager. Because such authority is specific or concerns certain functions only, it is called functional authority. It may be granted by either a line or a staff manager to another manager, who may be either line or staff. Where functional authority is authorized to operate, it restricts to a very large extent the normal authority in that area.

Figure 16–4 shows functional staff authority relationships in the

FIGURE 16–4. Functional authority in organization structure

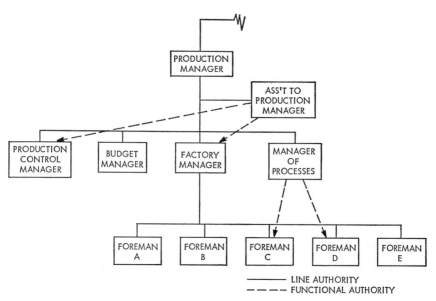

production segment of an organization structure. For certain activities dealing with production and some dealing with production control, the production manager has authorized his staff man, the "assistant to" the production manager, to deal directly with the factory manager and the production control manager.[3] With functional staff authority the "assistant to" need not submit his recommendation to the production manager. Likewise, for specific activities, the manager of processes, a staff position, can work directly and with the authority of a line manager with foremen C and D. On activities outside the specified ones and in all mat-

---

[3] The status of the "assistant to" is that of a staff manager and is discussed in the following pages of this chapter.

ters concerning foremen A, B, or E, the manager of processes counsels and gives his recommendations to the factory manager, who is free to accept or to reject them.

Functional staff authority is limited, or restricted, authority and usually is confined to how the particular activity is to be performed and at what time. If functional staff authority was not limited, it could damage vital line authority, destroy organizational departmentation, and bring chaos to organizing efforts. But the extent to which functional staff authority should exist poses real difficulties. Some issues because of their specialized nature appear to require a competent staff man to interpret and presumably to administer in order to insure proper handling. Functional staff authority probably should be kept at a minimum so that the strength of line managers is maintained.

THE "ASSISTANT TO" MANAGER

This manager is of a personal staff authority type. The "assistant to" manager has no formal line authority but commonly has functional staff authority over a number of activities conferred upon him. He can be viewed as a personal assistant with a limited set of duties and no major supervisory responsibilities. His chief purpose is to extend the superior line manager's capacity for handling a large volume of work. Typical of the work of an "assistant to" are the following: assisting in formulating plans, interpreting plans to others, seeking the opinions of others on matters of interest to his superior, and developing a departmental budget. Some of his work is a regular continuing activity, and some is diversified, varying in type and duration.

However, the interpretation and use made of "assistant to" is not fully comprehended by all concerned, and misuses on the part of the superior or misunderstandings by the subordinate line managers appear to be more common than necessary. Some feel that the "assistant to" is unnecessary; what is needed is more delegation of authority to a line manager by the superior line manager. Others fear that the "assistant to" may in the name of the principal take over the duties that rightfully belong to others. He might even tend to create the impression that *he is the superior* rather than one who *is acting for the superior*. In addition, improper assignments or work within the scope of someone else might be assigned the "assistant to." Such a situation leads to misunderstanding and poor cooperation. No "assistant to" should be assigned work when he must rely on others for the fundamental execution of the assignment; the work should be assigned to the others.

It is the belief of many that the title "assistant to" is inadequate. They suggest the establishment of a staff unit or units with designation explanatory of what the unit or units are supposed to do. Titles suggested and used include "special assistant," "executive assistant," "staff assistant," and "administrative assistant."

Generally speaking, it appears that the need for an "assistant to" arises from a number of situations, such as (1) a large quantity of routine correspondence or documents must be processed; (2) understanding of technical material outside the experience of the superior is required; (3) many outside contacts are necessary; (4) the superior attends many committee meetings in which arise complex circumstances that require analysis and evaluation; (5) positions are needed for older, experienced executives requiring less strenuous managerial jobs; and (6) a training ground for the younger executives is desired. These situations are self-explanatory, but under the fifth, it should be added that the "assistant to" job should not deteriorate into a dumping ground for executives no longer needed. Also, many feel that the "assistant to" position has limited value for training purposes. They point out that it provides intimate knowledge of the inner organization workings but little, if any, vital line experience.

THE ASSISTANT MANAGER

Because the "assistant to" is frequently confused with the assistant, discussion of the latter at this time is appropriate. Unlike the "assistant to," the assistant manager is a line manager reporting directly to his line superior. When this line superior is the president of an enterprise, the title "executive vice president" may be given the assistant manager. In such cases the work might be divided, with the president handling overall planning, outside contacts, and public relations, and the executive vice president actually supervising the operations of the enterprise. Typically, the assistant manager does just what his title implies—he assists his superior in his total duties, directly supervises the subordinates, and acts for his superior. But frequently limitations are placed on the assistant manager's action, for example, to act for his superior only in the latter's absence, and to directly supervise subordinates in certain activities only.

Probably the best conditions under which the assistant manager can be used advantageously include those when the duties of the superior are heavy and the internal affairs to be handled are dynamic. Here the assistant can contribute effectively toward maintaining a fast output of heterogeneous work. Also a manager with direct line authority is available to keep the operations going during unavoidable absences of his superior. In addition, managerial work that necessitates much concentrated mental effort might best be handled by a manager with an assistant. The former can devote most of his energies to this type of work and avoid the interruptions caused by hour-to-hour affairs in his department—the assistant administering the normal operating affairs of the department. Finally, the assistant gains excellent training for the manager's job. He has line authority and is literally the one in charge.

In the opinion of many, the assistant manager unit is undesirable because it adds another organization level, thus hindering communication, and frequently it creates the situation of two rather than one doing a job without proper differentiation of activities. Also, by having an assistant, the principal may lose touch with his unit's activities, but this need not necessarily follow. The manager can keep himself up to date by means of spot checking and periodic reports concerning key activities. There is also the question of cost, and critics of the assistant manager arrangement maintain it increases administrative costs. On the other hand, it might make possible a greater number of subordinates reporting to a superior and thus result in a reduction of costs by keeping the required number of managers at a minimum.

THE GENERAL STAFF

A second classification of the personal staff authority is the general staff. The military has used the general staff concept quite extensively, whereas in business the concept is relatively uncommon. General staff is a coordinated group which acts through its chief. Like other staff units, general staff may be advisory, service—usually in the sense of getting and supplying information—control, or functional, through supervisory activities. Action is taken and orders given in the name of the top executive or his office. In the general staff of the United States Army, for example, are G-1 Personnel, G-2 Intelligence, G-3 Operations, G-4 Supply, and G-5 Controller.

The general staff concept grew in response to a need to bolster a top manager's ability to handle large-scale operations. It has been employed with great success; yet in many instances it has proven very ineffective. A deciding factor apparently is the attitude and use the top manager makes of the general staff. Experience demonstrates that a practice of rotating general staff members to other areas and levels in the organization structure fosters their understanding for the line problems at lower levels. Staff members must keep aware of the ultimate results of their work. They should never be permitted to develop an immunity and sort of ivory-tower isolation to the realities of the situation.

CHARTS SHOWING ORGANIZATION RELATIONSHIPS

As indicated in Chapter 14, for any given enterprise an organization chart is itself useful in showing major formal organization relationships. A chart helpful in revealing the relationships embodied in a formal organization chart is an activity chart. When the organization chart is tied to the procedural flowchart for a selected procedure, a fuller meaning of organization relationships is provided. Both these charts will now be discussed.

ACTIVITY CHART

Use of an activity chart improves the visualization of the relationships of functions and the obligations embodied in a formal organization structure. Instead of the detailed information concerning a specific position, the activity chart outlines for a given objective the actions required along with the obligations of each person participating in the attainment of that objective. Figure 16–5 shows a portion of an activity chart. Note the objective is shown at the top with the required actions for this goal shown immediately below on the left side of the chart. The actions are segregated into major and minor classes. Opposite each action at the right of the chart are shown the obligations for that action.

The chart can be broad and include personnel of several different organizational units, or it can be confined to one unit, depending upon the objective being analyzed. It can also be drawn for one person within an organization unit. Such a chart has considerable value especially for a manager operating under a results management approach. In such a situation the activity chart assists him in determining what other departments and people in the organization will be involved, and in what way, in his reaching the objectives he sets for himself.

ORGANIZATION CHART AND PROCEDURAL FLOWCHART

Figure 16–6 shows the organization and the procedural flowchart for a purchasing procedure. Such an illustration helps clarify the relationships among the various organization units with respect to a given actual work performance.

FIGURE 16–5. An activity chart (showing actions and obligations required for the attainment of a given objective)

Objective: Produce and ship products according to customers' requirements					
Actions		Obligations			
Major	Minor	Department	Division	Section	Position
1. Design and test products		Production			Vice president of production
	1.1 Research and plan the design and general processes required		Engineering		Chief engineer
	1.2 Conduct thorough study to see that product meets trade requirement of efficiency and appearance		Product development		Product development engineer
2. Produce approved products		Production			Vice president of production

The various functions and personnel involved in purchasing are highlighted on the organization chart. They include the purchasing agent, the cash disbursement, the accounts payable, the receiving department, and stores, as shown in the upper portion of the illustration. The purchases procedural flowchart occupies the bottom portion of the illustration and depicts the various steps, in sequence, that take place in the purchasing procedure. To interpret the flowchart, follow the arrow lines and read each horizontal level, progressing downward on the chart. Beginning under stores, the requisition is made in duplicate, one copy going to accounts payable and the other to the purchasing agent. Competitive bidding is required. When the successful bidder is known, the purchase order (five copies) is made out, with two copies sent to the vendor, one to stores, one to accounts payable, and one to receiving. Continuing down the chart in this manner gives the entire purchasing procedure.

There are considerable advantages in using a procedural flowchart

FIGURE 16–6. Procedural flowchart for purchasing drawn in relation to organization chart to portray the interrelationship between the two

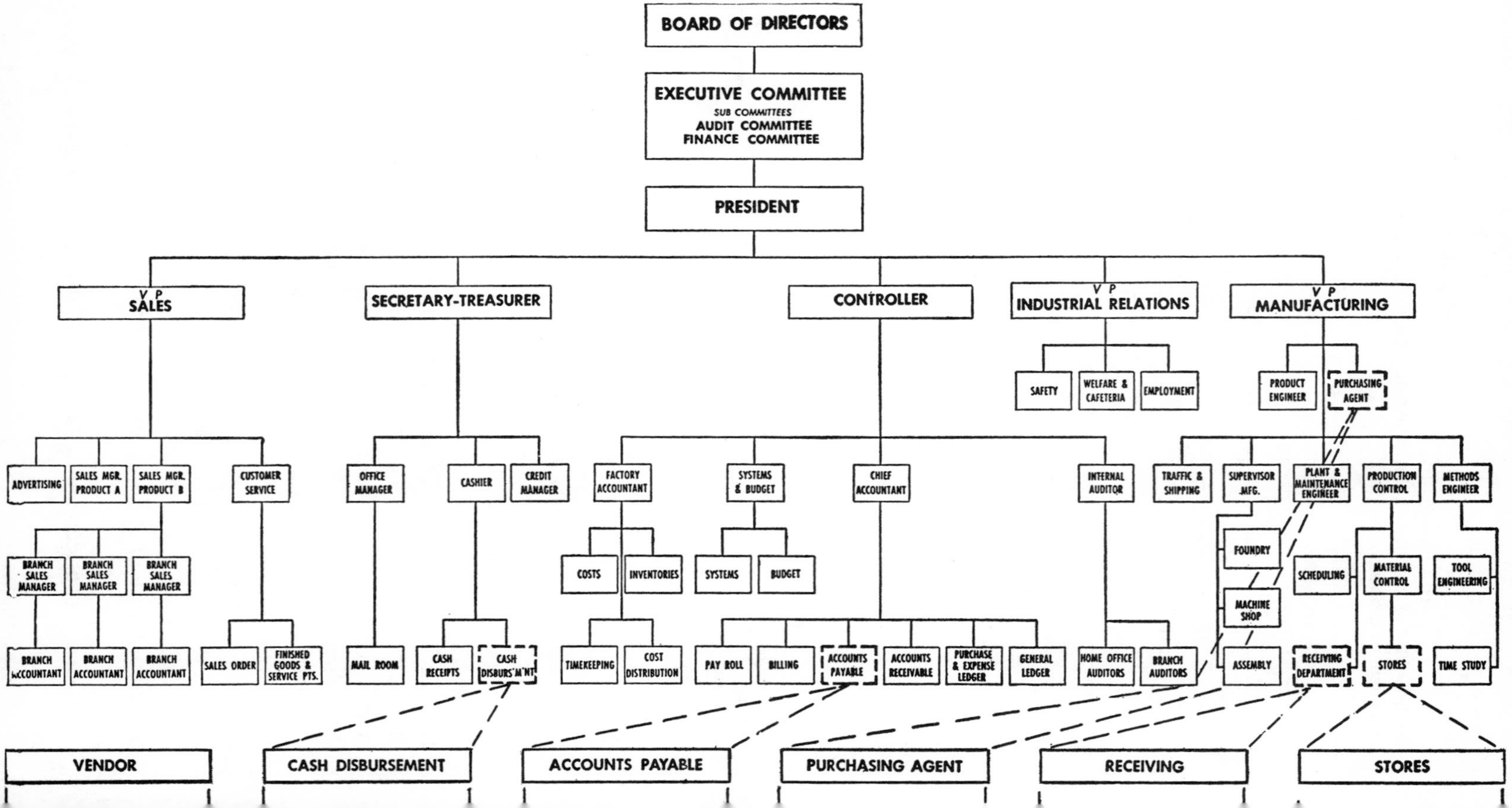

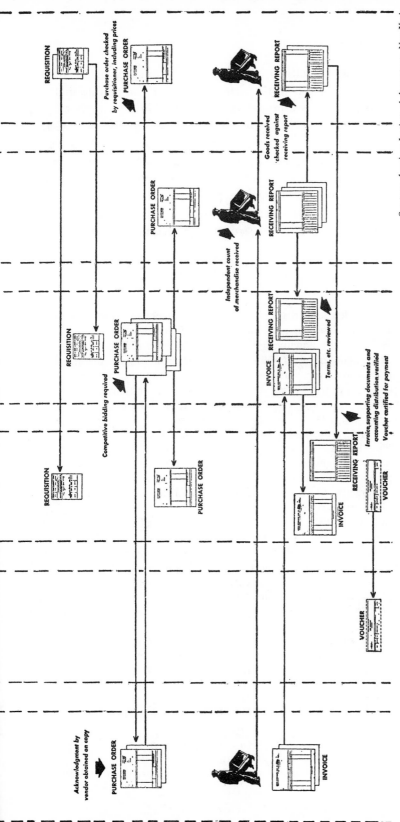

Courtesy: American Institute of Accountants, New York

with an organization chart. By this combination, an idea of the amount and the character of the work performed in each organizational unit can be visualized and ascertained. Also, by drawing such a chart for an organization unit alone, it is possible to observe clearly the interrelation of activities within this unit and to determine what, if any, unrelated activities are being handled. Lastly, the practice of tying procedural flowcharts to organization charts more closely relates procedural improvements to organizational improvements. From the managerial viewpoint this is especially desirable, because in many cases improvements within the organization structure are required in order to improve procedures.

QUESTIONS

1. Justify the viewpoint that it does make a difference in organizing whether a manager is identified as having line or staff authority.
2. For each of the following, indicate what kind of authority is being used: (1) the manager of computer operations explaining to the purchasing agent how bids for purchase are to be filled out, (2) the manager of inspection approving reworked parts for use on the assembly line, (3) the purchasing agent ordering needed materials for the production control manager, and (4) the market research director informing the assistant marketing director the results of a recent consumer study.
3. Back in chapter 9 we discussed communicating. Which type of authority do you feel might tend to hinder effective communication? Which type to help attain effective communication? Justify your answer.
4. Would practice of results management eliminate the need for line, staff, or all authority? Why?
5. Define each of the following: (1) the general staff, (2) staff authority, (3) procedural flowchart, and (4) personal staff authority.
6. Would you say the functional staff authority concept probably developed from formal organization or from a modification of the formal organization? Repeat for service staff authority. Give reasons for your answers.
7. Draw a simple organization chart to show the difference between the "assistant to" manager and the assistant manager. Describe the difference in the type of duties that each one performs.
8. Enumerate some of the more common problems in line-staff relationships in organizing. Suggest ways in which these problems might be solved.
9. Discuss the concept and use of the general staff in organizing.
10. Indicate, along with your reasons, whether you are in favor of having compulsory staff service. Of having complete staff work doctrine.
11. What is an activity chart and for what purpose is it used in organizing?
12. Explain the meaning of Figure 16–5.
13. Point out the differences between a manager having control staff authority and a manager who is an "assistant to."
14. Drawing from an organization with which you are familiar, enumerate

some activities managed with advisory staff authority. Explain the operation of each one.

CASE 16–1. VECTOR MANUFACTURING COMPANY

Russell Mead, general foreman, decided to proceed immediately with the punching of some special parts for a Navy order. The production of this order has been delayed due to reworked tooling required and was already five weeks behind schedule. While the machine setter was installing the die for performing this work, Dennis Saines, the director of safety, walked by and noticed the die that had been rejected because of safety reasons, was being installed in the machine. He checked with the machine setter and confirmed that it indeed was the die he rejected two months ago. At that time it was found from a trial run that the sheet metal tended to flip upward and Mr. Saines requested that it be reworked to avoid any accident which might injure the operator. The organization chart including the locations of the general foreman and the director of safety is shown in the accompanying drawing.

Mr. Saines telephoned Mr. Mead and told him not to use that non-approved die. Mr. Mead explained that he had to use it. He is way behind schedule and the office is screaming at him to get the Navy order completed. Mr. Saines retorted that the die is unsafe and if used, could cause trouble.

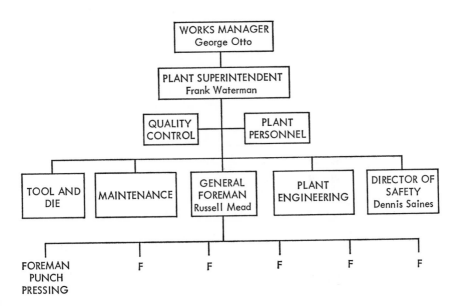

MEAD: What do you mean?

SAINES: I mean a man may get hurt—lose an eye, maybe.

MEAD: Oh come on. It's not that bad. I'm putting one of my best men on it and we'll be finished in less than one day.

SAINES: No, I can't go along with you. If you use that die, I'll have to report it to Frank (Frank Waterman, the plant superintendent).

MEAD: Frank wants the order out of the shop. And I'm tried of having that lot of material setting out there on the floor. It's in the way. You fellows are getting pretty choosy.

Russell Mead told his punch press foreman to go ahead with the order and get is out as soon as possible. He told him it would probably be best not to say anything to anybody about it, just get it completed. However, word reached Mr. Saines after the punching work with the rejected die had been in progress about two hours.

Questions

1. What is the problem?
2. Comment fully on the action by Mr. Mead.
3. As Mr. Saines what action would you take? Why?
4. Assuming Dennis Saines sends a report to Frank Waterman, what should Mr. Waterman do? Why?

CASE 16–2.   KENYON-WERNER COMPANY

Helen Snelling is executive secretary to Mr. Evans, a cautious, retiring, and quiet man. She was transferred to his office about four months ago when the Louisville regional sales office of the company was closed. Top managers hoped to provide Mr. Evans with expert help by assigning Miss Snelling, whose personnel record showed her to be capable, highly efficient, ambitious, somewhat impatient, and the possessor of a quick temper. She is 28 years old and has never been married.

Reporting to Mr. Evans are James Root, head of accounting; Mrs. Hortense Higgins, head of order writing; Francis Green, head of production scheduling; Miss Beth Cooper, chief of switchboard operators and receptionists; and Henry Schwartz, chief of the mailroom. James Root, age 46, knows accounting very well, but he is not too good an administrator. He is inclined to let chores other than accounting work be unduly delayed and seems to have little perception of human relations problems within his unit. Well-liked and accommodating, he is accepted by his employees, but the top managers do not view him as a heavyweight to assume higher management responsibilities of the company.

In view of delay and uncertainty displayed by Mr. Evans, Helen Snelling is inclined to take action on those matters that, in her opinion, need attention. Usually her decisions have proven quite effective, but other members of the department object to her grabbing authority that doesn't belong to her. To illustrate, about two weeks ago, Mrs. Higgins, age 50, and Miss Snelling got into a verbal scuffle about priority in completion of the order writing for certain customers. The issue was settled by Mr. Evans, who decided it in favor of Mrs. Higgins. Then he had a talk with Miss Snelling about taking it easy and the folly of being too aggressive in business relationships. Only two days ago, during the lunch hour, Miss Snelling answered Mr. Root's telephone, took a request for some records to be sent to the purchasing director, secured the wanted records from the file, and sent them to the purchasing director. Mr. Root found out about the request yesterday and spoke with Miss Snelling about it. He stated that she was overstepping her prescribed duties and the least she could have done would have been to tell him about it or leave a note on his desk. Miss Snelling said she did write him a note and was only trying to help. Mr. Root emphasized that he would not tolerate any interference by her and that he intends to report the incident to Mr. Evans. Later, in searching through papers on his desk, he found the note referred to by Miss Snelling.

It is the opinion of Miss Snelling that the people reporting directly to Mr. Evans are taking advantage of him and have been doing so for a long time. He is so buried in details that he delays many financial decisions. She is certain that the management personnel of the finance group are going in all different directions and that Mr. Evans doesn't realize this. In her own mind, Miss Snelling is positive that her dealings with various heads within the finance group are for the best interests of the company. She also feels certain that the subordinates of Mr. Evans go ahead and decide issues, sometimes poorly, when the final decision should come from Mr. Evans, or at least with sanction by him and knowledge of what decision has been made.

Questions

1. What is the problem as you see it?
2. What important factors do you believe contributed to the present state of affairs? Elaborate on your answer.
3. What plan of action would you recommend to remedy the problem stated above? Discuss.

17

Organizational structure and departmentation

The great achievements have always been individualistic. Indeed, any original achievement implies separation from the majority. Though society may honor achievement, it can never produce it.

GEORGE CHARLES ROCHE

AN ORGANIZATION STRUCTURE can be considered the framework within which managerial tasks are performed. A sound structure is the goal of organization efforts and it has high priority in effective management. The framework can be any one of many different configurations depending upon what is to be accomplished, the preferences of the top managers, and the attention and effort given to organizing.

"To deal effectively with opportunities that lie ahead" or "to secure our production leadership in each of our diversified product lines" are typical reasons for striving to obtain the best possible organization structure. An organization structure is sought that includes an adequate number of organization units related in such a manner that top cooperation, efficiency, and satisfaction from personal work efforts are gained for the individual circumstances and conditions.

CENTRALIZATION AND DECENTRALIZATION

The relating and ranking of organization units form a hierarchy which represent both the concepts of centralization and of decentralization. Decision making and responsibility are centralized in that au-

374

thority and formal activities are concentrated in fewer and fewer managers as the organization structure is reviewed from the lower to the higher organization levels. At the very top, all decisions and responsibilities theoretically emanate from the apex or chief manager. In contrast, proceeding from the top to the bottom levels, decision making and responsibility are decentralized in that they are dispersed among an increasing number of management members, the greatest number usually being at the lowest organization level.

Briefly, we can state that when authority is concentrated, centraliza-

FIGURE 17–1. An organization structure featuring centralization

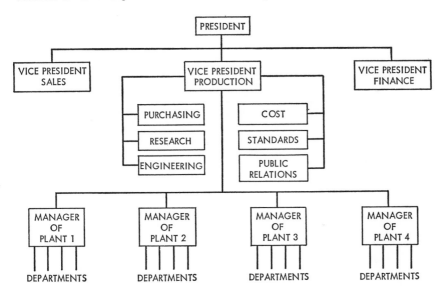

tion is present; when authority is dispersed, decentralization is present. Both centralization and decentralization are intimately tied to the delegation of authority. The controlling issue is how much authority is delegated to subordinates.

To clarify the meaning of centralization and decentralization, Figures 17–1 and 17–2 have been included. The organization structure shown by Figure 17–1 is centralized. Assisting and reporting to the vice president in charge of production are six experts heading, respectively, units of purchasing, research, engineering, cost, standards, and public relations. The operative managers reporting to the vice president in charge of production are the plant managers of the four respective plants. In turn, department managers report to each plant manager.

Under a more decentralized arrangement, the organization structure of the enterprise would appear like that shown in Figure 17–2. Each plant is now set up to operate more as a self-contained unit. For example, the manager of plant 1 has his own purchasing, engineering, costs, and standards departments reporting to him as well as his departmental operating units. But note that the units decentralized are not the same for each plant manager. This decision will depend in part upon the plant managers themselves and also how efficiently it is believed these activities can be performed at and for the particular plant. In Figure 17–2, plant 1 has a standards organizational unit, whereas plant 2 does not have such a unit, but plant 2 has a research unit which 1 does not have. Plant 4 has both standards and research units. Although not shown in the illustration, the organization level of some of

FIGURE 17–2. An organization structure featuring decentralization

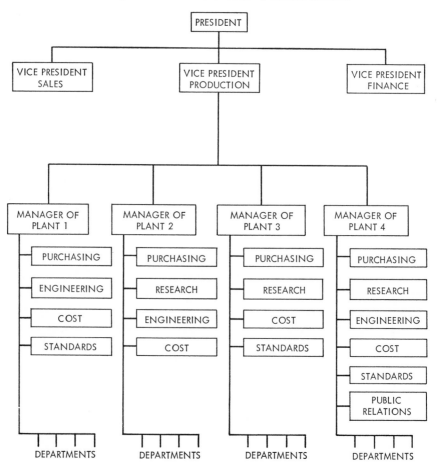

the new units under each plant manager can vary somewhat with the different plants. This is due to the relative importance given these activities by the respective plant managers.

Actually there is some decentralization of authority in every organization structure; otherwise the structure could not exist; that is, all authority would remain vested in the top manager of the enterprise. Likewise a manager cannot delegate all his authority, for by so doing he ceases to be a manager and as far as he is concerned would not be a part of the organization. Hence, centralization and decentralization are opposites and can be thought of as two theoretical extremes, neither of which are found in actual practice; but the concept of each one is helpful in the study of organizing. What helps formulate the organization structure is the degree or tendency to which either centralization or decentralization is practiced.

ADDITIONAL MEANING OF CENTRALIZATION AND DECENTRALIZATION

As employed in the above discussion it would be more precise to use the terms *authority centralization* and *authority decentralization* because we have implied that the condition of centralization or of decentralization depends, respectively, upon the concentration or the dispersion of authority. However, the terms centralization and decentralizations are commonly used to designate the concentration or the dispersion, respectively, of employees and physical facilities. Hence, from this view the centralization of purchasing may mean the grouping of the employees performing purchasing and their desks, chairs, and files into one organizational unit. Likewise, centralization of inspection may mean all inspection work is located in one section of a factory building, or a centralized manufacturing enterprise may mean all buildings of the company are clustered in one section of a city. In contrast, decentralization may mean the dispersion of the employees and physical facilities of an enterprise.

It is entirely possible for centralization of employees and physical facilities to exist with decentralization of authority and, vice versa, decentralization of employees and physical facilities with centralization of authority. Generally speaking, when employees and physical facilities are centralized, authority probably is likewise, but when employees and facilities are centralized, authority can be either decentralized or centralized. For example, in a grocery chain with stores scattered over several states, a store manager has no authority over his company's advertising or purchasing. In another case, a manufacturer has employees and plants scattered throughout the United States, with each plant doing its own purchasing, advertising, cost, and product research work.

EVALUATING CENTRALIZATION AND DECENTRALIZATION

Most enterprises start out with a centralization of authority arrangement. This stems from quite normal causes. The top executives may feel that they are in better touch with activities and can apply their special abilities more forcefully under a centralized setup. Cost also enters the picture, for mistakes made by subordinates may prove quite serious financially. Then too the duplication of functions is minimized in the centralized arrangement. The disinclination to delegate authority also contributes in some degree to the following of a centralized arrangement.

Size of enterprise apparently plays a major role. If the enterprise is large, decentralization probably exists. The scope and amount of managerial work contribute to this arrangement. Also many advocates of decentralization point out that this arrangement encourages good human relations among employees and helps to give them status, freedom, and an opportunity to manage and earn promotions. The argument is that people are developed more under a decentralized than a centralized arrangement. In fact, a test of managerial decentralization is the extent to which one man or small group rule of the enterprise is eliminated and the enterprise management members of the lower organization levels are permitted to make and enforce decisions.

Despite all the interest and discussion in management circles about decentralization, many chief executives continue to employ the centralized arrangement. For example, a well-known transportation equipment manufacturer changed from a centralized to a decentralized plan. Much publicity was given this move, but the hoped-for benefits did not materialize, and after three years a swing back to centralization was made. This is not to imply that decentralization offers no advantages for this is definitely not true. Just where between the two extremes of centralization and decentralization an enterprise should be organized depends upon the individual circumstances. Some experts claim that the use of automation, permitting large outputs in a concentrated area, favors centralized operations. Computers, for example, tend to centralize organizational authority over much paperwork processing. However, the greater availability of terminal units tied to the computer has emphasized a decentralized arrangement. Additional considerations could be cited, but the selection is managerial in that some managers with certain goals and available resources prefer the centralized arrangement, while others sincerely believe the decentralized is superior.[1]

To provide some evaluating basis, Figure 17–3 has been included. A listing of the major advantages from centralization and likewise those from decentralization are shown.

FIGURE 17–3

Important Advantages of Centralization
1. Power and prestige are provided the chief executives.
2. Uniformity of policies, practices, and decisions are fostered.
3. Full utilization of the main office specialists is promoted, due in large part to their proximity to the top-management level.
4. High qualified specialists can be utilized because the scope and volume of their work are sufficient to support and to challenge topnotch managers.
5. Duplication of functions is maintained at a minimum.
6. The danger of actions drifting and getting off course is minimized.
7. Elaborate and extensive controlling procedures and practices are not required.
8. A strong coordinated top-management team is developed.

Important Advantages of Decentralization
1. A decentralized organization structure stresses delegation of authority and relieves the top managers' load.
2. The development of "generalists" rather than specialists is encouraged, thereby facilitating succession into positions of general managers.
3. Intimate personal ties and relationships are promoted, resulting in greater employee enthusiasm and coordination.
4. Familiarity with important aspects of special work is readily acquired.
5. Efficiency is increased since the structure can be viewed "as a whole" so that trouble spots can be located and remedied easily.
6. For multiunit enterprises keyed to geographical dispersion, full advantage of respective local conditions can be obtained.
7. Plans can be tried out on an experimental basis in one plant, modified, and proven before being supplied to similar plants of a company.
8. Risks involving possible losses of personnel, facilities, and plants are spread out.

An interesting organization is that of the mammoth General Motors Corporation. Its guiding genius, the late Alfred P. Sloan, conceived in the formative days of GM "to divide it into as many parts as consistently can be done, place in charge of each part the most capable executive that can be found, and develop a system of coordination so that

---

[1] For literature on this subject see: Rodney H. Brady, "Computers in Top-Level Decision Making," *Harvard Business Review,* July–August 1967, pp. 67–76; William E. Reif, "Computer Technology and Management Organization," Iowa City: Bureau of Business and Economic Research, 1968; Alfred P. Sloan Jr., *My Years with General Motors* (Garden City, N.Y.: Doubleday & Co., Inc., 1964), pp. 46–55; Harold J. Leavitt and Thomas Whisler, "Management in the 1980's" *Harvard Business Review,* November–December, 1958, pp. 41–48.

each part may strengthen and support each other." This has been termed "decentralized organization with centralized control." The units exercising major controls are centralized, and in the case of General Motors, financial controls play a prominent role. Buick competes with Oldsmobile, and likewise Frigidaire competes with Harrison Radiator; yet they are all coordinated by the central domestic office in Detroit. On this concept GM has grown into a gigantic corporation, building and selling approximately one half of the total volume of cars and trucks in the United States.

COMMON BASIC ORGANIZATION UNITS

The overall pattern of most organization structures is built around three fundamental activities performed: producing, selling, and financing. The terminology may differ, but essentially these are the activities carried out. They are necessary for the operation and survival of the enterprise. In business enterprises these three activities are clearly visible, but in other types of undertakings one or more of the activities may be obscure. To illustrate, for a manufacturer of automobiles the basic organizational units are production, sales, and finance; but for an airlines company, the use of operations (production), traffic (sales), and finance is common; and for an insurance company, the following is frequently found: underwriting and actuarian (production), general agencies (sales), and claims and investments (finance).

Why these three fundamental activities? Because most companies are concerned with the producing of a product or service for use by others. Since it is produced for use by others, it must be distributed or marketed; that is, people must be found who want the product or service and are willing to accept it at mutually agreeable terms to the seller (enterprise) and the buyer. Also to produce and to distribute the product or service necessitate the raising and the maintaining of sufficient capital; that is, the financing activities must be performed by some members of the enterprise.

ADDITIONAL ORGANIZATION UNITS

The scope of the three fundamental organization units and the complexity of the enterprise give rise to numerous types of additional organization units. These types will result mainly from such things as the nature and amount of the work to be done, the degree of specialization practiced, and the people and the work places available for the work.

To illustrate, under the fundamental unit of sales the scope of the work may be so broad that it is believed advantageous to divide the work into advertising, sales promoting, and selling. Hence, the manager in charge of sales splits off the advertising and sales promoting activities and for each places a subordinate in charge. A sales manager is appointed to manage the selling work in the field. These three additional units will appear in the organization structure at the level immediately below that of the fundamental organizational unit of sales. In a similar manner, assume the manager in charge of production established a unit of engineering and research, of factory work, and also of purchasing. These concepts are illustrated graphically by the chart shown in Figure 17–4.

FIGURE 17–4

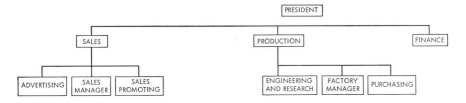

Now assume that the products and services of the enterprise continue to grow and conditions become such that further additional units are deemed necessary for efficient operation. Accordingly, from the advertising unit is spun off the two subordinate units of (1) television and radio and (2) magazines and newspapers, both of which are placed in the organization level below that in which advertising is located. This is illustrated by Figure 17–5. In addition, other units are established, as indicated by the figure. They include two sales units—one for the eastern and one for the western territory. Under the eastern sales unit are four units added to handle sales, respectively, to (1) institutions, including hotels, hospitals, and schools; (2) wholesalers; (3) government; and (4) manufacturers. Likewise under production, two units have been created. One is designated to include metal products, the other to encompass products made of plastics. Under the former, five units composed of punching, heat treating, welding, assembling, and finishing have been added as subordinate units. It can be readily seen

FIGURE 17–5. Showing the vertical growth of an enterprise from that illustrated in Figure 17–4

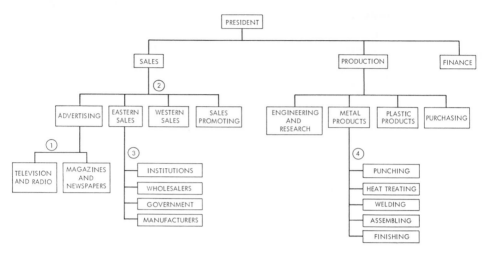

that as the enterprise continues to expand, more units will probably be required.

DEPARTMENTATION

The division of authority and responsibility among managers at the same organization level gives rise to departmentation in organization. Normally each organization level below the very top or apex is departmentized and likewise each succeeding lower level is further departmentized.

As pointed out in Chapter 14, departmentation is followed in order to distribute the work, take advantage of work specialization, obtain units of manageable size, and utilize managerial ability. It is usually carried out by dividing the work to be done into semiautonomous units. Managementwise, the net effect is a setting forth of managerial authority and responsibility along with operating activities for each organization unit.

Departmentation helps shape the organization structure significantly. And departmentation is closely related to the centralization or decentralization followed. When centralization is predominant, relatively little departmentation is followed and vice versa, when decentralization is followed, a relatively large amount of departmentation is practiced.

MEANS OF DEPARTMENTATION

The chief means of departmentation include by (1) function, (2) product, (3) territory, (4) customer, (5) process, (6) task force, and (7) matrix. An organizer is free to use any means of departmentation in constructing an organization structure. In fact, in any given structure several means are typically used.

Departmentation by Function. This means is usually followed for the top and for the bottom organization levels. As implied by its name, the departmentation is by function or activity and it results in units, each one of which deals with a separate function or a group of similar activities. Referring again to Figure 17–4, departmentation by function has been followed for the top levels, i.e., sales, production, and finance, and also for the next level as indicated by advertising, sales manager, sales promotion, engineering and research, factory manager, and purchasing.

Departmentation by Product. This arrangement is quite common for it is readily understood, stresses the utilization of specialized knowledge, and encourages a sensible degree of specialization. Examples include the departmentation of a department store which is segregated by products; loans of a commercial bank wherein commercial, personal, and industrial are common organizational units; and the organization of certain governmental executive departments, such as the Department of Interior, which has major organizational units of fish and wildlife, parks and marine reserve, mineral resources, public land management, water and power development, water quality and research, and solicitor (legal adviser). In Figure 17–5, departmentation by product is illustrated by the left portion marked with a "1" in which under advertising, the two units (1) television and radio, and (2) magazines and newspapers, are established.

Departmentation by Territory. This is followed where nearness to local conditions appears to offer advantages, such as low cost of operation and opportunities to capitalize upon attractive local conditions as they arise. Territorial departmentation is especially popular for sales where the division according to some geographical market segregation appears feasible. It also provides a good arrangement for training and developing in that the executive can demonstrate his ability in a certain territory and thus merit promotion to a more important area. In Figure 17–5 establishing the sales unit for eastern sales and one for western sales illustrates departmentation by territory, located by a "2" on the figure.

Departmentation by Customer. When the major emphasis is upon being better able to serve buyers of the enterprise's products or services, a departmentation by customer is suggested. The teen-age shop in the department store is illustrative, as is also a large bank's unit for loans to customers. A common breakdown is loans to retailers and wholesalers and loans to manufacturers. Under this latter unit are breakdowns such as (1) loans to manufacturers of primary metal, glass, and machinery; (2) loans to manufacturers of chemicals, petroleum products, paper, and transportation equipment; (3) loans to textile, apparel, and furniture manufacturers; and (4) loans to food processors and miscellaneous manufacturers. Departmentation by customer can usually be justified when a product or service of wide appeal is offered through numerous marketing channels and outlets. However, this organizational arrangement has a tendency to remain rigid, thus posing adjustment problems during widely fluctuating periods of enterprise activity. With reference again to Figure 17–5 the four organization units under eastern sales, marked by a "3" on the figure, depict departmentation by customer.

Departmentation by Process. This provides a logical means when the machines or equipment used require special skill for operating, or are of a large capacity which eliminates organizational dividing, or have technical facilities which strongly suggest a concentrated location. Economic and technologic considerations are the foremost reasons for adoption of process departmentation. It is most commonly found in production and frequently at the operative levels. Note the five units under the production unit for metal products in Figure 17–5, marked by a "4."

Using process as a guide, there are three basic patterns available: (1) serial, (2) parallel, and (3) unit assembly. The pattern followed will determine, in part, the organizational units adopted. In few instances will any of these patterns be used in its pure form. More commonly, part of the work will be processed under one pattern, part under another, and so forth.

Under the serial pattern, work moves through a single channel or assembly line and progresses step by step to completion as it passes the various work stations. This arrangement permits employees to be highly specialized by process and usually requires a brief breaking-in time for attainment of satisfactory output. However, the "cycle time," or total elapsed time from the beginning to the ending of a unit of work, may be great, and there is also the possibility of reduced employee interest under the serial arrangement.

The parallel arrangement designates concurrent handling and provides for a number of different work steps to be performed within an organizational unit or by one employee. Actually the work divisions can be made on any of several bases, as long as the same work steps, or nearly so, remain in each segment. For example, operation Nos. 1, 2, 3, and 4 may be done by operator A on brass couplings while the same operation Nos. 1, 2, 3, and 4 may be done by operator B. Under the parallel arrangement, cycle time is reduced, movement of the work in process is minimized, and employee interest is promoted. But training time for the employee may be increased since several work steps must be mastered.

Simultaneous handling is another way of expressing the unit-assembly arrangement. Here different employees perform different work steps upon the same work at the same time. To illustrate, the work to be done is divided among employees A, B, and C. Simultaneously, employee A performs his particular operation on his batch of work, B his operation on his batch, and likewise C on his batch of work. At appropriate times the different batches of work are shifted among the employees so that completion of the total work is accomplished. Under the unit-assembly pattern process, specialization is followed, yet the cycle time is minimized. Training is quite likely not to be excessive. The work, however, must be divided and routed to the various employees.

Departmentation by Task Force.   This arrangement includes the assigning of a team or task force to a definite project or block of work which extends from the beginning to the completing of a wanted and definite type and quantity of work. A task force is usually relatively small, perhaps not over a dozen members. It exists for the life of the project and is then disbanded. It has a leader, is self-contained, and includes all the necessary knowledge and skill for performing the work. It is a preferred means whenever a well-defined project must be dealt with, or the task is bigger than anything the organization is accustomed to. Sometimes called project organization or project management, it is in keeping with the newer decision-making theories which are inclusive in their scope of operations, it encourages objective-mindedness, it gives the members somewhat of a free hand to accomplish the objective, and it emphasizes each member's developing and utilizing his own initiative and creativity in his work efforts.

Departmentation by task force has gained favor for many research projects outstanding of which are those of the missile or weapons system and outer space projects. It is widely used in public accounting firms, advertising agencies, and management consultant firms.

Task-force departmentation does have shortcomings, however, such as some members feeling frustrated, having a sense of insecurity, and complaining of unstable organization. Who determines their promotion possibilities, and future careers may also give rise to knotty problems. To help minimize these drawbacks, certain factors should be kept in mind. These are given in Figure 17–6.

FIGURE 17–6. Factors aiding successful task force departmentation

1. The basis for project is sound. Commitment to supporting the task force must be thorough. And the project should be designed for each specific project and company. Borrowing the format from another may not give desired results. Generally speaking successful task force departmentation requires more managerial attention than does normal functional activities.
2. The tasks are defined adequately. Sufficient time and effort are required to define the objectives and the tasks to be performed. Network plans and work breakdown structures are the type of techniques to assist in spelling out this required information. The project manager should participate in the project design and also, if possible, several members of top management so that the obligations of all are clearly understood. Both large and complex projects as well as small projects should be defined.
3. The task force has a competent leader. The task force leader has considerable influence upon the project. Ability to work with members of different organization levels representing various disciplines, and providing an overall view are mandatory. The continuing trade-off conflicts between schedules, technical performance, and costs require that an effective planner and organizer serve as the leader.
4. The regular company management is supportive to the task force. A project manager survives difficulties if he receives cooperation of the managers of the functional departments. Top managers must see to it that proper authority is given the task force, that project funds are released as agreed upon, and that some flexibility will be followed in making changes required by recommendations and decisions of the task force.
5. A definite project termination date is established. Best results stem from planning a definite period to complete the project, otherwise it may continue indefinitely. For morale purposes, it is advisable to tell each task force member his next assignment before the project ends. Further, no member should suffer adverse effects on his progress with the company such as promotion, or pay increase because of leaving his regular job and serving on a task force team.

Departmentation by Matrix. This is one of the important newer concepts of organization featuring not only departmentation on a highly technical basis, but also on a management basis as well. The supervision is dual, being technical from the technical chief and administrative from the administrative chief. This concept using a matrix form is shown by Figure 17–7. For example, in this figure five groups, A, B, C, D, and E represent five different technical skills. Each technical unit has a chief who reports to the manager of technical services. Simultaneously and cutting across these technical services are administrative groups made up of the technicians from the different technical groups.

FIGURE 17–7. Matrix departmentation concept

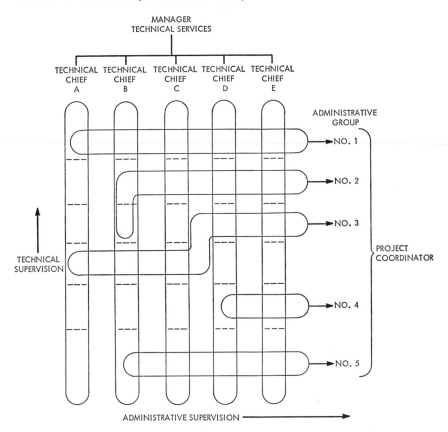

Administrative group No. 1, for example, consists of one technician from each of the five technical groups while administrative group No. 2 has none from technical group A, two from group B, and one each from C, D, and E.

The matrix departmentation, known also as grid, or lattice work organization patterns, emerged as an answer to the growing complexity and size of enterprises which required an organization structure more flexible and technically oriented than the traditional line and staff. By means of multiple reporting systems and interweaving authority lines a more balanced form of organization is achieved and one which tends to reconcile a company's breadth with its depth. If the task requires broad, problem-solving know-how, that can be supplied; on the other hand, if specialized advice in depth is needed, that can be offered. Among the well-known companies successfully using matrix departmentation are Caterpillar Tractor Company, American Cyanamid Company, and TRW, Inc.

Care should be exercised in adopting matrix departmentation. The "one man, one boss" honored management practice is severely modified into one-man, one-boss relationship plus other relationships. The line and staff may be primarily for one aspect of a man's job, then eventually several superiors may be coequal for other aspects of his job. The matrix arrangement requires extensive communication and preferably it should meet internal company needs and not simply be grafted onto the existing organization in hope of demonstrating progressive management thinking. Decision making may be slowed down by following matrix departmentation and the amount and type of authority of each manager must be clearly delineated. In addition, all managers must understand the rules of the game and this usually necessitates an educational effort so that none feel their authority is threatened and non-management members learn how to function with two managers.

SPAN OF AUTHORITY[2]

Organization structure is also affected by another major factor, namely, span of authority. It conditions the number of organization units, their arrangement, and their relationships. *Span of authority is the number of immediate subordinates that report to a manager.* Wide spans or a manager having a relatively large number of immediate subordinates usually results in few organization levels and a "flattening out" of the structure. A small number of organization levels expedites communication, but wide spans are challenging to a manager inasmuch as his scope of operation is broadened and he has the opportunity to grow and show what he can do. In contrast, narrow spans calling for a relatively small number of immediate subordinates, expedite more personalized manager-subordinate relationships, perhaps more effective managing of the subordinates, and a "tall organization," i.e., one with relatively many levels.

The question arises: What is the proper number of persons to be subordinated to any executive? Proper span is basically a behavioral question and varies with such things as the ability of the manager, his relative location in the structure, fear of possible rivals, faith in subordinates to perform satisfactorily, and the degree of teamwork that is present. However, the type of work is also important. For example, enterprises in which the work remains essentially the same and is re-

---

[2] This is called span of control by many. However, the term "span of authority" is more meaningful of the concept and is employed here in the interest of clarity.

peated over and over again with slight, if any, change are usually successful in employing greater spans of authority than are those enterprises dealing with highly dynamic and volatile activities. Also, the necessity for frequent and involved communication usually requires a short span.[3]

Among well-known enterprises one finds a wide variety of practice. As Supreme Commander of the AEF in World War II, Dwight D. Eisenhower had three operating subordinates reporting directly to him. In a well-known hotel chain the president has a total of six executives reporting to him, and the organization structure of a prominent university shows no less than 18 men of executive status immediately subordinate to the president. In one unit of this university's organization structure, a college, a total of 37 report directly to the dean.

To improve understanding of span of authority, it is helpful to differentiate between span of authority of executive supervision and that of operative supervision. The former is predominately mental, strong on leadership, and requires ability to solve a variety of different nonrecurring problems. Relatively short spans of authority are common at the top management organization levels. On the other hand, at the middle and lower levels, the decisions required are not of a high pioneering type, contacts are direct with subordinates, and the areas of operation are fairly well defined and limited. Under such conditions the span of authority may be relatively greater than that in the case of management members at high organizational levels.[4]

QUANTITATIVE SPAN OF AUTHORITY

A quantitative approach to this subject reveals that the preferred span of authority is six subordinates to one superior under the conditions of (1) the time spent by the superior with a subordinate is one-half hour (called service time), (2) the time between such conferences (called service sessions) is seven and one-half hours, and (3) the number of superiors is one. If the service time is reduced to one-fourth hour, the span increases to nine or ten employees to one superior.[5]

The span of authority affects significantly the number of organiza-

[3] Critical variables affecting the span of authority have been stated as (1) dependence of subordinates on their superior, (2) interdependence of subordinates' activities, and (3) interdependence of the work units with other units. See Robert G. Wright, "An Approach to Find Realistic Spans of Management," *Arizona Business Bulletin,* Nov., 1970, pp. 20–28.

[4] See Ralph C. Davis, *Industrial Organization and Management* (3d ed.; New York: Harper & Bros., 1957), pp. 72–73.

[5] Lawrence S. Hill, "The Application of Queuing Theory to the Span of Control," *Academy of Management Journal* (March 1963), pp. 58–69.

tional relationships between the superior and the subordinates. Observe first that the number of these relationships is greater than the number of persons directly supervised because there are also relationships between the persons directly supervised. Thus, a superior with three subordinates is concerned not only with the three direct relationships, that is, to subordinate No. 1, to No. 2, and to No. 3, but also with the six cross-relationships among the three subordinates that include No. 1 to No. 2, No. 1 to No. 3, No. 2 to No. 1, No. 3 to No. 1, No. 2 to No. 3, and No. 3 to No. 2. There are also nine direct group relationships possible; that is, the superior to each possible combination of subordinates, for example, the superior to No. 1 with No. 2, to No. 1 with No. 3, to No. 2 with No. 1, to No. 3 with No. 1, and so forth.

FIGURE 17–8. The effect of the number of subordinates upon the number of organization relationships

Number of subordinates	Number of Relationships			
	Direct	Cross	Direct Group	Total
1...................	1	..	..	1
2...................	2	2	2	6
3...................	3	6	9	18
4...................	4	12	28	44
5...................	5	20	75	100

The quantitative approach to the number of organizational relationships was developed by V. A. Graicunas, a French consultant in management.[6] He developed mathematical formulae with which to calculate and to show the rapid increase in executive-subordinate relationships as the number of subordinates increases. The formula is

$$R = n(2^{n-1} + n - 1)$$

where

$R = $ Relationships
$n = $ Number of subordinates

Figure 17–8 shows data based on these mathematical findings. Observe that when a fourth subordinate is added, the total relationships jump from 18 to 44, an increase of over 140 percent. While there may be differences in opinion regarding the application of his work to a given

[6] V. A. Graicunas, "Relationships in Organization," *Papers on the Science of Administration* (New York: Institute of Public Administration, Columbia University, 1937), pp. 183–87.

situation, Graicunas' efforts serve to emphasize the multiplicity of relationships induced by the adding of subordinates. This means, of course, that the tasks of supervision multiply rapidly as subordinates are added.

PRINCIPLE OF INCREASING ORGANIZATION RELATIONSHIPS

As additional persons or units are added to an organization structure, the number of organization relationships increases at a much greater rate than the number of persons or units added.

ADDITIONAL CONSIDERATIONS OF DEPARTMENTATION

In quite a few instances, the organizer is faced with the problem of where to place a specific activity in a specific organization structure. Neither the degree of decentralization, various means of departmentation, nor spans of authority seem to point to a definite organization location. For such cases, the following considerations can prove helpful:

1. Place Activity in Unit Having Most Use for It. Frequently, this proves effective even though the unit's activities and the newly assigned activity are quite dissimilar. Engineering, for example, in some business enterprises is under production; in others it is a part of sales. If the engineering activity is performed mainly to meet customers' requirements and requests, it might well be placed under sales. In contrast, if engineering concerns essentially problems of production and is used extensively by the production personnel, then engineering logically belongs under production.

2. Consider Splitting an Activity between Two Units. Most activities are best performed by one organizational unit; but for some the nature of activity may suggest dividing it between two organizational units. Checks or audits on the work done by other organizational units are illustrative. Generally speaking, the proofing of work should be done by someone other than the performer of the work. Inspection, for example, is commonly located within an organization so that its work will not be unduly influenced by operative managers and nonmanagers. Likewise, in accounting, the auditor of accounts is an independent unit—frequently outside the entire enterprise.

3. Inject Competition between Units. In some instances the greatest opportunity for development occurs when certain activities are disassociated. The purpose is to provide a stimulus to greater achievements. Competition and the introduction of rivalry in an organization spurs managers to make the best possible showing in their respective efforts. The classical example in this respect is the organization of the General Motors Corporation, in which separate units are established and competition among them is consciously applied and encouraged. In effect each unit strives to outperform the other units within the same overall organization. Further examples of injecting competition between units is the dividing of the sales management activity into foreign and domestic, or by types of products, or by territories.

4. Emphasize Harmony and Cooperation. Sometimes the departmentation has the prime purpose to achieve harmony and cooperation. Competitive effort within a segment of the organization structure is avoided. To illustrate, industrial engineering might include wage administration and plant maintenance in order that unnecessary managerial friction, arising if the activities were separate, can be avoided. Or in the case of a large retail distributor having branch stores and a strong mail-order division, one sales manager was placed in charge of all sales—both retail and mail order—for the purpose of preventing one type of selling to dominate at the expense of the other.

The practice of emphasizing harmony in the departmentation efforts of organizing must be handled carefully and discreetly; otherwise the urge to create, excel, and accomplish are stifled. Harmony is desirable but not at the cost of dulling initiative and suppressing the development of an aggressive and astute management team. If the harmony and cooperation theme is carried to excess, there is real danger of having spineless "yes-men" constituting the management members of the organization.

5. Follow Manager's Interest. Where to locate a particular activity is sometimes suggested by the interest of a manager. The assignment of a new activity or the transfer of an old one to an interested manager generally works out satisfactorily because having interest in the unit frequently but not always means he will strive to see that it is performed well. In a large beverage company, one of the industrial engineers was insistent that the company establish an operations research unit. No action was taken on the matter for nearly two years, but the engineer continued to urge the creation of the new activity. Finally, the unit was established, the industrial engineer was placed in charge, and extremely favorable results have been achieved.

GROUP FUNCTIONS IN ORGANIZATION

Up to this point we have discussed organization structure and departmentation in terms of composition and relationships of organization units as being among individuals. However, there are functions assigned to a group rather than an individual. These group functions are quite important in organization and they are present in practically every structure. Committees, plural executives, and boards of directors are the three group functions that will be discussed here.

COMMITTEES

Committees are common yet controversial in most organizations. They can and do exist at any organizational level, serve in various capacities and for different purposes, are known by many different names, and enjoy wide degrees of acceptance among management members. Extremely important work is accomplished via the committee route. Typically, educational enterprises are loaded with committees, and they are common in government and in business. In trade associations and most professional societies, the major portion of the organization structure is made up of committees.

Literally the word "committee" means those to whom some matter or charge is committed. It can be defined as *a body of persons elected or appointed to meet on an organized basis for the discussion and dealing of matters brought before it.* This is a committee from the formal viewpoint. Such a committee usually has a formally recognized and permanent place in the organization structure. Its makeup, duties, membership, and decision-making power may be carefully spelled out. For example, some business enterprises have at the top level, a planning and policy committee, or a general management committee made up of selected company executives. The committee meets regularly—perhaps weekly—makes decisions, sees that they are enforced, and participates in the management affairs of the company. Likewise, in other types of enterprise, typical top committees are in the organization of the Atomic Energy Commission, the Tennessee Valley Authority, and state public utility commissions.

In addition, there are formal committees of a temporary nature. They are put together to discuss a particular problem and to determine either what action to take or suggest possible actions that might be taken. Further, what can be termed informal committees exist. They consist of an informal gathering of people, perhaps executives at luncheon, and discuss some aspect of company business. Such an informal committee has no formally designated purpose, authority, or organization, yet it does have influence and in some respects serves the equivalent function of a formal committee.

Why are committees used? Basically for two reasons. First, the interaction of members serving as a group should produce superior results in contrast to those achieved by an individual. Both idea generation and deliberation to improve an action are among the benefits believed possible by committee use. Second, the complexity of organization with its large number of functions and various levels necessitates periodic exchange of information. A committee is an effective medium to meet this need and in this capacity serves not only as a communicative aid, but also as an effective coordinative medium.

COMMITTEE EVALUATION

To some managers, committees are highly effective and represent an indispensable tool of organizing. Other managers honestly feel committees are a great source of frustration and an excellent means for wasting time. This latter group like to recite:

> In all our towns and all our cities
> There are no statutes to committees.

Committees have a place in organization, but since they are a part of organization, they are subjected to all the influences of good or bad organization. A committee serves neither as a substitute for a good manager nor as a device that corrects poor organization. Committees have legitimate functions in organization; the challenge is to use them properly.

A key consideration in evaluating a committee is the type of authority it has. Much of the criticism leveled at committees stems from a lack of identifying the authority of the committee. For example, if it has staff advisory authority, it is supposed to suggest ideas and counsel regarding how a project should be accomplished and not implement the actual actions.

Figure 17–9 outlines the main reasons for the widespread use of committees. In essence, these are advantages resulting from committee usage.

In contrast, there are disadvantages in the use of committees. The most frequent criticism is that the cost of committees is greater than the benefits received from them. A committee provides the medium for people to assemble and talk over various matters. Admittedly, this is a time-consuming process, and of course while a committee is in session, its members cannot transact their important day-to-day duties; hence the possible loss of time is compounded. The cost of a $20,000-a-year manager is about $10 per hour. If a committee of five such

FIGURE 17–9. Reasons for the extensive use of committees

1. Expert and collective knowledge can be concentrated upon a specific problem. A wide range of experience can be tapped, exchange of ideas fostered, and effective give-and-take discussions encouraged. Employed is group judgment, which is believed superior for certain type problems and situations.
2. Coordination is assisted. Different views can be unified and integrated, agreed prescribed courses of action established, and maximum understanding among committee participants achieved. The receiving, relating, interpreting, and channeling of information makes this coordination feasible.
3. Too much authority of one person is prevented. By its very nature, a committee tend to distribute its authority among the committee members, who can watch and check each other's actions. This check on authority is most prominent in government, religious, and educational organizations. In the latter, for example, the president of a university is usually restrained by the committee, or board of regents, that appoints him, as well as by faculty committees and other university committees that, among other activities, determine operating policies, curriculum, salaries, and tenure.
4. Social values are provided. Committee membership provides prestige, permits recognition as an equal with other members who have status, and tends to satisfy the human desire to belong and to do something worthwhile.
5. Motivation is supplied. People like participation, and committee use encourages it. Cooperation is enhanced in the execution of a proposed action and is reasonably assured if the committee develops the plan. There is also knowledge acquired by the committee members and possibly pride of authorship gained by a member. Such characteristics have strong motivational value.
6. Education of members is promoted. Each participant's viewpoint is broadened; he gains an appreciation of the other unit's problems as well as those of the entire enterprise. Placing at least one young manager on a committee and asking him to express himself first at each meeting can be practiced.

executives meets one hour each week the salary cost alone is about $2,500, to which secretarial expense and other expenditures must be added. The yearly accomplishments of the committee can be evaluated in comparison to its annual cost in an attempt to determine whether the committee should be continued.

Another disadvantage of the committee is its lack of accountability. All members of a committee are theoretically accountable for the committee's action, yet this is extremely difficult to assess, especially if the committee's final position was reached by compromise. No one member, including the chairman, can be held accountable for the committee's action, since he has no effective control over the individual members of the committee. This lack of accountability makes committees ineffective where the assignment calls for taking action. Also, in some instances, committees are used by a manager as an alibi or escape from responsibility. If the decision is likely to be unpopular, he can escape the consequences by diffusing the responsibility via the committee route.

Another drawback is that a committee's decision frequently is one of compromise. The belief seems to persist among committee members that their decision should reflect a unanimity of opinion. Harmony is sought. This is understandable, since the committee members are also members within the company who must work together in many different capacities. Furthermore, they usually have some responsibility in implementing their collective decision and a dissatisfied or recalcitrant committee member might sabotage the committee's action by not cooperating in the implementation efforts. In addition, there is the situation of control by a minority when the tradition of unanimous action is present. The only decision possible is one of compromise. Also, certain issues may be avoided when all committee members know bringing them up for discussion and a decision will cause endless discussion and no decision.

ACQUIRING COMMITTEE EFFECTIVENESS

In addition to what has been said, there are additional suggestions to follow in acquiring committee effectiveness. Like all practitioners of management, a member of a committee should have a clear idea of what he is to consider. The objective must be definite. It is relatively easy for the members to get off the beam and delve into areas not intended for their consideration. A satisfactory approach is to provide written specifications outlining the purpose and scope of the committee, its authority, its responsibility, and its relationships with the organizational units of the enterprise.

The decision-making task of a committee should be defined and known to all concerned. This is a major prerequisite for successful committee work. A clear statement of whether the committee is to decide and take action, or advise and counsel, or simply serve as a sounding board for the chairman is necessary for efficiency. In addition, the duties of each member should be pointed out. After all, serving on a committee is a job, and it is paramount that a person will do better on a job when he knows what the work is and what is expected of him. Spelling out the decision making and the duties also makes for better organization relationships.

To expedite discussion and exchange of ideas the committee size should be from 3 to 17 members as the most practical limits, with perhaps 3 to 7 as the preferred number. The committee members need to have a mutual respect for each other's interests, to understand the several possible viewpoints presented about an issue, to express themselves clearly and concisely, to think independently, and to integrate, as well as compromise, tentative conclusions presented for action. Many feel that for best results the members should be of about equal status. This avoids the tendency for one member, superior in position, to dominate or sway the thinking of the committee members unduly.

The chairman is usually the key to successful committee work. Through his leadership he can promote helpful sessions. Careful planning and preparing of an agenda, seeing that each member is supplied with appropriate data well in advance of the meeting, and keeping the discussions on the subjects at hand and moving along with each member given an opportunity to express himself are among the "musts" for a good committee chairman. In some enterprises, questionnaires are filled out after each meeting to rate the chairman's effectiveness. In other cases, the chairmanship is rotated in order to develop leadership and increase each member's interest in the committee.

The subject matter is another important consideration which affects a committee's effectiveness. Generally speaking, subjects pertaining to objective evaluations, broad means for achieving stated objectives, and evaluating past activities from an overall viewpoint are among those best suited for committee work. Basic issues, not masses of data, are best handled by committees. Experience shows that committees are not especially effective in collecting data for a particular project.

Finally, it is well to have adequate follow-up to the work of a committee and to review periodically its contributions. The follow-up is accomplished by a designated committee member taking the appropriate action—presenting the recommendation to an officer, distributing notes of the meeting to designated members, or instituting the action decided. Committees often become self-perpetuating; their need and contributions should be evaluated from time to time. Basic in this effort is to determine whether the purpose of the committee is still valid and if the committee is effective in terms of the purpose.

PLURAL EXECUTIVE

Although the term, plural executive, can be used to identify a committee, the common meaning of plural executive is two or more executives usually with line authority at the top levels of organization. The specific area of operations may be a phase of the enterprise activities of one or more of the fundamental management functions. Plural executive is commonly found in planning, especially policymaking. Controlling in its broader phases may also be included to a somewhat limited extent. The plural executive also is especially effective for settling questions of jurisdictional dispute and for the formulation of objectives.

The plural executive will no doubt increase in usage. Decision making is more and more being shared. This is not a matter of generosity, but simply a matter of sound management practicality. There is too much happening too fast in too many fields for one man to handle successfully all these diverse activities. Some companies such as General Electric, General Mills, Mead, and Chase Manhattan Bank have set up "offices of presidents."[7] By such means it is hoped that the needed broader scope of company operations at the top will be gained, top management in depth will be provided, and excellent development work for succession will be expedited.

The use and the position of the plural executive in any given case is influenced by such things as tradition, the type of enterprise, the caliber of the executives making up the plural executive, and the prominence through leadership or other influence by any one member of the group. True, there is more than one, but the group is strongly influenced by the leader, perhaps the president, so that the lead and pace are actually set by him—the other parts of the plural executive are followers for the most part. Theoretically, the plural executive has no person in charge and no one possessing ultimate authority to gain compliance with decisions, if necessary. Responsibility is not fixed with an individual; decisions may be delayed, and considerable time spent in determining what action to take. In these respects the plural executive encompasses new concepts, i.e., those not included in traditional management organizing.

BOARD OF DIRECTORS

A board of directors is legally created by the papers of incorporation of a corporation, and by them it is given the authority to exercise the powers of the corporation, limited by any conditions set forth in the corporation's bylaws. It is by means of a charter, as stipulated in state statutes called incorporation laws, that the corporation comes into existence.

It must be remembered that board of directors' decisions are group decisions. The board is a group; it acts jointly as a board—never as an individual. Opinions and actions result from several persons whose

---

[7] "The New Management Finally Takes Over," *Business Week,* August 23, 1969, p. 60.

background, experience, knowledge, and attitude condition what is done by any board. Some boards determine decisions that virtually affect the life of the corporation while others serve basically as approval bodies for the actions of the top management group. Between these two extremes are a number of activities that can be considered typically performed by a board of directors.

Many items come to a board of directors for consideration and action. For convenience we will classify them under four headings: (1) objectives determination, (2) selection of top managers, (3) financial structure of the corporation, and (4) review and appraisal. A board of directors acts as a steward of the assets that belong to the corporate owners. Because of this stewardship, the board has the legal right and the obligation to determine the objectives of the corporation. These objectives are quite broad and are made primarily in the light of protecting and watching over the assets of the corporation for the benefit of its stockholders. Also, in a number of instances, the board plays an active role in formulating basic corporate policies. This is in keeping with suggestions on how the broad objectives are to be accomplished.

The president of a corporation is almost always selected by the board of directors, but the selection of other top managers by a board varies widely. Commonly followed is the practice of the president nominating his top associates, subject to approval and confirmation of the board. In addition, compensation questions of base salary, bonuses, and expense allowances are answered by the board.

Financial matters such as approving or initiating changes in capital structure, the distribution of earnings, and the financial expansion or contraction by the corporation are decided by the board of directors. Seldom are these financial responsibilities turned over to other members. For example, almost without exception the board decides what portion of earnings should be paid to stockholders in the form of dividends, what portion used to decrease corporate indebtedness, and what portion to be plowed back into the corporate operations. Review and final approval of budgets dealing with overall corporate affairs are another common activity of a board.

The accomplishments of the management team is reviewed periodically by the board of directors. This is followed not only to find out if the objectives are being met, but also to motivate key managers by making suggestions helpful to them. This action commonly called "conscientious deliberation" involves asking pertinent questions designed to force the proponent of a particular action, commonly a corporate executive, to justify his proposed or past action and to bring out possibilities perhaps not thought of previously. In the case of new proposals this board action tends to promote only completed and well-thought-out programs being submitted. At the same time the board members can keep the corporation in tune with changing environment and conditions by their questioning and suggesting techniques. Frequently because of their positions, they are able to make worthy contributions along this line.

It should also be noted that a board member performs many activities on an informal basis. Not all of his corporate work is performed while attending a formal board meeting. He may, for example, talk informally with different executives of the corporation, or have lunch with managers not associated with the corporation to get their reactions to new ideas that the corporation contemplates using. Further, he may arrange to have interviews with technological experts, attend special meetings, and in various other ways seek information that may be of benefit to his corporation.

What is the proper size of a board of directors? Opinions vary, but probably a minimum of five and not more than fifteen is most satisfactory for most corporations. The membership should be large enough to be representative, but not so large that it becomes unwieldly. If the board is merely a façade used basically for status and prestige, the question of size is not important.

Likewise, the composition of the membership will vary among boards. Among the principal occupations of the members are top executives of the corporation, retired corporate executives, bankers, attorneys, prominent businessmen, investment and financial counselors, and educators.[8] The board makeup can be either from (1) inside members, i.e., employees of the corporation, resulting in an *inside board,* or (2) from inside and outside members (outside the corporation) resulting in an *outside board.* Inside boards bring satisfactory results when a sufficient number of qualified employees can be selected, the board's experience will help mature the members' thinking, and a relatively high technical knowledge is requisite for the decision-making process. Family-owned corporations commonly have inside boards, sometimes called *family boards,* because the owners believe outside help is not necessary or they fear having outsiders' participation. The chief advantage of using an outside board is to gain the benefits of members with diverse backgrounds, fulfill a sense of obligation to a community

---

[8] Jeremy Bacon, "Corporate Directorship Practices," *Business Policy Study No. 125* (New York: National Industrial Conference Board, Inc., 1967), pp. 14–16.

or to society, and promote good public relations. However, if an outside member lacks the time and interest to acquaint himself thoroughly with the corporation's aims and operations, the advantages accruing to the corporation from his being a board member may be greatly diminished.

Regarding frequency of meetings, some boards meet once or twice a week. However, many meet about once a month, but quarterly meetings are popular, and some meet only once or twice a year. The law requires one board meeting a year. The boards of smaller corporations tend to have fewer meetings than do larger corporations.

QUESTIONS

1. What is the meaning of the term centralization as applied to a company's formal organization? What is meant by the term, decentralization? Give an example of each.
2. Refer to Figure 17–1 and list the different means of departmentation used. Give the respective location of each means.
3. How do you account for the widespread use of committees in organizing today?
4. Have you ever worked in an organization where departmentation by task force was used? If so, describe the arrangement followed, and how successful it appeared to be. If not, do you believe the task-force arrangement would have improved the organization? Why?
5. Make a drawing illustrating the parallel basic arrangement under process departmentation.
6. With reference to a board of directors, discuss (1) the number and composition of its members, (2) the meaning of a family board, and (3) informal activities performed by its members.
7. What is matrix departmentation and what managerial considerations are important in its use?
8. As a manager would you be inclined to favor decentralization? Why?
9. In an enterprise with which you are familiar, enumerate the activities which are centralized from the organizational viewpoint and those that are not. How do you account for this arrangement?
10. Discuss under what conditions you as a manager would be inclined to use a wide span of authority in your organization structure.
11. Of the various duties of a board of directors, which one do you feel is most important in today's management? Why?
12. Define, point out probable future usage, and give advantages of having plural executive in an organization.
13. Relate an experience wherein the use of a committee was not effective. In your opinion discuss what could have been done to make the committee's use satisfactory.
14. Is it a good departmentation practice to establish, within an organization structure, units that are competitive? Explain, citing an example.

CASE 17–1. SEBO CORPORATION

As a large supplier of automobile accessories, lighting equipment and plastic parts, this company enjoyed favorable growth on its reputation to supply superior products at competitive prices and in keeping with buyers' schedules. Each year tooling for new models of automobiles requires millions of dollars and rearrangement of the factory floor plan. This work necessitates a large force, the management of which is given very close attention.

CHART 1

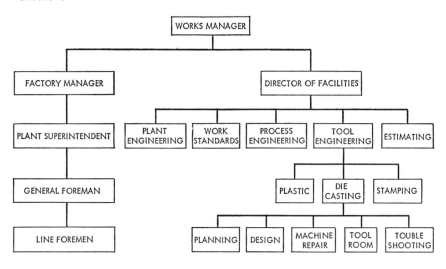

Until two years ago, the formal organization of the production plant was as shown by accompanying Chart No. 1. This is a portion of the formal organization including tooling, rearranging, and producing work. The belief behind this organization arrangement was that definite functionalization was needed. For example, if a problem arose in die casting, one person or a group of persons in die casting was responsible and stayed with the problem until a satisfactory answer was found. Experience showed, however, that too much time was spent in the shop by nonproductive personnel, who as a consequence did not have sufficient time for designing and developing work. The transaction from the floor to the office took up too much time. And it was not possible to perform satisfactorily the necessary estimating, following-up on tooling, and trouble shooting.

As a result the organization structure was changed to that shown by

Chart No. 2. This took place two years ago. The change was triggered by the new works manager who joined the company at that time. Of course, the unsatisfactory results from the then existent organization made the suggested move to improve it highly acceptable. The new works manager believed emphasis upon specialization and industrial engineering were what was needed. A comparison of Chart No. 2 with Chart No. 1 reveals that immediately below the works manager a department of industrial engineering was established with units of

CHART 2

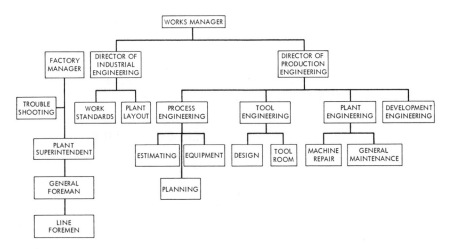

work standards and plant layout. In addition, production engineering was established with four engineering departments—process, tool, plant, and development. This represented some shuffling around of activities that had been under the director of facilities.

To date, this arrangement (Chart No. 2) has not resulted in solving the problem that existed before its adoption. The specialist approaches a problem from a relatively narrow viewpoint. Feedback and communication are poor. Estimators and planners were not aware of production or design problems. In several instances the designers were putting this year's mistakes into next year's tools. Further, the production man's problems were not being reflected in the new cost estimates being prepared.

Personnel from industrial engineering gave extra effort to locate and analyze the various production problems being encountered, but in general their efforts were late and, in a number of cases, duplicated the efforts of specialists from tool engineering design and also process engineering.

The works manager is very much concerned about the present situation and especially so since the president of the company told him that for the first two months of this current model year just concluded, the company, in order to maintain its reputation for meeting buyers' schedules, has spent over $165,000 in air shipments and nearly $900,000 in overtime.

Questions

1. What is the problem faced by Sebo Corporation?
2. Other than those of organizing, what factor would you feel might have influence upon the problem faced by this company? Discuss.
3. Point out the major changes made in the company going from the organization structure shown in Chart No. 1 to that in Chart No. 2.
4. What action do you recommend the works manager take? Why? What action the president take? Why?

CASE 17–2. STARR SNACK STORES, INC.

Twenty-three stores of this corporation located in four different states specialize in food snacks and party supplies including such items as potato chips, pretzels, cheese, beverages, place mats, napkins, and novelty items for favors. The central office is in Fort Wayne, Indiana.

Charles Cooper, president of "Triple S," as the corporation is commonly called, is a strong believer in decentralized operations. He feels the strength of the corporation lies in the competency of each store manager operating a sound retail store as the respective manager sees it. As a result, the local store manager decides what items will be carried in his store, prices charged, the number of employees, wages paid, hours the store is open, and the arrangement used for displayed products. Until recently, this latter item was handled out of the main office. Prominent among the activities handled by the central office are purchasing, accounting, including the analyzing and consolidating of records and reports performed by each store manager and sent to the home office, advertising, and store location.

The stores of the corporation enjoyed good acceptance by the public. The corporation had attained its present size within a period of four years. Although a loss was incurred the first six months, operations then became profitable, but for the past six months, there has been a sharp decline in profits. Mr. Cooper is quite concerned. Reports from his assistant, Mike Miller, show that each store appears to be busy, based on the number of people visiting the store. Also, the traffic count is high in each of the shopping centers where most of the stores are located. Mr. Miller states that many of the store managers complain to him about the reports they are required to turn in saying they take too much time and they could better spend their time in selling in the store.

Mr. Cooper talked with his accounting executive who said, in his opinion, the store managers needed closer supervision. They are not managing, otherwise their stores would show profitable operations. The current financial position of seven stores is critical. Another eleven stores are not quite realizing their total expenses. He stated, "In some of our stores, I personally have observed items displayed that are not authorized or purchased from us. What we need is a more rigid audit. These fellows would like complete freedom and have nothing at all to do with us in the central office."

After considerable thought, Mr. Cooper decided the present poor showing was probably due to competition. Hence, in a letter to each store manager, he set forth his views urging competitive pricing, improved service, and use of better store displays. Also announced was a stepped-up advertising program for which each store would be assessed an additional one third over its present advertising budget for the next six months.

Four months later, there has been no improvement in the profit picture of the corporation. Telephone communication between Mr. Cooper and several of the store managers reveal that they are not pleased with the advertising material and help given them. They feel it should be directed more toward building up their respective stores than to improving the image of Starr Snack Stores to the public. And they point out that they are paying more for advertising, but have no voice in how the funds are being used.

Questions

1. Evaluate the company's organization and the managerial activity of Mr. Cooper.
2. In general, what are your reactions to the thoughts and behavior of the store managers? Discuss.
3. What action do you recommend Mr. Cooper take? Justify your answer.

18

Organization dynamics

Spend some time alone and learn to develop your personal resources.

ALEXANDER REID MARTIN

ORGANIZING is a continuous activity which makes the manager question, appraise, and possibly change his organization structure in order to better achieve the goals which he and his associates seek. Since organization is so intimately associated with people, it is a living, vibrant entity. All living things change, none remains static. Hence, organizations change and the wise manager uses the dynamics of organization to his advantage.

In these efforts to make the organization a better means to achieve sought ends, the manager should include effective late practices available and incorporate the best current thinking found in writings about organization. At the same time he should neither permit himself to be carried away by a fad which has not yet been proven effective nor resist progressive organization ideas which are in tune with modern and growing accepted practices. Basically the requirements are to be aware of organization dynamics, constantly seek better ways, and develop the skill to know when and how to use organization change to enhance teamwork and take advantage of both social and technical improvements.

ORGANIZATION DYNAMICS

Why do organizations change? There are a number of reasons. Foremost is because of the handiwork that organizing creates. It emphasizes, or at least it should emphasize, interdependence among various necessary units. It is made up of components, relationships, and their inter-actions upon one another. These interactions actually create and main-tain an organization and at the same time condition the activities of its various parts. In other words, in an organization there are numerous, mutually dependent variables that are active, and each is affected by the collective effect which all the variables help maintain.

With time, the shortcomings of an existent organization show up and changes to correct these deficiencies are taken. Typical shortcom-ings include inadequate communication, slowness in decision making, misunderstanding of organization relationships, and poor committee work. The specific remedy followed varies in keeping with the indi-vidual circumstances prevailing, but most experienced managers agree that organizational deficiencies such as these mentioned will not correct themselves with the passage of time; corrective managerial organiza-tion action is required.

Fluctuation in the demand of products or services provided by the organization is also important. This results not only in the buildup or reduction of the number of employees, but also of changes in the makeup and even of the existence of certain organization units. For example, "coordinators" of various and sundry descriptions, assistants, and staff people change with the demands placed upon an organization. Certain units are needed at a given period, but subsequent develop-ments may make them superfluous.

Obsolescence of functions is another major contributor to organiza-tion dynamics. Change in objectives brings about change in functions to be performed; but even when objectives remain constant, the means of achieving them change with time, and this brings about dropping of old and adding of new functions. During boom business times, produc-tion requirements multiply, sales increase, and activities flourish. Under such stimuli many companies add new functions to their organization structure; new organizational units are formed; and departments spread in all directions, usually with little guidance. Later, it is discovered that some of these functions are not essential. Sometimes a reduction "across the board" is followed; that is, for each organizational unit, 10 or 15 percent of its personnel are eliminated. The result of such action is commonly a weakening of the essential and efficient organizational units, with the marginal units and overstaffed departments being per-mitted to continue their inefficient operation. A closer and more careful look at the activities from the viewpoint of organizational dynamics would help bring about a more effective answer to the problem.

In keeping with the above, we could say that technological changes are another contributing factor to organization dynamics. New equipment or new materials in the office or shop may call for pronounced changes in work procedures and skill requirements. In the office, for example, the installation of a computer can make for drastic organizational changes. Office units that were formerly separate are now combined, and other office units are completely eliminated. Or consider the case of technological changes in the factory. Changes in processes make for different organizational unit makeups and relationships. What constitutes a satisfactory organizational arrangement for certain methods of production may be wholly inadequate under new processes. Both the grouping of activities and their organizational location may be altered. Automation, for example, may completely eliminate former functional divisions of production and place more emphasis on maintenance and material handling, less on production scheduling and order control.

There is also the tendency to "keep up with the Joneses" in organizational changes. If a strong competitor reorganizes along certain lines, the urge to do likewise seems to prevail. A fad to establish a certain type department may spread rapidly among companies. At one time, the fashion was to adopt decentralization as a way of life. Some companies followed the trend without any assurance that decentralization was best for their individual circumstances.

Change is also brought about in an organization by the personnel. Employees retire, quit, get married, die, are transferred, promoted, demoted, and fired. The human element in organization is a dynamic concept, and it must always be considered as such. Human beings change in their characteristics; for example, a job providing complete satisfaction for a young man of 22 may not suffice 8 years later when that man is 30 years of age. To ignore organization dynamics as it affects the personnel of an organization is to court ultimate disaster and failure in organizing work. Usually training and developmental efforts are used to minimize this difficulty.

Lastly, a considerable amount of organization dynamics comes about due to a change in top management personnel. It is taken for granted that an incoming top executive has the right and is expected to reorganize his organizational unit. No doubt in some instances this reorganizing to impose his preferences and way of operation is justifiable, but there are other times when the changes appear to be arbitrary and without adequate investigating and planning.

PRINCIPLE OF DYNAMIC ORGANIZING

Organizing is dynamic; it should take into account changes in the enterprise.

WHO PLANS AND IMPLEMENTS ORGANIZATION CHANGE

Some companies have organization departments to help top managers in their organization efforts. Usually such a department has from three to ten members headed by a manager who reports to the president. This department arrangement, however, is by no means universal. In fact, a great many companies follow the belief that organizing is the manager's job and he should perform this function for his specific unit in order to fulfill his managerial job requirements satisfactorily. The separate organization plans are coordinated by the president or another top manager. He also counsels the manager doing the organizational work and offers him suggestions and aids. In still other companies, the president along with a committee study, recommend and adopt reorganization plans. The managers affected by the change are active in participating and in implementing the revised organization. There is also the arrangement of assigning organizing activities to the personnel department. This has merit because proper placement, motivation, and employee work-satisfaction are closely related to his job assignment, location in the organization, and his relationships with others within the organization structure.

In addition to developing organization plans, the various tasks performed by an organization group include clarifying the approved organization by means of charts, job descriptions, manuals, and other devices. Also, they study the present organization to determine its adequacy, propose changes, and review changes suggested by others. In addition, some have jurisdiction over certain expenditures, wage and salary structures, promotions, and key appointments. In such instances, it is believed that these activities are really inseparable from the updating of an organization.

WHEN TO CHANGE

From the viewpoint of timing the organizational change, either of two extremes or some compromise between them can be adopted. The two extremes are (1) to make the changes within a relatively short period—the so-called earthquake approach—or (2) to make the changes on a continuing basis spread out over a relatively long period. The approach followed is conditioned mainly by the personal choice of the manager and the pertinent considerations of the individual case.

The earthquake approach is quite common. It may coincide, but not necessarily, with the appointment of a new manager who wishes to make a fresh start or "to do things his way." It is decisive; yet it may destroy harmonious and productive relationships, curtail employee participation, and damage morale. However, it minimizes the suspense of employees wondering what is going to happen next and affecting their work output adversely as a result of their suspicions and fears. The earthquake approach has its place and in certain situations is undoubtedly the practice to follow.

In contrast, organizational changes can be brought about over extended periods of time. For example, a manager may take 3, 6, or 12

FIGURE 18–1. Four major factors suggesting change in an organization

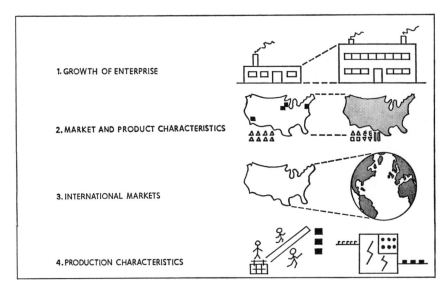

months to accomplish an organizational change. This extended period of time has its favorable aspects in that it permits ample consultation with managers about the changes and their suggestions regarding them. Then too it provides time for thorough indoctrination about contemplated changes. It represents the conservative, let's-be-sure-before-we-go-ahead attitude and is in keeping with the current practice of giving serious consideration to employees' viewpoints. It appears that the majority of managers favor this infiltration approach, or accomplishing the change over a period. Yet it may take too long to do the more or less obvious. And swift action may be called for. Do it and get it over with might prove superior, especially in terms of cost and time expenditures.

Certain concrete considerations, such as indicated by the following four factors, will assist in deciding when a change is indicated and should be made. The precise timing, however, is still a matter of the manager's judgment. Figure 18–1 lists and illustrates these factors, discussion of which follows.

1. Growth of Enterprise. As an enterprise grows, additional organizational levels are added, functions multiply, more products are taken on, and spans of authority widen. Action tends to slow up, becomes inflexible and cumbersome, and decision making is retarded. In a well-known national hospital supply company the story is told that the president called a meeting to discuss a major problem concerning a product of the company. Attendance by 17 executives was required to consider all aspects of the issue. When the president realized that such a large number had to be consulted to settle one issue, he recognized that his original functional type of organization was outmoded and a change was in order. Organizational dynamics had made his current organizational structure obsolete.

2. Market and Product Considerations. Changes in the markets and products of an enterprise commonly suggest changes in the organizational structure. Market characteristics such as size, location, number of potential consumers, outstanding preferences of buyers, pricing problems, and channels of distribution help determine what type of organization structure should be attempted. In some instances there are marked differences among local markets, with the organization being constructed to meet best these specific requirements. When there is a variety of products, the problem of decision making and coordination can become quite complex. In such cases, divisionalization in organization may help supply the solution. For the marketing efforts of each product to succeed in its own competitive market, expeditious decisions by executives completely familiar with the unique marketing problems of that particular product are commonly required. Diversification of products appears vital in this area. For example, a manufacturer of many different types and sizes of hose lines, straps, couplings, and fittings divisionalized his organization when total sales reached $25 million, whereas an aircraft manufacturer having little product diversification operated effectively under a functional organization with sales volume of nearly $900 million.

3. International Markets. Normally foreign sales and frequently foreign manufacturing are handled by different units than those of domestic sales and production. This is due primarily to the market characteristics, the mode of performing sales and production efforts, and the location of buyers. When production is performed in foreign countries, the tendency is to divisionalize by a territory basis. Other considerations, such as taxes, currency control, import-export restrictions, and quota systems suggest the desirability of keeping foreign operations separate, and this, in turn, results in separate organizational units for foreign operations. The ramifications of international operations are many, and in brief, they are reflected in the organizational structure set up to cope with them.

4. Production Characteristics. When the raw materials utilized in the production process are readily accessible, bulky, or heavy, or freshness of products to consumer is important, then adoption of a divisionalized organization by territory is often helpful. In contrast, products requiring relatively high capital investment, unique processes for manufacturing, and a great deal of engineering skill usually indicate product divisionalization. The choice, or as a matter of fact the change, is not always clear cut. Separation of the physical production facilities offers one approach, or, as an alternate, the use of separate cost systems for each product or group of related products can be followed. When separation is not feasible, a common practice is to have one production unit sell to other production units at competitive prices or to distribute production costs on some predetermined and equitable basis.

BASIC CONSIDERATIONS OF ORGANIZATION CHANGE

Any reorganization is costly. There is always a period of adjustment and modification before the employees and their organization relationships are rearticulated. Hence, it is advisable to weigh the probable gains and probable losses from any organizational change to determine if it is desirable or is the best available. In this respect, a reaffirmation of the objective is helpful, an appraisal of the proposed change in keeping with what is to be accomplished is desirable, and an honest evaluation of the personnel available to do the work is fundamental.

At the same time it should be noted that many reorganizations are prompted by the need to reduce expenses. Usually this takes the form of getting along with fewer management members, eliminating organization units, or transferring the work to another unit. However, this is not to infer that the least expensive reorganization arrangement is the best and should always be adopted. Rather, the manager must decide whether the more expensive arrangement provides additional benefits in keeping with the sought objectives. Cost is always to some degree a consideration in reorganization.

It is essential to recognize that usually too much organization change too soon is disturbing to those affected by it. While organization dynamics is a reality, there is also a need for organization stability. Most of us accept a certain amount of change as inevitable, but when the amount becomes what we consider excessive we are disturbed, may become frustrated, and our work attitudes change in ways that are not helpful to our work efforts. To the reorganizer the proposed changes may seem trivial, but to others the change may mean working with or for a superior they do not want to work for, a possible reduction in job security, or a loss of prestige or title. It is vital, therefore, to keep organization changes within reasonable limits.

In addition, certain self-vitalizing mechanisms should be present and active within the organization. These mechanisms include an organization environment conducive to the free exchange of ideas, stimulation of creativity, and the resolution of differences promptly. Such measures frequently minimize the need for organization changes; and where modifications in existent organization structure or personnel are imperative, these mechanisms help to insure success in the new arrangement and relationships.

Emphasis should be given preventive organizational changes. This means that periodically efforts are taken to detect areas where change is going to be needed to avoid serious organization trouble. It is erroneous to confine organization change to situations that currently exist, i.e., to concentrate upon remedial organization changes. Normally, what is called for is either an analysis in depth of the situation under question or a survey to uncover the broad contributing factors.

USING ORGANIZATION DYNAMICS ADVANTAGEOUSLY

The dynamics of organization supply opportunities for improvement. Changes make progress feasible and provide the organizer with a set of circumstances conducive to obtaining improvement. Important considerations to keep in mind include:

1. Maintain an Environment in Which Uncomfortable Questions Can Be Asked. After a period, a person with authority or with power runs the danger of self-deception in that in many cases, he is not adequately self-critical. Failing to see or refusing to see the problem eventually takes its toll. The dynamics of organization offers tremendous opportunities, but they must be seen. One medium to identify them is by welcoming criticism, not forbidding it.

2. Utilize the Dynamics to Motivate Personnel. Motivation of personnel is essential in effective organizing. Every employee must sincerely believe that it really makes a difference whether he does his work well or poorly and that what he achieves as an individual means something to the entire organization. High motivation is required to accept change and break through the rigidities and waste of an old organization.

3. Have a Program for Recruiting and Developing New Members. In the final analysis, people are the source of organization renewal. Dynamics makes it feasible to have a recruitment plan that brings in a steady flow of competent, highly motivated individuals as well as constructive and effective programs of career development.

4. Combat Vested Interests and Procedural Red Tape. These exist throughout an entire organization, in nearly every department, unit, or work group. Change threatens someone's status or someone's authority. But in the long run the idea must be accepted that change overrides these vested interests in the continuing vitality of the organization itself. Man becomes a prisoner of his own procedures and becomes a slave to his customary ways of doing things. But again the dynamics of organization provides opportunities to break away, to eliminate useless procedures and to improve the organization arrangement followed.

5. Concentrate on What Organization Can Become, Not What It Is or Has Been. In essence, this is developing and maintaining a way of looking forward, of practicing positive thinking. Looking ahead habitually with optimism is important in improving an organization and when this attitude exists the opportunities for improvement made feasible by organization change will result in progress maximization.

GROWTH PATTERNS OF ORGANIZATIONS

As an enterprise expands, its organization structure normally grows (1) vertically, (2) horizontally, and (3) from a functional to a divisionalized type. Let us consider each of these growths.

In most cases, the increase of an organization structure starts with vertical growth only. This can be illustrated by considering a man, Mr. Doe, going into business for himself. At the beginning Mr. Doe will perform all the fundamental activities himself. He will produce the product, sell it, supply and maintain his necessary finance. As his business increases, Mr. Doe finds the amount of work too great for him to handle; so he secures help by employing one who can handle one of the three fundamental activities and retains the other two for himself. Assume this helper is Mr. Brown to handle production. Greatest efficiency is obtained by having the helper concentrate on one activity instead of spreading his efforts over all three activities.

As the workload continues to increase, additional helpers are obtained. That is, a Mr. Miller and a Mr. Smith may be secured to handle the fundamental activities of sales and finance, respectively. Mr. Doe, the owner, now concerns himself with the overall managing and the major issues only; he is assisted by three subordinates. Progress of the enterprise persists, and the amount of work becomes greater and greater, until a further segregation of the activities appears desirable. Accordingly, three helpers are obtained for production, two for sales, and two for finance. This situation is illustrated in Figure 18–2. The

FIGURE 18–2.

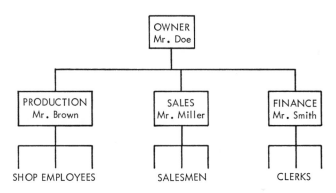

organization structure has grown vertically and now consists of several organizational levels. It has also grown horizontally. This will be discussed in the following paragraphs.

HORIZONTAL GROWTH OF ORGANIZATION STRUCTURE

As the amount of work increases, the complexities of the activities performed are quite likely to grow. This condition is brought about mainly by the nature of most work and the vertical growth of the organization. By way of illustration consider the production organizational unit only. Assume by vertical growth that there are several distinct production departments beneath the fundamental production unit and that there are seven or eight employees in each production department. It will be found that in order to get out the work the foremen must perform many different types of activities, but that among the foremen some of these activities are more or less similar in their basic nature. For example, each foreman probably is required to schedule his work;

to train, place, and promote production employees; and to see that the products manufactured are of acceptable quality and meet customers' specifications. In the interest of efficiency, it may be reasoned that the grouping of common activities and having them performed by a specialist in that particular work would be beneficial. Hence, the activity of scheduling work would be transferred to a unit such as shop scheduling with an expert scheduler in charge. Likewise, a unit of personnel to handle training, placing, and promoting of all shop employees and another unit to handle the inspection work of all products manufactured by the company may be established. This arrangement is shown in Figure 18–3.

FIGURE 18–3. Showing the horizontal growth of the production department from that shown in Figure 18–2

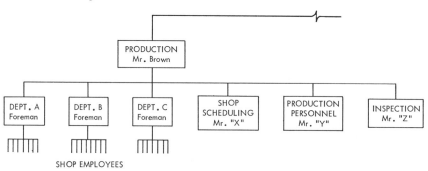

As a result of this arrangement, the organization structure has been expanded horizontally. A continuation of vertical growth has been checked, in part, by avoiding duplication, wasteful competition, overlapping of work among organizational units. However, the addition of a horizontal unit must be justified by sufficient work in that particular category added. If the work of shop scheduling, for example, is insufficient to keep at least one scheduler fully occupied, the wisdom of taking this work from the foremen and establishing the new unit may be questioned. The same evaluation applies equally to vertical growth units, but the justification for vertical units appears to be more tangible and evident than that of horizontal additions.

FUNCTIONAL TO DIVISIONALIZED GROWTH

Most companies grow *from a functional type;* that is, the beginning organizational structure is departmentized by major functions, *to a divisionalized type* of organization which is usually *on either a product or a territory basis*.[1] At the same time, centralization of authority tends to become decentralized. The functional organizational structure is used at the start because it is direct, economical, and a simple way to organize. Eventually, with growth, the divisionalized organization structure is adopted because it better meets the basic organizational needs of the enlarged, diversified company. A graphic portrayal of the common pattern for organizational growth is shown by Figure 18–4.

The divisionalized type of organizational structure breaks the functional organization into relatively small, self-contained organizational

FIGURE 18–4. The common pattern for organizational growth

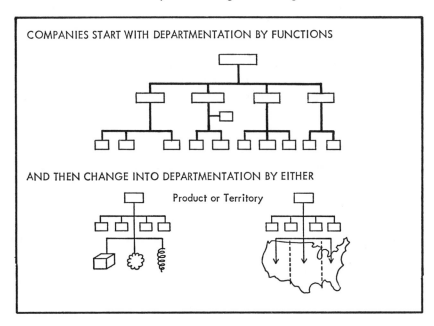

units. Each such unit is set up so that it can compete in the open market against outside enterprises as well as other divisions inside the same enterprise. The various units are tied together at the top by a central headquarters and staff. Thus, an organization is formed that can compete with dynamic smaller companies and is flexible. Growth and diversification, either in the form of new products or new territories, can be accomplished without distorting basic structure.

---

[1] Reference is made here to the departmentation at the top levels of organization. As explained in Chapter 17, other means of departmentation are usually not employed at the top levels.

IMPROVING ORGANIZATION EFFECTIVENESS

As inferred in comments above, unless sufficient managerial efforts are continuously applied to organizing, defects will appear and develop in an organization. The severity, type, and location of the difficulty will vary somewhat with the individual case, but one common mistake is to spend little or no effort toward improving the structure in light of what is currently to be accomplished. The objectives may have been changed, but the organization structure remains status quo. Another common defect is that the organization is not reviewed periodically. In essence, the fundamental function of organizing is ignored. Also, changes in organization are erroneously considered to consist exclusively of personnel replacements. New men are placed on a faulty structure. Further, the breakdown of activities may be carried too far. The organization units are so small that the volume of work is insufficient to permit economic workloads. Along with this excessive activities breakdown is usually found a complicated pattern of authority relationships among the many organizational units. Simplicity of the organization structure is ignored. Frequently, too, needless duplication of work is permitted to continue within a department or among different departments. In addition, authority may not be properly delegated and may be greatly unbalanced among the various organizational levels. And it is not uncommon to find management members devoting their full time to assignments not requiring their special training and experience. Such organization defects offer a challenge to the alert manager.

What can be done? Recommended is a three-point program consisting of (1) evaluate overall existent organization, (2) conduct an organization audit, and (3) change personnel of organization. Discussion of each immediately follows.

EVALUATE OVERALL EXISTENT ORGANIZATION

Recognition and utilization of organization dynamics can be applied to improve an organization and to make it more in keeping with current needs. For this purpose, any one or all of several approaches can be followed, depending upon the judgment of the evaluator.

The first may be termed the *packaged* approach. Here the organization is analyzed for violation of pragmatic beliefs concerning what an effective organization should be. For example, areas having too great a span of authority or a lack of a continuous chain of command would be noted.

The *informal* approach consists of asking short, pertinent questions to uncover possible areas for improvement. To illustrate, Figure 18–5 has been included. Answers to questions such as these revel areas requiring remedial action. To utilize the informal approach effectively may require considerable firsthand knowledge of the structure and the various relationships existing therein.

Or the approach of *comparison* can be utilized. In it, the organization is compared with those of competitors and others of somewhat similar enterprises. Care must be taken to obtain sufficient information about the others so that comparisons are valid. Diagrams of competitors' structures are insufficient because the actual content of many organizational units may not be revealed by the diagrams, and the influence of the respective personnel upon the work being accomplished with the respective structures is unknown.

Another approach is the *ideal* approach. In this case the ideal organi-

FIGURE 18–5. Typical questions for use in evaluating an organization

1. Are the stated objectives the proper ones to be sought by the enterprise?
2. Are the main efforts being directed toward obtaining the stated objectives?
3. Are the management members completely qualified by training and experience to achieve these major goals? If so, are these members in proper organizational positions?
4. Is the overall organization pattern adequate? Are the various activities logically related and grouped for maximum effectiveness?
5. Are all necessary activities specifically assigned to individuals in the proper organization units?
6. Is the authority for each management member properly identified, and is it placed as closely as possible to the point where action originates?
7. Does every management member fully understand his own work, his authority, and his relationships to other management members?
8. Is authority adequately delegated?
9. Is there proper integration among the various units, or do any departments appear to operate too independently?
10. Can project organization be used advantageously?
11. Are there any management members who direct too many subordinates? If so, lack of managerial planning, actuating, and controlling is quite likely.
12. Are there probable replacements for management members at different levels for the next five years? For the next 10 years?
13. Does the enterprise have an effective program for replacing needed management members?
14. Are present management members being developed for greater efficiency and effectiveness?
15. Are periodic evaluations used to measure management members' progress and potential?
16. Does the enterprise have an organization chart and manual showing present formal organization conditions? Probable conditions five years hence? Ten years hence?
17. If there is an organization chart and manual, is there a provision for its regular review?

zation is visualized and conditions for its existence assumed. Questions like the following might be asked: What is new in organization thinking that we might use advantageously? What structure would be best? What should each manager do? What authority is necessary? What responsibility should exist? The ideal is then compared to that being evaluated, and areas for improvement noted.

There is also the *quantitative* approach. This employs the use of measurements, especially those obtained by calculating various ratios. For example, the ratio of managerial to operative employees, the amount of staff to line people, the number of organizational units for the number of employees, enterprise and industry comparisons of each ratio data, as well as industry and national comparisons, are among the types of quantitative data that may be used. The quantitative approach is effective where it can be used. Reliable data for its use, however, are not always available.

CONDUCT AN ORGANIZATION AUDIT

This provides a somewhat detailed analysis or differentiation of the organization. It reveals, for example, the extent to which the formal organization permits and encourages the attainment of sought goals, the utilization of capable performances, and the growth of individuals. Further, under it, a revised organization is evolved. Any of a number of procedures can be followed, but the following actions usually bring excellent results.

First, bring together all available written materials dealing with the organization. This includes the statement of purpose and scope of the organization and each unit of it, job descriptions, performance appraisals of management members, and qualifications needed as well as those not needed or used by each of these members in their present positions. Next, review these materials, carefully noting whether they are consistent, non-overlapping, and directed to the major goals of the organization. Following this, develop job requirements to accompany the position description of each management member's job. Likewise, analyze each manager's apparent qualifications and relate his education, experience, knowledge, and skill to his job requirements. Fifth, for each management member compare job requirements and individual qualifications. Underscore in pencil any job requirement not possessed adequately by the manager; underscore in ink any qualification that apparently is not needed by the manager on his current job. Segregate those pencil underscored areas that normally can be acquired through development work from those that cannot be acquired to assure acceptable performance within reasonable time limits. Analyze the ink underscored areas, showing unused abilities, and relate them to other requirements of other jobs. Lastly, design various possible organization patterns and positions breakdowns, using existing managerial personnel, but noting the type of personnel needed if not presently within the organization. The proposed alternatives are subsequently evaluated against criteria selected by the top manager or group performing the audit.

After the revised organization is decided upon, it is advisable to provide revised operational procedures to expedite changes within the organization. These revised operational procedures (ROP) outline what specific activities are to take place in the performance of specific work. In writing and using ROP, concentrate on the changes that are required. This is the information the employee really needs to know to carry out the change. Also, the precise timing of putting ROP into effect should be carefully planned so that a coordinated change is secured. Extreme care should be taken to see that the ROP is inclusive and shows all details. It should not be considered a temporary stopgap but a carefully thought out change. Flexibility and adjustments, in keeping with how it works out and with the suggestions of the employees, should be honored. Further, the flow of the work must be maintained. Proper standards of work output should be established and adequate records kept to insure that this flow is not impeded. Usually this necessitates special activities during the transition period.

CHANGE PERSONNEL OF ORGANIZATION

Organization dynamics alone brings about changes in organization personnel, but these changes are accelerated when improvement in the organization effectiveness is sought. Of particular importance is the fact that the individual manager himself changes with time. Typically, he will not be aware of it, but his associates are. The individual may have grown tremendously and now possesses much managerial knowledge and skill. On the other hand, he may have become overconservative, inflexible, negative in his viewpoints, or emotionally unstable. Also, job requirements change. During the past, the present incumbent could perform competently, but with the addition of new or complex duties, he seems unable to perform the work effectively. "Executive obsolescence" is becoming increasingly common with the wide, sweeping changes taking place in our economy. In other instances the individual apparently has been moved up too fast, such a move being dictated by an emergency, inadequate management development, or excessive pushing by a sponsor. Or the individual may simply be over his head on his current job. He doesn't have the necessary qualifications to do the work. Overestimating his ability, present and potential, is a common cause of this situation.

Recommendations as to what to do to help the incumbent acquire the needed competency range from quiet means of assistance to the extreme of terminating employment. The method followed should be tailored to suit the particular circumstances. Any decision should include not only consideration for the effect of the action upon the individual concerned, but also for the effect upon the group of which the individual is a member.

Specifically the following alternatives can be used:

1. Hire New Managerial Members. Such members usually bring new ideas, new ways of carrying out the managerial functions, and a fresh viewpoint on problems. A recent managerial addition is usually nonbiased, does not belong to a special click, and has no vested interests. Objectivity and enthusiasm are usually gained by hiring new managerial members.

2. Give Counseling. For the superior to talk things over with the incompetent subordinate and suggest possible actions to improve performance is especially effective for temporary periods of incompetency brought about by additional duties, a crisis, or adjustments either of a social or economic nature. As a result of counseling, better understanding between the two parties is promoted, areas in which help is needed can be spotted and the assistance given, and needed encouragement can be provided.

3. Transfer the Incompetent Executive. For this approach to be followed there must be flexibility in the organization and "open" managerial positions at various levels. Certain transfers designate changes to insure technical training and the development of managerial skill, while other transfers take place essentially to find out where the particular individual fits into the organization. The distinction is not always clear, but generally speaking, transfers for incompetency are characterized by an excess of transfers within the same organizational level, failure to move vertically within reasonable time periods, or lack of attaining a certain organizational level by the time the transferee has arrived at a certain age range.

4. Use Staff Positions. To provide for required executive changes in an organization, an executive can be moved from a position of line authority into one of staff authority, usually that of advisory staff. To make the change attractive, the staff job is commonly at a higher organizational level than the present line job. Commonly the transferee is told that there is a difficult problem in the new area and that the executive is wanted to help straighten it out. The change can be accomplished quite painlessly, especially if the staff position carries prestige and no reduction in salary. This method maintains relatively high morale and loyalty. It successfully removes incompetents from important line authority decisions where great damage might be done; yet it retains the benefits of executive experience and knowledge for special problems. However, the method may prove expensive in that overhead costs are high and the reputation of the true worth of a staff manager may suffer—the erroneous viewpoint developing that staff is a graveyard for line managers who do not make good.

5. *Terminate the Employment.* This is the most extreme way to handle incompetency. Commonly when this means is used the termination is indirectly applied, that is, the executive either resigns under force applied in numerous different ways. Or the direct method can be followed by simply informing the person that "his work is not up to expectations" or "things haven't worked out," with the expectation that he will leave the company. The indirect method takes many interesting forms including giving the manager very little, if anything, to do so that, in time, he will voluntarily resign. Another technique is withholding important facts from the manager, omitting his name on important memoranda, and excluding him from conferences. Also, there is always the method whereby the top manager makes himself unavailable to a management member for consultation.

RECRUITING AND SELECTING MANAGEMENT MEMBERS

The changing of organization personnel brings up the subject of recruiting and selecting managerial members. Recruiting is the fountain feeding the potential executive pool; without adequate recruitment the executive manpower dries up and the survival of an enterprise is threatened. Today, the best men no longer hunt jobs; the jobs hunt them. To get desirable candidates an enterprise must aggressively let its interests and wants be known to likely candidates. The watchful and enthusiastic cooperation of present executives, alumni, and nonmanagement members in locating such talent should be tapped. It is necessary to keep an almost constant lookout for candidates. Perhaps the best five sources are:

1. Other Companies. Commonly used for managers, this source gets candidates with new ideas and different approaches. Executive inbreeding of poor decision making is thus minimized. However, outsiders may not bring special results to the company. Reliable standards in judging applicants' qualifications are required.

2. Promotions from Within Company. This source is popular with employees, emphasizes opportunity in line with service to an enterprise, frequently serves as a strong incentive, and offers a pool of potent managers to the enterprise. However, for this source to be productive, aggressive efforts to ferret out likely candidates are necessary. In addition, an unbiased means for evaluating candidates in line for advancement should be established. Viewed quite realistically, many employees are neither hired for possible future managerial work nor are they interested in assuming the task of making the decisions and having the obligations inherent in managerial work. Yet they are competent, faithful, satisfied employees and essential to the company's success, even though their managerial potential may be low.

3. Graduates from Universities and Special Schools. Such graduates by virtue of their specialized training are believed to possess a satisfactory background upon which further training and experience pertinent to the future management of the enterprise can be based. Many young men and women are now receiving higher formal education emphasizing managerial subjects, but college graduation alone does not ensure a candidate of management caliber. When this source is used, the skill of the recruiter and the reputation of the company are important. The recruiter's knowledge of his company, of the university, and especially of the job are highly significant. He should be able to supply all pertinent information requested in a simple, forthright manner. Recruiting from many schools is superior to that of dealing with one school. Two candidates from each of ten universities normally provides a better group than twenty candidates from one university.

4. Advertisements. This source reaches candidates who otherwise probably would not know of the vacancies; it is a democratic process. However, it is quite impersonal and relies on either the candidate or his friend seeing the notice. A number of candidates are usually found by this means, but many probably will be unqualified; hence, effective selection devices must be employed for these candidates. Also the media employed influences the results obtained.

5. Employment Agencies. Many of these perform creditable work and give entirely satisfactory results. However, most agencies are not equipped to screen applicants to the individual criteria of the hiring company, and hence careful selection of such candidates by the enterprise is usually in order. On the other hand, some agencies offer quite extensive personnel services.

Selection of the executive candidate can follow several approaches, but the format visualized in Figure 18–6 is recommended. Beginning at the top of the figure, the candidates recruited are subsequently appraised for ability, personality, and social factors by means of biographical data, interviews, observations, and tests. The appraisals need not necessarily be in this order, since they are integrated, and from the results the candidate is either rejected or selected. Observe that at any

FIGURE 18–6

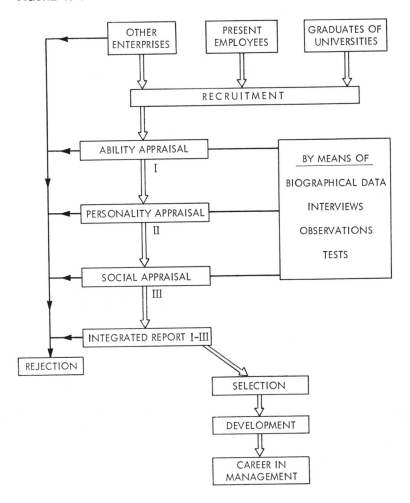

of the appraisals or at the integrated report, the candidate may be rejected.

The ability appraisal takes into account the candidate's education, training, experience, technical skill, and achievement as well as mental ability, imagination, and similar basic abilities necessary to perform the job. Personality factors are those attributes of the candidate required to get along with people and to stimulate them to work willingly toward a definite goal. Ability to adjust to situations, to operate under pressure or adverse conditions, to take criticism, and to maintain emotional stability are included under this major heading. Social factors include the applicant's manners, general appearance, grooming, willingness to travel, marital status, and willingness to relocate his home geographically. Few, if any candidates, are tops in all desirable qualities. The composite score is what is important.

As shown in Figure 18–6, the first means for appraisal is biographical data which reveal the candidates past accomplishments, personal background, employment record, and outstanding past successes. Certain of these data are most helpful for selection work. From considerable research, the Life Insurance Agency Management Association, for example, believes the following items most significant.

1. The applicant's total number of dependents.
2. Specific work done in recent years.
3. Whether presently employed.
4. Length of present or last employment.
5. Organizations of which applicant is an active member.
6. Offices held in the above organizations during the last five years.
7. Approximate net worth of applicant.
8. Minimum monthly living expenses.
9. Amount of life insurance carried.

Interviews, observations, and tests are also used. Carefully conducted interviews can be exceptionally helpful. The applicant's background, training, and education can be thoroughly explored and pertinent questions asked in a forthright manner. Some insight to his aims, interests, and activities can also be gained. In contrast, the candidates may be brought together as a group along with the interviewers. An extended informal social meeting lasting through a day and an evening might be arranged, during which time detailed observation of the candidates takes place in order to judge reactions to situations, ideas advanced, and ability to communicate effectively. Qualities usually considered paramount are a firm belief by the candidate in his own ultimate success and energy or drive tempered by tactfulness and interest. The question is not only how much ability and knowledge does the candidate possess but also how willing is he to use his abilities and knowledge. Psychological tests are available to measure a number of traits, such as interest, personality, mechanical aptitude, emotional maturity, and leadership. The chief difficulty in using tests for management personnel is the lack of agreement on what qualities are necessary for competency. Furthermore, the requirements may differ from one enterprise to another. Also, the number of executives may be relatively small so that in formulating an executive test the psychologist is faced with two prime obstacles: (1) lack of uniformity in the pattern of the attributes and in the attributes themselves to be tested and (2) an insufficient sample to validate the test. However, present tests are helpful, but not as significant as the recruiter might like them to be. If the score is sufficiently low, they suffice to disqualify a candidate, but success in the present tests does not predict success in the management job. Experts in tests for executives agree generally in recommending total appraisals of tests rather than just three or four tests on selected attributes.

QUESTIONS

1. Discuss the subject of who plans and implements organization change.
2. Discuss the consideration for market and product as a factor bringing about change in an organization.
3. What are the four major reasons for the existence of organization dynamics?
4. Is it possible for a manager to make organization dynamics work to his advantage? Discuss.
5. From your own creativity, suggest a plan that will provide adequate preventive organizational change.
6. Tell what is meant by each of the following: (1) earthquake approach, (2) executive obsolescence, and (3) revised operational procedure (ROP)
7. Typically what four concrete factors suggest when an organizational change is indicated?
8. Describe in some detail what approach you believe you would follow for determining whether an existent organization is relatively good or bad.
9. Distinguish between the two concepts in each of the following pairs: (1) vertical organization growth and divisionalized growth, (2) the comparison approach to organization evaluation and organizational audit, and (3) organization evaluation and using staff positions for improving managerial competency.
10. Discuss Figure 18–6 in your own words.
11. Enumerate the major steps taken in performing an organization audit.
12. Evaluate each of the following suggestions for trimming a business organi-

zation to meet a recession in business: (1) eliminate what appears to be the least needed staff units, (2) cut personnel in all existing units by a fixed percentage to reduce the organization to desired size, and (3) fire high-salaried executives and replace them with much lower-salaried executives.

13. Enumerate three alternatives that can be followed in changing the personnel of an organization in order to improve it. Discuss one of these alternatives fully.

14. Figure 18–5 lists 17 questions on the subject of organization evaluation. Select any three and relate how the answers to these questions would help you improve an organization.

CASE 18–1. MANAGER FREDERICK MUTCHLER

WILLIAM CAMS (Executive Placement Services): Are you employed now?

FREDERICK MUTCHLER: No, sir. I lost my job four weeks ago.

CAMS: Who were you with?

MUTCHLER: With Top Foods. I was brand manager for their new and small consumer products division, Ace-High Products.

CAMS: Will you tell me something about this last job you had. Anything you feel I should know.

MUTCHLER: All right. I went with them about a year ago at the Ace-High main office on the West Coast. My immediate superior, an excellent vice president of sales and marketing, says my position was eliminated. His boss, president of our division, came up via production, is brilliant, and hard working. He got the president's job due to his excellent record in handling an overseas subsidiary when he increased sales from something like $10 to $100 million in seven years.

CAMS: That's quite a record.

MUTCHLER: Yes. Quality was the major consumer benefit on which the overseas business was built. The corporation hoped to duplicate the success story here in the domestic market. But as I see it, competition here is much stronger. There are several competing quality products that equal Ace-High and further, distribution in the United States is more difficult.

I was hired as a brand manager with responsibility for determining how to market our product, what variations to permit, what pricing to follow, and how much advertising and sales promoting efforts we should adopt. I recruited two experienced assistants from the East Coast, luring them by pointing out the opportunity to get in on the ground floor of a well-financed company and a chance to avoid winter.

CAMS: So what went wrong?

MUTCHLER: A number of things in my opinion. In fact, they fore-warned of a final termination. About ten months ago I got my brand group together and held meetings with the manufacturing managers to learn of their problems and to expose them to the list we were developing, giving definition to the limits of possible changes we might suggest. I thought the meetings went well, but within a week I received a memo from our president that in the future all manu-facturing-brand meetings were to be held with the president in at-tendance. Other clues followed. For example, we received reports on product testing when the results were favorable to the company, but they were withheld when results were not satisfactory. And from time to time, meetings on Saturday mornings were held by the president and top departmental people, but the brand group was excluded.

CAMS: I see.

MUTCHLER: The last two months there were rough. I talked with each of my assistants, trying to decide what I could do to correct the situa-tion. Our department was unable to fulfill its mission; our people were disappointed because we could accomplish so little. And they were getting anxious about their future. Actually we had no power to initiate investigations, to serve as a rallying point for product development, or to go ahead with broad studies we believed essential. I was successful, however, in getting my immediate superior to talk with about five people in our unit including my two assistants.

CAMS: Then what happened?

MUTCHLER: About two weeks later my boss called me in on Saturday and advised me that the whole brand unit would be eliminated at once. With it went my job, but my two assistants and a few of the office staff would be transferred mostly to staff marketing and coordi-nating work.

CAMS: Do you believe brand management is a requisite for survival of Ace-High?

MUTCHLER: Yes, I'd say that it was. On the other hand, for a short-line single technology firm, it is not. I feel I got into trouble because I tried to establish brand management as an initiator for change and in so doing a frontal attack on management already in existence took place. And I lost.

Questions

1. Do you agree with Mr. Mutchler that certain clues forecast his forthcoming termination? Discuss.

2. If you were asked to help this company would you be guided by the belief that consumer needs and product benefits are more important than an intimate knowledge of manufacturing process? Justify your answer.
3. With the limited data that you have, do you feel that Ace-High Products will be a successful endeavor of Top Foods? Why?
4. What recommended action do you suggest for the president of Ace-High Products? Why?

CASE 18–2. DILLMAN COMPANY

Dillman Company was recently acquired by Kamack Corporation whose executives are well aware of the inept management team of their new subsidiary. Mr. Paul Wood, the principal owner and president of the acquired company, had been the real genius and spark plug back of Dillman's remarkable record. Now 69 years of age, Mr. Wood is happy to retire and let somebody else take over. Associates of Mr. Wood had let him run the show since he was very successful and wanted to do it. They answered his beck and call, always agreed with him, made few decisions, and kept themselves busily occupied on minor activities and of little consequence in the total viewpoint of the company.

Kamack's executive committee decided that the best way to clean house and get an aggressive, hard hitting management group for the new Dillman division was to hire an outsider for one year and let him trim and revitalize the management personnel. Neither the limited appointment nor the objective of this new general manager was to be publicized. Accordingly, Mark Yost was appointed to the general manager's post of Dillman, an act which came as a total surprise to all employees, customers, and the public.

Mr. Yost immediately sought to evaluate the management team with whom he was now associated. He requested various progress reports, one-year plans, cost estimates, and the like. He held meetings and voiced disapproval of many past activities and asked for programs to be drawn up to achieve goals which he spelled out in some detail. After two months, the consensus was that the pressure was on, Mr. Yost was a very demanding person, was difficult to please, and was trying to make a name for himself with the top brass of Kamack. Two managers had quit, one was asked to leave, and it was rumored that the employment of five more were to be terminated. Over half of the twenty-one top and middle managers indicated they would leave if successful in finding another job. One department was eliminated and three other small organizational units were consolidated into one large unit.

At the end of eight months under Mr. Yost, Dillman's operations were beginning to show definite signs of increased efficiency and lower unit costs on many of its products. The executive committee members of Kamack were well pleased. Profits, in fact, were increasing. However, they realized Mr. Yost was not well liked by most of the management members of the old Dillman Company, but he was getting a job done and had very successfully incorporated four new managers Kamark had recommended that he hire. They offered Mr. Yost an extension of his one-year contract, but he turned it down, explaining it did not give him adequate compensation for what he was accomplishing. At the end of the year, announcement was made that Mr. Yost was resigning and a new general manager would be named in the near future.

Questions

1. As you see it what was the problem of Dillman Company and what factors contributed to it? Discuss.
2. What major alternatives were available to Kamack Corporation after acquiring Dillman Company?
3. Do you believe a results management approach by Kamack Corporation would have proven successful in this case? Discuss.
4. What recommendations are in order to the executive committee members of Kamack Corporation? Why?

part V

Actuating

The third fundamental function of management to be discussed is actuating. Dealing intimately with the human being, actuating offers tremendous challenge and appeal. A person's beliefs, hopes, ambitions, behavior, satisfactions, growth, interaction with other persons are all involved in the actuating effort.

Many feel that actuating is probably the most important fundamental function of management. It is vital and pervasive. It conditions and is a part of every managerial action taken. And it exists at every level, location, and operation throughout an enterprise. Proficiency in actuating is a must for continued success in management. The four chapters included in this section are:

19. *Management actuating*
20. *Leading*
21. *Creating and innovating ideas*
22. *Evaluating, developing, and compensating managers*

19

Management actuating

*If there is any great secret of success in life, it lies in the
ability to put yourself in the other person's place and to see
things from his point of view—as well as your own.*

HENRY FORD

THE THIRD fundamental function of management to be discussed in
some detail is actuating. We can plan and organize, but no tangible
output is achieved until we implement the proposed and organized activities. This requires actuating, which literally means the putting or
moving into action. Actuating emphasizes working with people to win
their enthusiasm, desire, and energy toward achievement of mutual objectives. The following definition is helpful. *Actuating is getting all the
members of the group to want to achieve and strive to achieve mutual
objectives because they want to achieve them.*

CHALLENGE OF ACTUATING IN MANAGEMENT

Getting members of a company to work together more efficiently, to
enjoy their work, to develop their skills and abilities, and to be good
representatives of the company, presents a major challenge to the managers of that company. Basic to effective actuating is enlightened management—managers must demonstrate by their behavior and decisions
a deep concern for members of their organization. Fundamental to management success is an awareness of current conditions affecting personnel, belief and trust in each employee, and acceptance of the fact that
the willingness and capacity for each person to perform enthusiastically
conditions the success of most endeavors.

435

The truth is that many enterprises depend upon human beings and every problem and every decision involves the human element. The potential for improving human resources is terrific because most people are lucky if they use 25 percent of their potential. Managerial planning is successful because *people* put together the right combinations of activities; organizing proves effective because *people* adopt it in order to work together effectively; and controlling is effective because it helps *people* to reach their goals competently.

It is also well to keep in mind that all enterprises are built to serve people—both within and without the enterprise. Man in his dignity and in his sanctity is the center about which all material things revolve. This human-element-centered approach further emphasizes the importance of actuating in management work.

Basically, actuating starts within one's self and not with actuating others. A manager who is not motivated for success and progress makes it almost impossible to actuate others. However, it is difficult to become self-actuated. It stems from a strong desire, an intense feeling, and an enthusiastic willingness to pursue a goal regardless of the hurdles which must be overcome.

Although actuating stresses the importance of people, it should always be objective in its determination and use. To do this it helps to focus on the behavior, not on the person behaving. Concentrate on what the person does, how he acts, and his responses and reactions to certain events. Observations, not inferences, reporting, not judging, and interpreting behavior in terms of more or less, not either/or, are further requirements for valid objective insight so important in actuating.

Actuating efforts are highly personalized and herein lies much of the challenge. We should not try to stimulate efforts in an attempt to increase equally everyone's satisfaction or try to make everyone equally happy. People differ like fingerprints. Performance will not be equal; neither will their rewards and satisfactions from their work.

HUMAN WANTS

To reiterate, when we talk about actuating in management we are referring to employees wanting to achieve mutual objectives because they want to achieve them. Why does a human being want to achieve anything? Basically to satisfy his human wants. We all have wants—physical, economic, social, political, and so forth—and we consciously or unconsciously, by our behavior, seek to satisfy them in order that we live the life we believe we want to live, or the life that somebody we believe in tells us we should live. From the viewpoint of management, the satisfaction of these wants is related to the individual and his work, his superior, his associates, and his work environment.

PRINCIPLE OF ACTUATING

Favorable actuating efforts are normally obtained by treating employees as human beings, encouraging their growth and development, instilling a desire to excel, recognizing work well done, and insuring fair play.

The question is: What wants are satisfied by an employee during his work life; i.e., his forty hours each week on his particular job? The theory is that if he can satisfy many of his wants, he will be enthusiastic about his work, will give his best efforts willingly, and will be a happy, satisfied, and content person. As Chester I. Bernard stated, the test of an organization's success is its ability to provide values to its members in order to compensate them for the burdens imposed.[1]

Hence, in actuating, we are concerned with ascertaining and satisfying human wants. The task is not easy. Typically, the employees of a company have different backgrounds, experiences, hopes, desires, ambitions, and psychological makeups. They see events in different terms, and their reactions to each other, to their work, and to their surroundings are subject to considerable variations. Psychologists have developed different classifications of human needs ranging from one basic need to some twenty-five needs. The sex drive, power, and desire for individuality are examples of well known single motives.

The importance of the various needs or wants which motivate man was expertly expressed by the late Professor Douglas McGregor in these words:

> Man is a wanting animal—as soon as one of his needs is satisfied, another appears in its place. This process is unending. It continues from birth to death. Man continuously puts forth effort—works, if you please—to satisfy his needs. . . . A satisfied need is not a motivator. This is a fact which is . . . ignored in the conventional approach to management of people.[2]

A very useful classification of needs developed by the psychologist, A. H. Maslow, recognizes five basic human needs which make up a hierarchy of needs.[3] They include:

---

[1] Chester I. Bernard, *The Functions of an Executive* (Cambridge: Harvard University Press, 1951), pp. 92–4, 177–81, 252–56.

[2] Paul R. Lawrence, et al., *Organizational Behavior and Administration* (Homewood, Ill.: Richard D. Irwin, Inc., 1961), p. 224.

[3] A. H. Maslow, "A Theory of Human Motivation, *Psychological Review*, July, 1943, pp. 370–96.

1. *Physiological needs,* exemplified by hunger and thirst; these needs are the basic or starting point for most needs. Their satisfaction is necessary for the preservation of life. Once satisfied they cease to operate as a prime motivator of behavior.

2. *Safety needs* constitute the second level of needs. They consist of the need for clothing, shelter, and having an environment of a predictable pattern such as job security, pension, and insurance.

3. *Affection needs* include the need to belong, to be a wanted member of a group, not only of a family, but a work group as well.

4. *Esteem needs* are represented by needs for self-respect, achievement, and for recognition by others. The desire for prestige and status is an important aspect of the drive for achievement. Esteem needs represent the fourth level of basic human needs.

5. *Self-actualization needs,* the capstone of the hierarchy of needs is represented by self-fulfillment, a man doing what he can do—his ultimate in his contribution to his fellowmen. It represents the complete realization of one's full potential.

In contemporary society the needs lower in the hierarchy are more completely satisfied than the higher needs. Many, for example, have the great majority of their physiological and safety needs fulfilled. It is the affection needs and the esteem needs that require satisfying and, for the top, or self-actualization needs, relatively still fewer people gain satisfaction for them. However, this hierarchy of needs is not always followed in a rigid pattern. There are reversals and substitutions. A research chemist, for example, may neglect to eat and sleep (physiological needs) in the midst of creativity. Likewise, some persons center on esteem needs—the acquisition of wealth, for example, almost to the exclusion of affection needs—the need to belong to a group. In many cases such a situation may have developed due to a suppression of affection needs early in life with a resultant emphasis on esteem needs as a substitute. Needs are relative in their strength and are individualistic. A "lower" need does not necessarily have to be fulfilled before a "higher" need emerges.

In addition, the so-called preference-expectation theory advanced by Victor Vroom in 1964 offers additional assistance worthy of inclusion here.[4] This theory is based on two premises:

1. A person subjectively assigns values to the expected outcomes of various courses of action and therefore has preferences among the expected outcomes.

2. Any explanation of motivated behavior must take into account not only the ends that people hope to accomplish but the extent to which they believe that their own actions are instrumental in producing the outcomes they prefer.

---

[4] Victor Vroom, *Work and Motivation,* (New York: John Wiley and Sons, Inc. 1964), pp. 17–33, 121–47.

The theory makes no attempt to identify differences among preferences and expectations among individuals, but to use the theory we must know the preferences and expectations of the person concerned. A person may place a high value on bringing about a certain outcome, but if he does not believe that any act of his will affect what happens, he will not act. If he anticipates to a great degree that a highly valued act depends on his own actions, he will become highly motivated to act. In some cases, the various aspects of a situation may balance each other so that neither the value of the total outcome nor the probability of occurrence alone will increase his motivation to act. For example, having a high value on achieving a promotion is negated if he believes there is no probability that greater performance on his part will bring it about.

ACTUATING PREMISES

Human behavior is conditioned by the cultures in a society. As pointed out in Chapter 2, culture refers to learned behavior. It influences what is desirable and conditions what is possible.[5] Cultures include past achievements and provide a practical means for a person to cope with his present environment; that is, man stores and carries over knowledge and accepted behavior patterns from one generation to another. Different societies have different cultures. For example, either beef or pork is used in some cultures to satisfy hunger, but in other cultures, fish or seafood is the only accepted means.

Cultural variations give rise to differences in human motives. What will arouse greater effort and interest in one culture may fail completely in another. Some will encourage individual effort while others place emphasis upon group effort; some bless certain kinds of economic endeavor while others condemn it or at least make the endeavor very difficult to attain. In the United States, for example, our cultural heritage causes us to question authoritarianism more than is the case in a number of other countries. Likewise, the democratic approach in religious and economic affairs further illustrates this state of affairs. Hence, the cultures of a society can be said to condition human behavior and provide a part of the background against which actuating must take place.

But observe also that actual social behavior is not always in harmony with the social sanctions. Man's capacity to reflect and think bring about changes. A person can chose to be a nonconformist and follow behavior patterns that differ from those of his society. From the overall viewpoint

---

[5] See page 26.

this has advantages in that different concepts are tried out. Thus progress is possible, a person can be himself, do his own thing, and pioneer trails are blazed. Furthermore, people with different motives and behaviors are made available to fit diverse tasks that are necessary.

Another and highly important premise of actuating is the fundamental viewpoint that top managers have toward their manpower. A popular and effective statement illustrating opposite views is that provided by Theory X and Theory Y.[6] The chief characteristics of Theory X are:

1. Most employees of a firm work as little as possible and are by nature resistant to change. Basically the employee will do only what he has to do; work is disliked and hence, trouble is common in trying to achieve goals.

2. Most employees must be persuaded, rewarded, punished, and controlled to modify their behavior to fit the needs of the organization. They are self-centered, and indifferent, passive, and even resistant to the needs of the organization.

3. Most employees want direction supplied by a formal manager and they want to avoid job responsibilities whenever possible. Employees therefore must be led and directed by a recognized manager in authority within the company.

In contrast, Theory Y includes:

1. Most employees of the firm do not inherently dislike work. They expect to expend physical and mental efforts in performing their jobs.

2. Most employees have the capacity for assuming responsibility and the potential for development, but management by its action must make them aware of these characteristics. When committed to specific objectives, an employee will exercise self-control in trying to attain that objective.

3. Most employees want to satisfy social, esteem, and self-actualization needs. The employee wants to use his intellectual potential, imagination, and judgment in performing his work in the best way. Management should achieve an environment in which employees can achieve their objectives best by directing their efforts toward objectives of the company.

It is easy to see that a manager predominantly of a Theory X type presents a climate and an attitude which is the direct opposite of a manager following Theory Y. In this day and age and for practically all cases, Theory Y should be adopted and aggressively followed for it will give the better actuating results.

---

[6] Douglas McGregor, *Leadership and Motivation* (Cambridge, Mass.: M.I.T. Press), 1966.

IMPORTANCE OF WORK IN ACTUATING

Work itself is an extremely important consideration in actuating and could have been included under the heading of actuating premises just concluded. However, the work is so vital in actuating that it warrants a separate and complete heading and discussion. As indicated under Theory X above, it is assumed that work is disliked by employees. In contrast, in Theory Y, work is liked and is not viewed as a punishment to man, but as his glory, strength, and pleasure.[7]

The question can be asked, "Why do men and women work so hard if they don't like work?" One simple answer is that people have wants that cannot be satisfied without money. Work is a way to get money. Hence, they work to satisfy wants in terms of goods and services or what they can attain with financial assets.

However, some persons who are well fixed financially continue to work hard and maintain a punishing schedule of activities. Others work hard, but not for material gains. Missionaries, teachers, clergymen, government workers, and some scientists are examples. Probably they could make more money in some other field of endeavor but they are passing this up, at least for the present, for nonmonetary returns or rewards. What is motivating these hard workers? Is it desire for power, is it pride, is it a set behavior pattern, or is it love of action? It could be any one or all of these—or any of a number of other considerations.

A person balances one reward against another, one possible gain or result against another. Work is regarded differently by different persons. Few really revere work for its own sake, but it is performed essentially for what the worker believes he is getting from it; that is, doing the work is related to the personal goals which the person is trying to achieve. He tends to work with zeal if the satisfaction from the work is high and in keeping with what he wants. In essence, the reasons a man gives much of himself to his work is that the work gives to him much of what he is seeking.

It is helpful to think of job satisfaction as something that is likely to result from performance behavior rather than as the cause of good or bad behavior. Satisfaction comes from and is the result of performance. The behavioral scientist, Frederick Herzberg, has stated that achievement leads to motivation, it is not the reverse, i.e., motivation leading to achievement.[8]

---

[7] People disliking work are sometimes referred to as those of the "Mediterranean ethic" while those who like work are of the "Protestant ethic." See Chapter 2, pp. 25–6 for discussion of each of these ethics.

[8] Herzberg, Mausner, and Snyderman, *The Motivation to Work,* (New York: John Wiley and Sons, Inc. 1959), pp. 5–22.

JOB CONTENT AND JOB CONTEXT

Job content concerns the work itself. To the person performing work, this area has the potential for strong determinates that provide satisfaction from working. It includes such concepts as acquiring a sense of achievement and gaining recognition, personal growth, and advancement. Job content factors are frequently referred to as being intrinsic because they belong to or are a property of the work itself and the employee.[9]

On the other hand, job context concerns company policy and administration. This area has the potential for great dissatisfiers. Included are such concepts as the technical aspects of the supervision received, the environment under which the work must be performed, and the interpersonal relationships with peers and superiors. Job context factors are commonly called extrinsic because they are outside the main thing that is being considered, namely the work itself and the employee.

Of the two concepts, job content and job context, the former, or job content, is of relatively more importance. It is most desirable to have effective job content, but job content is never entirely satisfactory unless job context is reasonably satisfactory and effective. The two are obviously closely related in most work situations. But observe that job content is always timely and acts to reinforce behavior as it occurs. It must be correct if motivation efforts are to reach their zenith. In contrast, job contexts are relatively of short duration in that normally they meet cyclical needs. The conclusion to be drawn here is that the work itself should be designed so as to stimulate and challenge the employee and provide the opportunity for him to be creative. When the work offers the employee no more satisfaction than a paycheck, a comfortable place to work, and an agreeable boss, apathy and minimum effort are quite likely to be present.

ACTUATING AND CHANGE

From what has been stated it follows that in many cases success in motivation requires change—especially change in behavior on the part of the person being motivated. Too many times the actuating effort is just words—complete agreement exists regarding the end results, but nothing really takes place to move in the direction of the desired change. Successful actuating requires change.

To induce change we need to remember that any kind of personality

---

[9] Ibid, pp. 87–94.

behavior represents a sort of equilibrium. Further, a person is not likely to change; he tends to stay with what he now possesses; in fact he may resent any attempt to change him because it will require new adjustments of him. Stated briefly, the task of changing human behavior requires the necessity of understanding more fully the psychological mechanisms that have to be set in motion.

Part of the difficulty is that when behavior is changed it is an admission by the person changing that what he had been thinking and doing he now admits to be erroneous. And he reasons, he should have been more intelligent and discovered his own error. So there is a very strong face-saving element present in most major behavior changes.

Help can be given a person in changing his behavior. Persons are influenced favorably or unfavorably by examples provided, experiences permitted, frames of reference supplied, encouragement of certain motives, and the discountenance of other forces. An existing behavior represents the outcome of motives supporting that behavior. Some motives exert a stronger influence than others. To change the behavior it is frequently helpful to weaken the supporting influences to certain motives. To use a frontal attack in an effort to substitute a new motive for an old one is usually ineffective. Removal of accustomed influences meet resistance and arouses defenses.

The weakening of supporting influences can be attempted in various ways. Among the more common is to provide facts and knowledge which can be evaluated. The attempt here is to stress greater rational consideration than emotional. Supplying expert or authoritative explanations or viewpoints along with the reasons for such viewpoints can also be employed. In some instances it is effective to get the individual to review his experience, to become more aware of what it means, and to try to reevaluate it. Frequently it is effective to alter the relationship of the individual with the reference group, that is, to reduce the ego-involvement by lowering the favorable respondence of the group to the behavior. An effective way is to talk with the group, point out major reasons for the change with emphasis given to possible gains to be realized by the group's members, request their cooperation and support, and appeal for a favorable decision.

ACTUATING AND ATTITUDE

Attitudes are important in actuating effort. An attitude is a way a person tends to feel, see, or interpret a particular situation. An attitude is intangible; it is determined by another from the way a person acts or responds to a situation, person, group, event, or institution. It is well to point out that an attitude is neither (1) a motive nor (2) a response. Attitude refers to probable direction, not the behavior itself. Attitude is not a drive or force, as a motive is, but simply a state of readiness to respond. For an attitude to exist, it is necessary that a person be motivated with respect to the given object and that his motives regarding this object have a common direction, thus providing a so-called motive pattern. It follows that attitudes do not necessarily lead to expression or action. A person can have an attitude concerning an

FIGURE 19–1. An excellent creed for developing favorable attitudes

THE OPTIMIST CREED

Promise yourself—
To be so strong that nothing can disturb your peace of mind.
To talk health, happiness, and prosperity to every person you meet.
To make all your friends feel that there is something in them.
To look at the sunny side of everything and make your optimism come true.
To think only of the best, to work only for the best, and to expect only the best.
To be just as enthusiastic about the success of others as you are about your own.
To forget the mistakes of the past and press on to the greater achievements of the future.
To wear a cheerful countenance at all times and give every living creature you meet a smile.
To give so much time to the improvement of yourself that you have no time to criticize others.
To be too large for worry, too noble for anger, too strong for fear, and too happy to permit the presence of trouble.

CHRISTIAN D. LARSON

Courtesy: Optimist International, St. Louis, Mo.

enterprise or another person without taking any action with respect to either of them. In fact, most people have experienced this particular state of affairs.

A common classification of attitudes is (1) positive or constructive and (2) negative or destructive. A positive attitude emphasizes success and encouragement. In contrast, a negative attitude stresses possible hurdles or the viewpoint that in a given case the objective cannot be attained. Most objectives are accomplished far more effectively when positive attitudes prevail. Optimism is a matter of attitude. Managers must first think they can before they can. Success and victory thrive under the influence of positive attitudes. The kind of atmosphere in which managers are going to live is determined more by their attitudes than anything else. Figure 19–1 gives an excellent creed to follow for developing favorable attitudes.

Attitudes are learned or acquired during daily life experiences. They are founded perhaps more on an emotional than on a rational basis. People are not born with attitudes. From infancy on, a person acquires traditions, beliefs, opinions, and knowledge, all of which help to formulate his attitudes. Attitudes are acquired in one or a combination of three ways (1) past experience, (2) acceptance of the attitude of the group of which a person is a member, and (3) a statement of an authoritative source. While all three of these sources are important, that of experience is probably most common. To a significant degree, a person feels and thinks toward an object as he has personally witnessed that particular object. An arbitrator's attitude toward settling collective bargaining disputes will probably differ from that of a retired businessman in Florida.

The influence of experience upon attitude is brought out by a popular Mother Goose rhyme which goes—

> Pussy-cat, pussy-cat, where have you been?
> I've been to London to look at the Queen.
> Pussy-cat, pussy-cat, what did you there?
> I frightened a little mouse under the chair.

What would you expect a cat to do? It performed those actions which from experience the cat had grown accustomed to do. Likewise, an employee sees only what his mind has been trained to observe and does what his firsthand experience suggests should be done—this experience sets the stage for many of his attitudes.

MOTIVATORS TO USE

Diligent application of the following ten modern motivators provide good results in management actuating. Included are:

1. Multiplier Manager. Seeing himself primarily as a multiplier of others by the work they accomplish promotes actuating. A multiplier manager acts in context of how what he does can assist others in his work group to do a better and more effective job. He asks of each of his subordinates, "How good have I made you look?" He strives to make others look good in their own eyes, for he knows that then he will look better to himself.

An advantage of being a multiplier manager is that individuals are led to develop fully and completely their own talents. Also, there is a very close relationship formulated between the interests and skills of each subordinate and the requirements of the enterprise. Further, evaluation of management personnel is enhanced. Questions answered include:

How complete and fresh are his plans? Is he letting obsolescence overtake him? What activities are being performed to improve his management knowledge and skills?

2. Results Management. Initially discussed in Chapter 3, we have mentioned results management as the recommended modifier to the process approach to management throughout this book. The participation of each employee in determining his own objectives and how he intends achieving them, with final approval given by his superior and the evaluation of the subordinate's efforts based on results using his objectives as the standard, has tremendous built-in motivational qualities. The subordinate becomes results-minded, as well as practical with respect to how and when certain tasks can be completed. He must, of course self-appraise his abilities carefully, and realize where he is strong and where weak.

We say a great deal in management about a manager knowing precisely what his objectives are, having unity of effort, possessing adequate authority and responsibility to do his job properly, and receiving a feedback on "how he is doing." Results management provides all these things. They are built right into the approach. In essence, each employee is made the manager over his own work affairs. The results are up to him. He takes over, manages, and is judged on the results he achieves. This appears to be the ideal managerial arrangement, the zenith of true and effective actuating efforts.

3. Participation. Participation encourages and permits contributions to decisions, goals, and plans along with suggestions as to how these can be implemented. It can be formally defined as *both mental and emotional involvement of a person to make contributions to the decision-making process, especially on matters in which personal involvement of the person exists, and to assume his share of the responsibility for them.* The motivational basis is that people like to be asked their opinion and know that their ideas and beliefs have some weight in the ultimate management action taken. The underlying assumptions are: People derive satisfaction from being a part of the management action, from doing as effective a job as practical, and having self-control rather than organization control utilized. By using participation greater acceptance to change is accomplished. Most people more readily accept what they in part helped create than something entirely foreign to them. Also, participation supplies the feeling of belonging and being wanted. It inflates or at least recognizes a person's ego and provides a needed sense of importance. In addition, it encourages better decision making, gets people to accept responsibility, promotes teamwork, and emphasizes the use of creativity.

Participation cannot be universally applied to all people. Like other actuating efforts it must be used skillfully and must suit the individual circumstance. Fundamentally, participation in management gives the best results when employees are interested in and ready to assume responsibility, are keyed in with the objectives of the enterprise, and have adequate knowledge to deal with the problems at hand. For example, it is foolish to expect fruitful results from participation when the employees do not have the know-how about the subject in which participation is encouraged. Also, (1) there must be time to participate, (2) participants must be familiar with the constraints to be observed (legal requirements, company policies, etc.), (3) effective communication must exist, and (4) each participant must know his position and status will not be adversely affected by his participation.

4. *Realistic Human Relations.* To grant the typical employee extreme permissiveness in encouraging him to do anything he feels like doing does not contribute to his satisfaction of wants or to his desired development. Following a "hands-off," no direction, universal agreement, harmony-at-any-price managerial role is an unrealistic approach and usually does not result in effective actuating.

Many a manager has found that following a program of "make the employees happy and try to be liked, then they'll produce more" just isn't always effective. This does not mean that a manager should be dictatorial, operate as a lone wolf, be unfriendly, and make himself difficult to get along with. He need not be a "hard-boiled" boss; neither does he have to be a "soft-boiled" boss. The latter is as bad as the former. "Soft-boiled" managers stress the belief that no one should be asked to do anything that he or she does not want to do. They operate on a "management by consent" basis—the manager waits long enough for employees to arrive at the idea themselves. Trouble arises if they do not want to do what must be done. If it is imperative that it be done, the manager had better get it done. "Soft-boiled" managers usually indicate to the employees that management has abdicated, the enterprise is wishy-washy, there is no firm direction, and inefficient performance will be tolerated.

The great majority of employees want to contribute and accomplish work that to them is satisfying. Inherently they want to please their superior and at the same time gain satisfaction from their work efforts and relationships. They respond to a sense of fairness, duty, and work. They resent being manipulated by any means, direct or indirect, and prefer a forthright answer to a forthright question.

5. *Environment of Accomplishing Work.* This includes a work climate which has the presence of a pressure to get things done. When this exists to a high degree, the success of actuating efforts is usually high. The need to achieve, getting projects finished, and the value of time are prominent attributes that make for a high work accomplishment environment. Employees are directly and indirectly influenced by the presence of such an environment and usually are willing to do better and more work.

When there is no spirit urging the purposeful pursuit of a demanding goal, actuation is quite likely to be low. Generally speaking, this environment factor is relatively low in certain offices and in some universities. The work pace and urgency to achieve are not high. The attitude may be described as "If we do not get it accomplished this morning, we will do it this afternoon or perhaps tomorrow." Variations in the environment exist not only by type of company, but also by department. In other words, some departments in a university, for example, might have a high environmental factor, while in others it may be low. But there is no question that the degree of environment work accomplishment factor influences the organization's way of life, characterizes its management team, and mode of performing work.

6. Job Enrichment and Rotation. To a great extent the approach of simplifying jobs, hiring people to do these very simple jobs, and permitting each employee to perform only one of several of these very simple tasks is going by the board. We know with reasonable certainty that this is the road to smother any interest or challenge in the job and to generate apathy, boredom, and fatigue. The degree to which these undesirable concepts are reached depends upon the individual. Also with the average employee having a higher education than years ago, with the unions and their demands, and with the changing attitude toward authority, we have discovered that slicing the work into very thin strips just doesn't fit modern job requirements.

Job enrichment tends to relieve this poverty of job satisfaction. The possibility that effective actuating efforts can be accomplished ranks high when the job is deliberately enriched to encompass greater responsibility, broader scope of activities, and more challenge.

Job rotation is also winning favor. Under this arrangement an employee is rotated from one job assignment to another. Periodically job switches take place, thus hopefully minimizing boredom and disinterest. The practice of job rotation can be followed without redesigning the job as is the case with job enrichment and it further permits a job switch to occur at the most opportune time for management.

7. Power of Mind. It was Emerson who wrote, "What you are speaks so loudly that nothing you say can be heard." We become what we think. This implies an enormous challenge and is vital in management actuating. A manager should know what his subordinates really think, if he hopes to motivate them. Further, the manager should know what is needed to improve the value of the mind that each of his subordinates brings to work each day. Having information of this sort will help in getting answers to what changes and improvements in the thinking of a group should take place. Progress along this line will assist significantly in improving motivation.

Further, management by example can be employed. A manager can search his mental capacities, know what he can be, and then be what he says he is which should be the product of the best individual developments he can undertake. A manager tends to extract the best from others when he strives to do the best that he can do.

Trying to motivate employees who spend too little time in environments where they are exposed to the sort of people, information, and actions that will help them, is part of the problem of motivation. What a person's mind attends to continually, he believes. Employees come to believe that their work environment, the caliber of their top management, and so forth, mediocre though it be, is par for the course—it is what work environment and top management are in their minds and they accept it for what it is. And the same holds true for employees working under good environment and effective top management in that this type of work life becomes the accepted condition.

8. *Effective Criticism.* This can be a springboard for improving an employee's behavior and performance. Adopting a positive approach makes criticism less difficult as well as more effective. The superior should examine his own motives before he criticizes. He should be sure that what he plans to say is actually intended to help the situation. It is also helpful to know whether a consistent behavior pattern or merely a one-time occurrence is being dealt with.

The most effective criticism features a mutual exchange of beliefs, ideas, and suggestions. It is well to point out that mistakes are a part of growth, and progress is more likely if mistakes are brought out in the open. Further, that although there are faults in the present behavior and performance, there are also good points about what is being done. Keep the criticism on use of personal efforts for improvement now, not next week or next month. Resolve mutual immediate and realistic goals. Try to set up specific time schedules for improvements.

An effective plan to follow is, first, establish the basic problem. Then, say the negative things you have to say. Be specific in examples of unsatisfactory behavior. Next, ask the subordinate for specific ways in which he believes he can improve the unsatisfactory behavior. Help by suggesting ways yourself and work them out with the subordinate. Following this, point out the subordinate's outstanding good points and how they demonstrate his potential for improvement. Lastly, close the conversation, but do not do this until you believe the problem and its solution has been fairly discussed.

9. Zero Defects. Designed to actuate employees to adhere consistently to high standards of work excellence, Zero Defects (ZD) programs have been extremely effective. The goal is to make the defects

FIGURE 19–2. General observations pertinent to satisfying employee wants

1. People differ in their basic wants, and they expect to be treated as individuals.
2. The acceptance of new ideas and changes is more likely to take place if people are prepared for them; normally the instituting of sudden changes should be avoided.
3. Habit and emotion are of major importance in explaining people's behavior; reason is of secondary importance.
4. People want credit for work accomplished when they deserve it.
5. A sense of belonging to an acceptable group and of feeling important are strong motivating forces to most people.
6. Fear is a strong motivating force, but it is negative in effect and normally diminishes with time.
7. Employees want to use their highest abilities and enjoy a sense of accomplishment on their jobs.
8. Employees want to achieve things of which they can be proud.
9. Employees prefer supervisors whom they respect and trust.
10. Giving information to employees about matters that concern them helps formulate an effective team.
11. A person is affected by the group of which he is a part and, in turn, affects the group's behavior.
12. Criticism or unfavorable comparison of an employee's work in public is resented by most employees; they dislike "losing face."
13. When doing their work incorrectly, employees want to be told about it along with the correct way.
14. Reprimands and remedial actions are expected by most employees when they violate established and known means of operations; most employees prefer not to have the soft, "good Joe" type of superior.

zero by avoiding mistakes, oversights, unreliable products, and delivery delays. ZD programs rely upon recognition of the importance of the human element and the self-will of personnel to want to give outstanding quality work performance. It emphasizes self-motivation to acquire pride of workmanship and to manufacture acceptable quality parts and products.

In establishing a ZD program it is best to give it positive identification from the top to the bottom of the entire organization. A manager of the program should be appointed, comprehensive training about it provided, and a dramatic kickoff date established. Promotional efforts are normally needed to maintain a high rate of interest in the program. Along this line, the following is recommended: displays of posters throughout the work areas, awarding of ZD pins to all who pledge to support the program, handing out of ZD stickers for car windows, a "ZD Special" on the company lunchroom menu, and wide publicity to ZD accomplishments.

Success stories about ZD programs are abundant. Some users term it PRIDE (Production of Reliable Items Demand Excellence), but by whatever name it is known, favorable results predominate. To illustrate, in a sheet metal shop, weekly data revealed that of a total of 13,800 production man-hours expended, 82 man-hours were spent on correcting production errors. After the ZD program was in effect, these 82 man-hours for correction were reduced to only 16 man-hours, a reduction of over 80 percent.

10. Proven Practices in Dealing with People. To actuate successfully, the wise manager follows proven successful practices in dealing with people. An appropriate list of observations to assist in this respect is shown by Figure 19–2. Managers utilizing these observations in their daily work are practically certain to improve their management.

GROUP INFLUENCE

Up to this point we have directed the discussion to the individual and actuating. But we know that actuating is also effected by the group's influence. Considering the individual only as an individual does not give us the true picture for the individual is commonly a member of a group. When satisfying group demands we also satisfy in various degrees the wants of individuals making up the group. We know, for example, that each individual does not set out alone to satisfy his wants irrespective of others in the group. Rather he seeks to satisfy his wants by working together with others as a group. Every member contributes something toward the accomplishment of the common group goal. Each depends on the other, and the entire group is united in this mutual interest in order to achieve the predetermined objective.

Figure 19–3 is an attempt to show these concepts graphically. At the top of the drawing are spaces indicating five individuals, A, B, C, D, and E. Each works toward the Goal shown at the bottom of the drawing for which he hopes to receive in return the satisfaction of his individual wants, as indicated by the arrows and their identifications. The contribution of individual A to the goal is indicated by the area marked A_1.

FIGURE 19–3

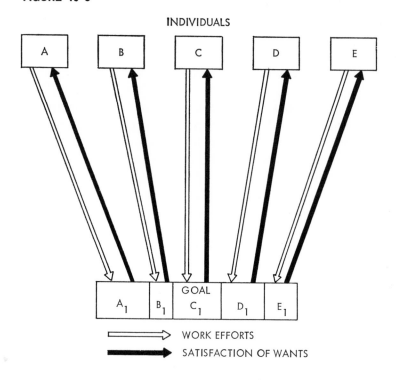

INDIVIDUALS

Likewise that of B, C, D, and E is marked B_1, C_1, D_1, and E_1, respectively. These contributions are not necessarily equal, but they are vital to the entire goal achievement and are interrelated. A_1, for example, depends somewhat on the success of B_1, and the achievement of E_1 contributes to the entire goal which affects A_1, etc.

Frequently in the integration of individuals' efforts into a smooth working group, the individual loses some of his individual personality and characteristics. When this transition occurs, the individual's former personal wants are changed and become mainly those of the group. Common goals, beliefs, and motivations of the group predominate. The members usually have a set of values, a certain way of doing things, and acceptable behavior patterns. This welding of individuals into an operating unit makes for teamwork characterized by the mutual dependence of the members upon one another.

GROUP BEHAVIOR

Group behavior is gaining prominence and becoming a specialized subject. For purposes here we shall brief some of the more important fundamental knowledge.[10] Group behavior is an entity of its own; it is not simply a summation of the behaviors of the individuals making up the group. Generally, a group can be influenced more effectively by dealing with the group as a unit rather than with the components of the group or the individuals singly. There are several reasons for this. First, it is frequently less difficult to sway a group than an individual. This is true for several reasons. First, when members of the group change their attitude, the individual can see that a change on his part will not reduce his relative ego-involvement. Second, changes or acceptance of persuasive efforts are often more effective on a group than on an individual, the influence of mob psychology and group motivations being exercised. Third, the attainment of an atmosphere of high enthusiasm, helpful for inducing changes, can best be reached with a group.

The values and behavior of an individual are related to the group to which he belongs, and the group's characteristics assert themselves in numerous situations. To illustrate, an individual who is affiliated with a definite group will not normally change his behavior from that of the group if such a change sets him apart or deviates from the accepted behavior of the group. Selecting one individual from a group, indoctrinating him with specialized training, and then returning him to the group may result in trouble rather than in hoped-for progress. The trained individual has the problem of remaining or perhaps reinstating himself as a part of the group and yet retaining and applying the training that was given to him. The better application of group human relations to bring about the change would be to establish the need for the change among certain members and have them suggest and promote the change for the group. Members of a group are more likely to listen and believe what a member of his group says in comparison to what an outsider says. In fact, anyone working with a group soon realizes that he must share the group's values and beliefs, perhaps feel like a member of the group, in order to accomplish aims by means of the group's efforts.

Most employees spend more of their time in their work group than in any other group. The problem of such things as the acceptance or rejection of an individual to a group, the extent and effect of friendship within the group, and the compatibility of group and individual person-

---

[10] For information on group behavior see the following: Alan C. Filley and Robert J. House, *Managerial Process and Organization Behavior* (Glenview, Ill.: Scott, Foresman and Company, 1969); A. Paul Hare, *Handbook of Small Group Research* (New York: The Free Press of Glencoe, 1962); G. C. Homans, *The Human Group* (New York: Harcourt, Brace & World, 1950); H. T. Leavitt, *Managerial Psychology,* (Chicago: University of Chicago Press, 1964); J. G. March and H. A. Simon, *Organizations* (New York: John Wiley and Sons, Inc., 1958); R. M. Stogdill, *Individual Behavior and Group Achievement* (New York: Oxford Press, 1959).

ality are considerations of genuine concern to management members. Being able to recognize a bad situation and shifting a misfit from one group to another or of knowing what factors to consider in forming groups are basic in obtaining effective group action.

The group leader's statements made in introducing a new member to a group condition considerably the group's acceptance of the newcomer. Not all barriers, however, can be dissolved by introductory remarks. Favorable introductory comments elicit favorable group acceptance while opposite clues given in the introduction evoke relatively low group acceptance. Likewise, a group's cohesiveness and productivity is higher when the members are permitted to form or select their own work groups. Under such conditions the job satisfaction of each member tends to increase. The members of the group fit together, adjustment in behavior is a minimum, and each individual works with fellow employees he likes and with whom he prefers to work.

QUESTIONS

1. In your opinion can work that a man does be motivating? Substantiate your answer.
2. Discuss your reaction to and the importance to you of the following statement: "Actuating is challenging and this is especially so since effective actuating efforts are highly personalized."
3. Relate a personal experience in which you were motivated by striving to achieve an esteem need.
4. Define each of the following: (1) zero defects, (2) job enrichment, (3) hierarchy of needs, and (4) multiplier manager.
5. Relate the help and the relative benefits a manager in his actuating efforts can gain by giving careful consideration to job content and job context.
6. What is the preference-expectation theory and of what importance is it in actuating?
7. As a manager you are fairly certain that a basic want of employee Philip Kimbrough is recognition as an individual. How would you go about meeting Mr. Kimbrough's want?
8. Discuss fully an actuating premise that you feel is important for a manager to keep in mind.
9. Why does the typical member of an organization tend to resist changing his behavior? Of what importance is this in actuating?
10. What is the meaning of and what are some useful suggestions for using participation as a motivator?
11. State a clear definition for each of the following: (1) affection needs, (2) theory Y, (3) attitude, and (4) Protestant ethic.
12. Discuss the importance of group behavior in managerial actuating work.
13. Discuss the use of effective criticism as a means of motivating.

14. Enumerate eight points to keep in mind in order to satisfy human wants of either a management or nonmanagement member.

CASE 19–1. JAVES COMPANY

Leonard Hart, director of engineering design and research, joined Javes Company right after receiving his M.E. degree. He started as a trainee. Winning promotions from time to time, he has now been with the company twenty-seven years. For the past four years, he has been been in his present capacity as a major officer of the company. Leonard Hart likes his job and he likes the Javes Company. Ambitious and a very hard worker, he is well thought of by his compeers in management and has the reputation of running a good department. Now 50 years of age, he well realizes that he has reached the top of his bracket, that there are no future promotions for him at Javes, and that no further financial incentive is available to him. By staying with the company for the next fifteen years, he will retire with an attractive pension.

His wife, Lenora, is active in church and several community associations. She likes the small town where the company is located and enjoys her large number of friends. Their younger of two daughters is getting married next month and Lenora is looking forward to increasing her social activities in the future and expects to continue residency at their present address.

Elsworth Rieter, president of Javes Company, has observed that Mr. Hart is losing some of his enthusiasm and willingness to take on extra company assignments that he used to request. Arranging for the company's annual picnic and handling contributions for United Charities are illustrative. It's not that Mr. Hart is not as energetic as he once was. He jogs a mile every morning, plays golf twice a week, and spends considerable time in his workshop at home making all sorts of gadgets. He is in excellent physical condition. Mr. Reiter has informally discussed Mr. Hart's behavior on special occasions with the vice president of finance, who says, "Leonard has changed somewhat. He realizes he has reached his peak and is starting to level off." What neither Mr. Reiter nor the vice president of finance know is that for the last year, Mr. Hart has attempted to find a better job, but to date has been unsuccessful in locating one. He is beginning to accept the idea that there probably isn't a better job for him than the one he has and he should remain where he is.

Questions

1. Assuming Leonard Hart spends the rest of his work life with Javes Company, do you feel problems will arise in motivating Mr. Hart? Discuss.
2. What actions do you recommend the company take? Why?

CASE 19–2.   THE LANE COMPANY

SALES REP. NO. 1.: Gordon Allison runs the show. He writes all letters to customers and to the home office. Since I have to come in the office at the end of each day, which is another of his silly ideas, I don't understand why I can't handle correspondence with my own customers. The office would have a copy so they would know what's going on.

SALES REP. NO. 2.: Gordon keeps saying we're in business for ourselves. That's all bunk. He keeps close tab of where you are, what you said to the customer, and when you come in the office. He is like radar. It's far worse than a strict parent who never lets his young teen-ager out of the house.

SALES REP. NO. 3: He (Gordon) makes all the decisions that have any importance at all. If I have a big deal pending, he calls on the account, usually with me, but he does all the talking and if we close the deal, he calls the home office in Memphis telling them he landed another big order. I griped to him about the big FW order we got last week that was handled this way. He explained, "It's from Los Angeles office and they know you are working on this account." Frankly, I do not believe that they do.

SALES REP. NO. 4.: Reporting in every night is the biggest waste of time ever. Frequently, I have to start returning to the office around 3:30 P.M. to see "Mr. Establishment" during the 4:30 to 5:30 P.M. confession period when you give a verbal account of each call you made during the day. It is not needed. The office receives a written report that I make out on each call on a customer.

SALES REP. NO. 5.: I've been with Lane for eleven years. If I could find another sales job paying me the same money, I'd quit this job. Gordon Allison is critical and most of it is intended to put fear into you. It is not helpful. Yet I believe Gordon is fair. He treats all of us exactly alike. If Gordon moves up and goes to Memphis, I'd be the one in line and I'd like very much having the regional job in L.A.

Mr. Gordon Allison is Los Angeles regional sales manager for the Lane Company of Memphis. He has five salesmen, an office staff, and two men in the warehouse. Each salesman calls in right after 9:00 A.M.

giving his itinerary for the morning. Then again around noon each salesman calls in to find out if any calls have been received for them. At 4:30 P.M. each salesman is required to return to the office, fill out a separate report sheet for each call made, and talk over the important highlights of each case with Mr. Allison. From these written reports and conversations, Mr. Allison writes the home office for additional information needed or writes the customer in the form of a quotation, a thank-you follow-up, or a complaint settlement. In addition, Mr. Allison makes calls with his salesmen. He estimates about one half of his time is spent in working with his salesmen in the field and he enjoys this part of his job as he gets to see the customer, observes his salesmen in action, and enjoys the change from being in the office.

Questions

1. What is the problem?
2. Recap the major points made by the sales representatives. Discuss.
3. Do you feel results management could be used successfully by this company? Why?
4. What action and plan of implementation do you recommend for the Lane Company? Justify your answer.

20

Leading

To be what we are, and to become what we are capable of becoming, is the only end of life.
ROBERT LOUIS STEVENSON

LEADING HUMAN BEINGS is an important part of actuating efforts. The relationships between the leader's mode of activities and the way his followers perform tasks significantly affect the satisfaction of the followers as well as the material results achieved. Effective leading triggers a person's "will to do" and transforms lukewarm desires for achievements into burning passions for successful accomplishments. It is highly helpful in getting plans put into action and is a necessary ingredient of management.

MEANING OF LEADERSHIP

Changes in organizations, history, and society result from efforts of a relatively few superior individuals. These individuals may dedicate their lives to a certain mission; they may desire power and influence over others; or they may possess boundless energy and willpower to accomplish certain values which to them have supreme significance.

Leadership has been defined in various ways. It has, for example, been referred to as a process of influencing the actions of an organized group in goal setting and accomplishment; also as an influence under which followers accept willingly the direction and control by another person or the leader. For purposes here, we can state that *leadership is the relationship in which one person, or the leader, influences others to work together willingly on related tasks to attain that which the leader desires.* Observe that leading has to do with one person *influencing* others in

458

his group. Further, this influence comes about from the relationship between the leader and a group member or members, i.e., there is *interaction* or reciprocal reactions of people in a group to each other. These two words, influence and interaction, are basic in any discussion of leadership.

The influence of a leader is of two different types. First, there is his own performance that directly affects the group level of work. Second, there is the behavior and actions he takes to affect the group's stability and members' satisfaction. Likewise, interaction is of two different types, including first, those between the leader and the group, and second, those between and among individual members of the group.

FIGURE 20–1. Comparison between leadership and nonleadership

Leadership	*Nonleadership*
1. Inspires the employee.	1. Drives the employee.
2. Accomplishes work and develops the employee.	2. Accomplishes work at expense of employee.
3. Shows employee how to do his job.	3. Instills fear in employee by threats and coercion.
4. Assumes obligations.	4. Passes the buck.
5. Fixes the breakdown for loss in production or sales.	5. Fixes the blame on others for loss in production or sales.

A leader leads, he does not push. He pulls his followers to heights of accomplishment they may not have believed were possible. A leader knows the individual characteristics of his key followers, knows what qualities will elicit their best efforts, and is a developer of at least some of his followers. The consequence and satisfaction to those being led are of prime importance. A leader serves at the same time he leads. He has an ability to awaken emotional as well as rational powers of the follower. He can incite others. In fact, leadership appears to be more emotional than intellectual or rational. The leader realizes this and seeks to cultivate the emotional nature of the followers. He knows that power comes from dedication, not knowledge alone. An interesting comparison between leadership and nonleadership practices is clearly illustrated by Figure 20–1.

To many, a mission or a goal to achieve is the important consideration in any discussion of a leader. People of this belief point out that a leader may write off his whole life as a sunk cost to achieve this cause he feels is worthy and vital. The leader is "for something" and commonly his objective is ahead of those of his contemporaries. The importance of a cause is also borne out in the literal meaning of leader as "one who goes." Where does he go? To seek his worthwhile goal. And in doing this, the leader explains the objective clearly and forcefully in terms that show it is to the follower's best interest for this goal to be achieved.

INFLUENCE AND LEADING

Stated above was the fact that influence is a key word in the meaning of leading. It will be helpful at this point to note the bases upon which a leader influences a subordinate or a group of subordinates. A fivefold framework of power, defined in terms of influence is offered by John French and Bertram Raven.[1] They identity: (1) *coercive power,* which relies on fear and is based on the expectation of the subordinate that punishment is given for not agreeing with superior's actions and beliefs; (2) *reward power* sees that rewards are granted for compliance with superior's actions and wishes; (3) *legitimate power* is derived from the supervisor's position in the organization; (4) *expert power* stems from an individual's possessing some special skill, knowledge, or expertise; and (5) *referent power* which is based on identification of a follower with a leader who is admired and held in high esteem by the follower.

This framework supplies distinction among the possible power bases and is helpful in knowing from whence the power arises and something of its nature. Actually the first three powers—coercive, reward, and legitimate—are primarily of organizational factors, while the last two—expert and referent—are of individual factors.

INTERACTIONS AND LEADING

Interactions between a leader and members of his group and among the group members are, as stated above, essential for effective leadership. The leader is related to the group members in some way and likewise the group members are related to the leader. Overall these relationships are conditioned by the active forces present in the environment within which the leader and group operate. These relationships vary and are frequently quite dynamic. These changes are brought about in part by the reactions of the people (the leader and his group) to one another.

How much interaction should take place for good leadership to exist depends upon what is to be achieved, the behavior of the people in-

---

[1] John R. P. French and Bertram Raven, "The Bases of Social Power," in *Group Dynamics,* D. Cartwright and A. F. Zander (eds.) (Evanston, Ill.: Row, Peterson, and Co., 1960), pp. 607–21.

volved, the knowledge and ideas that each one can contribute toward solving a problem, and the permissiveness of the general environment. If the whole affair is somewhat routine and takes place with some degree of regularity, little interaction is required. On the other hand, if the issue calls for new ideas, is constantly changing, and affects seriously the leader and many members of the group, the need for interaction is great, if not critical.

FUNDAMENTALS OF MANAGERIAL LEADING

Our current understanding and knowledge of managerial leading point to certain fundamentals that are well to keep in mind. For con-

FIGURE 20–2. Leadership is a complex relationship

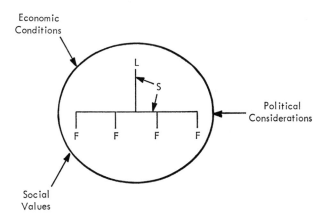

venience, these fundamentals have been condensed to five, the first of which is *leadership is a complex relationship existing between the leader, the led, the organization, and social values and economic and political conditions.*[2]

To be precise we should add that it is the characteristics of each of these four components that make up the complex relationship we are discussing. This leadership fundamental is extremely important and is diagrammed in Figure 20–2. Shown at the top by the letter "L" is the leader and his characteristics. Followers are represented by the four "F's," while the "S" points out the organization structure with the type

[2] See Douglas McGregor, *Leadership and Motivation* (Cambridge, Mass.: M.I.T. Press, 1966), pp. 73–77, for full discussion of this fundamental.

of tasks to be performed. Encircling the entire structure and affecting each part of it are social values, economic and political considerations.

A leader influences others or those led by his qualities of confidence, communicative ability, and awareness of his impact on others as well as his perceptions about the situation and his subordinates. The degree of confidence the group has in the leader appears vital, as is also the willingness of the group to do what the leader tells them. Those who are led want their goals and needs satisfied by the leader through his structuring of the group's interactions. The leader must have the ability to sense the group's needs and traditions, then operate within the constraints of the group's norms. In addition, the work situation or organization constraint within which the members work must be taken into account. The qualities for successful leadership vary with the particular work situation. This evinces the leader's genuine skill and ability to adopt his leadership to the particular conditions and relationships involved. The fact that a leader gained success in one situation does not necessarily mean he will be successful in another. We will say more about this under the fifth fundamental several paragraphs below. In addition, social values from the outside, such as social legislation and education of followers, economic and political conditions, including standards of living, change in markets, and modifications in taxes, bring about changes that subsequently lead to a redefinition of acceptable and effective leadership.

Second, *the leader's role and the degree of its acceptance by the group condition the leadership.* Shared information and close emotional and knowledge ties between the leader and his group contribute to both the leader's and the group's effectiveness. The leader should give high priority to gaining the understanding and confidence of the group members. Likewise, followers must believe in their leaders. The leader should take the leadership role defined by the formal organization or if from an informal organization, he should assume the leader's role expected of him. There is leadership by acceptance of the group which comes into existence informally similar to the emergence of authority by acceptance discussed in Chapter 15. The authority the formal organization vests in a leadership position is important. What is the leader to decide? Can he hire, fire, promote, grant wage increases, and decide major issues? Over a period, the leader's formal role may become diluted, and he may have to rely upon his informal situation to maintain adequate leadership.[3]

---

[3] The means by which one becomes a leader include by (1) inheritance, (2) personal power, (3) appointment by a superior, (4) elected by his peers, or (5) recognized by his subordinates.

It should also be noted that followers expect practical help from their leaders. Hence the successful leader makes himself known as one who can and does satisfy the needs of the group, assists in having desirable working conditions, and helps set realistic goals. In return, followers normally support such a leader and make it easier for him to be a leader.

Also, *the extent to which tasks are spelled out has significant influence.* The leader has more influence when he can tell a follower what to do and how to do it. This is typical of those types of jobs where the work is highly structured with standard operating instructions and detailed manuals. Such work is programmed in detail; little is left for the group member to decide. In contrast, work dealing with research projects, committee assignments, new product development, and managerial policies do not lend themselves to predetermined detailed tasks for their successful accomplishment. As such, the influence and the type of leadership given employees doing such work differs from that when the tasks are spelled out in detail.

The fourth leadership fundamental is *the leader has the ability to determine what actions will best help accomplish the group's goals.* This necessitates an understanding of how his actions as a leader will affect the work of the group as well as the members of the group. It involves effective decision making and its implementation. What a leader decides is usually closely related to his perception and analysis of the group's problems within the framework or background of the entire organization. This is more than the ability to make effective decision in the ordinary meaning of that wording, because commonly the leader must stress unique situational and interactional factors so that the best action is initiated and unfavorable results are minimized.

Lastly, *the style of leadership and the situation affect the results obtained.* The same leadership behavior will not be equally effective in all situations. And, as stated above, the situation, or environment, varies. Few individuals excel as leaders in every situation. In essence, there is no such thing as an effective leader or an ineffective leader. More correctly we need to state, for example, that leader A is effective in situation 10 and ineffective in situation 25. This leads to the conclusion that either the leader's style or the organization structure, or both, require modification in a case where the current leadership leaves much to be desired. It is a common happening for a leader to become involved in different work environments which call for different types of leadership behaviors. Some leaders are flexible and do adjust to each situation, but many others apparently cannot. Yet, we cannot afford to discard a leader who is a specialist simply because he does not perform effectively in a particular leadership job. On the one hand, we try, through training, to get flexibility in the leader and, on the other hand, to adjust the situation, through organization changes, to fit better the leader's behavior pattern. This suggests the possibility of tailoring the manager's job to his leadership style rather than struggling to change his style to that of the job requirements. But as a leader progresses, changes necessitated by each successive job can become burdensome and costly.

How can the manager's job be changed, yet retain its major essentials? A few suggestions will show possible ways. Variations in authority are possible, such as giving the leader final and complete authority over his department or limiting it, or perhaps requiring that all decisions be approved by the leader's superior before they are put into action. Also, to a degree the task structures can be modified. Some can be spelled out while others are defind in broad outlines with assignments left to the initiative and imagination of the leader. Further, the homogeneity of the group the manager works with can be altered, thus changing his work efforts and his relationships to the new group.

THEORIES OF LEADERSHIP

Leadership has been subjected to considerable research and study and, as a result, there are today numerous theories of leadership being expounded. They include differences in opinions, methodologies, explanations, and conclusions. Each has its group of advocates who profess their particular theory as the right and proper one. Interpretations from the various theories have given rise to controversies; by no means is there complete harmony among the concepts advanced by the various leadership theorists. Although more is known today about leadership than ever before, we still do not have complete and integrated theories about it that represent the totality of leadership. There is no known one best way of leading people. Leadership practice and style constitute a complex web of factors. Such things as the leader's personality, skill, experience, confidence, awareness of self, type of followers, interactions, and organization climate influence the leader's behavior and what he does or does not accomplish. However, the importance of empirical findings in developing leadership theories is beginning to be emphasized. Progress in this direction may assist in consolidating, as well as filling in the voids existing in the present theories to supply several complete leadership theories.

For convenience, we will discuss eight leadership theories which represent collectively a large portion of the thinking being done in this area and also illustrate diverse and valid approaches to the study of leadership. Included are (1) the autocratic theory, (2) the psychologic theory, (3) the sociologic theory, (4) the supportive theory, (5) the laissez-faire theory, (6) the personal-behavior theory, (7) the trait theory, and (8) the situational theory.

AUTOCRATIC THEORY

Leadership as envisioned under this theory features commands, enforcements, and somewhat arbitrary actions in the leader's relationships with subordinates. The leader tends to be work-centered; he closely supervises to ensure that designated work is performed and utilizes rates of production to help in this effort. The formal organization structure is respected at all times for which economic security as steady employment, promotions along prescribed paths, and status symbols to denote relative formal rank are granted. Orders and directives are employed, but frequently an explanation or reason for them is not given. However under the autocratic theory, the leader is not viewed as an inflexible autocrat always making decisions without regard to human values, but the preponderance of his leadership behavior tends to have these characteristics.

The autocratic leader uses commands generally supported by sanctions of which discipline is among the most important. Discipline may either bring about the giving of rewards or the establishing of a system of penalties, as, for example, giving a pay increase or penalizing for excessive defects in the quality of the product. Enforcement by the autocratic leader depends on his power to reward or punish. He believes that most humans work better in a climate where the sanction of discipline prevails, that is, acceptance of a prescribed habit of obedience exists. Accordingly, both the contentment and the productivity of an employee are aided when the employee knows where he stands and what is expected of him—a modus operandi helped by the sanction of discipline.

PSYCHOLOGIC THEORY

Perhaps better identified as the psychological overview, this approach to leadership advocates that the major function of a leader is to develop the best motivation system. The leader stimulates his subordinates to contribute to organizational objectives as well as to satisfy their own personal goals. Leadership that motivates gives considerable attention to the subordinate's attributes such as recognition, emotional security, and opportunity in keeping with his desires and needs. The satisfaction of these needs in a manner that aids organization to be more successful represents what the psychologic theory leader must perform.

The needs of human beings were discussed in the previous chapter. The hierarchy of needs as suggested by Maslow included in the last chapter offers excellent direction in what constitutes the various needs to be satisfied. Programs to satisfy these needs are the challenge of the leader and inclusion of all five levels of needs makes for better motivating success than that of concentrating on a partial program including only one or two levels.

This theory of leadership is quite broad and general. The techniques for motivating are many and success is usually associated with applying the correct technique for the particular individual circumstances. There is no one best consistent motivational plan that a leader can follow.

SOCIOLOGIC THEORY

Others view leadership as made up of work efforts that facilitate the activities of followers and strive to reconcile any organizational conflicts between followers. The leader establishes goals with participation by the followers in the final decision making. Goal identification gives direction that followers often require. They know what performances, beliefs, and behaviors are expected of them. But the efforts to accomplish the goal influence the interactions among the followers, sometimes to the degree that disruptive conflict within or between groups exists. Under such a condition, the leader is expected to take corrective measures, exercise his leadership influence and reinstate harmony and cooperative effort among the followers.

From the practical viewpoint, a leader does attempt to facilitate the activities of his followers, but in some cases goals are set for him and, further, he may find conflict resolution almost beyond his power to influence. Again, the particular situation, the individual differences of group members, and the competency of the leader are the underlying causes.

SUPPORTIVE THEORY

Here the leader takes the position that his followers want to do their best and that he can lead best by supporting their efforts. To this end, the leader creates a work environment which promotes the desire by each follower to perform to the best of his ability, cooperate with others, and develop his own skills and abilities. Suggestions about how better to do the work, what improvements in working conditions can be made, and what new ideas should be tried out are encouraged. The leader gives general managerial overseeing and encourages his subordinates to use their creativity and initiative in handling the details of their jobs. Decision making by the leader includes consideration for the followers' opinions and recommendations which they aggressively seek.

The supportive theory is termed "participative theory" by some. This follows due to the leader encouraging followers to participate concerning decisions to be made. Others call it "democratic theory of leadership" and while it does have democratic aspects, it neither implies rule by the majority or by vote. On the other hand, in the supportive theory the leader considers his subordinates as social equals and has respect for their knowledge and ideas.

On the plus side, proponents of the supportive theory claim the practice of helping the follower and treating him as an individual with human dignity and rights, makes for a cooperative, productive, and satisfied employee. The leader wins acceptance and his enlightened mode of operation prevails. Further, unilateral authority is rejected, and unwarranted special privileges are minimized. In contrast, there are opponents to the supportive theory. They object on the grounds that group influence on decision making leads to confusion, a great waste of time, and "watered-down" decisions. Further, they state that individual rights and dignity are entirely possible without sharing in what amounts to managerial activities by nonmanagement members. Also, it is claimed the theory violates traditional tenets of private enterprise where the owner or his authorized agent is endowed solely with the decision making process.

LAISSEZ-FAIRE THEORY

Under this theory a leader, if he can be called a leader, gives complete freedom in determining activity to his followers. He does not participate, or if he does, very little. This approach is the direct opposite to the autocratic theory. Various data and material are submitted by the laissez-faire leader either voluntarily or by request to the followers, but he takes no part in work discussions. It is complete nonparticipation by the leader. He communicates essentially when he is communicated to, making very infrequent comments on activities by followers unless questioned.

Laissez-faire groups tend to develop informal leaders and frequently from a group whether formally designated or not. Groups seem to prefer some guidance along with much participation on their part, as exemplified by the supportive theory. In general, groups want help, but object to being told precisely what to do. Laissez-faire raises the question of what does the leader do, if the followers do all the work. And the followers may be limited in what they can suggest and decide due to their lack of experience and knowledge, especially in a technical area. Nevertheless, the laissez-faire theory appears to have interesting possibilities. More research on it may reveal that it holds the key to the dynamic adjustment required in leadership among the leader, the followers, and the internal and external environmental factors.

PERSONAL-BEHAVIOR THEORY

Leadership can also be studied on the bases of the personal qualities or behavioral patterns of leaders. This approach emphasizes what the leader does in leading. An important contribution of this theory is that a leader neither behaves the same nor does he take identical actions for every situation he faces. He is flexible, to a degree, because he feels he must be to take the most appropriate action for handling a particular problem. This suggests a leadership continuum whereby the leader's actions and amount of authority used are related to the decision making freedom or participation available to the subordinates.[4]

Figure 20–3 illustrates the leadership continuum concept. The top of the figure represents boss-centered leadership, the bottom, subordinate-centered leadership. In going from top to bottom, less and less authority is used, and more and more freedom for subordinates. Seven different levels of leadership between the top and bottom are indicated. They are identified by the managerial actions stated at the level, for example, at the top, for boss-centered leadership, the manager makes and announces decisions. In contrast, at the next to the bottom level, more freedom for subordinates and less use of authority are present. At this level the manager defines limits and asks for the group's decision.

This means that different styles of leadership can be employed depending upon the leader's evaluation of the situation, his capabilities, desire to decide the issue, and the amount of control he wishes to exercise. In brief, he must be flexible in order to cope with the task of being a leader.

Another example of personal-behavior theory is that where the leader

---

[4] Robert Tannenbaum and Warren H. Schmidt, "How to Choose a Leadership Pattern," *Harvard Business Review,* March–April, 1958, pp. 95–101.

is subordinate-centered. As indicated in Figure 20–3, such a leader permits much freedom to subordinates. He may, for example, give his subordinates participation in the setting of their work goals, decide how they are going to achieve them, communicate with them on all matters affecting their work, and ask their opinions on controversial organizational and departmental problems.

We mentioned under the discussion of autocratic theory, the tendency

FIGURE 20–3. Continuum of leadership behavior

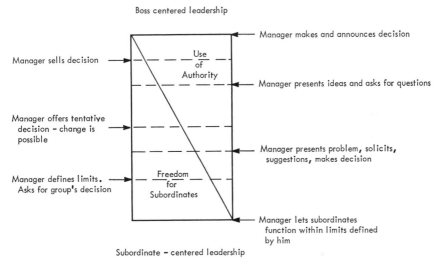

Boss centered leadership

Manager makes and announces decision

Manager sells decision

Use of Authority

Manager presents ideas and asks for questions

Manager offers tentative decision – change is possible

Manager presents problem, solicits, suggestions, makes decision

Manager defines limits. Asks for group's decision

Freedom for Subordinates

Manager lets subordinates function within limits defined by him

Subordinate – centered leadership

Source: Adapted from Robert Tannenbaum and Warren H. Schmidt, "How to Choose a Leadership Pattern," *Harvard Business Review*, March–April 1958, pp. 95–101.

to be work centered. How do the results of work-centered leadership compare with those of subordinate-centered leadership. Research indicates that the high-producing groups are led by managers who are characterized by subordinate-employee-centered leadership.[5] In addition, absenteeism, labor turnover, and defective workmanship were found to be lower when employee-centered leadership was utilized. Hence, it appears that the wise manager will use and develop employee-centered leadership wherever possible.

A third and last example of personal-behavior theory to be offered is that of the autocratic leader who is benevolent. Such a description may sound contradictory, but he exists in reality and, in fact, is not exactly scarce. The benevolent autocratic leader possesses much power and pres-

---

[5] Rensis Likert, *New Patterns of Management* (New York: McGraw-Hill Book Co., Inc., 1961).

tige, has much interest in the welfare of his subordinates, is anxious to help solve their problems, and usually is able to take prompt remedial action whenever required. He is and remains the "chief." While vitally concerned about the attitudes and feelings of his subordinates, he structures all work activities, decides policies, and uses rules and regulations.

Why does the benevolent autocrat exist? In some business companies, the founder or his relatives have worked extremely hard to attain their enterprise's current position and they feel strongly about continuing to control its destiny. They wish to make all major decisions and justify this mainly on the difficulty of reaching these decisions, the impact of what is decided upon the company, and their past successful record. With all the recent behavioral and human value developments in management, it would seem that a weakening in the utilization of the benevolent autocratic leader might take place. But he is found and is successful in the modern company.

TRAIT THEORY

Much work has been done to identify the traits of leaders for use in describing and predicting success in leading. Many engaged in the selecting and developing of managers feel that the trait approach, while open to criticism, is as valid as any available leadership theory. Actually among the trait advocates there is no universal list of traits that make one a successful leader, rather it is a syndrome of the characteristics that are believed to be required.

Among the more common traits are the following:

1. *Intelligence.* It is generally believed that the level of intelligence of an individual gives a reasonable approximation of his chances for succeeding as a leader up to a certain intelligence level. Above this level, which is relatively high, success is less likely. Possibly this can be explained by the fact that individuals with very high intelligence levels find leadership activities and challenges insufficient; they prefer to deal with abstract ideas and basic research work. Sometimes judgment and verbal facility are included under this trait.

2. *Initiative.* Made up of two parts: (1) the ability to act independently and start actions, and (2) the capacity to see courses of action not seen by others. This trait is usually sought in a managerial candidate. Studies show it is outstanding among upper management members, but declines in managers at the lower and operating levels.[6]

---

[6] Edwin E. Ghiselli, "Managerial Talent," *American Psychologist,* October 1963, pp. 638–41.

3. Energy or drive. Many contend that one of the outstanding characteristics of a leader is that he is more energetic in achieving his goal than the nonleader. Both mental and physical energy are required. A leader has stamina to see the work through; he is able to withstand the rigors demanded of his position, overcome all obstacles, and sustain drive for continuous achievement.

4. Emotional maturity. Included in this trait are dependability, persistency, and objectivity. The leader can be counted on to do what he says he will do and accomplish it. He is willing to work long hard hours, give intense application of self, and spread enthusiasm among his followers. Consistent in his actions, he refrains from use of anger and is understood by others. He has a purpose in life and gives full cognizance to what he is trying to achieve. He knows what he wishes to accomplish

FIGURE 20–4. Approaches in persuading

1. Make suggestions and allow time for them to ripen in the minds of followers.
2. Point out reasons why following your point of view is beneficial to the follower.
3. Meet the other fellow halfway—compromise if this seems appropriate.
4. Avoid pet peeves and denouncing "sacred cows" of the other fellow.
5. Ask questions when the answers will help the follower to the conclusion that your point of view is the one to follow.
6. Cite similar situations when your recommendation proved successful.
7. Request rather than order certain action.

today, next year, or five years from today. Detours may be necessary from time to time, but the leader gets back on the beam as fast as he can.

5. Persuasive. There is no leading without the consent of those led. To gain this consent a leader usually must resort to persuasion. Efforts are made to get the subordinate to develop a certain attitude, to induce convictions about certain beliefs, or to be convinced about a certain state of affairs. The means used are many. Figure 20–4 lists the more common approaches.

6. Communicative skill. A leader is able to talk and to write clearly and forcefully. He has an ability to brief accurately the opinions of others and to pick out the real essence from the statements of others. A leader uses communication skillfully for persuasive, informative, and stimulative purposes.

7. Self-assurance. This is the extent to which the leader perceives himself to be effective in solving problems that he faces. It can be expressed as confidence in his leadership skills. The effective leader is well adjusted and has few, if any, antisocial attitudes. He believes he can meet successfully most situations that will confront him. Self-assurance is greatest among high-level managers, lowest among low-level managers.[7]

8. *Perceptive.*   This trait refers to the ability to perceive characteristics and behavior of other persons and especially of his followers in the case of a leader. It also includes the ability to utilize empathy or the capacity to project oneself mentally and emotionally into the position of another person. When one is empathetic, he knows what makes the other fellow think as he does, even though he does not necessarily agree with the other fellow's thoughts.

9. *Creativity.*   The capacity for originality, to think up new ways, and to blaze a brand new way of solving a problem represents a highly desirable trait of a leader. Progress and improvement depend in large measure upon creativity. This one trait alone can give a leader a decided advantage over his peers and competitors.

10. *Social participation.*   A leader understands people and knows their strengths and weaknesses. He adapts to various groups and has the ability to meet people from different walks of life and converse on a wide range of subjects. He conducts himself so that he gains the confidence and loyalty of his group. People cooperate willingly with him. He is approachable, friendly, and helpful.

The trait theory has serious shortcomings in its assistance to understand leadership. It emphasizes what a leader probably possesses in personality rather than what he does as a leader. He may possess a lot of drive but the real question is, does he use it and if so, for what purpose? Also, are we talking about traits to acquire a leadership job or to maintain one? Further, the trait approach assumes that personality is a composite of discrete traits rather than a sort of integrator of characterisics that shift and change in their respective strengths and importance. Both the followers and the situation or environment are ignored except in a remote and indirect way as they influence the traits of the leader based on past behavior. In addition, no relative importance of the traits is usually specified. No weights are assigned. For example, is initiative or self-assurance more important? Finally the traits are not mutually exclusive. There is commonly some overlap and possibly some conflict among several of the traits in most lists. However, this may not be a deficiency, and may accurately represent leadership traits as they are. But it does raise problems in how the traits are used.

---

[7] Ibid, pp. 577–83.

SITUATIONAL THEORY

This approach to the explanation of leadership suggests that there must be enough flexibility in the leadership to adjust to different situations. Leadership is multidimensional. In this theory, leadership is made up of three ingredients: the leader, the followers, and the situation. Of these, the situation is considered most important, because it contains the most variables. However, adjustments to the leader and to the followers also take place. A common problem for which this theory can be helpful is determining whether an applicant for a leadership job is competent. Is he, for example, available because the particular situation of his former position did not permit him to lead even though he tried to adjust to it? In contrast does his former position indicate his inability to lead, as such?

Research on adaptive leadership suggests that there is a type of leadership that is most appropriate in different situations. In studies by Fiedler, three dimensions were used to measure the leader's effectiveness, including (1) the degree of confidence the followers have for their leader, (2) the degree to which the followers' jobs either are routine or are ill-structured, and (3) the degree of power inherent in the leadership position. It appears that permissive leaders (considerate and fostering effective interpersonal relations) obtain optimum group performance in situations that are known and where the tasks are well structured, but the leader must be diplomatic. Also, the permissive leader is effective where the situation is ambiguous and the task is unstructured, providing the leader is well liked by the followers. Further, when the situation is ambiguous and the task is structured, directive (work-oriented and controlling) leadership is more effective.[8]

ADDITIONAL CONSIDERATIONS OF LEADERSHIP

It is appropriate to mention some additional considerations of leadership which may help one understand it more fully. First, some irritations are almost always present in leader-follower relationships. It is simply in the nature of people's behavior. Many are not well organized or self-motivated. They elect, accept, or recognize others to get them to do what they know should, but will not be done unless leadership is present. The leader can be liked or disliked, but he must have the respect of his fol-

---

[8] Fred E. Fiedler, *A Theory of Leadership Effectiveness* (New York: McGraw-Hill Book Co., Inc., 1967).

lowers. They may not be overcome with affection for him, but they are glad to have the leader they have because they are getting somewhere.

Leadership requires followers. Leaders come into being as the result of legal, formal, or informal actions. Whatever the reason, to be effective the leader must retain and develop the continued acceptance and the confidence of the group members. They remain willing followers primarily because the leader satisfies their needs, stands for a cause they believe in, or is probably the best leader they can hope to get under the prevailing circumstances. The leader, however, does not practice blind followership simply to get followers, for to do so would lead to stagnation, failure, and ultimately to chaos. To get followers, he stresses achievement of mutual objectives from his leadership, uses the drawing power of his personality, and emphasizes the causes he is trying to advance. He seeks to give the impression of a person capable of complete understanding of their difficulties, a man of action, and an achiever of aims that will help them.

Time influences leadership. For example, most leaders are influenced somewhat by the time in which they live, as revealed by the opportunities which either exist or can be created during their active work life. We are all conditioned to a greater or less degree by the general modus operandi of the time in which we live. Furthermore, a time of emergency seems to bring about a greater emphasis upon leadership. In an emergency, people look for a leader to lead them out of their difficulties. An awareness of leadership tends to get lost in the orderly, methodical achievement of the group's aims. Few ships' captains prove their worth in a calm sea, and it is the same with enterprises. To the leader, emergencies are opportunities to serve. On the other hand, it is also true that in emergencies people tend to blame the leader for their troubles, pointing out that he led them into difficulties. Hence, leadership has its penalty, or price to be paid.

Finally, a leader operates in the light of publicity; people know his achievements or failures. When successful, many will emulate his achievements, but a few will envy his accomplishments. The more outstanding a leader is, the more he becomes a target for the envious few. If a leader is mediocre, he is let alone. The reasons for this appear to lie in the interaction of human relations and in the operations of groups. No leader is perfect in the eyes of all. A leader is probably assailed because he is a leader, and concerted efforts to equal or excel him are added proof of his leadership. There are always a few who delight in clamoring denial of a leader's achievements. However, the successful leader is not deterred from his appointed goal by these minority cries. He continues to lead and remains a leader.

QUESTIONS

1. Discuss the existence and the need for interactions of the leader and his group members.
2. As a member of an organization, give an example you have experienced of a leader's behavior and action that affected the members' satisfactions.
3. What are the four components, the characteristics of which make leadership a complex relationship?
4. What is meant by each of the following: (*a*) leadership continuum, (*b*) referent power, (*c*) democratic theory of leadership, and (*d*) laissez-faire leadership.
5. What is your reaction to the following statement: "The tremendous amount of attention and study devoted to leadership during the past decade points to the one best way of leading people. It is known as supportive leadership and every manager would profit by using it."
6. Enumerate five theories of leadership and discuss one of these fully.
7. As you see yourself and as a manager, what type of leadership would you probably use most of the time? Why?
8. Based on contributions by the subordinate-centered personal behavior theory and the situational theory, what leadership guides for obtaining optimum group performance can you suggest?
9. What is a benevolent autocratic leader? In what type of environment or under what circumstances would you expect to find him?
10. Discuss Figure 20–3 in your own words.
11. Since the trait theory of leadership has serious shortcomings, how do you account for the fact that it is so widely known and prominent in many discussions on leading?
12. Discuss autocratic leadership pointing out its meaning, characteristics, and means of enforcement.
13. Discuss the influence of time upon leadership.
14. Select two leaders about whom you know something and for each name the traits, from those included in this chapter, in which you feel each leader is especially outstanding. Discuss the conclusions you draw from your answer.

CASE 20–1. McGRATH FURNITURE CORPORATION

Earl Raymond accepted the presidency of McGrath Furniture Corporation last week. Formerly he was executive vice president of a large magazine publishing firm in the New York City area. When this corporation was purchased about six months ago by another corporation, Mr. Raymond was informed that there was no suitable place for him in the merged setup, but he could remain for three months with pay and seek to relocate himself. Accordingly he talked with friends and also Executive Placements, a firm specializing in locating employment for top executives. Without solicitation, he received an attractive offer from a publishing house competing with his former employer, but he turned it down. He did not feel it was the thing to do; he could not work enthusiastically for a former competitor. From Executive Placements the offer of the presidency of McGrath Furniture came about. The challenge of being in a different industry, in the top spot, and making new friends appealed to him. His wife urged him to accept. She wanted to get out of New York City and pointed out that the small town in South Carolina where McGrath is located would be ideal for raising their two sons, ages 9 and 12, and a daughter, age 14.

McGrath Furniture Corporation was owned by the Burleigh McGrath family. When Burleigh McGrath, the president, died, the survivors decided there was no one in the employ of the corporation able to assume the presidency. They believed the corporation had an excellent sales manager and also a splendid factory manager, but neither had the broad vision of the total corporation's operations to assume the presidency. Mrs. Burleigh McGrath, an accountant, supervised the finance, accounting, and tax activities of the corporation.

Earl Raymond's personal history showed him to be an outstanding graduate student in college. He earned majors in both business administration and marketing, believing that with two specialties he could always use one or the other to gain advancement. He made a good appearance and projected the image of one who knows where he is going and how he is going to get there. He always engaged in administrative work, never in that requiring technical specialist ability and knowledge. One of his top qualities is his persuasiveness—an uncanny ability to win others to his way of thinking. But some think he acts too much as an independent, overwhelms others, decides too quickly, even giving the impression of being impulsive. It was generally agreed, however, that Earl Raymond was fearless; he'd tackle a complicated problem and stay with it to a conclusion. He also has a sense of humor and typically, after giving an order involving some knotty situation, would add some humor to make the order more palatable.

Things appeared to go quite well at McGrath for Mr. Raymond but a certain environment perturbed him. Work was performed on time, costs were in line, and sales orders were received in a satisfactory volume. His management compeers were friendly and cooperative, yet distant. He learned a great deal from them about the furniture business and they seemed most willing to help. But after four months, Mr. Raymond felt he was not getting full and enthusiastic cooperation. He did not feel that he or his family were fully accepted by the management team. There was a tendency for them to go to Mrs. McGrath with problems that he thought should be handled by him. He wasn't quite certain where he stood, but during visits with Mrs. McGrath certain statements were made by her indicating everyone seemed pleased that he was with them.

Mr. Raymond involved himself in the project of acquiring some factory machines and rearranging a portion of the factory layout, but he quickly sensed that this activity caused resentment in his factory superintendent. Several attempts by Mr. Raymond to change the superintendent's attitude about this were futile, so he withdrew. Sales were being maintained and since he realized he knew very little about the marketing of furniture he decided to stay out of this area. Besides it entailed considerable traveling and his wife wanted him to stay home.

Seven months after Mr. Raymond was hired, installation of a computer system began. This had been ordered prior to Mr. Raymond's employment with the company. There were a great many problems to be worked out. Mrs. McGrath was overwhelmed with the tasks to be completed so that the records and reports would be computerized. She informed Mr. Raymond of her problem and suggested that perhaps he might like to assume direction of the computer installation and it would give him first-hand insight into the operations of the company.

Questions

1. Evaluate Mr. Raymond's decision to join McGrath Furniture Corporation as president. Discuss fully.
2. What is the problem faced by Mr. Raymond?
3. What recommended action do you suggest Mr. Raymond take? Justify your answer.

CASE 20–2. BOVEE COMPANY

Charles Scott has become the big enigma of Bovee Company. Promoted to the job of assistant production manager almost a year ago, he hasn't measured up to expectancies, and the company's top managers agree that something must be done to correct this situation. To date, production has not seriously suffered, but it is believed that unless managerial action is soon taken, serious production problems will be commonplace. The plant is not unionized.

Among possible candidates for the job opening of assistant production manager, Charles Scott appeared best qualified, was offered the promotion, and he accepted. Mr. Scott has been with the company seven years, starting as an assembler and working his way up to assistant foreman and then to foreman of the final assembly department. His production record was good, he appeared to be well liked by his fellow employees, and he had the most seniority of any of the candidates.

The top managers were dissatisfied with the handling thus far of a proposed materials handling project by Mr. Scott. A consultant suggested certain changes be made in the present handling of raw materials and the subsequent three production operations on a major production process. Estimated savings were $87,500 annually, a substantial sum. Mr. Scott has personally discussed this recommendation with each of his several foremen involved, and it has also been a major topic of discussion at each of three monthly production departmental meetings. According to Mr. Bruce Knightberry, production manager, "Mr. Scott has gone over the recommendations a hundred times; and the whole project has been taken apart and put back together again; alternatives have been created and then destroyed; and suggestions representing minor improvements are held in abeyance awaiting disposition of the overall plan the consultant gave us. I'm certain Charley means well, but he just doesn't come up with the go-ahead signal or the order to toss the whole project aside. He's got to live with whatever he approves so, as of now, I haven't got on him about it."

The personnel manager had some difficulty with Charles Scott in determining a vacation schedule for the men in his department. Mr. Scott asked each of his foremen, and they, in turn, asked each of their employees for preferences for their vacation time. The result was overlaps in periods requested. Following this, Mr. Scott and his foremen individually spent much time talking with small groups of their employees in an effort to eliminate the overlaps and conflicts. Several employees complained informally to the personnel manager that "the company asks you when you want your vacation; you tell them; then they say you can't have the time for which you have put in."

It is known that Charles Scott is, above everything else, keenly interested in getting production out. This is his common theme and he keeps repeating it to members of the production department. He insists that work schedules be achieved. In keeping with this sense of dedication, Scott frequently makes repairs on equipment and machines to avoid any delay or interruption in production. This is a practice he started as a foreman. The maintenance men have never objected to Charles Scott doing this repair work. They state that Mr. Scott is very competent in making repairs and keeping machines running. His ability to do this has, in many instances, lessened the emergency nature in connection with much of the maintenance work on production machines.

Questions

1. What is the problem as you see it?
2. Evaluate the work of Charles Scott.
3. What action do you recommend be taken? By whom? Discuss.

21

Creating and innovating ideas

What man can imagine, man can do.

JOHN F. MEE

MANAGEMENT REQUIRES hundreds of applied ideas to operate an enterprise. In many endeavors, the margin of success and in some instances survival itself depend upon the ability to evolve a new workable idea and put it into practice. There is no adequate substitute in management for creating and putting into use practical ideas.

By creating and innovating ideas a manager seeks new combinations, better goals, and improved ways of accomplishing goals. Along with this is required the will to destroy the outmoded and inefficient and to replace with the new and better, even if it means violating convention and stepping out of the pattern. This does not imply that caution and good judgment are eliminated, but that open-mindedness, new approaches, and recognition to challenges stressing progress are emphasized.

Creativity deals with the generation of ideas, innovating with the application of ideas. From the managerial viewpoint, creativity alone is insufficient, the idea must be implemented too; that is, both the creating and the innovating of ideas are essential to progressive management. One of the big problems is to create the right idea and apply it in the right manner and at the right time.

WHO PERFORMS CREATING AND INNOVATING

Both management and nonmanagement members can and should perform creating and innovating for management to progress and be most satisfactory for all concerned. From the manager's viewpoint the demands to which he is subjected cannot be met by striving to repeat past successes. Making "either/or" analyses, comparing possibilities and making a choice, or reviewing evidence and rendering a verdict may not provide the best answer. The manager needs more than a judicial mind; he also needs a creating and innovating mind.

To the extent that the nonmanager is encouraged to participate, to have an interest in, and take a formal or informal part in, managerial affairs, he too needs creative and innovative power. Nonmanagers can contribute significantly in problems dealing with product improvement, stabilizing cost, and employee work satisfaction. Much of this contribution comes from his observations and work experience.

Every manager, as well as nonmanager, is born with creative potential. Certain managers do not have a monopoly on it. The challenge is to keep from inhibiting creativity. The capacity of most managers and nonmanagers to think up new ideas and to implement them can be doubled within a short period if they develop attitudes freeing their minds from the mental chains of pattern, conformity, and culture. The four main blocks of impediment include (1) lack of self-confidence, (2) fear of criticism and failure, (3) desire to conform, and (4) inability to concentrate. Overcome these hurdles and you release the ability to create and use ideas. We are all habit-prone. Certain time-tested methods of performing certain tasks become ritual.

Being able to create and apply ideas is one of the greatest actuators. This aspect of a job puts new life and challenge into it and makes work an interesting and satisfying experience. When results management is followed, for example, the employee may face the challenge of how to achieve certain objectives he has set for himself in ways that are most agreeable to him. His answer will be found in his using his own creating and innovating. They are the key to both his personal and work satisfactions.

ENCOURAGING CREATIVITY

A work climate conductive for creating should exist. To provide such an environment, the first step is to announce that evidence of creativity is wanted and start to inject creative stimuli to all employees through distribution of appropriate literature, suggestions, and encouragement to think about their work in abstract terms. Subsequently, their thoughts are discussed at monthly meetings, the establishing of which is the second step. These meetings can either be focused on the attendees being given either unsolved company problems to study and discuss or selected problems for them to offer solutions. The former works better in a small company, gets many employees involved, and opens up communication. The latter is more formal, more directed, and indicates somewhat the confidence of the attendee in his own judgment.

It is also possible to encourage creativity of one person by counseling and coaching. In certain situations, these means are very effective. Generally speaking, however, group interactions produce more and better ideas because the members stimulate each other. Questions and suggestions focus each participant's attention on the process of creativity and make him aware that ideas exist, that they must be sought, and that many are not the result of genius, but of long, hard work.

Typically the creative person looks at things in divergent ways. He may feel some dissatisfaction with things as they are or believe strongly that present ways of doing things can be improved. Characteristically he (1) observes situations and problems that have previously escaped attention, (2) relates ideas and experience encountered from many different sources, (3) tends to have many alternatives on any given subject, (4) defies precedent and is not constrained by custom, (5) utilizes and draws readily from all his emotional, mental, and preconscious forces, and (6) maintains a high degree of flexibility in his thoughts and actions.

TYPES OF THINKING

Most ideas start with thinking of which there are several major types. Some of these types are more productive than others. For purposes here, the following five will be considered: (1) creative, (2) causative, (3) inductive, (4) deductive, and (5) problem-solving. The first, or creative thinking, deals with deeply impressing a problem upon one's mind, clearly visualizing it, contemplating it, all toward the formulation of an idea or concept along new or different lines. Facts are used, but some of the facts are recognized as missing. In other words, creative thinking is performed with the understanding that only a partial knowledge of the situation is available and is utilized. Elimination of some and combination of other available facts help to clarify the idea that is new. Insight thus gained feeds the imagination with the sought new idea. It is imagination, not logic, that is the source of the new idea. Many competing hunches are evaluated and related in order to arrive at the best idea, but the thinking process is creative. Frequently the image comes as a flash of inspiration and is sometimes referred to as seeing "the light."

Causative thinking emphasizes the shaping of future events and achievements instead of waiting for destiny to decide them. The future reality is conceived and made the cause of each action event. The imagined future situation is conceived of as a series of related events which will bring about the desired future situation. The imagined future effect becomes a causative factor in the series of events which are then planned and carried out. Hence, causative thinking is characterized by thinking in reverse, so to speak, in that results are derived by converting nonproductive present actions into related events leading to the desired future situation. For creativity, causative thinking is extremely helpful. It depends upon creative imagination; it is closely related to creative thinking.

Inductive thinking is reasoning based on building up to a general principle or conclusion from various particulars. It is reasoning from parts to a whole or from the individual to the universal. In the process of synthesis it is used. Here the components are put together to form a whole. Inductive thinking is characterized by a settled disposition to follow an established behavior.

Deductive thinking is the direct opposite of inductive thinking. From general conclusions to reason down to particular ideas, or from the whole to the part, typifies deductive thinking. For this type of thinking, analysis, or breaking down the entirety into its components, is employed. Deductive thinking provides explicit knowledge, not implicit or general knowledge. It is logical and is used extensively.

Problem-solving thinking, as suggested by its name, is a judicial type of thinking. It is concerned with securing facts about a situation, ascertaining the problem, analyzing and evaluating the facts logically to determine meaningful relationships among them, and finally evolving the decision to the problem. It is greatly influenced by powers of judgment, past experience, and tradition. In some instances habit plays an important role. Problem-solving thinking typifies the factual "analyze-evaluate-select" approach, is highly useful, and is practical.

THE CREATIVITY PROCESS

The generation of ideas normally follows a process which is made up of closely related, yet distinct, steps. These will be discussed in the next several pages. They can be listed as follows:

1. Develop favorable attitude toward ideation.
2. Exhibit problem sensitivity.
3. Prepare for creativity by acquiring needed raw materials.

4. Apply idea fluency.
5. Allow incubation or unconscious brain action to take place.
6. Permit illumination of new idea.

Develop Favorable Attitude toward Ideation. For one to realize maximum creative potential, it is necessary to have a positive attitude
toward freedom of ideas, regardless of any initial unfavorable reactions
that one may receive. Many ideas will seem impractical at first, but the
creative thinker must not permit this predisposition to influence him
and give up in despair. Premature judgment can choke the seed of a new
idea, and emotions can build hurdles in the pathway of progress and
newness. Mental laziness and cultural blocks are also responsible. The
former needs no explanation, but the latter, cultural blocks, include
those elements in our cultural environment which are not conducive to
ideation. They can include past experience, education, friends, and companies from which patterns of habit are developed. People, things, and
ideas that violate the pattern of habit are either condemned or ignored.
To illustrate, an architect showed a friend a picture of a proposed circular exhibition hall utilizing new materials and new building concepts.
The friend exclaimed that it did not look like an exhibition hall. When
asked why, he explained, "Because it does not have walls and vertical
columns." The architect explained that it didn't need them. The friend
replied that could be, but it should have walls and vertical columns to
look right. The pattern is set; this retards creative thinking.

However, the creative thinker firmly believes new ideas are possible
and can be used advantageously. He seeks change; he believes in trying
to find better ways and means. Seldom does he stick to safe, tried,
prosaic approaches. He believes that every article, business operation,
and human relations technique can be improved. No matter how many
times it has been met and handled before, an opportunity exists to find a
better way.

Exhibit Problem Sensitivity. Basically this is the ability to recognize that a problem exists. It entails being able to cut through mis-
conception, lack of facts, and misunderstanding and identify the real
problem. The creative thinker determines first what he wants to accomplish—this is the focal point. A carefully worded statement of the
objective sets the right stage for the creative efforts. Creativity can be
effective when the reason or need for ideas is recognized. Merely looking for new ideas is a hopeless task. The idea must be tied in with a
specific goal. Like all efforts, those of a creative nature require general
directions to be of greatest value. To be creative, start with picking and

defining a problem; then stay with the problem until a solution is reached.

If the problem seems too large or complex, break it down. It is essential that the creative thinker sufficiently understands the problem before trying to solve it. To clarify thinking, it is helpful to state the same problem different ways or explain the problem to someone completely unfamiliar with it.

A break from emotions and conventions may be necessary to state precisely what really is the problem, its boundaries, and the essential rules which must be followed. The story is told that when Dr. Walter Reed arrived in Cuba as the chairman of the Yellow Fever Commission, he found upon questioning his associates that a recent victim of yellow fever was a man in a guardhouse for six days with several other men, but none of the others had contracted the disease. From this simple fact, Dr. Reed reasoned that there must be a carrier of the disease—something must have crawled or flown through the window, bitten the prisoner, and thus infected him with the fever. Other tentative aims suggested for finding the cure and prevention of the disease were laid aside, and now all efforts were concentrated on the one aim that led ultimately to the solution.

Problem sensitivity also helps to acquire concentration which is an essential of the creative process. Efforts should be centered on relatively small areas; otherwise the creative thinker is spreading himself too thin and seriously retarding creativity. It is an excellent practice to devote some 20–25 minutes each day to complete concentration on a specific problem. This period should be free of interruptions.

Prepare for Creativity by Acquiring Needed Raw Materials. Ideas are created from raw materials which include primarily knowledge, other ideas, and experiences. These materials are obtained from personal observations, talks with informed people, reading, radio and television, and travel. The search for facts should cover a broad field and deal with every facet of the problem. This broad fund of information forms the foundation upon which the mind can evolve ideas.

In brief, ideas are not created out of a vacuum. To perform creative work, it is helpful to have a broad, rich background which can be called upon in forming ideas; to experience a labyrinth of situations from which the idea may evolve; to observe, see, and feel the meaning of events; and to possess a keen imagination and curiosity about people and things in general. The thing to be created as well as the urge to do something about it must be keenly felt. For example, because of hardships and family needs, Irving Berlin, creator of many song "hits," worked during his early life as a singing waiter in a restaurant in New York's Chinatown. But as a waiter he grew rich in firsthand experience and observed people and their interests from a vantage point. He once said: "You can't write a song out of thin air. You have to know and feel what you are writing about."

This step in the creative process is not easy. It requires much time, effort, self-discipline, and tenacity of purpose. Some material is difficult to obtain; much is incomplete; but it is well to remember that, if all the facts were known, the need for the creativity would be nil. In addition, the raw materials should be classified so that future reference and use of them are expedited.

Apply Idea Fluency. Idea fluency means an ability to pile up a quantity of ideas about a given problem. The value of this is that the more ideas available, the greater the chance for disclosing a usable one.

In other words, idea volume is what is wanted. Also, a deadline for these ideas stimulates creativity. The human tendency is to procrastinate. In addition, judging the ideas should be held as a separate step. Idea evaluation tends to stop the creating of new ideas; hence it is better to evaluate them after there is a quantity of ideas on which to work.

PRINCIPLE OF CREATIVITY

Strive for a quantity of ideas within a given time and abstain from evaluating them during the idea-getting step of the creativity process.

Personal mental habits control idea fluency and they can be improved or developed in nearly every individual. A number of specific devices and aids are available to develop idea fluency. The more effective are the ten included in this list.

1. *Make Notes.* The use of notebooks, or "idea traps" as they are called, is a common practice for jotting down ideas as they occur. Small 3×5 cards can also be used. An idea is the most fleeting thing in the world; it comes and goes within a fraction of a second. Don't expect to bring back an idea and examine it carefully at your discretion. What is perfectly clear today may be a complete blank tomorow. The best time to capture an idea is when it occurs. Hence, it is well to note in writing ideas or fragments of ideas as they appear. Tests have established that for information of average interest either read or heard, about 25 percent is forgotten within the first 24 hours and 85 percent within a week. If the idea appears to have no particular use at the time, it can be filed in an "idea file" for future reference.

2. *Pick a Time to Be Creative.* This time will vary with individuals;

some will find early morning most productive, and others produce best late at night. The point is to find out which period is most productive and reserve it for the specific task of creative thinking. There is also usually a special location which seems superior for ideating. If so, effort should be made to utilize both the best time and location.

3. *Employ Curiosity and Questioning Ability.* Ask questions such as: Why is this done this way? Is this really necessary? Why won't this work? This means is one of "challenging the obvious." A checklist made up of operational questions that challenge the obvious aspects of a problem is especially helpful.

4. *Utilize Relationship of Ideas.* Most ideas are related to other ideas. The power of association is especially consequential in the creating of ideas. The manager who aspires to create can start with known facts and build, step by step, upon them until the resemblance and relation of things suggest a new concept which is the signal for a new idea. Centuries ago this relationship of ideas was observed by Aristotle, who suggested to "hunt for the next in the series, starting our train of thought from what is now present or from something else, and from something similar or contrary or contiguous to it."

Among the best ideas are those which represent improvements over other ideas. The history of the development of a current idea might well reveal that idea as the last of a chain or series which has been thought about for a long time. Most inventions are in this category. They evolve slowly over a period and are improved step by step.

5. *Changes Existent Form.* The clue for an idea might be found by changing the existent form. There are a number of ways in which this can be accomplished, including (*a*) *rearrange*—will it work inside out, backwards, upside down. A golfer's ball rolled into a paper bag on the fairway. To remove the ball from the bag would cost him a penalty; so he rearranged his thinking, deciding to remove the bag from the ball by burning the bag; (*b*) *substitute*—what happens if a different process is used, a different sequence, women rather than men employees, a new material in place of the traditional metal, glue for nails; (*c*) *add*— duplicate the training program in the branch plants; make the product bigger; add more units to a package; (*d*) *subtract*—make fewer units to the package; reduce the car height; offer a smaller desk; leave something out, and (*e*) *switch*—turn the present arrangement around by having the employees offer suggestions instead of the managers; have the employees rate their foreman; let the retailer call on customers at their homes. Figure 21–1 offers suggestions for design changes in materials.

6. *Obtain Help from Attribute Listing.* Here the characteristics or parts of a concept or object are listed. For example, for desk, the list would include top, drawer, pedestal, wood, steel, file space, size, and so forth. Now association between these attributes is made, such as top and file space, pedestal and size, in the hope that a new idea helpful in desk use or manufacture can be created. A modification of this technique can also be followed. This consists of forcing or bringing together two objects or ideas never previously associated in order to evolve an idea from this new relationship. Commonly a list of objects or ideas that may have possible relationships is compiled, then one item is related to every other item on the list to find the idea.

FIGURE 21–1. Checklist for improving design changes in materials

Can you	
Change	size, shape, weight?
Reduce	weight, scrap, loose parts?
Eliminate	waste, frills, backtracking?
Improve	quality, delivery, packaging?
Substitute	new, stronger, or cheaper material?
Simplify	by using pallets or letting supplier do it?
Standardize	parts, routes, size, weight, finish?
Utilize	scrap, rejected parts?

7. *Use Brainstorming or Free-Association Technique.* This approach emphasizes the use of thinking that is ungoverned, visionary, erratic, or wild. It utilizes any thoughts which happen to come to mind on a problem. The mind is purposely permitted to "free wheel" about the problem and come up with all possible ideas, some of which will seem impractical and downright silly. In brainstorming, a group of about fifteen is given a problem and each member is encouraged to contribute ideas. Emphasis is on quantity of ideas. It is usually desirable to have the group with a wide diversity of backgrounds and to include some persons with little experience in the problem area. The intent of brainstorming is to supply leads and possible ideas for the problem solution. Evaluation of the ideas is done after the brainstorming session. However, this technique can be used in various ways; for example, a large group can be divided into smaller brainstorming groups, each one of which thinks up a quantity of ideas, then evaluates them and offers their No. 1 selection as the best idea from that group. Or reverse brainstorming can be used in which all the possible shortcomings of a product or service are evolved. A manager can also practice solo brainstorming

with himself. Actually many managers do this to meet at least certain requirements of their work.

8. *Read between Lines.* A lucrative source of practical ideas is reading between the lines of letters and reports. Various tips on what will help improve the product, achieve goals, contribute to better understanding, and build public relations can be acquired from this source. To illustrate, Figure 21–2 shows the report of a department head to the merchandising manager of a large retail store. After reading this report the manager might note from the first paragraph, "Our paint clerks need education and training," and from the second paragraph, "How to give proper care to painted surfaces." "What is paint?" "Explanation of

FIGURE 21–2. Report of department head to the merchandising manager of a large retail store

In my opinion, the biggest problem in the paint department is teaching the clerks how to sell paint properly. The specific service for which the paint will be used is frequently not considered. A customer is allowed to buy cheap paint for outside use when we know that it isn't going to last. Only a few of our clerks know that the surface must be properly prepared so that it is clean, smooth, and free from all loose old paint.

And we don't tell the customers how to take care of a painted surface because we do not know what to tell them. I doubt that any of our clerks know what the basic ingredients of paint are and how to explain to the customer why one quality costs more or less than another.

different grades." Interpreting reports in terms of sales opportunities is simple, but it requires open-mindedness and the use of ideas.

9. *Reverse Positions.* An excellent source of ideas is simply put yourself in the other fellow's place. Think creatively of what you would do if you had the various goals, problems, and wherewithal to accomplish the end results that the other fellow possesses. There is an old adage that it is well to know your competitor and never discount his intelligence.

10. *Make Use of Accidental Events.* The clue to the sought idea might be an accidental event. An unusual happening or a sudden surprise has been known to start the creative process toward productive directions. Such events appear to give a new twist or angle to a person's thinking and afford the outlet to the sought solution.

This fourth step in the process for the generation of ideas—apply idea fluency—should continue until a feeling of frustration appears. This may be sensed by restlessness, general emotional conflict, or a feeling that further creative effort is fruitless; that is, efforts to evolve further ideas do not seem to be productive. When this point is reached, a forced relaxation usually follows, during which time a recall of the efforts may involuntarily be made, and out of this mental and physical preoccupation the creative work emerges. This leads to the next step.

Allow Incubation or Unconscious Brain Action to Take Place. When frustration appears after laboring diligently over a problem, the best thing to do is get away from the problem—rest the conscious mind. However, the conscious mind is but a small part of the total mental power of a human being. There are many, many memory cells holding an infinite number of facts and associations, and this unconscious mind is now given a chance to help find a solution to the problem. This incubation period is commonly referred to as "sleeping on the problem." Actually there is little that one can contribute to this step directly. Rest, diversion, or thinking about another problem are the alternatives to follow.

Permit Illumination of New Idea. The beginning of this last step is determined by the individual circumstances. In some instances it may follow the previous step in a matter of minutes, hours, or perhaps days, or it may not come until years later. It appears that the thinker cannot force his ideas to emerge, but being receptive, opportunistic, and alert helps the creative step to take place. The shutting out of distracting influences may be helpful. Many creative people feel that in the creative step some power outside themselves is trying to find expression through them.

A most difficult question to answer is: When does the idea or the creative material begin to flow? The illumination frequently takes place when least expected. The right idea may come while one is walking, looking out an airplane window, watching flames in an open fireplace, listening to music (without words), attending concerts, sitting in church, or sailing. Usually with little or no warning the creative person "starts clicking," and the ideas and creative suggestions begin appearing.

HEURISTIC COMPUTER PROGRAMS

In addition to the human mental process just discussed, there are other means that have been demonstrated as possible important contributors of new ideas and information. One of these is heuristic computer programs, which could become prominent in the future. The word "heuristic" means "aiding or guiding in discovery." By putting masses of information and data into a computer and then processing them according to a prescribed sequence of operations, new relationships are obtained suggesting ideas heretofore unknown.

In a formal thought process, a man organizes myriads of simple information processes into an orderly sequence. For example, he may look for certain similarities with which he is familiar. What he finds suggests a subproblem; he pursues this subproblem, discovers it leads nowhere, and so discards it; he then thinks of opposites or differences, and so forth. Finally, he assembles the results and tries to fit them together into possible usable information. We can synthesize a great deal of this work with a computer if the work is of a simple and routine nature.

THE INNOVATIVE PROCESS

As in the case of creativity, the adoption of a formal program is recommended for satisfactory progress in implementing ideas. No matter how good the idea, it does not implement itself. Ideas have to be put out in the open and used if they are going to be helpful. Hoarding ideas seldom brings about any needed improvement. One does not run out of ideas by using them. Ideas multiply if you let them grow and put them to work. It can well be that a certain idea cannot be put into immediate and complete action, but the chances are strong that something can be done with it. At least, the idea should be recognized as being in existence, christened, and some planned efforts followed to see what future it might change advantageously.

The applying of new ideas is a major activity; it is an enormous task. Innovation is frequently a slow and tedious process. A single basic idea, for example, may necessitate exhaustive study, thorough investigation, and complete examination. Furthermore, to apply a basic new idea usually requires many additional little ideas in order to achieve ultimate success. People of various degrees of capacities, interests, and attributes must be directed, assisted, and encouraged in many ways before the new idea is adopted.

The proponent of an idea that is rejected should not receive simply a "no" as his answer. He deserves to be told why the idea is being rejected, what the major opposition to the idea is, and if any part of the idea is salvageable.

New idea implementation requires faith on the part of managers—faith to listen to the idea; to consider its possibilities; to study the various ramifications of its implementation, carefully noting reasons which might mean success and, likewise, which might mean failure; to keep the idea alive through both human and technical difficulties; and to formulate a wise decision concerning it. Normally, in the typical enterprise these attributes do not come "in the nature of things." They must be conscientiously applied. To assist in this effort, these five helpful suggestions are included:

1. Have the new idea worked out in detail. Make sure it is complete.
2. List the potential benefits to be received from the use of the new idea and indicate who will receive what benefits. Help to someone else and in terms of improved service, lower cost, or reduction in waste are usually most acceptable.
3. Make the new idea easy to understand. Avoid unusual and trick words in communicating it.
4. Condition the new idea by talking it over with several people to disclose possible weaknesses that need correction; then adjust to rectify the weak points.
5. Present the reworked idea at an appropriate time—when the need for it is great or when it will be given adequate consideration.

Meetings similar to those suggested above for encouraging the creativity of ideas are effective and should be followed, but in addition, other means should be considered. If the idea answers a possible solution to an acute problem at hand its chances for implementation are excellent. But usually the idea must be brought through existing constraints. This suggests the practice of requiring each manager, say twice a year, to submit a written report to his immediate superior. This report should detail (1) the operational effectiveness of his unit's operation and (2) recommend changes that will lead to better realization of his unit's objectives. In essence this opens the door for idea implementation by targeting possible areas of application for new ideas. The superior can accept or reject the ideas, and if the former, he can proceed to implement them.

However, a better practice is to route the improvement reports through the respective supervisor, so that he knows what is going on, or to a committee whose expertise is in the same area as the type of recommendations being made. This committee serves as a clearing house for what ideas probably can most readily be used. Inappropriate ideas are weeded out, potential benefits are estimated, and technical feasibility is judged. In addition, opinions of the managers and of the supervisors are given the committee, but the clearing house for ideas and the determination of the ones upon which to concentrate, and where, are questions resting with the committee.

Next, the ideas passing the review tests are tried out on an experimental or limited basis under the guidance of the committee or a designated manager. The point here is to ascertain the soundness of the idea—

whether better results are obtained, the idea's practicality, skills required, and cost. Also measured is the effect of variables external to the new idea. In a large enterprise, personnel proficient in experiments, data collection, and analysis can be used.

If tests show successful results, the next step is to implement the idea. This work entails acquiring raw materials and equipment; hiring, transferring, and training personnel; and establishing work patterns along with the necessary controls.

Last, is evaluating the results. Here the effort is to determine the gain by using the idea. An estimate of the idea's payoff is made available to the person who originated it. This serves as an incentive to continue creative thinking. Pay increases, promotions, and other recognitions will take place as a consequence of the favorable results from ideas that prove effective in the working environment.

OPPOSITION TO INNOVATION

The late Charles W. Kettering, famed research executive of General Motors, once said, "The greatest durability test in the world is getting a new idea into a factory." Why does the habitual answer to trying out a new idea tend to be a resounding, "No"?

One possible reason is that the manager, already burdened with work, has more ideas than he can see how to use. And the idea submitted gives inadequate information on the time, cost, manpower, and risk factors utilized by its possible adoption. On the other hand, some experts in creativity argue that the idea submitter or creator is seriously handicapped when held responsible for spelling out the implementation details. But as implied above, an answer here is to develop ways to implement the idea by group effort.

Another reason for opposing new idea implementation is that the enterprise is operating successfully, the work is being accomplished, employees appear satisfied, and customers are getting what they want. There is no need in upsetting things. Let well enough alone. Maintain the status quo. The old ideas are working all right. All ideas are potential threats to the established order of things.

Rejection might take place simply because the management members to be convinced lack the vision and imagination to appreciate fully the possibilities in the idea. They simply do not understand the new idea. They may be bound by tradition—the new suggestion reverses the way the activity is usually done, and its adoption may mean cherished feelings will be trampled. Sometimes insufficient effort is spent in presenting and explaining the idea, or a prescribed manner of applying it has not been thoroughly prepared.

The opposition might be conveyed in these words: less effort is required to follow the leader. The general management practice may be to "Let the other fellow think up and pioneer. If successful, we will follow and adopt the idea to our operations." This view can connote a degree of mental laziness which may develop into a dangerous lethargy.

Also to be reckoned with is the risk of possible failure by applying the idea. Few want to be associated with an idea that proves impractical. They fear failure and dislike receiving adverse criticism. It is safer and more comfortable to stay with the "tried and proven."

Furthermore, the timing of the idea may be illogical. The old saying that there is a right and a wrong time for everything applies equally to the implementing of ideas. For example, an idea for recruiting college graduates may be scorned if offered at the time the company is retrenching and has a surplus of qualified college-trained employees.

SUGGESTION SYSTEMS

Suggestion systems are a popular and important means for getting ideas implemented. Employees are encouraged to submit their ideas for improving operations and working conditions. Suggestions adopted reward their creator, usually in the form of cash awards.

It is imperative that managers give the suggestion system of their enterprise enthusiastic support and explain it thoroughly to all employees. Success in suggestion systems requires continuous promotion and publicity. Too frequently a system starts with a burst of enthusiasm and interest only to fade away to practically nothing within several months because of the fallacious belief that the system would be self-generating and continue right along. Employees should be encouraged to make suggestions and given help in how to write them. Figure 21–3 lists what the manager can do in this respect.

Experience shows that conveniently located suggestion boxes, an adjacent place to write, plenty of suggestion forms handy, regular pickup of suggestions, and prompt acknowledgment of suggestions are especially helpful in maintaining keen interest in a suggestion system. Likewise, the decision on suggestions should be determined within a reasonable period of time. It is helpful to maintain a catalogue of suggestions so that reference can be made to previous suggestions and their respective disposition. If a suggestion requires more than a normal time to judge, the suggestor should be informed of this situation, for it is

FIGURE 21–3. Practices helpful to a manager in receiving and improving suggestions

---

1. Encourage the contributor by listening carefully to his suggestion.
2. Compliment the contributor on his initiative in making the suggestion, thus demonstrating managers want new ideas.
3. Seek the basic idea and approach being offered; details and additional information, if needed, can be secured later.
4. Point out the weakness of suggestion precisely and diplomatically so that the contributor is helped in any necessary modification.
5. Permit contributor to keep control of suggestion while it is being developed or amended.
6. Find out if best suggestions are coming from the same people, and if so, offer them increasingly difficult problems about which they can make suggestions.

---

perfectly normal for an employee to want to know what happened to his idea or the status of his suggestion. Decisions, along with reasons and amounts of awards, if any, should be made known by postings on a bulletin board or insertions in the company publication. In many instances, it is believed helpful to mask the suggestor's name in order to eliminate any personal influence in judging, to improve the accuracy of rewards, or for any of a number of reasons in an individual circumstance. Figure 21–4 shows a suggestion form in which identity of the

FIGURE 21–4

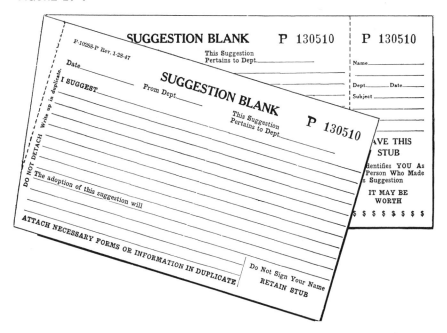

suggestor is masked. The number stub is retained by the person making the suggestion, which is written in duplicate.

The awards should be paid without delay, the suggestion put into effect as soon as possible, and a follow-up made of installed suggestions. The amount of the award will vary, but an effective range to follow is from a minimum of $10 to a maximum of 10 percent of the savings for the first year resulting from adoption of the suggestion. The award must be worthwhile to retain the employees' interest and active participation. Prompt activation of an approved suggestion is desirable, for many employees are more interested in seeing their suggestions put into effect than they are in receiving the award. Follow-up of suggestions demonstrates a continuing interest by managers and reveals the degree to which the suggestion is followed and the long-range benefits which are being derived.

QUESTIONS

1. Do you believe that creating and innovating ideas can be motivating? Elaborate on your answer.
2. Discuss ways by which creativity is encouraged among both management and nonmanagement members.
3. If innovating ideas is highly beneficial, how do you account for so many ideas being opposed and never put to use?
4. Enumerate six aids to develop your idea fluency. Discuss one of these in detail.
5. Give a satisfactory definition for each of the following: (1) brainstorming, (2) causative thinking, (3) innovating, and (4) inductive thinking.
6. In your opinion what problems in your community are in need of creativity being applied to them? Discuss.
7. For each of the following three situations, point out as many possible consequences as you can: (*a*) In making his rounds in a chemical plant, an elderly night watchman discovers a fire. Rushing to turn in an alarm, he observes that the connecting wire of the telephone has been severed. (*b*) While remodeling an apartment in Chicago, a carpenter finds a stamped but unmailed letter on the shelf of an old closet. On his way home that night, he mails the letter. (*c*) Alexander Parave, a research chemist, claims to have found a new chemical that when taken daily in the form of a pill (costing 13 cents a piece) will enable a man to get all the sleep he needs by sleeping only two hours a day.
8. Daleville Products Company is formulating plans for the installation of a suggestion system for its total work force of 900 employees. You have been asked to suggest what the plans should include relative to the management of the suggestion system. What is your answer?
9. Suppose as a result of circumstances you find yourself with no employment and stranded in a city of 25,000 population with a suitcase of clothes and

$250 in cash. You are not to see or write any friend or relative. You are to achieve "success" by the end of four years. Explain what you would do and why.

10. Discuss the importance of problem existence and recognition in the generation and application of ideas.

11. Give as many reasons as you can for each of the following statements which are assumed to be true. (*a*) Women of today go to the beauty shops 15 percent more often than did their grandmothers. (*b*) There are proportionately more houses painted white in San Francisco than in San Antonio. (*c*) The women of Minnesota have more perfect vision than the women in any other state of the United States.

12. Relate an experience wherein you encountered rejection of your idea. As you now see it, what should you have done to have your idea accepted?

13. Give two examples of creativity by changing the existent form by means of each of the following: (*a*) rearranging, (*b*) substituting, and (*c*) subtracting.

14. What future do you envision for heuristic computer programs? Why?

CASE 21-1. TALLMAN ALUMINUM FABRICATORS, INC.

Conrad Clark, president of this company, is vitally interested in civic affairs. Recently he was named chairman of the local city's Transportation Advisory Board. Its prescribed duties are to represent the public's ideas in a portion of the forthcoming project of establishing an adequate low-cost inner-city transportation system. It is fully agreed by all concerned that a modern transit system is required. The use of private automobiles and public buses has created huge traffic snarls. During most of the day hours the existing expressways and streets, especially those within the central core of the city, are jammed and traffic moves at 5 to 8 miles an hour.

The engineering aspects of location, terminal points, station spacing, and the like will be handled by the local Rapid Transit District. The Transportation Advisory Board is to concern itself with features of an advanced rapid transit car which will incorporate the ideas of what passengers would like in a modern transit vehicle.

Mr. Clark's personal opinion was that the new car should offer riders a level of comfort, convenience, and safety never before achieved by a public transportation system. He favors high-speed aluminum cars, high-structured integrity for safety purposes, and a brushed exterior appearance featuring no fasteners of any kind. Two double doors on each side of the car are desirable to handle the traffic in and out of the car quickly. Another member of the board believed air conditioning and foam-padded seats were a must. He also mentioned that the car should be noiseless and might use rubber or composition wheels, similar to the cars in the Mexico City subway.

It was Mr. Clark's desire to get as many ideas as possible from the board's total membership of eleven. To achieve this end, he proposed to hold an extended brainstorming session of the board's members. He also believed it mandatory that ideas of the general public be obtained and included in the report to be written. But he wasn't certain how to proceed in this effort.

Questions

1. Suggest ways that ideas of the general public regarding desired features of the new transit car may be obtained. Which way do you prefer? Why?
2. List some additional ideas you feel might be forthcoming at the board's brainstorming session.
3. Outline the general format of the report you believe the board should follow.

CASE 21–2. MATTHEWS COUNTY DEVELOPMENT

An industrial development committee for the acquisition of new industrial plants to locate within Matthews County consists of two county officials, two industrialists of the county, and a lawyer. One of the industrialists is also president of the Chamber of Commerce of Matthews County and chairman of the committee. He is extremely enthusiastic about new industrial plants. At the committee's last meeting, the following took place:

MR. AGNEW (Chairman): In keeping with our last meeting, the Chamber of Commerce has assembled data on the following:

1. Availability of water, its composition (indicating its hardness), cost, and existent water pipeline system within the county.
2. Natural resources within a radius of approximately 200 miles of the county. Coal, for example, is available at relatively low cost.
3. Existent transportation rates, by commodities and by type of carrier.

Basil, you have information on taxes, do you not?

MR. BASIL TITUS (lawyer member of committee): Yes, I do. Per your request last month, gentlemen, I have here (holds up papers) information on the taxes in Matthews County compared with that of other counties in the state and regional area. I would say our rates look attractive.

MR. ARTHUR GETZ (industrialist on committee): Are they lower?

TITUS: Yes, they are lower considering what is included. However, you can go over to Burke County, for example, and get a lower tax rate, but there is a minimum of services—such as police and fire protection, transportation, zoning, and the like.

GETZ: But their taxes are less than ours.

TITUS: On a strictly dollar basis, yes.

AGNEW (*addressing Arthur Getz*): Art, what additional data do you think we need?

GETZ: You mean on taxes?

AGNEW: Well, yes. If you have any thoughts on it. What I really had in mind were any major areas other than taxes or, for example, on what I offered.

GETZ: Seems to me a prospect will be very interested in labor, including its availability, skills, attitude toward new industry coming into the county, rates, and productivity.

A COUNTY MEMBER: Rates and productivity—they're the same, aren't they?

GETZ: Oh no. No, not at all. Rates have to do with what a man is paid, like $2.50 per hour, whereas productivity is what he produces or accomplishes for that $2.50.

COUNTY MEMBER: If you are talking about labor costs, they will be difficult to get.

GETZ: Direct labor cost could be one way to express it, but not the only one. Sure, you're going to have trouble getting some of this information, but labor productivity is something a prospect is going to be asking about.

COUNTY MEMBER: Should this type of data be held confidential?

AGNEW: Personally, I don't think so.

TITUS: Well, I wouldn't make it public. Seems to me the prospect ought to be screened quite well before divulging certain types of data such as these would be.

GETZ: You can't be too secretive or you'll lose the prospect.

Questions

1. Using your creativity, make general suggestions regarding how the committee should proceed with its work.
2. Considering the data on labor, how would you suggest they be obtained for showing (*a*) the availability of labor, (*b*) the labor rates, and (*c*) the labor productivity? Discuss.
3. What other types of information do you feel will be helpful to induce industrial plants to locate in Matthews County? Discuss.

22

Evaluating, developing, and compensating

No person was ever honored for what he received. Honor has been the reward for what he gave.

CALVIN COOLIDGE

AMONG THE FOREMOST AREAS of managerial actuating are evaluating, developing, and compensating management members. Demonstrating a genuine interest in a manager's performance, telling him how he is doing, and helping him develop his skills in order to qualify for bigger jobs are highly motivating. The typical manager wants to know where he can improve. Further, he is interested in his compensation because of what money can acquire for him.

EVALUATING MANAGERS

Appraisal has in itself beneficial attributes. When a top manager with the help of others seeks to appraise the performance and potential of the executives reporting to him, he will acquire a new and helpful understanding about them. He will become more aware of what they are doing, in what possible ways they can be helpful, and what can be done to speed their growth. He also becomes more conscious about his own values and growth. Even in cases where the appraisal is done by outsiders, the executives within the company become more aware of their relative merits, get to know themselves better, and develop greater interest in self-improvement.

A subordinate's performance is always a consideration of a superior who typically appraises in some fashion how well each member of his management team is doing. While not found in every organization, a formal performance appraisal program is recommended so that uniform practices are followed, all managers know how they are appraised, and the importance given to these efforts by top management. Our discussion will center around these major considerations: (1) the purpose of the appraisals, (2) the criteria or standards of performance used, and (3) the appraisal interview.

PURPOSE OF APPRAISALS

There are two major reasons for evaluating performance. The first is to appraise the manager in his present job. We are inventorying our executive power to know what we have. This is the basis for other evaluating purposes we may have in mind. But we start with what we have now. If our purpose is to appraise future candidates for managerial jobs, we are really dealing with a placement problem, a part of which is appraising the candidate. This can probably best be handled by starting with appraisal of his present efforts.

The second major purpose is to determine his developmental needs, if any. The difference between required and present performance represents the developmental need which is fulfilled by self-development, in-plant programs, or external courses of study. We want to pinpoint present developmental requirements accurately, to catch poor management practices before they snowball into costly errors, and to find out in what areas help can be given to spur the manager to do a better job.

Are justifications for salary increases another purpose of evaluating performance? Yes, this is a usage. However, experience indicates that if the goal is a salary consideration, the performance appraisal should not be mixed with either of the two major purposes stated above. To justify this viewpoint, note that performance is only one factor among many to be considered in granting salary increases. Salary ranges, relative position of executive within range, and available funds must also be taken into account. Also where the decision to give or not to give a salary increase is based heavily upon the performance appraisal, there is a tendency to distort the appraisal in order to justify the increase. This is a friendly gesture, but certainly is not discriminatory. And in the case of promotions, similar arguments hold true. Briefly then, the recommendation is that decisions concerning salary or promotion should be made at a separate time from appraisals for present performance and for determining developmental needs.

THE CRITERIA USED

Usually one person does the performance appraisal, although in some instances a group of three may appraise separately, and combine their ratings into a composite value of the group. The appraiser should have first-hand information and knowledge of the manager being rated and of the work or results being accomplished. Frequently this means the immediate supervisor should do the appraising. However, he may feel that he is too busy with other tasks or is not competent to do the appraising. In such cases, a person trained in appraisal work may perform the task.

Appraising accurately is difficult. Having to state capabilities and accomplishments in writing necessitates keen observation, good judgment, and objectivity. To some degree what is stated as the subordinate's performance reflects the appraiser's concept of performance adequacy and his most outstanding personality characteristics. He tends to describe the appraisal in terms of his values and of what he understands. Actually at the present time the relationship between capabilities and performance is not fully known. This is another reason for limiting performance appraisals to current performance.

In a number of companies the standards of performance against which the ratee is evaluated are expressed in terms of selected traits or performance factors. Included, for example are job knowledge, judgment, creativity, initiative, drive, self-expression, and stability. Actually, by using such factors, a measurement of traits probably influential upon the subordinate's behavior is derived, and the assumption is with such-and-such behavior he accomplishes a certain level of management work. In other words, it is assumed that his behavior is directly related to his work performance, for example, how well he uses judgment on his present job. There is a question in the minds of many whether the trait approach is effective in appraising a manager's performance. As implied above, what the appraiser thinks of the ratee is present to some degree in the evaluating and, as a result, prejudice and favoritism may influence the answer. However, this influence may be very minor and not nearly as important as some critics suggest.

The trend in appraising is toward "measured appraisals." This is especially true for managers. Under this arrangement performance is evaluated in realistic and quantitative terms, such as reduce scrap loss by 5 percent, raise quality production runs to 98 percent "acceptable," and sell 125 percent of quota. Performance is measured in terms of the ratee's accomplishment of these goals. Measured appraisals minimize subjective judgment and express performance in universally understandable terms. However, they may tend to stress certain goals excessively and introduce too much rigidity into the individual's efforts as a team member of the organization. Further, the goals and work must be measurable.

This measured appraisal approach is in keeping with the concept of results management which places emphasis upon the results. Quantitative work should be evaluated first followed by qualitative tasks. Quantitative tasks can be *measured;* qualitative tasks can be *judged.* Figure 22–1 shows the performance goals for a director of personnel.

FIGURE 22–1. Performance goals for director of personnel

DIRECTOR OF PERSONNEL PERFORMANCE GOALS

The following are required this year to meet company goals.

Quantitative targets:
1. Reduce cost of recruitment by 2.5 percent.
2. Increase the Research and Development unit from present 10 to 14 employees.
3. Reduce personnel department total costs by 7 percent.

Qualitative targets:
1. Develop actuating program for the Research and Development personnel.
2. Improve the present grievance system so that complaints can be processed more quickly and accurately.
3. Work out transition requirements in transferring manual clerks resulting from computer installation this forthcoming October.

Note that both quantitative and qualitative targets are spelled out, they are clearly stated, and within the control of the manager.

There is some practice of blending the trait and measurable approaches, thus certain attributes of an employee's performance must be judged, while others can be evaluated in terms of specific measurements. In addition, all are related to a definite period and to the overall goals of an enterprise.

Interviews are helpful in ascertaining specific information and obtaining answers to questions, all of which combined with observations and consultation of records of achievement assist in formulating the performance appraisal. In some instances, printed forms are used to assist and guide the evaluators.

In some companies a practice found advantageous is to appraise each manager's performance on a specific date such as his birthday or the day he joined the company. This tends to spread out the evaluation work. On the other hand, it can be concentrated by appraising all at a given period each year.

THE APPRAISAL INTERVIEW

When measured appraisals are used, the comparison between what is achieved and what is expected is relatively simple. Prior to the interview, the subordinate knows fairly well how he rates in terms of results achieved. Hence, the discussion with his superior is structured and directed to those areas where possible improvement is mutually believed possible. However, where traits are used and much judgment is involved, a sensitive situation may be present. Careful handling is required for a superior to state the performance appraisal of his subordinate, who is expected to listen and understand fully. Sharp differences of opinion may arise.

In preparing for the interview, it is recommended that for either the measured or trait appraisal, the superior observe these suggestions: (1) outline the points you wish to cover, (2) emphasize the purpose is to help the manager to improve his performance on his present job, (3) concentrate on strengths, (4) ask him where he believes he could improve to get into the discussion of his weaknesses, (5) give specific examples and means for improvement, (6) encourage him to talk, to express his beliefs and feelings—you listen, (7) do not make reference to other management members to him.

During the appraisal interview it is best to refrain from any criticism for it is quite likely to have no motivational effect upon future efforts and may possibly put the subordinate on the defensive with attempts to discredit parts of the appraisal or to sit silently through the interview and thus prevent good communication. Likewise, giving praise during the interview seems to be disliked by both superior and subordinate. In many cases it is a mere formality, but it appears necessary when the subordinate wants to know what his appraisal is.

Seldom is complete agreement reached, and differences may be scattered over several points. But with time at least part of the differences may diminish. Hence, the appraisal interview may be looked upon as a period to get the appraisal to the subordinate along with some explanations. Then terminate it and let the subordinate "think it over." Later, get together again and discuss it more openly. Justification for this delayed approach is that typically when there are significant differences, the first stage of the subordinate's reaction is that his rater has been unfair, expects too much, doesn't have all the facts, or fails to realize that the fault is really with someone else—another manager or a subordinate. Later, perhaps within a week or so, the second stage starts wherein the manager rated begins to think that perhaps the rating in correct, or at least a portion of it. It could just be that he has not been doing as well as is expected of him. Finally, in the third stage and some time later, he recognizes and admits to himself that the rating is correct. He recalls situations and observes some of his present efforts that reveal he is not operating at par or achieving the results he set for himself. Further, he now begins to realize that to get ahead in this particular enterprise he would be wise to correct the deficiencies enumerated by the appraiser.

DEVELOPING MANAGERS

Development is vital to managerial actuating; much of the work of this basic activity is performed with the hope that managers will improve their particular work. And a definite program is needed. Most modern managers are developed; few are "born managers." Present-day qualifications are far more than matters of natural endowment. Depending solely upon informal association with immediate superiors is slow, incomplete, and frequently ineffective. It pays to have the very best managers and formal developmental efforts to this end are an investment that pays excellent returns.

The supply of qualified managers is seriously limited. This stems from many causes. Probably foremost is the growth in the economy, with the resultant need for more managers in business, government, schools, and other enterprises. Also, changes in the economy—new products, new methods, and new technology have increased the demand. In addition, the emphasis on specialization makes for cencentration in limited areas so that the opportunities to acquire a broad background of experiences are distinctly limited. As greater specialization is practiced, the tendency is for young executives to remain specialists in their fields. The executive shortage is also due in part to the relatively slow process of conventional promotional systems, especially in the relatively stable enterprises, and the scarcity of executive development efforts in many of the rapidly growing enterprises.

As employed in this book, the development of managers is thought of as *the application of planned efforts to assist in maintaining and improving managers at or intended for the middle and top organizational levels in order that they can more effectively attain the objectives of the enterprise.* This definition is in keeping with common usage of the term, although it is also used to include all levels of management, specifically supervisory. The justification for separating supervisory development from the development of managers is primarily that of convenience.

Managerial developmental efforts are established for a number of reasons. They include: to improve sales, lower production cost, acquire better teamwork, instill greater enthusiasm, and add confidence. More precisely, however, the types of benefits commonly cited by managers as expected and received are:

1.   Improved communication among management members and better use of informal discussions about their work.
2.   Identification of broad, inclusive problems which affect several operating departments and which require managerial attention.
3.   Evaluation of adequacy and suitability of company policies.
4.   Keeping up to date on current managerial developments.
5.   Revealing certain weaknesses of superiors hindering subordinate efforts, and suggest possible remedial actions to be taken.
6.   Securing better cooperation and teamwork among management members.
7.   Stimulating managers to appraise and develop their subordinates.
8.   Encouraging the promotion of qualified managers.
9.   Uncovering poorly placed management members, and bringing about needed transfers for mutual advantage.
10. Assisting in college recruitment efforts.

CURRENT CONCEPTS ON MANAGEMENT DEVELOPMENT

Programs designed to help develop managers are so varied and difficult to define that any significant trends in their makeup and application defy expression in a few simple terms. Management development programs are changing. To a great extent the rigid, highly systematized developing procedures have been abandoned. In their place, management members are performing more informal training or development work. The program is sustained by top managers and line managers. Management courses dealing with technological advances together with changes in the business environment have expanded; yet there is also growth in the practice of placing capable men in demanding jobs. This latter approach develops and tests men quickly and at the same time produces profits for the enterprise.

The true objective is to see that the learner leaves the group able to do certain specific things or to mull over concepts and formualte ideas and thoughts helpful to him in performing his job. The objectives have changed from that of developing *learned* managers to *learning* managers. The latter is the real need of today and of the future. With all the evolutionary change and growth around us, the modern manager must cope with this highly dynamic state of affairs and relate his knowledge and skill to the projected tomorrows. Problems are viewed more as opportunities than threats of failure, and the manager is becoming more of a finder of answers than a giver of answers. In brief, he is learning along with his group; he is finding out with them how best to meet certain situations and what decisions should be made. The learning manager stresses participative learning, interacting with other people, and working with problems meaningful to him and his work.

There is, of course, need for knowledge transfer, and programs for this purpose are and should be utilized. These are the familiar "how-to" courses. But usage of these, namely straightforward lecture presentations of explicit and prescribed policies and practices has revealed the need for an awareness of others and a recognition of the setting into which the knowledge must be placed. In essence, this helps move management development efforts into an unstructured laboratory situation. The highly structured classroom situation is not typical of the condition faced by the manager. Continuing this trend, the course that presents the identity and feedback on managers' current attitudes is gaining more and more acceptance. This is justified by the fact that the knowledge and skill of a manager are strongly conditioned by his attitude.

While as yet not an accepted practice, there is more and more thought being given to providing time for needed management development from the manager's work period. No longer is a weekend or a night a week sufficient to keep abreast of the lengthy and special education that the manager of today requires. Much is known and available to those who want to learn about management and its application. Sometime in the future a leave of absence with pay so that a manager can go to the proper source for developing and refueling may be an accepted custom. If nearly all enterprises would do so, there would be no competitive disadvantage to anyone following such a practice, and the improvement of management would be terrific.

FUNDAMENTAL CONSIDERATIONS

Management development should produce changed behavior which is more in keeping with the organization's goals than the previous behavior. This change frequently consists of a number of small steps resulting from the training, but the cumulative effect is considerable and is the end result sought. It is also basic that a terminal behavior is identified before the development efforts start.

Essential to a developmental program is genuine top-management support in the form of leadership and the providing of rquired resources willingly and enthusiastically. Requirements, potentials, and limitations of the development work must be recognized by the top managers and realistic goals approved. Benefits are usually slow in being realized; hence, top managers should not expect quick favorable gains.

To supply the needed basic information for development programs a complete description of each managerial job should be written. The duties, responsibilities, to whom the manager reports, who reports to him, and organization authority are typical information to be secured. Complete information is necessary.[1] A good, formal organization chart and manual will greatly assist in this step. Furthermore, the personnel specifications for each management job should be precisely stated. This includes what is generally considered necessary for satisfactory performance of the job. Included are such things as education, experience, personal qualities, and ability deemed necessary to fill the job. Printed forms are helpful in this task but they are not mandatory. These managerial job descriptions and personnel specifications can be prepared mainly by the present managers of the enterprise. Most managers will write quite accurate and complete personnel specifications for their own and those positions immediately subordinate to them.

A schedule of estimates for executive replacements showing the approximate number, location, and time should normally be prepared. This can be based on the composite judgment of the best informed minds. For small and medium-sized companies the most practical approach is position analysis, which is primarily a careful review and analysis of each executive position and its incumbent in view of present and future needs of the company. In the case of large companies a mathematical approach can be used. Figure 22–2 shows, for different organization levels, the number of executive positions, the cumulative number of executive positions, the *average* age for retirement at the top level, and the *average* age for hiring in the intermediate and middle levels. Since the *average* length of service between top and middle levels is 20 years (65–45) and the cumulative number of executive positions for all the levels is 100, an *average* of $\frac{1}{20}$ of 100, or 5, executives must be promoted to the middle level each year to maintain the

---

[1] See Chapter 14 for further discussion of this point.

status quo of the organization. Likewise, the promotions from the middle to intermediate level are equal to $\frac{1}{10}$ of 20, or 2, executives. This approach is based on important assumptions, including the following: average ages are used, all promotions are made from within, the enterprise remains approximately the same size, and the enterprise enjoys a relatively uniform level of activity throughout each year.[2]

No program develops a management trainee; he develops himself. The program simply makes him aware of his growth possibilities and helps him to help himself. The urge to acquire knowledge and skill must be strong *within* the individual trainee. No amount of organized executive training will succeed unless the individual's desire, ambition, and will to achieve are present. The self-directed approach should guide

FIGURE 22–2. Pertinent data on executive personnel of an enterprise

Organization level	Number of executive positions	Cumulative number of executive positions	Average age (years)
Top	4	4	65 for retirement
Intermediate	16	20	55 for hiring
Middle	80	100	45 for hiring

the development efforts with high value being placed on personal initiative and self-sufficiency. The program should emphasize improving his work on his *present job*. Normally this is the beginning of a manager increasing his efficiency and of preparing for greater responsibility.

Managerial development programs are pervasive and represent a continuing process. No one individual or one department is completely responsible for management development. The ultimate responsibility is shared, and it requires constructive action and thought by all the management members at all levels. Furthermore, management development flourishes only when it is given a property of continuity. It should not be turned on and off like water from a faucet. The most successful programs provide either carry-over assignments to the trainees requiring application of knowledge to the day-to-day needs of their jobs or regular meetings at periodic intervals. A seminar one year, nothing the

[2] This technique for analyzing promotional possibilities has been taken from H. A. Simon, D. W. Smithburg, and V. A. Thompson, *Public Administration* (New York: Alfred A. Knopf, Inc., 1950), pp. 344–52.

next, and several meetings the next contribute little toward genuine management development. The planned efforts should be permitted to run their course.

The program offered should take into account that a manager usually must grapple with several problems at the same time. Problems of different intensity arise in a disorganized manner. The executive cannot work with one problem till solved, then move on to another problem, and then to a third. He tends to work on the most urgent problem. Men with multiple-track minds—those who can move swiftly from one problem to another and derive good decisions for each problem— are scarce. This dearth is one which effective management development can help alleviate.

Upon completion of a course, management trainees may have to wait some time before trying out their new knowledge and skill. This "delay gap" can cause frustration and sometimes even loss of the trainee, who may find employment with another company. All promises of promotion should be withheld until the job opening is known to be definite and the trainee has completed the program successfully. The reward should come after performance is demonstrated, not before; nor should the development program be used as a hurdle to managers. It should be viewed as an opportunity and a privilege to attend and to participate.

MEDIA FOR MANAGEMENT DEVELOPMENT

The following 25 different ways, segregated by participative and non-participative means, show the variety available and the most common ones used.

Participative means include:

1. Learning on the Job. This is a common and effective means for training executives. Nothing can replace the actual experience of meeting problems and situations as they really are, coping with various personalities, and witnessing the outcome of various personal efforts. Observation *and participation* are necessary for learning on the job. Suggestions, assistance in difficulties, the sharing of facts, and explanations of reasons for certain decisions by a senior executive are usually helpful to the trainee.

2. Problem Solving. The trainee is given a written description of a situation or "case" that necessitates managerial action. Either as an individual or a member of a group, the trainee is required to (1) identify the problem, (2) analyze the facts and conditions leading to the problem, (3) state his recommended plan of action to solve the problem, and (4) justify his particular plan of action. The cases should be carefully selected and pertinent so that their use meets the developmental requirement of the trainee.

3. Conferences, Seminars, and Special Meetings. The exchange of ideas, discussions bringing out the many facets of a problem, and practice in analyzing situations and determining what should be done are typical of the advantages from conferences and seminars. A good leader of the discussion is paramount. Discussions can be centered around such subjects as past and current methods of company operations, promotional ideas, and new product suggestions and developments. Activities other than executive training as such commonly constitute a portion of the program.

Special meetings are formal and administered by company officers. Basic information covered includes company policies, services, and problems encountered.

4. Business Game. Trainees are divided into teams which make business decisions dealing with a given set of conditions of an enterprise, commonly expressed by an initial operating statement. Each team starts with exactly the same financial position and with identical choices available. The format may vary somewhat; but in a typical game each team makes decisions for quarter-to-quarter operations, covering such areas as pricing, make-or-buy decisions, purchasing new equipment, borrowing from the bank, disposing of plant, and investing in research and development. Each team is in direct competition with the other teams. The goal is to achieve the greatest improvement in the financial position of the company in a given number of quarters. The results are quantitative, not qualitative. Games permit trainees to broaden their viewpoints, to visualize interrelated activities, to gain experience in decision making, and to comprehend the results of their decisions.

5. In-basket Exercises. This is a type of business simulation in which the trainee playing the role of a manager receives a packet of background information and several items of correspondence and memos that are placed in his "in basket" and necessitate his managerial action. Within a prescribed period, he reads the papers, determines the problems, establishes priorities, and decides what actions to take. After the time period, a general discussion is held among the group on how the various situations were handled, and a consensus is usually reached on the most effective ways of dealing with the situations presented.

6. Role Playing. Realistic face-to-face conflict encounters between two persons, such as between a superior and a subordinate or a management member and a customer, are simulated by use of this medium. The trainee learns how to cope with a variety of situations and to apply his knowledge of handling affairs and dealing with people. Background information necessary to play the role is provided, and participants gain valuable insights not only from their actions but also from a feedback session where they can listen to a tape recording of what they said, note the outcome of their actions, and profit from comments of observers.

7. Special Assignments.   A trainee is given complete freedom to handle a special assignment, and from his efforts an opportunity is gained to see how well he handles himself and what he accomplishes. Typical special assignments include supervising the development of a new product, determining plans for increased distribution in "Territory T," establishing additional dealer outlets, and representing the company in local civic associations.

8. Job Rotation and Use of Strategic Jobs.   Service with carefully selected successive jobs, or job rotation, throughout the major portions of an enterprise provide broadening, balancing, and enriching experience. A general idea of what the trainee is to acquire from each job should be established, and the trainee should be made aware of the respective goal before each job. Job rotation is probably most effective for jobs of the lower and middle levels and the rotation should consist primarily of lateral moves if possible and include both line and staff positions to maximize experience. About four to six months should be spent on each job. A couple of weeks on each job furnishes orientation and acquaintance only, not managerial training. But too long a period on each job impairs the training value.

A special variation of job rotation is the use of strategic jobs which hold unusual opportunities for self-development. Factors identifying strategic jobs are (1) key decisions are made and carried out, (2) opportunities to solve difficult problems are present, (3) contacts with top managers and personnel outside the company are required, and (4) effective leadership is needed to fill the job.

9. Committees.   Serving on an active committee as chairman or some other responsible post has definite training value. By this means the learner gains a wider perspective, experiences situations involving the resolution of conflicting ideas, learns to adjust to others' viewpoints, and gains practice in reaching decisions and getting work done by and through the efforts of others. Committees are good media to stress organizational relationships and help the member to visualize the operations of each major organization unit. Preferably a major committee with line authority should be selected.[3]

10. Sensitivity Training or T-groups. The goal of sensitivity training is to increase a person's awareness of his effect on others and of his own subconscious motivations. It is an experience through one's emotions of interpersonal relationships, frequently resulting in a change in feelings and attitudes toward one's self and toward others. T-groups are motivational during the initial "unfreezing" step, followed by "changing" and "refreezing" steps during which respectively the group seeks to improve its effectiveness and to make permanent its new form of group participation. The training takes place under controlled laboratory conditions.

11. Team Task Forces. These groups are set up to meet specific, nonrecurring problems. They give trainees the opportunity to analyze actual situations and participate in decision making. Practice in acting constructively in a group situation is demonstrated, and a chance to evaluate the trainee's ability to think is provided.

12. Farm System. This means applies only to companies having branches or subsidiary operations. A man can be developed for an executive job in the parent company by first placing him on a similar and relatively smaller scale job in the branch. The candidate has the opportunity to become acquainted with the company's mode of operations, the work climate, and the methods of doing business.

13. Decentralized Organization Structure. The more decentralized the organization structure, the greater the need and the opportunity to learn by managing. Basically this means opens up the opportunities to learn by doing, and the precise means of development can be any of a number of the means discussed above. Decentralization, viewed as a means of management development, assumes that qualified men are given managerial duties and that they will receive help from their superiors. However, complete dependence upon the man above is undesirable for its discourages individual initiative and confidence.

14. Second Team. In most group athletic contests it is helpful to have a strong second team to back up the first team. The same holds true for most companies and their management men. This medium places emphasis upon a reserve *team,* not separate individuals, to take over at regular intervals and relieve the first team of managers. The second team is considered and trained as a unit and operates as a unit.

15. Junior Board of Directors. An effective but as yet not widely

---

[3] See also Chapter 11, for discussion of committees and their use.

adopted practice in training executives is the establishing of "junior boards," who operate somewhat in a managerial capacity just like a regular board of directors. The junior board is, however, primarily for training purposes. This medium makes possible participation in an atmosphere closely resembling actual conditions. Its use is limited more or less to training with reference to policy making, administrative practices, getting along with other executives, and obtaining a broad viewpoint of the various activities of the enterprise.

16. Community Activities.   Trainees can get valuable experience in managing when they occupy key positions in civic, fraternal, and church groups. Management experience in one type of enterprise is helpful in working with another type of enterprise. Participation in community activities is not only the right and duty of the management trainee, but it gives him a feeling of inner satisfaction, prestige, and valuable management experience.

Nonparticipative means include:

17. Lectures.   One of the oldest means for developing managers, lectures permit concise presentations of knowledge by a recognized expert and qualified speaker. This medium is personal and can be highly effective. Visual aids make a lecture more effective, and the inclusion of models and demonstrations helps provide a forceful presentation.

18. Programmed Instructions.   Sometimes referred to as teaching machines, this approach focuses the trainee's attention on the significant points while he learns. Questions are asked in a sequence that advances from the simple to the difficult and complex. A response by the trainee is required at each step in the sequence. The programmed sequence is presented in a series of "frames," or separate views on the screen of a machine. Each frame requires response by the trainee. Any knowledge or skill that can be specified can be programmed. Advocates of programmed instruction claim learning time can be reduced from 30 to 50 percent, retention is greatly improved, self-pacing by the trainee is emphasized, and a high level of achievement is attained.

19. Special Courses.   When the need is for specialized knowledge having a direct bearing on his present job or the one for which he is being developed, a special study course may be prescribed. Such a course may be designed to provide specific factual information and the trainee enrolls in such a course offered by a special school or a university.

20. Planned Special Readings.   If the need is primarily to extend the cultural background of the executive and give him a better understanding of the world in which he lives, it is usually effective to use special reading assignments. Selected topics, articles, and books dealing with management techniques, current affairs, or present-day problems can be used. In some instances the trainee is requested to report to the trainer and discuss the particular assignment, or written answers to specific questions relative to the reading may be required.

21. Observation Posts. This method stresses learning by observation. "Assistant to" positions make good observation posts in the development of managers.[4] Candidates holding assistant-to positions are close enough to their superiors to observe managerial activities which can be employed for future use by them.

22. Coaching. By means of coaching, the manager is trained in the use of the best methods for his work and is made familiar with the makeup of his job assignment and the policies and procedures affecting his work. For greatest effectiveness, coaching should be provided by the trainee's superior and conducted on a continuous or regularly scheduled basis. Permitting long periods of no coaching at all is a common error and nullifies many of the training benefits. Coaching is essentially helpful when applied during the early training period of an individual. With the passage of time, less coaching is usually required.

23. Counseling. Support to an executive trainee in a temporary period of difficulty can be supplied through counseling. An emotional crisis, adjustment to the work, or some hurdle in filling the job successfully can frequently be overcome by talking over the problem with one skilled in listening, questioning, and observing, and capable of offering pertinent suggestions to alleviate the difficulty. The objective is to help the counselee gain a better understanding of himself. Followed is either (*a*) directive counseling in which the counselor finds that he can and should apply the answer to the trainee, or (*b*) nondirective counseling in which the counselor facilitates the trainee's adjustment by helping him understand his own difficulties arising from problems on and off the job and has the trainee solve his problem himself.

24. University Management Development Programs. Many universities now offer or sponsor conferences, institutes, workshops, special courses, and "programs" especially designed to help in the development of executives. The scope of these offerings differs widely. Some include a concentrated and specialized course extending for several weeks; others offer more extensive work in the form of 8-, 10-, and 13-week courses. Some are on a one-day-a-week basis; in other instances the course is operated on a part-time basis, with participants working on their regular jobs in the morning and attending classes in

---

[4] The "assistant to" is discussed in Chapter 16, "Organization Relationships."

the afternoon or at night. The approach and material content differ among sponsors. Some stress use of basic management, functions, others stress skill in leadership, communication, and group relations, others point their efforts toward quantitative methods and decision making.

25. Professional Association Membership. Active membership in a truly professional group can assist management development through attendance at meetings, informal discussions with other members, and the reading of the association's journal or official publication. Some associations stress individual self-improvement; others promote workshops, seminars, and study groups. These experiences help to promote the important "develop yourself" philosophy.

COMPENSATING

Another major area of actuating is compensating, which becomes especially effective when the individual wants money or what money can do or buy for him. Managerial actuating by means of compensation is an intriguing, interesting, yet highly complicated subject. Compensation makes its contribution as a sort of "all-purpose" motivation that has various values to different people. For example, the purchasing power of money received may be critical to one manager, while to another money acquisition is not wealth but a symbol of achieving recognition and status, while to another it is symbolic of gaining individual economic freedom.

For compensating to have motivational value, certain basic conditions appear necessary. They include: (1) the goal of high compensation should be mutual and rank high with both the company and the individual, (2) the manager must be convinced that the application of his energy and skill will lead to achievement of the goal, that his performance improvement will be rewarded with greater compensation, and (3) the manager believes he is able to and will improve his present results achieved, that improvement is attainable and within his capability.

BASIC CONSIDERATIONS IN COMPENSATING

Compensation for managerial work, particularly at the higher levels, is the result of many different forces. Foremost are three basic considerations: (1) the size of the company, (2) the industry, and (3) the contribution of decisions made.[5] These are interrelated. The first, size of

---

[5] Arch Patton, *Men, Money, and Motivation* (New York: McGraw-Hill Book Co., Inc., 1961), p. 43.

company, has been studied quite thoroughly and is confirmed by statistical studies and surveys. The large company has relatively greater assets and usually greater profits, and decisions put into action have more scope and greater impact than do those in a small company. Secondly, the industry appears to be significant. Certain industries appear to be high-paying, while others are low-paying enterprises. The mode of operation, facilities, growth, degree of competition, whether currently propelled or running on past momentum, and policies followed are among the most influential factors accounting for differences. The third consideration, the contribution of decisions made, reaffirms the truism that a manager is paid for managing. More enlightening is the fact that higher managerial compensation seems to be associated with enterprises that deal in products and services that change rapidly, where a high degree of creativity is required, where the effect of decisions is quickly translated to statement of profit and loss, where there is no sheltered competitive life, and where there is individual- not group-centered environment.

Fundamentally we can base a manager's compensation upon (1) his time only, (2) his performance only, or (3) a combination of his time and performance. The first is illustrated by a straight salary per year to a director of research. This means is common and is usually followed when it is difficult or costly to measure performance. The second, paying for performance only, is represented by the sales manager who is paid a percentage of total net sales. The third, a combination of time and performance, can be thought of as the base compensation for time only and incentive pay for how well the job is done, that is, job performance. There are numerous combinations of these three bases used.

Much of the motivational effect of compensation is in the relativity of the amounts being paid. For example, $30,000 a year paid to a manager in Company A may be highly motivational because it is well above that being paid to most managers in Company A. In contrast, $30,000 a year in Company B may not be motivational because it is not above that paid most managers in Company B.

This relativity factor has given rise to compensation plans termed (1) shallow or (2) steep. In the former the differentials of base compensation among the managers are relatively small and commonly indicate the condition where managers tend to be conservative and make major decisions very slowly. For the latter, or steep arrangement, a great differential between the top managers and the middle and lower manager groups exists. Usually this reflects great emphasis on aggressive and dominant leadership and decision making at the top.

There is also the condition of geographical location. Managerial compensation is relatively high in certain areas and low in others. Highest managerial salaries tend to be paid for jobs located in the larger cities, but there are notable exceptions.

Compensation from the viewpoint of actuating appears to be related to the age of the executive. A manager's wants change with time. While no two managers are alike even in the same age group, it is possible to generalize on the basis of age. Figure 22–3 shows possible relationships in this respect.

FIGURE 22–3. Possible relationships between manager's age and characteristics of compensation

Age in years	*Characteristics affecting compensation*
20–30	Is ambitious and aggressive, needs self-esteem, seeks opportunity, wants chance to make good.
31–45	Has demonstrated definite accomplishments, seeks more current, not deferred, compensation, wants challenging compensation arrangement.
46–55	Current compensation still important, but deferred and fringe benefits are attractive.
56–65	Visualizes forthcoming end of career, deferred compensation and fringe benefits wanted, longs to "do something" nonfinancial for fellowmen that employs his mature experience and judgment.

BASE PAY

Total compensation is made up of base pay plus a variety, if any, of extra payments including bonus, profit sharing, financial incentives, and fringe benefits. The base pay is normally adjusted periodically in keeping with the results achieved by the manager, the length of service, inflation, and the cost of living. The foundation upon which total compensation is built is base pay. It also determines, in effect, the amount of (1) the cash bonus, (2) company-paid life insurance coverage, (3) the pension the employee will receive, and (4) the deferred compensation. Furthermore, it is base pay that is publicly known if compensation is revealed; and it provides the status symbol and the measure of approval for an individual among his associates.

Base pay represents the stable long-term value of a position. Different job requirements are reflected by different base pays. Normally, a person is motivated by these differentials. This is one reason why the ambitious manager seeks a better job, that is, one of a higher compensation and therefore one that requires more and pays more. Base pays differ primarily because of tradition and the knowledge, skill, and responsibility requirements of the work.

BONUS AND COMMISSION

Bonus and commission are payments over and above base pay. They are based on performance. Any factor or set of factors can serve as a basis for award, but commonly the amount of base salary or an appraisal of performance are employed. In some cases, bonus and commission are related to profits, but this is not mandatory. Also, a graduated scale, not a fixed percentage, is sometimes used to determine the amount of bonus. From the managerial viewpoint, a bonus payment is a one-time action with little future commitment. If paid each year, the employee may develop the notion that the bonus is a "sure thing." However, there is no obligation to pay it, and the basis on which it is paid should be clearly understood by the recipient.

A common formula is to put 6 or 7 percent of profits in excess of a determined amount into a bonus fund and to divide this fund among bonus recipients. Opinions differ to what amount of bonus adequately motivates. Many feel a figure of about 10 percent of base pay is a minimum for annual base pays up to $20,000. Above this amount something like a 20 percent bonus appears to be in line. But there is no widely accepted range. And payment of a bonus has disadvantages. Usually its payment is fairly far removed from the time of actual accomplishment, and associating the bonus with excellent work may be difficult for the person receiving it. Also, giving the recipient a large sum of money at one time may result in his spending it unwisely. In addition, an employee may be disinclined to stand up for a minority opinion, disagree, or exercise management boldness when he knows his superior has the power to give or deny a sizeable bonus.

Commissions are actually a type of bonus. They are directly related to the recipient's performance and are influenced by what he alone is directly responsible for doing. Hence, commissions are an effective form of incentive.

PROFIT SHARING

This is one of the oldest types of compensation used by business enterprises. Profit sharing is a broad subject and has many ramifications. It is included here to indicate that such a plan is used and to indicate some highlights of it. The basic compensation should be sound before profit sharing is used, because profit sharing will not correct an unsound, but will strengthen a sound, basic plan. Different patterns can be followed; however most include payment of a portion of net profits into a fund that is credited to the account of each participant, commonly in proportion to his base salary or in keeping with his performance. Most profit sharing features retaining or investing the funds for payment to participants at some future date. Thus a future "nest egg" is built up. There are usually certain tax advantages too.

Profit sharing emphasizes a single and meaningful objective and results in a company paying when it can best afford to pay. Managers receive a valuable compensation supplement. On the other hand, opponents claim that many managers cannot directly influence profits very much by their own performance, that the pay and performance are widely separated, and that morale may suffer when profits sink or investments of profit sharing funds decline.[6]

DEFERRED COMPENSATION

Pensions, contractual payments, and stock options feature deferred compensation. These means are used because it is believed that they can do for the individual employee what he cannot or will not do for himself because he lacks fortitude, determination, knowledge of finance, or knowledge of tax laws.

Pension plans are popular. Over 90% of the larger companies have pension programs, but there are significant differences in their makeup. The trend is very definitely toward the noncontributing type, meaning all payments to the pension fund are made by the employer, but in many plans the employee pays into the pension fund. Retirement at age 65 is a common provision, but earlier retirement on a selective basis is possible. However, the cost of the pension program is nearly 50 percent higher for retirement at age 60 in comparison with that at age 65. Many of the pension funds are what is known as a trusteed pension plan, meaning that the dollars set aside for pensions are invested in a trusteed plan. Also many pension funds are insured pension plans meaning the funds for the pensions are provided by means of insurance. Here surety of payment to recipient is certain because of built-in features found only in insurance. When the insurance method is followed, it is common for the policy to be written on the life of the individual and made payable to the company, which, in turn, pays the

---

[6] The Council of Profit Sharing Industries, 400 W. Madison St., Chicago, Ill. 60606, has many informative booklets on profit sharing available to the public.

insured a stated sum annually after his retirement. Payments to survivors in the event of premature death are commonly provided. In many instances the insured coverage is accomplished by means of a group policy.

Pension plans have actuating value in that (1) employees are provided economic security at retirement, (2) older employees are retired on an orderly basis, thus giving younger employees an opportunity to advance in the organization, and (3) the employee receives more deferred compensation because the employer can get more benefits at a lower cost due to his larger purchase and income tax structure, and (4) the employee feels the company is a good place to work. In contrast, certain disadvantages of company pension plans exist: (1) the employee is frequently required to remain in the company's employment to retain full pension benefits, (2) pensions represent a cost which eventually is paid by consumers in the form of higher prices, (3) the economic security can be lost or seriously reduced if the company fails or goes out of existence, and (4) due to inflation, the employee may receive small *real* economic purchasing power.

A contractual payment is an agreement between employee and employer whereby the employee, after retirement or term of employment, is paid a stated amount of money periodically over a stated period. The method of deferred compensation can be mutually beneficial. It enables the sales manager, for example, with fluctuating earnings to level and spread them out, thereby reducing taxes on current earnings. To the employer, contract payments represent a known expense over a definite period. It is possible to renegotiate contract payments from time to time. However, all such agreements must be in keeping with government regulations concerning such matters.

A stock option grants the right to buy common stock of a corporation at a stipulated price within a stated future period. Stock options are highly motivating. With them, a manager, by achieving good results, can increase the price of a company's stock by increasing its earnings, exercise his stock option to purchase shares at a relatively low price, and then sell them at the current high price, thus realizing a handsome profit.

FINANCIAL INCENTIVES

Financial incentives normally provide extra compensation in return for accomplishment over a mutually agreed base or standard. Earnings are related with accomplishment according to a specific plan or formula.

Financial incentives offer recognition in the form of extra compensation for extra effort. While similar to other compensating plans discussed above, financial incentives are more exacting and more closely tie together extra compensation with performance above an agreed performance level.

For management members an incentive compensation plan should restrict eligibility to those who make nonroutine decisions and exercise judgment that affect the attainment of stated company goals. Reasonable guides to clarify participation or nonparticipation should be pro-

FIGURE 22–4.   Important observations of managerial financial incentives

1.   The participants must have a strong desire for extra earnings.
2.   A measurable output, mutually understood, should be utilized.
3.   Temporary bases as standards of reference should be held to a minimum and be clearly designated as such.
4.   The standard of reference must be current and in keeping with present levels being followed.
5.   A known and identifiable relationship must exist between the effective effort of the manager and the measured accomplishment.
6.   Effective effort of the manager must be proportional to the monetary reward paid.
7.   Extra pay rewards should go to those making extra performance.
8.   Quality contributions over the work output must be established.
9.   Accuracy and fairness should take precedence over simplicity—difficult calculations can be reduced to convenient formulas or tables of data.
10.   A three-, six-, or twelve-month's period is usually an effective length for which incentive pay is calculated.

vided as a part of the plan. Further, the total incentive amount should be carefully defined and closely tied in with the financial goals of the enterprise. The amount paid to a participant should be related to what the manager accomplished or contributed during a given period (usually a year) and be in keeping with a distribution formula known to all participants. Finally, alternatives of payment should be provided, that is, a choice between current or deferred income, cash or stock. The opportunity to choose increases the incentive value.

No incentive is self-operating. Proper guidance and attention must be provided so that the program is modern, vibrant, and a top-notch force in actuating. An incentive program is only as effective as its administration. General observations of help in this respect are shown in Figure 22–4.

PRINCIPLE OF FINANCIAL INCENTIVE

The urge to do more work output for more pay is influenced mainly by the relative importance of more money to the recipient and his evaluation of the fairness of the plan under which he receives the extra pay.

A famous and highly successful financial incentive plan has been followed for several decades by the Lincoln Electric Company of Cleveland. This plan covers all employees, managers as well as nonmanagers. During the past decade, the company has paid annually a cash bonus of about $16 million to its nearly 2000 employees, or an average of over $8,000 per employee. In addition, over $1 million was paid for employee retirement annuities. The bonus payment represented the 38th consecutive year that the company paid a cash bonus. The plan operates as follows: Each year a target is set for cost reduction. Then all employees help to achieve it and to give highly efficient performances. Annual turnover of employees is less than 1 percent, and annual absenteeism averages 1.5 percent. Incentive pay is calculated by multiplying the base wage rate by the merit rating of performance by the incentive factor. This factor is the value of total incentive paid divided by the total number on payroll. Each recipient is constantly reminded that the incentive pay is not a gift, but a result of his outstanding results achievement. Due in part to the high effectiveness of its incentive plan, the company has been able to reduce continually the selling price of its products, which are welding equipment and electric motors.

NONFINANCIAL INCENTIVES

In a discussion of compensation, nonfinancial incentives should be included. These are symbols of achievement and are important at all levels, but especially so for executives. We have indicated in the previous three chapters that actuating need not include money payments. Men strive for recognition, prestige, and pride of accomplishment. Basically, every employee expects respect for work well done. If he receives respect when he earns it, his energies are almost limitless. The compensation program that respects work well done, rewards excellence in performance, and keeps money payments in line with these intangible factors develops and maintains a superior company team.

Titles are an excellent example of nonfinancial incentives. Many, if not all, managers will work harder and more objectively for a wanted title than they will for monetary reward. Why is this? Because the title gives them prestige, the sense of having arrived, of being somebody among their fellow men. The student of management should never underestimate these qualities. Or consider special furnishings supplied an executive in his office—a special conference table, carpeting on the floor, a private secretary. Granted these mean much more to some executives than to others; but they are important, and their motivating power depends in large measure upon the value which the superior places upon them and which, in turn, is accepted by members of the enterprise. Pins, awards, and certificates are additional examples. The monetary value of such items is negligible. It is what these items represent that is vital. Recognition for work well done, for having completed a difficult assignment, or being selected for a special mission are the true motivating power that is encompassed in such nonfinancial awards.

Principle of Nonfinancial Incentive

Nonmonetary rewards for extra achievements have strong incentive value.

Incentive merchandise is one of the most effective means ever devised to stimulate sales people. It consists of giving, free of cost, standard-brand merchandise selected from a catalog to those whose job performance equaled or exceeded a stated goal. Sometimes an all-paid vacation trip is offered. Frequently the array of offered merchandise is publicized to the participant's wife and family, who supply additional motivating stimuli for the head of their family to accomplish the goal and receive the merchandise. Incentive merchandise has a record of outstanding success in both large and small enterprises. Some argue that in the final analysis incentive merchandise is actually a financial incentive since the merchandise can be expressed in money terms. This may well be, but the point is that improved results or extra effort is exerted for the reward of the incentive merchandise. This is important in any compensation plan.

FRINGE BENEFITS

These have become the miscellany catch-all of compensation. They include various and sundry types of payments—some current, some deferred, some small, some large, some individual, some group, some financial, some nonfinancial. Figure 22–5 shows a listing of some of the more common fringe benefits extended managers.

What, if any, motivation is derived from these expenditures? The great majority of fringe benefits are socially desirable, but the actuating impact seems to be lost in many instances. There is a lack of personalizing the benefits and for the most part they are viewed as expected

FIGURE 22–5. Types of fringe benefits to managers

1. Contribution to group insurance plans.	9. Paid sick leave.
2. Counseling, financial advice, legal aid.	10. Reserve military duty.
3. Discounts on purchases.	11. Scholarships.
4. Termination pay.	12. Time spent at seminars and conferences.
5. Use of company library.	ences.
6. Medical and dental care.	13. Travel and moving expenses.
7. Military service allowance.	14. Vacation pay.
8. Paid club memberships, magazine subscriptions.	15. Voting time.
scriptions.	16. University courses.

assistance. Little or no weight is given job performance. Then too, there is no competitive edge, the manager can obtain the same benefits with any of several employers, and he acquires them automatically. It appears that fringe benefits are in the nature of socially desirable upward adjustments in base pay and ensure that certain benefits are provided.

QUESTIONS

1. Discuss the major reasons for evaluating performance.
2. Discuss the appraisal interview, giving what it is, preparing for it as a manager, and actually conducting it.
3. What significance do you attach to the statement that a management trainee develops himself—no program will do this for him? Elaborate on your answer.
4. As a director of executive training, would you favor the use of in-basket exercises? Why? The use of lectures? Why? The use of business games? Why?
5. What is the meaning of each of the following: (*a*) programmed instruction, (*b*) multiple-track minds, (*c*) strategic jobs in management development work, and (*d*) T-groups.
6. Relate your understanding of a learning manager. Is this type important today? Discuss.
7. Of the 26 available means for developing managers offered in this chapter, select 5 that appeal most to you. Give reasons for each of your selections.
8. What are the differences between coaching and counseling? Between profit sharing and stock option? Between measured appraisal and financial incentive?
9. What qualifications would you make for the statement, "Compensating has motivational value"? Why?
10. Discuss the subject of base pay as a part of the total compensation picture.
11. As a management member do you favor pension funds under a trusteed plan? Why? Under an insured plan? Why? Built up by contributing payments? Why?

12. In your opinion do fringe benefits have incentive value? Discuss.
13. Discuss the importance and usage of nonfinancial incentives in modern management.
14. What type of future form of compensation would you like to see adopted? Discuss your suggested plan pointing out its advantages as you see them.

CASE 22–1. UPPER STATE UNIVERSITY

PROFESSOR ZIEGLER: It certainly is a pleasure to see you again Dean Bolnick. And you are looking great.

DEAN BOLNICK: Thank you. It's nice to see you, Dr. Ziegler.

ZIEGLER: I hear you are making some changes in your Graduate School of Business. Will you tell me about them?

BOLNICK: Certainly. Glad to. Let's talk about curriculum first. Business schools generally are of one of two categories—those developing students as general managers and, at the other extreme, those developing specialists. Like most others, we at Upper State have found that the product turns out either as a generalist who lacks depth of knowledge in any area or a specialist with insufficient overall vision. On his first job the generalist is usually given a specialized task to do, special company training is given, and his chances of ever getting the more general management role is jeopardized. Meantime, the specialist gets off to a better start, but he is less able to see the whole picture. Each discipline looks at its own problems. There is not enough interplay. It's business, not a portion of business that we must be interested in.

ZIEGLER: Yes, I agree. What are you going to do about it?

BOLNICK: We are going to turn out only one type of graduate—the general manager armed with a specialty. That's what they do over in the Med. School—a great body of general understanding is required usually before the person can begin to become a specialist. I believe right now we have too many pat devices for decision making. Solving a problem should be measured in progress rather than finality.

ZIEGLER: Yeah.

BOLNICK: Our new curriculum in the two-year graduate program will begin with general courses in management. Also more technical courses will be required. The intent is to give the student a broad idea of what management is all about. Then, in the second year, the student will be required to select an area of specialization such as finance, accounting, or marketing.

ZIEGLER: It sounds good. I suppose you have had internal problems getting such a program accepted.

BOLNICK: Sure. But that's to be expected. The biggest problem right now, and I don't think it has anything to do with the curriculum change, is to develop a plan for appraising the performance of our faculty.

ZIEGLER: A performance appraisal plan?

BOLNICK: Right. At present we do not know how competent each professor is in instructing. If we don't receive any complaints, we assume he is O.K. But there is a difference among professors. At the end of five years service, a faculty member can be promoted to the next higher rank—from associate to full professor, for example. A committee consisting of the dean, department heads, and three full professors at large recommend who should be promoted. These recommendations are then submitted to the university's administrative council who consider and make the promotions.

ZIEGLER: On what basis does your School of Business committee make its decisions?

BOLNICK: That's a good question. Really, that's the problem. Some feel the candidate should have completed some writing and have it published. Others stress activity in local community affairs. Others give weight to the candidate's contacts and business executives he personally knows. Some insist that the candidate have his Ph.D. or D.B.A. Now all of these considerations have validity and are important. I look upon them favorably. But I think we should remember that usually the person was originally hired to teach.

ZIEGLER: You have faculty members who are nonteaching?

BOLNICK: Yes, such as our Director of Business Relations and our Director of the Research Bureau.

ZIEGLER: I see what you mean. To me, it is unrealistic to assume that a professor can be proficient in all these areas.

BOLNICK: I couldn't agree with you more.

ZIEGLER: Sounds like there are politics in your present practices.

BOLNICK: Yes, I guess I would have to say there is. Surprisingly, they come up with a fairly good selection. And it gives some of our faculty participation, which is what they want. I think there will be politics in any approach we devise, but I feel we can make improvements over what we're doing now.

ZIEGLER: How do you handle pay increases while a professor remains within his given rank?

BOLNICK: Each year he is given an increase of $500 up to a maximum of five years. This is automatic. Also, we have a cost of living adjustment that varies from year to year. In addition we have ranges of compensation for each rank from instructor to full professor.

Questions

1. What are your reactions to the curriculum changes stated by Dean Bolnick? Discuss.
2. From the viewpoint of management study, what interpretation do you give Dean Bolnick's statement, "Solving a problem should be measured in progress rather than finality." Discuss.
3. Present a plan you recommend for handling the promotion of faculty members. Justify your answer.

CASE 22–2. EDENS LIFE INSURANCE COMPANY

The director of personnel, under whose jurisdiction all training programs are conducted, had long harbored the idea of the company providing a special development program for its top- and middle-level managers in the nonsales areas. He believed that development for these managers should be started not only to improve the caliber of the company's management but also to offer equal training opportunities and to maintain a desired balance in managerial competency between nonsales and sales management personnel. For a number of years the company has offered training assistance to its various sales agencies. This help is offered at the local location of the agency. Subjects such as finding the prospect, selecting the proper insurance policy, closing the sale, and adequate follow-up were treated in some detail. Also, all new employees are put through a special Edens indoctrination program; clerical employees are provided training opportunities to increase their skill and promotional possibilities; and from time to time special courses which are suggested by changes in existing policy writing, processing, or terminating are offered.

In his interview with the president regarding the nonsales management development program, the director of personnel proposed a two-week conference or seminar to be held at Camp Apache Grove, an exclusive location some 75 miles from Albany, New York. The facilities offered there were excellent, and it was believed that locating the conference away from the office would minimize interruptions and provide a desired exclusiveness and status to the proposed program. Candidates would be limited to 30 and would be selected by a committee headed by the director of personnel. The conference would be designed to provide each trainee with a broader understanding of (1) the life insurance business and Edens' present and proposed future in it, (2) how to work effectively with individuals and groups of people, and (3) the economic, political, and social scene in which Edens operates. Succinctly stated, the objective is to help the trainee develop himself.

The president stated he favored such a program, but before recommending its approval by the Executive Operating Committee, he wanted the answers to these questions:

1. What subjects and type of sessions would be offered?
2. Who will conduct the sessions?
3. What will the proposed program cost?
4. What follow-up to the program should be undertaken to evaluate the results of the program?

The president believed that the meetings must be practical and the trainees given ample opportunity to ask questions and be a part of the discussions.

Questions

1. Outline in general the contents of the program you feel the director of personnel should offer.
2. Propose an itemized estimate of the cost of the two-week program, assuming cost data that in your opinion appears to be reasonable.
3. What answer do you feel the director of personnel should give the president regarding the follow-up to the program. Why?

CASE 22–3. EMPIRE MANUFACTURING AND SALES CORPORATION

Mr. Raymond Jensen, chief engineer, is dissatisfied with the salary he is being paid by his company, Empire Manufacturing and Sales Corporation. Believing he is underpaid in comparison to the salaries other managers of the company are receiving, he arranged to talk the matter over with the president, Mr. George B. Dart. During this interview, Mr. Jensen discovered that the entire management compensation arrangement was undergoing study, no current adjustment would be made until the study was finished, and no idea of his compensation under a new plan, if adopted, could be given at this time.

Currently, Empire Manufacturing and Sales Corporation pays its management personnel on a straight salary basis. In the president's opinion, the present arrangement makes reasonable differentiation among the various jobs within the company, and the rates are well in line with industry practices. However, he is not satisfied with the straight salary plan in effect. He believes it provides little motivation and fails to recognize an executive's unusual contribution in a given year. Furthermore, the present salaries are inflexible costs and can't be lowered effectively if the company's sales and profits decline.

Mr. Dart is considering three possible plans but is undecided which one he favors or will try to get adopted if and when the subject comes before the Salary Committee. The three plans are (1) profit sharing, (2) pension, and (3) savings investment.

Under a profit sharing-plan extra income is paid each year, depending upon the profits of the company. In Mr. Dart's opinion, this is the best plan to provide incentive. He reasons it makes each manager feel as if he were in business for himself and encourage a profit-making viewpoint, an essential factor in the company paying higher salaries. To start this plan, Mr. Dart believes average profits of the last four years might be the level at which the current pattern of total compensation would be paid, but it would be made up of 80 percent base salary plus 20 percent derived from profits. In other words, a current base salary of $20,000 would be changed to $16,000 base plus $4,000 from profits. The percentage of profits would be determined to make up this 20 percent manager salary payment. In subsequent years, the percentage of profits could well be a greater number of dollars, depending upon the company's profits.

Next is a pension plan. Several managers of the company have expressed concern about their income after they have retired, but Mr. Dart is of the opinion that most of them have amply provided for their retirements. Still he believes the protection and tax advantage of a pension plan to the managers to be worthwhile. Counsel supplied him indicates the contemplated pension plan would probably be "qualified," or approved, by the U.S. Treasury. Some 47 percent of the company's present managers are over 50 years of age, and from this Mr. Dart reasons that a pension plan would be relatively expensive. He believes there is a popular trend toward pensions, but he doesn't know what the consensus is toward pensions among the company's management personnel.

The third plan is a savings investment plan whereby the managers would contribute regularly 5 percent of their base pay and the company would contribute an equal amount, both contributions being turned over to a trustee for investment in bonds and stocks. Again, advice given Mr. Dart is that the company contributions will be deductible for tax purposes. A manager would not be permitted to withdraw any company contributions until he had been in the plan 10 years or attained the age of 65 years. However, he could withdraw at any time his own deposits. The manager's own deposits have already been taxed, Mr. Dart is interested in finding out whether a savings investment plan would be motivating to his managers.

Questions

1. If you were Mr. Jensen, what would you do? Why?
2. Which of the three compensation plans under consideration by Mr. Dart do you favor? Why?
3. What action should the company take regarding its managerial compensation plan? Discuss.

part VI

Controlling

The fourth and last fundamental function of management to be discussed is controlling. With this discussion of controlling the modified management process of planning, organizing, actuating, and controlling is completed.

The modern meaning of controlling, why it is used, and benefits derived from it, start our discussion of this important function. Subsequently the need to develop self-controlling, the importance of updating controlling techniques to be followed, and the application of controlling to quantity, quality, time use, cost, and budgetary action are presented. The four chapters comprising this section are:

23. *Management controlling*
24. *Overall managerial controls and audits*
25. *Quantity and quality controlling*
26. *Time use, cost, and budgetary controlling*

23

Management controlling

In your area of responsibility, if you do not control events, you are at the mercy of events.

HARLAND SUARE

TO DETERMINE whether the managerial efforts are resulting in the desired goal achievement requires evaluation of the results. If the results are not in keeping with expectancy, then corrective measures are applied. This following up or evaluating and correcting, if necessary, constitute the work of management controlling.

CONTROLLING DEFINED

To many laymen the concept of controlling is synonymous with that of management. To them, one who checks to see what's being accomplished, decides if it is satisfactory, and enforces decisions personifies a management member. This concept, however, is only partially true, for as already stated, controlling is only a part, but an important part, of the entire concept of management.

Controlling is *determining what is being accomplished, that is, evaluating the performance and, if necessary, applying corrective measures so that the performance takes place according to plans.* Controlling includes the active policing of an operation to keep it within defined boundaries and is in the nature of follow-up to the other three fundamental functions of management. It helps to insure that what is planned for is accomplished.

We can view controlling as being made up of a mechanism for detecting and correcting significant variations from the results obtained from planned activities. It is in the nature of things that some errors, loss of efforts, and misdirected directives take place and make for unwanted deviation from the intended goal. So the function of controlling is necessary. But it is important to keep in mind that the purpose of controlling is positive—it is to make things happen, i.e., to achieve the goal within the stated period, or to increase the product's profitability. Controlling should never be viewed as being negative in character—to keep things from happening. Such a view is erroneous in that it is repressive and lacks helpful direction. Controlling is a necessity and a help, not an impediment and a hindrance.

CONTROLLING AND THE MANAGEMENT PROCESS

If the other fundamental functions of management, that is, planning, organizing, and actuating, were performed perfectly, there would be little need for controlling. However, very rarely, if ever, is there planning that is perfect, organizing above any possible reproach, and actuating 100 percent effective. Controlling, in the formalized management meaning of the term, does not exist without previous planning, organizing, and actuating. Controlling cannot take place in a vacuum. It is related to and a part of the outputs of the other three fundamental functions of management. The determination of corrective action, such as improving motivation, or supplying additional capital, are, in essence, practical applications of adjusting the management process in a given case to accomplish the given goal. In other words, the corrective action includes revisions in the planning, organizing, and actuating efforts.

This means that controlling established independently of the broader needs of planning, organizing, and actuating is destined to be ineffective. Controlling must be linked with the other fundamental managerial functions and the more vital the linkage, the more effective the controlling. Since control is essentially the examination of results, it is intimately related to planning, organizing, and actuating which are performed to achieve results.

Planning bears special close relationship to controlling. As already discussed, planning identifies commitments to actions intended for future accomplishments. Controlling is performed to help in seeing to it that the commitments are carried out. Failure of controlling means sooner or later failure of planning, and success of planning means success of controlling. When controlling clearly demonstrates that the planning cannot be implemented, a modified or new plan must be developed. When unacceptable performance under a plan becomes common, the controlling tends to trigger thinking of how best to alter the plan or even to abandon it. Also, to reiterate it is well to note that a plan should identify and specify the controls needed, otherwise it is not a viable plan.

PRINCIPLE OF CONTROLLING

Effective controlling assists in the effort to regulate the planned performance in order to assure that performance takes place as planned.

This close dovetailing of planning and controlling is illustrated in a number of management devices and techniques. Budgetary control is an excellent example. Here the planning or budget figures are developed and then the data on actual operations are added and compared to the budget or planned figures. From this comparison, what corrective action, if any, is determined.[1]

It should be added that controlling helps unify understanding of policies. Consistency in the use of policies is aided by the controlling efforts followed. To illustrate, a sales manager may have a policy that any change in price from the published prices must be authorized in writing by him; no field salesman is permitted to change any price. In effect, this gives clarification of the existent policy and provides control to the sales manager and permits him to know what is going on and exercise regulation and restraint over it.

THE CONTROL PROCESS

Controlling consists of a process made up of several definite steps. Regardless of the activity these same basic steps apply:

1. Measuring the performance.
2. Comparing performance with the standard, and ascertaining the difference, if any.
3. Correcting unfavorable deviation by means of remedial action.

Stated in a slightly different manner, controlling consists of (1) finding out what's being done, (2) comparing results with expectancies, which leads to (3) approving the results or disapproving the results, in which latter case applying the necessary remedial measures should be added.

The concept of the control process is shown graphically in Figure 23–1. At the top, the performance is measured. Then comparison is

---

[1] Budgetary control is discussed thoroughly in Chapter 26.

FIGURE 23–1. The control process

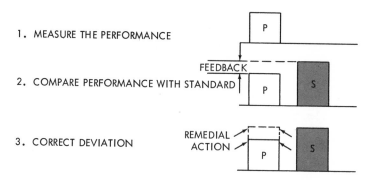

1. MEASURE THE PERFORMANCE

2. COMPARE PERFORMANCE WITH STANDARD

3. CORRECT DEVIATION

made between performance and the standard which is obtained from planning as discussed in Chapter 11. From the comparison of performance to standard, it is determined whether performance is above, below, or the same as the standard. In the figure, the performance is less than that of the standard. From this comparison, the difference between what is done—the performance—and what is expected—the standard —is determined. This differential is termed "feedback," which sets forth the amount of correction necessary to provide satisfactory performance. The last step is to correct the deviation by action deemed proper by the manager.

The place of controlling in the whole management process and the concept of feedback and its relationship in controlling are clearly set

FIGURE 23–2. Controlling and feedback with relationship to planning, organizing, and actuating

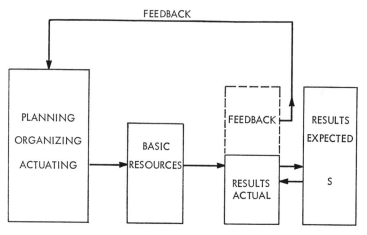

forth in Figure 23–2. Beginning at the left, planning, organizing, and actuating are directed to basic resources with "results actual" being realized. This entity is compared with the results expected, or the standard. The difference between these two (a deficiency in the case illustrated) or feedback shows the amount of correction to be made if the present plan is to be successful. This feedback is directed to planning, organizing, and actuating in order to improve their performance or to modify them so that the actual results equal the expected results.

MEASURING THE PERFORMANCE

The first step of controlling, measuring the performance, starts with a consideration for the problems of measuring. Succinctly stated, measurement is the ascertainment of the quantity or capacity of a well-defined entity. Without measurement, a manager is forced to guess or employ rule-of-thumb methods which may or may not be reliable. Measurement requires a measuring unit and a count of how many times the unit is contained by the quantity of the entity under consideration. In Chapter 11, we discussed the major considerations in measurement under the heading of standards—their establishment and feasibility.[2]

In measuring an entity there is always the question of what characteristics to consider. This can be a challenge that taxes the best imagination. In many cases the most helpful characteristics are (1) output—what specific activities are expected to be performed, (2) capital expenditure—what amount is needed, and what is its relative effective utilization, and (3) cost—what dollar layout for staff people and direct-operative people is reasonable, and how much is it worth to forego opportunities.

In management the entities being measured can be classified into two groups: (1) those concerned with the achievement of a complete program or total accomplishment and (2) those concerned with output per unit of applied direct labor. The former is broad in scope, deals in terms of overall progress, and is normally of most concern to members of the higher organization levels. For such cases the measurement is commonly by objectives. Frequently these are stated in general terms, for example, a research manager developing a particular new product within a stated period or a controller formulating and implementing a cost accounting system within a stated total expenditure. However,

---

[2] See page 239.

results management with its emphasis upon objectives achievement has increased the popularity of using measurement of results at all organizational levels.

Also for top and intermediate levels, profit centers and cost centers can be used. The former measures performance in terms of profits which are generated and achieved by a manager having complete and overall responsibility for the management of a specific organization unit, such as a subsidiary or a division. A profit center is a segment of an enterprise with a designated manager responsible for its income or revenue, expenses, and assets used to sustain operations. It is regarded as an independent firm, its use expedites the application of accounting techniques for measuring the performance of smaller manageable segments. The cost center approach is similar, but here the manager's performance is measured by his achieving a specific quantity of work, such as units produced or sold, at a designated cost.

In the second group or those concerned with output per unit of applied direct labor, a more detailed and precise measurement is normally applied. Why is this? Because it is easier to measure such output than the performance embodying a complete program. For direct-operative employees the performance is confined within a relatively small area and covers direct productivity in its own right. Work which is highly repetitious, requires little judgment, flows at a fairly steady rate, and is entirely objective can usually be measured quite accurately. In contrast, work of a creative nature, irregular in occurrence, and varying considerably in its makeup is difficult to measure. Hence, due to the relative difficulty of measurement, some work is more difficult to control than is other work.

Sometimes it is helpful when confronted with measurement problems for control purposes to think in terms of tangible and intangible achievements. Units produced, cards filed, and samples distributed are tangible measurements. They indicate the count of a number of like units whose total gives a value of relative standing to a known entity. We have given such data considerable attention, subjected them to a great deal of manipulation for analytical purposes, and used them for controlling extensively with a certain surety of validity and fairness. On the other hand, there are many intangible results in the typical enterprise. Data on them cannot be gathered directly, hence dependence upon such means as judgment and indirect clues are used. The development of executives, the building of employee morale, the effectiveness of communication, and the efficiency of purchasing may be cited as a few of the more important intangibles, the activities of which should be under control, yet pose measuring difficulties.

The actual carrying out of measurement of performance is achieved in many different ways. Discussion of some of the more common ways will be deferred until several pages later. At the moment we will proceed to the second step in the controlling process.

COMPARING PERFORMANCE WITH THE STANDARD

Step No. 2 of the control process is comparing performance with the standard. In effect this evaluates the performance. When there is a difference between the performance and the standard, judgment is frequently required to resolve the significance of the differential. To establish a rigid absolute variation or even a range for what is satisfactory is inadequate. Relatively small deviations from the standard merit approval for the performance of some activities, while in other cases a slight deviation may be serious. The manager performing the controlling work must therefore analyze, evaluate, and judge the results as a definite part of this step of the control process.

In this respect, written summaries highlighting what activities are out of line—that is, the spotting of feedbacks—are especially helpful. Further, suggestions from those performing the work or those close to it indicating what control efforts might be taken are pertinent. Usually such information can be written in not more than one page; its effectiveness is in its simplicity. Also, any trend data for the subject showing current, week ago, month ago, year ago, actual with estimated, and percentage of expected performance are helpful. In addition, the indicating of controllable, as differentiated from noncontrollable, items should be included.

Generally speaking, this controlling step of comparing performance with the standard should be done as close to the point of performance as possible. This expedites controlling efforts and assists in locating areas to be corrected and usually results in minimum losses. However, in cases where judgment is a big consideration in determining the meaning of any variation, some delay may be necessary in order to get the control information to the party in authority for the control decision.

In comparing performance with the basis of control, it is *the exception* to which managerial attention should be directed. The manager does not need to concern himself with situations where performance equals or closely approximates the expected results. On the other hand, when a significant variance occurs, control is in order, or at least an evaluation of the situation to determine what, if anything, should be done. Furthermore, concentration on the exceptions necessitates less work, for normally the number of items having significant variances is small compared to the total. This brings up the subject of the managerial principle of exception.

PRINCIPLE OF EXCEPTION

Controlling is expedited by concentrating on the exceptions, or outstanding variations, from the expected result or standard.

This principle is important in controlling. It means that much of the controlling effort is directed to the exceptional cases, or those that do not conform adequately with the standard or basis of control. It is only the exceptional cases that require remedial action. To illustrate, controlling the prices at which 100 items are purchased will probably reveal but 5 prices out of line; that is, these 5 are the exceptions and can be investigated further. Much time and effort are saved in controlling by applying the principle of exception which is always followed by competent managers.

Closely akin to controlling by the exception principle is to control by concentrating on the use of key points only. The innumerable activities of an enterprise preclude the control of every activity. Any attempt to include all facets of an enterprise into a control system results in too many figures to compile and watch, too many details, and too much time spent on attempting to control relatively minor activities. An effective answer is to confine control to activities around key points. This approach is simple yet adequate. The points selected will vary with the type of enterprise but are normally those areas or activities about which other activities tend to cluster. In some instances, so-called bottleneck operations provide adequate key control points. Examples include one person signing all checks (also providing excellent control over expenditures), designating an individual to handle all purchasing, compiling a daily record in dollars of total orders received and total shipments made, and requiring all pay rates and their adjustments, if any, to be authorized and cleared through a particular employee. Also, in a certain large manufacturing company the president concentrates his controlling efforts on five key points: (1) shipments, (2) customers' orders, (3) inventories, (4) production efficiency, and (5) forecasts.

Simple ratios can be worked out among selected key points to provide a quick, meaningful review.

CORRECTING DEVIATION BY MEANS OF REMEDIAL ACTION

This is the third and last step of the control process. It can be viewed as enforcing the seeing-to-it that operations are adjusted or efforts are made to achieve results in keeping with expectancies. Wherever significant variances are uncovered, vigorous and immediate action is not only called for but imperative. Effective control cannot tolerate needless delays, excuses, endless compromises, or excessive exceptions.

The corrective action is put into effect by those having authority over the actual performance. As indicated above, it may involve modification of the planning as, for example a change in method or a new way to check the dimensional accuracy of parts being manufactured. In some instances, an organizational modification may be in order, while in other cases a change in motivation might suffice. Reestablishment of the objective in the employee's mind or a review of a policy and its application may be all that is necessary.

For maximum effectiveness, the correcting of the deviation should be accompanied by fixed and individual responsibility. Holding a particular individual responsible for this work is one of the best means of achieving expectancy. Fixed individual responsibility tends to personalize the work. It becomes his job, his responsibility to take the necessary action to reach satisfactory performance—his responsibility to make any correction which might be necessary. In short, somebody does something about it and that somebody is definite and known.

Remedial action is preferable to corrective action. That is, this last step of the control process implies more than ferreting out trouble and correcting it. The real cause of the difficulty should be uncovered and efforts taken to eliminate the source of the discrepancy. In this way, genuine assistance and cooperation are obtained. In addition, a favorable attitude toward control is achieved, and this is especially important.

OBTAINING DATA ON ACTUAL PERFORMANCE

Let us return now to step No. 1, measuring the performance, and review the means commonly followed in obtaining data for this step. The discussion will be confined to personal observations, oral reports, and written reports. For any of these sources, the precise form may vary. For example, personal observations may take the form of a cursory examination, a concentrated and planned watchfulness over an extended period, or a spot check at random intervals. Written reports may be either compiled individually by manual means or periodically by means of a computer.

PERSONAL OBSERVATIONS

Going to the area of activities and taking notice of what is being done represents one of the oldest means of finding out what is being accomplished. The methods being followed, the quality and quantity of work, attitude of employees, and the general operation of the area are among the types of things which might be observed. There are many who feel that there is no adequate substitute for firsthand direct observation. Advocates of this method believe that the use of direct contacts gives an intimate picture of what is going on and a certain feeling or sense of satisfaction in seeing the work being done and in talking with those doing it.

Many sales executives visit their various sales offices periodically in order to get firsthand information on how sales performance is going and what lines of products are not selling as well as expected. On-the-spot checks can be made with the salesmen, and their reasons for sales surplus or deficiency from the established goal can be obtained. In many instances, calls are made with the local sales supervisor and individual salesmen to check market reactions, advertising effectiveness, and the approach and selling techniques of the salesmen, and to keep in touch with customers.

Personal observation is especially helpful for checking and reporting intangibles. There is probably no satisfactory substitute for observing firsthand the morale of a work group, for watching training efforts being directed upon new recruits, for listening to a prospective customer's reactions to a recently developed product, or for talking over the problems confronted by the junior executives of the enterprise. The personal contact makes for a realistic appraisal and for greater understanding and appreciation of what's behind the data used to measure the particular entity.

On the other hand, use of the personal observation approach has its disadvantages. Foremost is that it does not provide accurate quantitative values, and the information acquired is in broad and general terms. Precision is not obtained. Also, personal observations are time-consuming and take the executive away from his other tasks. Situations requiring immediate attention and decision might be delayed because the executive is somewhere in the shop or in the sales territory. Also, there is the possibility that the good intentions of the executive might be misunderstood by the employees. The practice of having to see for himself might be interpreted as mistrust or lack of confidence in the employees. The practice might even be viewed as unnecessary snooping. Lastly, direct contact at best is limited in many instances to a few employees and happenings; it is neither possible to talk with all employees nor to see all that is going on.

ORAL REPORTS

Another means of measuring performance is oral reports. This may take the form of either a series of interviews or one large group meeting in which informal discussions are held. One common example of oral reports is the practice of salesmen reporting personally to their immediate manager at the close of each business day on the accomplishments, problems, or customers' reactions encountered during the day. The manager not only learns what is going on but also is able to give suggestions and other help to the salesmen. Frequently, oral reports are supplemented with direct observations and personal calls upon customers.

Oral reports maintain certain elements of the personal observation method in that information is transmitted orally and personal contact is included. The facial expressions, tone of voice, and general evaluation of the performance by the reporter can be observed, and questions can be asked at the most opportune time in order to clear any misunderstandings or to gain additional information. Tentative answers to conditions needing remedial action can also be worked out at the time of discussion. Furthermore, oral reports can provide wide and complete coverage, a condition not always possible under the personal observation method.

WRITTEN REPORTS

In all enterprises, but especially the larger ones, written reports are used to provide information on performance. These reports lend themselves to comprehensive data and are adaptable for statistics which are somewhat involved and detailed. Written reports also supply a permanent record, should comparison or study at a future date be desirable.

Frequently, written reports are supplemented by oral reports and direct observation.

There are numerous types of written reports; some are primarily descriptive, others are statistical; some cover limited areas of operations, others deal with the entire enterprise. Figure 23–3 gives some ideas as to the type of control reports used. Reference here is to written reports in general. Discussions of the well-known balance sheets and profit and loss statements are deferred to the following chapter dealing with overall controls.

A written report used for controlling factory work is shown by Figure 23–4. Information is shown by departments on the amount of work, the rate of accomplishment, and the number of employees and

FIGURE 23–3. Various types of control reports are used by a typical company

Report Type	*Information Shown*
Daily machine	Idle machine time, its cause, and cost per hour of operation.
Production control	Factory work ahead of schedule, factory work behind schedule with brief explanations of each. Data are shown by days for four-week period. Possible corrective actions for each lot of work are included.
Area sales	Planned and accomplished sales by territories, products, and salesmen are issued monthly with comparable figures for six months, and for one year ago.
Delivery performance	Actual and planned quantities of undelivered units at end of each day are prepared daily and also in a cumulative weekly and monthly report.
Daily quality	Includes for each inspector the quantity of units inspected, hours worked, units inspected per hour, and quantity of rejected units along with brief comments on reasons for rejection.
Daily accounts receivable	Shows number of sales invoices held for needed additional information, number of nonposted remittances, and number of credit sales not yet posted to customers' accounts.

man-hours. For example, for the week ending February 7, as indicated, in the cutting department there were 7,621 units of work on hand at the beginning of the week. During the week 6,280 units were received and 6,550 units were completed, leaving the amount of work on hand at the end of the week of 7,351 units. More units were completed than received, and so the backlog of units was reduced. To accomplish this, six full-time employees working 240 regular hours and 18 overtime hours were employed. For control purposes these data might be reduced to units produced per man-hour worked and compared with the standard for this type of work. The output and personnel data for the other departments listed are read in the same manner as those of the cutting department. It should be observed that the work output of one department is not necessarily the work received by the next department in the list; that is, the cutting department completed 6,550 work units, but the coiling department received only 784 units. This is attributed to several reasons: (1) the units were not transported to the coiling department during the week and (2) the measurement or meaning of a work unit is not necessarily the same for both departments. In this latter instance, the work unit is determined by the characteristics of the particular work. After the product is completely assembled, the measurement probably will be one unit of the product. This is true in the illustration beginning with the soldering and assembly department, when the various parts are brought together into the finished product.

Measurement of performance reports must be timely. Sometimes

FIGURE 23–4

OUTPUT AND PERSONNEL REPORT							
						Week ending: Feb. 7, 197-	
Department (listed in production sequence)	Work units at beginning of this week	Work received	Work output	Work units on hand at end of week	Number of full-time employees	Total hours worked	
						Regular time	Over-time
Cutting	7,621	6,280	6,550	7,351	6	240	18
Coiling.	845	784	500	1,129	4	152	27
Soldering and assembly	1,012	815	712	1,115	12	474	..
Testing	427	712	805	334	2	80	..
Finishing	714	800	760	754	6	220	8
Shipping	305	700	818	187	4	157	..

preciseness must be sacrificed to supply the report when it is needed and in order to provide maximum assistance. If effective control is to be achieved, excessive delays, lack of material, or shortage of help must be quickly identified. Promptness in receiving performance information assists in determining the difficulty and doing something about it. Allowing too much time to elapse gives the impression that controlling is of secondary importance, persons responsible for an unsatisfactory situation cannot remember critical details, and the real source of the trouble becomes more difficult to uncover.

Reports should be reviewed periodically as to their need. Too frequently the preparation of useless controlling reports is permitted to continue. Also, it is a good practice to include the preferences of the receiver and to keep in mind the use to which the report is put. A receiver usually can utilize most efficiently that which is in keeping with his ideas of what data should be included, how it should be arranged, and the frequency of publication. The sequence of data should be determined by the intended purpose.

A report is intended to inform the reader. Hence, a short interpretation or summary about the performance data is effective. Only pertinent data should be included; as too many data cause confusion and hinder the control work rather than help it. Some advocate the use of whole numbers and the omission of the cents figure in dollar data in order to simplify the report. Such a practice merits consideration.

RESULTS MANAGEMENT AND CONTROLLING

As pointed out in Chapter 3, under results management the employee participates in establishing his own objectives and determining how he intends to achieve these objectives. All this is done with knowledge and participation by his superior so that the objectives are mutually agreed upon. Further, the expected results serve as the standard against which the performance is evaluated.

This approach gives a new concept to controlling. It is not simply an authoritarian follow-up, but becomes viewed as a tool to assist in guiding his efforts and an aid to help in achieving the objectives he has set for himself. Controlling becomes more meaningful and acceptable to the employee under results management. It is something he can use to his advantage as well as to the advantage of the company.

Results management includes appraisal by results. This is a strong motivator. Results are tangible, easily understood, and self-informing—the employee knows "how he is doing." And he can find this out easily on his own and be self-directed. Further, he can self-modify his efforts in a manner that he believes in and will strive to make successful.

Appraisal by results is preferred and used by the true professional. Consider a star big league baseball player. He is big league because of the results he achieves, not the activities he performs. Getting the home run when it is needed, striking out the heavy hitter, or completing a sensational fielding play are illustrative of results and appraisal on that basis is what makes such a player valuable and motivates him to do his best at all times.

CONTROLLING AND THE HUMAN ELEMENT

The human response to controlling is vital. The best controlling is a positive activity enthusiastically demanded by the employee. As stated above, the use of results management makes this condition possible. But if not using the results approach, the enlightened manager should recognize and promote the idea that controlling helps employees to do their work better, to win respect, to contribute to the progress of their work unit. Admittedly checking and reviewing work can bring grim news, but this can serve as a challenge and an opportunity to improve what is being accomplished. Most people gain much satisfaction from doing a good job, and one of the best ways of motivating employees is to expect them to do a good job. This positive element of controlling should always be emphasized.

Specifically what can a manager do? For one thing, he can be aware of the employee's need to know what is expected of him. This is fundamental in any motivational effort to have the employee meet or exceed the expectancy. Also, the astute manager will explain the controls in terms of the need and importance of the activity, its consistency, effect upon co-workers, and so forth. True, such logical arguments may not change the employee's attitude, but a basis for self-rationalization by the employee is provided.

Another suggestion is that the manager should explain the control measurement used. For controlling to succeed, complete understanding of the standard used by both manager and nonmanager should exist. And the same is true for the steps of comparison and the evaluation of results. Any contemplated changes should be thoroughly explained, and the opportunity to discuss them should be given each person to be affected by such changes. Where all parties are qualified and understand the technique of the measurement being used, participation in determining the measurement process can be extremely effective.

Furthermore, in the controlling effort, the manager should take into account specific local factors; that is, some flexibility is necessary, but not to the degree that every gripe results in a change or that sound management practice is evaded. Integrity in the controlling must be maintained. Where it is known, for example, that changing work volume or shifting quality standards directly affect the controls by a known amount, provisions for adjusting them can be made automatically. This adds to the reality and fairness of the controlling.

It is also recommended that "the bottom of the pyramid" approach be followed. This means that the feedback data be given first to the manager and nonmanagers of the bottom units so that they have a chance to take action on how the results are being achieved before those in the higher levels get into the act. Actually this makes for enriching jobs and gives employees some degree of control over their own situation. In some instances reports on a day's work (quantity and quality) are given to nonmanagement members only, who decide and implement the corrective actions, if needed. If the same problem is reported the following day, the information is relayed to the manager of the group and together they (manager and nonmanagers) decide what's to be done about it.

A number of firms have also successfully used relatively unsophisticated arrangements to bring the operative employees into the controlling efforts. In one instance, free coffee and doughnuts for a week are supplied to employees of a department producing 98 percent or more of its total operations in accordance with the established controls, i.e., the feedback is minimal—no corrective actions are required. Contests have also proven successful and can be significant in motivating the use of controls positively.

MAJOR GUIDES TO EFFECTIVE CONTROLLING

It is helpful to recognize the basic characteristics of controlling so that this fundamental function of management can be used advantageously. Controlling results from derivative action and it is nonpermanent. It must be continued to provide current valid data. It provides future-shaping assistance. The orientation is of the future, control reports, for example, are not merely reports of the past. The question to be asked is not only "What did they do in cutting and shaping today?" but also "What are they going to do differently tomorrow?" Furthermore, controlling is concentrated at points or interfaces where change occurs. The control process does not cover an operation in total. This suggests that the location of control points should be selected carefully with especial attention given to avoid strain among organizational relationships. In addition, the mere creating of certain controlling does not guarantee its working successfully. The inception and adoption of the controlling must contain reasonable certainty that it will work. It must be practical and it must have a purpose which is that it is required for fulfillment of a known and stated objective. Another characteristic is that controls must be enforceable. If the controlling effort is directed toward what is really a fantasy, it is likely to produce much resentment by the people involved in it.

Also, it is well to keep in mind that the standard is the key in controlling. This is the basis for the evaluation and the standard should employ some form of measurement—quantitative if possible. Controlling diminishes in effectiveness as standards become inexact. Furthermore, controlling is needed and should continue as long as a plan is being implemented and causing action. When the plan is achieved or discarded, the controlling can be stopped. Lastly, it is the consensus of most managers that multiple controls, not a single one, should be utilized. While the controlling followed should be simple, the use of one type only is commonly inadequate. Economic, financial, social, and technical controls appear necessary.

Actually, managerial controlling consists of what managers believe is necessary for a specific case. Among the more common controls are so-called functional controls such as inventory control, production control, maintenance control, quality control, salary control, sales control, advertising control, and cost control.

Any activity can be controlled with respect to any or all of the following factors (1) quantity, (2) quality, (3) time use, and (4) cost. In fact, these are the controlling factors included in any functional type. To illustrate, sales control deals with controlling sales and this is accomplished by controlling with reference to quantity of sales and to cost of sales. Figure 23–5 shows the interrelatedness between controlling by function and by factor.

Controlling should be subjected to controlling. Actually controlling differs widely in effectiveness and cost. It is entirely possible to have good controlling at low cost and also poor controlling at high cost. The situation is found from time to time where $3,000 is being expended to ensure that 1,000 losses of $1 each are avoided. This is uneconomical. The cure is worse than the disease. In this case, the controlling should be improved so that it is economically sound. Probably a part of the required action is a modification of the existent planning, organizing, and actuating, bringing about the unfavorable current condition.

Adequate authority for the person doing the controlling is also important. Taking the proper corrective action necessitates sufficient authority to accomplish this task. This in turn requires in formal organization the delegation of authority. A person controlling must be free to control; and this means freedom from being buried in details, yet keeping in close touch with what is going on. Usually the person with line authority should handle any corrective measures taken, the staff authority manager being involved only in the control steps of measurement and comparison of performance.

Where it is possible and legal to do so, some companies have found that intercompany comparisons are helpful in overall top-level controlling efforts. By this approach, companies exchange key ratio figures—

not dollars and cents figures—for mutual enlightment. For example, information on machine efficiency, capital requirement to sales ratio, and net worth to fixed assets ratio might be used. For best results, comparison should be on a continuing basis, say from year to year. Deviations indicate departure from the practices of others, but this is not necessarily a danger signal. Conformity need not exist. The devia-

FIGURE 23–5. Controlling by factors or by functions is interrelated

Factors	Functions			
	Production	*Sales*	*Finance*	*Personnel*
Quantity........	Is factory output satisfactory?	Is sales volume up to expectancy?	Is the working capital sufficient for the needs of the enterprise?	Is the work force adequate?
Quality.........	Are specifications for raw materials, dimensions, and test runs being met?	Do the products being sold represent a satisfactory balance among the company's total line of products?	Should bonds, preferred stock, or common stock be utilized?	Are the proper skills available within enterprise and are they utilized?
Time use........	Are the finished products completed within proper periods and shipped on time?	Are salesmen making a sufficient number of calls per day?	Should short-term or long-term borrowing be utilized?	Are individual tasks adequately and fairly measured?
Cost............	Are the dollar expenditures for raw materials and direct labor satisfactory?	Is the cost of advertising, sales promotion, and the sales force satisfactory for the sales being obtained?	Are the interest payments for use of borrowed funds in line with current market?	Does the enterprise's wage structure meet "going levels" of the community?

tions point out areas that might warrant close scrutiny and possible alterations.

Another consideration is to provide predetermined control data, commonly expressed in dollars to operate a unit, to the individual in charge of the work being done. To illustrate, if the expenditures of a department are not to exceed $25,000 for the next quarter, the manager of that department would be informed of this fact and given complete control information to help maintain costs within the predetermined amount. Predetermined amounts of expenditures are usually arrived at by means of a budget which is discussed in Chapter 26.

QUESTIONS

1. Discuss the close relationship between planning and controlling.
2. What is meant by feedback and of what importance is it in controlling?
3. Give several examples of managerial controlling of activities by key points.
4. What is meant by the control process?
5. Discuss the problem of measurement from the viewpoint of controlling achievements of a complete program.
6. Does the use of results management eliminate the use of managerial controlling? Why?
7. Describe the meaning of using the principle of exception in controlling efforts by a manager.
8. Elaborate on the statement, "Managerial control has no single type."
9. Discuss ways the manager might use to obtain a favorable human response to controlling.
10. Enumerate some of the basic characteristics of controlling.
11. Distinguish carefully between the concepts in each of the following pairs: (*a*) bottom of pyramid approach and time use as a factor of controlling, (*b*) controlling and managing, and (*c*) profit centers and measuring intangible achievements.
12. Referring to Figure 23–4, as a manager what control activities would you take based on these data? Explain. Assume the following standards: cutting, 35.4 units per hour; coiling, 2.5 units per hour; soldering and assembly, 1.9 units per hour; testing, no standard; finishing, 3.5 units per hour; and shipping, no standard. Based on these additional data, what control action do you feel is in order? Why?
13. From your experience give an illustration where the principle of exception either should be or is being applied in the controlling of work.
14. For what types of work do you favor the use of personal observations by a manager in order to find out what is being accomplished? Defend your viewpoint.

CASE 23–1. HARRY'S HAMBURGER, INC.

Mr. Harry Kielmann started his first hamburger retail restaurant three years ago. With much work and determination he has, by being quite frugal, built the business to its present size of seven stores. He has had little training in management. His drive and intense desire to be in business for himself has brought him to the level that he is today. Competition is keen, but "Harry's Hamburger" stores have successfully competed. They have always stressed high-quality food, good service, a cheerful atmosphere, and reasonable prices.

Mr. Kielmann feels that he doesn't get enough feedback as to just where his business stands financially, what stores are most profitable, how accurate his information is, how proficient his help is, and similar questions. At the present time he receives a daily "Food Sales Report" from each store manager showing (*a*) dollar sales today, (*b*) total dollar sales this day a week ago, (*c*) total dollar cumulative sales this week. These data for each store are entered on a daily composite sales report which is totaled giving the information for the entire business.

In addition, each store manager prepares daily a "Food Purchases Report." A representative copy of this report is shown in the accompanying illustration, Chart 1. Also, a "Weekly Personnel Report" is prepared by each store manager and mailed to Mr. Kielmann to reach him by Tuesday afternoon of each week. Chart 2 is illustrative of this report.

What amounts to his central office is maintained at store No. 1. Mr. Kielmann manages this store and also the office. He has one female clerk helping with the office work. An outside firm is engaged to prepare accounting statements and to calculate his taxes. The central office handles all purchasing, all hiring of personnel, and specifies how all food is to be prepared and served. In all other matters, the store manager manages his store. He is compensated by a base wage plus a

CHART 1

Store No. __3__		DAILY FOOD PURCHASES REPORT		Manager _Hank Page_ Date ___10/16/7-___	
Items	Purchased	Opening Inventory	Closing Inventory	Sold	Comments
Ground Beef (lbs.)	200	27	135	92	
Hot Dog (units)	60	21	50	31	sales increasing
Potatoes (lbs.)	20	7½	25	2½	
Cheese (lbs.)	5	2	6	1	
Milk (units)	100	83	142	41	
Coffee (lbs.)	—	14	12	2	
Coca-Cola (gallons)	2	6	7	1	
Pepsi-Cola (gallons)	—	7	6	1	
Ice Cream (gallons)	—	13	12	1	sales slow
Other (specify) Napkins (large box)	2	—	1½	½	

percentage of sales over a stated dollar sales amount. For example, the manager of store No. 4 is paid $135 a week plus 2 percent of dollar sales over $1,000 a week. For example, if sales for the week reach $4,000, the manager receives a total gross compensation of $195 ($135 plus 2 percent ($4,000 — $1,000)).

Mr. Kielmann believes he has good managers for his stores and is of the opinion that he has to trust them to be honest in handling money

CHART 2

Store No. 5	WEEKLY PERSONNEL REPORT							Manager Elmer Botts Date 10/19/7-		
Employee	Job	S	M	Tu	W	Th	F	S	Total Hours	Comments
Elmer Botts	Manager	2	9	8½	9	8	5	6	47½	
Bryce Brooks	Cook and Counter Man	8	—	8	8	8	—	8	40	
Ken Early	Counter Man	—	8	8	8	8	—	8	40	
Wm Chamlley	Counter Man	4	8	—	—	—	8	4	24	
Fred Ultzig	Dishwasher	5	7	2		8	8	8	38	
Arturo Cutauro	Utility	—	8	6		8	8	4	34	
Mills Newman	Utility	7	—	4	8	—	8	8	35	

and in making out the reports. From time to time he has attempted to relate data of food purchases with dollar sales, but he finds this most difficult and not at all conclusive. He tends to be guided by and relies heavily upon his experience and knowledge, especially that gained from current operations of the store he is managing.

Questions

1. In general, what types of controls do you feel Mr. Kielmann should have? Explain how he would design and implement one of the controls you suggest.
2. Evaluate the control reports now being used by Mr. Kielmann.
3. What is your reaction to Mr. Kielmann's attitude toward his store managers? Discuss.

4. What recommendations for obtaining improved controlling can you make for Harry's Hamburger, Inc.? Discuss.

CASE 23–2. KAVANAUGH SALES CORPORATION

Last year sales of this corporation were $4.3 million, on which $283,000 profits before taxes were realized. Mr. Kavanaugh, president of the corporation, decided to take measures to improve both sales and profits. After talking with several close business friends at the Oruro Country Club and with his corporation counsel, for whom he had considerable respect, Mr. Kavanaugh formulated his plans to put the corporation in better financial condition. He called a special sales strategy meeting for all of his 42 salesmen.

In several sessions at this meeting, Mr. Kavanaugh made these announcements:

1. The company needs more sales, and more aggressive efforts by the salesmen are imperative.

2. To assist in sales growth, the company has established a market research department headed by Dr. Don Kamura, an experienced researcher in the sales areas in which the corporation now operates.

3. The present schedule of costs of products to salesmen will be adjusted. This is necessary because certain charges now being made for products of the company do not cover their costs. However, in other cases, some reductions in charges by the company may be put into effect.

4. The present sales contract under which each salesman works will remain intact. The company will continue to recognize each salesman as an independent businessman—independent in all his actions and considered an individual, not an employee. Specifically, salesmen will continue to negotiate the price paid by the customer. Whether the margin received by the salesman will remain within the present range of 23 to 25 percent of the selling price to the customer will depend on what price the salesman gets for the product. As mentioned above, the salesman will be billed at a higher price for certain products.

5. A new line of products will be added to those now handled by the company. This new line may be considered by some salesmen as too sophisticated for them to handle. It will require new product knowledge and good, hard selling. This new product line will represent entry by the company into a market which is huge and unit sales for which are much larger than any of the company's present products.

The last two hours of the meeting were given to answering questions by the salesmen. After this, the meeting adjourned.

Six months later the records showed that both sales and profits have seriously declined. The situation is especially critical as the company is operating at higher overhead costs due primarily to the expenditures for market research and promotional efforts for the new product line. Recently Mr. Kavanaugh talked with several key salesmen about making a pro rata charge on each sales order to cover the expenses for market research which is, in the final analysis, being conducted to assist the salesmen make more sales. The salesmen voiced vigorous opposition to such an arrangement. Also, two months ago, in order to compile a manual, the company requested each salesman to describe in writing an experience showing how a new customer was gained, a sales objection overcome, or an old customer reinstated. To date, only one reply has been received by the company.

Dr. Kamura expressed the opinion that the salesmen did not seem interested in improving their compensation and was at a loss to know what to do. Mr. Kavanaugh indicated that if improvements were not soon shown, he would be forced to make some drastic changes.

Questions

1. What is the problem faced by the company?
2. What are your reactions to Mr. Kavanaugh? Discuss.
3. Relate your recommendation to the company managers.

24

Overall managerial
controls and audits

*Opportunities for distinction lie in doing ordinary things
well and not in erratically striving to perform grandstand
plays.*

WILLIAM FEATHER

A POPULAR TYPE of managerial controlling is that of overall controlling, in which the entire enterprise, or a relatively large portion of it, is
considered as a unit. The concept is that of large segments of an enterprise being utilized; it is not confined or applied to a particular activity
or single function. Overall controls provide simple, yet effective, bench
marks for measuring and evaluating performance by major areas of
an enterprise.

Akin to overall controlling and appearing in increasing numbers is
the management audit. It includes a review and evaluation of management either overall or of areas selected for analysis. Usually, certain
selected attributes are employed as guides; the control process is not
followed. Since these audits are closely related to overall controlling,
their inclusion here appears justifiable.

The work of overall managerial controls and audits goes beyond
rendering an opinion on financial statements. More effectiveness
throughout the organization is the modern goal. Recommendations for
managers and their use of basic resources are wanted. Also the degree
to which projects and programs achieve their objectives with what expenditure of time, effort, and money has gained favor. We will discuss
overall controlling first and follow this with comments pertaining to
audits.

CONTROLLING OVERALL PERFORMANCE

The normal tendency is for a manager to get deeply engrossed in a certain specific type of controlling and to concentrate his control efforts on activities in which he has the greatest personal interest. However, keeping a watchful eye upon the overall performance helps a manager to maintain the needed broad viewpoint of management, to see the interrelation of the various activities, and to foster a desired balance among goals and efforts. Further, it helps the manager to see "the forest, not simply the trees."

In the case of a national enterprise having many plants and sales offices throughout the country, the need for overall performance controlling is apparent. Accepting control over each separate unit as being sufficient can lead to autonomy of the enterprise so that it eventually will consist of a series of small units rather than a completely integrated large unit. Furthermore, viewing the entire enterprise as a unit and controlling its action from a single vantage point usually results in maximum coordinated work. Certain activities, like the raising of necessary capital funds, frequently can best be handled and controlled from an overall viewpoint of the entire enterprise.

In addition, controlling overall performance supplies a manager with quick checks on all operations and can save much managerial time and effort. The controlling work is simplified, in that the overall performance is evaluated to determine if the total setup is bringing about the desired end results. Of course, it is possible for the overall performance to be satisfactory while some of the elements of the performance may require remedial action. That is to say, controlling overall performance is helpful but not necessarily conclusive. Controls over limited areas are also needed in order to keep the respective elements of performance within the desired limits.

MAJOR AREAS OF OVERALL CONTROLLING

In the great majority of cases there are eight major overall areas in which controlling should be set. These include (1) market standing of the enterprise, (2) profitability, (3) materials acquisition and usage, (4) employee performance (both managerial and nonmanagerial), development, and attitude, (5) capital or financial resources, (6) productivity, (7) physical resources, and (8) public responsibility. Applying controlling to these broad areas helps to minimize unexplained losses in sales, material, time, profit, manpower, capital, and facilities.

By way of explanation, let us elaborate upon one of the major areas just stated—for example, No. 3, materials acquisition and usage. In what activities of this area is it probably most important to set up and implement controls? First, in purchasing, to insure that competitive bids are sought and accurately recorded, that material specifications, promised delivery dates, and quality are maintained. Second, in receiving, to check authorization to accept materials, identity of materials, quantity by count or weight, damage to materials, packaging, units of shipment, and grade or quality of materials received. Third, in the factory, to determine when to replenish supply of a given material, to prevent distortion of production records leading to faulty material needs, to clear batches of finished production or parts in machine areas when work shift changes, to prevent and discourage waste of materials, and to provide safe, temporary storage for materials on the factory floor and to provide a place where such material is free from pilferage and damage.

COMPARATIVE BALANCE SHEETS

Especially helpful in controlling overall performance is the comparative balance sheet. This is an important accounting document made up of the data from one or more balance sheets of a corporation and for consecutive periods, as quarters or years. A balance sheet is a financial picture of a corporation at a given moment. It itemizes three elements (1) assets, (2) liabilities, and (3) capital, in an accounting statement. Assets are the value of the various items owned by the corporation, liabilities are the amounts owed to various creditors by the corporation, and capital or stockholders' equity is the amount accruing to the corporation's owners. The relationship among these three elements is: Assets equals liabilities plus capital. This is called the balance sheet equation.

Figure 24–1 shows a comparative balance sheet. In this figure it can be observed that during the year the company has grown as a result of enlarging its building and acquiring more machinery and equipment by means of long-term debt in the form of a first mortgage. Additional stock was sold to help finance this expansion. At the same time accounts receivable were increased and work in process reduced. Observe that total assets ($3,053,367) equals total liabilities ($677,204 plus $618,600) plus stockholders' equity ($700,000 plus $981,943 plus $75,620).

A summary of balance sheet items over a relatively long period un-

FIGURE 24–1

COMPARATIVE BALANCE SHEET FOR THE YEARS ENDING DECEMBER 31

ASSETS	*This year*	*Last year*
Current Assets:		
Cash	$ 161,870	$ 119,200
U.S. Treasury bills	250,400	30,760
Accounts receivable	825,595	458,762
Inventories:		
Work in process and finished products	429,250	770,800
Raw materials and supplies	251,340	231,010
Total Current Assets	$1,918,455	$1,610,532
Other Assets:		
Land	157,570	155,250
Building	740,135	91,784
Machinery and equipment	172,688	63,673
Furniture and fixtures	132,494	57,110
Total Other Assets	$1,202,887	$ 367,817
Less accumulated depreciation and amortization	67,975	63,786
	$1,134,912	$ 304,031
Total Assets	$3,053,367	$1,914,563
LIABILITIES		
Current Liabilities:		
Accounts payable	$ 287,564	$ 441,685
Payrolls and withholdings from employees	44,055	49,580
Commissions and sundry accruals	83,260	41,362
Federal taxes on income	176,340	50,770
Current installment on long-time debt	85,985	38,624
Total Current Liabilities	$ 677,204	$ 622,021
Long-Term Liabilities:		
Fifteen-year, 5 per cent loan, payable in each of the years 1958 to 1971	210,000	225,000
Five per cent first mortgage	408,600	
Registered 5 per cent notes payable		275,000
Total Long-Term Liabilities	$ 618,600	$ 500,000
Capital:		
Common stock: authorized 1,000,000 shares, outstanding last year 492,000 shares, outstanding this year 700,000 shares at $1 par value	700,000	492,000
Capital surplus	981,943	248,836
Earned surplus	75,620	51,706
Total Liabilities and Capital	$3,053,367	$1,914,563

covers important trends and gives a manager further insight into overall performance and areas over which adjustments should probably be made. For example, Figure 24–2 shows a 10-year summary of the consolidated financial condition of an enterprise. Data arranged in this manner increase their managerial value.

FIGURE 24–2. Ten-year summary of consolidated financial condition (in thousands of dollars)

	Cash and government securities	Accounts receivable	Inventories	Plant and equipment (net)	Current liabilities	Long-term liabilities	Total stock-holders equity
This year	8,421	9,970	10,500	6,411	5,120	4,800	23,900
Last year	6,491	6,022	9,440	5,820	5,375	5,100	17,130
2 years ago	4,904	4,010	7,780	3,075	3,845	4,200	14,600
3 years ago	3,570	5,320	7,940	3,995	2,427	5,500	12,160
4 years ago	2,322	5,455	7,026	3,112	3,822	2,900	11,740
5 years ago	2,961	4,485	4,951	3,180	2,704	1,750	10,250
6 years ago	2,943	5,148	4,093	2,965	3,193	3,600	8,900
7 years ago	2,153	4,160	5,130	2,687	4,440	3,555	6,775
8 years ago	2,411	2,472	4,190	2,251	4,800	2,270	4,450
9 years ago	2,945	1,540	2,707	1,040	2,272	2,430	3,600

PROFIT AND LOSS STATEMENTS

These statements are another means of overall performance controlling. A profit and loss statement is an itemized financial statement of the income and expenses resulting from the corporation's operations during a stated or accounting period of time. Basically it shows income less expenditure; that is, the income before and after taxes (net income). Figure 24–3 illustrates statements of profit and loss arranged to

FIGURE 24–3

STATEMENT OF PROFIT AND LOSS FOR THE YEAR ENDING JUNE 30			
	This year	Last year	Increase or decrease
Income:			
Net sales	$253,218	$257,636	$ 4,418*
Dividends from investments	480	430	50
Other	1,741	1,773	32*
Total	$255,439	$259,839	$ 4,400*
Deductions:			
Cost of goods sold	$180,481	$178,866	$ 1,615
Selling and administrative expenses	39,218	34,019	5,199
Interest expense	2,483	2,604	121*
Other	1,941	1,139	802
Total	$224,123	$216,628	$ 7,495
Income before taxes	$ 31,316	$ 43,211	$11,895*
Provision for taxes	3,300	9,500	6,200*
Net Income	$ 28,016	$ 33,711	$ 5,695*

* Decrease.

expedite data comparison for two consecutive years. In this illustration the net sales for the enterprise have decreased while expenses have increased, resulting in a lower net income. From comparative statements of this type, a manager can locate troubled areas and set out to correct them. Some managers draw up tentative profit and loss statements as plans and use such statements as goals toward which to strive. Performance is measured against these goals which amount to standards for control purposes.

Controlling by profit and loss is applied most commonly to an entire enterprise or, in the case of a consolidated corporation, to its subsidiaries. In any of these cases, it is of prime importance that whoever is in charge of the overall controlling has adequate authority to control. As mentioned in the last chapter, adequate authority is needed to make controlling effective, but especially is this true when profit and loss statements serve as the control media.

When departments of an enterprise are the units used for controlling, a profit and loss statement is drawn up for each department. Thus, the contribution of each department to net income of the entire enterprise is ascertained. In essence, this approach amounts to each department's output being measured along with charging so much cost, including overhead, to each department's operation. The department's achievement of showing a net income of an expected amount is considered a standard for measuring its performance. To illustrate, suppose a manufacturer has three departments: punching, welding, and assembling. The punching department produces and sells its products and services to the welding department, which in turn sells its products and services to the assembling department. Each department is thought of as a separate enterprise with its own applicable profit and loss statement. This approach works out satisfactorily for departments that produce tangible or physical results. However, where a department's output is predominantly intangible, as for example with certain staff and service units, control by profit and loss statements is unsatisfactory and other media should be used.

CONTROL REPORTS

There are also a variety of additional reports which serve to expedite the control process. For purposes here we have termed them "control reports." Illustrative is Figure 24–4, which shows pertinent data on production and shipments, factory operations, and finances. By studying the data and comparing them with other like control sheets in this

FIGURE 24–4. An effective form for periodic report used for control purposes

No._____	CONTROL SHEET				
Year._____	THE MARK MERRIMAN MANUFACTURING CO.				
				Week ending:_____	

PRODUCTION AND SHIPMENTS:

	This Week		Cumulative This Month		Same Period Last Year	
	Amount (Dollars)	Percentage of Expectancy	Amount (Dollars)	Percentage of Expectancy	Amount (Dollars)	Percentage of Expectancy
Orders.						
Production.						
Shipments						
Orders unfilled . . .						

FACTORY OPERATIONS:

	This Week	Cumulative This Month	Same Period Last Year
Total direct man–hours.			
Total indirect man–hours.			
Percentage of plant capacity			
Material scrapped (dollar value).			
Number of employees added to payroll. .			
Number of employees subtracted from payroll			

FINANCE:

Cash on hand	Accounts payable . . . .
Balance in bank	Bank loans. . . . .
Deposited in bank	Other payments or loans. . . . .
Accounts receivable.	_____ . . . .
Accounts past due	_____ . . . .

series, a manager can know what is going on. On items warranting further investigation, other written reports showing the source and more detailed information would be consulted. For example, under material scrapped, it might be helpful to find out what departments are responsible for the loss and the reasons for the spoilage.

KEY RATIOS OF TOTAL ACTIVITIES

Helpful checks on overall performance of an enterprise can be obtained by the use of key ratios. This technique has been employed by many managers for some time. Most of these ratios are determined from selected items in the balance sheet and the profit and loss statement. A ratio is the numerical relationship between two numbers. Analysis by ratio is the process of determining the relations of selected items in accounting statements. Some ratios have wide recognition and acceptance. Many are helpful in indicating possible weaknesses in a corporate operating structure. Any ratio must be interpreted and evaluated to give it meaning and this must take into account its sources, the accuracy of the factors from which the ratio is calculated, and its probable relative value and meaningfulness to the operations of the company. In other words, the limitations of any ratio used in controlling must be recognized. The precise identity of a factor used in a ratio is always important. For example if investment is being considered, the questions arise, "What is investment? Is it the total amount or should it be reduced by reserves?" Those who do not reduce investment by depreciation justify their position by pointing out that write-offs represent funds available and, in most cases, used in other fixed assets. On the other hand, to reduce investment by reserves eliminates possible fluctuation in operating investment and prevents possible ensuing distortion in the ratio results.

Many managers use comparisons of ratios of various types to measure results and to reveal emerging problem areas. Comparisons within a company or among comparable companies are sensible, for such comparisons are pertinent and valid. On the other hand, when a company's ratios are compared to those of a dissimilar company or to those of an unknown and arbitrary industry classification of companies, the analyses are meaningless because the samples are neither representative nor comparable.

There is danger in calculating too many ratios—for to interpret too large a number for a given corporation may pose extreme difficulty and a complicated maze of probabilities that almost defy application. Ratios are not ends in themselves but possible indicators of what has taken place. And they always should be affiliated with the setting from which they were determined. Some managers, reluctant to use ratios for overall controlling, state that such ratios place too much emphasis on certain concepts and place excessive rigidity into a manager's work. Too much emphasis upon the ratio of sales to inventory, for example, may relegate other considerations, quite important, to a secondary position. That is, such things as research, product development, managerial development, and progressive personnel practices may not be given sufficient attention. Such viewpoints appear to have merit, and in the interest of adequate balance the manager may temper his use of ratios with other control media.

FIGURE 24-5. Balance sheet and other pertinent data

PEGGY LYNN PRODUCTS COMPANY
BALANCE SHEET
December 31, 197–

Current assets:

Cash:			
Cash in bank..........................	$ 32,846.85		
Petty cash fund......................	300.00	$ 33,146.85	
Accounts receivable...................	$173,465.30		
Less: Reserve for doubtful accounts.....	6,118.25	167,347.05	
Inventories:			
Raw materials........................	$123,655.40		
Work in process......................	60,521.62		
Finished goods.......................	177,831.70	362,008.72	$562,502.62
Fixed assets:			
Land................................	$ 28,500.00		
Building............................	$156,620.00		
Less: Reserve for depreciation.......	22,050.00	134,570.00	
Machinery and equipment.............	$248,300.00		
Less: Reserve for depreciation.......	40,500.00	207,800.00	370,870.00
Deferred charges....................	$ 2,380.00		
Unexpired insurance.................	6,750.40	9,130.40	
			$942,503.02

Current liabilities:

Notes payable:			
Bank...........................	$50,000.00		
Trade..........................	13,925.00	$ 63,925.00	
Accounts payable....................		87,058.77	
Accruals............................		11,571.25	
Federal income tax..................		87,000.00	
Other taxes.........................		16,948.00	$266,503.02
Funded debt:			
First mortgage 4½% bonds...........			100,000.00
Capital stock:			
Common stock—par value $1.00 per share; authorized 500,000 shares, issued and outstanding 400,000 shares............			400,000.00
Surplus.............................			176,000.00
			$942,503.02

Tangible net worth.................	$ 576,000.00	
Net working capital................	295,999.60	
	$562,502.62	
	266,503.02	
Total sales........................		2,100,000.00
Earnings...........................		175,000.00
Average number of employees........		100

RATIO ANALYSIS ILLUSTRATED

Representative of the more common ratios are (1) current assets to current liabilities, (2) sales to inventory, (3) revenue created per employee, (4) transaction time, (5) fixed assets to tangible net worth, (6) current liabilities to tangible net worth, (7) funded debt to net worth capital and (8) return on investment. We will show how these ratios are calculated and discuss each briefly, but ratio analysis is too vast a subject to be treated here in any detail. Figure 24–5 shows the balance sheet of the Peggy Lynn Products Company for the year ending December 31, 197–. The following ratios are calculated from data given in this figure and are shown in Figure 24–6.

1. Current Assets to Current Liabilities. This ratio is sometimes called the "net working capital ratio." It provides an indication of the extent to which current assets may decline and still be adequate to pay current liabilities. In the illustration, the ratio is 2.11, which is generally considered satisfactory. Some analysts place a ratio of 2 to 1, or 2.00, as the desirable minimum.

FIGURE 24–6. Ratios determined from data in Figure 24–5

1. Current assets to current liabilities:
$$\frac{562,502.62}{266,503.02} = 2.11$$

2. Sales to inventory:
$$\frac{2,100,000.00}{362,008.72} = 5.80 \text{ times}$$

3. Revenue created per employee:
$$\frac{\frac{2,100,000}{12}}{100} = \$1,750$$

4. Transaction time:
$$\frac{362,008.72 \times 365}{2,100,000} = 62.8 \text{ days}$$

5. Fixed assets to tangible net worth:
$$\frac{370,870.00}{576,000.00} = 64.4\%$$

6. Current liabilities to tangible net worth:
$$\frac{266,503.02}{576,000.00} = 46.3\%$$

7. Funded debt to net working capital:
$$\frac{100,000.00}{295,999.60} = 33.8\%$$

8. Return on investment:
$$\frac{175,000}{942,503.02} = 18.6\%$$

2. Sales to Inventory. This ratio does not reflect true inventory turnover because sales are at selling price and inventory is at cost. Furthermore, the data are for the year end; they are not average figures for the year. A value of 5.80 times, as found in the illustration, is probably lower than it should be. Either sales should be increased or inventory reduced. This latter course merits further analysis. For example, current assets exclusive of inventories are only about 75 percent of current liabilities, a situation which might prove serious if inventories become difficult to dispose.

3. Revenue Created per Employee. This is for a definite period, usually one month, and is calculated by dividing the dollar shipments by the average number of employees. To illustrate, monthly shipments can be considered as total sales, $2,100,000 divided by 12, or $175,000, which amount divided by the average number of employees, 100, gives $1,750 per employee per month. What constitutes a satisfactory ratio depends upon the type of enterprise, but most analysts believe that the range is between $1,500 and $2,000 per employee per month. If the revenue per employee is too low, it usually signals that there is idle production time, methods are poor, sales are being missed, or incorrect sellings prices are being used.

4. Transaction Time. This is the time required to carry out the entire operation of providing form and place utility to the products and services by the enterprise. Transaction time is found by dividing the average inventory by the net shipments. Frequently a time period of one year is used to avoid wide fluctuation in this value. In our illustration we will use the inventory amount at the end of the year, which is the only inventory figure available and consider sales equal to shipments. The transaction time is then equal to inventory, $362,008.72, multiplied by 365 (number of days in one year), divided by net shipments, $2,100,000, or 62.8 days. Transaction time varies considerably with the type of enterprise. For meat packers and foundries, the value may be around 20 to 25, whereas for canneries it may be as high as 100. When transaction time of an enterprise is excessively high for its particular industry, it frequently means inadequate control over the amounts produced, too much paper work, excessive delays, or incomplete inventory control.

5. Fixed Assets to Tangible Net Worth. If this ratio is too high, it indicates that too much of the firm's net worth is tied up in fixed assets, that is, land, building, and machines. Comparisons with past experience of the enterprise and with others in the same general business are desirable. When this ratio is too high, it means probably that the firm is short of capital for current assets and will be obliged to borrow. In this illustration, the ratio figures 64.4 percent, which seems higher than it should be. Based on this ratio alone, either the fixed assets should be reduced or the tangible net worth increased.

6. *Current Liabilities to Tangible Net Worth.* For the business illustrated, this ratio is 46.3 percent, an amount which appears reasonable and satisfactory. With the information from ratio No. 5 above, that fixed assets are probably out of line with tangible net worth, either current liabilities or funded long-term debt may be out of line, since both current liabilities and funded debt plus tangible net worth constitute the entire right side of the balance sheet and equal total assets on the left side. Ratio No. 6 shows current debt is satisfactory so that the funded or long-term debt probably is the one needing adjustment and could be increased in the case illustrated.

7. *Funded Dept to Net Working Capital.* When this ratio is excessive, the working capital might be depleted to amortize the funded debt. In this illustration a value of 33.8 percent is obtained. There is no apparent danger in this case; as a matter of fact, the funded debt could be a little higher without hindering the company's operations.

8. *Return on Investment.* Many managers have adopted the use of this ratio in their overall controlling. It is a rate of return from capital, not an amount or rate of profits. It can be viewed as a ratio of profit to capital employed. The ratio can be calculated for any base, be it a group of machines, an organizational unit, or the entire company. However, it is most satisfactory for a large organization unit and preferably for the entire company. It is difficult, for example, to determine the earnings derived from sales, and their cost, from the output of one machine.

Advocates of return on investment believe it is the best single measurement of performance. It can be compared with opportunities elsewhere and it focuses attention upon how successful the results are in making the best use of capital employed or how effective assets are to generate profit. A single comprehensive figure is derived and from year to year such data are useful in comparing and noting trends. In addition, a manager can quickly detect factors affecting return on investment; and direct efforts to remedy the situation can be undertaken intelligently. In general, it is beneficial to do any of the following (1) increase sales, (2) reduce costs, or (3) reduce the amount of invested capital, while holding the other two constant.

On the other hand, it should be recognized that return on investment is not a perfect ratio. Many feel it should be used along with other performance measurements. One problem is that the measurements used in return on investment are difficult to come by. Valuing long-lived assets or inventory is illustrative. An exact measurement of total investment is likewise difficult. In addition, the investment decisions should be made by the same manager against whose efforts the return on investment is being used. If he does not have control over investments the validity of the ratio is open to question. Furthermore, return on investment is valid at the planning stage, but not in the short-range responsive control process. When it is decided to keep an operation active, it makes little difference whether 1 percent or 30 percent is earned. The commitment has been made. What does matter is this: Are the results better or worse than the plan anticipated? Finally, the question can be raised whether it is reasonable to expect all assets to show similar returns since the nature of the enterprise and objectives differ considerably among enterprises.

The return on investment, R, is equal to E, the earnings, divided by I, the total investment. Expressed algebraically:

$$R = \frac{E}{I}$$

An alternative and popular means of calculating the ratio is to multiply the turnover of sales, or sales divided by investment, by the earnings divided by sales. Expressed as a formula:

$$R = \frac{S}{I} \times \frac{E}{S}$$

For our illustrative company, the return on investment is found by dividing earnings ($175,000) by investment ($942,503.02) giving 18.6 percent. This appears reasonably satisfactory. Some companies attain 25–28 percent, while many are in the 10–12 percent bracket.

Based on these various ratios as a group and reviewing Figure 24–6 it can be stated that the Peggy Lynn Products Company is in a reasonably satisfactory condition. The net working capital appears adequate, current liabilities are not excessive, and the company is not in need of funds. The funded debt could be increased without harm to the company. The fixed assets may be slightly larger than desirable; but with time and due to depreciation, they will decrease. In contrast, the tangible net worth should increase as continued favorable operations are maintained and surplus is increased. The present level of sales appears reasonably good but if possible should be increased through price adjustments or greater output with existent facilities.

RETURN ON MACHINE INVESTMENTS

Although not a return on investment from the overall view of the entire enterprise, another somewhat similar, but special type of return is that of return on machine investment. Discussion of this type of return will be included here.

Labor cost reduction is a major consideration in machine selection, but translating the estimated savings into a return on machine investment poses a real problem. However, the arrangement shown by Figure 24–7 offers an effective approach. In the illustration the cost of the new

FIGURE 24–7. Computing return on machine investment

WORK SHEET
The cost of the new machine is $9,000

	Old Machine	New Machine
Direct labor costs per hour	$1.50	$1.70
Extra direct labor costs per hour	0.27	0.20
Total	$1.77	$1.90
Divided by number of parts produced per hour	110	200
Total direct labor cost per piece	$0.0161	$0.0095

The new machine produced *1,500* pieces per day (7½ hours running time per day)

At *0.0161* per piece on old machine, they would cost	$24.15
At *0.0095* per piece on new machine, they would cost	14.25
Labor savings per day	$ 9.90
Annual savings, labor (5-day week, 50 weeks per year)	$2,475.00

Desirable annual rate of recovery of capital invested in the new machine, assuming it has a 10-year* profitable life (1/10 of cost) ... $ 900.00
Amount recovered annually tax-free by 20-year* depreciation schedule (½ of above) ... $ 450.00
Additional amount to be recovered annually out of excess of income over cost ... $ 450.00

Earnings required annually before taxes (at 43%) to recover above amount (above figure divided by 0.57) ... $ 789.47
Annual capital recovery required over the 10-year period; *$450.00* from depreciation plus *$789.47* from profit before taxes ... $1,239.47

Total annual savings ... $2,475.00
Required annually for recovery of capital ... $1,239.47

Annual net return on investment ... $1,235.53
Rate of annual return on capital invested; annual net return of *$1,235.53* divided by *$9,000.00*, the cost of the new machine ... 13.73%

* These periods vary, of course, depending on the nature of the machine and the product.

Source: Format of work sheet through Courtesy of National Machine Tool Builders' Association.

machine is $9,000, with direct labor cost per hour of $1.70, extra direct labor costs per hour estimated at $0.20, and a machine capacity of 200 parts per hour. Comparable data for the old machine are direct labor, $1.50; extra direct labor, $0.27; and capacity, 110 pieces. This information is shown at the top of the illustration; and by simple arithmetic, the value of the total direct labor cost per piece for the old machine and for the new machine are shown. Next the direct labor savings in using the new machine are calculated. In this case the amount is $9.90 per day, or $2,475 per year.

Consideration for depreciation allowance and federal income taxes is now made. Experience shows that, owing to design changes and improvement, many machines have relatively short lives; hence the investment should be entirely recoverd from earnings before a later model or new type of equipment brings obsolescence to existent machines. In the illustration, a 10-year straight line period is used. At the same time, the U.S. government may not allow this rate of recovery, and for tax purposes the period defined by the government must be used. For depreciation, the figure of 20 years is arbitrary and is used in the illustration. Should the company elect to use the now permitted "fast write-off," the period is shortened considerably from the 20 years. Referring again to Figure 24–7, the desirable annual rate of recovery of capital invested is one tenth of the original machine cost, or $900. The amount recovered tax free, based on a 20-year depreciation, is one half of $900, or $450. Assuming the company is in the 43 percent income bracket, the earnings required annually to recover $450 or $789.47, which added to the depreciation cost of $450 equals $1,239.47, the total amount required for recovery of capital. The difference between this figure, $1,239.47, and the total annual savings to be realized from the machine, $2,475, represents the annual net return on investment. In the illustration this amount is $1,235.53, which based on the machine cost of $9,000 represents a 13.73 percent return on machine investment. Or stated another way, over a 10-year period, the investment in the machine will be fully recovered and at the same time $1,235.53 will be earned annually, representing a return of 13.73 percent per year.

In some instances it may appear advisable to rebuild the present machine rather than to replace it with a new one. To determine whether such a course should be followed, an analysis similar to that just discussed can be utilized. Usually significant gains in the output per hour are not realized from a rebuilt machine.

It is suggested that the work sheet illustrated in Figure 24–7 be used in cases where (1) obsolete machines are not fully depreciated and (2) fully depreciated machines are still operating. In the former case, the amount of unrecovered investment can be charged to the company's profit and loss account. If the used machine is sold, the amount received can be used to reduce the loss. To charge unrecovered investment to the price of a new machine tends to decrease the rate of return on the new machine investment. Likewise, in the second case, that of a fully depreciated but still operating machine, the amount realized by its sale should not be deducted from the price of a new machine because such a practice tends to increase the rate of return on the new machine investment. An alternate practice is to consider the difference in investment required. Under this practice the unrecovered cost of the old machine is not added to the cost of the new machine but net receipt from the old machine when sold is deducted from the cost of the new machine.

ACCOUNTING AUDITS

Verification of the array of reports and statements such as those discussed above is accomplished by accounting audits. The periodic inspection of accounting records, to see that they have been properly prepared and are correct, assists in overall controlling. Checks are made of the accuracy of records, and at the same time review and appraisal of projects, activities, and procedures can be made. Comparisons between what was expected to be accomplished and what actually is being accomplished can be made, any deviations revealed, and suggestions offered for remedial action. Unfortunately, suggestions by accounting auditors are commonly not given sufficient attention by the operating manager, usually because he doesn't fully understand the reasons for the particular recommendations or the auditor fails sufficiently to impress the manager that remedial action is needed. The auditing of accounting records and reports is performed by members of an outside firm of public accountants. To know that the records are accurate, true, and in keeping with approval accounting practices forms a reliable base for sound overall controlling purposes.

THE MANAGEMENT AUDIT

The periodic assessment of a company's managerial planning, organizing, actuating, and controlling compared to what might be called the norm of successful operation is the essential meaning of management audit. It reviews the company's past, present, and future. The areas the company covers are examined with a view to determine whether the company is achieving maximum results out of its endeavors. A management audit cannot be conducted until the company has been operating a sufficient time to establish its behavior pattern.

1. A check on new policies and practices for both their suitability and compliance.
2. Identification of major areas needing shoring up.
3. Promotion of better use of company staff organizational units, especially when audit is conducted by company personnel.
4. Improved communication that informs all employees on the "state of the company."
5. Measurement of extent to which current managerial controls are effective.

Management auditors concern themselves with the broad scope and deal with the interrelatedness of activities and the absence of needed activities—all in their proper relation with set objectives. They do not appraise individual performance. Results discovered are given in an audit report which is written from a viewpoint and style designed to set forth clear statements of results and recommendations and to make them as impersonal as possible. The job of the auditor is to audit; implementation of his recommendations is the prerogative of the manager having the particular authority for the activity under question. The custom is to provide one inclusive audit report from each audit. In addition, however, it is an excellent practice to provide an audit report covering a specific area direct to the manager who can make the change recommended. In other words, if a manager can make a desired change, an audit report should go to him.

Any attempt to audit an activity as pervasive, important, and dynamic as management is certain to be fraught with great difficulty. Imponderables must be overcome, concepts created, and new management trails blazed. Among the management needs is knowledge of value formulation, what relative importance do we and should we attach to people, new products, opinions of customers, attitudes, and so forth.

IDENTIFYING AREAS FOR AUDIT

A number of techniques can be followed by the management auditor to identify areas warranting a penetrating examination. We will briefly consider here some of the more common means. First is the reviewing of internal reports that managers utilize to obtain data on progress, accomplishment, and present status of work. Of special interest are disclosures of projects upon which management has not acted. Inquiries about such inaction and its justification may point out weaknesses that need correction.

Second is to select key systems or procedures used by the company and follow them from start to finish. This approach provides an insight into the present efficiency and the way the work is being done. For example, by noting the capabilities of the personnel involved, the usefulness of the prescribed systems and procedures, and the degree of participation by employees in what areas and in what manner, the audit can uncover possible inadequacies and suggest possible areas or improvement.

Also, interviews with managers and nonmanagers are an important source of valuable information. Discussion with responsible personnel must be handled carefully. Prior to any formal interview, the interviewer should have some background and knowledge of the company so that constructive and pertinent questions can be asked. Also, the atmosphere should be conducive to response. Whom to talk with is significant and the selection should be made only after appropriate thought has been given to this consideration.

ATTRIBUTES USED IN AUDITING

To perform a management audit it is necessary first to set up a list of qualifications desired with the credit valuation attached to each. The selection and respective weights given these qualifying factors are highly flavored with judgment and in many cases, quite controversial. The audit itself assesses (1) what the company has done for itself and (2) what it has done for its customers or recipients of the products or services provided. To reach these assessments, evaluations on a number of factors may be deemed necessary and include attributes dealing with financial stability, production efficiency, sales effectiveness, economic and social affluence, personnel development, earnings' growth, public relations, and civic responsibility.

Figure 24–8 shows a list of twelve qualifications for use in the management audit of an advertising agency. The attributes are divided into three main groups and under each one are listed specific qualifications. The maximum points assigned to each attribute are indicated. For example, the highest value is accorded creative services with a maximum of 215 points.

FIGURE 24–8. Attributes and relative weights for use in a management audit of an advertising agency

MANAGEMENT AUDIT

Maximum Points

1. Overall
   a. General reputation.. 50
   b. Financial stability.. 60
   c. Increase in billings of 15 percent per year....................... 65
   d. Retention of clients... 75
2. Work within agency
   a. Objectives stated and sought..................................... 100
   b. Policies and practices pursued................................... 60
   c. Employee relations... 90
   d. Vendor relations... 50
3. Outside work with clients
   a. Creative services.. 215
   b. Contact work with client... 90
   c. Contact work with trade.. 70
   d. Advertising budget and media recommendations.................... 75
   Total... 1000

When an intelligent buyer of a manufacturing company seeks to evaluate a possible purchase, he normally looks into a number of factors concerning the prospective company. Although his purpose and proposed action differ from that of the management auditor, it is of interest

FIGURE 24–9. Some factors considered in evaluating a potential acquisition

1. The history of the business.
2. Present audited financial statements.
3. Summary of financial statements for past ten years.
4. Estimated operating statements.
5. Trend in total number of employees, by skills.
6. Labor relations history and present status.
7. Appraisal of working conditions.
8. Compensation methods used.
9. Personnel policies followed.
10. Present formal organization chart and manual.
11. List of machines including age and condition.
12. Production work load for past year.
13. Principal materials used and purchasing methods.
14. Amount and description of inventory.
15. Trends in product sales performances.
16. Forecasts, both short- and long-term, of sales expectations by product lines.
17. Ten-year forecast for industry of which company is a member.
18. Review of competitive practices including products, share of market, pricing practices, and channels of distribution used.
19. List of research and engineering facilities.
20. Credit report from banks.

to review quickly some of the considerations which a buyer investigates for whatever help and suggestions they may provide in planning a management audit. Figure 24–9 lists common factors considered in investigating possible acquisition. The list is suggestive only and would be modified depending upon the individual case and conditions.

AUDIT BY FOUR PUBLICS

The efforts of most managers are judged by the four publics: customers, employees, community, and suppliers. How they rate their impressions of the enterprise provide clues to the effectiveness of the general

FIGURE 24–10

An Enterprise Is Believed Well Managed by—	
Customers when—	*Employees* when—
1. Products are up to standard. 2. Salesmen call regularly. 3. Deliveries are made when promised.	1. Effective supervision is supplied. 2. Good work facilities and environment are provided. 3. Participation is practiced in matters affecting them.
Community when—	*Suppliers* when—
1. Managers contribute some of their time to community affairs. 2. Facilities are attractive. 3. Cultural projects are supported.	1. Bills are paid promptly. 2. Orders are stated clearly. 3. Standard or regular merchandise is utilized whenever possible.

management, especially in controlling. Figure 24–10 suggests factors that these publics commonly consider.

AUDIT BY AIM

AIM stands for the American Institute of Management, which appraises the management of enterprises by means of comparative audit or examination. For this purpose, ten basic categories are used, having a total value of 10,000 points. The categories include economic function, corporate structure, health of earnings growth, fairness to stockholders, research and development, directorate analysis, fiscal policies, production efficiency, sales vigor, and executive evaluation. Different maximum attainable ratings are given these categories; for example, a maximum of 2,400 points is assigned to executive evaluation.

The Institute's personnel perform the evaluation. To guide their efforts, several hundred questions are used. For example, under the factor "economic function," the evaluator seeks to answer questions such as the following:

1. Has the competitive standing of the company in its industry risen since the company was founded?
2. What important changes have occurred in management since the company's inception and why did these occur?
3. What contribution do the company's operations make to the national economy, regardless of the size of the company?

The analysts secure answers not only from sources within the enterprise, such as executives, but also from sources outside of the enterprise. Ratings based on facts are preferred, but where the rating involves judgment and interpretation, confirmation of the available information used in this connection is sought.

Efforts to appraise the management of an enterprise deserve laudation. The proper basis for such appraisal, terminology, difficulties, and appropriate standards poses problems and elicits differences of opinion. But one of the first steps toward improvement is to measure current achievements. The effort to appraise management is commendable; in itself it helps locate areas where improvements in management can be made.

QUESTIONS

1. As a manager do you feel you could do a reasonably good job of controlling without the use of overall controls? Justify your answer.
2. For the ratios of total activities included in this chapter, would you say that they are related or unrelated? Explain your answer.
3. What are the trouble spots of areas needing attention as revaled by the data of Figure 24–3?
4. Distinguish between the two terms in each of the following pairs: (*a*) profit and loss statement and current liabilities to tangible net worth, (*b*) an overall control and the validity of a control ratio, (*c*) accounting audit and management audit.
5. Enumerate some advantages and some disadvantages in using ratios for overall controlling purposes. Do you favor the use of ratios for such purposes? Justify your answer.
6. As president of a manufacturing company would you favor the use of return on investment in your overall controlling? Why?
7. Enumerate six major areas for which overall controlling is usually desirable.
8. Justify the identifying of Figure 24–4 as a "control report."
9. Elaborate on the overall controlling of the major area of productivity

pointing out in what activities of this area you feel it would be important to set up and implement controls.

10. Discuss some common means for identifying areas for a management audit.

11. Name four benefits derived from a management audit. Discuss one of these in detail.

12. What is indicative to the manager of the ratio, fixed assets to tangible net worth? Of the ratio, return on investment?

13. Discuss the selection and use of attributes in making a management audit.

14. How effective do you feel audit of an enterprise by the four publics is? Why?

CASE 24–1. MADDEN CORPORATION

April 3, 197–

Dear Fellow Madden Stockholder:

You have now received Madden Corporation's Annual Report for 197–. In it the statement is made that Madden is improving its public image and that during the year, working capital was conserved, common dividends paid, and a retirement of part of the corporation's debt was paid.

We submit that it is time to make a change in the management of our company. A committee has been formed to elect a new Board of Directors which is essential to realize Madden's potential. As a stockholder we ask your support and help in bringing about this badly needed change. Incidentally, I personally own 500 shares of Madden.

To support our viewpoint, may we call your attention to some important facts. By examining the data of the annual report recently received you will find that net operating income *per share* decreased. The increase in net income, as shown by the report, is fallacious as a portion of it was realized from returns from capital derived from additional sales of common stock. Also, sales of certain physical facilities were made. Had this not been done, there would have been a decrease in working capital instead of the increased $7.4 million shown in the report. The additional sales of common stock also account for the increase in stockholders' equity of some $4.4 million which otherwise would have shown a decrease of about one-half million dollars.

Furthermore, paying dividends of 40¢ when the corporation earns only 32¢ a share places your company in jeopardy. This dividend was not fully earned from net operating income. No company can indefinitely maintain dividend payments based partly on extraordinary items or retained earnings from prior years.

I am sure you are aware of the fact that the market value of the common stock of your company is now at the lowest level it has been in the last six years. From a range of $64–33 per share six years ago, the range has steadily decreased until during the past year it was $31–14 with a close at the end of last month of 15½.

Yet the present managers keep making favorable statements regarding the rosy future of Madden. For example, in the annual report two years ago, Mr. Culpepper, our president, wrote, "Looking ahead, we view the future with keen anticipation of maintaining a high rate of growth in sales and profits." Last year, Mr. Culpepper stated, "Continued cost reduction programs and the introduction of new products should make this year the best ever in all Madden's history." Then this year, "We will look forward with confidence to the future progress of the corporation."

We invite you to join us in expressing dissatisfaction with the present management. Sign, date, and return your *blue* proxy. The latest dated proxy returned by you is the one that counts. You can change your mind so send in your *blue* proxy now.

Thank you very much.

Richard M. Kettler (s)
Chairman
Committee for Stockholders Protection

Excerpted material from the recent annual report follows:

Five-year financial summary (dollars in thousands)

	This Year	*Last Year*	*Two Years Ago*	*Three Years Ago*	*Four Years Ago*
Net sales	$600,243	$602,569	$587,180	$505,371	$471,840
Income					
Before taxes	14,954	27,631	32,258	30,803	39,517
Net	12,280	11,468	20,926	19,155	24,163
Earnings per share	.32	.79	1.21	1.16	1.44
Dividends paid	.40	.40	.40	.40	.40
Capital expenses	24,592	21,275	39,348	36,037	29,161
Current assets	285,280	296,649	271,332	227,436	232,157
Current liabilities	82,451	101,237	117,073	80,185	59,629
Working capital	202,829	195,412	154,259	147,251	172,528
Net property, plant and equipment	233,281	238,524	240,149	215,375	186,603
Total assets	561,120	573,954	532,573	475,637	434,513
Long-term debt	133,863	141,276	105,762	97,428	77,364
Equity of stockholders	294,091	290,470	285,391	276,145	263,436

Questions

1. Based on the limited data available, are you inclined to feel a change in management of Madden Corporation is in order? Justify your viewpoint.
2. Other than financial data, what type of information would you like to have in order to reply to Mr. Kettler's letter. Discuss.
3. As a stockholder of Madden Corporation, what is your general evaluation of the management of the corporation? Why?

CASE 24–2. DOUGLAS CORPORATION

The balance sheet for the year just ending is:

BALANCE SHEET
December 31, 197—

ASSETS

Current Assets:		
Cash in banks or on hand		$ 5,462,377.24
Accounts receivable, less reserves		1,812,390.65
Inventories—at cost or market, whichever lower:		
Raw materials, parts, and supplies	$1,833,345.12	
Work in process	747,772.50	
Finished goods	381,600.31	2,962,717.93
Total Current Assets		$10,237,485.82
Fixed Assets:		
Machinery and equipment	$ 606,370.05	
Furniture and fixtures	284,917.80	
Improvements to leased property	177,650.00	
Tools, dies, jigs, fixtures	42,606.64	
	$1,111,544.49	
Less: Reserves for depreciation	270,271.84	
Total Fixed Assets		841,272.65
Total		$11,078,758.47

LIABILITIES

Current Liabilities:		
Accounts payable		$ 1,533,776.35
Accrued items:		
Payroll, commissions, etc.	$ 151,463.36	
Interest	18,925.16	
Federal and state taxes	457,593.60	$ 627,982.12
Total Current Liabilities		$ 2,161,758.47
Long-Term Notes Payable		2,800,000.00
Capital Stock and Surplus:		
Common stock—par value $1 per share; authorized, 5,000,000 shares; issued and outstanding, 4,000,000 shares	$4,000,000.00	
Paid-in surplus	2,117,000.00	
Total Capital Stock and Surplus		6,117,000.00
Total		$11,078,758.47

For the same year, a net earnings of $1,320,714.35 on net sales of $23,164,357.60 was shown by the company. This is more clearly indicated by the following:

STATEMENT OF EARNINGS
FOR YEAR ENDING DECEMBER 31, 197–

Net sales....................................	$23,164,357.60
Less: Cost of goods sold......................	14,007,861.19
Gross Profit on Sales.........................	$ 9,156,496.41
Selling, general administrative expenses.........	6,355,782.06
Profit from operations........................	$ 2,800,714.35
Provisions for federal and state taxes...........	1,480,000.00
Net earnings.................................	$ 1,320,714.35

The executive committee of the corporation believes that the net earnings figure is relatively low for the amount of the company's net sales and is of the opinion that some overall controls should be instituted. The average number of employees for the year is 1,427.

Questions

1. Calculate each of the following ratios: (*a*) current assets to current liabilities, (*b*) fixed assets to tangible net worth, (*c*) funded debt to net working capital, and (*d*) return before taxes on investment.
2. Evaluate each of the above ratios in terms of what it means to the Douglas Corporation.
3. As a member of the executive committee, what are your specific recommendations for improving the operations of the corporation?

25

Quantity and quality controlling

The secret of success is the consistency to pursue.
HARRY F. BANKS

MANAGERS of most enterprises must deal with problems concerning the quantity or amount of products or services supplied or obtained. Also, they deal with problems of the quality of these products and services. In this chapter we deal first with controlling quantity, followed by controlling quality.

CONTROLLING QUANTITY

In the typical business enterprise, materials from various and widely dispersed suppliers are procured, processed into completed or partially completed products, and sold to customers located in various geographical areas. The ideal situation is to have the flow moving in an orderly fashion from start to finish and utilizing the full capacity of the processing equipment. But this is not easy to attain. With many different materials being used, a variety of machines employed, various skills utilized, and sales fluctuations in amount and type of products being the rule not the exception, the complexity of quantity controlling is quickly perceived.

The typical flow is illustrated by Figure 25–1. For simplicity, only three raw materials and one finished product are depicted. Beginning at the left, the securing of materials from various suppliers can be termed *Input*. Where required, flow of these materials is physically regulated by means of utilizing a storage facility, *S,* as shown in the figure. The materials are processed, that is, subjected to manufacturing operations transforming them into a desired product. This can be termed *Process.* Lastly, the finished products are distributed to customers, either by sending direct to customer or by utilizing a warehouse facility, *W,* from whence shipment is made to the customer. This phase of business can be termed *Output.* Hence, the physical quantity flow of material is regulated when needed by means of a storage facility and a warehouse facility. In addition, there is a controlling unit which determines what materials, when, and where will be permitted. In other words, this unit

FIGURE 25–1. Quantity flow of materials in a manufacturing enterprise

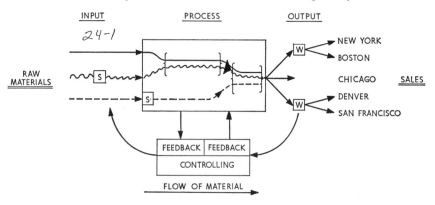

controls the quantity of material for the entire system, *Input–Process–Output,* by measuring the performance or flow, comparing it with prescribed standards, and determining the amount of correction or feedback, if any. It is performing the control process dealing with quantity. Its action plus usage of storage and warehouse facilities implements the quantity controlling work.

SALES AND QUANTITY CONTROLLING

The ultimate regulator of the flow of materials through the manufacturing cycle is effective consumer demand. In the final analysis, this is the real reason for the existence of the entire system. Usually over a period, there are inevitably variations in consumer demand. To a great degree, both the flow of *Input* and *Process* can be controlled to harmonize with these demand variations of *Output.*

Quantity control is intended to bring about an orderly and smooth flow of products and services. Like all controlling, it follows the basic control process. The scope of operations which quantity controlling covers depends upon the individual situation. Some include relatively small areas, while others are quite extensive in scope. In the interest of clarity, it is desirable to select an area which is important, basic, and about which there is usually some knowledge. Hence, the subject of quantity controlling as applied to sales has been selected or what might be viewed as that depicted by the right portion of Figure 25–1.

QUANTITY CONTROLLING OF SALES

The amount of products or services moving to markets is regulated or controlled, in the final analysis, by the acceptance and purchase of these products and services by buyers or consumers. From the viewpoint of an enterprise, the fundamental requirement is sales in sufficient quantities at satisfactory prices and accomplished within reasonable limits as set forth by the manager. Good control over sales efforts assists immeasurably in acquiring good quantity controlling of products and services.

Without adequate sales control, certain conditions tend to exist. Foremost perhaps is unbalanced sales—those products are being sold that are easiest to sell. It is also common to find that only certain accounts are being sold. Some buyers are called on regularly, while others are called on infrequently or not at all. Without sales control there is also the tendency for some sales areas to be much stronger than other areas, and the gap between the good and the bad areas will tend to increase unless managerial efforts are made to correct the situation. In addition, in the absence of sales control, some areas will be undermanned, while others have a surplus of sales personnel. To be sure, quantity controlling can be applied to products and services moving to markets no matter where these markets are, but the most effective quantity controlling is possible when effective sales control exists. Hence, we will point our discussion to sales control realizing this, in turn, is intimately connected with quantity controlling.

BASIS OF SALES CONTROL

Measuring and evaluating sales performance are not especially difficult. Before applying the familiar control process, however, it is mandatory to determine the basis of control which will be used. For sales, the determination of the basis of control is the hard-core problem. Actually, this is a standard evolved from planning. However, a somewhat detailed treatment of the basis of sales control appears warranted because of its importance and also for the reason that it includes features not previously discussed. The basis of sales control commonly consists of (1) a sales control unit, (2) the sales potential for this unit, and (3) the characteristics of the sales outlet being employed for the distribution of the product or service. Discussion of each will be given.

SALES CONTROL UNIT

A sales control unit is normally a geographical area to which sales can be identified. Its use expedites such things as ascertaining the trend of sales, new accounts acquired, size of orders, and comparisons between sales and costs.

A number of factors enter into the selection of the control unit; but among the most important are the product or service, the sales methods used, and the extent to which the company markets its products. The control unit should be practical and as small as necessary in order to reveal pertinent data concerning sales flow. That is, the unit should not include too many products or too great a geographical area. The unit selected should reflect self-contained areas of normal sales operation or of a usual line of products so that the results by control units are meaningful to the particular company using them. Artificial barriers or undue influence on sales either in one area or of one product should be minimized by the proper selection of the control unit. Comparisons between costs and sales accomplishments should be expedited by the control unit selected; otherwise the record keeping, sales analysis, and control work are made unnecessarily more difficult.

Common sales control units include (1) political units, such as states, counties, and cities; (2) marketing areas, such as consumer trading areas, wholesale trading areas, and sales territories; and (3) areas in which certain industries or technical processes are concentrated, that is, textiles, chemical, aircraft, and electric motor manufacturing. In many instances, a state is too large a unit for effective control. If Ohio sales increased, it would be difficult to tell whether Dayton, Cincinnati, Cleveland, or another area or areas were mainly responsible for the change. However, states may prove useful control units for products where state regulations or taxation are involved, for example, in the sale of gasoline, margarine, and cigarettes. Counties and cities as control units provide a smaller and more self-contained unit; they are easily understood and especially helpful for companies selling in a limited territory.

For consumer goods, the consumer trading area as a control unit offers many distinct advantages. A consumer trading area is a region about an important trading center from which buyers normally perform the major portion of their purchasing. The boundaries of a trading area are predicted upon the flow of trade, purchasing habits of consumers, size of trading center, nearness of other trading centers, and transportation facilities.

Figure 25–2 illustrates the characteristics of consumer trading areas. The scope of these areas is indicated by the lines extending from the major trading centers. The trading center of Memphis extends into many counties as well as into several states. Notice that the trading area of Union City, Tennessee (upper right center of figure), extends across the state line into Kentucky. Likewise, buyers in the adjoining county of Weakley trade in the Union City area. In the lower left of the illus-

FIGURE 25–2. Consumer trading areas

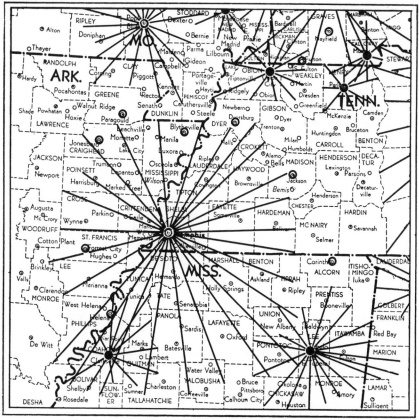

Courtesy: Hagstrom Co., Inc., New York, Map Makers, and Editor and Publisher Co., Inc., New York

tration, it should be observed that the consumer trading area of Memphis overlaps that of Clarksdale, Mississippi. Consumers in Tunica, Mississippi, for example, may buy in either Memphis or the Clarksdale trading areas.

In the case of industrial product sales, the best control unit might constitute selected areas in which buyers of the product are located. The market for industrial products tends to be concentrated; hence, logical areas for control purposes must be selected accordingly. For example, bearings are not sold in all markets, as is the case with candy and chewing gum. The areas in which bearings are marketed make up the logical control units for that product. Similarly, the buyers of wood pulp are concentrated in certain areas, and these areas appear to be the logical choice for control areas of that product.

SALES POTENTIAL

Sales control requires an acceptable sales level or par which sets up the objective of the selling activities. Decisions whether to promote more vigorously in one area than another, to accept sales obtained for a product as satisfactory, or to hire more salesmen can best be reached when there is a sales potential—an established sales goal covering a definite period.

To establish these potentials equitably necessitates considerable data, judgment, and experience. The work can commence by dividing the entire market to be served into the greatest number of sales areas that the available funds for selling will provide. Next, estimate the total company sales for the next period. This involves considerable judgment, based on an evaluation of the general market conditions, the ability of the company to produce, and its requirements. The subsequent step is to pro rate the total sales figure among the individual sales areas. This is based on the inherent characteristics which are known or believed to influence sales areas. Some areas are capable of buying more than others, for example, the Chicago area compared to the Rockford, Illinois, area. How much more the potential in Chicago is over that of Rockford depends upon the factors considered and the weights attributed to each one. The factors used must have a causal relationship to the product being sold. For a product like pencils, the factors might include statistical data on the percentage of literate population, sales of the company during the past several years, numbers of persons gainfully employed, consumer buying power index, and general level of retail sales. The selection of these factors might be justified as follows. The percentage of literate population gives emphasis to those who can write and, hence, are most likely to buy pencils; company's past sales are indicative of what has been accomplished in the past; the latter three factors give consideration to the ability and willingness of people to buy. It should be observed that past sales of the company are not necessarily an indication of what will happen or can be accomplished in the future.

FIGURE 25–3. Sales potential based on six factors

SALES POTENTIAL				
Area: Rockford				
Factor	Amount	Percentage of Total Market Area Served by Company	Weight Assigned	Weighted Percentages
Literate population over 12 years of age. .	95,342	0.902	1	0.902
Sales 197–	8,755	1.250	2	2.500
Sales 197–	9,420	1.206	2	2.412
Number of persons gainfully employed . .	54,612	0.715	3	2.145
Consumer buying power index	. . . . .	1.164	3	3.492
Percentage of retail sales	. . . . .	2.352	3	7.056
Totals.			14	18.507

$$\frac{18.507}{14} = 1.322\%$$

Figure 25–3 shows for the Rockford sales area these six factors and the percentage of each in the total market area served by the company. The weights assigned each factor are also indicated. Multiplying the percentage value by its respective weight, adding the weighted percentage values so obtained, and dividing this sum by the total weights assigned, or 14, gives a market potential for this area of 1.322 percent. This means that 1.322 percent of the company's total sales should be obtained from the Rockford area. If the company expected to do $1 million sales, 1.322 percent of this amount, or $13,220, should be acquired from the Rockford area. An adjustment of this figure might be made based on knowledge of the business, the company, the Rockford area, and the judgment of the analyst.

CHARACTERISTICS OF SALES OUTLETS

The third consideration in the establishing of a basis for sales control is the characteristics of sales outlets. Not all outlets are identical in makeup; they differ in regard to size, type of ownership, management, methods of purchasing, and, in the case of industrial goods, the use of which products are bought. Any program of sales control is affected by these outlet characteristics, and their influence should be taken into account whenever possible.

Figure 25–4 shows an interesting breakdown of sales data of retail

FIGURE 25–4

			BOSTON SALES DISTRICT BREAKDOWN								
Sales District Code	Broker-age Area Code	All Retail Outlets		Total Grocery		Total Independents		Total Chains		Popula-tion 1970
		Stores	Sales ($000)	Stores	Sales ($000)	Stores	Sales ($000)	Stores	Sales ($000)	
Orange County										
2	203	240	$11,740	62	$3,439	57	$2,557	5	$882	21,614

Independent Split—By Volume Group

Under 10M		10-50 M		50-100 M		100-300 M		Over 300 M	
Stores	Sales ($000)	Stores	Sales ($000)	Stores	Sales ($000)	Stores	Sales ($000)	Stores	Sales ($000)
6	$19	32	$960	16	$1,162	3	$416	—	—

Courtesy: A. C. Nielsen Company, Chicago

outlets in a Boston sales district. In this area, there are a total of 240 retail outlets with total sales of $11,740,000. Of these outlets, a total of 62 are grocery retail outlets, accounting for $3,439,000 of sales. A further breakdown of these 62 grocery outlets shows that 57 are independents (independently owned) and 5 are chain stores. Furthermore, the independents vary considerably by sales volume: 6 independents do less than $10,000 annual sales, 32 stores from $10,000 to $50,000, 16 stores from $50,000 to $100,000, only 3 from $100,000 to $300,000, and none over $300,000. These data are included in the lower half of the illustration. If a company found that it paid to concentrate its sales efforts on outlets doing a sales volume of over $50,000 per year, only

19 independents and 5 chains would be visited by the company in the particular sales area discussed.

In addition, characteristics of the buyer, including his attitude toward the company, extent of cooperation in use of display material, care taken in informing his salespeople of the product's superior features, and interest in promoting sales, are also significant in establishing and carrying out sales control work. In some instances, these somewhat intangible, yet powerful, forces of the outlet's makeup are decisive factors in the ultimate success or in the failure of the controls instituted.

Some sales managers have found it desirable to make up route sheets for salesmen so that important outlets are not overlooked, calls are not wasted on outlets that are too small, a proper spread between independent and chain stores—in the case of retail outlets—is maintained, and promotional material is distributed to provide maximum coverage.

MEASURING SALES PERFORMANCE

With the basis of control established, the common control process of (1) measure performance, (2) compare performance with standard, and (3) correct deviation can be followed. We prefaced this with a discussion of establishing the standard because the measuring of performance must be in the same units as those of the standard, thus making valid the comparison between performance and the standard.

In measuring and comparing sales performance, the unit is commonly dollar sales, although product units, number of calls, number of prospects interviewed, number of displays set up, cities covered, or miles traveled may prove satisfactory and are easy-to-measure units. The choice depends upon the individual circumstances. Most sales activities are highly personalized—the human element is of great significance. Hence, the measuring of sales performance may stress information concerning the sales personnel activities. Figure 25–5 shows a weekly report which provides for summary information of salesmen's activities and important analysis and ratios. This type of information is helpful in knowing what sales work is going on in the field and, when compared with the basis of control, whether sufficient calls are being made, orders being secured, and promotional work in the form of displays being carried out.

Data for such a weekly summary report are obtained from salesmen's reports which are mailed daily to the sales office. The makeup of these reports varies considerably among different enterprises. Some require

FIGURE 25–5. Form for securing data used in sales control work

SUMMARY OF SALESMEN'S ACTIVITIES

Week ending:_____

1. Total days reported:
2. Total calls on wholesalers:
3. Total orders from wholesalers: _____ $_____
4. Total calls on retailers: (Number)   (Dollars [approx.])
5. Total orders from retailers: _____ $_____
6. Displays set up: (Number)   (Dollars [approx.])
   Window:
   Island:
   Other.............:
   _____:
   _____: _____

   Total

ANALYSIS	WHOLESALERS	RETAILERS
1. Average calls daily......................		
2. Orders-to-calls ratio.....................		
3. Average-size order in dollars............ $		$
4. Displays-to-calls ratio.................. xxxxx		

quite elaborate and detailed information, while others are simple statements of who was called on and the results of the interview. Generally speaking, it is advisable to confine the salesmen's reports to pertinent data only. Too much detail tends to bog down the sales control efforts and dampen the salesmen's enthusiasm for such a program. On the other hand, sufficient data should be requested to gain all the information deemed essential to the control work. To illustrate, this might require from each salesman a daily report including the name and address of each dealer called upon; what, if any, sales orders were secured; the conditions of the dealer's stock; whether a display was installed; general comments about the sales interview, and an evaluation of future business prospects with each buyer.

ACTIVITIES OF COMPETITORS

The measuring of sales performance, as well as comparing it with the standard, must take into account how and what competitors are doing. Special promotional deals by competitors might call for a change in sales strategy by a company, with corresponding adjustments in its control pattern. The nearness of a competitor to a particular market might require special efforts by a company—efforts arranged and implemented through a sound sales control program. Although a competitor's efforts might be uniform throughout a large region, it is seldom that the effects of these efforts are uniform. What the effects are, segregated by small well-defined areas, furnishes the most useful information.

Some companies have their salesmen write informal reports every week or month outlining information on such subjects as the activities of competitors including the apparent results of their (competitors) special promotional efforts, including exhibits, samples, trade shows, and advertising campaigns. The content of such reports vary considerably. Their use is particularly helpful when competition is intense and such information aids the improving of sales control.

COMPARING SALES PERFORMANCE WITH STANDARD

By comparing the sales being accomplished with the standard or basis of control, the degree of market penetration is determined. This penetration is an indication of how successful a sales job is being done within the area considered. It is entirely possible to believe that area A with sales of $100,000 for the past year is doing a better job than area B with sales of $60,000. However, the true measurement of effectiveness takes into account the respective sales potentials of the two areas. Should the sales potential in area A be $200,000 and in B, $75,000, the degree of market penetration in A is 50 percent ($100,000/$200,000), while in area B, the penetration is 80 percent ($60,000/$75,000). In this illustration, area B is actually doing a better sales job, based on sales potentialities, than is area A. Information of this sort for all territories of a company is extremely valuable in controlling the sales efforts.

As already mentioned, units other than dollar sales can be used in sales control work. For example, the number of calls made by salesmen compared to a predetermined number could be used to determine the degree of efficiency. When this is done, comparisons of performance to standard cover such considerations as the number of sales calls and the sales orders-to-calls ratio.

CORRECTING THE SALES DEVIATION

When the sales performance is significantly less than its respective standard, the correcting of the deviation may take many different forms. The product or service may need revamping, price may require adjustment, or the use of different marketing outlets may be suggested. In many cases, however, improvements in the salesmen's effectiveness is sought. The better selection of salesmen, more thorough sales training, improved motivation through sales contests, sales meetings, and incentive pay may be followed. Sometimes the sales standard or basis of control is adjusted. In any event, if sales are below expectancies, the proper quantity of goods or services moving through the normal channels of business is lacking and merits managerial attention. The need is for proper and effective quantity controlling efforts as reflected by adjustments and improvements in the managerial planning, organizing, and actuating being used.

CONTROLLING QUALITY

Another major type of controlling is that exercised to achieve a specific quality. Due primarily to the closer tolerances required for high-precision products, the demand for higher speeds of production, and the increasing demand for "trouble free" products, quality control has become a major consideration in today's industry. To most people the word quality means high quality and a consistent quality. But the more accurate and practical use of the term is that the quality is satisfactory for the intended purpose, is the best in terms of what price is acceptable for the product or service to which it applies, and is of a level that gives dependable results; i.e., the product or service always satisfies the need about quality. To help assure the proper quality, either or both (1) inspection and (2) statistical quality control are employed.

INSPECTION CONTROL

By inspection a manager seeks to determine the acceptability of the parts, products, or services. The basis for inspection control is usually a specification commonly referred to as an inspection standard. Inspection is made by comparing the quality of the product to the standard by means of a visual or a testing examination. Sometimes inspection reverts to a sorting procedure that classifies acceptable from unacceptable parts. Ingenious devices and machines have greatly simplified what formerly were difficult inspection tasks. The heaviest responsibility for inspection lies with manufacturing personnel—they make the product. Whether a product is acceptable or not is influenced chiefly by the operative personnel, whether they are concerned and want to make certain that proper quality is achieved. The inspector checks what has been made. But he should also serve as a helper in suggesting ways to improve or maintain the quality. His role is not all passive.

The question arises regarding how often inspection should be made. Usually the answer resolves to a consideration of what it costs to inspect versus what it costs not to. The challenge is to keep inspection costs minimum, yet insure desired quality. In some cases every part is inspected. This is called 100 percent inspection. When the inspection is less than 100 percent, it is termed partial or sampling inspection. Parts having high value or those showing from experience to have a tendency to run to a large number of rejects, are commonly subjected to 100 percent inspection.

In general, it is desirable to inspect (1) raw material to ensure manufacturing efforts are starting with proper materials, (2) finished parts and products to know that correct parts are to be assembled or products are right when shipped, (3) before a costly operation to make sure you're adding this operation on a proper base, (4) the output of automatic machines periodically so that possible errors are confined to small quantities, (5) before an item is covered as in an assembly so you know parts to be covered are right, and (6) before an operation that cannot be undone, for example, in mixing paint.

STATISTICAL QUALITY CONTROL

Statistical quality control (SQC) seeks to assist in controlling the process that produces the parts. In other words, it is preventive as well as remedial. It is based on the statistical theories and methods of probability to sample testing. Many of the efforts to insure proper quality have always been done on a sampling basis; that is, a relatively few of the entirety are inspected. However, with statistical quality control the risk involved in assuming the sample has the same characteristics as a lot is known, and better quality control with minimum inspection costs can be achieved. The risk is not eliminated, but the probability of the reliability of the samples is expressed in numerical terms.

Why use statistical quality control? As stated above, one important reason is because it can help prevent defects from being made. In operation, accurate measurements of the parts at the machines are taken, compared to predetermined standards, and the decision reached whether the operation should continue or not. When and where to look for sources of trouble are revealed. Costly errors can be located and corrected before large scrap and rework losses due to quality deficiency occur. Another important reason for using statistical quality control is to supply an audit of quality regarding the producer's products. A universally understood measurement is supplied. In addition, the reasonableness of the quality standards established are checked. Frequently this is a "free extra" but in some cases quite important information to have.

THE BASIS OF STATISTICAL QUALITY CONTROL

When man attempts to make many identical parts, some are a little large and some a little small, but most will be approximately the same. The middle or average will be the most frequent, with smaller and larger sizes as extremes from the average. When the frequency or count of the items by size is plotted with size on the horizontal scale and count on the vertical scale, what the statistician calls a normal, or bell-shaped, curve is obtained. A measure of the dispersion or spread of the sizes from the average or central tendency size is indicated by the standard deviation, which is a statistical concept calculated by (1) finding the difference between the arithmetic means of all sizes and the value of each size, (2) square each difference, (3) add the squared numbers and divide the sum by the number of items, and (4) take the square root of the quotient. For a normal distribution of sizes illustrated by a normal curve, 68.27 percent of the sizes will be between one standard deviation on either side of the arithmetic mean size, 95.45 percent between two standard deviations, and 99.73 percent between three standard deviations. Figure 25–6 illustrates these concepts. The bottom portion of the figure indicates ideal measurement, or average size, and the lower and upper control limits are located, respectively, three standard deviations below and three standard deviations above the average.

The variations in size between 0.995 and 1.005, with most of the sizes at 1.000, can be considered due to chance. It is in the nature of things resulting from the process employed—the machine used and the part made—that this variation will take place within the pattern indicated. However, when from this same process a size is manufactured outside the limits indicated, it is not due to chance or expected variation but to an assignable cause. Stated differently, it is not normal, referring to Figure 25–6, for a size 1.007 to be made from this particular process. If a size 1.007 occurs, something has gone wrong in the process because this size out of normal limits is due to an assignable cause. Such a cause may be traced to such things as internal temperatures and friction changes of the machine parts, a dull tool, improper dimensions of raw material, or the setting of machine being changed unintentionally. Knowing when an improper size is made as a result of an assignable cause makes it feasible to stop the machine and find and rectify the cause.

FIGURE 25–6

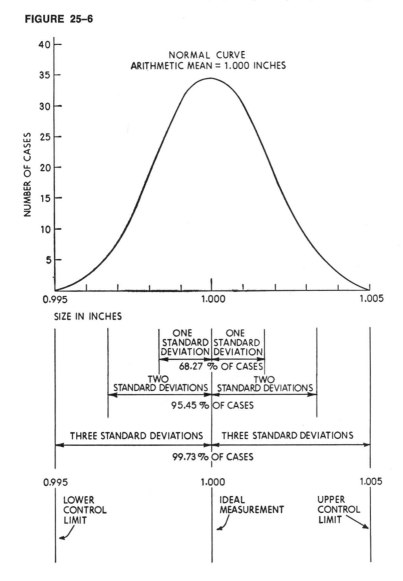

CONTROL CHARTS

In actual practice, control charts are constructed so that an operator can tell whether the process is performing in a consistent, satisfactory manner. To construct a control chart, on-the-job data are collected from which an average and standard deviation values can be calculated. These values are then compared to the specifications or desired limits. If the actual values are within the specification limits, the process is all right or the limits can be narrowed since production already is concentrated in a narrow range. In contrast, if outside the specification limits, the process must be improved or the specifications loosened.

The general format of control charts shows time horizontally and the quality variations vertically. Samples of production are inspected periodically, perhaps hourly, every two hours, or daily, and the results plotted on the chart. If within the control limits, all is well; if without, corrective action is taken. Figure 25–7 shows a control chart with production values plotted on it. Based on this illustration, the work being done is of a satisfactory quality since all the plotted values are within plus or minus three standard deviations of the arithmetic average. Each plotted

FIGURE 25–7. Control chart for statistical quality control

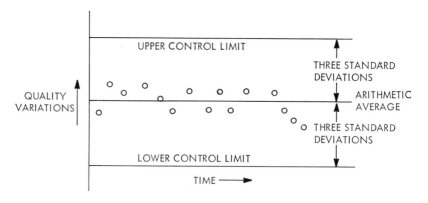

value is obtained by averaging several specimens taken at the time indicated. (Frequently for each value the spread of these specimens is plotted on a range or bar chart which is not illustrated here.)

Some SQC men would state that a possible danger is indicated by the trend of the plotted values at the right of the chart in Figure 25–7. If successive readings continue this downward trend, a future reading could be below the lower control limit, thus signaling the quality is unsatisfactory and due to an assignable cause. In such an event, the process would be stopped; the assignable cause determined and corrected. The value of the limits establishing the width of the acceptance band can be calculated by several different statistical formulas, but in each case the fundamental basis is predicated upon the theories of probability and sampling. It is common practice to post the control chart near the site of the operation, not only for convenience but also to promote interest in quality work.

The above discussion is based on what is termed "variable inspection"; that is, the *measurement* of a characteristic is included. The average of measurements and deviations from this average are vital. In contrast, attribute inspection is concerned with whether a product is acceptable or not. An inspection of a finish on a product illustrate attribute inspection. The vital consideration in attribute inspection is the percentage of products rejected or with ratios, usually expressed as the number of defects per 100 items. The average defective percentage or ratio along with the upper and lower limits are determined, similar to the method described above. Likewise, the interpretation of the chart is the same.

QUESTIONS

1. Briefly discuss what constitutes the basis of sales control.
2. Explain how data derived from Figure 25–5 could be used for controlling sales performance.
3. Discuss the influence of competitors' activities upon sales controlling efforts of company A and relate what the sales manager of company A can do about such activities.
4. What differences, if any, are there between standards and sales potentials? Explain.
5. Distinguish carefully between the two concepts in each of the following: (*a*) control chart of statistical quality control and a standard deviation, (*b*) sales control unit and *Input,* and (*c*) *Output* and a bell-shaped curve.
6. List the common types of sales control units, and illustrate each one along with a product or service you feel is appropriate for that control unit. Discuss.
7. Suggest ways in which deviation from a sales standard may be remedied. Discuss one of these ways in some detail.
8. Justify the statement that among several sales areas the basis of sales control can have relatively different dollar sales expectancies and yet be utilized effectively for sales control purposes.
9. What is the widely accepted meaning of quality? Is it in keeping with practical quality control? Why?
10. Enumerate five recommendations as to where and when inspection is desirable.
11. Explain the significant differences between inspection and statistical quality control.
12. Do you agree with this statement, "Controlling, no matter how carefully devised, will not ensure that satisfactory quality products are being manufactured." Justify your answer.
13. Interpret the meaning of a statistical control chart where all the recorded values taken every half hour for the past 24 hours have been between one and two standard deviations below the arithmetic average.
14. Do you agree with this statement, "Statistical quality control is limited to phenomena that can be measured. There are no exceptions"? Why?

CASE 25–1. SETTLE MANUFACTURING COMPANY

A special unit made of plastic and wood has been supplied to Everett Electronics Corporation for the past 17 months. To date, six different orders, each for 5,000 units, have been supplied at a selling price of $10 each. Material cost for each unit is $1.10, labor cost for each unit is $2.85.

The sales representative of Settle Manufacturing Company has tried to get the purchasing agent at Everett Electronics to place a contract for these units with his company and has offered a selling price of $8.90 each for a contract specifying a minimum of 15,000 units to be delivered over a six-months' period. However, the purchasing agent claims he doesn't know how many of these units, if any, of this design he will need in the future. The sales representative says the purchasing agent has been telling him this since the second order was placed some 15 months ago. In the opinion of the sales representative, it is probably a 50–50 chance that Everett Electronics Corporation will continue to buy the unit for at least the next nine to ten months.

Another purchase order for 5,000 of the units was received today. The vice president of production favors making 15,000 of these units in his production run. To justify his view, he points out that the setup cost for the machines to make the units is $12,500, the reduction in material cost would amount to 10 percent, and the past usage by Everett of about 5,000 units every three months appears reasonable. However, more importantly, he sees greater profitability in manufacturing the unit, if Settle Manufacturing Company produces them in larger quantities.

The accounting department estimates that it will cost 8 cents per month per unit for storage and that the salvage value is $1.00 per unit.

Questions

1. Calculate the following: (*a*) for 5,000 unit manufacturing lot, the difference between the total revenue and total manufacturing cost; (*b*) for 15,000 unit manufacturing lot, the difference between the total revenue and total manufacturing cost assuming buyer purchases 5,000 units now, 5,000 units in three months, and 5,000 units in six months, (*c*) same as (*b*) except buyer purchases only 5,000 units now, (*d*) same as (*b*) except buyer purchases only 5,000 units now and 5,000 units in three months.
2. What alternatives are available to Settle Manufacturing Company? Elaborate on your answer.
3. What decision do you believe the management of Settle Manufacturing Company should reach? Why?

CASE 25–2. SIBSON INSURANCE COMPANY

For the past five months, trouble has been experienced in getting insurance proposals typed accurately and within the time limits requested by the field or sales department. At first, it was believed the situation might rectify itself, but instead of improving, it appears to be getting worse.

"Policy Writing–A" is the official designation of the organizational unit whose work is typing proposals used in connection with the selling of life insurance policies of $75,000 and over. In most cases, these proposals are in the nature of a written estate plan, individualized for the prospect. These proposals appeal to a select and highly sought clientele. The sales manager insists that these proposals be letter-perfect, make a favorable impression, and reflect the integrity, dignity, and responsibility of the company. He forbids his salesmen to use any proposal which is not typed to meet these requirements.

Rough estimates showed that some 22 percent of the proposals were returned by the sales department to Policy Writing–A for rewriting. The more common complaints include:

Cause of rewrite	*Percent of total**
Misspelling	41
Typed insert not centered	28
Uneven key strokes	39
Erasures	13

* Includes multiple causes so total exceeds 100 percent.

Shirley Bishop, supervisor of Policy Writing–A, has been trying to turn out the caliber of work demanded, but the difficulty has become acute during the past five months. She has been with the company 16 years and supervisor of "Unit A" for the past 5 years. She is considered by the Director of Personnel to be an "average to above" supervisor. At one time, the supervisor of Policy Writing–A checked the work for possible errors before sending it to sales. This practice was discontinued some eight or nine months ago because the supervisor did not have time to do it and those in the sales department appeared to have sufficient free time to do this checking work. Furthermore, some parts of the proposal were rather technical and had always been checked by the salesman, regardless of the inspection by the personnel of Policy Writing–A unit. It has long been the custom for each typist to check her own work.

In the supervisor's opinion, the nine girls in her department should be permitted to perform additional types of work, that is, not be confined to typing insurance proposals. Miss Bishop believes errors and carelessness are caused by the present work specialization which makes the work too confining and monotonous. When confronted with the fact that insurance proposals have always been typed by a designated group who do no other type of work and that no serious difficulties were experienced until now, Miss Bishop states that employee wants and working conditions have changed with time. Things are not what they used to be.

In part, Miss Bishop was referring to an increase in the number of proposals each typist was expected to complete each day. The increase amounted to about 12 percent and was the result of a cost reduction program the company started about six months ago to keep Sibson Insurance Company competitive. At the same time the increase in work expectancy became effective, salaries of the typists were increased from an average of $95 per week to $100 per week.

Joan Derby, who works in Policy Writing–A, has told her brother, Jack Derby, one of the company's salesmen, that her typewriter is just about worn out and she can't do better work with it. When she mentioned this to Miss Bishop, Joan was told that the company has an excellent typewriter maintenance service and all typewriters are in good operating order. Miss Bishop is also reported to have stated to Joan, "You cannot excuse yourself for doing sloppy work by blaming it on poor equipment. There is nothing wrong with our typewriters."

Jack Derby reported what his sister had told him to his superior, the sales manager. He also mentioned that he cannot understand why they don't use automatic typewriters. The proposals could be standardized, in part, and thus expedite the use of modern office equipment. The superior's only comment was, "O.K. Thanks. Jack, I want to tell you something. Just remember it is our job to make the sale. Getting the proposal typed correctly is not our responsibility. Let's concentrate our efforts on what we are supposed to do. Understand?"

"Yes, sir," answered Jack Derby.

Questions

1. Who do you believe is responsible for correcting the problem of this case? Justify your answer.
2. What types of controlling would probably be of help to the Sibson Insurance Company?
3. What's your general opinion of Miss Bishop? Of the sales manager? Discuss.
4. What actions do you recommend be taken? Why?

26

Time use, cost, and budgetary controlling

Those who have most to do, and are willing to work, will find the most time.

SAMUEL SMILES

TIME IS a unique resource of mankind. The supply is not only totally inelastic, but it is also totally perishable. Time cannot be stored and it cannot be regained. It is always in very scarce supply. Hence, its use, or time use, is a cardinal factor of much controlling and is a challenge faced by most management members.

PERSONAL TIME USE BY MANAGER

Controlling time use starts with a manager's efficient use of his own time. He should strive to employ his minutes and hours purposefully and take measures to minimize any waste of his time. Effective personal time use by a manager starts with information of the present pattern of his time expenditure.

To get the facts, it is an excellent idea for the management member to keep a daily log by 15-minute intervals as to what activity is performed and whether it is basically managerial or not. A form like that shown in Figure 26–1 is helpful. For the appropriate period, the activity is written in, a checkmark made in the proper column whether managerial or nonmanagerial, and comments added. At the end of the day, the totals and respective percentages are calculated. Similar log sheets are made out for each working day for a period of 12 weeks,

FIGURE 26–1. Daily log sheet

| TIME | ACTIVITY | IS ACTIVITY | | COMMENTS |
		MANAGERIAL	NONMANAGERIAL	
8:30				
8:45				
9:00				
9:15				
9:30				
9:45				
		%	%	
TOTALS				

which is sufficiently long to supply a representative picture of the various activities.

These fundamental data are then analyzed with a view to what a manager should be doing with his time. Improvements are sought; time robbers are eliminated. Interruptions, trivia, and nonessential activities are reduced. The manager may have to say "no" more frequently to nonessentials seeking his attention. The really essential activities are identified, but in this work it is best not to be too ambitious. Reasonable goals achieved are more satisfying.

Having decided what to do, the next step is to schedule the events by proposed time expenditures. If possible, assignments should lead into one another. Varying the types of work helps maintain interest in it. Expect interruptions and allow for them in the schedule, but don't let them get out of hand. A manager should know when he works best—at the beginning of the day, at the end, first of week, or whenever it is. Then schedule the toughest jobs for this period. It is helpful to take the 15 minutes at the end of each day to firm up the schedule for the following day.

TIME USE AND NEW PRODUCT INTRODUCTION

An interesting example of time-use controlling is found in new product introduction. One of the chief characteristics of modern marketing is the number of new products appearing on the marketplace. It has been estimated that a general store of 100 years ago handled less than 5 percent of the products offered in a modern supermarket. The development of new products reflects material progress in a world of explosive change. Since the birth of the youngest person reading this sentence, more new products have been offered on the market than had been offered between the time he was born and the birth of Christ.

The present situation is such that many companies are dependent upon new products for continued growth and in some cases for their very existence. Too little time devoted to developing and testing a new product can limit its success and likewise too much time can result in losing a potential market advantage. The need is to utilize time-use controlling over product installation activities so that the proper amount of time is taken. Studies in this area show the following approximate averages values:

Step	Average time required in months
Product inception	8
Development of satisfactory product	6
Packaging	3
Test marketing	3
Production readiness	4
Trial before product is success or failure	12
Total	36

In other words, from the time of initial product inception to that of market evaluation as a product success or failure requires 36 months.

TIME USE AND PRODUCTION CONTROL

Another example of time-use controlling is that included under the common term of production control. With respect to a given production order, this control is performed to assist in utilizing designated materials, machines, and men for the proper amount of time and at the right time. Production control, as the term is commonly used, is not restricted to time use controlling only.

Production control data normally includes the amount, type, and kind of materials required for each manufacturing order released to the factory. The necessary material must be on hand or be delivered by a definite date in order that production can be started and continued. To expedite material requirements, notices or requisitions to purchase showing complete data on required material and when needed are sent to the purchasing department. Commonly such data are called bills of materials.

The manufacturing process, made up of various sequential production operations, is determined by production planning. But the meshing together of all production orders so that the best total pattern of activities is followed is the contribution of production control. By best pattern is meant that dovetailing of various requested production efforts which supply the finished products when desired at a minimum of time and cost. This usually entails maximum machine utilization, full use of operators' skills, adequate material available and ready for use, and efficient intraplant materials handling. For purposes of this discussion and also in the interest of clarity, we can consider the essential production data utilized in production control as consisting of (1) routing, (2) scheduling, and (3) dispatching. The first two, routing and scheduling, are basically planning efforts. They supply production expectancies and are included here to provide the needed background for the third activity, or dispatching, which is essentially a controlling function.

ROUTING

Routing concerns the establishment of the path which the production will take in its travel through the plant. The route sets forth the operations to be performed and the sequence to be followed. The machines, attachments, and work areas to be utilized at each production step are indicated. In some cases, the specific machine to be used is designated, while in other cases only the machine division is named, in which case the foreman determines which particular machine will be used. Routing also provides data on the time allowed to complete each respective operation. These values are usually obtained from the use of time standards. Figure 26–2 shows a route sheet in which six different operations are required in the sequence as listed. Frequently, the route sheet is supplemented by drawings, blueprints, instruction sheets, or any information helpful in the handling of the order.

SCHEDULING

Scheduling is the assigning of time values (clock or calendar) for carrying out the various operations in an orderly and synchronized manner. Figure 26–3 shows a popular type of chart used for this purpose. Its general appearance is that of a large visible file with over-

FIGURE 26–2

ROUTE SHEET
THE PARKER AND WILLIAMS MANUFACTURING CO.

Part No. _D227_   Item: _Base Support_   Quantity: _200_
Material: _3/4" CR steel rod_   Used on: _Rocker Mechanism_   Date Issued: _6/14/197-_
_(1140)_

Dept. No.	Oper. No.	Operation	Machine	Machine No.	Equipment	Standard Hours per 100 Pieces	No. Opera- tors	Total Hours per 100 Pieces for Scheduling
32	1	Cut rods to length	Cutter	. . . . . .	Regular	0.60	1	0.60
32	2	Grind rough ends	Grinding wheel	. . . . . .	8" Diameter $\frac{3}{4}$" face, medium No. 414 wheel	0.45	1	0.45
57	3	Form rods	Forming machine	H–2	Regular	1.30	2	0.65
25	4	Drill 4 No. 36 holes	Drill press	D–11	Carboloy ground 32°	3.40	2	1.70
84	5	Weld part to rod	Welder	M–7	. . . .	1.75	1	1.75
84	6	Brush and clean unit	. . . . . .	. . . . . .	. . . .	1.60	1	1.60

lapping pockets hanging vertically. At the extreme left, cards similar to those used in regular visible files are inserted in the visible margins, a separate card being used for each order. Pertinent data covering the order are written on the card. In the extension of the visible margin to the right, a "loader card" is inserted for each operation indicating the scheduled starting and total time to complete the operation. Time is shown horizontally. The length of the card represents the scheduled time for an operation. For example, on the top line, order No. 17542, the first operation is shear and is scheduled to start at period 5; the time scheduled is 40 periods, so the card extends from 5 to 45.[1] The next operation is blank, requiring 30 periods. It is scheduled to follow the previous operation immediately, or from 45 to 75. The next operation, form, begins at 85. Nothing is scheduled between periods 75 and 85 on this order, and so a blank or white space appears in the visible margin. Different color stripes on the bottom of the loader cards are used to indicate different operations. In Figure 26–3 these are shown by different designs and crosshatching.

The controlling aspects of the chart are the indications of the produc-

---

[1] On the scale of periods of the chart the segment identified by number 1 means 0 to 10 units, so that unit 5 is midway of this segment. Likewise, unit 45 is midway of segment identified with a 5 on the chart.

FIGURE 26-3. A chart illustrating scheduling of orders by operations

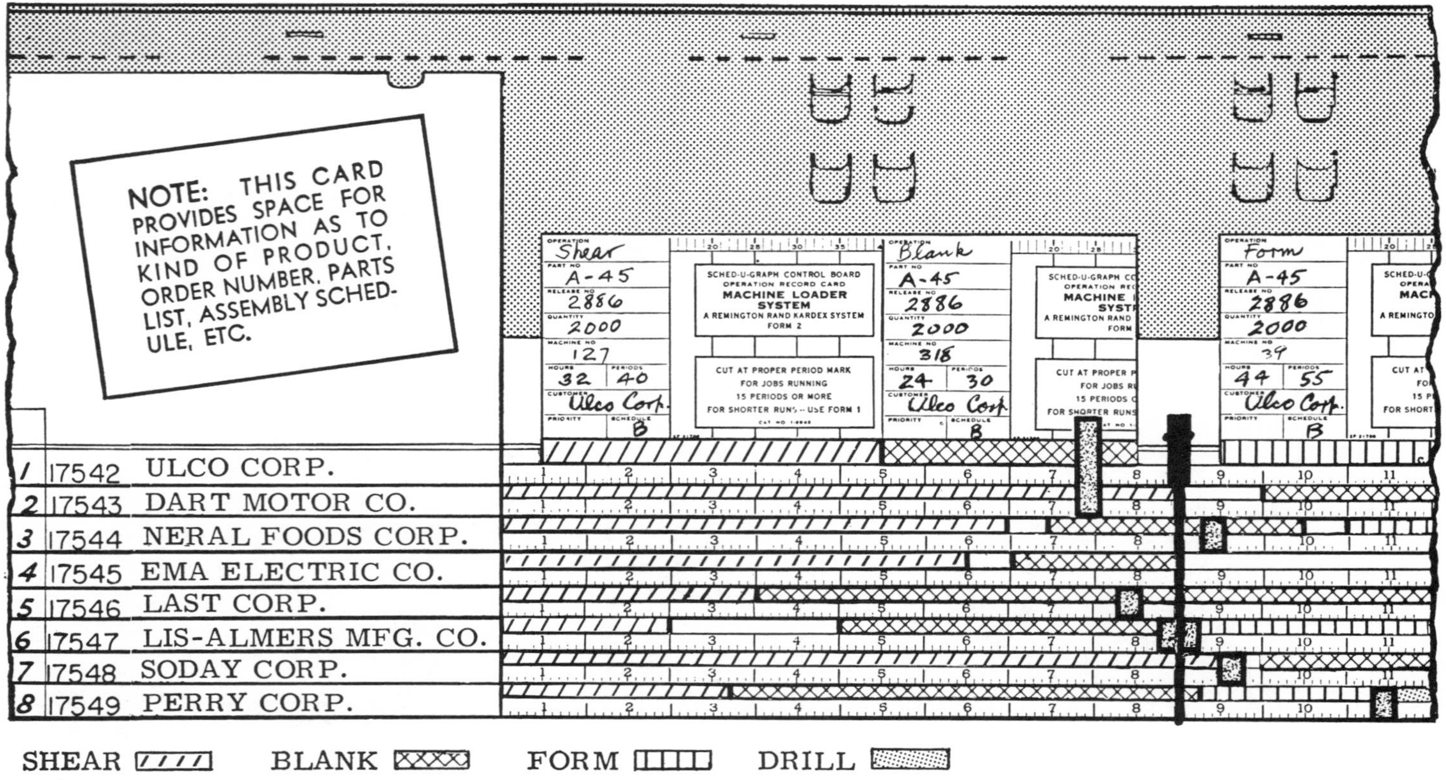

Courtesy: *Sperry Rand Corp., New York.*

SHEAR ///   BLANK XXXX   FORM |||| DRILL ▓▓

tion progress of each operation. This is accomplished by means of a color signal, moved across the margin of the card as the work progresses (vertical mottled spaces on chart). For order No. 17542 the signal is approximately at period 68, and it is the same for order No. 17543. The vertical line transcribing all margins at period 85 is the "Today" or present time. Comparing the signals on each order with the "Today" line shows whether the order is behind, on, or ahead of schedule. In the illustration, order Nos. 17542, 17543, and 17546 are behind schedule, order No. 17547 is on schedule, and order Nos. 17544, 17548, and 17549 are ahead of schedule.

Orders should not be completed too far in advance of the time scheduled, otherwise extra handling and storing are required. In contrast, orders completed after the scheduled time may cause costly delays and possible disruption of the smooth flow of subsequent operations.

DISPATCHING

This last part of production control emphasizes conformity with plans and correction of the deviation, if any. Dispatching provides the authority to move what materials where and when. It maintains the scheduled movement of materials through the plant. Dispatching includes securing reports on work progress, informing on the progress at each key production step, and handling of emergency situations, such as machine breakdown, shortage of help, and excess waste of

FIGURE 26–4. A move ticket

Mfg. Order No. S29735	Quantity 1500	Part No. ZV22R8	Class 2

Style Regular	Spec. No. 383S54	Design R-13	Special Notes

Specifications of Material XXND-59 Plastic Sheet 0.320" x 9/32" wide 1/4" Blank	None

Deliver to _____   Delivery time _____   Receiving time_____
Dept. No. __44__   Date __1-/5/7-__   Date
Machine No. __12__   Clock time __11:05 A.M.__   Clock time
Area No. __—__   Delivered by _____   Received by_____

               (Signed)   (Signed)

material. These reports might take the form of cards upon which operators report their time, a trucker's card that material has been moved to another area, or a message telephoned by the foreman to the dispatching unit. Figure 26–4 on page 609 illustrates a dispatching move ticket which serves as written authority to convey a specific lot of material to the next department and machine at which the immediately successive operation will be performed.

CONTROLLING OF COST

The use of cost as a factor for controlling is generally recognized as an indication of managerial efficiency. The capability and quality of managers to get out the work is important, be it selling or producing, but this achievement *at what cost* is a further consideration of managerial effectiveness. In the case of most enterprises, over the long period of time, total costs must be covered by total income; otherwise the enterprise will cease to exist.

Cost, represented by dollar expenditures, must apply to a known physical unit which determines the quantity and the identity of the part, and operations. Trade practices, experience, and desires of management members are among the important factors affecting the choice of the cost unit.

It is also necessary in any given case to specifiy the particular type of cost being used. Four common types of cost are (1) material, (2) labor, (3) selling, and (4) overhead. The names of these types are self-explanatory, with the possible exception of overhead, which is sometimes called "burden." In the case of material, labor, and selling, the costs are commonly segregated under the headings of (1) direct and (2) indirect. Figure 26–5 shows the principal cost types classified by direct and indirect costs and some examples of each group.

These four principal costs are interrelated. For example, the following equations are helpful to remember:

Direct material cost *plus* direct labor cost *equals* prime cost.
Prime cost *plus* factory overhead *equals* manufacturing cost.
Manufacturing cost *plus* selling expense *equals* total manufacturing and selling cost.
Total manufacturing and selling cost *plus* general administration cost *equals* total cost.

How are cost data on current activities collected? There are several sources. For example, direct material cost is ascertained by means of

FIGURE 26–5. Common types of cost segregated as direct or indirect

	Expenditures	
	Direct	*Indirect*
Material	Expenditures for materials which are or become a part of the product or service.	Expenditures for materials not a part of the product or service but required in executing the work.
	Examples: Sheet metal, cloth, wire, and wood which are allocable to the specific product or service.	*Examples:* Cleaning compound and sandpaper.
Labor	Expenditures for labor which has a bearing straight upon the product or service.	Expenditures for labor which does not have an immediate or a straight connection to the product or service.
	Examples: Machine operator, assembler, and packer.	*Examples:* Trucker, cost clerk, and methods man.
Selling	Expenditures for sales activities which are immediate and without an intervening influence upon the sales of the product or service.	Expenditures for sales activities which are not of an immediate or straight influence upon the sales of the product or service.
	Examples: Commission payments to salesmen and salesmen's salaries.	*Examples:* Advertising, market research, sales offices, and cost of training salesmen.
Overhead	Expenditures for all activities which are not allocable exclusively to material, labor, or selling. Overhead costs are in addition to material, labor, and selling costs and considered as one group, i.e., not segregated into direct and indirect.	
	Examples: General managerial costs, legal expenditures, depreciation, insurance, rent, light, power, and telephone.	

adequate records maintained as a part of normal purchasing practices. The invoice price, less discounts, transportation, and special charges are known for every item purchased. In many cases, these net purchase prices are reduced to cost per selected unit and posted on the records of the storeroom. Normally, material is issued by the storeroom or stores department only upon receipt of a properly signed requisition, and this practice provides an allocations record so that the proper amount and kind of material can be charged to the proper cost unit.

The direct labor cost data are obtained by having the employee keep a record of the job order number worked on, the operation performed, and the time spent on each operation. These data are written on a labor time card such as illustrated by Figure 26–6. Observe that such records are simply an accounting by the employee of how his time was spent. The validity of the data depend upon the employee's understanding of the purpose and use of such information, the desire to

FIGURE 26–6

			Time		Total Time		
		TIME CARD					
CLOCK NO.				DATE			
Shop Order Number		Operation	Start	Stop	Hours	Min.	✓

cooperate, the importance attached to such information by managers, and the effectiveness of supervision.

To the direct material and labor costs per cost unit must be added factory overhead cost. This is calculated in a number of ways, but taking a certain percentage of either material or labor, or both, is a common practice. However, the allocated estimates of factory overhead made to separate cost units must add up to the actual total factory overhead costs; otherwise each cost unit is not supporting its proper burden. To meet this requirement, adjustments in overhead sometimes must be made.

Selling expense is obtained from records maintained by the sales department. When selling expense is added to the total factory cost, the total manufacturing and selling cost is obtained. To this, general administrative expense (really overhead cost) is added to arrive at the total cost.

OVERHEAD COST

More needs to be said about overhead cost because it does significantly affect cost information. Actually, overhead costs do not vary in direct proportion with either material or labor costs but are determined by numerous influences, including the circumstances surrounding a given enterprise, the product or service manufactured or sold, and the manner of managerial operations. Overhead costs are an individual consideration and must be evaluated for each enterprise. For example, some units probably require more of the activities going to make up overhead costs than do other units. The majority of an executive's time might have been devoted to solving the problems in producing and selling product X, and little, if any, attention was given to products Y and Z. Also important is the extent and action of competition. Most enterprises have the problem of keeping their prices competitive but at the same time of securing their overhead costs as required for survival. To allocate too much overhead on a product might result in "pricing themselves out of the market." Competition might permit more overhead on certain items and less overhead on others.

Generally speaking, rates dealing with time are preferable to those dealing with dollars. This follows from the fact that most elements making up overhead costs are functions of time, that is, depreciation, insurance, salaries, and rent; hence, time rates are likely to move in step with overhead charges.

Overhead costs are rarely uniform throughout an entire organization; they will be greater in some areas than in others. This suggests the desirability of establishing various overhead costs for different areas in keeping with their respective overhead requirements. With this in mind, overhead cost rates can be based on any of three major bases: (1) on the plant as a whole, (2) on each department, and (3) on each cost center.

METHODS OF DISTRIBUTING OVERHEAD COSTS

How are overhead costs distributed? Figure 26–7 gives six different ways. No one basis is ideal for all products of an enterprise; selection should be made on what is believed will result in the most accurate and useful cost control.

The first, or *direct labor hours,* is popular and simple to apply. It is useful where labor is the main productive element or represents a large portion of the total cost. However, this method ignores variations in size and type of equipment. An hour of direct labor might mean a man operating a simple lathe in one case; while in another instance it might include a huge and complicated punch and forming machine. The second, *direct labor costs,* or hours times rate per hour, is similar to direct hours, except the hours are weighted according to the wage rate structure. Where the variances in wage rates are small, the results from direct labor costs and direct labor hours are nearly identical. The use of *direct material costs* assumes that variations in direct material are in

FIGURE 26–7

Method of distributing overhead costs	Formula	Expressed in terms of
1. Direct labor hours	Total overhead costs ÷ Total direct labor hours	Dollars per direct labor hour
2. Direct labor costs	Total overhead costs ÷ Total direct labor dollars	Percentage of overhead per direct labor costs
3. Direct material costs	Total overhead costs ÷ Direct material costs	Percentage of overhead per direct material dollar
4. Product unit	Total overhead costs ÷ Total number of product units	Dollars per product unit
5. Machine rate	Overhead for machine ÷ Machine hours	Dollars per machine hour
6. Cost center	Overhead for selected group of machines ÷ Machine hours	Dollars per selected group of machine hour

direct proportion to variations in overhead costs. This is true for some continuous manufacturing processes. The fourth, *product unit,* is easy to use, and it provides satisfactory results for large-volume manufacturing of a single product or of a few that are quite uniform and similar. Fifth, *machine rate,* is most helpful where machines are an important productive element and overhead costs are influenced far more by machines than labor time or cost. Lastly, *cost center* is the machine rate method extended to include several machines which are normally used as a unit or center in the production process. This method simplifies the distribution of overhead costs but like the machine rate requires extensive records and competent clerical personnel.

COMPARING COST PERFORMANCE WITH STANDARD

Comparing cost results with cost expectancies, or the second step of the familiar control process, reveals whether any cost variances exist. In most cases, the expectancy, or the standard, for cost control is the standard cost which is expressed in dollars and is a predetermined cost computed by an analyst. Standard cost is supposed to represent the normal amount of total expenditures, including material, labor, and overhead, for the accomplishment of the work. Strictly speaking, a standard employee using standard materials and methods should represent an expenditure equal to the standard cost.

From the practical viewpoint, another type of standard cost, called *basic standard cost,* is used. It is in the nature of a predetermined standard from which actual costs can be expressed as relative percentages with the basic standard cost as the base. For example, a basic standard cost might be $1; but under conditions of high material cost and labor rates, the actual cost might be $1.50. Knowing the variance and evaluating its amount, the basic standard cost is a perfectly valid basis of control, although it does not represent the standard cost, that is, the one under normal prevailing circumstances.

CORRECTING COST DEVIATIONS

Spotting the cause of a cost variance and taking steps to correct it are, of course, helpful. However, one of the most effective means for keeping costs in line is to acquire a cost consciousness among the entire work force. This is exemplified by helping every employee to think in terms of cost expenditures, to plan for keeping costs minimum, and for each employee to regulate his work action so that the costs incurred are acceptable. That is, every employee should have the responsibility to control costs on all activities over which he or she has charge or has intimate influence in the normal sequence of the work.

From the practical viewpoint, implied in the meaning of cost controlling is usually cost reduction, even though current performance costs are well within the limits of cost expectancies. The constant challenge facing most managers is to reduce costs. For the most part, cost reduction is achieved by (1) preventing waste in materials and time, (2) improving the operational processes and methods, and (3) encouraging new ideas for more effective operations.

Cost reduction, however, is not too salable. The typical employee is not enthusiastic about lowering costs. It is usually necessary to explain why reductions are in order and how they will probably affect the employee. In many instances employee job security is improved through the lowering of costs. An employee should be informed regarding whether his costs are satisfactory or not. In addition an employee needs to be informed about the effect of cost reduction upon his job and that of his buddy. If loss of job is probable there is reasonable certainty that an employee cost reduction program will not be entered into heartily. If loss of job is involved, explanations of how necessary adjustments will be handled and the disposition of such things as lay-offs, transfers, process changes, and the like should be covered in detail. It should also be pointed out that normally it is easier to find many small cost reductions than a few big ones, but the aggregate of the former make up sizable savings.

COST-EFFECTIVENESS METHOD AND VALUE ANALYSIS

Two additional concepts in cost reduction merit discussion. They are (1) cost-effectiveness method and (2) value analysis. There are instances where the allocating of a firm's resources cannot be measured entirely in monetary terms. An example is the allocation of funds for research facilities. The return or the worthwhileness of one research and development endeavor over another can only be measured in terms of its long-range contribution to the implementing of scientific experiment and the adding to scientific knowledge. Likewise, institutions such as hospitals and colleges face similar cost control questions because the value of their "product" is only partially economic.

An interesting form of cost effectiveness is planning-programming-budgeting-system (PPBS). It is an effort or a means to promote greater efficiency and economy by developing more rational approaches to decision making. Initiated by the U.S. Department of Defense, PPBS consists of identifying objectives and alternative methods of meeting the objectives being subjected to systematic analysis comparing projected costs with benefits. Focus is made on the output of a program and its judged values in relation to its projected cost. It is helpful in trying to arrive at a rate of return for a planned action. In addition, it helps identify what may have to be foregone when one action is selected over another. In the case of the U.S. Department of Defense, for example, it became clear several decades ago that improvements in a weapons performance capability did not embrace its utility per se. Many other considerations, it was reasoned, should be taken into account and most of them cannot be expressed precisely in terms of dollars. However, the value of the added performance can be estimated with respect to the requirements of the units it is supposed to support. And this is what PPBS assists the manager in accomplishing.

Value analysis is a technique utilizing an organized creative approach to identify unnecessary costs in a product or service and subsequently substituting different materials and methods to obtain equal performance at lower cost. This technique, sometimes referred to as value engineering, can be used to reduce the cost of existent products or to assist in designing products before they are manufactured. The meaning of "value" as used in value analysis is established by comparison. It can be of two different types (1) *use* value or the properties and qualities that accomplish an activity and (2) *esteem* value which is the attractiveness and features that stimulate a buyer to own or to prefer the given product. Hence, by means of value analysis the objective is to achieve the lowest cost of providing acceptable performance and features the buyer's or user's wants.

The three basic steps of value analysis are: (1) identify the function, (2) evaluate the function by comparison, and (3) develop value alternatives. In performing these steps, answers are sought to these key questions: What is the item? What does it cost? What does it do? What else will do the job? What will that cost? By applying these questions to each part of a product, unnecessary costs are identified, alternative ways are discovered, and the cost of these alternatives are ascertained. From this, the alternative giving the best value can be selected and utilized.

FIXED AND VARIABLE COSTS

An additional important concept in cost controlling is the use of fixed and variable costs and their subsequent analysis in so-called break-even charts. Costs for any enterprise can be segregated into (1) fixed and (2) variable with respect to the volume of work output. Fixed costs are expenditures which *tend to remain fixed* or relatively constant regardless of the volume of work output for a period. There is no absolutely fixed cost for all times. Items such as executives' salaries, depreciation, and interest on borrowed money are examples of fixed costs. On the other hand, variable costs are expenditures which *tend to change directly* and are related to the volume of work output. Direct material costs and salesmen's commissions are examples of variable costs.[2]

Analysis of fixed and variable costs provides a picture of how the enterprise is set up costwise for operations, what volume of work is necessary to break even, that is, where total income equals total expendi-

---

[2] A third classification, semivariable costs, is also sometimes used in cost behavior analyses. Semivariable costs vary with the volume of work output but not in direct proportion to it. When the volume is zero, some semivariable costs exist—they are never completely eliminated.

tures and there is no profit, and what the profit possibilities are at various levels of sales.

SOLVING BREAK-EVEN POINT PROBLEMS

In solving break-even point problems it is helpful to keep four fundamental constraining factors in mind:
1. Sales equal fixed cost plus variable cost plus or minus profit.
    or

$$S = FC + VC + P$$

2. At break-even point: sales equals fixed cost plus variable cost.
    or

$$S_{BEP} = FC + VC$$

3. Variable costs and profits vary with sales.
4. Fixed costs remain fixed within the range of the sales being considered.

Assume a company has sales of $3 million, variable costs are 40 percent of sales, and fixed costs are estimated at $1.5 million. The problem is to find the profits, if any, at this level of sales and the break-even point. Also, the profits, if any, at sales of $4 million and at $2 million are to be calculated.

The variable costs are 40 percent times $3 million, or $1.2 million, which added to the fixed costs give a total of $2.7 million. The difference between total sales, $3 million, and total costs, $2.7 million, is $300,000, or the profits when sales are $3 million. At the break-even point, profits are zero and fixed costs are $1.5 million (since fixed costs remain fixed), which represents 60 percent (100 percent total less 40 percent variable) of total costs, so break-even point sales equal $1.5 million divided by 0.60, or $2.5 million. To find profits, if any, when sales equal $4 million, calculate the variable costs, which are 40 percent of $4 million, or $1.6 million. At this same sales level, fixed costs are $1.5 million, and so total costs are $3.1 million, leaving a profit of $900,000. In similar manner, when sales are $2 million, a loss of $300,000 is incurred.

ALGEBRAIC SOLUTION

To solve this same problem by algebra, first substitute values in formula 1 as given above.

$$S = FC + VC + \text{Profit}$$
$$\$3,000,000 = \$1,500,000 + 40\% \text{ of } \$3,000,000 + \text{Profit}$$
$$\$3,000,000 = \$1,500,000 + \$1,200,000 + \text{Profit}$$
$$\$300,000 = \text{Profit}$$

To determine the break-even point, use formula 2 given above.

$$S_{BEP} = FC + VC$$
$$= (100\% - 40\%) S_{BEP} + 40\% S_{BEP}$$
$$= \$1,500,000 + 40\% S_{BEP}$$
$$60\% S_{BEP} = \$1,500,000$$
$$S_{BEP} = \$2,500,000$$

For profit at sales of $4 million using formula 1:

$$\$4,000,000 = \$1,500,000 + 40\% \text{ of } \$4,000,000 + \text{Profit}$$
$$\$900,000 = \text{Profit}$$

For profit at sales of $2,000,000 using formula 1:

$$\$2,000,000 = \$1,500,000 + 40\% \text{ of } \$2,000,000 + \text{Profit}$$
$$-\$300,000 = \text{Profit (loss)}$$

GRAPHIC SOLUTION

Figure 26–8 shows the graphic solution to the same problem. The horizontal axis of the chart represents volume or output; the vertical axis is used to show dollars representing sales cost and profit. To construct the chart, we first draw the fixed cost line which is the horizontal line, *AF*, on the chart. It is $1.5 million above the base line and has this same value regardless of the amount of output, since fixed costs are fixed. Using this line, *AF*, as a base, line *AV* is drawn representing variable cost between lines *AF* and AV. This line will pass through point A and since variable cost equals 40 percent of sales dollars, the line will slope upward to the right at a rate of 40 to every 100 increase in sales. At sales of $3,000,000, fixed cost is equal to $1,500,000, variable cost $1,200,000, and profit $300,000. These values locate point *T* which in on the sales line, *RS*. Another point on this sales line is the break-even point which we will determine and then draw in line *RS*. The break-even point dollar value is determined by recognizing that the fixed cost, or $1,500,000, is equal to 100 percent minus 40 percent of the sales at the break-even point. Hence, if 60 percent is equal to $1,500,000, then 100 percent is equal to $2,500,000, which equals sales at the break-even point, or the total dollar value of the dotted vertical line on the chart through the break-even point. As indi-

FIGURE 26–8. Break-even chart

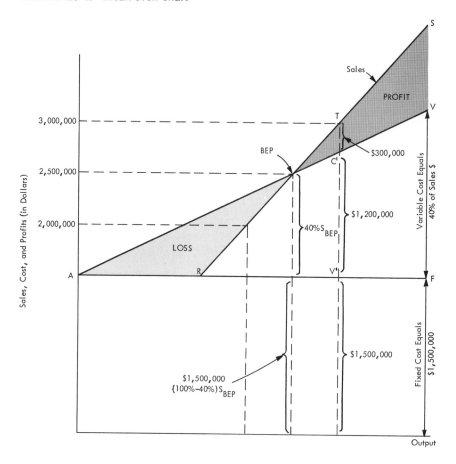

cated above, by joining points *T* and the break-even point, the sales line *RS* is determined. Subsequently, cost and profit value patterns can be read directly from the chart. At $2 million sales, for example, fixed cost is $1.5 million, variable cost is $800,000, with profit showing a deficit or loss of $300,000.

UTILIZING BREAK-EVEN POINT ANALYSIS

It behooves managers to arrange the setup of an enterprise in keeping with a reasonable range of sales expectancy. In the above example, if the sales were likely to be between $2 million and $2.5 million, it is apparent that this company will be profitless. It is geared to handle a larger sales volume. On the other hand, if there were reasonable certainty that sales will maintain a fairly high-volume range, say from $6 million to $10 million, it can be shown that greater profits will be realized if some of the present variable costs are converted into fixed costs through mechanization or some other means.

Consider the data in Figure 26–9. In this illustration the level of sales has been assumed equal to $6 million; that is, profits are identical at this sales level in either the original or revised setup. Comparing the revised with the original, fixed costs have doubled and variable costs reduced from 40 to 15 percent of sales. As a result, profits change also.

FIGURE 26–9

Original setup

Sales	Fixed costs	Variable costs (40 percent)	Total costs	Profits
$ 4,000,000	$1,500,000	$1,600,000	$3,100,000	$ 900,000
6,000,000	. . .	2,400,000	3,900,000	2,100,000
8,000,000	. . .	3,200,000	4,700,000	3,300,000
10,000,000	. . .	4,000,000	5,500,000	4,500,000

Break-even point $2,500,000

Revised setup

Sales	Fixed costs	Variable costs (15 percent)	Total costs	Profits
$ 4,000,000	$3,000,000	$ 600,000	$3,600,000	$ 400,000
6,000,000	. . .	900,000	3,900,000	2,100,000
8,000,000	. . .	1,200,000	4,200,000	3,800,000
10,000,000	. . .	1,500,000	4,500,000	5,500,000

Break-even point $3,529,412

The results are typical and lead to an important principle which will now be stated.

PRINCIPLE OF VARIABLE-COST AND FIXED-COST RELATIONSHIPS TO PROFIT POTENTIAL

For a given enterprise, the lowest variable and highest fixed costs consistent with a break-even point which is less than the smallest probable total sales result in the maximum profit potential.

Over the past several decades, many companies have increased their break-even point by two major actions: (1) the increasing of fixed costs so that relatively they represent a greater proportion of total costs and

(2) the increasing costs of items making up fixed and variable costs. These enterprises with high break-even points must secure high sales volumes in order to survive. Various means of easing this pressure or of operating effectively with present facilities are listed in Figure 26–10.

From the viewpoint of fixed- and variable-cost relationships, many companies are presently in a position that if their respective sales decline 20 to 25 percent, they are in serious difficulty to match total income to total costs. The flexibility of the operations has been lessened—rigidities in the form of fixed costs have become more dominant, as illustrated by

FIGURE 26–10

To ease demands of high break-even point, an enterprise can—

1. Increase the number of units sold.
2. Add new products or services which indicate reasonable sales volumes. Give particular attention to items smoothing out seasonal fluctuations.
3. Redesign present products to provide a wider margin.
4. Increase selling price to acquire a larger dollar sales volume, if demand is constant.
5. Lower selling price to attract a broader market, if demand is elastic.
6. Eliminate slow-moving, nonprofitable items when research and sales efforts clearly show little improvement is likely.
7. Consolidate departments or functions to reduce costs.
8. Modernize methods used in production and selling processes.
9. Install more efficient machines and equipment in factory and in office, the capacities of which are within the economic limits of reasonable sales expectancy.
10. Watch carefully the costs of sales promotion and advertising efforts to help insure maximum effectiveness in these fields.

---

greater and greater automation. As fixed-cost items increase, it takes more dollars, obtained from sales, to cover these fixed costs.

BUDGETARY CONTROLLING

Budgetary controlling is one of the most widely recognized and used means of managerial controlling. It encompasses the planning-controlling combination approach referred to in Chapter 23. Precisely it can be stated that *budgetary controlling is a process of finding out what's being done and comparing these results with the corresponding budget data in order to approve accomplishments or to remedy differences.* Budgetary controlling is commonly termed budgeting.

FUNDAMENTAL BUDGETARY CONSIDERATIONS

In private industry, budgetary control begins logically with an estimate of sales and the income therefrom. This follows, since the ultimate controller is sales. However, in the case of governmental enterprises, the amount appropriated serves the same purpose as sales in private enterprises. In determining the sales estimates, the forecasting should be based on sound research to as great an extent as possible. Guesses should be confined to those areas in which no factual information is available. To expedite the forecasting work, at least in the initial stages, it is advisable to concentrate on the key items. Trying to do a complete study on every single item can result in doing a haphazard job on all items. Final estimates are a result of judgment plus careful analysis and interpretation of available factual information.

FIGURE 26–11. A sales-expense budget

	January		February		March	
	Expectancy	*Actual*	*Expectancy*	*Actual*	*Expectancy*	*Actual*
Sales............	$1,200,000		$1,350,000		$1,400,000	
Expenses						
General overhead	310,000		310,000		310,000	
Selling..........	242,000		275,000		288,000	
Production......	327,000		430,500		456,800	
Research........	118,400		118,400		115,000	
Office..........	90,000		91,200		91,500	
Advertising.....	32,500		27,000		25,800	
Estimated Gross						
Profit.........	80,100		97,900		112,900	

Likewise, the probable selling expenses in attaining the estimated levels pose another problem of forecasting and require firsthand information and knowledge of the particular marketing activities.

Figure 26–11 shows a budget with estimates for sales and expenses for the first three months of the year, January, February, and March. Space is provided for entry of the actual accomplishments so that comparison by each item between expectancy and actual is expedited. Note that the total expenses plus estimated gross profit equals the total sales expectancy.

Budgeting is based on data which are either of (1) a constant or (2) a variable classification. Constant means the budget standards are for a fixed or constant level; that is, the targets remain constant, and the estimates are believed to be based on a high degree of accuracy. In contrast, variable includes budgeted estimates at several levels so that variations in sales, production, cash, or other key data can be recognized. In other words, estimates are made for total sales at different levels, for production at different levels, etc.; and as actual happenings take place, the budget figures corresponding to the most appropriate level actually reached are used.

Budgeting can be supplied to the total or any segment of an enterprise. It is not confined to matters of finance. Units other than dollars are commonly used. For example, budgeting of production in physical units and of labor by different skills is extensively employed by industry.

It requires time to achieve a level of effective budgetary control. Too much should not be expected of budgetary control within too short periods of time. It requires time-consuming experience, judgment, and a desire to make budgeting effective before tangible and good results are attained. Habits are not changed overnight. Experienced managers neither expect to correct deep-seated difficulties instantly nor to witness sudden miracles as a result of budgetary control.

Also, estimates are alterable; they should not be considered rigid and infallible. The most helpful estimates are generally those which are responsive to political and economic changes and are sufficiently flexible to meet rapid shifts and turns. Too much rigidity defeats the possible advantages of budgeting because of failure to acknowledge realities. At the same time, alterations should not be too freely accepted, lest stability and integrity of budget data become jeopardized.

In connection with budgeting and the action of taking corrective measures, it is recommended that specific approval be required for nonbudgeted items. From time to time, unforeseen items not included in the budget arise and require immediate disposition. They should be specifically approved by the person in charge of the work. This fixes responsibility and makes the manager aware of these nonbudgeted items. To ignore them can result in diluting the benefits of budgeting and in losing effective control.

FORMULATING THE BUDGET

The practice is growing of performing preplanning prior to the budget preparation in order to determine the broad assumed operating plan of an enterprise. This preplanning is developed from two basic sources of data: company objectives and environmental factors. Included are trends in buyers' demands, company's competitive position, and potential in relation to economic trends. The availability of such a plan provides helpful guides and constraints in the formulation of the budget which, as stated above, starts with the sales forecast.

Normally a member of top management serves as the chief executive and coordinator for drawing up the budget and using it. He need not necessarily be concerned with the details but should resolve conflicting interests, recommend adjustments when needed, and give official sanction to budgetary procedures. In the case of large enterprises, the development of the budget estimates may be guided and carried out by a specially designated executive. In some instances the job of budget controller is created. More commonly, the treasurer, controller, or chief accountant is charged with these duties.

In most instances, a budget committee exists to formulate and to assist in implementing the budgetary work. Such a committee is made up of the executives in charge of the respective major functions or departments, such as sales, production, purchasing, research, finance, and personnel. These executives are thoroughly familiar with their respective units and are in a position to know what the requirements are to operate their departments efficiently. Meetings of the committee, at which the budget director serves as chairman, offer an excellent medium for coordinating the various functions, securing greater cooperation, and encouraging participation by active line officers in budgeting work. Major departmental objectives and constraints are determined and this information is disseminated by the committee members to their respective interested members.

The tentative estimates of each respective organization unit is prepared. Clues, key figures, and all possible information are supplied so that plans are prepared in keeping with the general demands outlined by the top management. Participation by department heads is followed because these individuals are familiar with their respective particular type of work, and greater acceptance and use of the final budget will probably result if they have an active part in its formation. In turn, the department heads consult with various members of their respective units.

Within due time, the various departmental estimates are completed and submitted to the budget director. A series of meetings then follows during which the plans are discussed, adjustments suggested, and possible changes indicated. Sometimes preliminary meetings between the director and each department head are held. Finally, all the departmental estimates are evolved in their final approved form. They are then consolidated by the budget director and submitted to the top-management member for final approval.

A graphic presentation of this budget preparation is shown by Figure 26–12. Under the first heading of "Established Expectancies," there are seven steps, starting with the estimate of sales and ending with the approval of the budget and its publication. In addition, the chart indicates the efforts for budgetary controlling. The second heading of

FIGURE 26–12. The drawing up of budgets

	PRES-IDENT	V.P. SALES	V.P. MFG.	V.P. R.&D.	SEC'Y-TREAS.	BUDGET DIRECTOR
I. ESTABLISH EXPECTANCIES						
1. Set forth broad plan of company and estimate sales						
2. Prepare programs for next period						
a. Sales						
b. Inventory						
c. Research						
d. Costs and expenses						
3. Submit finished programs for next period						
a. Capital investments						
b. Cash requirements						
4. Translate into budgets						
5. Review, adjust, and return budgets to Budget Director						
6. Coordinate budgets						
7. Approve, publish, and distribute budgets						
II. BUDGETARY OPERATIONS						
8. Prepare reports comparing performance to budget date						
9. Review, analyze, and explain variances						
III. CORRECTIVE ACTION						
10. Take corrective action and if necessary revise budgets						

"Budgetary Operations," consisting of two steps, encompasses those portions of the control process dealing with finding out what is being accomplished and comparing it with the expectancy. The last heading, "Corrective Action," made up of one step, is the familiar, correcting deviation, if this is necessary.

APPLYING BUDGETARY CONTROL

Comparisons between budgeted activities and actual performance should be carefully reviewed and interpreted; and recommendations, if any, should be made for future action. Variances are almost certain to appear and should be expected within reasonable limits. Any operation which is clearly out of line should be noted and possible reasons for the difference ascertained.

Usually the budget director sends copies of all budget reports issued to various department heads and to his superior or the top-ranking executive over all budgeting activities. This not only keeps the chief executive informed but also helps assure proper backing on corrective actions recommended by the director. Simple, yet concise and complete reports can be issued with ease. Such reports should be issued regularly and as frequently as the situation warrants. Information must be timely, since too long a delay for results of actual operations depletes the interest and lessens the vitality to correct the condition. In fact, delay commonly increases the difficulty of achieving the needed correction. Reports should include comparisons to previous comparable periods and, if possible, show the efficiency of the department. Such information helps to orient the respondent and provides a meaningful basis of control which assists in deciding when and what action should be taken.

It is the duty of the budget director to review the results with the responsible operating heads or department heads concerning matters relating to their particular activities. Assistance should be given the person in charge of the activity to discover and to curb unfavorable departures or trends. Suggestions are in order as to what remedial actions might be taken; information and assistance in seeking improvements should be stressed.

Normally, periodic conferences are held between the chief executive and the budget director to discuss the present budgeting status, forecast probable future developments, and decide what action should be taken. Also, from time to time and as the occasion requires, meetings are arranged to discuss the specific subjects. The interested parties to these meetings include the following persons: chief executive, budget director, members of the budget committee, department heads, and supervisors. These meetings are of great assistance in ironing out differences of opinion and in reaching mutual agreements on what should be done.

TYPES OF BUDGETING

There are many types of budgeting available. First is a simple *sales budget* providing for sales estimates and accomplishments by months for various sales areas. Frequently a breakdown by product is included. Records are also kept of quarterly and yearly totals.

Another common type deals with *production.* Expressed in physical units, it indicates when products must be completed to meet scheduled sales forecasts and helps in determining the material and labor requirements to meet the production scheduled. The equipment and capacities of machines, their availability and working order, and the most economic quantities to produce are among the basic information which must be available to budget production successfully. Frequently, the cost of production is also included either as a part of the production budgeting or separately in what might be termed *cost production budgeting.* Sometimes the cost of production figures are compared with the sales price to ascertain whether satisfactory margins are being obtained, that is, items being sold at too low a price or items costing too much to produce. The term *step budget* is frequently used when the production budgeted estimates include various steps or levels of production. In short, a step budget is another name applied to budgeted estimates which are classified as variable.

To have suitable material at the proper time, place, and cost is the goal of *purchasing budgeting.* Excessive stocks and depreciation of inventories are minimized; yet sufficient materials of the proper quality and quantity are available. Help in avoiding the tying up of purchasing funds and buying in markets when prices are declining constitute major advantages in the use of purchasing budgeting.

Although not as common as some of the other types, *labor budgeting* assists in determining the number and type of skills or people required during the budget period. Labor demands can be forecast fairly accurately from the production estimates, and any surplus or shortage of particular skills can be noted. Recruitment and training programs can be scheduled accordingly so that turnover is minimized and adequate selection and training techniques are followed. In periods of labor scarcity, expansion, construction, or conversion from one line of products to another, the budgeting of labor can prove especially helpful.

Cash, or financial, budgeting is a necessity for every business enterprise. Estimates for this budgeting are most convenient to prepare after all other budget estimates are completed. The anticipation of cash problems and the possible means of meeting them are the major purposes of cash budgeting. This type of budget shows the anticipated receipts and expenditures along with the financial requirements of the business so that the amount of working capital needed to conduct the various activities can be determined. The extent to which outside financing might be required, the time and method of paying obligations incurred, probabilities of funds available for equipment purchases, extent to which capital is kept in productive channels, and periods of cash availability and also of cash deficiency are among the major benefits which can be gained from the cash budget estimates and budgeting. If cash from the anticipated operations of the business is insufficient and borrowing is unavailable, it is necessary to revise the operations so that the financing can be adequately handled.

Figure 26–13 illustrates the work of cash budgeting for a manufac-

FIGURE 26–13. Work of cash budgeting

Cash budget

	Jan.	Feb.	March	April	May
Estimated sales.............	$130,000	$120,000	$170,000	$175,000	$160,000
Receipts:					
Cash sales...............	$ 8,000	$ 5,000	$ 12,000	$ 10,000	$ 8,000
Accounts receivable........	132,500	100,000	85,000	108,000	117,000
Notes receivable..........	40,000	40,000	35,000	40,000	40,000
Total..............	$180,500	$145,000	$132,000	$158,000	$165,000
Disbursements:					
Direct labor..............	$ 45,000	$ 49,000	$ 49,000	$ 49,000	$ 51,000
Indirect labor.............	18,500	18,500	18,500	18,500	20,000
Purchases................	24,000	57,000	72,000	55,000	50,000
Overhead salaries..........	9,000	9,000	9,000	9,000	9,000
Taxes...................	10,000	10,000	63,000	10,000	12,000
Insurance................	...	...	...	2,800	...
Dividends................	22,000	...	...	22,000	...
Total...............	$128,500	$143,500	$211,500	$166,300	$142,000
Excess or deficiency (*)......	$ 52,000	$ 1,500	$ 79,500*	$ 8,300*	$ 23,000
Cash balance					
at start of month........	27,500	79,500	81,000	50,250	41,950
Borrow...................	...	...	48,750	...	...
Repay....................	...	...	...	...	...
Cash balance					
at end of month...	$ 79,500	$ 81,000	$ 50,250	$ 41,950	$ 64,950

turing company. Estimated sales for January are $130,000, with total receipts forecast at $180,500, some receipts being received from sales of former months. Disbursements during the same month are figured at $128,500, leaving an excess of $52,000 ($180,500 — $128,500). Since the cash balance at the beginning of the year is $27,500, the cash balance at the end of January will be $52,000 plus $27,500, or $79,500. During March the company will borrow $50,000 from the bank at 5 percent interest for six months. Interest charges will therefore amount to $1,250 for this period; the amount advanced to the company will be $48,750 ($50,000 — $1,250), which will be repaid in six months (during September) in the full amount of $50,000.

Another type of budgeting warrants inclusion in this discussion because of its value to managers; this includes estimates of all major activities and is commonly referred to as the *master budget*. As the name suggests, a master budget is a principal, or supreme, budget. It brings together and coordinates all the estimates of other budgets. In a sense the master budget can be thought of as a "budget of budgets." Sales estimates are coordinated with those of production so that minimum risk, ample financial funds, and sufficient material and labor will be available. The master budget and its use tie together the programs of the various units. Customarily it does not show sufficient details from which operating departments can guide their respective activities. For working purposes, one or several of the above-mentioned types (sales, production, purchasing, labor, cash) is employed.

BUDGET PERIOD

Another consideration of budgeting is the budget period. All budgets are prepared for a definite time period. Many cover one year; but some are for longer periods, such as 5 or even 10 years, while others are for several months or several weeks. Probably the most common budget periods are 1, 3, 6, and 12 months.

The length of time selected depends upon the main purpose of the budgeting. If quarterly checks are desired, the time period will be three months. On the other hand, if more frequent checks are deemed necessary, one- or two-month periods might be selected. The period chosen should include the complete normal cycle of activity for the enterprise. For example, seasonal variations should be included and also periods of both production and sales. To have a budget plan covering primarily the productive period only and another the sales period only neither makes for meaningful budgeting comparisons nor reveals the true interrelations of all the activities. For convenience and uniformity, it is desirable to make the budget period coincide with other control devices. If managerial reports, balance sheets, and statements of profit and loss are issued semiannually, a like period, or six months, is suggested for a budget period. In addition, the extent to which reasonable forecasts can be made should be considered in determining the budget period. Comparisons used in budgetary control are dependent somewhat upon the accuracy and validity of estimates. Too long a period reduces the dependability and usefulness of the budgeting. Although forecasts for shorter periods would seem fairly easy to determine, it is entirely possible to have the periods too short so that continuous operations of a long cyclical nature become difficult to estimate accurately for a short period.

The common practice followed in modern management is to revise and adjust the budget estimates as developments take place and more data and information become available. Many different approaches can be used, although most procedures involve a periodic review or some sort of a progressive moving average approach. To illustrate, an enterprise might forecast for the next 12-month period in March, June, September, and December. In March, 1973, the estimate would cover March 1973–March 1974; in June, 1973, for June 1973–June 1974; etc. Progressive adjustments are possible in connection with each forecast. An alternate is to make a yearly forecast in January with revised forecasts in March, June, and September for the remaining months of the year. Some companies follow what can be termed "moving budgeting." A yearly forecast is set up; then as each month is completed, another month is added to the period. For example, at the completion of November 1972, a forecast for November 1973 is added so that a moving 12-month forecast is maintained. Regardless of the practice adopted, revisions are made at any time when believed necessary.

ADVANTAGES AND DISADVANTAGES OF BUDGETARY CONTROL

It will be helpful to list the more common advantages of budgetary control and follow this with a list of the more common disadvantages. Among the advantages are:

1. The overall managerial viewpoint of the entire organization and adequate recognition of the existence and importance of many different activities are fostered.
2. Efforts are directed in most profitable channels, a constructive influence is supplied, and achievement of common goals is enhanced.
3. Use of the principle of exception is emphasized. Time and effort of managers are focused upon areas where most helpful results are possible.
4. Responsibility is fixed. The person in charge of an activity is expected to make things happen in accordance with the budget plan.
5. Actions are likely to be based on study and careful considerations —snap decisions and hasty judgments are attenuated.
6. Weaknesses in the organization, managerial ability, and personnel

are revealed; possible means for improving and correcting such deficits are provided.

7. Waste reduction is promoted; needless spending is minimized.
8. Use of labor and equipment is stabilized and improved; future efforts in what amounts, where, and when are known.

On the other hand, budgetary control has its disadvantages including:

1. Budgetary control is only a tool; it is subject to human judgment, interpretation, and evaluation.
2. The courses are charted, but budgetary control in itself does not prevent deviations from appearing. It neither ensures satisfactory results nor controls automatically.
3. Good and adequate standards are mandatory and in some cases these are difficult to come by.
4. Forecasting is required and it is fraught with uncertainties. It is all tentative.
5. The data must be interpreted and proper evaluation given them.
6. The information from budgetary control must be communicated adequately to all concerned—no small task in most instances.
7. Skill and experience are required to make budgetary control work successfully. Success in its use is not acquired quickly.
8. Budgetary control requires expenditure of time, money, and effort. It must itself be "kept in line."

HUMAN BEHAVIOR AND BUDGETING

When it is all said and done, the ultimate purpose of budgeting is to direct and control human behavior of managers and of nonmanagers. Unfortunately, the belief is common that budgeting is employed to utilize best a company's dollars and direct effectively the actions of its management members. In too many cases it does not serve as a means in attaining a company's ends, but has become a tool emphasizing ends within itself. The fault lies mainly in the top managers' failure to recognize the human behavior inherent in controlling. Managers and nonmanagers want budgeting to do something *for* them, not something *to* them.

The question is not whether budgetary controls are necessary, but are they being administered in a manner that makes them really effective. To those requested to abide by them, the requests or directives may not carry the importance or make the same sense as they do to the issuing party. Under such conditions the recipient cannot be enthusiastic about budgeting and may adopt an acquiescence or a grudging acceptance of it. Or he may adopt a behavior of quiet subversion. The result is that he subconsciously absolves himself from responsibility for the budgeting results and makes it appear he is abiding by the rules when in reality he is busy minimizing them. The outcome is the loss of the effectiveness of budgeting.

Budgetary controlling handled in light of today's management knowledge does not lead to conflict. But certain beliefs about employees are necessary to achieve the most from budgetary controlling. Most managers and nonmanagers can relate their activities to company goals if they are told what the company goals are. They can follow a preferred controlling means if they know why it is preferred and they had a voice in selecting it. They can answer budgeting questions if they have helped formulate the budget. Both top and lower level managers can be satisfied if both participate in formulating the controlling whereby they will be managed. Budgets and budgetary controlling is not a one-man operation, with a manager issuing orders and insisting that certain steps be followed. Budgetary controlling helps all management members do their jobs better. The ideas of nonmanagement members concerning budgeting, especially those relating to costs, should be sought. Everyone in the enterprise should participate and feel that the budgeting practices are assisting him and making the enterprise a better place in which to work.

QUESTIONS

1. Discuss the meaning and function of dispatching in production control.
2. With reference to Figure 26–3, answer the following:
   a) What was the scheduled time for shearing on order No. 17544?
   b) Has the forming operation started on order No. 17549?
   c) Is the order for the Ulco Corporation ahead or behind schedule?
   d) Is the time period from 2 to 4 of Lis-Almers Manufacturing Company available for work? Why?
3. What is value analysis and how is it performed?
4. Are overhead costs usually uniform throughout a manufacturing plant? Why? Discuss in what ways your answer affects the controlling of costs.
5. Distinguish between the concepts in each of the following pairs: (a) basic standard cost and variable cost, (b) a constant and a variable type of budget, and (c) fixed cost and cash budgeting.
6. Is the break-even point equal to the sum of the fixed and variable costs at any volume of sales? Explain.
7. Referring to Figure 26–9, under the revised setup, show the calculations to determine the data given on the break-even point and on profits when sales are $10 million.

8. List and explain three methods for distributing overhead costs. Explain their validity and importance in establishing a basis of control.
9. In your own words describe the meaning of Figure 26–12.
10. Enumerate five prominent advantages of budgetary control. Five disadvantages.
11. Farley-Berkshire Company, a medium sized distributor of hardware items, has never used budgeting. Relate how you would attempt to get budgeting adopted by this company's managers.
12. Referring to Figure 26–13, explain how the cash balance, $64,950, at the end of May is calculated.
13. Suggest several ways in which budget estimates can be revised and brought up to date. Which method do you prefer? Why?
14. Discuss the subject "Human Behavior and Budgeting," carefully pointing out the salient features in this area as you see them.

CASE 26–1. THE MITCHELL COMPANY

Mr. James J. Mahoney, president of the Mitchell Company, has received an offer to purchase the Watford Company at a price of $2.5 million, to be paid and financed in ten annual equal installments. Mr. Mahoney is convinced that his company needs more sales and in view of experience during the current year, believes his company should reduce its fixed cost and gear its present operations to reasonable sales expectancies over the next several years. His compeers confirm that present fixed costs of the Mitchell Company can be reduced by $500,000 as a result of a strict and thorough cost reduction program. The offer to purchase Watford Company, a strong competitor, intrigued Mr. Mahoney and he felt that purchase of this company might be the means for securing the sales he believes he needs.

From marketing studies, it is estimated that annual sales between $4 and $7 million are a reasonable range for the Mitchell Company over the next three to four years. At the present time the company's fixed costs are $2.6 million with sales equal to $5.5 million. The Watford Company's comparable data are fixed costs of $2.0 million with sales of $3.0 million. Mr. Mahoney estimates his company will retain 70 percent of Watford Company's sales should this company be purchased. Also, he believes his present variable costs of 40 percent of sales could be reduced to 33⅓ percent for the new, merged company. Records show present variable costs of Watford Company are 30 percent of sales. In addition, it is believed that fixed costs of Watford Company could be reduced $500,000 as a result of its purchase by the Mitchell Company.

Questions

1. Calculate (*a*) current profits of the Mitchell Company, (*b*) current profits of the Watford Company, and (*c*) current profits of a merged Mitchell Company and Watford Company.
2. Calculate the data (costs, profits, or losses) for the several alternative actions open to Mr. Mahoney.
3. Based on cost, what decision should Mr. Mahoney reach? Discuss.
4. Other than cost, what considerations do you feel Mr. Mahoney should take into account? Why?

CASE 26–2.   UNITED UNIVERSITY

Vincent P. Fitzmaurice, assistant business manager of United University, claims that a major need of his university is not more classrooms but better utilization of classrooms it now has. He estimates that the current utilization is somewhat less than 50 percent and that the distribution over the available school day hours is particularly bad. For example, Saturday morning, utilization is extremely low, and on Tuesdays and Thursdays, there is a relatively small amount of classroom space utilization. He feels efforts should be made to improve this general situation. To bring this about, he admits many adjustments will be necessary, especially in schedules of classes, room preferences, and the like. But awareness of the problem is the first step toward its solution.

To justify his viewpoints, Mr. Fitzmaurice compiled data on current classroom usage in one building of the university. See following page. In other words, room 100 has a student capacity of 20 and is currently being used for 3 hours each Monday, Wednesday, and Friday. No other classes are officially scheduled in it for the current school period. University classes are held hourly from 8 A.M. to 5 P.M. with no classes between 12 noon and 1 P.M. and on Saturday from 8 A.M. to 12 noon. A 10-minute break between classes is permitted to enable students to get from one room to another.

Questions

1. Classify the data into four arbitrary groups including (*a*) rooms up to and including 25-student capacity, (*b*) from 26- to 45-student capacity, (*c*) from 46- to 65-student capacity, and (*d*) over 66-student capacity. For each group, determine the percentage of utilization.
2. Do you agree with the general statements made by Mrs. Fitzmaurice? Substantiate your answer.
3. What do you recommend Mr. Fitzmaurice tell the university's governing board or top management group? Discuss.

Room number	Capacity	Hours used					
		M	T	W	Th	F	Sat
First Floor:							
100............	20	3	...	3	...	3	...
101............	20	2	4	2	4	2	...
102............	35	5	3	5	3	5	...
103............	35	5	3	5	3	5	1
104............	25	6	5	6	5	6	...
105............	110	2	...	2	...	2	1
106............	45	7	4	7	4	7	...
107............	45	5	4	5	4	5	...
108............	40	6	2	6	2	6	2
Second Floor:							
201............	12	4	1	4	1	4	1
202............	12	2	...	1	1	...	1
203............	35	6	2	6	2	6	3
204............	25	5	1	5	1	5	...
205............	65	6	5	6	5	6	2
206............	65	7	3	7	3	7	...
207............	45	6	2	3	2	6	...
208............	40	7	2	4	2	7	...
Third Floor:							
303............	35	4	6	2	6	2	...
304............	25	1	2	1	2	1	...
307............	45	6	3	3	3	3	...
308............	40	7	4	3	4	3	...

CASE 26–3.   THE BARTON CLUB

The Barton Club has a current membership of 1,500 members who reside in Los Angeles County, California. Mr. J. Blair Lane is the executive secretary and receives a salary of $17,500 a year. He has been promised a $2,500 increase for the forthcoming year. Each member pays $45 dues a year. The club holds ten monthly meetings during the year, beginning with September and ending with June. An outside speaker talks on a subject of particular interest at each of these meetings. For this he is paid $75 to defray part of his expense.

To encourage good turnouts and also help balance the budget, an annual charge of $10 is made of each member for the dinners at the ten meetings. About 40 percent of the members attend each meeting and the club pays $3 for each meal, but this charge will be increased 10 percent beginning next year.

The Barton Club publishes a bulletin for which members pay $5 a year, entitling them to receive the four issues—one published in each quarter, winter, spring, summer, and fall. This $5 is in addition to their membership dues and dinner fee. The printing and mailing of the bulletin cost $9,540 this year, but next year the printer has advised that a $1,760 increase will be effective due to his higher labor and material costs. Editing of the material for the bulletin costs $750 per year, and contributors of accepted articles and papers received $6,000 this year. It is believed that these amounts will increase 20 percent for the next year. In addition to the club's membership subscription, past experience shows that approximately 700 extra copies of the bulletin are sold throughout the year. Single copies sell for $1.50 per copy.

In addition to his salary, Mr. Lane receives a $50 monthly travel allowance. He manages the activities of the club, giving direct supervision to a secretary receiving $400 a month, a statistician receiving $550 a month, two clerks each at $350 a month, and another clerk at $300 a month. Since money payments and receipts are handled by the employees, they are bonded on a comprehensive coverage basis, a protection costing the club $250 a year. A public accounting firm audits the club's books for a fee of $400 yearly. However, notice has been received that the fee will increase to $450 yearly beginning next year.

Additional expenses of the club include rent, $2,800 a year; postage, $160 a month; telephone, $35 a month; stationery and supplies, $150 a month; and office equipment maintenance, $30 a month. The club has received notice that the rent will be increased 15 percent for the next year. In addition, hospitalization insurance costs the club $95 per quarter, and miscellaneous expenses, including legal and unappropriated costs, amount to $1,200 a year.

Questions

1. Draw up the club's budgets for the current year and for the next year.
2. Do the budgets reveal any areas requiring managerial action? Explain.
3. What specific recommendations for future actions can you offer the club? Substantiate your answer.

part VII

Forthcoming
developments
in management

In this closing Part VII, are given ideas pertaining to the future of management. Significant current trends seem to point out a number of developments that we can reasonably expect tomorrow to bring. The makeup of future management thinking, new roles that management will play, the solving of the managerial challenges of technology and social environment, the characteristics of the new organization structure, the type of work being accomplished, changes in the needs of management manpower, and the handling of manager obsolescence are among the major issues of more than average interest.

The future of management is bright. It is on the move and will reach new peaks of accomplishment beyond our present most optimistic predictions. The opportunities are vast and the future manager will play a dominant part in achieving an improved quality of living for all and the opportunity for each human being to rise to his highest destiny. One chapter is included:

27. *Management in the future*

27

Management in the future

A Profile of the Liberally Educated Man

He is intellectual rather than bookish
He is competent rather than competitive
He is committed rather than captured
He is informed rather than opinionated
He is discriminating rather than prejudiced
He is compassionate rather than condescending.

Lloyd J. Averill

Any attempt to make precise predictions about the future developments of management is filled with much risk and difficulty. The future is not an immense jump toward a distant moving destination; the future begins with the present. Study of where we are today in management thought, and how we got there, gives clues to what concepts and practices may be terminated, continued, or initiated during the years ahead.

The role of those performing management of the future will be challenged by powerful forces developing in a changing environment. A number of our current managerial concepts will fall by the wayside and, in addition, many will be significantly altered. New ideas, new techniques, and new frames of reference will evolve to develop a way of management thinking that both serves and survives the new society that calls for symbiotic relationships among all kinds of organizations —economic, political, educational, governmental, and philanthropic. Important questions demanding answers will be numerous. Representative are: Can the managers cope with the forces that are changing the environment in which they operate? Can the effectiveness of management be continued? On what basis should managers of the future be judged? Can management education keep pace with the demands placed upon it?

MANAGEMENT THOUGHT

Management thought has been, is now, and will continue to be highly dynamic. New theories will be developed and expanded, old theories will be modified, and some will be discarded. Certainly there will be consolidation among the many present management theories. In the realm of possibility is the development of several frameworks about which portions or all of several present and separate schools of management thought can be integrated. Continued dynamic management thought is to be expected because a discipline as vital as management—with its involvement in fundamental issues affecting human wants, values, and technology—is certain to attract scholars and practitioners to contribtute to a viable, modern, and meaningful theory.

Today, too much managerial knowledge is available to manage arbitrarily. On the other hand, insufficient knowledge is available to manage with certainty. In some managerial areas we can predict results from selected actions with an acceptable degree of certainty, but in other areas we are still in what can be termed the descriptive stage. That is, we can apply certain managerial knowledge, but we are not positive that specific results will ensue from such action. To illustrate, we can predict quite reliably in situations pertaining to organizational relationships. In contrast, prediction of the consequences of using management development programs is, in most cases, almost totally inaccurate and unreliable. In the distant future, the ultimate status of management thought will be for a manager in a given case to be able to prescribe accurately and consistently what should take place to attain stated objectives. In other words, once the manager has the symptoms identified, he can then prescribe exactly what to do, with assurance that the desired results will be forthcoming. When this realm is achieved, we will have reached the high peak of managerial knowledge and implementation.

MORE INVOLVEMENT

The fundamental issues of participation, self-actualization, and a democratic work environment are not theoretical abstractions. They are basic in man's day-to-day work experience and relationships of human beings. Man desires and will shape his management destiny. He wants more involvement in management affairs and we shall see more of this in the future.

Participation will increase and take on many different forms. More nonstructured, informal group activities will appear and be utilized because they are in keeping with the desire for more involvement and at the same time more freedom. For people to have a part of the action will become the standard and accepted practice.

It is this trend that will make results management more widely used. When the results management approach modifies the process of management, which gives structure, continuity, and completeness to the efforts, an effective modern format of management is provided. Such an approach gives the participant the satisfactions he needs and wants. Results are what count, getting them is what management is all about. The employee of tomorrow will want more and more to achieve the results directly in accordance with how he envisions the work should be done. Accomplishment indirectly by achieving specified activities will decline in usage. The results management-process approach to management will thrive during the decades ahead, or until something better is discovered.

All of this means, of course, that the working environment will become more democratic. The ideas of a subordinate will be listened to more carefully and he will be "more on his own." The superior will be less authoritarian in his dealings with subordinates, but authority—being essential to group accomplishment—will exist. It will be in a form that stresses acceptance and willingness of subordinates.

This desire on the part of participants to have greater influence has been with us for the last several decades. Witness the growth of labor unions, demands of teachers and government employees, and requests of students of universities. Taking place is a narrowing of the gap of power differentiation between the manager and the nonmanager. The formal organization structure of the future will place less stress on its hierarchical structure and more on equalitarian efforts. This does not mean that management by consensus, with everyone deferring to the member with the best idea or greatest knowledge, will be followed. Some direction appears essential and the superior-subordinate relationship will remain although in quite a different context than is prevalent today. Man has always demanded structure in his life. He depends on human relationships, some routine, and some of habit to survive. Complete human autonomy is a romantic ideal. But the increasing emphasis on human resources and the quest to maximize their contributions will bring about significant changes in the working relationships of people. An adaptive rather than a mechanistic structure seems to be the order of the future.

MANAGEMENT AS A RESOURCE

Gaining increasing acceptance during the years ahead will be the concept that management is the important resource which is basic to most achievement. This is the normal outgrowth of (1) management maturing, and (2) management knowledge and skill being practiced by more and more people, whether officially designated as management or nonmanagement members. With the development of management it has become evident that management is purposive, is concerned with obtaining results, and is the effective applicator of knowledge including that of many sciences and disciplines. In its broadest meaning, it is a means toward achievement and is fundamental in man's efforts to progress. The current problems of blighted cities, polluted rivers, bankrupt business enterprises, and crises of universities will be solved only by management. By its use, the required actions to eradicate these problems will be evolved and implemented. Likewise we will continue our leadership as a nation and as a people as long as our managerial efforts are effective. Management knowledge and skill are now recognized as one of the important resources of any nation. There are no nations that are undeveloped, there are only nations that have a dearth of competent management.

With every member of an enterprise performing more or less managerial activities to accomplish his goals, realization will spread rapidly that management indeed is the important resource basic to accomplishment. Management to more and more people will be the means to gain their goals and to satisfy their needs. Hence, the trend toward more involvement by members of an organization in its management plus experience in utilizing management will accelerate the concept of management as a basic resource. The older and limited concept of management being a system of decision making or of authority will fall by the wayside.

Emphasis on management as a resource will in time sharpen our means to solve just about any problem we set our minds to solving. Some, in fact, feel that we already have a surplus of management means. But this ability to use the management resource effectively will stimulate thinking on, for what purposes should this means be used. In this light, the future could bring much more on the determination and evaluation of goals deemed worthwhile. What objectives should we be seeking as a person, as a company, as a nation, as a society? In turn, this emphasis on end-results will stimulate thought on values, philosophy, and more consideration for the cultures in which we operate. We will see more attention given these areas by the manager of the future.

MANAGEMENT SCOPE BROADENED

Management as a separate and recognized subject area can be considered to have emerged at the beginning of the present century, when efforts later known as scientific management were codified. In general, early managerial efforts were concentrated upon factory work and where the economic objectives of high productivity and low cost were supreme. The analysis centered on the work of one person, the methods he followed, his output, and his relationship with his superior. With time, attention was focused upon the firm as a whole rather than upon production alone. Concepts of the ideal organization design, group effort, and spans of supervision were stressed. The importance of the human resource began to gain formal recognition and values of a human being and of society were included in management thinking.

The trend toward a broader and broader scope of operations for management continued until currently it encompasses not only an enterprise, but an entire industry, and even an entire economy. This has brought into the management fold consideration for the forces of the environment in which an enterprise operates such as the impact of technology, government, social thrusts, and interfacing among enterprises. Clearly the scope of management has broadened and in the future a manager will be more and more concerned about these so-called external forces. He will develop new concepts and techniques to apply management to these new conditions which will offer tremendous challenges to him.

The environment has been, and during the foreseeable future will probably continue to be, disorderly. It is doubtful that the future manager will be blessed with a placid environment. Expansion of technology, growth of government, vast information accessibility, and strong aspirations of people to control their surroundings, will give rise to dynamic processes. This means the future manager must have skill in attaining dynamic flexibility and a responsiveness to change in all his efforts. He will learn to manage in what amounts to almost a constant confusion, a state of affairs that is ever dynamic.

Technology will continue to offer discoveries and developments that the human mind will find difficult to believe. New material resources far ahead of anything available today will become commonplace and challenge the new manager's innovation to utilize effectively. Automation will increase and big improvements in task performance in all fields—production, sales, and various services—will be widespread. Computerized operations, affecting both information processing and the decision-making process, will dominate the work in many enterprises especially those in service areas such as universities, libraries, and hospitals where, for instance, electronic equipment will eventually alter the entire enterprise as we know it today.

With these technological changes, the manager of the future will have to be able to judge their value and benefit to his enterprise and make the needed changes to acquire the advantages they offer. He may find that due to technology the nature of the enterprise's activities changes rather rapidly, greater investments in machines and equipment are required, greater standardization is promoted, and mass markets must be acquired. There are, of course, technical limitations. Future managers will plan in quite a sophisticated manner. The dynamic technology of their time, with its ever changing bundles of opportunities, strong appeal for progress, requirement for expensive machines, and close tie-in requirement between production levels and market demands, places a premium on efficient planning efforts. New approaches and techniques of planning will be developed to meet these needs.

Government and labor unions are additional environmental influences worthy of mention here. It seems reasonably certain that government influence will not be diminished in the future, at least not to any appreciable degree. Some feel that it will increase. In any event, government will continue to be important in both its service and its regulatory functioning and as a result it will condition the environment in which every enterprise must be managed. The future manager will be vitally interested in what government does and does not do. Government actions have major effects upon the environment within which the manager works including the influence upon employment, prices, wages, standards of living, ecology, international trade, product standardization, and taxes.

Labor unions are quite likely to remain in the total picture of "things to come." Their influence could shift to different areas than at present and the collective bargaining as now carried out may evolve into agreements reached by national arbitration. Some feel that changes in the present collective bargaining process will take place, giving government more control over labor unions. In any event tomorrow's manager will work in an environment where labor unions or an advanced substitute for them, exist.

SOCIAL ENVIRONMENT

Special forces making up and affecting our social environment will continue to be present, will probably increase in intensity, and will continue to be of major importance to the future manager. As pointed out in this book, we are committed to improving social conditions and there is nothing on the horizon to indicate that continued efforts in this direction will slow down or cease. The trend is strong and will continue toward viewing enterprises not solely as economic entities, but also as entities of the broad sociocultural environment. Society affects organizations through a host of influences—custom, law, institution, and so forth—and in turn, organizations affect society. The future manager will be well aware of this reciprocity action.

It is quite probable that our desire for social betterment via management may be enhanced by technology. Some disagree, suggesting that more and more technology will mean less and less social improvement. We feel that future managers facing up to their responsibility and challenge cannot and will not shortchange social considerations in their work. They will maintain a desired balance between technological and sociological activities and further will make them complementary forces in the total environment. There is evidence to justify this viewpoint. It is the old question of being smart enough to use technical knowledge advantageously and of man being master of science rather than science being master of man.

To illustrate, technology has contributed and can deal effectively with urban redevelopment, education, and medical care. Consider that the redesigning of cities to handle concentrated populations (technology means) can be effective in solving urban redevelopment problems. Or we can try to induce people to stay on farms and enjoy rural living (sociology means). The technology approach is a good short-run solution and is fairly easy to apply. The sociological approach of getting people to behave differently from what they have in the past requires much time and many individual decisions, but it can be very effective and may be the preferred way. In the final analysis, human technology is a means to an end and that end is for man's benefit. It is created by man and ultimately serves man's needs. Future managers must and will preserve both technological and social values.

ORGANIZATION OBSERVATIONS

The present trend toward large organizations is very likely to continue for some time. Increase in specialization, new interrelationships, greater performance complexity, and additional structural relationships have contributed to this growth pattern. New technology, goal enlargement, and "expansion of domain" are contributory causes. Expansion of domain includes the propensity of a going company to expand and bring within its structure those outside and needed activities creating uncertainties for the company. It is a decision based on what functions the company will perform for itself and what activities it prefers to depend upon others to do. We see this taking place in all categories of organization. The movement toward large-scale conglomerates in business is illustrative. Through mergers and purchases very large organizations have been formed. Typically these organization structures are complicated and require more flexibility in their managing than the smaller one-product line enterprise.

In the opinion of many, a considerable number of current large organizations are nearing the size of being unmanageable. The question to be decided is whether the gains accruing from size—economies of volume and financial resources—outweigh the losses—low productivity and poor morale. We might say that the economic and social size of diminishing returns is needed. But it should be pointed out that management is changing and this, in part, is due to the need to manage large, complex organizations. With management know-how as it was in 1950, many of the present very large organizations are unmanageable. But the modern manager of today uses different techniques and the manager of the future will improve and add to these approaches. Utilizing expertise more effectively at all levels, such as by means of project organization, group decision-making processes, and results management, are illustrative.

Small organizations will continue to occupy key positions and will be viewed with respect. Their managers will have many of the problems of their compeers of large organizations. In many cases, the techniques followed may be similar but the means of application may differ. Small organizations fulfill a definite role in that they supply a needed balance to the economy, provide a choice to the prospective employee and the purchasing agent, and take care of the inevitable interstices resulting from operations of the very large organizations.

Another observation concerning organization is a decline in the self-sufficient, fully integrated enterprise. Such an enterprise in business is one manufacturing all its own parts, selling all its products, and financing all its own needs. It will become a less popular type of organization in the future. The company that purchases parts from outside companies is not new; this practice is quite common and will expand. But it will spread to the elimination of certain major functions of an organization. For example, more and more companies are having their accounting and data processing work done by an outside organization. Research and development work is another function that might be farmed out. Others are plant maintenance, plant security service, and janitorial service. In general, the better candidates to farm out are services which the company's top managers feel are extraneous to their major activities or that they do not want to or cannot afford to provide the necessary manpower and facilities to perform themselves. An additional reason for the decline of self-sufficient companies is that it simplifies the management of the company. Bothersome specialized activities are removed from the manager's direct responsibility. Also, costs of these discarded activities can be better controlled since the work by the outsider is handled on a contract basis. In addition, it is taking advantage of a development of our time, for example, the specialized service bureau for data processing.

MASS NONROUTINE TASKS

One of the significant challenges to the future manager will be the efficient accomplishment of mass nonroutine tasks. For convenience, work can be divided into two large categories, routine tasks and nonroutine tasks. Routine tasks, familiar to most of us, are repetitive, relatively simple, identifiable tasks. Amenable to machine operation, automation has been employed extensively to perform much of this work and new peaks of accomplishment have been won.

In contrast, nonroutine tasks require a new order of solution. Typical are problems dealing with environmental control, crime, transportation, and space exploration. Characteristically nonroutine tasks have few end products in contrast to mass routine tasks where the output is large in volume. Also, nonroutine tasks are individual; their solutions are not applicable in total to other problems. To illustrate, the water pollution problem in Cleveland is unique to Cleveland and the solution cannot be applied in total to another city. The solution is tailored for Cleveland only. In addition, nonroutine tasks frequently are broad in scope and may involve not only private industry, but the community, government, and university efforts. Another characteristic is that nonroutine tasks are complex and commonly have no widely accepted solution. Often considerable individual creativity and judgment must be used to supplement current managerial tools and techniques. Further the management of these tasks requires the use of large amounts of information covering many subjects and necessitating the services of social scientists, engineers, technicians, and professional aids. It appears that more and more time of future managers will be devoted to the solving of nonroutine tasks.

CHALLENGE OF MANPOWER USE

People differ in their attitudes, aspirations, wants, like, behaviors, and potentials. It has ever been thus and differences will continue to exist in the future. Therein lies one of the greatest challenges in attempting to answer the question, "What will management of the future be like?"

During the period 1975–85 the majority of the U.S. population will be persons less than 25 years old. Statisticians tell us that the increase in 18-year-olds will be well over one million every year during this period. This heavy youth segment will have to be reckoned with simply by virtue of its number. But more importantly, these young people are socially aware and they are eager to achieve. Industry and government will have to find jobs for them—jobs which challenge their intellect. Future managers will be heavily involved in these efforts.

Also, managers of the future must make better fits of the misfits. Suitable jobs for minority members, nonskilled, and the disadvantaged must be found and, further, equitable arrangements for their upgrading and promoting must be made available and practiced. As yet the ideal solution to this vexing problem has not been found, but future managers hopefully will find a reasonable answer.

High turnover is likely to continue to be a problem in the future. The reasons are many, including the fact that the better educated employee is more restless. He not only changes jobs, but he changes careers. He has found that one way to improve his lot in life is job shopping. He does not hesitate to change jobs because he has little fear of failure. In addition, people today are more mobile. Having the same address for more than four years is becoming the exception, not the rule.

Future effective leadership will help supply the answers to the difficult manpower problems. As our knowledge of leadership grows we should, in the years ahead, have many leaders with the sensitivity, as well as the toughness and the skill, to assist in finding answers to the additional human-value problems that then will arise. Employees expect more from employment than money and both their breadth of interest and of experience are expanding and will continue to do so. Television, the automobile, travel abroad, and higher education are all contributing to greater expectations of life.

Our leaders of tomorrow must have the ability to penetrate the heart of any situation and assess it adequately. Decisions will be made, yet the options must be kept open as far as possible so that the number of choices do not diminish too quickly. In addition, future leaders must maintain and enlarge the dialogue between those making decisions and those at a lower level who assist in the decision making or who carry out the decision. And further, an environment must be developed and maintained within an enterprise that is conducive not only to change but which permits the individual to satisfy his personal needs from his work efforts. As indicated above, a favorable environment beyond the corporation affects the manager's work. To strive to improve this environment is mandatory because all managers and nonmanagers are required to work with it. We know how life can be lived, not only in terms of living standards, but also in the quality of living. Will it be there in the future? Dynamic, competent future leadership will play a large role in answering this question in the affirmative.

MANAGER OBSOLESCENCE

The obsolescent manager is with us now and his number is destined to increase. Manager obsolescence is brought about by a manager failing to recognize that his preemployment education and skills will not serve him through his work life without periodic updating learning effort. Management changes, and the one practicing it must change in order to maintain his status, as a manager. How best to handle manager obsolescence will plague the future manager. Some have the illusion that if they just work hard now, the future will take care of itself. The truth is that it does not.

The problem has been debated, researched, and analyzed. From these activities certain recommendations have been forthcoming. They represent current thinking; they will be changed somewhat in the future as we learn to cope with this problem better. To minimize the effect of manager obsolescence, follow these suggestions:

1. Acquire Maximum Flexibility. Normally this suggests acquiring a broad education, maintaining interest in many different areas, and keeping up not only with a specialty, but also with general fields of contemporary leading activities. For example, an accounting executive should have in addition to his own expertise, some basic, up-to-date knowledge of business law, economics, and computer data processing, if he is to share a common perspective with his associates.

2. Continue Education for Life.   Refresher courses, in-service programs, and evening university courses assist a manager to avoid obsolescence. Likewise, the scanning of pertinent periodicals will help in knowing what is going on, what subjects are mentioned most frequently, and toward what forces research is being directed. In effect, the objective is to have not only a major, but also a minor, field of interest. In this way a practicing manager can become expert in several fields. Further, such a position is advantageous both to himself and to his employer. In addition, this dual competency increases a manager's sense of independence and gives him greater confidence in his present job.

3. Realize Own Feelings Are Vital.   The two outstanding factors conducive to creating obsolescence are fear and passivity. Every man in this day and age must fight them if he is to survive. He must believe he is doing useful work contributing to a worthwhile activity, and participating constructively in solving current problems. This includes not only the proper personal attitude, but also the ability to maintain consistent interaction with helpful superiors. It is for this reason that many employers practice systematic reassignment, i.e., they follow a planned change of moving executives from job to job with the specific intent on increasing the man's breadth of knowledge and understanding as well as improving his confidence in himself.

It is altogether possible that in the future we shall see more organizations in which men work at specific tasks for only a few years and then are shifted to other jobs or leave the organization. This may become the accepted program to follow and it has certain advantages. For example, such a program would recognize the limits of a job in the context of a man's increasing age and experience. Also, it would limit the incumbent to the period in which the job remains challenging. In addition, the program would provide a needed stimulus to prevent a man suffering from his own procrastination, which is an ally of obsolescence.

MANAGER OF THE FUTURE

What sort of manager will be needed to guide our corporations and institutions of the future? The intensive technologies, programming of many jobs, information proliferation, and automation will change the composition of many managerial jobs. In order to coordinate the multiplicity of disciplines and functional efforts, the manager of the future will become a generalist, secure in his own background and area of competency, but intelligently committed to broader areas and goals. In brief, the future manager will unlearn his parochialism and extend his vision and efforts beyond the horizons of his discipline.

A common career pattern will be that of a manager-statesman who functions equally at ease heading a private corporation, a major foundation, a university, or a governmental agency. He will be able to operate effectively at the critical juncture between private and public interest. He will have empathy with specialists; a grasp—with some sophistication—of technical methodologies, and a workable knowledge of most functional tools. His managerial skill will be transferable and his experience will be relevant across most organizational lines. He will be a man of all organizations and will manage with confidence and in detail.

The ability to cope with problems of pressure will be an outstanding characteristic. His mind will be orderly and capable of absorbing quickly enormous amounts of knowledge and data, classifying them in a rational sequence, and deriving and implementing good decisions from them. But knowledge will be more widely distributed throughout the organization. It will not be concentrated within a relatively few management members. Information will be available to decision centers via a network of information flow that is inclusive and sophisticated.

Although there are many managerial difficulties ahead, the future for management not only looks bright, but also essential for mankind. The makeup of management and its implementation will change considerably, but constant improvements directed toward the best life to be lived in terms of quality of living will prevail. Difficult management problems will be mastered, achievements beyond our fondest expectations will be won, and fundamental questions will be resolved. At long last, man will possess the managerial techniques and abilities that provide him the opportunity to fulfill his highest destiny.

QUESTIONS

1. In your opinion will managers of the future be able to cope with the changing environment in which they must operate? Explain your answer.
2. Has management reached its peak so that decline in its importance can be looked to or, in contrast, will management become more important and be more widely applied? Justify your answer.

3. Elaborate on the statement: "Too much managerial knowledge is available to manage arbitrarily."
4. From your own experience give an example showing the narrowing of the gap of power differentiation between the manager and the nonmanager.
5. Will the environment in which the future manager operates probably be more orderly than that of the past ten years? How will your answer affect the manager of the future?
6. As you see it, will the day ever come when a manager will be able to prescribe accurately and consistently? Why?
7. Are we likely to see more and more organizations of the future becoming self sufficient, fully integrated enterprises? Why?
8. Discuss in general what characteristics, training, and mode of operation, the manager of the future probably will have.
9. What is your reaction to this statement: "Technological and social forces are destined to clash even more in the future than we have witnessed during the past. This basic conflict has given rise and will continue to increase in intensity and thwart many efforts of the future manager." Why?
10. What future do you envision for the results management-process approach to management? Discuss.
11. If enterprises continue to get bigger and bigger will we arrive at a point where, because of size, they are unmanageable? Justify your answer.
12. What is meant by mass nonroutine tasks and of what significance are they to management of the future?
13. What are your feelings about the influence of government in the future and its effect upon managerial actions in the years ahead?
14. Enumerate several ways to minimize the effect of manager obsolescence. Discuss thoroughly one of these ways.

CASE 27–1. NEFF CORPORATION

The managers of Neff Corporation are highly respected in various trade circles for their competency, fairness, and progress. Specialists in metal and plastic fabricated parts, their output serves primarily the home building, automobile, and home portable appliances industries. The corporation is in a very strong financial position. Over the years, it has accumulated quite a large surplus.

The president and his chief associates believe it desirable to appraise the corporation's future possible developments with respect to direction, speed, and future goals. Currently, its long-range planning efforts cover a ten-year period, but the proposed efforts would be for the period beyond. For example, what changes might exist 25 years from now in the trades now served and which changes probably will require alterations in the corporation's present mode of management? Also, should the corporation get into any different trades from those it now serves? What new developments on the market should the corporation be considering? What changes in management should they be preparing for now?

"Perhaps we should commence by defining what needs we are now meeting and go on from there," was suggested by the president in a recent address. Continuing, he stated, "Maybe it is to our best interests to develop diligently the trades we are now in. On the other hand, perhaps we should be getting into others which offer good promise. Maybe we ought to use a part of our surplus to purchase other companies. Or possibly we ought to be starting new divisions. I just don't know."

Questions

1. What alternatives are open to the corporation? Discuss.
2. What important managerial changes do you envision the corporation will face within the next 25 years? Elaborate on your answer.
3. Outline in general form what actions you recommend the Neff Corporation top management take. Justify your answer.

annotated bibliography

Annotated bibliography

The sources are listed alphabetically by author's name. Each source is coded by a bold-face number shown in parenthesis indicating for what management area the source is especially helpful. The code numbers correspond to the main sections of this book, *Principles of Management, 6th edition,* and are as follows:

Code No.	Especially helpful for:
I	Approaching the study of management
II	Facilitating managerial activities
III	Planning
IV	Organizing
V	Actuating
VI	Controlling
VII	Forthcoming developments in management

ACADEMY OF MANAGEMENT. *Academy of Management Journal.* Eugene, Oregon: University of Oregon. (Quarterly.) Excellent articles on current management topics written by well-qualified authors. (I)

ACKOFF, RUSSELL LINCOLN. *A Concept of Corporate Planning.* New York: Wiley-Interscience, Inc., 1970. A basic book on planning, dealing with the nature and content of planning, policies, design, organizing the planning, and controlling the planning efforts. (III)

ALBERS, HENRY H. *Principles of Management: A Modern Approach,* 3d ed. New York: John Wiley & Sons, Inc., 1969. Concerned with the basic elements of executive action, this book is interdisciplinary in approach, drawing from many fields of learning. The psychological and social foundation of authority is discussed at length. (I)

ALEXIS, M., and WILSON, C. Z. *Organizational Decision Making.* Englewood Cliffs, N.J.: Prentice-Hall, Inc., 1967. A well-written and documented interdisciplinary approach to the study of decision making in organizations. (IV)

ALLEN, LOUIS A. *The Management Profession.* New York: McGraw-Hill Book Co., Inc., 1964. Supplies a complete and enlightening picture of how successful managers think and act today, and plan for tomorrow. (I)

AMERICAN FOUNDATION FOR MANAGEMENT RESEARCH, INC. *Management 2000.* New York, 1968. Speeches given at the dedication of the AFMR Management Learning Center, Hamilton, N.Y. Many contain ideas and forecasts of what management at the beginning of the 21st century will be like. (VII)

AMERICAN MANAGEMENT ASSOCIATION. *Control Through Information.* New York. A series of pertinent articles emphasizing practical examples to show the importance and need of information for controlling to be effective. (VI)

———— *General Management Series.* New York. (Periodic.) Management information consisting of papers presented at conferences and ensuing floor discussions of the General Management Division of the Association. (I)

————. *Management News.* New York. (Monthly.) A six-page pamphlet giving timely information on management activities. Special sections are devoted to business conditions and forecasts. (I)

————. *Management Review.* New York. (Monthly.) A digest of articles selected from several hundred different publications. The articles are of special interest to managers. (I)

————. *Personnel.* New York. (Bimonthly.) An excellent source of articles by leaders in the field of personnel.

————. *Personnel Series.* New York. (Periodic.) (V)

————. Special research reports. New York. (Irregular.) Special studies on various management subjects which are of interest to practitioners and students of management. (I)

American Standards Association. *American Standards Yearbook.* New York. (Yearly.) The official annual publication of the association, which serves as a clearinghouse for the coordination and development of standards. Informative literature on the subject and a listing of the standards developed are included in the publication. (VI)

ANTHONY, ROBERT N.; DEARDEN, JOHN; and VANCIL, RICHARD E. *Managerial Control Systems.* Homewood, Ill.: Richard D. Irwin, Inc., 1965. Excellent text and cases on subject of management control. Emphasizes cost control areas with control profit centers and capital acquisition. (VI)

ARGYRIS, CHRIS. *Interpersonal Competence and Organizational Effectiveness.* Homewood, Ill.: Richard D. Irwin, Inc., and the Dorsey Press, Inc., 1962. Describes a successful change of top executive behavior and integrates the interpersonal relations theory with laboratory education. (V)

BARNARD, CHESTER I. *Organization and Management.* Cambridge, Mass.: Harvard University Press, 1948. The essentials of how groups function together, principally from the viewpoint of intuition, not logic, are expressed in this informative book. (IV)

BASSETT, GLENN A. *The New Face of Communication.* New York: American Management Association, 1968. About 200 pages on the elements of the nonmanager and the organization's influence on communication provide an informative presentation. The material is presented in a popular style. (II)

BELLMAN, RICHARD E., and KALABA, ROBERT. *Dynamic Programming and*

Modern Control Theory. New York: Academic Press, 1965. Presents an introduction to the mathematical theory of the planning-controlling process. Demonstrates the bewildering array of special factors frequently present and shows how dynamic programming takes them into account. (VI)

BERGEN, GARRET L., and HANEY, WILLIAM V. *Organizational Relations and Management Action.* New York: McGraw-Hill Book Co., Inc., 1966. Organizational behavior and decision making as they pertain to organizational relations of a manager is the core of this book. Well written and there are also interesting cases included. (IV)

BIERMAN, HAROLD, ET AL. *Quantitative Analysis for Business Decisions.* Rev. ed. Homewood, Ill.: Richard D. Irwin, Inc., 1965. Describes and explains quantitative techniques and models used in solving business problems. (II)

BITTEL, LESTER R. *Management by Exception.* New York. McGraw-Hill Book Co., Inc., 1964. Systematizing and simplifying the manager's controlling efforts are demonstrated in this volume by effective use of management by exception. (VI)

BONINI, CHARLES P. *Simulation of Information and Decision Systems in the Firm.* Englewood Cliffs, N.J.: Prentice-Hall, Inc., 1964. An award winner of the Ford Foundation Doctoral Dissertation Series, this volume describes a simulation model of a hypothetical firm which is subjected to informational, organizational, and environmental factors affecting the decision making of the firm. The book reflects excellence in research and competency in writing. (II)

BOWEN, EARL K. *Mathematics: With Applications in Management and Economics.* Rev. ed. Homewood, Ill.: Richard D. Irwin, Inc., 1967. Well written and incisive, this book presents the mathematical approach to management and economics decision making in an admirable manner. (II)

BOWER, MARVIN. *The Will to Manage.* New York: McGraw-Hill Book Co., Inc., 1966. Offers many useful analyses of corporate management and performance and shows how they can be used and meshed into a strong unity. (I)

BRANCH, MELVILLE. *The Corporate Planning Process.* New York: American Management Association, 1962. A critical analysis on what is currently being done in corporate planning with the objective of pointing up problems in this area and suggesting ways to strengthen planning efforts. (III)

————. *Planning: Aspects and Applications.* New York: John Wiley & Sons, Inc., 1966. A well-prepared book on this important area of management. Illustrations included are especially effective. (III)

BROWN, RAY E. *Judgment in Administration.* New York: McGraw-Hill Book Co., Inc., 1966. Informative book pointing out causes of failure in administration along with suggestions for eliminating them. Based on practical experience, the material is helpful for the decision maker. (II)

Business Horizons. Bloomington, Ind.: School of Business, Indiana University. (Quarterly.) Helpful articles, timely and well written, on subjects of interest to the management member or trainee are featured by this excellent publication. (I)

California Management Review. Berkeley, Calif.: Graduate School of Business Administration, University of California. (Quarterly.) Features articles bridging creative thinking and management thought. It is an excellent source of ideas and information. (I)

CARZO, ROCCO, JR., and YANOUZAS, JOHN. *Formal Organization: A Systems Approach.* Homewood, Ill.: The Dorsey Press, 1967. New thinking applied to organizing is effectively presented in this book. (IV)

COLLIER, ABRAM T. *Management, Men, and Values.* New York: Harper and Row, 1962. A delightful book, written in dialogue, and raising issues of philosophy and values that may arise in implementing management from day to day. (II)

COLLIER, JAMES R. *Effective Long-Range Business Planning.* Englewood Cliffs, N.J.: Prentice-Hall, Inc., 1968. An excellent book on planning including both the practical considerations for planning and the process of planning. The book is well written and the coverage is adequate. (III)

CRAWFORD, ROBERT P. *The Technique of Creative Thinking.* New York: Hawthorn Books, Inc., 1954. A helpful text in a subject that is rather difficult to present and in which increasing interest is being shown. (V)

DALE, ERNEST. *Management: Theory and Practice.* 2d ed. New York: Mc-Graw-Hill Book Co., Inc., 1969. Describes current management skills and techniques in a well-written book. Has chapters on management of foreign operations and future management trends. (I)

————. *Organization.* New York: American Management Association, 1967. New concepts in organization are discussed based mainly on in-depth study of organization practices in 166 companies. (IV)

————. *Readings in Management.* 2d ed. New York: McGraw-Hill Book Co., Inc., 1970. Selected articles in management are provided by this volume. (I)

DAVIS, KEITH. *Human Relations at Work: The Dynamics of Organizational Behavior.* New York: McGraw-Hill Book Co., Inc., 1967. The basics of human motivation and the influence of both leadership and of formal organization are included in this presentation of an integrative theory of organizational behavior. Well written, this book includes examples of ways to improve managerial relationships among compeers, superiors, and subordinates. (IV)

DAVIS, KEITH, and BLOOMSTROM, ROBERT C. *Business, Society, and Environment.* New York: McGraw-Hill Book Co., Inc., 1971. The responsibilities that business has toward society and its total environment are expertly handled in this excellent book. A system framework is used for the organization of the material. (II)

DONNELLY, JAMES H. JR.; GIBSON, JAMES L.; and IVANCEVICH, JOHN M. *Fundamentals of Management: Functions, Behavior, Models.* Austin, Texas: Business Publications, Inc., 1971. Different theories of management as applied to various institutions—business, government and schools are discussed to show that the contemporary manager can benefit by blending the various approaches. (I)

DRUCKER, PETER F. *The Age of Discontinuity.* New York: Harper and Row, 1969. Interesting reading directing attention to the new forces that are creating the society of tomorrow and their possible implications upon management. The book provides guidelines to our changing society. (I)

DYCKMAN, THOMAS R. *Management Decision Making under Uncertainty.*

New York: Macmillan Co., 1969. A complete and thorough writing directed to an introduction to probability and statistical decision theory in the solution of managerial problems. (II)

Dun's Review and Modern Industry. New York. Dun & Bradstreet Publications Corp. (Monthly.) Informative articles on important current management subjects are featured by this outstanding magazine. (I)

EELLS, RICHARD, and WALTON, CLARENCE. *Conceptual Foundations of Business.* Rev. ed. Homewood, Ill.: Richard D. Irwin, Inc., 1969. Presents the major concepts underpinning business in a democratic order, stresses the meaning and the importance of social and ethical responsibilities of managers, and reviews critically our values in the modern business world. (I)

EMORY, WILLIAM, and NILAND, POWELL. *Making Management Decisions.* Boston: Houghton Mifflin, Inc., 1968. The basic concepts and techniques enabling one to make better decisions and to do this more effectively is the core idea of this well-written book. The newer concepts of managerial decision making along with the older and widely used techniques are included in this volume. (II)

EWING, DAVID W. (ed.). *Long-Range Planning for Management.* Rev. ed. New York: Harper and Row, Inc., 1964. A book of readings which are helpful in assisting the reader to think through planning problems and to understand better their basic function of management. (III)

————. *The Practice of Planning.* New York: Harper and Row, Inc., 1968. A basic book on planning that is well written and the material is modern and adequately organized. (III)

EWING, DAVID W., and FENN, DAN H., JR. *Incentives for Executives.* New York: McGraw-Hill Book Co., Inc., 1962. A comprehensive text in an important modern management area. (V)

FAYOL, HENRI. *General and Industrial Management.* London: Sir Isaac Pitman & Sons, Ltd., 1949. A pioneer treatise in management literature brought forth in a new English printing from the original appearance in French in 1916. An important volume which reemphasizes the background against which managerial developments have taken place. (I)

FIEDLER, FRED E. *A Theory of Leadership Effectiveness.* New York: McGraw-Hill Book Co., Inc., 1967. A good book on leadership containing the highlights of some 15 years research of this area. A theory of leadership effectiveness is propounded. (V)

FLIPPO, EDWIN B. *Management: A Behavioral Approach.* 2d ed. Boston: Allyn and Bacon, 1970. The traditional and behavioral managerial approaches are presented by discussing one, then the other, covering the methods and philosophies of each, and following the general plan of the major management functions. (I)

GABRIEL, H. W. *Techniques of Creative Thinking for Management.* Englewood Cliffs, N.J.: Prentice-Hall, Inc., 1961. Explains how to become creative by means of a mental process consisting of simple, orderly steps. (V)

GANTT, H. L. *Industrial Leadership.* New York: Association Press, 1921. This volume is a classic in the management field. The book constitutes addresses delivered in 1915 before the senior class of the Sheffield Scientific School,

Yale University, and includes chapters on industrial leadership, training workers, principles of task work, results of task work, and production and sales. (**V**)

————. *Organizing for Work*. New York: Harcourt, Brace & Howe, 1919. Stresses the need for managerial ability operating with the view of rendering service for getting work accomplished. (**V**)

GARDNER, B. B., and MOORE, D. G. *Human Relations in Industry*. 4th ed. Homewood, Ill.: Richard D. Irwin, Inc., 1964. People and the relations among them in their places of work are discussed thoroughly and interestingly in this popular volume. (**V**)

GELLERMAN, SAUL W. *Motivation and Productivity*. New York: American Management Association, 1963. Gives the reader a clear perspective of the relation between environment and individual productivity. (**V**)

GEORGE, CLAUDE S. *The History of Management Thought*. Englewood Cliffs, N.J., Prentice-Hall, Inc., 1968. An outstanding and scholarly work on a most interesting subject—the history of management thought. Certain to be enjoyed by all who are interested in how management started, developed, and expanded into what it is today. (**I**)

GILBRETH, F. B., and GILBRETH, L. M. *Applied Motion Study*. New York: Macmillan Co., 1919. A pioneer book in the field of motion study and one which still offers valuable information to the present-day reader. (**III**)

GINZBERG, ELI. *The Development of Human Resources*. New York: McGraw-Hill Book Co., Inc., 1967. Sets forth and discusses the case for the human resource factor being the key determinant of economic progress and the present status of our skills economy. (**V**)

GOETZ, BILLY E. *Quantitative Methods*. New York: McGraw-Hill Book Co., Inc., 1965. An excellent volume on the application of quantitative methods for decision making. (**II**)

GREENWOOD, W. E. *Management and Organizational Behavior Theories*. Cincinnati: South-Western Publishing Co., 1965. A book of readings organized to make a comparative analysis between traditional management theory and that of the behavioral scientists. Well-organized and pertinent articles are a feature of the book. (**I**)

GREGORY, CARL E. *The Management of Intelligence*. New York: McGraw-Hill Book Co., Inc., 1967. Scientific problem solving and creativity are exceptionally well handled in this excellent text. (**V**)

GRILLO, ELMER V. *Control Techniques for Office Efficiency*. New York: McGraw-Hill Book Co., Inc., 1963. An all-inclusive book showing how to raise office procedures to high efficiency. The sections on controlling are very well done and merit reading. (**VI**)

GUEST, ROBERT H. *Organizational Change: The Effect of Successful Leadership*. Homewood, Ill.: Richard D. Irwin, Inc., and the Dorsey Press, Inc., 1962. Stresses the industrial sociology viewpoints followed by a new manager in improving performance of a large plant. (**V**)

GULICK, LUTHER, and URWICK, LYNDALL. *Papers on the Science of Administration*. New York: Institute of Public Administration, Columbia University, 1937. A classic in management literature pointing out sound and fundamental concepts along with their application in the field of administration. (**I**)

HANEY, W. V. *Communication and Organizational Behavior.* Rev. ed. Homewood, Ill.: Richard D. Irwin, Inc., 1967. Well-written and thorough, this book focuses on what happens inside the communicator before and as he writes or talks. Valuable suggestions are offered for improving communication. (II)

HARE, VAN COURT. *Systems Analysis: A Diagnostic Approach.* New York: Harcourt Brace & World, Inc., 1967. Highly recommended book on systems for management personnel. Includes system definition, analysis, diagnosis, and treatment. (II)

Harvard Business Review. Cambridge, Mass.: Graduate School of Business Administration. (Bimonthly.) Outstanding articles on business subjects of unusual interest for the management practitioner or student are offered by this publication. (I)

HAYNES, W. WARREN, and MASSIE, JOSEPH L. *Management: Analysis, Concepts, and Cases.* Rev. ed. Englewood Cliffs, N.J.: Prentice-Hall, Inc., 1969. Thought-provoking and effectively written, this book supplies basic concepts and sound philosophy about management. (I)

HENRY, HAROLD W. *Long-range Planning Practices in Forty-Five Industrial Companies.* Englewood Cliffs, N.J.: Prentice-Hall, Inc., 1967. Good coverage of the entire subject of planning with examples taken from different companies and industries to expedite understanding. Will prove helpful to the management planner. (III)

HERZBERG, FREDERICK. *Work and the Nature of Man.* New York: The World Publishing Co., 1966. Thought-provoking book on the general theory of work and man's behavior gives new considerations and possibilities to managerial action and to the psychological contributions that are feasible. (V)

HICKS, HERBERT G. *The Management of Organizations.* New York: McGraw-Hill Book Co., Inc., 1967. Directed to organizations and their managements, this book discusses what organizations are, why they exist, and how to make them more efficient. The coverage is basic and broad. (IV)

HIGGINSON, M. VALLIANT. *Management Policies.* 2 vols. New York: American Management Association, 1966. Books devoted to policies—how formulated, administered, and stated. Interesting and informative volumes on this vital aspect of management. (III)

HILTON, PETER. *Planning Corporate Growth and Diversification.* New York: McGraw-Hill Book Co., Inc., 1970. Spells out the fact that corporate growth can be effectively planned. Draws from case histories and makes planning a live subject. Well written and coverage is quite satisfactory. (III)

HODNETT, EDWARD. *The Art of Problem Solving.* New York: Harper and Row, Inc., 1955. A clear-cut discussion of problems, covering their diagnosis and how and why to attack them. Very helpful material is provided that can be put to good use in management. (II)

HOLDEN, PAUL E.; PEDERSON, CARLTON A.; and GERMANE, GAYTON E. *Top Management.* New York: McGraw-Hill Book Co., Inc., 1968. Reveals the management policies and practices of 15 leading industrial corporations. It is well written and informative. (I)

HOROWITZ, IRA. *An Introduction to Quantitative Business Analysis.* New York: McGraw-Hill Book Co., Inc., 1965. Covers decision-making theory, mathematical programming, game theory, and inventory controlling in simple, easy-to-understand language. (II)

HOUSTON, GEORGE. *Manager Development: Principles and Perspectives.* Homewood, Ill.: Richard D. Irwin, Inc., 1962. A thought-provoking re-examination and reevaluation of the needs and opportunities for the development of managers. (V)

JENNINGS, EUGENE E. *An Anatomy of Leadership.* New York: Harper & Bros., 1960. An interesting and well-written book on the meaning and importance of leadership; the thesis is presented that ours is a society without leaders. (V)

JOHNSON, R.; KAST, F.; and ROSENSWEIG, J. *The Theory and Management of Systems.* Rev. ed. New York: McGraw-Hill Book Co., Inc., 1967. A provocative and thorough presentation of the systems concept and its use in management. (II)

Journals of Business. Chicago: University of Chicago Press. (Quarterly.) One of the better journals dealing with business, economics, and trade subjects. (I)

JUCIUS, MICHAEL J. *Personnel Management.* 7th ed. Homewood, Ill.: Richard D. Irwin, Inc., 1971. A well-known and comprehensive text in the area of personnel management. All facets of the subject are covered, and the book is well organized. (V)

KAST, FREMONT E., and ROSENSWEIG, JAMES E. *Organization and Management: A Systems Approach.* New York: McGraw-Hill Book Co., Inc., 1970. An excellent book, providing a better understanding of the managerial role in a complex and dynamic organizational society. Organization is viewed as a sociotechnical system made up of subsystems: goals and values, technology structure, psychological, and managerial. (II)

KOLASA, BLAIR JOHN. *Introduction to Behavioral Science for Business.* John Wiley and Sons, Inc., 1969. An informative and complete presentation of the breadth of the behavioral field, concepts followed, and some results of research in this area. Profitable reading for the manager and the nonmanager. (V)

KOONTZ, HAROLD, and O'DONNELL, CYRIL. *Principles of Management.* 4th ed. New York: McGraw-Hill Book Co., Inc., 1968. A comprehensive volume on the theory of management, its meaning, and application. The principles are clearly stated. (I)

————. *Management: A Book of Readings.* 2d ed. New York: McGraw-Hill Book Co., Inc., 1968. A well-selected group of readings pertinent to management are offered by this book. The articles are presented in keeping with a logical outline and are easy to locate and to read. (I)

LAWRENCE, PAUL R. and LORSCH, JAY W. *Organization and Environment.* Cambridge: Harvard University Graduate School of Business Administration, 1967. The ways in which the internal structure and processes of an organization relate to its different external environmental conditions are included in this book. Also found in this volume is helpful information concerning response to changing technology and organizing for innovations. (IV)

LeBRETON, P. P., and HENNING, D. A. *Planning Theory.* Englewood Cliffs,

N.J.: Prentice-Hall, Inc., 1961. An integrated approach to the work of planning, providing complete treatment for each step in this important managerial area.

LEONARD, W. P. *The Management Audit*. Rev. ed. Englewood Cliffs, N.J.: Prentice-Hall, Inc., 1962. Points out the means and the performance of an audit of management in a given enterprise. (**VI**)

LEVINSON, HARRY. *Executive Stress*. New York: Harper and Row, Inc., 1970. Mental health and the meaning of work are the two basic concepts about which this book is written. Sound advice to aid the manager—emotions or stresses to cope with—and how to function at his best on the job are discussed thoroughly. (**V**)

LEWIS, RONELLO. *Profit Planning for Management*. Englewood Cliffs, N.J.: Prentice-Hall, Inc., 1960. An adequate treatment of an important type of planning, this book suggests ways to improve profits and tells it in an easy-to-understand manner. (**III**)

LIKERT, RENSIS. *New Patterns of Management*. New York: McGraw-Hill Book Co., Inc., 1962. Presents and discusses the major findings from an extensive research program on organization and management by the Institute for Social Research. Well written and comprehensive, this book is filled with provocative ideas concerning management theory and practice. (**IV**)

LINCOLN, JAMES F. *Incentive Management*. Cleveland: Lincoln Electric Co., 1951. The use of incentives as a main core in managerial work is advanced and substantiated in this detailed and well-organized book. (**V**)

LINDGREN, HENRY C., and BYRNE, DONN. *Psychology: An Introduction to a Behavioral Science*. 3d ed. New York: John Wiley and Sons, 1971. An accurate understanding of human behavior and an overall view of psychology as behavioral science is made feasible by this well-organized and well-written book. (**V**)

LIPPITT, GORDON L. *Organizational Renewal*. New York: Appleton-Century-Crofts, 1969. An interesting and well-written book in which are presented the ways for initiating and maintaining constructive, flexible response to contemporary attitudes regarding an organization's social and economic responsibilities. (**IV**)

LITTERER, JOSEPH. *The Analysis of Organizations*. New York: John Wiley & Sons, Inc., 1965. An interesting treatment of organization, pointing out the technical, economic, and social factors both within and without the organization, is supplied by this book. (**IV**)

———— (ed). *Organizations: Structure and Behavior (Vol. I.)* and *Organizations: Systems, Control and Adaptation (Vol. II.)*. New York: John Wiley and Sons, 1969. Selected readings provide an array of thinking about organization. The coverage is quite extensive and the book is helpful to the management student. (**IV**)

LONGENECKER, JUSTIN G. *Principles of Management and Organizational Behavior*. 2d ed. Columbus: Chas. E. Merrill Publishing Co., 1969. Attention is focused upon the behavioral and systems nature of the managerial role with helpful discussion on the complexity of organizational relationships, system operation, and the human aspects of management and organization. (**I**)

McCLELLAND, DAVID CLARENCE. *The Achieving Society.* Princeton, N.J.: D. Van Nostrand Co., Inc., 1961. Basic concepts in motivation discussed by an expert in this complex field. (V)

McDONOUGH, A. M., and GARRETT, L. J. *Management Systems: Working Concepts and Practices.* Homewood, Ill.: Richard D. Irwin, Inc., 1965. A basic and helpful book on systems and their use in managerial work. (II)

McGREGOR, DOUGLAS. *The Human Side of Enterprise.* New York: McGraw-Hill Book Co., Inc., 1960. A strong convincing presentation of the importance of people in an enterprise. (V)

McMILLAN, CLAUDE, and GONZALEZ, RICHARD. *Systems Analysis.* Homewood, Ill.: Richard D. Irwin, Inc., 1965. Excellent coverage of systems and their contribution in management study and application. (II)

McNICHOLS, THOMAS J. *Policy Making and Executive Action.* 3d ed. New York: McGraw-Hill Book Co., Inc., 1967. Although a casebook on business policy, the introductory pages, as well as the cases, highlight the importance of policy making in carrying out management work. (III)

MAIER, NORMAN R. F., and HAYES, JOHN J. *Creative Management.* New York: John Wiley & Sons, Inc., 1962. The interaction between man and the organization and the compartmentalizing of value systems through unilateral judgments are among the many facets giving rise to management problems discussed in this book. Suggested means for coping with them are also included. (V)

Management Science. Providence, R.I.: The Institute of Management Sciences. (Monthly.) Excellent articles on the theory and practice of quantitative measurements in management. (II)

MARCH, J. G., and SIMON, H. A. *Organizations.* New York: John Wiley & Sons, Inc., 1958. A classic in the area of behavioral study—motivation, conflict, and rationality upon managerial organizing. (IV)

MARGULIES, STUART, and EIGEN, LEWIS D. *Programmed Instruction Applied.* New York: John Wiley & Sons, Inc., 1962. An excellent source for comprehensive treatment of programmed instruction as a medium of training. (V)

MARTINDELL, JACKSON. *The Appraisal of Management.* Rev. ed. New York: Harper & Bros., 1965. Effectively presented by this book is a system of management appraisal by which defects can be spotted and overall performance rated. (VI)

MASSIE, JOSEPH L. *Essentials of Management.* 2d ed. Englewood Cliffs, N.J.: Prentice-Hall, Inc., 1971. The elements of management are summarized in this compact book. Management is viewed as an interdisciplinary study and contributions to management by the behavioral and quantitative science are included in the text. (I)

MEE, JOHN F. *Management Thought in a Dynamic Economy.* New York: New York University Press, 1963. A concise, thought-provoking presentation of management thought development and probable future trends in management study. (I)

MEGGINSON, LEON C. *Personnel: A Behavior Approach to Administration.* Rev. ed. Homewood, Ill.: Richard D. Irwin, Inc., 1972. The importance of the human factor and of interpersonal relations in administration are stressed in this well-organized text. (V)

MILLER, DAVID W., and STARR, MARTIN K. *Executive Decisions and Opera-*

tions Research. 2d ed. Englewood Cliffs, N.J.: Prentice-Hall, Inc., 1970. Excellent treatment of role mathematical approach can play in determining decisions. (II)

MOORE, FRANKLIN G. *Manufacturing Management.* 5th ed. Homewood, Ill.: Richard D. Irwin, Inc., 1969. A complete, concise volume on management as applied to production. Gives reasons why as well as the practices in this important field. (I)

NATIONAL INDUSTRIAL CONFERENCE BOARD. *Studies in Personnel Policy.* New York. (Irregular.) Nearly 100 separate studies dealing with the identification, establishment, and adjustment of policies pertaining to the field of personnel. (III)

————. *Perspectives for the '70's and '80's.* Report of distinguished experts who identify the major trends now emerging and likely to create major public problems in the 1970's and 1980's. Also included are research results of how aware the public is of these trends and possible problems. (VII)

NEWMAN, WILLIAM H. *Administrative Action.* Rev. ed. Englewood Cliffs, N.J.: Prentice-Hall, Inc., 1963. The techniques and application of administration are competently handled in this well-written book which is a significant contribution in its field of endeavor.

NEWMAN, WILLIAM H.; SUMMER, CHARLES E., JR.; and WARREN, E. KIRBY. *The Process of Management.* 2d ed. Englewood Cliffs, N.J.: Prentice-Hall, Inc., 1967. A well-presented integration of viewpoints from the behavioral science and decision-making theories with fundamental ideas presented regarding the scope, meaning, and operations of management. (I)

O'CONNELL, JEREMIAH J. *Managing Organizational Innovation.* Homewood, Ill.: Richard D. Irwin, Inc., 1968. A helpful volume on the important subject of organization design and change. The planning and controlling required for organization innovation are given special in-depth attention. (IV)

ODIORNE, GEORGE S. *Management by Objectives.* Rev. ed. New York: Pitman Publishing Corp., 1970. The thesis that effective management aided by precise definition of both corporate and personal goals is developed. The material is well presented. (I)

————. *Personnel Management by Objectives.* Homewood, Ill.: Richard D. Irwin, Inc., 1971. An effective book on personnel management, stressing the management by objective viewpoint. (I)

Operations Research. Baltimore, Md.: Operations Research Society of America. (Bimonthly.) Articles detailing methods, as well as results by operations research, are stressed by this publication. Stimulating and thought provoking characterize most of the papers included. (II)

PATTON, ARCH. *Men, Money, and Motivation.* New York: McGraw-Hill Book Co., Inc., 1961. A well-written, inclusive, and interesting book on compensation and its motivating influences. (V)

PAYNE, BRUCE. *Planning for Company Growth.* New York: McGraw-Hill Book Co., Inc., 1963. Planning is brought into a realistic focus, and its importance in all enterprises is clearly demonstrated. (III)

PEACH, PAUL. *Quality Control for Management.* Englewood Cliffs, N.J.: Prentice-Hall, Inc., 1965. Describes probability theories, statistical methods, and sampling techniques and places emphasis upon statistical quality control. (VI)

Personnel Journal. Swarthmore, Pa.: Personnel Journal, Inc. (Eleven times a year.) Special articles of interest to those in personnel, résumés of personnel research projects, and notes on activities in this field are featured. (V)

PETRULLO, LUIGI, and BASS, BERNARD M. *Leadership and Interpersonal Behavior.* New York: Holt, Rinehart & Winston, Inc., 1961. A group of experts on leadership present the findings of their research revealing the interactions of person and situation in leadership. A wide range of leadership information is presented effectively. (V)

PORTER, LYMAN, and LAWLER, EDWARD E. *Managerial Attitudes and Performance.* Homewood, Ill.: Richard D. Irwin, Inc., 1968. The job attitudes of managers and their performance are the center of attention. The material is approached by developing a conceptual model and presenting relevant empirical data. Well written and presented. (V)

PRINCE, THOMAS R. *Information Systems for Management Planning and Control.* Rev. ed. Homewood, Ill.: Richard D. Irwin, Inc., 1970. Basic treatment of information approach presented in understandable language. The book contains excellent cases for discussion. (II)

RADAMAKER, TED (ed.). *Business Systems.* Cleveland: Systems and Procedures Association, 1963. Excellent material on systems in management and data processing work. A useful bibliography is included. (II)

REEVES, ELTON T. *The Dynamics of Group Behavior.* New York: American Management Association, 1970. Offered is very readable and easy-to-comprehend material on the importance of group dynamics and its use by a manager. (V)

RICHARDS, MAX, and GREENLAW, PAUL. *Management Decision Making.* Homewood, Ill.: Richard D. Irwin, Inc., 1966. Business organization is viewed as an information-decision system—the decison made representing the focus of managerial activity. Contains interesting discussion and examples of the quantitative measurement approach to management. (I)

ROWLAND, VIRGIL K. *Evaluating and Improving Managerial Performance.* New York: McGraw-Hill Book Co., Inc., 1970. One of the better books providing practices of managers from many different companies. The practices have been assembled, classified, explained, and evaluated. There is a good group of chapters on evaluation of management performance. (V)

RUBENSTEIN, A. H., and HABERSTROH, C. J. *Some Theories of Organization.* Homewood, Ill.: Richard D. Irwin, Inc., 1966. Supplies a selection of papers dealing with organization theory classified by structure, leadership, change, communication, control, and decision making. (IV)

ST. THOMAS, C. E. *Practical Business Planning.* New York: McGraw-Hill Book Co., Inc., 1965. Gives planning information needed to replace judgment and guesses erroneously employed in some types of planning. (III)

Sales Management. New York: Sales Management, Inc. (Monthly.) Excellent articles dealing with management problems in the field of distribution are offered by this well-respected periodical. (I)

SCHEIN, EDGAR H. *Organizational Psychology.* Englewood Cliffs, N.J.: Prentice-Hall, Inc., 1965. Stresses a system analysis of psychological problems which arise within organizational structures. Both individual and group functioning are included. (IV)

SCHLEH, EDWARD. *Management by Results.* New York: McGraw-Hill Book Co., Inc., 1962. A stimulating presentation on the theme that management will make its important contribution to society when the objectives of the enterprise are harmonized and meet the needs of its employees. This theme is expanded to show that it is the effective means for tying all management levels together. (I)

SCHLENDER, WILLIAM E.; SCOTT, WILLIAM G.; and FILLEY, ALAN C. *Management in Perspective: Selected Readings.* Boston: Houghton Mifflin, 1965. A very good selection of readings that are helpful to the management student. Readings provide good cross-section of current management thinking. (I)

SCHODERBEK, PETER P. *Management Systems.* Rev. ed. New York: John Wiley and Sons, 1971. A book of well-selected articles covering such major topics as systems, measurement, management information systems, computers, systems design, PERT, and real-time systems. (II)

SCOTT, BRIAN W. *Long-Range Planning in American Industry.* New York: American Management Association, 1965. Describes and examines the techniques of major U.S. companies followed in their managerial planning. (III)

SCOTT, W. G. *Organization Theory.* Homewood, Ill.: Richard D. Irwin, Inc., 1967. An excellent presentation of the use of behavioral sciences as the formulation for explaining organization and management processes. (IV)

SEILER, JOHN A. *Systems Analysis in Organizational Behavior.* Homewood, Ill.: Richard D. Irwin, Inc., 1967. Good reading pertaining to human behavior in organization. The input of social, technical, and organizational influences are well handled. (IV)

SISK, HENRY L. *Principles of Management—A Systems Approach to the Management Process.* Cincinnati: South-Western Publishing Co., 1969. An offering of basic management organized essentially around the functional approach with an overall emphasis upon systems in management. (I)

SMITH, GEORGE ALBERT; CHRISTENSEN, C. ROLAND; and BERG, NORMAN A. *Policy Formulation and Administration.* 5th ed. Homewood, Ill.: Richard D. Irwin, Inc., 1968. One of the best books available on the subject of policies and their use by managers. (III)

Social Research. New York: New School of Social Research. (Monthly.) Interesting articles offering the social aspects of some current-day problems, many of which affect the work of the manager. (I)

SPURR, W. A., and BONINI, C. P. *Statistical Analysis for Business Decisions.* Homewood, Ill.: Richard D. Irwin, Inc., 1967. Statistical methods as scientific tools in the analysis of business problems is the core of this book. From simple analysis to simulation and Bayesian decision theory are included. (II)

STARR, MARTIN K. *Inventory Control: Theory and Practice.* Englewood Cliffs, N.J.: Prentice-Hall, Inc., 1962. A modern and thorough treatment of an old problem area of business. (II)

STERN, MARK E. *Mathematics for Management.* Englewood Cliffs, N.J.: Prentice-Hall, Inc., 1963. Mathematics required for an understanding and use of quantitative measurements in management are supplied by this excellent text. (II)

STEINER, GEORGE A. (ed.). *Managerial Long-Range Planning.* New York: McGraw-Hill Book Co., Inc., 1963. Describes in detail how successful long-range planning is performed by some major companies and government agencies. (III)

―――――. *Top Management Planning.* New York: Macmillan Co., 1969. Extensive coverage of planning by top managers including in-depth discussion of major problems encountered in planning efforts are clearly set forth in this well-written and well-organized book. (III)

STOCKTON, R. STANBURY. *Introduction to Linear Programming.* Rev. ed. Boston: Allyn and Bacon, Inc., 1963. A complete, yet concise, presentation of linear programming and its uses in business. The book is well organized and the concepts presented in an effective manner. (II)

STOKES, PAUL M. *A Total Systems Approach to Management Control.* New York: American Management Association, 1968. A practical and helpful presentation of controlling which offers much material of value to the operating manager. (VI)

STOODLEY, BARTLETT H. (ed.). *Society and Self.* New York: Free Press of Glencoe, 1962. A book of readings which emphasizes the major forces to which an individual reacts. The sociological forces stimulating or diminishing a person's creative powers and belief in himself are well presented. (V)

SUTERMEISTER, ROBERT A. *People and Productivity.* 2d ed. New York: McGraw-Hill Book Co., 1969. Selected readings integrating the findings of current behavioral research studies dealing with employee productivity and job performance are featured by this book. (V)

TANNENBAUM, ROBERT; WESCHLER, IRVING R.; and MASSARIK, FRED. *Leadership and Organization.* New York: McGraw-Hill Book Co., 1961. Very interesting and informative material on leadership and organization. The ideas presented are thought provoking and different viewpoints are included. Helpful in study of management theory and in contributions of psychology and sociology to management study. (V)

TAYLOR, FREDERICK W. *Scientific Management.* New York: Harper & Bros., 1947. This book combines the important managerial literature of Frederick W. Taylor, including *Shop Management, The Principles of Scientific Management, and The Testimony before the Special House Committee.* (I)

THOMPSON, JAMES D. (ed). *Approaches to Organizational Design.* Pittsburgh: University of Pittsburgh Press, 1963. Material in connection with seminar in social science of organizations make up this book. Good coverage and ideas are offered. (IV)

TIMMS, HOWARD L. *Introduction to Operations Management.* Homewood, Ill.: Richard D. Irwin, Inc., 1967. Competent treatment of a subject frequently not handled with the clarity and logic displayed in this book. Book informs and explains mathematical approaches in a style understandable to the layman. (II)

TIPPER, HARRY, JR. *Controlling Overhead.* New York: American Management Association, 1966. Emphasizing practical controlling overhead cost, this book is for the person who wants to do something about the cost of overhead. Suggests a program to follow and explains why and how to implement it. (VI)

TOWLE, J. W. *Ethics and Standards in American Business.* Boston: Houghton-Mifflin, Inc., 1964. Papers from a symposium on ethics and business make up this helpful volume. (III)

TURNER, ARTHUR N., and LOMBARD, GEORGE F. *Interpersonal Behavior and Administration.* New York: The Free Press, 1969. A worthy addition to the literature on interpersonal relationships, this book deals with the processes by which a person succeeds or fails in understanding another person when both are within the same organization and have some shared or common responsibility for certain work. (V)

U.S. DEPARTMENT OF COMMERCE, BUREAU OF STANDARDS. *The Standards Yearbook.* Washington, D.C. (Irregular.) This volume gives a picture of the activities and accomplishments of the federal government and of national technical societies and trade associations in standardization. (VI)

U.S. DEPARTMENT OF LABOR, BUREAU OF LABOR STATISTICS. *Monthly Labor Review.* Washington, D.C. (Monthly.) Official governmental publication containing pertinent data on labor and economic subjects along with timely articles in these fields.

WARNER, W. LLOYD. *The Corporation in the Emergent American Society.* New York: Harper & Bros., 1962. A distinguished sociologist views American society and identifies significant patterns of our national life and their possible effects upon our society. (V)

WHYTE, WILLIAM FOOTE. *Men at Work.* Homewood, Ill.: Richard D. Irwin, Inc., and the Dorsey Press, Inc., 1961. Discusses the problems of man adjusting to his work from the behavioral scientist viewpoint. The book is well written, provocative, and informative. (V)

―――. *Organizational Behavior: Theory and Application.* Homewood, Ill.: Richard D. Irwin, Inc., 1969. A comprehensive coverage of organization behavior employing an interdisciplinary approach, but strongly flavored of sociology. Excellent coverage is given of individuals and groups in the organization context and the introducing of change. (IV)

WOLF, W. B. *The Management of Personnel.* San Francisco: Wadsworth Publishing Co., 1961. A highly readable text covering the major topics of personnel management in an interesting and effective manner.

YODER, DALE. *Personnel Management and Industrial Relations.* 6th ed. Englewood Cliffs, N.J.: Prentice-Hall, Inc., 1970. A popular and standard text in the area of manpower management. (V)

ZALEZNIK, ABRAHAM. *Human Dilemmas of Leadership.* New York: Harper and Row, 1966. A psychological study of leadership based on clinical and theoretical concepts of psychoanalysis. Material is stimulating and new concepts are discussed in identifying and implementing leadership. (V)

indexes

Index To Cases

Index

*This book has been set in 12 and 10 point Gara-
mond No. 3, leaded 1 point. Part numbers are
in 18 and 30 point Helvetica. Part and chapter
titles are in 24 point Helvetica. Chapter numbers are in 30 point Helvetica. The size of the
type page is 27 by 46½ picas.*